Benefit–Cost Analysis
Volume I

The International Library of Critical Writings in Economics

Series Editor: Mark Blaug

Professor Emeritus, University of London, UK
Professor Emeritus, University of Buckingham, UK

This series is an essential reference source for students, researchers and lecturers in economics. It presents by theme a selection of the most important articles across the entire spectrum of economics. Each volume has been prepared by a leading specialist who has written an authoritative introduction to the literature included.

A full list of published and future titles in this series is printed at the end of this volume.

Wherever possible, the articles in these volumes have been reproduced as originally published using facsimile reproduction, inclusive of footnotes and pagination to facilitate ease of reference.

For a list of all Edward Elgar published titles visit our site on the World Wide Web at
www.e-elgar.com

Benefit–Cost Analysis
Volume I

Edited by

Richard O. Zerbe, Jr.

*Daniel J. Evans Distinguished Professor of Public Affairs and
Director, Benefit–Cost Analysis Center
Daniel J. Evans School of Public Affairs
and Adjunct Professor of Law
University of Washington, USA*

THE INTERNATIONAL LIBRARY OF CRITICAL WRITINGS IN ECONOMICS

An Elgar Reference Collection
Cheltenham, UK • Northampton, MA, USA

Published by
Edward Elgar Publishing Limited
The Lypiatts
15 Lansdown Road
Cheltenham
Glos GL50 2JA
UK

Edward Elgar Publishing, Inc.
William Pratt House
9 Dewey Court
Northampton
Massachusetts 01060
USA

A catalogue record for this book is available from the British Library

Library of Congress Control Number: 2008932885

ISBN 978 1 84720 964 1 (2 volume set)

Printed and bound in Great Britain by MPG Books Ltd, Bodmin, Cornwall

Contents

Acknowledgements

The editor and publishers wish to thank the authors and the following publishers who have kindly given permission for the use of copyright material.

American Economic Association for articles: Arnold C. Harberger (1971), 'Three Basic Postulates for Applied Welfare Economics: An Interpretive Essay', *Journal of Economic Literature*, **9** (3), September, 785–97; W. Michael Hanemann (1991), 'Willingness to Pay and Willingness to Accept: How Much Can They Differ?', *American Economic Review*, **81** (3), June, 635–47; W. Michael Hanemann (1994), 'Valuing the Environment Through Contingent Valuation', *Journal of Economic Perspectives*, **8** (4), Fall, 19–43.

Association for Evolutionary Economics for article: E.J. Mishan (1982), 'The New Controversy about the Rationale of Economic Evaluation', *Journal of Economic Issues*, **XVI** (1), March, 29–47.

Association for Public Policy Analysis and Management for articles: Dale Whittington and Duncan MacRae, Jr. (1986), 'The Issue of Standing in Cost-Benefit Analysis', *Journal of Policy Analysis and Management*, **5** (4), Summer, 665–82; Richard O. Zerbe, Jr. (1998), 'Is Cost-Benefit Analysis Legal? Three Rules', *Journal of Policy Analysis and Management*, **17** (3), Summer, 419–56.

Blackwell Publishing Ltd for articles: Lionel Robbins (1938), 'Interpersonal Comparisons of Utility: A Comment', *Economic Journal*, **XLVIII** (192), December, 635–41; Nicholas Kaldor (1939), 'Welfare Propositions of Economics and Interpersonal Comparisons of Utility', *Economic Journal*, **XLIX** (195), September, 549–52; J.R. Hicks (1939), 'The Foundations of Welfare Economics', *Economic Journal*, **XLIX** (196), December, 696–712; Tibor de Scitovszky (1941), 'A Note on Welfare Propositions in Economics', *Review of Economic Studies*, **9** (1), November, 77–88; Robin W. Boadway (1974), 'The Welfare Foundations of Cost-Benefit Analysis', *Economic Journal*, **84** (336), December, 926–39; Jinhua Zhao and Catherine L. Kling (2004), 'Willingness to Pay, Compensating Variation, and the Cost of Commitment', *Economic Inquiry*, **42** (3), July, 503–17.

Cato Institute for articles: Steven Kelman (1981), 'Cost-Benefit Analysis: An Ethical Critique', *Regulation*, **5** (1), January/February, 33–40; Gerard Butters, John Calfee and Pauline Ippolito (1981), 'Defending Cost-Benefit Analysis: Replies to Steven Kelman', *Regulation*, **5** (2), March/April, 41–2.

Econometric Society for article: Harold Hotelling (1938), 'The General Welfare in Relation to Problems of Taxation and of Railway and Utility Rates', *Econometrica*, **6** (3), July, 242–69.

Elsevier for articles: Daniel Kahneman and Jack L. Knetsch (1992), 'Valuing Public Goods: The Purchase of Moral Satisfaction', *Journal of Environmental Economics and Management*, **22** (1), January, 57–70; V. Kerry Smith (1992), 'Arbitrary Values, Good Causes, and Premature Verdicts', *Journal of Environmental Economics and Management*, **22** (1), January, 71–89; Daniel Kahneman and Jack L. Knetsch (1992), 'Contingent Valuation and the Value of Public Goods: Reply', *Journal of Environmental Economics and Management*, **22** (1), January, 90–94; John K. Horowitz and Kenneth E. McConnell (2002), 'A Review of WTA/WTP Studies', *Journal of Environmental Economics and Management*, **44** (3), November, 426–47; Richard O. Zerbe, Jr., Yoram Bauman and Aaron Finkle (2006), 'An Aggregate Measure for Benefit–Cost Analysis', *Ecological Economics*, **58** (3), 449–61; Jack Knetsch (2007), 'Biased Valuations, Damage Assessments, and Policy Choices: The Choice of Measure Matters', *Research in Law and Economics*, **23**, 345–58.

Oxford University Press for article: Paul A. Samuelson (1950), 'Evaluation of Real National Income', *Oxford Economic Papers*, **2** (1), New Series, January, 1–29.

Princeton University Press for excerpt: Theodore M. Porter (1995), 'U.S. Army Engineers and the Rise of Cost-Benefit Analysis', in *Trust in Numbers: The Pursuit of Objectivity in Science and Public Life*, Chapter 7, 148–89, notes, references.

Resources for the Future via Copyright Clearance Center for excerpt: Richard D. Morgenstern (1997), 'The Legal and Institutional Setting for Economic Analysis at EPA', in Richard D. Morgenstern (ed.), *Economic Analyses at EPA: Assessing Regulatory Impact*, Chapter 2, 5–23.

University of Chicago Press via Copyright Clearance Center for articles: John V. Krutilla (1961), 'Welfare Aspects of Benefit-Cost Analysis', *Journal of Political Economy*, **69** (3), June, 226–35; Daniel Kahneman, Jack L. Knetsch and Richard H. Thaler (1990), 'Experimental Tests of the Endowment Effect and the Coase Theorem', *Journal of Political Economy*, **98** (6), December, 1325–48.

Every effort has been made to trace all the copyright holders but if any have been inadvertently overlooked the publishers will be pleased to make the necessary arrangement at the first opportunity.

In addition the publishers wish to thank the Library of Indiana University at Bloomington, USA, for their assistance in obtaining these articles.

Introduction*

Richard O. Zerbe, Jr.

Two volumes cannot contain all of the worthy articles concerned with Benefit–Cost Analysis (BCA). There are undoubtedly others that should be included or substituted for those I have chosen here. These articles, nevertheless, constitute a useful collection. They will be valuable first and foremost to professionals who need a handy source for the best articles on BCA. Teachers will find here useful articles to assign for class readings, and those applying BCA will find useful guides and examples, perhaps especially in the companion volume, *Applied Benefit–Cost Analysis*, which is co-edited by Andrew Schmitz, who writes the Introduction for that volume.

In choosing articles we have kept in mind the major policy issues and themes in the use of BCA; many of these remain from the early period of BCA writings. To my mind these issues are (1) establishing a firm theoretical and ethical underpinning for BCA, (2) determining those institutional arrangements that will provide the best BCAs in a context in which they will be most useful to the policy and decision process, (3) working towards a set of principles and standards that will command wide agreement and serve to unify the methods for conducting BCAs, (4) determining unit values for non-market goods that are useful for BCA, (5) providing guidelines for how and when we should use general rather than partial equilibrium models, (6) providing procedures that encourage proper treatments of uncertainty and risk, and (7) addressing technical issues. These themes and issues are echoed or foretold in the articles collected here, and I hope that collecting them will provide a further impetus to address them. Along with issues and problems this first volume considers briefly the historical development of BCA as such development provides a framework to consider the role, future and usefulness of BCA.

Volume I

Parts I and II   Classic Historical Articles and History of Use

To affect beneficial changes in BCA it is useful to have an understanding of its history and development. The first two parts provide this perspective.

Part I, Classic Historical Articles, first notes those articles from the late 1930s and early 1940s that gave rise to basic concepts of welfare economics. It was during this time that the idea of applying benefit cost approaches to welfare was developed (Hotelling, 1938, Chapter 1), the problem of interpersonal comparisons of utility was clearly laid out (Robbins, 1938, Chapter 2), the concepts of the Kaldor–Hicks potential compensation measure arose (Kaldor, 1939, Chapter 3), and the concepts of the compensating and equivalent variations were developed and associated with the willingness to pay and accept (Hicks, 1939, Chapter 4).

What was and, to a considerable extent, is the mainstream form of BCA arose from a late 1930s controversy that began with Robbins' comment on the unscientific nature of making interpersonal comparisons of value. Before that time, it was generally assumed that each individual had an 'equal capacity for enjoyment,' and that gains and losses among different individuals could be directly compared.[1] Robbins' comments were seen as emasculating economists who would not be able to make professional or scientific judgments about such matters as taxes, tariffs, and policy matters in general. As Robbins notes (p. 640):

> And if it were a matter of personal defence [sic] against all accusations of imbecility, social indifference, and even sinister interest which have been made against their author, I certainly should not have thought it any more worth while writing now than at any time in the past.

Robbins' position was not, however, that the assumption of 'equal capacity for enjoyment' not be made. In fact he notes that the assumption 'counts each man as one … is less likely to lead one astray than any of the absolute systems … I do believe that, in most cases, political calculations which do not treat them *as if* they were equal are morally revolting' (p. 635). Robbins simply wished to separate normative assumptions from positive ones. Nicholas Kaldor accepted Robbins' advice and the assumption of equal marginal utility of income as a convenience for economists and proposed leaving decisions about equity to the politicians. Kaldor built on the foundation provided by Vilfredo Pareto. Pareto introduced a welfare criterion, the Pareto optimum, which became a foundational concept in welfare theory,[2] to the effect that a Pareto optimum is a state of affairs such that no one can be made better off without making someone else worse off.[3] A change in the economy is said to represent a Pareto improvement over what came before it, or to be Pareto superior to what came before it, if at least one person is made better off as a result of the change and no person is made worse off.[4] The Pareto criterion is not useful for most practical purposes for exactly the same reason that a criterion of unanimity is not useful in most voting situations.[5] The practical substitute for the Pareto criterion is the potential Pareto criterion, also known also as the Kaldor–Hicks criterion.

The Kaldor–Hicks (KH) is the standard for BCA.[6] Kaldor acknowledged the inability of economists to establish a scientific basis for making interpersonal utility comparisons but suggested that this difficulty could be made irrelevant. He argued that policies that led to an increase in aggregate real income are always desirable because the *potential* exists to make everyone better off:

> [T]he economist's case for the policy is quite unaffected by the question of the comparability of individual satisfaction, since in all such cases it is possible to make everybody better off than before, or at any rate to make some people better off without making anybody worse off.[7]

According to Kaldor, a project is desirable if the money measure of gains exceeds the money measure of losses. With regard to the *potential* compensation that could turn losers into winners in such situations, Kaldor notes that whether *actual* compensation should take place 'is a political question on which the economist, qua economist, could hardly pronounce an opinion.'[8] Hicks, perhaps the most prominent economist of the time, accepted the Kaldor approach, which eventually became known as the KH criterion.[9]

The KH criterion attempts to avoid interpersonal utility comparisons by separating equity from efficiency. Kaldor proposed that decision makers address equity through a process occurring outside the purview of BCA.[10] The change in aggregate gains was to be the measure of efficiency, so according to KH there is a separate consideration of efficiency and distributional effects, while economists should focus on efficiency effects.[11] Kaldor endorsed the procedure adopted by Pigou, which Kaldor describes as 'dividing welfare effects into two parts: the first relating to production, and the second to distribution.'[12] The KH approach produces outcomes that are equivalent to those produced by the assumption that the marginal utility of income is the same across all individuals, that is, that each dollar of benefit or cost is treated the same regardless of who receives it.[13] Hicks agreed also with this separation and noted, 'if measures making for efficiency are to have a fair chance, it is extremely desirable that they should be freed from distributive complication as much as possible.'[14] To Hicks, it would be '"rather a dreadful thing" to have to accept the view that welfare analysis was unscientific.' If it were, its conclusions would '… depend on the scale of social values held by a particular investigator. Such conclusions can possess no validity … one's welfare economics will inevitably be different according as one is a liberal, or a socialist, a nationalist or an internationalist, a christian [sic] or a pagan.'[15]

This separation of efficiency and equity has remained the common, though not universal, basis of normative economic analysis to this day. The more modern justifications for the separation are that changes in the income distribution are usually better effected through macroeconomic policy rather than through individual projects.[16] This defense, however, leaves unaddressed matters of equities for identifiable peoples or groups, or sentiments attached to particular projects that cannot be handled by macroeconomic policy; equity and justice are particular as well as general.[17] These articles, as well as early works by Pigou and Little, show that the earlier developers of BCA were fully aware of ethical and distributional issues that concern us today. The questions don't change, just the answers. The answers, however, show progress over time.

The article by Tibor Scitovsky in 1941 (Chapter 5) (original name de Scitovskzy) appeared to raise a major issue about the potential compensation criteria of Kaldor. Scitovsky showed that using the KM approach one could choose to move from one state of the world, state A, to state B, but then having arrived at state B, one could use the criterion to justify a move back to A. The possibility of preference reversals using cost–benefit analysis has concerned economists to some degree ever since. Scitovsky suggested that the paradox could be avoided by requiring a double test, using both the compensating variation (the KH test) and the equivalent variation tests. This would, however, leave some changes undefined in welfare terms. Lawyers and philosophers have fastened onto this possibility in an attempt to discredit, sometimes entirely, the use of cost–benefit analysis.[18] Scitovsky's main contribution can probably be seen as methodological, the creation of community indifference curves, often called Scitovsky curves, which have proved very useful in the hands of people such as E.J. Mishan in analyzing welfare propositions. As for the reversal proposition, in practice economists have acted as if or pretended that they were unimportant. They have been correct to do so according to a recent draft paper by Schmidt and Zerbe (2008).

We claim that Scitovsky reversals necessarily concern second-best situations. This means there will be states of the world that are Pareto superior to the status quo and to the proposed project. This raises the issue of why second-best positions are being considered if a Pareto superior position is available? In general, the domain of the paradox is severely limited. The paradox does not arise under the Pareto principle (actual payment of compensation) because this will produce a first-best situation. The paradox does not arise when one of the bundles being compared is of a first-best nature. Nor does the paradox arise when there is a rule rating the value of alternative income distributions. The reversal arises only when compensation principles are applied to a comparison of second-best bundles and when the Scitovsky curves cross in a particular manner.

Samuelson (1950, Chapter 6) contends that aggregate welfare comparisons that are consistent and free of ethics are impossible. Only in the case in which the utility possibility curves shift uniformly for the group can we say that aggregate welfare has increased or decreased. Even in this case, however, there is an ethical basis for such a conclusion; Pareto superiority must itself rest on the ethical assumption that preferences are the appropriate basis for welfare judgments. Ethics must be a part of any normative judgments so that the requirement of ethical freedom is neither appropriate nor possible. Nor is consistency itself a deciding factor. In a general sense, one can invoke Gödel's Theorem[19] to indicate that in a sufficiently complex system using first order logic, consistency cannot be shown to be proved within the system. But these issues are too abstract for our purposes, as is Samuelson's criticism. Our focus is on developing a criterion that is more useful and acceptable than other criteria. The ethical argument for the use of BCA must rest on the grounds that it is useful, has social acceptance and is consistent enough, not on grounds that it is an ethical imperative.

The 1961 article by John Krutilla (Chapter 7) builds on Hotelling's work but brings the question of distributional effects to the fore, as does E.J. Mishan's 1982 article (Chapter 10) on the ethical nature and basis of benefit–cost analysis. These works, as well as more recent work (e.g., by Goulder, Zerbe, and Zerbe *et al.*) suggests an answer different from that of Kaldor.[20]

These authors suggest that distributional and other ethical questions can be handled in the same manner as other goods; by determining the willingness to pay (WTP) or willingness to accept (WTA) for them. Both Goulder (2007) and Zerbe (2001) offer to expand to domain of BCA to include the sentiments of third parties. As Goulder says (p. 82):

> Since WTP may depend on individual characteristics such as age or income, the value of benefit attributed to a given policy impact (such as an improvement in safety) can differ depending on the age of income of the affected population. To many this is inequitable and calls in question the legitimacy of benefit-cost analysis. ... This paper offers a different option. It endorses a broader domain for the benefit calculation: including the WTP by third for the policy outcome in question.

A second major question that has been around from the early days is addressed by Arnold Harberger in 1971 (Chapter 8) in his three basic postulates. Harberger sounds the 'need for an accepted set of professional standards ... [which] should be obvious.' This need has yet to be fully addressed and cries out for attention. Harberger goes on the make the case for the usefulness of BCA and to point the way toward the incorporation of general equilibrium results. The premise of these two volumes is that we can, and should, begin to expand on the foundation Harberger and others have built.

The 1974 Boadway (Chapter 9) article introduces the relationship between potential compensation tests (PCTs) and compensating variation measures of welfare gain in a general equilibrium framework. In general, passing a BCA test does not ensure passing a PCT. Indeed, in the real economy (one with distortions), a positive sum of CVs is not even a necessary condition. (A positive sum of CVs is, however, a necessary condition only when the economy is undistorted.) The non-equivalence of the CV and the PCT test arises when price changes are sufficiently large. The PCT, however, is passed when the price changes are sufficiently small as Bruce and Harris (1982) have shown.

Part II on the History of Use, contains two articles. The Porter (1995, Chapter 11) article is valuable simply as history of practice in the United States. However, its main value for economists and policy makers is to illustrate how useful BCA can be when used by an agency (the Army Corps) with integrity, prestige, and with the support of Congress. Porter is able implicitly to raise two questions: (1) Why has the use of BCA by the Corps deteriorated? and (2) What are the lessons that can be applied to the future institutional arrangements for performing BCAs within the Federal government? The article by Morgenstern (1997, Chapter 12) was included for similar reasons although it examines a different agency, the Environmental Protection Agency (EPA). Morgenstern focuses on the uneven and inconsistent use of economics in environmental decision-making, the theme raised by Harberger much earlier. Morgenstern notes that the EPA has at best tolerated the goal of economic efficiency. This raises the issue of whether this has been due to limitations of BCAs that do not consider moral sentiments, or to other causes.

Part III   Philosophy and Foundation

Against this historical background, the following parts examine particular theoretical issues that have caused debate within the BCA community. The lead article in Part III by Kelman (1981, Chapter 13) is a popular attack on any significant use of BCA on the grounds that it is utilitarian is its roots, and that utilitarianism lacks or is missing certain moral values. Thus, in a readable manner this article raises concerns that lawyers and philosophers have raised broadly and for some time. (See for example the recent book by Ackerman and Heinzerling.)[21] Kelman's point is that BCA uses expedient values, of the sort to increase GDP, rather than considering the importance of moral values and the role that they might play. That is, BCA is missing important values. For those who would like to further explore, Elizabeth Anderson's (1993) book produces a scholarly treatment of these issues. A number of economists replied to Kelman; the reply included here by Butters, Calfee and Ippolito (1981, Chapter 14) makes the point that the purpose of BCA is simply to use information on preferences to inform decision-making and that BCA is not intended to be used on its own to make decisions. Expanding BCA in the manner suggested by Goulder (2007) and Zerbe (2001), however, vitiates most criticisms based on seeing BCA as utilitarianism.

Is it true that applied welfare economics is based on utilitarianism, where utilitarianism is seen in terms of narrow expediency? In practice, sometimes it is. However, maximizing utility is not utilitarianism but simply a heuristic for determining preferences and then aggregating them in a particular manner. Zerbe and others, argue that moral preferences should logically count in BCA to the extent to which they are supported by WTP or WTA measures. The philosopher, Mark Sagoff does not see preferences as values but this seems a non-starter (Zerbe *et al.*, 2006, pp. 14–16). Even a Kantian has a preference for the categorical imperative.

The arguments against including moral preferences are (1) they cannot be counted, (2) to count them is unnecessary given the invariance effect, (3) counting them can result in double counting and can also result in (4) a positive net present value that does not satisfy the potential compensation test and finally that (5) to include moral preferences requires counting immoral preferences as well.

Now in every BCA some sentiments and individuals or groups are not fully considered. Harberger has suggested to me, for example, that the national point of view is the appropriate one. A systematic approach is developed by Dale Whittington and Duncan MacRae who in 1986 (Chapter 15) introduced the concept of economic 'standing', which makes explicit what values and which persons' values will be included or excluded. BCAs are typically carried out by one municipality or state or other organization and may not consider effects on neighbors. Even in a federal analysis, effects on foreigners may be ignored, though this practice is less common than formerly. The concept of standing can also be used to connect BCA to the law. Zerbe (1998, Chapter 16) argues that a thief does not have standing to have her stolen goods counted since the law making theft illegal denies her standing. He suggests that a similar approach, relying on discussion and social norms, can be used to exclude immoral sentiments such as created by utility monster examples, such as murder, envy effects, and so on, from being counted. The foundational argument is that in a stable society benefit cost decisions have already been made that exclude such sentiments from having standing,

Zerbe, Bauman, and Finkle (2006, Chapter 17) show that the problems of invariance, double counting and failure to pass the potential compensation test (PCT) are, or at least should be, non-issues. The invariance effect applies to non-paternal altruism and points out that the net benefits to users must be positive for there to be altruistic values; but this claim is incorrectly extended to argue that therefore non-altruistic sentiments may be disregarded. This later part of the claim is not correct as (1) there may be groups other than the altruists and the objects of altruism so that the sign of the net present value (NPV) may change when including moral sentiments, and (2) including moral sentiments will affect the magnitude of the NPV when it does not affect the sign and this is relevant for comparison with alternative projects. With respect to the PCT, it is possible for this test not to be satisfied when net benefits are positive regardless of whether or not moral sentiments are included. Moreover, the issue only arises with respect to moral sentiments when they are trivial and weak. Finally the double-counting argument is just incorrect. Including moral sentiments does not result in double counting.

Part IV   Factors Affecting Willingness to Pay and Accept

Part IV examines a different set of issues, those that surround Willingness to Pay (WTP) and Willingness to Accept (WTA). What is owned is more valuable, ipso facto, than what is not. This is the familiar proposition that the WTA > WTP. But why? The difference apparently arises from income effects, substitution effects but also from purely psychological effects known as the endowment effects (Kahneman, Knetsch, and Thaler, 1990, Chapter 18). That the income effect will produce divergence has long been known, and measurements of the divergences indicate that they can be quite large (Horowitz and McConnell, 2002, Chapter 20). Hanneman (1991, Chapter 19), in an important result, points out that the divergence between WTA and WTP is also affected by the substitution effect, and that therefore the divergence will be greater the more unique the good. Also, Cohen and Knetsch (1992) and Zerbe (2001) point out that the concept of legal ownership contributes to psychological ownership. What one owns or feels one owns forms a reference point for measuring gains, measured by WTP. Losses are measured ideally by the WTA, which is also determined by ownership; one cannot lose what one does not psychologically have. The existence and importance of this effect is still contested to some extent. Certainly the evidence is overwhelming that the reference point for considering welfare gains and losses should value losses more than equivalent gains. At the market level presumably it is not so important, as indeed the authors admit, because the commercial owner of goods presumably does not take psychological possession. Such goods I have called 'commercial goods'.[22]

An interesting expression of this phenomenon is the 'endowment effect'. The endowment effect maintains that possession affects the value of the good. Jack Knetsch (2007, Chapter 22) and others have pointed out that the Coase Theorem, which holds that the final allocation between bargaining individuals is invariant to the initial distribution when transaction costs are zero, income effects aside, must be incorrect if the endowment effect exists. Let us consider an extension of the application of the endowment effect to the efficiency part of the Coase Theorem as well. Suppose that there are two parties, A and B, and there is a normal good (property) to which neither A nor B has psychological or legal ownership. Does it make any difference to whom the property (right) is given or sold in terms of economic efficiency? Assume further that all worthwhile trades are made. Suppose that the WTPa > WTPb and that for both parties their WTA > WTP. Then if A has the right she will not sell to B. The gain from giving the right to A is WTPa. The gain from giving it to B is WTPb. B will sell the right to A as long as WTAb < WTPa. The net social gains (NSG) from giving the right to A rather than B will then be:[23]

$$NSG = WTAb - WTPb$$

whether or not B sells the right to A. Now it is inefficient for the government to sell to B as, given the endowment effect, value is lost by sending the product to A by way of B and this loss arises because B would suffer from endowment effect loss (or a loss whenever the WTA and WTP diverge) in selling the good. In the case where it does not pay B to sell the good, A would suffer from not having it. In both cases the loss is as shown above. Thus the efficiency part of the Coase Theorem, as well as the invariance part, is violated if the endowment effect exists (Zerbe, 2001).[24]

Zhao and Kling (2004, Chapter 21) point out that the equivalent variation (EV) and compensating variation (CV) Hicksian measures are static and do not take into account *expectations* in buying and selling. Purchase decisions may, for example, be delayed while information is gathered, or it may be expected that time will soon bring forth new information and, in general, it is costly to reverse purchase mistakes. These uncertainties reduce the value of the WTP by the buyer at the current time and increase the WTA for the seller at the current time. The result is that even if the CV = EV, one can have:

$$WTP < CV = EV < WTA$$

The extent to which this explains the larger expected divergences between the WTP and WTA found in empirical results, has yet to be determined.

Commitment costs arise when (1) the agent is uncertain about the value of the good and (2) expects she can learn more over time and (3) has some willingness to wait and (4) expects a cost to reverse any current decision to buy or sell, and (5) is forced to make a trading decision now. In a related paper Zhao and Kling (2001) find that many experiments and surveys in general satisfy these five conditions.[25] This result should help to explain the greater than expected divergence between the WTA and WTP.

Part V   Contingent Valuation

One class of valuation used to capture moral sentiments as well as use values is contingent valuation methodology (CVM) in which respondents state their WTP for public goods. A good deal of discussion, some of it heated, has concerned whether or not CV is a reasonably useful method of collecting data concerning values. Kahneman and Knetsch (1992, Chapter 23) have suggested that the validity of CV is brought into question by the embedding effect by which moral values relevant to a larger class of goods are embedded in subsets of the class. Thus asking WTP questions about a member of the subset will overstate its economic value. The authors properly suggest that CVM studies should include a check for robustness and for the presence of embedding.

Kerry Smith (1992, Chapter 24) disagrees with all of Kahneman and Knetsch's embedding conclusions. His primary objections are that their results rely on flawed questions, improperly collected data, and overly small samples of experiments and surveys. He maintains their results can therefore be explained without recourse to embedding.

Kahneman and Knetsch (1992, Chapter 25) reply that Smith finds no fatal flaw in their work and that the existence of embedding is far from disproved. They go on to correctly point out that the implication of their work is to suggest better survey techniques. They cite their conclusion from Chapter 23: 'The conservative conclusion from our findings is that future applications of CVM should incorporate an experimental control: the contingent valuation of any public good should routinely be supported by adequate evidence that the estimate is robust to manipulations of embedding....'

As I suggested above, my speculation is that embedding is real but can be accounted for through sophisticated and well thought out surveys. If the effect of embedding moral sentiments for a particular subset of goods stops at the more general class for which embedding is relevant then asking first about the value of the general class and then subdividing into parts should be a method of accounting for embedding. For example, the value of the various subsets, whose sum is constrained to have a value equal to the total for the correct class, may properly capture the values of subsets. The existence of moral sentiments towards a subclass is not inconsistent with additional moral sentiments for the larger class. That is, an embedding effect is not properly seen as an argument for excluding moral values but rather as an argument for matching the moral sentiments with the correct good(s).

This conclusion finds support within the Report of the National Oceanic and Atmospheric Administration (NOAA) panel (1993, Chapter 26) and with Hanemann (1994, Chapter 27). Both support the use of closed-ended questions that specify prices rather than an open-ended question that simply asks 'what is the most you are willing to pay?' What is needed is a rich portrait of the interview. Robin Gregory, an experienced surveyor, has suggested to me that the whole interview process is not so much extracting numbers that already exist for a person but creating a context that allows the respondent to create numbers within the context of his value system. (At least this is my interpretation of his remarks.) Hanemann goes on to offer a critique of the more general controversy about whether or not CVM can be useful. He makes a strong case that it can be. Moreover, he offers useful suggestions for rules that should guide the conduct of surveys. The rules could be a starting point for the development of a generally agreed-upon set of principles for the conduct of surveys.

Volume II

Part I   Revealed Preference

Volume II begins with Kerry Smith's 1997/1998 article (Chapter 1) on valuation. This is an extended comparison and critique of different valuation methods. It has undoubted utility. What I like best about it is the following conclusion: 'Nonetheless, the needs for benefit measures are increasingly expressed in terms of some type of unit value. To meet these future needs, future research must begin to adopt strategies that parallel the theoretical and practical research that served to enhance the development of price indexes for marketed goods.' Smith goes on to suggest that this strategy seems feasible for environmental resources. The strategy has, however, much broader application, as Smith notes, for example in valuing outcomes in social programs. I can think of two problems that are associated with unit values: (1) they need to take into account income and substitution effects. One additional lake is worth less where there are many lakes, that is, where there are better substitutes. Also local incomes will affect both use and non-use values; (2) they will therefore need to be updated with time and for location.

The 2005 article by Palmquist (Chapter 2) is technical and relates to using the weak complementarity between an environmental good and a private good to derive an estimate of the value of a public environmental good. That is, there is often a (non-essential) private good that is consumed along with the environmental good. The non-essential good implies a choke price when demand is zero. By using compensated (Hicksian) demand it is possible to estimate the compensating variation for the public good. This method, however, will not necessarily give good answers when using Marshallian demand curves. It will do so only when a condition is satisfied, known as the Willig condition. However, in general it will be preferable to ignore the Willig condition and to specify an indirect utility function that satisfies the non-essentiality (has a choke price) and weak complementarity and derive compensated and uncompensated welfare measures directly. This allows greater flexibility in functional form.

Part II   General Equilibrium

Since the 1970s there have been a series of articles addressing the issue of whether partial equilibrium analysis will give different BCA results than general equilibrium (GE). The general answer is that they will give substantially different answers. The 1975 article by John Whalley (Chapter 3) is one of the earlier articles on this subject. Whalley concludes (p. 310) that '... although there is a considerable gain in computational simplicity in the use of partial equilibrium analysis, the reliability of results using more satisfactory general equilibrium techniques is considerably increased.'

Hazilla and Kopp (1990, Chapter 5) give another instance of the difference between the results of partial and general equilibrium analysis while criticizing government analyses of large environmental programs. They focus on cost estimates. First they point out what is now well accepted, that social costs are not the same as engineering costs. Social costs, for example, can be lower than private expenditures or exceed them due to household behavior in which leisure is substituted for consumption. The social costs of the Clean Air and Clean Water Acts were about $15 billion less than the EPA estimates of engineering costs. However, accounting for temporal effects of a reduction in savings on capital stock growth means that the longer run welfare effects shown by a general equilibrium analysis are much greater than shown by partial equilibrium due mainly to accounting for effects on economic growth in the GE analysis. They conclude that (p. 871) 'it is difficult to overemphasize the importance of approaching policy analysis from a general equilibrium analysis.'

A useful way to think about GE analysis, derived from Harberger, is to use reduced form equations to estimate changes in quantities of goods. These changes are then multiplied by the average size of distortions for all of the affected goods. Distortions in factor markets must also be included. The most important distortions are taxes, while changes in the quantities of those goods and associated inputs not subject to meaningful distortions can be ignored. Now one of the most taxed inputs is labor. Goulder and Williams (2003, Chapter 6) show that policies that change the use of labor can thus have a quite substantial welfare effect. They derive an equation implementing this approach as an approximation. The key data are an estimate for the labor supply elasticity and a labor tax rate. They test the results of their formula against a full general equilibrium approach and find that it works well as an approximation and is much more accurate than the simple excess burden formula. The authors thus provide a relatively simple formula that can be implemented and show the substantial significance of the labor tax.

Turnovsky, Shalit, and Schmitz (1980, Chapter 4) give a second particular application of general equilibrium analysis. The topic they consider is the welfare effects of price stability. Partial equilibrium analysis without considering risk aversion finds that price instability is preferable to intervention of buffer prices. The issue they examine is whether this preference for price instability is robust to a more general approach that also considers relative risk preferences. In particular they use an indirect utility function approach combined with measures of Arrow–Pratt relative risk aversion. When considering a single commodity, the preference for price instability depends on (1) the income elasticity of demand for the commodity, (2) the price elasticity of demand for the commodity, (3) the share of the budget spent on the commodity in question, and (4) the coefficient of relative risk aversion. These enter in an intuitive way. The desirability of instability increases with the magnitudes of the two elasticities and decreases with the degree of risk aversion but is indeterminate with respect to an increase in the budget share.

In considering GE effects of environmental amenities, such as cleaner air, location matters as does the ability to change location. Smith *et al.* (2004, Chapter 7) show that such effects can be taken into account. One of the advantages of disaggregation by location is that distributional effects can be estimated. These effects will depend on the initial level of air quality; relocation based on changes in ozone and price changes, and income levels of households. The general equilibrium welfare effects range from $33 to $2400 annually at the household level.

Part III   Discount Rates

The third part of Volume II explores another topic that has long generated intense debate within the BCA community. What is the right discount rate for public investment? The short answer is that no one knows. The longer and better answer is that we know enough to circumscribe, or perhaps more accurately to begin to circumscribe, the rate. Few suggest that, examined in terms of economic efficiency, the appropriate rate will be (except in unusual circumstances) greater than the opportunity cost of capital, say 7 percent to 10 percent in real terms. Few would suggest that it should be lower than the time preference rate, which is commonly estimated to be about 2–4 percent. Some argue that the rate should be about the same as the economic growth rate. This bounds the effective rate between about 2 percent and 10 percent in real terms. However, on ethical grounds some believe that the only ethically justifiable rate is zero. An exception to this is thought to arise on economic as well as ethical grounds when it is expected that future generations will be better off than the current generation. The expectation is that the marginal utility of income falls with income so that dollars accruing to future generations will be worth less to them, justifying a higher discount rate than otherwise.

In a now classic 1965 article Koopmans (Chapter 8) introduces both equity and efficiency considerations into the choice of rate. His approach is based on a preference ordering of alternative growth paths. The major suggestion is to use the 'Golden Rule' discount rate on both equity and efficiency grounds, a rate equal to the growth rate of the economy. Koopman shows that the golden rule path continually attains the highest indefinitely maintainable utility flow.

Bradford (1975, Chapter 9) examines the problem as a resolution first taking into account the argument for the use of the rate of time preference on the grounds that any public investment that yields a greater return will more than satisfy preference. Second, Bradford recognizes that government use of capital may displace private capital that will have rates higher then the rate of social time preference. His approach is similar to one recommended earlier by Musgrave and Musgrave (1973). Below I give a slightly different formulation of part of Bradford's work.

Bradford notes intuitively that a change in consumption should be evaluated using the social rate of time reference (SRTP). Thus:

$$dW = \sum_{t=0}^{T} \frac{\Delta Ct}{(1 + i)^t} \tag{1}$$

The total capital at time t from an initial investment of Ko will be:

$$K(t) = Koe^{srt} \tag{2}$$

Where,

Ko = original investment
$K(t)$ = the value of the investment at time t
S = the fraction of investment proceeds that are reinvested
r = the return to private capital
i = social rate of time preference

Then the amount of consumption per unit of capital in any t period will be:

$$C(t) = \frac{(1 - s)r\, Koe^{srt}}{Ko} = (1 - s)re^{srt}$$

whose present value over all time periods will be:

$$PVc = \sum (1 - s)re^{srt - it} \tag{3}$$

This will be infinite where $sr > i$. This is unlikely as the growth rate of the economy would be greater than the discount rate. It is more likely (a case Bradford did not consider) that the growth rate will equal the discount rate. In this case the *PV* would be just $(1 - s)r$. The discount rate would then be just r in the case where savings are zero, a situation that currently characterizes the United States economy. For any s less than 1 (and $sr = i$), the discount rate would be less than r. What Bradford shows is how much less in situations where $sr < 1$. Consider again equation (3). Using the formula for the sum of a geometric series, equation (3) converts into:

$$PVc = \frac{(1 - s)r}{i - sr} \equiv Vt$$

which assumes that s, r and i are constant over time. Let θc and θb equal the fraction of a dollar of public investment that displaces private investment and the fraction of a dollar from public investment that returns to private investment. Then, the NPV may be expressed as:

$$NPV = \sum_{t=0}^{T} \frac{Bt[\theta bVt(1 - \theta b)] - Ct[\theta cVt - (1 - \theta c)]}{(1 + i)^t} \tag{4}$$

where Bt and Ct are ordinary benefits at time t. I call the multiplier for benefits Mb and that for costs Mc. If $Mb = Mc$ then (4) reduces to:

$$NPV = \sum_{t=0}^{T} M \frac{(Bt - Ct)}{(1 + i)^t}$$

Thus the NPV is a multiple of the unadjusted NPV and will have the same sign. Given the large size of world capital markets most projects will not affect the interest rate and both Mc and Mb will be 1. In this case, the use of the SRTP as the discount rate would be required. Elsewhere Lesser and I have shown that under most scenarios an upward adjustment of costs of less than 10 percent would cover almost all likely cases so that one could use the SRTP with such an adjustment with some conference that if the NPV remained positive after costs are adjusted upward by 10 percent, the project was a good one.[26] Now Harberger suggests using a discount rate that is a weighted average of the SRTP and the return to private capital. The weights are determined by the amount of the capital that comes from private capital and from consumption. The Bradford result is however much more general. If we reduce the Bradford result to a two period model, the Harberger result is obtained. (This is not shown by Bradford, or others, but is an easy result to obtain.)

The ethics of Bradford's approach is the Golden Rule, though this is not the interpretation Arrow puts on it.[27] Arrow claims that the ethical time preference rate is zero. Yet, this is the result that you would obtain if the population at time zero lived forever and discounted future consumption based on expectations of increasing income and corresponding decreasing marginal utility of income. In considering whether to make an investment the decision maker considers her consumption loss now against the consumption later. That is, the consumption rate of preference should already incorporate the effects of declining marginal utility of income under a golden rule scenario. Future values are discounted but only if the extra consumption they receive would be worth it were the people making the investment to receive its rewards. Note that SRTP seems to be about the same as the economy growth rate. Thus a purely economic approach produces a similar result to that of Koopmans. In both cases the long run equilibrium requires the growth rate and the interest rate to be equal. The long-term growth rate of the economy is about 3 percent real.

Time inconsistency arises in long-term discounting in that if you assume that individuals at time zero will value consumption one year later in comparison to time zero, then they will value the same consumption at time 101 in comparison with time 100. This has been used to argue for lower discount rates for the longer term. Such an argument seems unacceptable for when the individual arrives at time 100 his time preference rate with respect to period 101 is, ceteris paribus, the same as it was in year zero. Weitzman (2001, Chapter 11) points out that for discounting of more distant values, it is the average of the discount factors that is relevant, not the average of the discount rates. This gives more weight to lower discount rates as time increases. The rate approaches a gamma distribution with respect to time. Weitzman uses as his range of rates the results of a survey of 2160 economists. He obtains a range from a negative rate (for three respondents) to 20 percent or above for eight respondents. He also constructs a rate from a panel of 50 high profile economists. The mean and standard deviation of the two groups are close at about 4 percent and 3 percent, with a median rate for the larger sample of 3 percent and a mode of 2 percent.

I suggest, however, that this is a questionable way to determine the best range of rates. The proper panel should not be either distinguished or undistinguished economists but those economists who have thought best and most about the subject. My speculation is that the mean and median rates of such a sample asking about the range of the SRTP probably would result in rates within the 2–4 percent range, which is also close to the reasonable range of rates for sustainable economic growth. For very long time periods, the lower bound discount rate would be the average of the discount factors and would approach, à la Weitzman, the lower bound of 2 percent. For example for a 500-year project, and a uniform distribution of discount rates of between 2 percent and 4 percent, the discount rate created by the average of the discount factors would be 2.14 percent.[28] No convincing argument has been advanced for adopting a much lower discount rate, not excepting the opinion polls cited by Weitzman.

Ethics should not be incorporated into the discount rate for convincing reasons suggested by Lesser and Zerbe in 1991, Zerbe and Dively in 1994, and most elegantly by Lind in 1995 and 1999 (Chapter 10). All of these authors suggest the impossibility of directly transferring income from generation zero to future generations and vice versa. There is no way the present generation can remotely guarantee that investment saved for a future generation will arrive there. The approach suggested for incorporating ethical sentiments into the valuation of future outcomes is to treat such sentiments as any other good and incorporate valuation based on ethical sentiments directly as part of the value attached to outcomes. This is not only consistent with the BCA approach generally, which should include all goods for which there is a WTP, but this approach also avoids the trenchant difficulty of adopting a discount rate on the basis of arbitrary categorical imperative. This leaves the practitioner in the untenable position of adopting a rule for society. In the 2004 article (Chapter 12, Volume II) Zerbe expands on previous work (Lesser and Zerbe, 1998; Zerbe, 2001, pp. 18, 291) to separate the value of ethical considerations from those of the choice of discount rate. This notion is also the main point of Lind's (1999) essay in which he considers the issue mainly in the context of long-term projects. This conclusion follows naturally or automatically from acceptance of what I have called ethical benefit–cost analysis that incorporates moral sentiments (along with other axioms). The approach suggested is shown by the following example from Zerbe (2007).

The following hypothetical[29] exemplifies the sort of problem that concerns critics of discounting:

> A nuclear project is being considered that produces benefits of about $100 billion at a cost of about $60 billion in real 2007 dollar terms but, in addition, produces a toxic time bomb that will cause enormous environmental costs sometime in the far future.[30] Suppose that waste-disposal technology will contain this waste for 500 years, after which it will escape its sarcophagus and generate environmental damage of $44,384 trillion in constant current-year dollars, an amount equal to the world's GDP in 2005. The present value of these damages discounted at a 3 percent real social rate of time preference (SRTP) is about $0.017 trillion. This amount is not insignificant, but it is far less than the damage that will occur in 500 years and far too small to affect the results of the benefit–cost analysis. Discounting these damages then results in the project going forward, as the benefits are determined to exceed the costs by almost $40 billion.

Critics say that this project would be unfair to future generations and therefore that the use of discounting in benefit–cost analysis is unethical. A commonly proposed solution to the problem of unethical harm to future generations is to use low, or even negative, discount rates or not to use discount rates at all.[31] This sort of argument is an ethical plea about what our ethical values should be towards future generations, but not an effective statement about what or whether discount rates should be used or even about the relevant actual ethical considerations. The proposed solution of using no or low discount rates is ad hoc and, if generally applied, will lead to other ethical problems; for example, the adoption of projects that provide less benefit to both present and future generations.[32]

Suppose we adopt an ethical benefit–cost analysis approach, that I have elsewhere called KHM for Kaldor–Hicks Moral. Under this approach we give standing to ethical considerations of the *present* generation about future generations. This provides a solution to the ethical dilemma of the discount rate problem by acknowledging the validity of ethical concerns, while also acknowledging the values that commend use of a discount rate and remains true to the willingness to pay approach of BCA. In Table 1, mitigation and compensation measures are assumed to completely eliminate future harm. However, mitigation does not enter the KH calculus, as the mitigation costs are less than the present value of the future harm. That is, mitigation does not occur under KH, as its costs are $7.5 billion and it eliminates only $0.018 billion in harm. This occurs because KH ignores the elimination of moral harm. Similarly KH does not consider compensation, as it ignores distributional effects and the costs of compensation.[33] Thus, the NPV under KH is the same under all scenarios.[34] KH misses values and information by ignoring moral harm and the cost of actual, as opposed to hypothetical, compensation.

Table 1   A comparison of KH and KHM

Benefits and Costs	[1] No compensation or mitigation occurs (PV billions)	[2] Compensation occurs (PV billions)	[3] Mitigation occurs compensation is not feasible (PV billions)
Ordinary benefits	100	100	100
Ordinary costs	60	60	60
Harm to future generations	0.017	0.017	[0.017]
Administrative costs of actual compensation	[10]	10	infinite
Mitigation costs	[7.5]	[7.5]	7.5
Moral harm to present generation	50	[50]	[50]
KH NPV	39.983	39.983	39.983
KHM NPV	−10.017	29.981	32.5
Conclusion	Neither compensation nor mitigation appears worthwhile under KH as moral harm is ignored. The project is not worthwhile under KHM	Compensation eliminates moral harm	Mitigation eliminates moral harm

Note: *A real discount rate of 3 percent is used to discount all figures. The 0.017 figure is the discounted value of future damage expressed in billions. Figures in brackets are costs not incurred in the given scenario. Note that not all figures are relevant to KH and that mitigation and compensation are substitutes so that one or the other but not both are included in the KHM calculation.

The analysis of the nuclear waste example is quite different using KHM as part of an ethical BCA; the NPV for a scenario without mitigation or compensation is negative, a negative $10 billion under KHM, instead of the positive nearly $30 billion under KH. This is because ethical considerations are included as required by KHM, but not included under KH. When compensation or mitigation occurs, the moral harm is eliminated and the missing values are now included under KHM. Some economists object, saying that moral harm cannot exceed the present value of the future loss.[35] They would ask, 'If the current generation can compensate future generations for $0.018 billion, then wouldn't this represent the maximum willingness to pay?' The answer is no, for two reasons. First, the costs of compensating are clearly not

$0.018 million. The administrative costs of providing compensation so far into the future must be included, and these may well be enormous, perhaps infinite. The ability to provide the required long-lived institutions that would carry out compensation has been found to be improbable.[36]

Second, the parties deciding on compensation may not be the same parties that suffer moral harm. That is, for goods supplied by the public, there is a distinction between those who would purchase ethical satisfaction and those who make the decision to purchase it. The transactions costs of actually persuading decision makers to compensate may be prohibitive, especially since any attempt at agreement may suffer from a free rider problem.[37] If no purchase of ethical satisfaction occurs, one must conclude that the transactions cost of purchase is at least as great as the moral harm to the present generations.

The highest NPV under KHM is $32.5 billion, which occurs with mitigation. The inclusion of the value of ethical considerations to reduce harm to future generations provides a justification for mitigation as long as its costs are less than the moral harm. Under KHM, rough estimates of moral harm might suffice for the correct decision. The KHM approach is superior, as it gives a truer and fuller accounting. In this example mitigation gives a KHM net present value of about $32 billion. The use of ethical BCA–KHM accounts for all relevant values and results in a valuable project, whereas KH results in a project with a $10 billion loss.

Moore *et al.* (2004, Chapter 13) commendably attempt to summarize existing information and to produce recommended rates in 'Just Give Me a Number!' They make a good start in narrowing the range of reasonable rates and furnishing a foundation to use to reach a consensus among knowledgeable scholars and practitioners about what rate or rates to use. They recommend using a discount rate of 3.5 percent real where there is no crowding out of private capital and the investment is intragenerational. This seems to me quite reasonable and is approximately consistent with my own recommendation of about 3 percent real. Adjustments are to be made to cash flows using the shadow price of capital in those rare cases in which investments are large enough to affect world rates, after which the 3.5 percent discount rate should be applied. Elsewhere, Lesser and Zerbe (1994) suggest that an adjustment of 10 percent to the cash flows is sufficient to cover virtually all of the likely cases, and this is also consistent with the Moore *et al.* recommendation; where costs displace private capital, costs would be adjusted upward by 10 percent and where benefits increase private capital, benefits would be adjusted upward by 10 percent. For long lived projects (more than 50 years), Moore *et al.* would use a time declining rate. This rate I believe should not fall below 2 percent, which I suspect the lower bound that economists who have thought about discount rates would choose.

Part IV   Risk and Uncertainty in Analysis

The 1970s saw a flurry of articles devoted to risk analysis and management. A simple, important one was by Fischhoff, Slovic, and Lichtenstein (1979, Chapter 14). One must both determine risks (risk analysis or assessment) and manage them (risk management). Answers to both are required to materially address the standard question, 'How Safe is Safe Enough?' Their essay is a state of the art survey for 1979. Important conclusions are that voluntary and involuntary risks are differently valued, the acceptable risk level is inversely related to the number of people exposed to the risk, and that the acceptability of risk is related to the third power of its measured benefits. As they go on to note, 'responsible management must ask not only which dangers are the worst but which are most amenable to treatment.' A final point that seems basic and important is that hazard management problems are too broad to be solved by any one discipline. We cannot expect to get the right answer, but we can come closer by reducing analytic mistakes.

By the late 1980s authors such as Plough and Krimsky (1987, Chapter 15) are talking about risk communication. As in many aspects of life, so in risk analysis and management; communication is perhaps 60 percent of the job, if policy is to be effectual – I call this the Procter and Gamble Rule. They note two changes in the modes of historical risk communication. First, more sophisticated analytic techniques that address underlying structural problems have been developed. These have not, however, solved the underlying issues over the social context of risk. Second, at the time of this article, little had been done to learn how to relate risks to non-experts in a way that promoted wise decision-making.

The brief excerpt (section 6.7 of Chapter 6) from my 2001 book considers a charming note by Paul Portney (1992) in which he presents a fantasy in which expert opinion and citizen opinion disagree and asks what should be done. If experts find no risk attached to a particular substance in the water, yet citizens of Happyville are willing to each pay $1000 to get rid of it, should it be eliminated? At least two issues are raised. One, if the residents themselves pay for the treatment, surely the argument for treatment is stronger. Yet the experts would presumably predict they would be happier in the short run but quite unhappy in the longer run, when the treatment did not work. How should this be analyzed and how decided? Should the residents' full WTP be included? This repeats the original conflict and question: how the experts' estimate of the future WTP of the residents differs from their own estimate. The Courts have generally taken a pragmatic view of this sort of situation; where the belief is widespread and common so that, for example, property values are affected, or likely to be effected, they side with residents or consumers; where this is not the case, the Courts side with experts. This approach is not always followed but it appears to be one reasonably consistent with an economic analysis.

What if now the town doesn't pay for it but, say, the whole County? Suppose the citizens outside Happyville believe the experts. They will especially resent paying for a program they believe is worthless. Should their resentment be counted as part of a BCA analysis?

Pollak (1996, Chapter 16) points out the conflict between scientific views of risk assessment and views that emphasize the cultural and personal aspects. He notes that to reduce the discretion of experts, the EPA has attempted to develop 'generic guidelines' that apply to all substances. These constitute a set of standards such as the following: no thresholds in dose–response functions, assume linearity in dose–response functions at low doses, cumulative lifetime exposure as measure of dose, and so forth. Pollak notes, however, that science does not resolve the issue of whether or not these rules are appropriate. Justice Breyer has suggested, as noted by Pollak, a bureaucratic structure to rationalize risk regulation across fields. But, Pollak notes, rationality in the form of 'scientifically determined' guidelines is not attainable. Rationalizing procedures and standards lead to procedures that are less subjective. More importantly, it is possible to achieve, 'procedural objectivity' by reducing discretion. I would add, as does Pollak, that in the long run, standards can lead to better decisions as they lead to pressure to improve the standards. Similarly, this approach can be a way to think about ways to bring credible reassurance to the public.

Continuing the theme, Wiener and Graham (1995, Chapter 17) ask how risk trade-off decisions can be made more intelligently. They suggest the answer lies in how the decisions are structured. First, many risk failures are intervention failures according to the authors. Why, that is, do decision makers act without accounting for the full consequences of their decisions? A major failure lies in the presence of 'omitted voices'. Politics (risk transfers and the inappropriate use of heuristics) contribute also to poor decisions. The basic solution suggested is more inclusive decision-making. The case of Beargrass Creek (2000, Chapter 18) gives a demonstration of how risk and uncertainty are accounted for in recent Corp of Engineers Studies.

Scott Farrow (2004, Chapter 20) shows how the foundational work by Dixit and others can be used to implement an economically based and sensible precautionary principle. Finally Richard Williams and Kimberly Thompson (2004, Chapter 21) present a process for combining risk assessment and benefit–cost analysis. The major obstacle to integration previously has been the use of point estimates and safe upper limits to risk, rather than risk distributions. As advanced techniques have made probabilistic techniques more available, economic analysts have been able to receive distributions of risk, and the natural use of BCA in risk assessment has become apparent. Thus BCA can now be better seen as part of risk assessment and assessment and risk management viewed as a more integrated process.

Part V   Select Methodological Articles

As an interesting application of the travel cost method for estimating WTP, Cicchetti *et al.* (1971, Chapter 22, Volume II) examine the 1969 Washington D.C. Mobilization to End the Vietnam War. The numbers of participants underestimates its economic importance. Examining the distance and costs involved in attending the march suggests that the aggregate WTP represented by the march is $10.1 million (1971 dollars) if the event is examined as a consumer purchase. The march could, however, be regarded as a political statement and therefore the consumer surplus represents an intensity of political feeling. In this case both the consumer surplus and the sum of individual expenses ($17.2 million) should be counted.

The article by Palmquist and Smith (Chapter 24, Volume II) is a 2002 summary of the use of hedonic property values for policy and litigation. As this is a summary itself, and a long one, it is redundant to summarize it here. The major focus of the article is on environmental effects on property. Not cited, as it was never submitted for publication, is my early work on hedonic measures of the effect of air pollution on property values for Toronto and Hamilton, Ontario, Canada. The results for Hamilton showed similar results to those found by Ridker (1967) and cited by Palmquist and Smith; the Toronto work first showed a positive correlation between air pollution and property values. Clearly some urban values were missing from the regression. Further work with the residuals suggested again results similar to those of Ridker.

Conclusion

Economic science, like other disciplines, proceeds bit by bit from the pre-existing foundations. Thus, this Introduction will need to be updated regularly. The survey here furnishes an overview of the subject of BCA that allows some imperfect but useful glimpses of the whole field. In addition, there may be useful information for those seeking to improve particular parts of it. This Introduction offers my own idiosyncratic point of view and raises issues that I hope will intrigue others. The subject of BCA is at heart one of practicality and usefulness as Arnold Harberger has always known and it with this in mind that these articles have been chosen and this Introduction written.

Notes

* I have had substantial help in choosing articles for these volumes although the usual caveat applies. Among those who made helpful suggestions were Sandra Archibald, Anthony Boardman, Ann Bostrom, Alison Cullen, Scott Farrow, Larry Goulder, David Greenberg, Robert Hahn, Al Harberger, David Layton, Ezra Mishan, Mark Plummer, Andrew Schmitz, V. Kerry Smith, Aidan Vining, and David Weimar.

1. *See* Ezra J. Mishan (1981), pp. 120–21; Peter Hammond (1985), p. 406. For example, Harrod argued that the net social benefit from a policy could be established on the assumption that the individuals affected were equal in their capacity to enjoy income. That is, an improvement can be assumed by looking at changes in income as long as, in modern terminology, the marginal utility of income with respect to income changes is the same for all individuals. *See* Harrod, p. 387. Harrod used this reasoning to justify the 1846 repeal of the English Corn Laws, a classic test case for British economists. In response, Lionel Robbins pointed out that interpersonal comparisons of utility couldn't rest on a scientific foundation since utility cannot be measured, and that the justification for such comparisons is more ethical than scientific. Harrod complained, perhaps rather plaintively, that in the absence of comparability of utility of different individuals, 'the economist as an advisor is completely stultified.' *See* Harrod, pp. 396–97.

2. *See* Vilfredo Pareto (1896).

3. In its strong form, Pareto efficiency states that state A is preferred to state B when state A is ranked higher than state B for one person and all other persons rank A at least as high as B. If the utility (well-being) of each individual is higher in state A, then state A is preferred according to the weak form of Pareto efficiency. *See* Robin W. Boadway and Neil Bruce (1984).

4. The attraction of the Pareto notion of efficiency is that it seems to eliminate interpersonal comparisons of welfare. Some economists feel that 'the inescapable conclusion' is that if one precludes interpersonal comparisons of welfare the only logically consistent foundation analysis is the Pareto principle. Its obvious limitation is that it is not very policy relevant; few policies have no losers. This limitation resulted in a search for a more applicable measure of welfare that continues to this day and of which this article is a part.

5. *See* Duncan Black (1970), p. 227 (who shows that such a rule did not work very well for the Polish legislature).

6. As envisioned by Kaldor, non-pecuniary effects were to be included in benefit–cost analysis. Kaldor (1939, Chapter 3), p. 551 n. 1: 'An increase in the money value of the national income (given prices) is not, however, necessarily a sufficient indication of this condition [the potential compensation test or Kaldor criterion] being fulfilled: for individuals might, as a result of a certain political action, sustain losses of a non-pecuniary kind, e.g., if workers derive satisfaction from their particular kind of work, and are obliged to change their employment, something more than their previous level of money income will be necessary to secure their previous level of enjoyment; and the same applies in cases where individuals feel that the carrying out of the policy involves an interference with their individual freedom. Only if the increase in total income is sufficient to compensate for such losses and still leave something over to the rest of the community, can the project be said to be "justified" without resort to interpersonal comparisons.' Clearly it is sentiments that are to be valued and not just objects.

7. *See* Nicholas Kaldor (1939, Chapter 3), pp. 549–50.

8. *See* Kaldor (1939, Chapter 3), p.550. It was thought that politicians or non-economists should make judgments and decisions about income distribution effects.
9. John R. Hicks (1939). A few years after the creation of KH, Scitovsky (1941, Chapter 5) introduced a parallel, but slightly different, criterion that states that a project is desirable if the losers are unable in the original state of the world to bribe the potential winners not to undertake the project. Both of these criteria are referred to as potential compensation tests. Shortly after this Sir John Hicks showed that the Kaldor and Scitovsky criteria are related to measures of willingness to pay for a good and willingness to accept payment for a good.
10. It cannot be said that this second assumption of equal marginal utility of income avoids interpersonal comparisons; indeed it embraces them in a very particular way: all people are treated equally in terms of the value they place on changes in income. A leading writer on welfare economics, Mishan, certainly was aware that questions of distribution belonged to welfare economics and recognized that the separation was useful, since there was less agreement about the income distribution issues. *See* Ezra J. Mishan (1952).
11. Kaldor (1939, Chapter 5), p.551.
12. The eagerness of economists to separate considerations of efficiency from those of distribution arose from a desire to put economics on a firm base as a policy instrument. Kaldor suggests, 'the economist should not be concerned with prescriptions at all ... For, it is quite impossible to decide on economic grounds what particular pattern of income-distribution maximizes social welfare.' Kaldor, Chapter 5, p.551; *see also* A.C. Pigou (1932).
13. *See* John Chipman and James C. Moore (1978), p.578; Kaldor (1939, Chapter 3), p.551.
14. Hicks (1939), p.712.
15. Hicks (1939), p.696.
16. *See* Mitchell A. Polinsky (1989), p.5.
17. For example, Boardman, Greenberg, Vining, and Weimer note that, 'Strict use of the Kaldor–Hicks test means that information on how benefits and costs are distributed among groups is ignored in decision making.' *See* David L. Weimer and A.R. Vining (1992), p.412. Friedman also notes, 'Some analysts would like to ignore equity altogether and use the compensation test as the decisive analytic test ... [A] second rationale for relying on the compensation test is the belief that concern for equity is simply unfounded.' *See* Lee Friedman (1984), p.170. Additionally, Posner notes that wealth maximization is simply the Kaldor–Hicks test and that wealth maximization ignores distributional effects. *See* Richard A. Posner (1986), p.13; Richard A. Posner (1987), pp.132–33. McCloskey incorrectly contends that the consumer surplus measure of social happiness is the same as the national income measure. *See* Donald McCloskey (1982), p.229. Of course, the national income measure contains no measure of income distribution. Posner's claim is, however, at variance with his acceptance of valuing moral sentiments by the WTP. *See* Posner.
18. *See*, for example, Coleman (1980) and Markovits (1993, 2008).
19. Gödel's 1931 work suggests that truth is more general than provability. For more on this see http://www.miskatonic.org/godel.html. *See* Kurt Gödel (1962 [1931]), pp.173–98.
20. Lawrence H. Goulder (2007); Richard O. Zerbe (2001); Richard O. Zerbe, Yoram Bauman, and Aaron Finkle (2007).
21. Frank Ackerman and Lisa Heinzerling (2004).
22. Zerbe (2001).
23. This result is shown in Zerbe (2001), pp.86–8.
24. Zerbe (2001).
25. *See* Zhao and Kling (2001).
26. Jonathan Lesser and Richard O. Zerbe (1994).
27. Kenneth Arrow (1999).
28. $(1/((1/(1.02)^{500} + 1/(1.04)^{500})/2)^{(1/500)}) - 1$.
29. This hypothetical is motivated by the nuclear waste problem at Rocky Flats, Colorado.
30. Cases in which this sort of issue have arisen include *Baltimore Gas & Electric* v. *Natural Resources Defense Council, Inc.*, 462 U.S. 87, (1983); and *Pacific Gas and Electric Co et al.* v. *State Energy*

Resources Conservation and Development Commission, 461 U.S. 190, (1991). *See also* 123 U.S. 45 (1999).
31. *See*, for example, Derek Parfit (1992; 1994); William D. Schultze *et al.* (1981); David A. Pearce *et al.*, *Blueprint for a Green Economy/a Report.*
32. For example, consider two projects with initial costs of $100. Project A has benefits of $150 in the first period. Project B has benefits of $150 in 100 years. With negative or sufficiently low discount rates, project B is preferred. Project A however may result in greater wealth in 100 years so that it is superior for both current and future generations.
33. Under KH compensation costs are hypothetical and are merely the present value of the costs of future harm, or $0.017 billion.
34. It is not the amount of compensation actually required for those injured that is directly relevant here; rather, it is the amount of compensation the current generation thinks is correct. This is information that is likely to be obtainable through a contingent valuation survey to determine, at least in principle, the WTP or WTA of 'others' who have ethical considerations about the project.
35. This was an objection raised when presenting this example at the Western Economic Association conference.
36. Thomas Leschine and Howard McCurdy (2003).
37. Critics of benefit–cost analysis suggest that the values individuals hold as private persons differ from those they hold for public decision-making (*See generally* Elizabeth Anderson (1993); Mark Sagoff (1988), p. 11). This works better as a caution to measure the actual values than as a criticism of the methodology of benefit–cost analysis. *See* Zerbe (2001).

Acknowledgement

We would like to thank the Center for Benefit–Cost Analysis at the Evans School of the University of Washington for support. The Center is funded by the John D. and Catherine T. MacArthur Foundation.

References

Ackerman, Frank and Heinzerling, Lisa (2004), *Priceless: On Knowing the Price of Everything and the Value of Nothing*, New York, New Press, distributed by W.W. Norton.
Anderson, Elizabeth (1993), *Values in Ethics and Economics*, Cambridge: Cambridge University Press.
Arrow, Kenneth (1999), 'Discounting, morality and gaming', in *Discounting and Intergenerational Equity*, Paul Portney and John Weyant (eds), Washington D.C.: Resources for the Future.
Black, Duncan (1970), 'On Arrow's Impossibility Theorem', *Journal of Law and Economics*, **12**, 227–48.
Boadway, Robin W. and Bruce, Neil (1984), *Welfare Economics*, Oxford: Basil Blackwell.
Breyer, Stephen G. (1993), *Breaking the Vicious Circle: Toward Effective Risk Regulation*, Cambridge, MA: Harvard University Press.
Bruce, Neil and Harris, Richard G. (1982), 'Cost-benefit criteria and the compensation principle in evaluating small projects', *Journal of Political Economy*, **90** (4), 755–76.
Chipman, John and Moore, James (1978), 'The new welfare economics, 1937–1974', *International Economic Review*, **19** (3), 547–84.
Cohen, David and Knetsch, Jack (1992), 'Judicial choice and disparities between measures of economic value', *Osgood Hall Law Journal*, **30** (3), 737–70.
Coleman, Jules L. (1980), 'Exchange and auction: Philosophic aspects of the economic approach to law', *California Law Review*, **68** (2), March, 221–49.
Friedman, Leo (1984), *Microeconomic Policy Analysis*, New York: McGraw Hill.
Gödel, Kurt (1962 [1931]), 'On formally undecidable propositions of Principia mathematica and related systems'. Translated by B. Meltzer, with introduction by R.B. Braithwaite, Edinburgh, Oliver & Boyd.

Translation of paper entitled 'Über formal unentscheidbare Sätze der Principia Mathematica und verwandter System I', published in the *Monatshefte für Mathematik und Physik*, **38**, 173–98, 1931.

Goulder, Lawrence H. (2007), 'Benefit-cost analysis, individual differences, and third parties', *Research in Law and Economics*, **23**, 67–86.

Hammond, Peter (1985), 'Welfare economics', in *Issues in Contemporary Microeconomics and Welfare*, George Feiwel (ed.), London: Macmillan, pp. 405–34.

Harrod, Roy F. (1938), 'Scope and method of economics', *Economic Journal*, **48**, 383.

Hicks, John R. (1939), 'The Foundations of Welfare Economics', *Economics Journal*, **49**, 696–98.

Leschine, Thomas and McCurdy, Howard (2003), 'The stability of long run institutions', Working Paper, on file at University of Washington.

Lesser, Jonathan and Zerbe, Richard O. (1994), 'Discounting procedures for environmental (and other) projects: A comment on Kolb and Scheraga', *Journal of Policy Analysis and Management*, **13** (1), Winter, 140–56.

Lind, Robert C. (1995), 'Intergenerational equity, discounting, and the role of benefit-cost analysis in evaluating global climate policy', *Energy Policy*, **23** (4/5), 379–89.

Markovits (1993), 'A constructive critique of the traditional definition and use of the concept of "The effect of choice on allocative (economic) efficiency" why the Kaldor-Hicks test, the Coase theorem, and virtually all law and economics welfare arguments are wrong', New Haven, Conn.; London: Yale University Press.

Markovits (2008), 'Truth or economics: on the definition, prediction, and relevance of economic efficiency', *University of Illinois Legal Review*, **485**, 512–15.

McCloskey Donald (1982), *The Applied Theory of Price*, New York: Macmillan.

Mishan, Ezra J. (1952), 'The principle of compensation reconsidered', *Journal of Political Economy*, **60**, 312–22.

Mishan, Ezra J. (1981), *An Introduction to Normative Economics*, New York: Oxford University Press.

Musgrave, Richard A. and Musgrave, Peggy B. (1973), *Public Finance in Theory and Practice*, New York, NY: McGraw-Hill Book Company.

Pareto, Vilfredo (1896), *Course d'Economie Politique* Vol. II, G.H. Bousquet and G. Bousino (eds), Lausanne: F. Rouge.

Parfit, Derek (1992), 'An attack on the social discount rate', in *Values and Public Policy*, Claudia Mills (ed.), San Diego CA: Harcourt, Brace, Jovanovich.

Parfit, Derek (1994), 'The social discount rate', in *Politics of the Environment*, R.E. Goodwin (ed.), Aldershot, UK, and Brookfield, US: Edward Elgar.

Pearce, David, Markandya, Anil and Barbier, Edward B. (1989), *Blueprint for a Green Economy/a Report* [1990 printing], UK Department of the Environment, London: Earthscan.

Pigou, A.C. (1932), *The Economics of Welfare*, 4th edn, London: Macmillan.

Polinsky, Mitchell A. (1989), *An Introduction to Law and Economics*, 2nd edn, Boston: Little, Brown.

Portney, Paul (1992), 'Trouble in happyville', *Journal of Policy Analysis and Management*, **11** (1), 131–32.

Posner, Richard A. (1985), 'Wealth maximization revisited', *II Notre Dame J.L. Ethics and Public Policy*, **85**, 103.

Posner, Richard A. (1986) *Economic Analysis of Law*, 3rd edn, Boston: Little, Brown.

Posner, Richard A. (1987), 'The Justice of Economics', *Public Finance and Public Choice*, **15**, 132–33.

Ridker, Ronald Gene (1967), *Economic Costs of Air Pollution*, New York: F.A. Praeger.

Sagoff, Mark (1988), *The Economy of the Earth*, New York: Cambridge University Press.

Schmidt, A. and Zerbe, R.O. Jr. (2008) (forthcoming).

Schultze, W.D., Brookshire, D.S. and Sandler, T. (1981), 'The social rate of discount for nuclear waste disposal', *Natural Resources Journal*, **21**, 811–32.

Weimer, David L. and Vining, A.R. (1992), *Policy Analysis: Concepts and Practice*, 2nd edn, Upper Saddle River NJ: Prentice Hall.

Zerbe, Richard O. (2001), *Economic Efficiency in Law and Economics*, Cheltenham, UK, and Northampton, MA, US: Edward Elgar.

Zerbe, Richard O. (2007), 'The legal foundation of cost-benefit analysis', *Charleston Law Review*, **2** (1), 93–184.

Zerbe, Richard O. and Dively, Dwight (1994), *Benefit Cost Analysis in Theory and Practice*, New York: HarperCollins College Publishers.

Zerbe, Richard O. and Lesser, Jonathan (1991), 'What can economic analysis contribute to the "Sustainability" debate', *Contemporary Economic Policy*, **13** (3), July, 88–100.

Zerbe, Richard O. and Lesser, Jonathan (1998), 'A practitioner's guide to benefit cost analysis', *The Handbook of Public Finance* (ed. by Frederick Thompson), Marcel Dekker.

Zerbe, Richard O., Bauman, Yoram and Finkle Aaron (2006), 'A preference for an aggregate measure: A reply to Sagoff', *Ecological Economics*, **60** (1), 14–16.

Zerbe, Richard O., Bauman, Yoram and Finkle, Aaron (2007), 'An aggregate measure for benefit-cost analysis, *Research in Law and Economics*, **23**, 223–46.

Zhao, Jinhua and Kling, Catherine L. (2001), 'A new explanation for the WTP/WTA disparity', *Economics Letters*, **73**, 293–300.

Part I
Classic Historical Articles

[1]

THE GENERAL WELFARE IN RELATION TO PROBLEMS OF TAXATION AND OF RAILWAY AND UTILITY RATES*

By Harold Hotelling

IN THIS PAPER we shall bring down to date in revised form an argument due essentially to the engineer Jules Dupuit, to the effect that the optimum of the general welfare corresponds to the sale of everything at marginal cost. This means that toll bridges, which have recently been reintroduced around New York, are inefficient reversions; that all taxes on commodities, including sales taxes, are more objectionable than taxes on incomes, inheritances, and the site value of land; and that the latter taxes might well be applied to cover the fixed costs of electric power plants, waterworks, railroads, and other industries in which the fixed costs are large, so as to reduce to the level of marginal cost the prices charged for the services and products of these industries. The common assumption, so often accepted uncritically as a basis of arguments on important public questions, that "every tub must stand on its own bottom," and that therefore the products of every industry must be sold at prices so high as to cover not only marginal costs but also all the fixed costs, including interest on irrevocable and often hypothetical investments, will thus be seen to be inconsistent with the maximum of social efficiency. A method of measuring the loss of satisfactions resulting from the current scheme of pricing, a loss which appears to be extremely large, will emerge from the analysis. It will appear also that the inefficient plan of requiring that all costs, including fixed overhead, of an industry shall be paid out of the prices of its products is responsible for an important part of the instability which leads to cyclical fluctuations and unemployment of labor and other resources.

A railway rate is of essentially the same nature as a tax. Authorized and enforced by the government, it shares with taxes a considerable degree of arbitrariness. Rate differentials have, like protective tariffs and other taxes, been used for purposes other than to raise revenue. Indeed, the difference between rail freight rates between the same points, according as the commodity is or is not moving in international transport, has been used in effect to nullify the protective tariff. While it has not generally been perceived that the problems of taxation and those of railway rate making are closely connected, so that two independent bodies of economic literature have grown up, nevertheless the underlying unity is such that the considerations applicable to

* Presented at the meeting of the Econometric Society at Atlantic City, December 28, 1937, by the retiring president.

taxation are very nearly identical with those involved in proper rate making. This essential unity extends itself also to other rates, such as those charged by electric, gas, and water concerns, and to the prices of the products of all industries having large fixed costs independent of the volume of output.

I. THE CLASSICAL ARGUMENT

Dupuit's work of 1844 and the following years[1] laid the foundation for the use of the diagram of Figure 1 by Marshall and other econo-

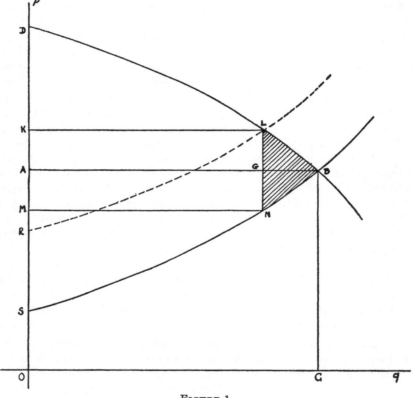

FIGURE 1

mists. A rising supply curve *SB* is used, and is sometimes regarded as coinciding with the marginal-cost curve. Such a coincidence would arise if there were free competition among producers, in the sense that each would regard the price as fixed beyond his control, and adjust

[1] Collected and reprinted with comments by Mario di Bernardi and Luigi Einaudi. "De l'Utilité et de sa Mesure," *La Riforma Soziale*, Turin, 1932.

his production so as to obtain maximum net profits. This condition is approximated, for example, in most agriculture. DB is a declining demand curve. The buyers are presumed to compete freely with each other. The actual quantity and price are the co-ordinates of the intersection B. Then it is supposed that a tax t per unit is imposed upon the sellers. Since this is a uniform increment to marginal cost, the marginal-cost curve SB is lifted bodily to the new position RL, at height $t = SR = NL$ above its former position.

Three conclusions have been derived with the help of this figure, all of which must be reviewed to take account of the interrelations of the particular commodity in question with others. One of these arguments has almost universally been accepted, but must be rejected when account is taken of related commodities. A second has been accepted, and is actually true. The third has been condemned and attacked by a long line of prominent economists, but in the light of the more thorough analysis made possible by modern mathematical methods must now in its essence be accepted. The first is the proposition that since the point L of intersection of the demand curve with the supply curve RL is higher by GL, a fraction of the tax rate NL, than the intersection B with the tax-free curve SB, therefore the price is increased as a result of the tax, by an amount less than the tax. That this conclusion is not necessarily true when account is taken of related commodities I have shown in an earlier paper.[2] The second proposition—whose conclusion remains valid under certain plausible assumptions[2a]—is that, since L is to the left of B, the quantity of the taxed commodity will diminish. With this diminution is associated an approximately measurable net social loss.

The third argument is based on Dupuit's, and is of primary concern here. Dupuit sought a criterion of the value to society of roads, canals, bridges, and waterworks. He pointed out the weakness of calling the value of a thing only what is paid for it, since many users would if

[2] "Edgeworth's Taxation Paradox and the Nature of Demand and Supply Functions," *Journal of Political Economy*, Vol. 40, 1932, pp. 577–616. Edgeworth had discovered, and maintained against the opposition of leading economists, that a monopolist controlling two products may after the imposition of a tax on one of them find it profitable to reduce both prices, besides paying the tax. However he regarded this as a "mere curiosum," unlikely in fact to occur, and peculiar to monopoly. But it is shown in the paper cited that the phenomenon is also possible with free competition, and is quite likely to occur in many cases, either under monopoly or under competition.

[2a] On p. 600 of the paper just cited the conclusion is reached that it is reasonable to regard the matrix of the quantities h_{ij} as negative definite. From this and equation (19) of that page it follows that a positive increment in the tax t_j on the jth commodity causes a negative increment in the quantity of this commodity.

necessary pay more than they actually do pay. The total benefit he measured by the aggregate of the maximum prices that would be paid for the individual small units of the commodity (a term used here to include services, e.g., of canals) corresponding to the costs of alternatives to the various uses. If $p = f(q)$ is the cost of the best alternative to the use of an additional small unit of the commodity when q units are already used, then, if q_0 units are used altogether,

$$(1) \qquad\qquad \int_0^{q_0} f(q)dq$$

is the total benefit, which Dupuit called *utilité*, resulting from the existence of the canal or other such facility making possible the commodity (service) in question. Since $p = f(q)$ is the ordinate of the demand curve DB in Figure 1, this total benefit is the total area under the arc DB. To obtain what is now called the *consumers' surplus* we must subtract the amount paid by consumers, namely the product of the price by the quantity, represented by the rectangle $OCBA$. Thus the consumers' surplus is represented by the curvilinear triangle ABD. There is also a *producers' surplus* represented by the lower curvilinear triangle SBA; this is the excess of the money received by producers (the area of the rectangle $OCBA$) over the aggregate of the marginal costs, which is represented by the curvilinear figure $OCBS$. The total net benefit, representing the value to society of the commodity, and therefore the maximum worth spending from the public funds to obtain it, is the sum of consumers' and producers' surpluses, and is represented by the large curvilinear triangle SBD. It is the difference between the integral (1) of the demand function and the integral between the same limits of the marginal-cost function.

Imposition of the tax, by raising the price to the level of KL, appears to reduce the consumers' surplus to the curvilinear area KLD. The new producers' surplus is the area RLK, which equals SNM. There is also a benefit on account of the government revenue, which is the product of the new quantity MN by the tax rate NL, and is therefore measured by the area of the rectangle $MNLK$. The sum of these three benefits is $SNLD$. It falls short of the original sum of producers' and consumers' surpluses by the shaded triangular area NBL.

This shaded area represents the net social loss due to the tax, and was discovered by Dupuit. If the tax is small enough, the arcs BL and NB may be treated as straight lines, and the area of the triangle is, to a sufficient approximation, half the product of the base NL by the altitude GB. Since GB is the decrement in the quantity produced and consumed because of the tax, and NL is the tax rate, we may say that the net loss resulting from the tax is half the product of the tax rate by the decrement in quantity. But since the decrement in quantity is, for small taxes, proportional to the tax rate, it then follows that the net loss is proportional to the *square* of the tax rate This fact also was remarked upon by Dupuit.

This remarkable conclusion has frequently been ignored in discussions in which it should, if correct, be the controlling consideration. The open attacks upon it seem all to be based on an excessive emphasis on the shortcomings of consumers' and producers' surpluses as measures of benefits. These objections are four in number: (1) Since the demand curve for a necessity might for very small quantities rise to infinity, the integral under the curve might also be infinite. This difficulty can be avoided by measuring from some selected value of q greater than zero. Since in the foregoing argument it is only *differences* in the values of the surpluses that are essentially involved, it is not necessary to assign exact values. The situation is the same as in the physical theory of the potential, which involves an arbitrary additive constant and so may be measured from any convenient point, since only its differences are important. (2) Pleasure is essentially non-measurable and so, it is said, cannot be represented by consumers' surplus or any other numerical magnitude. We shall meet this objection by establishing a generalized form of Dupuit's conclusion on the basis of a ranking only, without measurement, of satisfactions, in the way represented graphically by indifference curves. The same analysis will dispose also of the objections (3) that the consumers' surpluses arising from different commodities are not independent and cannot be added to each other, and (4) that the surpluses of different persons cannot be added.

In connection with the last two points, it will be observed that if we have a set of n related commodities whose demand functions are

$$p_i = f_i(q_1, q_2, \cdots, q_n), \qquad (i = 1, 2, \cdots, n),$$

then the natural generalization of the integral representing total benefit, of which consumers' surplus is a part, is the line integral

(2) $$\int (f_1 dq_1 + f_2 dq_2 + \cdots + f_n dq_n), \quad \cdot$$

taken from an arbitrary set of values of the q's to a set corresponding to the actual quantities consumed. The net benefit is obtained by subtracting from (2) a similar line integral in which the demand functions $f_1, f_2, \cdots, f_n$ are replaced by the marginal-cost functions

$$g_i(q_1, q_2, \cdots, q_n), \qquad (i = 1, 2, \cdots, n).$$

If we put

$$h_i = f_i - g_i,$$

the total net benefit is then measured by the line integral

(3) $$w = \int \sum h_i dq_i.$$

Such indeterminacy as exists in this measure of benefit is only that
which arises with variation of the value of the integral when the path
of integration between the same end points is varied. The condition
that all these paths of integration shall give the same value is that the
integrability conditions

$$\frac{\partial h_i}{\partial q_j} = \frac{\partial h_j}{\partial q_i}$$

be satisfied. In the paper on "Edgeworth's Taxation Paradox" already
referred to, and more explicitly in a later note,[3] I have shown that there
is a good reason to expect these integrability conditions to be satisfied,
at least to a close approximation, in an extensive class of cases. If they
are satisfied, the surpluses arising from different commodities, and also
the surpluses belonging to different persons, may be added to give a
meaningful measure of social value. This breaks down if the variations
under consideration are too large a part of the total economy of the
person or the society in question; but for moderately small variations,
with a stable price level and stable conditions associated with commodities not in the group, the line integral w seems to be a very satisfactory measure of benefits. It is invariant under changes in units of
measure of the various commodities, and also under a more general
type of change of our way of specifying the commodities, such as replacing "bread" and "beef" by two different kinds of "sandwiches."
For these reasons the total of all values of w seems to be the best
measure of welfare that can be obtained without considering the proportions in which the total of purchasing power is subdivided among
individuals, or the general level of money incomes. The change in w that
will result from a proposed new public enterprise, such as building a
bridge, may fairly be set against the cost of the bridge to decide
whether the enterprise should be undertaken. It is certainly a better
criterion of social value than the aggregate $\sum p_i q_i$ of tolls that can be
collected on various classes of traffic, as Dupuit pointed out for the
case of a single commodity or service. The actual calculation of w in
such a case would be a matter of estimation of vehicular and pedestrian
traffic originating and terminating in particular zones, with a comparison of distances by alternative routes in each case, and an evaluation

[3] "Demand Functions with Limited Budgets," *Econometrica*, Vol. 3, 1935, pp.
66–78. A different proof is given by Henry Schultz in the *Journal of Political
Economy*, Vol. 41, 1933, p. 478.

248 HAROLD HOTELLING

of the savings in each class of movement. Determination whether to build the bridge by calculation merely of the revenue $\sum p_i q_i$ obtainable from tolls is always too conservative a criterion. Such public works will frequently be of great social value even though there is no possible system of charging for their services that will meet the cost.

II. THE FUNDAMENTAL THEOREM

But without depending in any way on consumers' or producers' surpluses, even in the form of these line integrals, we shall establish a generalization of Dupuit's result. We take our stand on the firm ground of a system of preferences expressible by a function

$$\Phi = \Phi(q_1, q_2, \cdots, q_n)$$

of the quantities $q_1, q_2, \cdots, q_n$ of goods or services consumed by an individual per unit of time. If the function Φ, Pareto's *ophélimité*, has the same value for one set of q's as for another, then the one combination of quantities is as satisfactory to the individual in question as the other. For two commodities, Φ is constant along each of a set of "indifference curves"; and likewise for n commodities, we may think of a system of hypersurfaces of which one passes through each point of a space of n dimensions, whose Cartesian co-ordinates are the quantities of the various goods. These hypersurfaces we shall refer to as *indifference loci*.

It is to be emphasized that the indifference loci, unlike measures of pleasure, are objective and capable of empirical determination. One interesting experimental attack on this problem was made by L. L. Thurstone, who by means of questionnaires succeeded in mapping out in a tentative manner the indifference loci of a group of girls for hats, shoes, and coats.[4] Quite a different method, involving the study of actual family budgets, also appears promising.[5] The function Φ, on the other hand, is not completely determinable from observations alone, unless we are prepared to make some additional postulate about independence of commodities, as was done by Irving Fisher in defining utility,[6] and by Ragnar Frisch.[7] The present argument does not depend on any such assumption, and therefore allows the replacement of Φ by

[4] "The Indifference Function," *Journal of Social Psychology*, Vol. 2, 1931, pp. 139–167, esp. pp. 151 ff.

[5] R. G. D. Allen and A. L. Bowley, *Family Expenditure*, London, 1935.

[6] *Mathematical Investigations in the Theory of Value and Prices*, New Haven, 1892.

[7] *New Methods of Measuring Marginal Utility*, Tübingen, 1932. Dr. Frisch also considered the possibility of substitute commodities in his *Confluence Analysis*, and in collaboration with Dr. F. V. Waugh made an attempt to handle this situation statistically.

an arbitrary increasing function Ψ of Φ, such as sinh Φ, or $\Phi + \Phi^3$. The statements we shall make about Φ will apply equally to every such function Ψ. Negative values of the q's are the quantities of labor, or of goods or services, produced by the individual. It is with the understanding that this kind of indeterminacy exists that we shall sometimes refer to Φ and Ψ as utility functions.

Consider now a state in which income and inheritance taxes are used to pay for the construction of bridges, roads, railroads, waterworks, electric power plants, and like facilities, together with other fixed costs of industry; and in which the facilities may be used, or the products of industry consumed, by anyone upon payment of the additional net cost occasioned by the particular use or consumption involved in each case. This additional net cost, or marginal cost, will include the cost of the additional labor and other resources required for the particular item of service or product involved, beyond what would be required without the production of that particular item. Where facilities are not adequate to meet all demands, they are made so either by enlargement, or by checking the demand through inclusion in the price of a rental charge for the facilities, adjusted so as to equate demand to supply. Such a rental cost, of which the site rental of land is an example, is an additional source of revenue to the state; it must not be confused with carrying charges on invested capital, or with overhead cost. Some such charge is necessary to discriminate economically among would-be users of the facilities. Another example is that of water in a dry country; if demand exceeds supply, and no enlargement of supply is possible, a charge must be made for the water sufficient to reduce the demand to the supply. Such a charge is an element of marginal cost as here defined.

The individual retains, after payment of taxes, a money income m. At prices $p_1, p_2, \cdots, p_n$ determined in the foregoing manner, he can buy or sell such quantities $q_1, q_2, \cdots, q_n$ as he pleases, subject to the condition that

$$(4) \qquad\qquad \sum p_i q_i = m.$$

The combination he chooses will be such as to make his indifference function Φ a maximum, subject to the condition (4). We may put aside as infinitely improbable—having probability zero, though not impossible—the contingency that two different sets of values of the q's satisfying (4) will give the same degree of satisfaction. We therefore have that, if $q_1, \cdots, q_n$ are the quantities chosen under these conditions, and if $q_1', \cdots, q_n'$ are any other set of quantities satisfying (4), so that

$$(5) \qquad\qquad \sum p_i q_i' = m,$$

then

$$\Phi = \Phi(q_1, \cdots, q_n) > \Phi(q_1', \cdots, q_n') = \Phi + \delta\Phi,$$

say. Hence, putting $q_i' = q_i + \delta q_i$ in (5) and subtracting (4), we find that any set of values of $\delta q_1, \cdots, \delta q_n$ satisfying

(6) $$\sum p_i \delta q_i = 0,$$

and not all zero, must have the property that

(7) $$\delta\Phi = \Phi(q_1 + \delta q_1, \cdots, q_n + \delta q_n) - \Phi(q_1, \cdots, q_n) < 0.$$

Let us now consider an alteration of the system by the imposition of excise taxes and reduction of income taxes. Some of the taxes may be negative; that is, they may be bounties or subsidies to particular industries; or, instead of being called taxes, they may be called tolls, or charges for services or the use of facilities over and above marginal cost. There ensues a redistribution of production and consumption. Let p_i, q_i, and m be replaced respectively by

(8) $$p_i' = p_i + \delta p_i, \quad q_i' = q_i + \delta q_i, \quad m' = m + \delta m,$$

where the various increments δp_i, δq_i are not constrained to be either positive or negative; some may have one sign and some the other. The yield of the new excise taxes will be the sum, over all individuals, of the quantity which for the particular individual we are considering is $\sum q_i' \delta p_i$. (We use the sign $\sum$ to denote summation over all commodities, including services.) Since this person's income tax is reduced by δm, the net increment of government revenue

(9) $$\delta r = \sum q_i' \delta p_i - \delta m$$

may be imputed to him, in the sense that summation of δr over all persons gives the total increment of government revenue.[8] We neglect changes in administrative costs and the like.

The individual's budgetary limitation now takes the form $\sum p_i' q_i' = m'$, which may also be written

(10) $$\sum (p_i + \delta p_i)(q_i + \delta q_i) = m + \delta m.$$

[8] A friendly critic writes. "It is not clear to me why δp_i should be the exact per-unit revenue of the state from an excise tax which raises the price by δp_i from its old level. . . . I should expect (referring to Figure 1) an increase in price of GL, and a revenue to the state of NL." The answer to this is that the summation of δr over all persons includes the sellers as well as the buyers, and that the government revenue per unit of the commodity is derived in part from each— though it must be understood that the contribution of either or both may be negative. In the classical case represented by Figure 1, the buyers' δp is the height GL, while the sellers' is NG in magnitude and is negative. Since q' is positive for the buyer and negative for the seller, the product $q'\delta p$ is in each case positive. The aggregate of these positive terms is the total tax revenue from the commodity.

Subtracting the budget equation (4) corresponding to the former system and using (8) we find that

$$(11) \qquad \delta m = \sum q_i' \delta p_i + \sum p_i \delta q_i.$$

Substituting this in (9) we find that

$$(12) \qquad \delta r = - \sum p_i \delta q_i.$$

Suppose that, to avoid disturbing the existing distribution of wealth, the excise taxes paid by each individual (in the sense of incidence just defined; not in the sense of handing over the money to the government in person) are exactly offset by the decrement in his income tax. Then $\delta r = 0$. From (12) it then follows that (6) is satisfied. Except in the highly improbable case of all the δq's coming out exactly zero, it would then follow from (7) that this man's new state is worse than his old. The change from income to excise taxes has resulted in a net loss of satisfactions. Conversely, if we start from a system of excise taxes, or any system in which sales are not at marginal cost, this argument shows that there is a possible distribution of personal income taxes such that everyone will be better satisfied to change to the system of income taxes with sales at marginal cost. The problem of the distribution of wealth and income among persons or classes is not involved in this proposition.

This argument may be expressed in geometrical language as follows: Let $q_1, \cdots, q_n$ be Cartesian coordinates in a space of n dimensions. Through each point of this space passes a hypersurface whose equation may be written $\Phi(q_1, \cdots, q_n) = $ constant. The individual's satisfaction is enhanced by moving from one to another of these hypersurfaces if the value of the constant on the right side of the equation is thereby increased; this will usually correspond to moving in a direction along which some or all of the q's increase. The point representing the individual's combination of goods is however constrained in the first instance to lie in the hyperplane whose equation is (4). In this equation the p's and m are to be regarded as constant coefficients, while the q's vary over the hyperplane. A certain point Q on this hyperplane will be selected, corresponding to the maximum taken by the function Φ, subject to the limitation (4). If the functions involved are analytic, Q will be the point of tangency of the hyperplane with one of the "indifference loci." The change in the tax system means that the individual must find a point Q' in the new hyperplane whose equation is $\sum p_i' q_i' = m'$. If we denote the coordinates of Q' by $q_1', \cdots, q_n'$, we have, upon substituting them in the equation of this new hyperplane, $\sum p_i' q_i' = m'$. If the changes in prices and m are such as to leave the government revenue unchanged, (12) must vanish; that is,

HAROLD HOTELLING

$$\sum p_i q_i' = \sum p_i q_i.$$

Since $\sum p_i q_i = m$, this shows that $\sum p_i q_i' = m$; that is, that Q' lies on the same hyperplane to which Q was confined in the first place. But since Q was chosen among all the points on this hyperplane as the one lying on the outermost possible indifference locus, for which Φ is a maximum, and since we are putting aside the infinitely improbable case of there being other points on the hyperplane having this maximizing property, it follows that Q' must lie on some other indifference locus, and that this will correspond to a lesser degree of satisfaction.

The fundamental theorem thus established is that *if a person must pay a certain sum of money in taxes, his satisfaction will be greater if the levy is made directly on him as a fixed amount than if it is made through a system of excise taxes which he can to some extent avoid by rearranging his production and consumption* In the latter case, the excise taxes must be at rates sufficiently high to yield the required revenue *after* the person's rearrangement of his budget. The redistribution of his production and consumption then represents a loss to him without any corresponding gain to the treasury. This conclusion is not new. What we have done is to establish it in a rigorous manner free from the fallacious methods of reasoning about one commodity at a time which have led to false conclusions in other associated discussions.

The conclusion that a fixed levy such as an income or land tax is better for an individual than a system of excise taxes may be extended to the whole aggregate of individuals. In making this extension it is necessary to neglect certain interactions among the individuals that may be called "social" in character, and are separate and distinct from the interactions through the economic mechanisms of price and exchange. An example of such "social" interactions is the case of the drunkard who, after adjusting his consumption of whisky to what he considers his own maximum of satisfaction, beats his wife, and makes his automobile a public menace on the highway. The restrictive taxation and regulation of alcoholic liquors and certain other commodities do not fall under the purview of our theorems because of these social interactions which are not economic in the strict sense. With this qualification, and neglecting also certain possibilities whose total probability is zero, we have:

If government revenue is produced by any system of excise taxes, there exists a possible distribution of personal levies among the individuals of the community such that the abolition of the excise taxes and their replacement by these levies will yield the same revenue while leaving each person in a state more satisfactory to himself than before.

It is in the sense of this theorem that we shall in later sections speak of "the maximum of total satisfactions" or "the maximum of general welfare" or "the maximum national dividend" requiring as a necessary, though not sufficient, condition that the sale of goods shall be without additions to price in the nature of excise taxes. These looser expressions are in common use, and are convenient; when used in this paper, they refer to the proposition above, which depends only on rank ordering of satisfactions; there is no connotation of adding utility functions of different persons.

The inefficiency of an economic system in which there are excise taxes or bounties, or in which overhead or other charges are paid by excesses of price over marginal cost, admits of an approximate measure when the deviations from the optimum system described above are not great, if, as is customary in this and other kinds of applied mathematics, we assume continuity of the indifference function and its derivatives. Putting for brevity

$$\Phi_i = \frac{\partial \Phi}{\partial q_i}, \qquad \Phi_{ij} = \frac{\partial^2 \Phi}{\partial q_i \partial q_j},$$

we observe that the maximum of Φ, subject to the budget equation (4), requires that

$$(13) \qquad \Phi_i = \lambda p_i, \qquad (i = 1, 2, \cdots, n),$$

where the Lagrange multiplier λ is the marginal utility of money. Differentiating this equation gives

$$(14) \qquad \Phi_{ij} = \lambda \frac{\partial p_i}{\partial q_j} + p_i \frac{\partial \lambda}{\partial q_j}.$$

Expanding the change in the utility or indifference function we obtain, with the help of (13), (12), and (14),

$$(15) \qquad \delta \Phi = \sum \Phi_i \delta q_i + \tfrac{1}{2} \sum \sum \Phi_{ij} \delta q_i \delta q_j + \cdots$$

$$= - \lambda \delta r + \tfrac{1}{2} \lambda \sum \sum \frac{\partial p_i}{\partial q_j} \delta q_i \delta q_j - \tfrac{1}{2} \delta r \sum \frac{\partial \lambda}{\partial q_j} \delta q_j + \cdots$$

where the terms omitted are of third and higher order, and are therefore on our assumptions negligible. Their omission corresponds to Dupuit's deliberate neglect of curvilinearity of the sides of the shaded triangle in Figure 1. With accuracy of this order we have further,

$$\delta p_i = \sum_i \frac{\partial p_i}{\partial q_j} \delta q_j, \qquad \delta \lambda = \sum_i \frac{\partial \lambda}{\partial q_j} \delta q_j.$$

Upon substituting for these expressions, (15) reduces to

$$(16) \qquad \delta \Phi = - \lambda \delta r + \tfrac{1}{2} \lambda \sum \delta p_i \delta q_i - \tfrac{1}{2} \delta r \delta \lambda + \cdots.$$

If the readjustment from the original state of selling only at marginal cost, with income taxes to pay overhead, is such as to leave $\delta r = 0$ as above, (16) reduces to

$$(17) \qquad \delta \Phi = \tfrac{1}{2}\lambda \sum \delta p_i \delta q_i + \cdots,$$

where the terms omitted are of higher order.

As another possibility we may consider a substitution of excise for income tax so arranged as to leave this person's degree of satisfaction unchanged. Upon putting $\delta \Phi = 0$ in (16) and solving for δr we have, apart from terms of higher order,

$$(18) \qquad \delta r = \tfrac{1}{2} \sum \delta p_i \delta q_i + \cdots.$$

This is the net loss to the state in terms of money, so far as this one individual is concerned. The net loss in terms of satisfactions is merely the product of (18) by the marginal utility of money λ, that is, (17), if we neglect terms of higher order than those written. The total net loss of state revenue resulting from abandonment of the system of charging only marginal costs, and uncompensated by any gain to any individual, is the sum of (18) over all individuals. If the prices are the same for all, this sum is of exactly the same form as the right-hand member of (18), with δq_i now denoting the increment (positive or negative) of the total quantity of the ith commodity.

The approximate net loss

$$(19) \qquad \tfrac{1}{2} \sum \delta p_i \delta q_i$$

may be regarded as the sum of the areas of the shaded triangles in the older graphic demonstration. It should however be remembered that the readjustment of prices caused by excise taxes is not necessarily in the direction formerly supposed, that some of the quantities and some of the prices may increase and some decrease, and that some of the terms of the foregoing sum may be positive and some negative. But the aggregate of all these varying terms is seen by the foregoing argument to represent a dead loss, and never a gain, as a result of a change from income to excise taxes, or away from a system of sales at marginal cost. Any inaccuracy of the measure (19) is of only the same order as the error involved in replacing the short arcs LB and NB in Figure 1 by straight segments, and can never affect the sign.

It is remarkable, and may appear paradoxical, that without assuming any particular measure of utility or any means of comparison of one person's utility with another's, we have been able to arrive at (19) as a valid approximation measuring in money a total loss of satisfactions to many persons. That the result depends only on the conception of ranking, without measurement, of satisfactions by each person is readily apparent from the foregoing demonstration; or we may for any person replace Φ by another function Ψ as an index of the same system of ranks among satisfactions. If we do this in such a way that the derivatives are continuous, we shall have $\Psi = F(\Phi)$, where F is an increasing function with continuous derivatives. Upon writing the expressions for the first and second derivatives of Ψ in terms of those of F and Φ it may be seen that the foregoing formulae involving Φ are necessary and sufficient conditions for the truth of the same equations with Ψ written in place of Φ. The result (18) is independent of which system of indicating ranks is used. The fundamental fact here is that *arbitrary* analytic transformations, even of very complicated functional forms, always induce *homogeneous linear* transformations of differentials.

Not only the approximation (19) but also the whole expression indicated by (18) are absolutely invariant under all analytic transformations of the utility functions of all the persons involved. These expressions depend only on the demand and supply functions, which are capable of operational determination. They represent simply the money cost to the state of the inefficiency of the system of excise taxation, when this is arranged in such a way as to leave unchanged the satisfactions derived from his private income by each person.

The arguments based on Figure 1 have been repeated with various degrees of hesitation, or rediscovered independently, by numerous writers including Jevons, Fisher, Colson, Marshall, and Taussig. Marshall considered variations of the figure involving downward-sloping cost curves and multiple solutions, and was led to the proposal (less definite than that embodied in the criterion established by our theorem) that incomes and increasing-cost industries be taxed to subsidize decreasing-cost ones. He observed the difficulty of defining demand curves and consumers' surplus in view of the interdependence of demand for various commodities. These difficulties are indeed such that it now seems better to stop talking about demand *curves*, and to substitute demand *functions*, which will in general involve many variables, and are not susceptible of graphic representation in two or three dimensions. Marshall was one of those misled by Figure 1 into thinking that a tax of so much per unit imposed on producers of a commodity leads necessarily to an increase of price by something less than the tax.

Though the marginal-cost curve in Figure 1 slopes upward, no such assumption is involved in the present argument. It is perfectly possible that an industry may be operated by the state under conditions of diminishing marginal cost. The criterion for a small increase in production is still that its cost shall not exceed what buyers are willing to pay for it; that is, the general welfare is promoted by offering it for

HAROLD HOTELLING

sale at its marginal cost. It may be that demand will grow as prices decline until marginal cost is pushed to a very low level, far below the average cost of all the units produced. In such a case the higher cost of the first units produced is of the same character as fixed costs, and is best carried by the public treasury without attempting to assess it against the users of the particular commodity as such. Our argument likewise makes no exception of cases in which more than one equilibrium is possible. Where there are multiple solutions we have that sales at marginal cost are a necessary, though not a sufficient, condition for the optimum of general welfare.

The confusion between marginal and average cost must be avoided. This confusion enters into many of the arguments for laissez-faire policies. It is frequently associated with the calm assumption, as a self-evident axiom, that the whole costs of every enterprise must be paid out of the prices of its products. This fallacious assumption appears, for example, in recent writings on government ownership of railroads. It has become so ingrained by endless repetition that it is not even stated in connection with many of the arguments it underlies.

III. TAX SYSTEMS MINIMIZING DEAD LOSS

The magnitude of the dead loss varies greatly according to the objects taxed. While graphic arguments are of suggestive value only, it may be observed from Figure 1 that the ratio of the dead loss NBL to the revenue $MNLK$ depends greatly on the slopes of the demand and supply curves in the neighborhood of the equilibrium point B. It appears that if either the demand or the supply curve is very steep in this neighborhood, the dead loss will be slight. For a tax on the site rental value of land, whose supply curve is vertical, the dead loss drops to zero. A tax on site values is therefore one of the very best of all possible taxes from the standpoint of the maximum of the total national dividend. It is not difficult to substantiate this argument in dealing with related commodities; for the δq_i's corresponding to such a tax are zero. Since the incidence is on the owner of the land and cannot be shifted by any readjustment of production, it has the same advantages as an income tax from the standpoint of maximizing the national dividend. The fact that such a land tax cannot be shifted seems to account for the bitterness of the opposition to it. The proposition that there is no ethical objection to the confiscation of the site value of land by taxation, if and when the nonlandowning classes can get the power to do so, has been ably defended by H. G. Brown.[9]

Land is the most obviously important, but not by any means the only good, whose quantity is nearly or quite unresponsive to changes

[9] *The Theory of Earned and Unearned Incomes*, Columbia, Missouri, 1918.

in price, and which is not available in such quantities as to satisfy all demands. Holiday travel sometimes leads to such a demand for the use of railroad cars as to bring about excessive and uncomfortable crowding. If the total demand the year around is not sufficiently great to lead to the construction of enough more cars to relieve the crowding, the limited space in the existing cars acquires a rental value similar to that of land. Instead of selling tickets to the first in a queue, or selling so many as to bring about an excessive crowding that would neutralize the pleasure of the holiday, the economic way to handle this situation would be to charge a sufficiently high price to limit the demand. The revenue thus obtained, like the site value of land, may properly be taken by the state. The fact that it helps to fill the treasury from which funds are drawn to pay for replacement of the cars when they wear out, and to cover interest on their cost in the meantime, does not at all mean that any attempt should be made to equate the revenue from car-space rental to the cost of having the cars in existence.

Another thing of limited quantity for which the demand exceeds the supply is the attention of people. Attention is desired for a variety of commercial, political, and other purposes, and is obtained with the help of billboards, newspaper, radio, and other advertising. Expropriation of the attention of the general public and its commercial sale and exploitation constitute a lucrative business. From some aspects this business appears to be of a similar character to that of the medieval robber barons, and therefore to be an appropriate subject for prohibition by a state democratically controlled by those from whom their attention is stolen. But attention attracting of some kinds and in some degree is bound to persist; and where it does, it may appropriately be taxed as a utilization of a limited resource. Taxation of advertising on this basis would be in addition to any taxation imposed for the purpose of diminishing its quantity with a view to restoring the property of attention to its rightful owners.

If for some reason of political expediency or civil disorders it is impossible to raise sufficient revenue by income and inheritance taxes, taxes on site values, and similar taxes which do not entail a dead loss of the kind just demonstrated, excise taxes may have to be resorted to. The problem then arises of so arranging the rates on the various commodities as to raise the required sum while making the total dead loss a minimum. A solution of this theoretical question, taking account of the interrelations among commodities, is given on p. 607 of the study of Edgeworth's taxation paradox previously referred to.

IV. EFFECT ON DISTRIBUTION OF WEALTH

We have seen that, if society should put into effect a system of sales at marginal cost, with overhead paid out of taxes on incomes, inheritances, and the site value of land, there would exist a possible system of compensations and collections such that everyone would be better off than before. As a practical matter, however, it can be argued in particular cases that such adjustments would not in fact be made; that the general well-being would be purchased at the expense of sacrifices by some; and that it is unjust that some should gain at the expense of others, even when the gain is great and the cost small. For example, it appears that the United States Government can by introducing cheap hydroelectric power into the Tennessee Valley raise the whole level of economic existence, and so of culture and intelligence, in that region, and that the benefits enjoyed by the local population will be such as to exceed greatly in money value the cost of the development, taking account of interest. But if the government demands for the electricity generated a price sufficiently high to repay the investment, or even the interest on it, the benefits will be reduced to an extent far exceeding the revenue thus obtained by the government. It is even possible that no system of rates can be found that will pay the interest on the investment; yet the benefits may at the same time greatly exceed this interest in value. It appears to be good public policy to make the investment, and to sell the electric energy at marginal cost, which is extremely small. But this will mean that the cost will have to be paid in part by residents of other parts of the country, in the form of higher income and inheritance taxes. Those who are insistent on avoiding a change in the distribution of wealth at all costs will object.

One answer to this objection is that the benefits from such a development are not by any means confined to the persons and the region most immediately affected. Cheap power leads for example to production of cheap nitrates, which cut down the farmers' costs even in distant regions, and may benefit city dwellers in other distant regions. A host of other industries brought into being by cheap hydroelectric power have similar effects in diffusing general well-being. There is also the benefit to persons who on account of the new industrial development find that they can better themselves by moving into the Tennessee Valley, or by investing their funds there. Furthermore, the nation at large has a stake in eradicating poverty, with its accompaniments of contagious diseases, crime, and political corruption, wherever these may occur.

A further answer to the objection that benefits may be paid for by those who do not receive them when such a development as that of the Tennessee Valley is undertaken is that no such enterprise stands alone. A government willing to undertake such an enterprise is, for the same reasons, ready to build other dams in other and widely scattered places, and to construct a great variety of public works. Each of these entails

benefits which are diffused widely among all classes. A rough random-
ness in distribution should be ample to ensure such a distribution of
benefits that most persons in every part of the country would be
better off by reason of the program as a whole.

If new electric-power, railroad, highway, bridge, and other developments are widely undertaken at public expense, always on the basis
of the criterion of maximizing total benefits, the geographical distribution of the benefits, and also the distribution among different
occupational, racial, age, and sex groups, would seem pretty clearly to
be such that every such large group would on the whole be benefited
by the program. There are, however, two groups that might with some
reason expect not to benefit. One of these consists of the very wealthy.
Income and inheritance taxes are likely to be graduated in such a way
that increases in government spending will be paid for, both directly
and ultimately, by those possessed of great wealth, more than in the
proportion that the number of such persons bears to the whole population. It would not be surprising if the benefits received by such persons
as a result of the program of maximum total benefit should fall short
of the cost to them.

The other class that might expect not to benefit from such a program consists of land speculators. If we consider for example a bridge,
it is evident that the public as a whole must pay a certain cost of
construction, whether the bridge be paid for by tolls or by taxes on the
site value of land in the vicinity. There will be much more use of the
bridge if there are no tolls, so that the public as a whole will get more
for its money if it pays in the form of land taxes. But it will not in
general be possible to devise a system of land taxes that will leave
everyone, without exception, in a position as good as or better than
as if the bridge had not been built and the taxes had not been levied.
Landowners argue that the benefits of the bridge go to others, not to
them; and even in cases in which land values have been heightened
materially as a result of a new bridge, the landowners have been known
to be vociferous in favor of a toll system. Payment for the bridge by
tolls (when this is possible) has the advantage that no one seems to be
injured, since each one who pays to cross the bridge has the option of
not using it, and is in that case as well off as if the bridge did not exist.
This reasoning is not strictly sound, since the bridge may have put out
of business a ferry which for some users was more convenient and
economical. Nevertheless, it retains enough cogency to stiffen the resistance of real-estate interests to the more economical system of paying for the bridge by land taxes.

Attempts at excessive accuracy in assessing costs of public enterprises according to benefits received tend strongly to reduce the total

of those benefits, as in the case of the bridge. The welfare of all is promoted rather by a generous support of projects for communal spending in ways beneficial to the public at large, without attempting to recover from each enterprise its cost by charges for services rendered by that enterprise. The notion that public projects should be "self-liquidating," on which President Hoover based his inadequate program for combating the oncoming depression, while attractive to the wealthier taxpayers, is not consistent with the nation's getting the maximum of satisfactions for its expenditure.

V. DISTINCTION OF OPTIMUM FROM COMPETITIVE CONDITIONS

The idea that all will be for the best if only competition exists is a heritage from the economic theory of Adam Smith, built up at a time when agriculture was still the dominant economic activity. The typical agricultural situation is one of rising marginal costs. Free competition, of the type that has usually existed in agriculture, leads to sales at marginal cost, if we now abstract the effects of weather and other uncertainty, which are irrelevant to our problem. Since we have seen that sales at marginal cost are a condition of maximum general welfare, this situation is a satisfactory one so far as it goes. But the free competition associated with agriculture, or with unorganized labor, is not characteristic of enterprises such as railroads, electric-power plants, bridges, and heavy industry. It is true that a toll bridge may be in competition with other bridges and ferries; but it is a very different kind of competition, more in the nature of duopoly. To rely on such competition for the efficient conduct of an economic system is to use a theorem without observing that its premises do not apply. Free competition among toll-bridge owners, of the kind necessary to make the conclusion applicable, would require that each bridge be parallelled by an infinite number of others immediately adjacent to it, all the owners being permanently engaged in cutthroat competition. If the marginal cost of letting a vehicle go over a bridge is neglected, it is clear that under such conditions the tolls would quickly drop to zero and the owners would retire in disgust to allow anyone who pleased to cross free.

The efficient way to operate a bridge—and the same applies to a railroad or a factory, if we neglect the small cost of an additional unit of product or of transportation—is to make it free to the public, so long at least as the use of it does not increase to a state of overcrowding. A free bridge costs no more to construct than a toll bridge, and costs less to operate; but society, which must pay the cost in some way or other, gets far more benefit from the bridge if it is free, since in this case it will be more used. Charging a toll, however small, causes some people to waste time and money in going around by longer but cheaper ways, and prevents others from crossing. The higher the toll, the greater is the damage done in this way; to a first approximation, for small tolls, the damage is proportional to the square of the toll rate, as Dupuit showed. There is no such damage if the bridge is paid for by income, inheritance, and land taxes, or for example by a tax on the

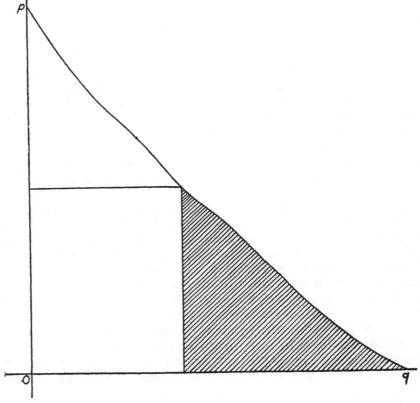

FIGURE 2

real estate benefited, with exemption of new improvements from taxation, so as not to interfere with the use of the land. The *distribution* of wealth among members of the community is affected by the mode of payment adopted for the bridge, but not the total wealth, except that it is diminished by bridge tolls and other similar forms of excise. This is such plain common sense that toll bridges have now largely disappeared from civilized communities. But New York City's bridge and tunnels across the Hudson are still operated on a toll basis, because of the pressure of real estate interests anxious to shift the tax burden to wayfarers, and the possibility of collecting considerable sums from persons who do not vote in the city.

If we ignore the interrelations of the services of a bridge with other goods, and also the slight wear and tear on the bridge due to its use, we may with Dupuit represent the demand for these services by a curve such as that in Figure 2. The total benefit from the bridge is then represented by the whole area enclosed between the demand curve and the axes, provided the bridge is free. All this benefit goes to users of the bridge. But if a toll is charged, of magnitude corresponding to the height of the horizontal line, the recipients of the toll are benefited to an extent represented by the area of the rectangle, whose base is the number of crossings and whose height is the charge for each crossing. But the number of crossings has diminished, the benefit to bridge users has shrunk to the small triangular area at the top, and the total benefit has decreased by the area of the shaded triangle at the right. This triangle represents the net loss to society due to the faulty method of paying for the bridge. If, for example, the demand curve is a straight line, and if the owners set the toll so as to bring them a maximum return, the net loss of benefit is 25 per cent of the total.

These are the pertinent considerations if the bridge is already in existence, or its construction definitely decided. But if we examine the general question of the circumstances in which bridges ought to be built, a further inefficiency is disclosed in the scheme of paying for bridges out of tolls. For society, it is beneficial to build the bridge if the total area in the figure exceeds the interest, amortization, and maintenance costs. But if the bridge must be paid for by tolls, it will not be built unless it is expected that these costs will be exceeded by the rectangular area alone. This area cannot, for our example of a linear demand function, be greater than half the total. We may in this case say that the toll system has 75 per cent efficiency in use, but only 50 per cent efficiency in providing new bridges. In each case the efficiency will be further diminished by reason of the cost of collecting and accounting for the tolls.

The argument about bridges applies equally to railroads, except that in the latter case there is some slight additional cost resulting from an extra passenger or an extra shipment of freight. My weight is such that when I ride on the train, more coal has to be burned in the locomotive, and I wear down the station platform by walking across it. What is more serious, I may help to overcrowd the train, diminishing the comfort of other travelers and helping to create a situation in which additional trains should be run, but often are not. The trivial nature of the extra costs of marginal use of the railroads has from the first been realized by the railroad managements themselves; indeed, it is implied in the amazingly complex rate structures they build up in the attempt to squeeze the last possible bit of revenue from freight and passenger traffic. If in a rational economic system the railroads were operated for the benefit of the people as a whole, it is plain that if people were to be induced by low rates to travel in one season rather than another, the season selected should be one in which travel would otherwise be light, leaving the cars nearly empty, and not a season in which they are normally overcrowded. Actually, our railroads run trains about the country in winter with few passengers, while crowding multitudes of travelers into their cars in summer. The rates are made high in winter, lower in summer, on the ground that the summer demand is more elastic than that of the winter travelers, who are usually on business rather than pleasure, and thus decide the question of a trip with less sensitiveness to the cost.

VI. COMPLEXITY OF ACTUAL RAILWAY RATES AND REMOTENESS FROM MARGINAL COST

The extreme and uneconomic complexity of railway freight and passenger rate structures is seldom realized by those not closely in touch with them. A few random examples will illustrate the remoteness of actual rates from what may be presumed to be marginal costs, which railway managements will find it profitable to cover even by the lowest rates. Prior to the last enforced reduction of American passenger rates the regular round-trip fare between New York City and Wilkesbarre, Pa. was $11.04. But at various times between 1932 and 1935 round-trip tickets good for limited periods were sold at $2.50, $6.00, $6.10, and $6.15. Between New York and Chicago the round-trip fare in the same period varied between $33 and $65 for identical accommodations. Between New York and Washington the ordinary round-trip fare was $18.00, but an "excursion rate" of $3.50 was applied spasmodically.

The lumber and logging activities of the country, which have been at a standstill for several years, are suffering from freight rates which in many important cases nearly equal, and even exceed, the mill price of the lumber. Thus from the large sawmills at and near Baker, Oregon, which produce lumber for the New York market, the freight amounts to $16.50 per thousand board feet. For No. 3 Common Ponderosa Pine, the grade shipped in largest quantities, the price of one-by-four inch boards ranged in the autumn of 1933 from $14.50 to $15.50 at the mill. Thus the New York wholesale buyer must pay more than double the mill price, solely on account of freight. The freight even to Chicago approximated the mill price. For No. 4 Common, also an important grade, the price was $12.50 per thousand board feet at the mill, but the New York buyer had to pay $29.00. A few months earlier, the prices were about $8 per thousand board feet less than those just given, so that the railroads received far more than the mill operators. It is hard to escape the conclusion that these high freight rates interfered seriously with the sale of lumber.

One advantage of the system of charging only marginal cost would be a great simplification of the rate structure. This is a great desideratum. It must not be assumed too readily that every purchaser distributes his budget accurately to obtain the maximum of satisfactions, or the most efficient methods of production, when the determination of the optimum requires the study of an encyclopedic railroad tariff, together with complicated trial-and-error calculations. Neither, from the standpoint of a railroad, can it be assumed that the enormously complex rate differentials have been determined at all accurately for the purposes for which they were designed. These complicated rate structures further contravene the public interest in that they enhance artificially the advantages of large over small concerns. When immense calculations are required to determine the optimum combinations of transportation with other factors of production, the large concerns are in a distinctly better position to carry out the calculations and obtain the needed information.

VII. MARGINAL COST DEPENDS ON EXTENT OF UNUSED CAPACITY

In the determination of marginal cost there are, to be sure, certain complications. When a train is completely filled, and has all the cars it can haul, the marginal cost of carrying an extra passenger is the cost of running another train. On the other hand, in the more normal situation in which the equipment does not carry more than a small part of its capacity load, the marginal cost is virtually nothing. To avoid a sharp increase in rates at the time the train is filled, an averaging process is needed in the computation of rates, based on the probability of having to run an extra train. Further, in cases in which the available equipment is actually used to capacity, and it is not feasible or is of doubtful wisdom to increase the amount of equipment, something in the nature of a rental charge for the use of the facilities should, as indicated above, be levied to discriminate among different users in such a way that those willing to pay the most, and therefore in accordance with the usual assumptions deriving the most benefit, would be the ones obtaining the limited facilities which many desire. This rental charge for equipment, which for passenger travel would largely take the place of fares, should never be so high as to limit travel to fewer persons than can comfortably be accommodated, except for unpredictable fluctuations. The proceeds from the charge could be added to the funds derived from income, inheritance, and land taxes, and used to pay a part of the overhead costs. But there should be no attempt to pay all the overhead from such rental charges alone.

Except in the most congested regions, there would, however, be no such charge for the use of track and stations until the volume of traffic comes to exceed enormously the current levels. An example is the great under-utilization of the expensive Pennsylvania Station, in New York City, whose capacity was demonstrated during the war by bringing into the city the trains of the Erie and the Baltimore and Ohio railroads. These trains are now required to stop on the New Jersey shore, constituting a wasteful nuisance which had existed before government operation, which was replaced by the more efficient procedure by the government, but which was resumed when the lines were handed back to their private owners.

VIII. THE ATTEMPT TO PAY FIXED COSTS FROM RATES AND PRICES CONTRIBUTES TO RIGIDITY AND SO TO INSTABILITY

One of the evil consequences of the attempt to pay overhead out of operating revenue is the instability which it contributes to the economic system as a whole. This is illustrated by the events leading to the depression. The immense and accelerating progress of science and technology led to the creation of new industries and the introduction of wonderfully efficient new methods. The savings from the new methods were so great that corporate profits and real incomes surged upwards. So large were the profits and so satisfactory the dividends that the operating officials of great industries did not feel under compulsion to push up the selling prices of their products to the levels corresponding to maximum monopoly profit. Because they kept their prices low, while paying relatively high wages, the physical volume of goods produced and transferred became enormous. The impulse to produce, with possibly some altruistic motives besides, tempered the desire for profits in many concerns. But under a profit system this could not last. As the prices of corporate shares rose, pressure developed to pay dividends equivalent to interest on the higher prices. This pressure would probably have led presently to gradual increases in the money prices of manufactured products, if the general level of prices had remained stationary. Such however was not the case. The general level of prices was declining.

And decline it must, according to the equation of exchange, when there was such a great new flood of goods to be sold. The vast increase in physical volume of goods, created by the new technology, called for a greater use of money, if the price level was to be maintained. This need was met for a time by increases in bank loans and deposits, and in the velocity of circulation. But neither bank loans nor velocities could continue to increase as fast as goods, and prices had to fall. The fall was not uniform. Corporations under increasing pressure to cover their overhead and pay high dividends out of earnings were strongly averse to reducing the selling prices of their products, when these selling prices were already below the points which would yield maximum profit. For several years prior to the crash, the prices of manufactured products stuck fast, while the proportion of national expenditure paid for these products continued to increase. This left a shrinking volume of money payments to be made for the remaining commodities, and these, including particularly the agricultural, had to come down in price. If, as the general price level fell, railroad, utility, and manufacturing concerns had reduced their selling prices proportionately, the prosperity of the years 1922 to 1928 might have continued. But such reductions in selling prices were not possible when an increasing volume of overhead charges had to be paid out of earnings. The intensified efforts to do this resulted in a pushing up of "real" prices of manufactured products—that is, of the ratios of their prices to the general price level—and of "real" transportation rates. Indeed, with a rapidly falling general price level, railroad freight rates, measured in money, were actually increased in 1931. This increase of 15 per cent on a large range of commodities, like the subsequent increases in suburban commuters' passenger rates, was obtained on the ground that the railroads needed the money to cover their overhead costs, though their operating costs had declined. Of course the effect was to make the depression worse, by stopping traffic which would have flowed at the lower rates. On the theory that bond interest and other such items must be paid out of operating revenues, the railroads were "entitled" to the higher rates, for their business had fallen off. But economic equilibrium calls for a rising rather than a declining supply curve; if demand falls off, the offer price must be reduced in order to have the offered services taken. This antithesis of rising railway rates, when general prices and the ability to pay are falling, well illustrates the disequilibrating consequences of the idea that overhead costs must be paid from operating revenues. There now seems to be a possibility of a repetition of the disastrous 15 per cent freight-rate increase in a time of decline.[10]

This explanation of the contrast of the prosperity of 1928 with the cessation of production in the following years rests upon the contrast of the system of prices which results from the whole-hearted devotion

[10] Since this was written the Interstate Commerce Commission has allowed a part of this proposed increase and postponed consideration of a request for a passenger fare rise.

of different concerns to their own respective profits, with the system of prices best for the economic organism as a whole. Under free competition, with no overhead, these two systems of prices tend to become identical. Where there are overhead costs, competition of the ideally free type is not permanently possible. Monopoly prices develop; and a system of monopoly prices is not a system which can serve human needs with maximum advantage.

IX. CRITERION AS TO WHAT INVESTMENTS ARE SOCIALLY WORTH WHILE

When a decision whether or not to construct a railway is left to the profit motive of private investors, the criterion used is that the total revenue $\sum p_i q_i$, being the sum of the products of the rates for the various services by the quantities sold, shall exceed the sum of operating costs and carrying charges on the cost of the enterprise. If no one thinks that there will be a positive excess of revenue, the construction will not be undertaken. We have seen in Section V that this rule is, from the standpoint of the general welfare, excessively conservative. What, then, should society adopt to replace it?

A less conservative criterion than that of a sufficient revenue for total costs is that *if some distribution of the burden is possible such that everyone concerned is better off than without the new investment, then there is a prima facie case for making the investment.* This leaves aside the question whether such a distribution is *practicable.* It may often be good social policy to undertake new enterprises even though some persons are put in a worse position than before, provided that the benefits to others are sufficiently great and widespread. It is on this ground that new inventions are permitted to crowd out less efficient industries. To hold otherwise would be to take the side of the hand weavers who tried to wreck the power looms that threatened their employment. But the rule must not be applied too harshly. Where losses involve serious hardship to individuals, there must be compensation, or at least relief to cover subsistence. Where there are many improvements, the law of averages may be trusted to equalize the benefits to some extent, but never completely. It will always be necessary to provide for those individuals upon whom progress inflicts special hardship; if it were not possible to do this, we should have to reconcile ourselves to greater delays in the progress of industrial efficiency.

Subject to this qualification of avoiding excessive hardship to individuals, we may adopt the criterion stated. In applying it there will be the problem of selecting a limited number of proposed investments, corresponding to the available capital, from among a larger number of possibilities. The optimum solution corresponds to application of our criterion to discriminate between each pair of combinations. The total amount of calculation and exercise of judgment required will not, however, be so great as might be suggested by the number of pairs of combinations, which is immense. Numerous means are available to shorten this labor. One of these is by the application of the line integral (3), namely

$$w = \int \sum h_i dq_i,$$

which provides a measure of value corresponding to the sum of consumers' and producers' surpluses. The part of w constituting the generalized consumers' surplus is (2); the validity of this line integral as a measure of an individual's increment of satisfaction corresponding to sufficiently small changes in the q's may be seen merely by replacing p_i in (13) by f_i, and noticing that for small changes the marginal utility of money λ changes little, so that f_i is very nearly proportional to the derivative of the utility function Φ. Hence the increment in Φ is proportional to the sum of the integrals of the f's, apart from terms of higher order; and the factor of proportionality λ is such as to measure this increment in money so as to be comparable to an increase in income. Similar considerations apply to the part of w corresponding to producers' surplus.

Defenders of the current theory that the overhead costs of an industry must be met out of the sale of its products or services hold that this is necessary in order to find out whether the creation of the industry was a wise social policy. Nothing could be more absurd. Whether it was wise for the government to subsidize and its backers to construct the Union Pacific Railroad after the Civil War is an interesting historical question which would make a good subject for a dissertation, but it would be better, if necessary, to leave it unsolved than to ruin the country the Union Pacific was designed to serve by charging enormous freight rates and claiming that their sum constitutes a measure of the value to the country of the investment. Such an experimental solution of a historical question is too costly. In addition, it is as likely as not to give the wrong answer. The sum of the freight and passenger rates received, minus operating costs, is not the line integral $w = \int \sum h_i dq_i$, which with some accuracy measures the value to society of the investment, but is more closely related to the misleading measure of value $\sum p_i q_i$. In other words, the revenue resembles the area of the rectangle in Figure 2, while the possible benefit corresponds to the much larger triangular area. The revenue is the thing that appeals to an investor bent on his own profit, but as a criterion of whether construction ought in the public interest to be under-taken, it is biased in the direction of being too conservative.

Regardless of their own history, the fact is that we now have the railroads, and in the main are likely to have them with us for a considerable time in the future. It will be better to operate the railroads for the benefit of living human beings, while letting dead men and dead investments rest quietly in their graves, and to establish a system of rates and services calculated to assure the most efficient operation. When the question arises of building new railroads, or new major industries of any kind, or of scrapping the old, we shall face, not a historical, but a mathematical and economic problem. The question then will be whether the aggregate of the generalized surpluses of the form (3) is likely to be great enough to cover the anticipated cost of the new investment. This will call for a study of demand and cost functions by economists, statisticians, and engineers, and perhaps for a certain amount of large-scale experimentation for the sake of gaining information about these functions. The amount of such experiment and research which could easily be paid for out of the savings resulting from operation of industry in the public interest is very large indeed. Perhaps this is the way in which we shall ultimately get the materials for a scientific economics.

Columbia University
New York, N. Y.

MANAGING EDITOR'S NOTE: Professor Frisch has written a brief criticism of Professor Hotelling's argument, but because of limitations of space it has had to be held over for publication in a later issue.—D. H. L.

[2]

INTERPERSONAL COMPARISONS OF UTILITY:
A COMMENT

In the course of his interesting paper on the " Scope and Method of Economics," Mr. Harrod raises once more the question of the status of interpersonal comparisons of utility. I do not wish directly to controvert any of his statements on this matter. But it occurs to me that a short account of the genesis of the views which I have put forward, and which form the subject of his friendly comment, might at once elucidate the nature of our differences and make clear to those who rejoice in the spectacle of disunity how very slender the practical implications of these differences actually are. I must apologise in advance for the personal nature of the argument. I am under no illusion concerning the interest of my intellectual difficulties in so far as they are purely my own. But, in so far as they can be regarded as typical, a brief explanation may perhaps facilitate mutual understanding.

My own attitude to problems of political action has always been one of what I might call provisional utilitarianism. I am far from thinking that thorough-going utilitarianism *à la Bentham* is an ultimate solution of any of the major problems of social philosophy. But I have always felt that, as a first approximation in handling questions relating to the lives and actions of large masses of people, the approach which counts each man as one, and, on that assumption, asks which way lies the greatest happiness, is less likely to lead one astray than any of the absolute systems. I do not believe, and I never have believed, that in fact men are necessarily equal or should always be judged as such. But I do believe that, in most cases, political calculations which do not treat them *as if* they were equal are morally revolting.

It follows, therefore, that when I came to the study of economics, I had the strongest bias in favour of a utilitarian analysis. The delicate balancing of gain and loss through intricate repercussions of policy which I found in such works as the *Economics of Welfare*, fascinated me; and I was powerfully attracted by the proposition, urged so forcefully by Edwin Cannan and others, that recent developments of the theory of value could be invoked to demonstrate the desirability of the mitigation of inequality. When I look back on that frame of mind, I find it easy to understand the belief of Bentham and his followers that they had found the open sesame to problems of social policy.

But, as time went on, things occurred which began to shake my belief in the existence of so complete a continuity between politics and economic analysis. I never thought of abandoning my provisional utilitarianism as a working political philosophy. But I began to feel that there were profound difficulties in a complete fusion between what Edgeworth called the economic and the hedonistic calculus. I am not clear how these doubts first suggested themselves; but I well remember how they were brought to a head by my reading somewhere—I think in the works of Sir Henry Maine—the story of how an Indian official had attempted to explain to a high-caste Brahmin the sanctions of the Benthamite system. " But that," said the Brahmin, " cannot possibly be right. I am ten times as capable of happiness as that untouchable over there." I had no sympathy with the Brahmin. But I could not escape the conviction that, if I chose to regard men as equally capable of satisfaction and he to regard them as differing according to a hierarchical schedule, the difference between us was not one which could be resolved by the same methods of demonstration as were available in other fields of social judgment.

This led me to a re-examination of the propositions of the text-books. It did not take long to see that the " law " of diminishing marginal utility, assumed by Cannan and others in the analysis of inequality, differed from the " law " of the same name invoked in the analysis of exchange and that the difference was precisely the introduction of this assumption of equal capacity for satisfaction. I did not see so quickly that the same assumptions were involved in most pronouncements relating to movements of the social dividend. But, gradually, reflection on the tariff problem and such-like matters forced me to this view. I found that this attitude was already maintained by a great number of continental writers : and further research on index-number problems only strengthened my conclusion. Mr. Harrod very properly draws attention to the fact that, if we do not make the assumption of equal capacity for satisfaction, we are precluded from asserting that the repeal of the Corn Laws tended to increase the general welfare. In lecturing upon these subjects for many years, I have continually used this self-same illustration. By the time I came to write the book to which Mr. Harrod has referred, I had acquired the settled habit of classifying the propositions of traditional political economy according as they did or did not involve this particular assumption.

Having reached this stage, however, I was confronted with a further question. The assumptions of the propositions which did not involve interpersonal comparisons of utility were assumptions which had been verified by observation or introspection, or, at least, were capable of such verification. The assumptions involving interpersonal comparison were certainly not of this order. " I see no means," Jevons had said, " whereby such comparison can be accomplished. Every mind is inscrutable to every other mind and no common denominator of feeling is possible." Would it not be better, I asked myself, quite frankly to acknowledge that the postulate of equal capacity for satisfaction *came from outside*, that it rested upon ethical principle rather than upon scientific demonstration, that it was not a judgment of fact in the scientific sense, but rather a judgment of value—perhaps, even, in the last analysis, an act of will ? Ought it not to be made clear, for instance, that theories of public finance which went beyond tracing the effects of given measures on prices, quantities produced and such-like measurable magnitudes, and which attempted to sum social gain or loss, were not, strictly speaking, economic science ? The analysis of the effects of a small tax on particular prices and quantities of particular products would rest upon scientific demonstration. But according as Maine's Brahmin or Bentham, Hitler or St. Paul, laid down the postulates of interpersonal comparison, the valuation of these effects in terms of social welfare would be different.

The answer seemed obvious. The distinction existed. It ought to be recognised. But I confess that at first I found the implications very hard to swallow. For it meant, as Mr. Harrod has rightly insisted, that economics as a science could say nothing by way of prescription. It could say whether a certain course of action could lead to a desired end. It could judge the consistency of different policies. But, in itself, it passed no verdict of good or bad. It was not possible to say that economic science showed that free trade was justifiable, that inequality should be mitigated, that the income tax should be graduated, and so forth. I attached high importance to these propositions ; and the realisation that I could not claim for them scientific justification was profoundly antipathetic.

Further thought, however, convinced me that this was irrational. I was bound to admit that what I was doing was simply to carry one stage further a very common and almost universally accepted practice. All economists recognised that their prescriptions regarding policy were conditional upon the acceptance of norms lying outside economics. All that I was doing was only to recognise that, in a field of generalisations hitherto thought to involve no normative elements, there were in fact such elements concealed. The traditional political economy, for instance, had taught that free trade increased social wealth. It had fully recognised that the prescription, built on this analysis, that free trade was a good thing, was contingent on the assumption that an increase of wealth was to be desired : if defence, for instance, was more than opulence, free trade had to go. All that I proposed to do was to make it clear that the statement that social wealth was increased, itself involved an arbitrary element—that the proposition should run, *if* equal capacity for satisfaction on the part of the economic subjects be assumed, *then* social wealth can be said to be increased. Objective analysis of the effects of the repeal of duties only showed that consumers gained and landlords lost. That such an arbitrary element was involved was plain. It seemed no less plain, therefore, that, here as elsewhere, it should be explicitly recognised.

Moreover, when I came to ask myself how much persuasive force was really lost to the principles of action which I valued so highly, I could not resist the conviction that my initial perturbation had been unnecessary, and even somewhat ridiculous. Of course I could see that, if I could prove scientifically that men were equally capable of happiness, that would be a great help in arguing with people who wished to treat them as if they were not. But although I had looked upon certain deductions from concealed assumptions of equality as scientific, I had never thought of claiming that particular status for the assumption of equality itself. If Maine's Brahmin had told me that members of such and such a caste or race were eligible for taxation ten times as heavy as others, since they were only one-tenth as capable of true happiness, the strength of my resistance would not have rested on belief in the social law of diminishing marginal utility. The belief that that helped could only rest on the prospect of putting up a smoke-screen of technical jargon to terrify an ignorant antagonist—surely not a very creditable manœuvre. Why should one be frightened, I asked, of taking a stand on judgments which are not scientific, if they relate to matters outside the world of science ? To recognise the claims of science in fields where scientific method was applicable was one thing ; to attempt to claim scientific sanction for judgments of questions not capable of scientific proof was another. The one was an obligation on rational man; the other, the stratagem of spiritual uncertainty. Was it not only the timidity of an age which had lost all confidence in ultimate values which led us to attempt to claim " scientific " justifications for attitudes which in the nature of things could not be justified (or refuted) by appeal to laboratory methods?

Arrived at this point, it was not difficult to see certain positive advantages in the course I had felt compelled to follow. It did at least make it possible to keep a whole range of intellectual questions free from squabbles concerning philosophical matters. I had no objection to philosophical squabbles. But it did seem to me that great harm had been done by their intrusion into spheres where they were completely irrelevant. It might be necessary to discuss the political philosophy underlying the prescriptions of the theory of public finance. But it was completely futile to discuss the political philosophy underlying the positive theorems relating to the effects on prices and quantities produced of the imposition of small taxes. Yet, because of failure to separate out clearly normative and positive elements, this kind of discussion was continually arising. No one who had ploughed through the turgid mass of German work in this field could doubt the desirability of keeping philosophy in its proper place.

At the same time it seemed to me that, if this procedure were adopted, the due place of philosophy in the general scheme of social studies would be all the better emphasised. Once it was recognised how completely neutral were the findings of economic science, it would surely leap to the eye how necessary it was, if these findings were to be applied to human improvement, that they should be supplemented by political philosophy. In the past, it seemed to me, a failure to recognise the arbitrary element in certain of the findings of traditional Political Economy had been conducive to too facile a use of these findings in framing prescriptions for action. The achievement of wealth seemed so obviously desirable that it was a temptation to imagine that the propositions of economics could be translated forthwith into prescriptions for action without much further regard for considerations of political philosophy. I was not at all desirous of preventing economists from giving prescriptions. I was, indeed, fully convinced that, if a man tried to talk much about the ultimate questions of politics without a knowledge of economics, it was something of a miracle if he talked sense. But I felt that anything which brought out the necessity for independent and systematic study of the ends which prescriptions based on economics might serve, had profound pedagogical and practical advantages. The postulate of equal capacity for satisfaction, for instance, about which all the trouble had arisen, needed much more refinement if it were to be applied sensibly : it was possible, indeed, that an equalitarian postulate involving no reference to satisfaction might prove in the end to be more suitable. At the London School of Economics, where I was trained, and in the Oxford School of Philosophy, Politics and Economics,where I was teaching when I did most of my thinking about these things, this necessity was recognised in the structure of the curriculum ; it seemed to me that what I was doing was simply to give it further emphasis. I confess I was very surprised when I found myself held up as advocating for economists the impossible and sterile virtue of never attempting to apply their conclusions— rapt astronomers of the social universe deigning no aid to navigators in search of the desired haven. All that I had intended— and it was certainly possible to cite the most explicit statements to this effect—was that they might better realise the exact connection between the normative and the positive, and that their practice as political philosophers might be made thereby more self-conscious.

This is a long story about the genesis of two or three pages in an essay that was written some time ago, and which was never expected to be the subject of much discussion. And if it were a matter of personal defence against all the accusations of imbecility, social indifference and even sinister interest which have been made against their author, I certainly should not have thought it any more worth while writing now than at any time in the past. But I am distressed that anything that I have said should give rise to recurrent dispute which suggests to the outside world a disunity among economists which I am persuaded does not exist : my essay was meant to defend economics from lay misunderstanding, not to provoke new confusion. Looking back, I do not feel that I have much to retract. I still cannot believe that it is helpful to speak as if interpersonal comparisons of utility rest upon scientific foundations—that is, upon observation or introspection. I am perhaps more alive than before to the extraordinary difficulties surrounding the whole philosophy of valuation. But I still think, when I make interpersonal comparisons (as, for instance, when I am deciding between claims affecting the satisfactions of two very spirited children), that my judgments are more like judgments of value than judgments of verifiable fact. Nevertheless, to those of my friends who think differently, I would urge that, in practice, our difference is not very important. They think that propositions based upon the assumption of equality are essentially part of economic science. I think that the assumption of equality comes from outside, and that its justification is more ethical than scientific. But we all agree that it is fitting that such assumptions should be made and their implications explored with the aid of the economist's technique. Our dispute relates to definitions and to logical status, not to our obligations as human beings. In the realm of action, at any rate, the real difference of opinion is not between those who dispute concerning the exact area to be designated by the adjective scientific, but between those who hold that human beings should be treated as if they were equal and those who hold that they should not.

LIONEL ROBBINS

London School of Economics.

[3]

WELFARE PROPOSITIONS OF ECONOMICS AND INTER-PERSONAL COMPARISONS OF UTILITY

IN the December 1938 issue of the ECONOMIC JOURNAL Professor Robbins returns to the question of the status of inter-personal comparisons of utility.[1] It is not the purpose of this note to question Professor Robbins' view regarding the scientific status of such comparisons; with this the present writer is in entire agreement. Its purpose is rather to examine the relevance of this whole question to what is commonly called "welfare economics." In previous discussions of this problem it has been rather too readily assumed, on both sides, that the scientific justification of such comparisons determines whether "economics as a science can say anything by way of prescription." The disputants have been concerned only with the status of the comparisons; they were—apparently—agreed that the status of prescriptions necessarily depends on the status of the comparisons.

This is clearly Mr. Harrod's view. He says:[2] "Consider the Repeal of the Corn Laws. This tended to reduce the value of a specific factor of production—land. It can no doubt be shown that the gain to the community as a whole exceeded the loss to the landlords—*but only if individuals are treated in some sense as equal.* Otherwise how can the loss to some—and that there was a loss can hardly be denied—be compared with the general gain? If the incomparability of utility to different individuals is strictly pressed, not only are the prescriptions of the welfare school ruled out, but all prescriptions whatever. The economist as an adviser is completely stultified, and unless his speculations be regarded as of paramount aesthetic value, he had better be suppressed completely." This view is endorsed by Professor Robbins:[3] "All that I proposed to do was to make clear that the statement that social wealth was increased [by free trade] itself involved an arbitrary element—that the proposition should run, *if* equal capacity for satisfaction on the part of the economic subjects be assumed, *then* social wealth can be said to be increased. Objective analysis of the effects of the repeal of duties only showed that consumers gained and landlords lost. That such an arbitrary element was

---

[1] "Interpersonal Comparisons of Utility: A Comment," ECONOMIC JOURNAL, December 1938, pp. 635–691.

[2] "Scope and Method of Economics," *ibid.*, September 1938, pp. 396–397. (Italics mine.)

[3] *Loc. cit.*, p. 638.

involved was plain. It seemed no less plain, therefore, that, here as elsewhere, it should be explicitly recognised."

It can be demonstrated, however, that in the classical argument for free trade no such arbitrary element is involved at all. The effects of the repeal of the Corn Laws could be summarised as follows : (i) it results in a reduction in the price of corn, so that the *same* money income will now represent a higher real income ; (ii) it leads to a shift in the distribution of income, so that some people's (*i.e.*, the landlord's) incomes (at any rate in money terms) will be lower than before, and other people's incomes (presumably those of other producers) will be higher. Since aggregate money income can be assumed to be unchanged, if the landlords' income is reduced, the income of other people must be correspondingly increased. It is only as a result of this consequential change in the distribution of income that there can be any loss of satisfactions to certain individuals, and hence any need to compare the gains of some with the losses of others. But it is always possible for the Government to ensure that the previous income-distribution should be maintained intact : by compensating the " landlords " for any loss of income and by providing the funds for such compensation by an extra tax on those whose incomes have been augmented. In this way, everybody is left as well off as before in his capacity as an income recipient ; while everybody is better off than before in his capacity as a consumer. For there still remains the benefit of lower corn prices as a result of the repeal of the duty.

In all cases, therefore, where a certain policy leads to an increase in physical productivity, and thus of aggregate real income, the economist's case for the policy is quite unaffected by the question of the comparability of individual satisfactions ; since in all such cases it is *possible* to make everybody better off than before, or at any rate to make some people better off without making anybody worse off. There is no need for the economist to prove—as indeed he never could prove—that as a result of the adoption of a certain measure nobody in the community is going to suffer. In order to establish his case, it is quite sufficient for him to show that even if all those who suffer as a result are fully compensated for their loss, the rest of the community will still be better off than before. Whether the landlords, in the free-trade case, should in fact be given compensation or not, is a political question on which the economist, *qua* economist, could hardly pronounce an opinion. The important fact is that, in the argument in favour of free trade, the fate of the landlords is wholly irrelevant : since the benefits of free trade are by no means destroyed even if the landlords are fully reimbursed for their losses.[1]

This argument lends justification to the procedure, adopted by Professor Pigou in *The Economics of Welfare*, of dividing " welfare economics " into two parts : the first relating to production, and the second to distribution. The first, and far the more important part, should include all those propositions for increasing social welfare which relate to the increase in aggregate production; all questions concerning the stimulation of employment, the equalisation of social net products, and the equalisation of prices with marginal costs, would fall under this heading. Here the economist is on sure ground; the scientific status of his prescriptions is unquestionable, provided that the basic postulate of economics, that each individual prefers more to less, a greater satisfaction to a lesser one, is granted. In the second part, concerning distribution, the economist should not be concerned with " prescriptions " at all, but with the relative advantages of different ways of carrying out certain political ends. For it is quite impossible to decide on economic grounds what particular pattern of income-distribution maximises social welfare. If the postulate of equal capacity for satisfaction is employed as a criterion, the conclusion inescapably follows that welfare is necessarily greatest when there is complete equality; yet one certainly cannot exclude the possibility of everybody being happier when there is some degree of inequality than under a régime of necessary and complete equality. (Here I am not thinking so much of differences in the capacity for satisfactions between different individuals, but of the satisfactions that are derived from the prospect of improving one's income by one's own efforts—a prospect which is necessarily excluded when a régime of complete equality prevails.) And short of complete equality, how can the

---

[1] This principle, as the reader will observe, simply amounts to saying that there is no interpersonal comparison of satisfactions involved in judging any policy designed to increase the sum total of wealth just because any such policy *could* be carried out in a way as to secure unanimous consent. An increase in the money value of the national income (given prices) is not, however, necessarily a sufficient indication of this condition being fulfilled : for individuals might, as a result of a certain political action, sustain losses of a non-pecuniary kind—*e.g.*, if workers derive satisfaction from their particular kind of work, and are obliged to change their employment, something more than their previous level of money income will be necessary to secure their previous level of enjoyment; and the same applies in cases where individuals feel that the carrying out of the policy involves an interference with their individual freedom. Only if the increase in total income is sufficient to compensate for such losses, and still leaves something over to the rest of the community, can it be said to be " justified " without resort to interpersonal comparisons.

economist decide precisely how much inequality is desirable—*i.e.*, how much secures the maximum total satisfaction ? All that economics can, and should, do in this field, is to show, given the pattern of income-distribution desired, which is the most convenient way of bringing it about.

NICHOLAS KALDOR

London School of Economics.

[4]

THE FOUNDATIONS OF WELFARE ECONOMICS [1]

1. THE subject of this paper is a matter of very fundamental importance, both for economic theory and for the proper attitude of economists towards economic policy. That being so, it is not surprising that it should have been a matter of controversy, controversy which has even tended to widen into a profound difference of opinion. During the nineteenth century, it was generally considered to be the business of an economist, not only to explain the economic world as it is and as it has been, not only to make prognostications (so far as he was able) about the future course of economic events, but also to lay down principles of economic policy, to say what policies are likely to be conducive to social welfare, and what policies are likely to lead to waste and impoverishment. To-day, there is one school of writers which continues to claim that economics can fulfil this second function, but there is another which (formally at least) desires to reject it. According to their view the economics of welfare, the economics of economic policy, is too unscientific in character to be a part of economic *science*. So long as economics is concerned with explanation, it can hope to reach conclusions which will command universal acceptance as soon as they are properly understood; but once it goes beyond that point, and endeavours to prescribe principles of policy, then (so they hold) its conclusions must depend upon the scale of social values held by the particular investigator. Such conclusions can possess no validity for any-one who lives outside the circle in which these values find acceptance. Positive economics can be, and ought to be, the same for all men; one's welfare economics will inevitably be different according as one is a liberal or a socialist, a nationalist or an internationalist, a christian or a pagan.

It cannot be denied that this latter view is in fact widely accepted. If it is intellectually valid, then of course it ought to be accepted; and I must admit that I should have subscribed to it myself not so long ago. But it is rather a dreadful thing to have to accept. No one will question the activity of some of our "positivists" in the criticism of current institutions; but it can hardly be denied that their authority to advance such

[1] Based on a paper read to the Economic Society of Stockholm, May 1939.

criticism *qua* economists is diminished by their abnegation, so
that in other hands economic positivism might easily become an
excuse for the shirking of live issues, very conducive to the
euthanasia of our science.

Fortunately there is no need for us to accept it. The way is
open for a theory of economic policy which is immune from the
objections brought against previously existing theories.

The standard representative of these existing theories is of
course Professor Pigou's *Economics of Welfare*. It is such, not
only in its own right, but as the culmination of a great line of
economic thought. A whole series of economists, among whom
Dupuit, Walras, Marshall and Edgeworth deserve particular
mention, had sought to find in utility theory a sure basis for
prescriptions of economic policy. In those of its aspects which
particularly concern us, the *Economics of Welfare* is essentially
a systematisation of this tradition.

I am not so much concerned in this paper with Professor
Pigou's conclusions (most of which are very readily acceptable,
and are abandoned with reluctance even by the positivists),
as with the grounds on which those conclusions are based. It is
not surprising that these grounds should have caused so much
trouble. Professor Pigou derives his prescriptions from the
postulate that the aim of economic policy is to maximise the real
value of the social income. In order to arrive at such a *real
value*, the quantities of the various commodities produced must
be weighted by a *given* set of prices—and the prices actually
selected are those ruling on the market in the actual circumstances
considered. In order to justify this procedure, a long argument
is needed, which occupies most of Part I of the book. There are
three steps in this argument which cause difficulty. The first
is at the very outset, when the reader is asked to accept a direct
correlation between economic welfare and social welfare in
general (whatever that may be). This is not easy to swallow;
in any case it is open to the positivist objection that it reflects a
particular social outlook, held by certain classes at certain times,
and never likely to be acceptable universally. At the next step,
we have to admit the possibility of comparing the satisfactions
derived from their wealth by different individuals. (This is
where Professor Robbins parts company; for my own part, I
go with him.) And then further, even if these things are admitted,
a third jump has to be taken.[1] Strictly speaking, the quantity
to be maximised is the sum of the consumers' surpluses derived

[1] *Economics of Welfare*, 4th edition, p. 57.

from the various commodities in the social dividend. This is too awkward to handle, so it is replaced by the real value of the dividend—which is not the same thing at all.

I do not think that anyone can be blamed for declining to entrust himself to a chain containing three links as weak as these. If there were no alternative foundations for the theory of economic welfare, it would be nothing more than the development of an interesting ethical postulate—the status Professor Robbins allows. Alternative foundations are, however, available. A way round the first difficulty has been shown by Mr. Harrod; [1] round the second by Mr. Kaldor; [2] while Professor Hotelling, in a most valuable and suggestive paper covering the whole subject, has provided a mathematical analysis in which all these difficulties are in fact overcome. [3]

Therefore my own task is mainly one of synthesis. I propose to set out briefly and simply the main lines of the new welfare economics. It will appear that the main propositions can be established quickly and easily, and at the same time their significance can be made perfectly clear.

2. The *positive* theory of economics exhibits a system in which people co-operate with one another in order to satisfy their wants. We assume each individual (each free economic unit [4]) to have a certain scale of preferences, and to regulate his activities in such a way as best to satisfy those preferences. As Pareto put it, in his famous masterpiece of generalisation, the economic problem consists in an opposition of " tastes " and " obstacles," each individual endeavouring to satisfy his tastes as far as is possible in view of the obstacles to satisfaction which confront him. Looking at society as a whole, the obstacles are technical obstacles—the limited amount of productive power available, and the technical limits to the amount of production this productive power will yield. Looking at a single individual, the obstacles which prevent him from attaining a fuller satisfaction of his wants are not only technical obstacles but also the wants or tastes of other people. He is prevented from being better off than he is, not only because total production is limited, but also because so much

---

[1] " Scope and Method of Economics," ECONOMIC JOURNAL, Sept. 1938, pp. 389–395.

[2] " Welfare Propositions and Inter-personal Comparisons of Utility," ECONOMIC JOURNAL, Sept. 1939, pp. 549–52. See also Viner, *Studies in the Theory of International Trade*, pp. 553–4.

[3] " The General Welfare in Relation to Problems of Taxation and of Railway and Utility Rates," *Econometrica*, July 1938.

[4] It would appear from Mr. Harrod's analysis that we ought to be prepared, on occasion, to reckon public and semi-public bodies among our " individuals."

of total production is at the disposal of persons other than himself. The same thing holds, of course, for any group or society of individuals, so long as that group is less than the totality of a closed community.

Now as soon as the economic problem is conceived in this way (and it is in some such way that all modern economists regard it), we are really obliged to go on and to consider as part of our business not only the objective consequences of this pursuit of satisfactions (the quantities of goods produced and exchanged, and the prices at which they are exchanged—the problems of positive economics) but also a further problem. We ought to examine how far these activities are effective in achieving the ends for which they are designed, to be able to examine the efficiency of any particular economic system as a means of adjusting means to ends. We are obliged to go so far, because the subject-matter of our study is something which is defined relatively to its purpose. We are not like geologists, comparing rocks laid down by natural forces; we are like archæologists, comparing flint implements made by man for a purpose, one of whose functions must be to compare the relative efficiency of these implements, and by tracing the ups and downs of that efficiency, to trace out the tortuous course of human evolution.

The task of examining the efficiency—in this sense—of any given economic organisation is thus one which we should like to regard as an integral part of economics. But before we can accept it as such, we have to face the second difficulty which lies in our way, the difficulty of inter-personal comparisons. Although the economic system can be regarded as a mechanism for adjusting means to ends, the ends in question are ordinarily not a single system of ends, but as many independent systems as there are " individuals " in the community. This appears to introduce a hopeless arbitrariness into the testing of efficiency. You cannot take a temperature when you have to use, not one thermometer, but an immense number of different thermometers, working on different principles, and with no necessary correlation between their registrations. How is this difficulty to be overcome?

We may list three possible ways of dealing with it, two of which have to be rejected as unsatisfactory. One is to replace the given thermometers (the scales of preference of the individuals) by a new thermometer of one's own. The investigator himself decides what he thinks to be good for society, and praises or condemns the system he is studying by that test. This is the method which is rightly condemned as unscientific. It is the way of the prophet and the social reformer, not of the economist.

Secondly, one may seek for some way of aggregating the reports of the different thermometers. This is the traditional method of Marshall, Edgeworth and Pigou. The fundamental reason why it cannot be accepted is that it is impossible to arrive at an aggregate without " weighting " the component parts; and in this case there is no relevant reason why we should choose one system of weights rather than another. (The equal weights, 1, 1, 1, . . . are just one possible system of weights like the rest.) As a matter of fact, when they are composing their aggregate, Marshall and Pigou pay no attention to variations of the marginal utility of money between rich and poor—a point which, on their own principles, ought plausibly to be taken into account.[1] Thus although their method can produce results, the significance of those results remains quite uncertain.

The third method is Mr. Kaldor's. It consists in concentrating attention upon those cases which have been admitted, even by some of the positivists,[2] to be an exception to their general rule that the impossibility of inter-personal comparisons prevents any estimation of the general efficiency of the economic system. Mr. Kaldor's contribution is to have shown that these cases are not the mere trifling exception they appear to be at first sight, but that they do actually offer a sufficient foundation for at least the more important part of welfare economics.

3. Let us go back to the Paretian scheme referred to a little while ago. For society as a whole, the only *obstacles* to satisfaction are the limited quantity of physical resources, and the limited quantities of products which can be got from those resources. For the individual, however, the wants of other people have to be reckoned among the obstacles which limit the satisfaction of his wants. There are usually some ways in which he can improve his position without damaging the satisfactions of other people; there are other ways in which an improvement in his position (an upward movement on his scale of preferences) involves a downward movement for other people on their scales. Now these latter movements, which make some people better off and some people worse off, cannot be reckoned as involving an increase in " social satisfaction " unless we have some means of reducing the satisfactions of different individuals to a common

---

[1] Cf. Kahn, " Notes on Ideal Output," ECONOMIC JOURNAL, 1935, p. 2.

[2] Cf., for example, G. Myrdal, *Das politische Element in der nationalökonomischen Doktrinbildung*, p. 288.

measure—and no unambiguous means for such reduction seems to exist. But the former movements, which benefit some people without damaging others, stand in another category. From any point of view, they do represent an increase in economic welfare— or better, an increase in the efficiency of the system as a means of satisfying wants, that is to say, in the efficiency of the system *tout court*.

Let us then define an *optimum* organisation of the economic system as one in which every individual is as well off as he can be made, subject to the condition that no reorganisation permitted shall make any individual worse off. This is not an unambiguous definition of an optimum organisation; it does not enable us to say that with given resources and given scales of preference, there will be one optimum position and one only. That is not so; there will be an indefinite number of different possible optima, distinguished from one another by differences in the *distribution* of social wealth.[1] In spite of this, we are able to lay down the conditions which must be fulfilled in order that a particular organisation should be optimum, and so we can test whether an actual organisation is optimum or not. If it is not optimum, then there is a definite sense in which its efficiency can be increased. Some at least of the individuals in the system can have their wants satisfied better, without anyone having to make a sacrifice in order to achieve that end.

The significance of this definition may be illustrated by taking the familiar case of comparative costs in inter-regional trade. Suppose that the supplies of two commodities are each derived from two regions, each region producing each commodity. Suppose that each commodity, in each region, is produced under diminishing returns, and that no migration of factors between the regions is possible. Then, as is well known, the technical possibilities of production in each region can be represented by a *substitution curve*.[2] The abscissa of each point on this curve represents a certain quantity of the one commodity, and the corresponding ordinate represents the maximum amount of the

---

[1] If we start from a given organisation which is not optimum, there will be several different optima which can be reached subject to the condition of no one being damaged, since the " increment of wealth " can be divided in different ways. In addition to these there will be many other optima which cannot be reached from the initial position, since they involve some people being worse off than they were initially. These are optimum positions all the same, although they could only be reached by a " permitted reorganisation " if we begin from some other starting-point.

[2] Haberler, *Theory of International Trade*, p. 176.

other whose production is consistent with the production of that amount of the first. A and B (Fig. 1) represent the substitution curves of the two regions. Under the assumed diminishing returns, each substitution curve will be concave to the origin.

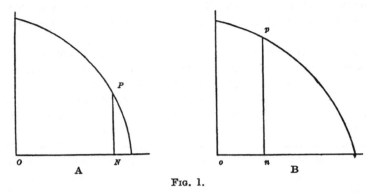

FIG. 1.

Suppose we start with a case where the quantities of the goods produced in the two regions are *ON*, *PN* and *on*, *pn*. Then, taking the two regions together, the total amounts produced of

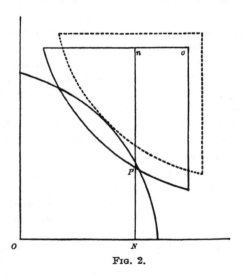

FIG. 2.

the two commodities are *ON* + *on*, *PN* + *pn*. These total amounts might be plotted on a third diagram, but a more instructive method of compounding is to " sit " the one curve on the other, keeping the axes parallel, as in Fig. 2. It will be observed that the curve *B* is reversed before being superposed,[1] so that it is the co-ordinates of *o* with respect to the *A*-axes which represent the total amounts produced. This reversal has a definite advantage, since it shows us at once what condition must be fulfilled in order for the distribution of production between the regions to be optimum. If, when the diagrams are superposed, the curves intersect, a reorganisation of production will enable the outputs of both products (in the two areas taken together) to be increased. It is only when the curves touch (as in the dotted position) that an optimum organisation is realised.

When two curves touch, their slopes are the same; and the slope of a substitution curve measures the ratio between the marginal costs of the two products. It is thus a condition of optimum organisation that the marginal costs of the two commodities should be in the same ratio in the two regions. If this condition is not satisfied, the position is not an optimum; for the production of both commodities can be increased by a suitable re-arrangement.

An exactly similar construction can be used for the case of exchange between two individuals. Here again we can construct a substitution curve (an indifference curve, as it is more commonly called), showing the various quantities of two commodities which would yield a particular individual the same amount of satisfaction. His whole scale of preferences can be represented by a series of such curves. Now if the first individual only moves from one position on his scale to another position by exchanging goods with the second, every movement of the first individual implies a movement of the second in the opposite direction. We can then draw the second individual's indifference map upon the same diagram as the first's, but his curves will naturally all turn the other way.[2]

Once again, if the amounts possessed by the two parties are such that their indifference curves through that point intersect, the position cannot be an optimum. For it will be possible for either party to reach a preferred position (a position on a higher indifference curve) while the other party remains on the same indifference curve as before. One party can be made better off without the other being worse off, so the position is not an optimum position. The position will only be an optimum if the curves touch—in this case, if the ratio of the marginal utilities of the two commodities is the same for both parties.

---

[1] I owe this device to Mr. Kaldor.

[2] Bowley, *Mathematical Groundwork of Economics*, fig. 1.

4. The general conditions for the attainment of an optimum organisation may now be set out in a formal manner.[1]

The first set of conditions are *marginal* conditions. They state—in the terminology I prefer—that the marginal rate of substitution[2] between any two commodities must be the same for every individual (who consumes them both) and for every producing unit (which produces them both) in the whole economy. In the older terminology, the ratio of the marginal utilities of the two commodities must be the same for every individual; the ratio of the marginal costs must be the same for every producing unit; and these ratios must be equal. Exactly similar conditions must hold between factor and product, and factor and factor, as between product and product. Thus the marginal product of labour in terms of a particular product must equal the marginal disutility of labour in terms of that product. And so on.

If these conditions are not fulfilled, some " tightening-up " (of the kind illustrated in our diagrams) will always be possible.

The second set of conditions are *stability* conditions. Their rôle is to ensure that the position established is one of maximum, not minimum, satisfaction. They can be defined in terms of the curvature of the substitution curves; but it does not seem necessary to elaborate them here, because their importance for the theory of the optimum is largely eclipsed by that of the third set of conditions—which we may call the *total* conditions.[3]

The function of the total conditions is to ensure that no improvement can be brought about by the complete abandonment of the production or consumption of some one commodity, either in one producing or consuming unit, or generally; and that no improvement can be secured by the introduction of new commodities, which could have been produced or consumed, but were not being produced or consumed, either partially or generally, in the initial situation. Similar conditions must hold for factors— thus conditions referring to the mobility of labour (occupational or local) arise in the form of total conditions.

[1] It should be observed that it is not at all necessary to raise the awkward problems about the definition of real income, which gave so much trouble to Professor Pigou. We can *proceed directly* to the analysis of the optimum. This is, of course, not to deny that a definition of real social income is wanted for other (statistical) purposes, and that the issues raised in the search for that definition are very cognate to those in question here. In my ideal *Principles of Economics* the theory of economic welfare and the theory of the social income would be the subjects of consecutive chapters—but they would not get into the same chapter.

[2] See my *Value and Capital*, pp. 20, 86.

[3] Compare the triple classification of the conditions of equilibrium in positive economics, given in *Value and Capital*, chap. 6.

The working of both these latter sets of conditions can be readily understood by reference to our diagrams. In Fig. 2 (the inter-regional trade case) both the stability condition and the

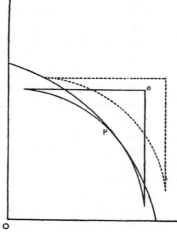

Fig. 3.

total condition were in fact assumed to be satisfied—as a consequence of the assumption of diminishing returns. Complications arise from increasing returns. In Fig. 3 the marginal

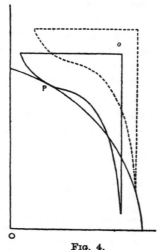

Fig. 4.

condition is satisfied, but neither of the other conditions. In Fig. 4 we have both the marginal condition and the stability condition, but not the total condition. In both these cases, it is only possible for an optimum position to be reached if production of one commodity is abandoned in one of the regions. (Optimum positions are such as those indicated by the dotted curves.) There must be specialisation in the inter-regional case; more generally, there must be a change in the kinds of goods produced or consumed somewhere.

5. These are the general conditions for optimum organisation; they are universally valid, being applicable to every conceivable type of society. No economic system has ever existed, nor (we may be sure) will any ever exist, to which they are irrelevant.[1] But for us the most interesting application which they offer still lies in their use as a means of criticising or testing the efficiency of production by private enterprise.[2] It is this which I shall take as my topic for the remainder of this paper.

When we are dealing with the system of private enterprise, there is one point which requires special attention, although it is (in a sense) nothing but the practical aspect of that theoretical difficulty which has concerned us all along. Under private enterprise, any ordinary change in economic policy involves a change in the price-system, and any change in prices benefits those on one side of the market, and damages those on the other. Thus no simple economic reform can be a permitted reorganisation in our sense, because it always inflicts a loss of some sort upon some people. Nevertheless, this does not prevent us from applying our criteria to the case of private enterprise, because we can always suppose that special measures are taken through the public revenue to compensate those people who are damaged. A " permitted reorganisation " must thus be taken from now on to mean a reorganisation which will allow of compensation being paid, and which will yet show a net advantage. The position is not optimum so long as such reorganisation is possible.

The critique of private enterprise naturally begins by pointing out the one conceivable case in which an optimum position may be attained by perfect *laisser-faire*. This occurs when competition

---

[1] Most of them are still relevant even if there is only *one* free economic unit.

[2] Another important application of Welfare Economics, which should perhaps be distinguished from this, is the application to Public Finance. Welfare Economics, defined as we have defined it, cannot lay down what is *the* optimum method of raising a given revenue—the " least sacrifice " method, as taxation theorists would call it. That is impossible without inter-personal comparisons. It can, however, distinguish between those methods of raising revenue which are consistent with optimum production and those which are not. In practice, this would seem to be a quite sufficient achievement.

On these questions of optimum taxation Professor Hotelling (*op. cit.*) has thrown particular light.

is *perfect* in all industries, so that every producer and every consumer takes for granted the prices of all those things he buys or sells, and contents himself with adjusting quantities to these (for him) given prices. If these conditions are realised, the *perfection* of the consumers' market ensures that each individual consumer equalises his marginal rate of substitution between every pair of goods to the ratio of their market prices; and the *perfection* of the producers' market ensures that each producer makes the marginal cost of every article he sells equal to its price. Thus the marginal conditions for the optimum must be satisfied. The fact that such universal perfect competition is only possible under universal diminishing returns [1] ensures that the stability and total conditions for the optimum must be satisfied too. Thus, so it appears, an optimum position must be reached.

There are, however, certain reasons why an optimum position may not be attained, even in these favourable circumstances of universal perfect competition and universal *laisser-faire*. The first is one which has been rightly emphasised by Professor Pigou.[2] It is of enormous importance that only some of the ways by which human beings affect one another's prosperity are controlled through the mechanism of the price-system. We are all of us affected by the economic activities of other people in ways for which we do not pay, or are not paid. Thus it is not necessarily to the social advantage (even in the narrow sense in which we are using that term) that a person should be able to acquire a particular product so long as he is willing to pay a price equal to the marginal cost of that product. This condition ensures that he can acquire it without making anyone else worse off because that person has to bear a part of the ordinary costs of production of that commodity; but there are other ways in which other people may be injured (or benefited). The ultimate implications of this exception are indeed very large. Hidden under this heading are some of the gravest philosophical issues about the relationship between the individual and society.

This qualification is generally admitted; but there are other qualifications, of a more dynamic character, whose place in the

---

[1] Since these particular technical conditions are necessary in order for universal perfect competition to be a possible state of affairs, the true basis for the criticism of monopolistic output is always to compare it with optimum output. not with competitive output (which may easily be a meaningless term in the state of affairs assumed). Whatever the technical conditions, an optimum output always exists.

[2] *Op. cit.*, pp. 172 ff.

theory is less generally appreciated. When they are taken strictly, the optimum conditions can only be interpreted *ex post*; it is only *after the event* that we can say whether an optimum organisation has in fact been achieved. Now even under perfect competition, producers only equate prices to marginal costs *ex ante*; it is anticipated marginal costs which are made equal to anticipated prices, so that if any of these anticipations are wrong, actual prices will not equal actual marginal costs, and the position achieved, though planned to be an optimum, will not turn out as such in fact. Of course, the utmost which can be done by wise economic policy is to secure equality *ex ante*—the planned optimum, but it is as well to remind ourselves that this does not necessarily imply a realised optimum, in order that we should be quite clear about the part played by foresight in economic efficiency.

Nor is this all; if the optimum conditions are interpreted *ex post*, they can make no allowance for risk, since risk is a phenomenon due to uncertainty of the *future*. On the other hand, the policy of the individual producer, being *ex ante*, is greatly influenced by risk; consequently prices always tend to exceed the relevant marginal costs by a risk-premium. Consequently production is carried less far in the more risky industries than is theoretically desirable.

If foresight is very bad, there may be little harm in this; for the refusal to embark resources in risky enterprises may prevent much mal-investment and waste. Indeed, so long as it confines itself to deflecting resources from more risky to less risky sorts of *production*, wo may not need to have much quarrel with the risk factor in practice, the trouble is that it may go beyond this. Liquidity-preference is only a form of risk-aversion; and the effect of liquidity-preference on the general activity of industry is well known. When liquidity-preference manifests itself in a large amount of " involuntary unemployment," a monetary policy directed to the reduction of interest rates, and even a public works policy which calculates the profitability of public enterprise at an " artificially " low rate of interest, may be measures which promote movement in the direction of the optimum as we have defined it.[1]

---

[1] In spite of the close dependence of actual interest rates upon risk factors (expressed by Mr. Keynes in his liquidity-preference theory), it must not be supposed that the payment of interest is itself inconsistent with optimum organisation. For a convincing demonstration of this, see Lindahl, " The Place of Capital in the Theory of Price " (*Ekonomisk Tidskrift*, 1929, appearing in English as Part III of his *Studies in the Theory of Money and Capital*). The

6. I do not propose to say very much in this paper about the welfare economics of monopoly and imperfect competition, for this is altogether too large a subject to be capable of useful treatment on the scale here available. A very large part of the established theory of imperfect competition falls under the head of welfare economics, and it is actually much the strongest part of the theory which does so. Considered as a branch of positive economics, the theory of imperfect competition is even now not very convincing; the assumption that the individual producer has a clear idea of the demand curve confronting him has been justifiably questioned, and the presence of intractable elements of oligopoly in most markets has been justifiably suspected.[1] When it is considered as a branch of welfare economics, the theory of imperfect competition has a much clearer status. Oligopoly and monopolistic competition fall into their places as reasons for the inequality between price and marginal cost, whose consequences are then a most fertile field for study along welfare lines.

It is perhaps rather to be regretted that modern theories of imperfect competition have not been cast more overtly into this form; for the general apparatus of welfare economics would have made it possible to state some of the most important propositions in a more guarded way than usual. Take, for example, the very important question of the optimum number of firms in an imperfectly competitive industry, which is so near the centre of modern discussion. Since (*ex hypothesi*) the different firms are producing products which are economically distinguishable, the question is one of those which falls under the heading of our *third* set of optimum conditions—the *total* conditions; we have to ask whether a reduction in the number of products would be conducive to a movement towards the optimum.

Suppose then that a particular firm is closed down. The loss involved in its cessation is measured by the compensation which would have to be given to consumers to make up for their loss of the opportunity to consume the missing product, *plus* the compensation which would have to be given to producers to make up for the excess of their earnings in this use over what they could

---

economy with perfect foresight and perfect competition, elaborately analysed by Professor Lindahl, is automatically an economy with optimum organisation and yet it has a rate of interest (of course a pure time-preference rate). The time-preference element in interest is that element which is consistent with the optimum, the liquidity-preference element is that which is not.

[1] Cf. Hall and Hitch, *Price Theory and Business Behaviour*, Oxford Economic Papers, Number 2.

earn in other uses. The loss is therefore measured by Marshall's *Surplus* (Consumers' Surplus [1] *plus* Producers' Surplus). Under conditions of perfect competition, this loss is a net loss. For when the factors are transferred to other uses, they will have to be scattered about at the margins of those uses; and (since the earnings of a factor equal the value of its marginal product) the additional production made possible by the use of the factors in these new places is equal in value to the earnings of the factors (already accounted for). Under perfect competition, the marginal productivity law ensures that there is no producers' surplus generated at the new margins; while, since the marginal unit of any commodity is worth no more than what is paid for it, there can be no consumers' surplus either. Thus there is nothing to set against the initial loss; there cannot be a movement towards the optimum if the number of products is reduced.

But if competition is imperfect, there is something to set on the other side. The earnings of a factor are now less than the value of its marginal product by an amount which varies with the degree of monopolistic exploitation; and therefore the increment to production which can be secured by using the factors at other margins is worth more than the earnings of the factors. There is a producers' surplus, even at the margin, and this producers' surplus may outweigh the initial loss. The general condition for a particular firm to be such that its existence is compatible with the optimum is that the sum of the consumers' and producers' surpluses generated by its activities must be greater than the producers' surplus which would be generated by employing its factors (and exploiting them) elsewhere.

The rule usually given is a special case of this general rule. If entry to the industry is "free," price equals average cost, and the producers' surplus generated by the firm as a whole can be neglected. If the products of the different firms are very close substitutes, or merely distinguished by "irrational preferences," consumers' surplus can perhaps be neglected as well. With these simplifications, the number of firms in an imperfectly

---

[1] This use of Consumers' Surplus is not open to any of the objections which have been brought against Marshall's concept; it does not involve either interpersonal comparisons or the measurement of utility. Consumers' surplus is the measure of the compensation which consumers would need in order to maintain them at the same level of satisfaction as before, after the supply of the commodity had been withdrawn. It is, however, not exactly equal to the area under the ordinary demand curve (see my *Value and Capital*, Appendix to Chapter II). This inequality (usually only a slight inequality) was responsible for the difficulties about the aggregation of consumers' surpluses which troubled Professor Pigou.

competitive industry is always excessive, so long as price is greater than marginal cost anywhere in the industry. (Or, if we can retain the identity of price with average cost, the number of firms is excessive until average cost is reduced to a minimum.)

These, however, are simplifications; it is not always true that the number of firms in an imperfectly competitive industry is excessive, though very often it may be. Before recommending in practice a policy of shutting down redundant firms, we ought to be sure that the full condition is satisfied; and we ought to be very sure that the discarded factors will in fact be transferred to more productive uses. In a world where the most the economist can hope for is that he will be listened to occasionally, that is not always so certain.

7. By adopting the line of analysis set out in this paper, it is possible to put welfare economics on a secure basis, and to render it immune from positivist criticism. That is a great gain in itself; but, as often happens in such cases, other gains are secured with it. The main practical advantage of our line of approach is that it fixes attention upon the question of compensation. Every simple economic reform inflicts a loss upon some people; the reforms we have studied are marked out by the characteristic that they will allow of compensation to balance that loss, and they will still show a net advantage. Yet when such reforms have been carried through in historical fact, the advance has usually been made amid the clash of opposing interests, so that compensation has not been given, and economic progress has accumulated a roll of victims, sufficient to give all sound policy a bad name.

I do not contend that there is any ground for saying that compensation ought always to be given; whether or not compensation should be given in any particular case is a question of distribution, upon which there cannot be identity of interest, and so there cannot be any generally acceptable principle. This being so, it will often happen in some particular case that the economist will find himself not at all anxious for compensation to be given [1]; but his personal feeling in that direction will be based either upon the non-economic ground that the persons damaged

---

[1] The typical hard-boiled attitude is, of course, to reject all compensation on the ground that such risks *ought* to have been allowed for. In view of the importance of foresight for economic efficiency, there is something in this; when applied to ordinary changes in data which promote productivity (such as inventions) it is probably a decisive consideration; nevertheless, if it is always regarded as decisive, the case for an active pursuit of economic efficiency in other ways is seriously weakened.

do not deserve much consideration, or upon the only quasi-economic ground that the loss inflicted on them is nothing but the materialisation of a risk they may be expected to have allowed for. Nevertheless we must expect that there will be many other cases where the redistribution, resulting from a sound measure carried through without compensation, would be regarded by him as deplorable; and then, if he considers the measure in isolation from the question of compensation, he will pay no more than lip-service to its productive efficiency, and probably reject it in practice. From this it is only a step to the state of mind which judges measures solely by reference to their distributive justice, without reference to their bearing on efficiency. If measures making for efficiency are to have a fair chance, it is extremely desirable that they should be freed from distributive complications as much as possible.

We can make this separation in our own minds if we accustom ourselves, whenever we can, to thinking of every economic reform in close conjunction with some measure of compensation, designed to render it approximately innocuous from the distributive point of view. Since almost every conceivable kind of compensation (re-arrangement of taxation, for example) must itself be expected to have some influence on production, the task of the welfare economist is not completed until he has envisaged the total effects of both sides of the proposed reform; he should not give his blessing to the reform until he has considered these total effects and judged them to be good. If, as will often happen, the best methods of compensation feasible involve some loss in productive efficiency, this loss will have to be taken into account. In practice, it is not unlikely that we shall have to reject on these grounds many measures which would be approved of by the traditional analysis, but which would only be reckoned by that analysis as offering a small gain. (It is not very surprising to find that some of the fine points in welfare theory are nothing but snares.)

Further investigations of such matters would lead us far beyond the " Foundations " which have been the subject of this paper. I have accomplished my end if I have demonstrated the right of Welfare Economics—the " Utilitarian Calculus " of Edgeworth—to be considered as an integral part of economic theory, capable of the same logical precision and the same significant elaboration as its twin brother, Positive Economics, the " Economical Calculus."

J. R. Hicks

[5]

A Note on Welfare Propositions in Economics

Modern economic theory draws a sharp distinction between positive economics, which explains the working of the economic system, and welfare economics, which prescribes policy. In the domain of welfare economics the impossibility of interpersonal utility comparisons has for a long time been believed to impose strict limitations on the economist, which kept this branch of economic theory in the background. Recently, however, there has been a reawakening of interest in welfare problems, following assertions that these limitations are less restrictive than they were hitherto supposed to be.[1] The present note attempts to analyse the problem in detail.

I

The aim of welfare economics is to test the efficiency of economic institutions in making use of the productive resources of a community. For analytical and historical reasons it is useful to distinguish between welfare propositions based on the assumption of a fixed quantity of employed resources and those that regard that quantity as a variable.

The former are concerned with the allocating efficiency of the system;[2] i.e. with its ability of best allocating a given quantity of utilised resources among their various uses in consumption and production. They can be conceived of as criteria for judging institutions and policy in a closed community whose potential resources are fixed and can be trusted to be fully employed, either because of the automatism of the system or because of the existence of a governmental policy aiming at full employment.

The latter, which may be called welfare propositions in the wider sense, are in addition to the above problems concerned also with the total quantity of resources available to an open group and the degree of utilisation of those resources. They are therefore relevant, first of all, to problems of international trade from the point of view of a single country; and secondly, to the general problem of employment.

II

All the welfare propositions of the classical economists—viz., perfect competition, free trade, and direct taxation—belong in the first category; a fact which has not always been realised. They are all based on the principle that

[1] Cf. N. Kaldor: "Welfare Propositions of Economics and Interpersonal Comparisons of Utility," *Economic Journal*, vol. 49 (1939), p. 549; J. R. Hicks: "Foundations of Welfare Economics," *Economic Journal*, vol. 49 (1939), p. 696. See also N. Kaldor "A Note on Tariffs and the Terms of Trade," *Economica* (N.S.), vol. 7 (1940), p. 377; and J. R. Hicks: "The Rehabilitation of Consumers' Surplus," *Review of Economic Studies*, vol. 8 (1941), p. 108. The present note is a criticism of the principle enunciated in Mr. Kaldor's first-quoted article and underlying the argument of the others. It is not presented in polemic form, in order to enable the reader not acquainted with the articles here quoted to follow its argument.

[2] This expression was suggested to me by Mr. George Jaszi to whom I am also indebted for reading the manuscript and making valuable suggestions.

THE REVIEW OF ECONOMIC STUDIES

given the total quantity of utilised resources, they will be best distributed among different uses if their rates of substitution are everywhere and for every person equal ; for only in such a situation will each person's satisfaction be carried to that maximum beyond which it cannot be increased without diminishing someone else's. Perfect competition, free trade, and direct taxation are one (probably the simplest) among the many ways of achieving this aim.

By limiting our universe of discourse to two commodities and two persons, we can illustrate this principle on a simple diagram. Let us draw the indifference maps of the two individuals superposed on each other, one of them reversed, with the axes parallel and in such a position that their intersection gives the quantities of the two goods jointly possessed by the two people. Every point of the rectangle enclosed by the axes corresponds to a given distribution of the two goods between the two persons, and the two indifference curves going through that point show their respective welfare positions. At some points, indifference curves do not cut but are tangential one to another. At these points the rate of substitution of the two goods is equal for the two persons, and they represent optimum situations, because once such a point has been reached no redistribution of the two goods can increase the welfare of either person without diminishing that of the other. The locus of all optimum points gives the contract curve.

We judge the allocating efficiency of economic institutions by the criterion whether or not they enable people so to redistribute goods and services among themselves (irrespective of their initial position) as to arrive on the contract curve. That perfect competition or, from the point of view of the universe, free trade are efficient in the above sense can be proved by showing that all pairs of offer (reciprocal demand) curves drawn from any point within the rectangle intersect on the contract curve. Similarly, excise taxes and, from the point of view of the universe, import and export duties are inefficient, because they can be represented as distortions of offer curves that make them intersect outside the contract curve. The arguments based on this diagram can be generalised for any number of persons and commodities.[1] It implies only one limitation : the quantities of goods available to the community as a whole must be fixed ; for they determine the points of intersection of the axes and the position of the contract curve. This shows that the propositions illustrated by the diagram are allocative welfare propositions ; and it also appears to limit their applicability to the problem of the exchange of goods whose quantities coming onto the market are given. It can be proved, however, that our arguments are equally valid when instead of these quantities those of the factors utilised in their production are considered to be fixed. For the formal proof of the geometrical arguments and their generalisations the reader is referred to the original sources and to textbooks dealing with the subject.[2]

---

[1] This also holds good for all arguments based on other diagrams in this note.

[2] Cf. F. Y. Edgeworth : *Mathematical Psychics*, London, 1881, and " The Pure Theory of International Trade," *Economic Journal*, vol. 4 (1894) ; Alfred Marshall : *The Pure Theory of Foreign Trade* (1879), London School reprint, 1930 ; and his *Principles of Economics*, Bk. V, Chap. II. Note on Barter and Mathematical Note XII ; A. P. Lerner ; " The Symmetry between Export and Import Taxes," *Economica* (N.S.), vol. 3 (1936) ; J. R. Hicks : *Value and Capital*, Oxford, 1939, etc. For the best analysis of the nature of this kind of diagram see A. L. Bowley ; *The Mathematical Groundwork of Economics*, Oxford, 1924.

A NOTE ON WELFARE PROPOSITIONS IN ECONOMICS   79

III

We have seen above that allocative welfare propositions are based on the criterion of economic efficiency. They state that of alternative situations, brought about by different institutions or courses of policy, one is superior to the other in the sense that it would make everybody better off for every distribution of welfare, *if* that were the same in the two situations. This is different from saying that one situation is actually better than the other from everybody's point of view, because a change in institutions or policy almost always redistributes welfare sufficiently not to have a uniform effect on everybody but to favour some people and prejudice others. It follows from this that economic welfare propositions cannot as a rule be made independently of interpersonal comparisons of utility.

It would hardly be satisfactory, however, to confine the economist's value judgments to cases where one situation is superior to the other from the point of view of everybody affected. It is doubtful if in practice any choice comes within this category ; besides, there would not be much point in soliciting the economist's expert opinion when everybody is unanimous, except in order to enlighten people as to their true interest.

Favouring an improvement in the organisation of production and exchange *only* when it is accompanied by a corrective redistribution of income fully compensating those prejudiced by it might seem to be a way out of the difficulty, because such a change would make some people better off without making anyone worse off. For instance, it might be argued that the abolition of the Corn Laws should not have been advocated by economists in their capacity of pure economists without advocating at the same time the full compensation of landowners out of taxes levied on those favoured by the cheapening of corn. Yet, in a sense, and regarded from a long-run point of view, such propositions are not independent of value judgments between alternative income distributions either. For, going out of their way to preserve the existing distribution of income, they imply a preference for the *status quo*.

There seem to be two solutions of the problem. First of all, in addition to admitting his inability to compare different people's satisfaction, the economist may postulate that such comparisons are impossible, and that therefore there is nothing to choose between one distribution of income and another. He may then make value judgments on the sole criterion of efficiency without bothering about concomitant shifts in the distribution of income, since he considers one income distribution as good as any other.[1] In this case, however, he cannot claim that his value judgments are independent of interpersonal utility comparisons, because they depend on the assumption of their impossibility.

Secondly, the economist may put forward his welfare propositions with due

---

[1] This, I think, was the attitude of the classical economists ; at least of those who did not, like Bastiat, impute ethical values to the distribution of income under perfect competition. It seems to be the correct interpretation of that fairly representative statement of Cairnes' : " . . . standards of abstract justice . . . are inefficacious as means of solving the actual problems of . . . distribution. . . . If our present system of industry (perfect competition) is to be justified, it must . . . find its justification . . . in the fact that it secures for the mass of mankind a greater amount of material and moral well-being, and provides more effectively for its progress in civilisation than any other plan."

80   THE REVIEW OF ECONOMIC STUDIES

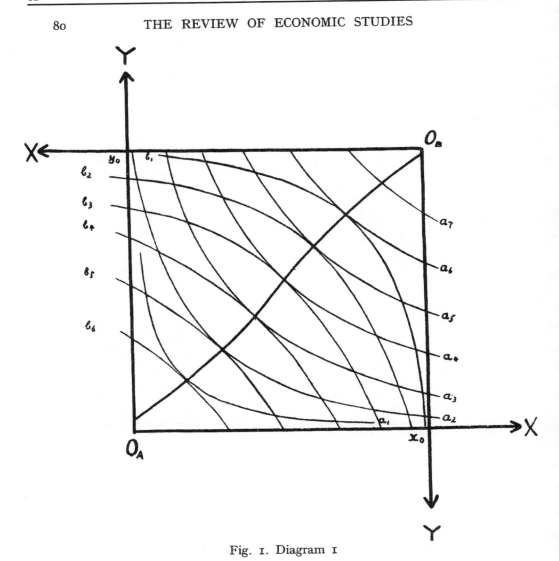

Fig. I. Diagram I

emphasis on their limitations, as being based on the sole criterion of efficiency. He may then point out the nature of eventual redistributions of income likely to accompany a given change, and stress the necessity of basing economic policy on considerations both of economic efficiency and of social justice.[1] Such an attitude, which I think is the only correct one, may diminish the force of the

[1] Or, of course, he may also renounce his claim to purity and base his own recommendations on both criteria.

A NOTE ON WELFARE PROPOSITIONS IN ECONOMICS   81

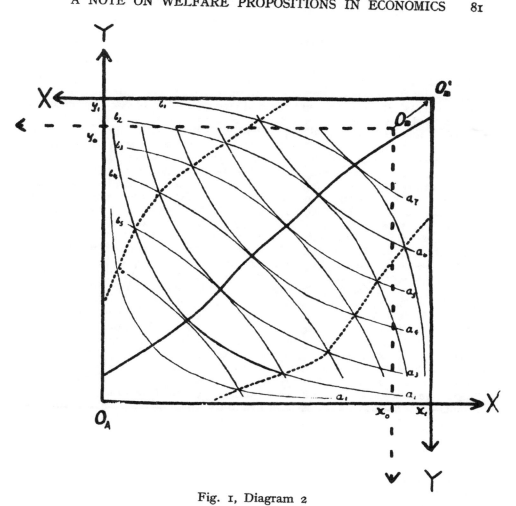

Fig. 1, Diagram 2

economist's welfare propositions but does not make them less useful. The above considerations qualify also the welfare propositions to be discussed below.

IV

When we come to the problem of welfare propositions in the wider sense, we can no longer illustrate a change in economic institutions or policy on a single diagram. For such a change will no longer mean a mere redistribution of income and alteration of the rules of production and exchange ; but may also involve a change both in the total quantity of resources available to the community, and in their degree of utilisation. The former may be due to the imposition of a duty on international trade, which from the point of view of an individual country alters the quantities of imports and retained exports available for home consumption ; while the latter may be caused by this or any other change, if it affects the propensity to save or the inducement to invest and thereby changes employment. Analytically there is no difference between the two cases. In both, the quantities of resources available for consumption are changed, hence the relative position of the indifference maps is altered ; whence it follows that welfare propositions in the wider sense must involve the comparison of two diagrams. Since these are constructed from the identical two indifference maps and differ only in the latter's relative position to each other, such comparisons are not the hopeless task they might seem at first sight. For we can represent some (not all) welfare positions on both diagrams ; and it is possible to represent on one diagram the welfare positions corresponding to all those points of the other diagram's contract curve that are inferior to its " own " contract curve. This follows from the fact that our diagrams admit the representation of all welfare situations that are inferior (worse from the point of view of at least one of the two persons) to their contract curve, while welfare positions superior to the contract curve cannot be represented on them.

Our welfare propositions may necessitate the comparison of points on the contract curves of the two diagrams, or of points suboptimal to them, or of a point on one contract curve with a point suboptimal to the other contract curve. The first case is that where the system's allocating efficiency is at an optimum both before and after the given change ; the second, where it is suboptimal both before and after the change ; the third, where the change affects allocating efficiency. Taking an example from the theory of international trade, the first case may be illustrated by the imposition of an import duty by a country in which taxation is direct and domestic markets are perfectly competitive ;[1] the second case can be represented by a duty imposed in a monopolistic world ; and the third by a duty which favours the formation of monopolies or is linked with an excise tax on the home production of import substitutes.

V

Let us draw two diagrams (Fig. 1), both consisting of the superposed indifference maps of individuals A and B, but with the difference that in the second, B's map has been shifted by $o_B o_B$; so that the joint possessions of A and B have increased by $x_0 x_1$ of X and $y_0 y_1$ of Y compared with what they were in the first. This shift will bring into a position of tangency indifference curves that in the first diagram have neither touched nor intersected, and will thus make the second diagram's contract curve superior to that of the first diagram throughout its range. This follows from that fundamental postulate of economic

[1] A tariff on foreign trade is not incompatible with the tariff imposing country's domestic trade and production being of optimum allocating efficiency. The reader must not let himself be confused by the fact that similar diagrams have been used for illustrating the waste caused by tariffs from the point of view of the universe as a whole. We are here solely concerned with the effects of a tariff on the welfare of a single country, consequently the indifference maps that constitute our diagrams belong to inhabitants of the same country.

A NOTE ON WELFARE PROPOSITIONS IN ECONOMICS 83

theory that indifference curves can never have a positive slope, and it will be the case whenever the shift in the relative position of the indifference maps represents an increase in the quantity of at least one of the two commodities without a diminution in that of the other. From the fact that the second diagram's contract curve is superior to that of the first, it follows that the latter can be represented on the second diagram by tracing the locus of the points of intersection of all the indifference curves that in the first diagram are tangential to each other. This will give us a curve on each side of the second diagram's contract curve, and the area between them represents welfare positions that are superior to the first diagram's contract curve. Hence, a change that brings the welfare of our groups from a point of the first diagram's contract curve onto a point of the second diagram's contract curve (or at least within the area between the broken lines), can be said to be desirable with the same generality and significance with which perfect competition or direct taxation are said to be desirable on the ground of their allocating efficiency. In other words, while it need not actually improve everybody's position, it would do so for every possible distribution of welfare if the change were to leave that distribution unaffected.

The above argument is an explicit formulation of the statement that getting more of some (or all) commodities at no cost of foregoing others is a good thing. This may be considered as overpedantic, since that statement seems to be obvious ; on the other hand, it is subject to the same limitations that qualify allocative welfare propositions (cf. section 3 above) ; and besides, it is not even always true. Increased plenty is a good thing only if it is not linked with a redistribution of welfare, too retrogressive from the point of view of social justice ; and if it does not lead to a serious deterioration of the allocating efficiency of the economic system. For the former there exists no objective criterion, but there is a simple test for the latter. To test whether a diminution in allocating efficiency has not obviated the advantages of increased plenty, we must see if after the change, it is possible fully to compensate people prejudiced by it out of funds levied on those favoured by the change, without thereby completely eliminating the latter's gain. From the geometrical argument above it follows that if this test is fulfilled for one initial income distribution, it will be fulfilled for all possible initial income distributions, and *vice versa*. Our test is completely general also in the sense that it is applicable whether or not the initial situation is of optimum allocating efficiency. (I.e. whether or not it lies on the contract curve).

VI

The kind of change contemplated above, where the quantity of some or all goods is increased without a diminution in others, is likely to occur as a result of increased employment, capital accumulation, technical progress, better utilisation of strategic advantages in international trade (by putting a duty on the export of goods for which foreign demand is inelastic), and the like. Another kind of change, especially important in international trade, is that where the quantity of some resources is increased and that of others diminished.[1] In

[1] This is the effect of import and export duties whenever the foreigners' reciprocal demand for exports is not inelastic and employment is given.

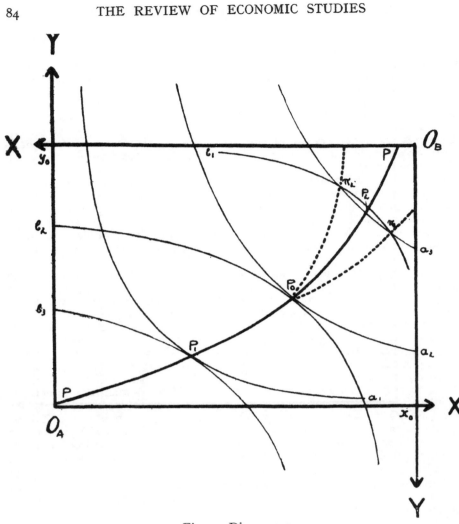

Fig. 2, Diagram 1

Fig. 2 this is represented by a parallel displacement of one of the two indifference maps in the negative direction ; so that the quantity of X is diminished by $x_0 x_1$ and that of Y increased by $y_0 y_1$. Nothing general can be said about the relationship of the two contract curves in this case without detailed knowledge of the shape of the indifference maps. It is possible that the change will result in superior welfare positions throughout the whole range of the contract curve, in the same way as was depicted in Fig. 1. This is especially likely to happen when the increase is large and the diminution small. When on the other hand,

A NOTE ON WELFARE PROPOSITIONS IN ECONOMICS   85

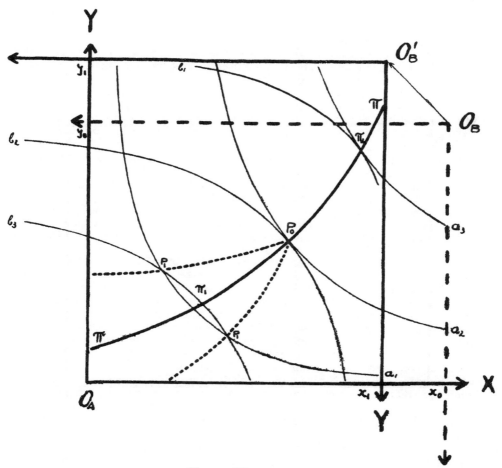

Fig. 2, Diagram 2

the diminution is large and the increase small, the change may result in inferior positions throughout the contract curve ; a situation which can be visualised by thinking of diagram 2 (Fig. 1) as showing the initial, and diagram 1 the new, position. Between these two extremes lies the more general case in which some sectors of the new contract curve are superior to the old one, while others are inferior to it. Its simplest example is illustrated in Fig. 2, where P_0 is a common point of the two contract curves, to the left of which the new contract curve, $\pi\pi$, represents welfare positions superior to the corresponding welfare positions of the old contract curve, PP ; while to the right of P_0, the old contract curve is superior to the new one. In each diagram the broken lines show the welfare positions corresponding to the other diagram's contract curve wherever that is inferior to the diagram's own contract curve.

The economic meaning of this is that the identical change in the composition of the national income would improve general welfare for some hypothetical welfare distributions and worsen it for others. Imagine members of a community divided into two groups according to their preference for goods Y and X respectively.[1] Then assume a change that increases the quantity of Y and diminishes that of X, but leaves the distribution of money income between our two groups unaffected. From the point of view of individuals, the change will appear as a shift in relative prices ; which, given the distribution of income, will be likely to make those with a special preference for Y better off, and those with a liking for X worse off, than they were before. Assume next that the members of our first group are rich and those of the second poor. Then the gain of the first group expressed in money (or in terms of any single commodity) will be greater than the money equivalent of the loss suffered by the second group. Therefore, if we so redistributed income as to restore approximately the initial distribution of welfare, there would be a net gain, making members of both groups better off than they were before. Conversely, if the people favoured by the change were poor, and those prejudiced by it were rich, the money equivalent of the former's gain would be insufficient fully to compensate the latter's loss, so that a redistribution of income tending to restore the initial distribution of welfare would result in a net loss of satisfaction for everybody.

What significance are we to attach to this case ? To refrain altogether, as the classical economists did, from making welfare propositions relating to it, seems unduly restrictive. It is true that as we have seen such a change would improve general welfare for some welfare distributions and worsen it for others ; on the other hand, we are not interested in all possible welfare distributions. There are only two distributions of welfare that really matter. Those actually obtaining immediately before and after the change contemplated.[2] It seems therefore sufficient to concentrate on these and to investigate how the change would affect general welfare if it were to leave the distribution of welfare unaffected and if that were both before and after it, first what it actually is before, secondly what it actually is after, the change. Whenever these two comparisons yield identical results, we can make welfare propositions of almost the same generality and significance as the allocative welfare propositions of the classical economists ; especially since the identical results for the two welfare distributions imply a strong presumption in favour of the same result holding for all intermediate welfare distributions as well.

We propose, therefore, to make welfare propositions on the following principle. We must first see whether it is possible in the new situation so to redistribute income as to make everybody better off than he was in the initial situation ; secondly, we must see whether starting from the initial situation it

[1] The term " preference " is used in a loose sense. It denotes the whole shape of indifference surfaces and not only their slope at the relevant point, which in equilibrium conditions is the same for everybody.

[2] The reader's attention is called to the fact that in reality the distribution of income is not *given* as we have assumed in the argument above. As a rule, the change will affect the distribution of welfare not only by shifting relative prices but also by boosting some industries and depressing others, and thereby redistributing money income.

A NOTE ON WELFARE PROPOSITIONS IN ECONOMICS 87

is not possible by a mere redistribution of income to reach a position superior to the new situation, again from everybody's point of view. If the first is possible and the second impossible, we shall say that the new situation is better than the old was. If the first is impossible but the second possible, we shall say that the new situation is worse ; whereas if both are possible or both are impossible, we shall refrain from making a welfare proposition.[1]

We can illustrate this procedure in Fig. 2 for the special case when allocating efficiency is at its optimum both before and after the change. Each situation can then be represented by a point on its respective contract curve and compared with the corresponding point on the other contract curve. If both points lie to the left of P_0 on their respective contract curves, the change will increase general welfare, because starting from the new situation on the second diagram's contract curve it is always possible to travel along that curve by redistributing income and arrive at a point which is superior to the initial situation from everybody's point of view ; whereas starting from the initial situation on the first diagram's contract curve, it is impossible by travelling along that curve to reach a position superior to the new situation. If on the other hand, both points lie to the right of the common point P_0, the change can be said to diminish general welfare on the same reasoning ; while if one point lies to the left and the other to the right, we can make no welfare propositions relative to our group.

VII

Our two criteria for making welfare propositions bear a close resemblance to Paasche's and Laspeyre's formulae in the theory of cost of living index numbers. There, just as here, the difficulty lies in comparing averages whose weighting is different ;[2] and the solution is sought in comparing the two real situations not one with another, but each with a hypothetical situation, which resembles it in weighting but is otherwise identical with the other real situation. In the theory of index numbers, budgets of different dates or places are compared each with the cost of the identical bundle of commodities at the prices of the other date or place ; and these two comparisons, expressed as ratios (Paasche's and Laspeyre's formulae), are the limits within which the true difference in the cost of living must lie.[3] In welfare problems, of course, we can aim neither at a " true " answer nor at its quantitative expression without measuring satisfaction and comparing different people's. But our two criteria are exactly analogous to Paasche's and Laspeyre's formulae. For we compare the first welfare situation with what general welfare would be if the satisfaction, yielded by the physical income of the second situation were distributed as it was in the first ; and contrast the second situation with the welfare that the first situation's physical income would yield to each person if it were so distri-

[1] It need hardly be recalled that in the situation discussed in section 5—that is, when the quantities of goods and services all change in the same direction—this last case can never occur, and we can always make welfare propositions.
[2] Because the general welfare can be conceived of as average welfare.
[3] Cf. Henry Schultz : " A Misunderstanding in Index Number Theory," *Econometrica*, vol. 7 (1939), p. 1 ; and A. A. Konüs : " The Problem of the True Index of the Cost of Living," *Econometrica*, vol. 7 (1939), p. 10.

88   THE REVIEW OF ECONOMIC STUDIES

buted as to make the distribution of welfare similar to that of the second situation.[1]

VIII

Mr. Kaldor and Professor Hicks have asserted that it is *always* possible to tell whether a given change improves general welfare, even if not all people gain by it and some lose. The test suggested by them : to see whether it is possible after the change fully to compensate the losers at a cost to those favoured that falls short of their total gain, is fundamentally identical with the first of our two criteria. The objection to using this criterion by itself is that it is asymmetrical, because it attributes undue importance to the particular distribution of welfare obtaining before the contemplated change. If the government had a special attachment to the *status quo* before the change and would actually undertake to reproduce that welfare distribution by differential taxation after the change, then Mr. Kaldor's test would be sufficient. For then, the economist could regard that particular welfare distribution as the only relevant one and would be entitled to use it as his sole standard of reference. But in the absence of such a governmental policy there can be no justification in attaching greater importance to the welfare distribution as it was before than as it is after the change.

To illustrate the pitfalls of this one-sided criterion, imagine a change, say the imposition of a duty on imports, that brings the welfare of A and B from P_1 (Fig. 2) on the contract curve of diagram 1 onto π_2 on the contract curve of diagram 2. According to Mr. Kaldor's test this change is desirable, because by redistributing income we could travel from π_2 along the $\pi\pi$ curve to π_1, which is superior to P_1. But once the tariff has been imposed and situation π_2 established, it will be free trade and the resulting (original) situation P_1 that will appear preferable *by the same test*, because starting from P_1, income could be so redistributed (travelling along the PP curve in the first diagram this time) as to reach P_2, which is superior to π_2. So the two situations can be shown each to be preferable to the other by the identical criterion : an absurd result, which can only be avoided by using our double criterion.

Washington, D.C.   T. DE SCITOVSZKY.

---

[1] We say that the distribution of welfare is similar in two situations if every member of the community prefers the same situation. A more exact definition would be unnecessary for our purposes ; besides, it is also impossible, since welfare cannot be measured.

[6]

EVALUATION OF REAL NATIONAL INCOME

By PAUL A. SAMUELSON

Introduction

1. Improved measurement of national income has been one of the outstanding features of recent progress in economics. But the theoretical interpretation of such aggregate data has been sadly neglected, so that we hardly know how to define real income even in simple cases where statistical data are perfect and where problems of capital formation and government expenditure do not arise.

In 1940 J. R. Hicks made an important advance over the earlier work of Professor Pigou. This has given rise to recent discussions between Kuznets, Hicks, and Little, but the last word on the subject will not be uttered for a long time. I have tried to treat the problem somewhat exhaustively in this paper, relating it to the modern theories of welfare economics of Pareto–Lerner–Bergson type. The result is not easy reading even to the author—but without such a careful survey I doubt that even the classical writings of Pigou can be adequately gauged.[1]

2. In Fig. 1, the point A represents observed consumption data for a single consumer in equilibrium at the indicated price-slope line through A. All the other points are each to be regarded as alternative to A and have nothing to do with each other. The following statements are immediate consequences of the modern theory of a single consumer's behaviour and are based on $\sum pq$ data such as the national income statistician might be able to measure:

    (a) We can immediately infer that B is on a lower indifference curve than A.

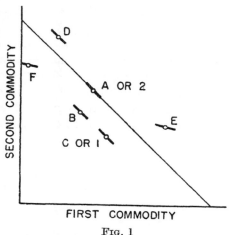

FIRST COMMODITY

FIG. 1

---

[1] The principal references are to J. R. Hicks, 'The Valuation of the Social Income', *Economica*, 1940, pp. 105–24; Simon Kuznets, 'On the Valuation of Social Income—Reflections on Professor Hicks' Article', *Economica*, Feb. 1948, pp. 1–16, and May 1948, pp. 116–31; J. R. Hicks, 'The Valuation of the Social Income—A Comment on Professor Kuznets' Reflections', *Economica*, Aug. 1948, pp. 163–72; I. M. D. Little, 'The Valuation of the Social Income', *Economica*, Feb. 1949, pp. 11–26; A. C. Pigou, *Economics of Welfare*, 4th ed. (1932), Part I, especially chaps. ii, iii, v, vi; P. A. Samuelson, *Foundations of Economic Analysis* (1948), chap. viii. Since writing this article I have benefited from reading two

4520.3   B

2   EVALUATION OF REAL NATIONAL INCOME

(b) Less directly, but with equal certainty, C reveals itself to be inferior to A.

(c) The point D reveals itself to be superior to A.

(d) The points E and A reveal nothing about their order in the consumer's taste-pattern.

(e) The point F is inconsistent with A. The consumer has changed his tastes, or he is not in equilibrium at the indicated points.

Problems of Inference from Group Market Data

3. Let us now regard Fig. 1 as applying to market data for two or more individuals, so that each quantity, q, represents the total of two or more individuals' consumption, $q'+q''+,...,$ &c. The slope through A or any other point represents the market-price ratio of the first and second goods, the only commodities in our simplified world.

What can we now say about our points? Advances in the theory of welfare economics since 1940—many of them growing out of Hicks's own researches—suggest that certain of the definitions and propositions then laid down need to be modified. I resurrect these matters only because most people who have seen the recent discussion between Kuznets, Hicks, and Little must find their heads swimming, and must be in considerable doubt as to what the proper status of this vital matter is.

4. First we may clear up one misunderstanding, in itself unimportant, but giving an initial clue that we cannot make any very sweeping inferences from aggregate price-quantity data. In 1940 it was held that a situation like that of A and F is quite impossible on the assumption that individuals preserve the same well-defined tastes and are in true equilibrium in competitive markets.[1] It was held that, for national totals,

$$\sum p_2 q_2 > \sum p_2 q_1 \quad \text{implies} \quad \sum p_1 q_1 < \sum p_1 q_2.$$

As stated earlier, for a single individual this would be a correct assertion; but it is definitely false for group data involving two or more individuals. Examples to show this can be given *ad lib*. No recourse need be made to the Kuznets case of necessaries and luxuries (understanding by the latter, goods which some individuals do not choose to buy at all)—but, of course, there is no reason why such examples should not also be used. Perhaps the very simplest example to illustrate the possibility of a contradiction would be one in which we keep the exact national totals of the point A, but reallocate goods between the individuals so that they come into final equilibrium with a new and different price ratio. Then already we are on

further papers by Little and from corresponding with him. See I. M. D. Little, 'The Foundations of Welfare Economics', *O.E.P.*, June 1949, and an addendum to his *Economica* article 'A Note on the Significance of Index Numbers'.

[1] See *Economica*, May 1940, pp. 112–13.

the borderline of a contradiction, and by making a slight change in the totals we can obviously get a strong outright contradiction.

Already we are warned that $\sum p_2 q_2 > \sum p_2 q_1$ cannot imply that the second situation represents an 'increase in social real income' over that of the first—since this implication would leave us with the real possibility that each situation is better than the other!

This should also warn us against thinking that we can save such a definition by applying it only where there is no such outright contradiction. For suppose that we consider a case which just escapes *revealing* itself to be contradictory; being so close to a nonsense situation, such a case can in no wise escape being subject to the same *fundamental* (as yet undiagnosed) difficulty, even though it may not be advertising the fact to us.

Inadmissibility of the 1940 Definition of Increased Real Income

5. This tells us already that either there is something inadequate about the 1940 definition of an 'increase in society's real income' or else there is something faulty about the logical proof that the index-number criterion $\sum p_2 q_2 > \sum p_2 q_1$ implies such a defined increase in real income.

The 1940 passage in question is so compact that one must be careful in interpreting it. In my judgement the root of the trouble lies more in the inadequacy of the definition enunciated than in the logic of the demonstration that the stated index-number criterion does imply an increase in defined real income. Although it has already been extensively requoted, the relevant 1940 passage is so brief that it can be given completely here.

'. . . What does it signify if $\sum p_2 q_2 > \sum p_2 q_1$?

'It should first of all be noticed that since this condition refers only to the total quantities acquired, it can tell us nothing about the distribution of wealth among the members of the group. There may be a drastic redistribution of wealth among the members and the aggregates will remain exactly the same. Thus what the condition $\sum p_2 q_2 > \sum p_2 q_1$ tells us is that there is *some* distribution of the q_1's which would make every member of the group less well off than he actually is in the II situation. For if the corresponding inequality were to hold for every individual separately, it would hold for the group as a whole.

'As compared with this particular distribution, every other distribution of the q_1's would make some people better off and some worse off. Consequently, if there is one distribution of the q_1's in which every member of the group is worse off than he actually is in the II situation, there can be no distribution in which everyone is better off, or even as well off. Thus if we start from any actual distribution of wealth in the I situation, what the condition $\sum p_2 q_2 > \sum p_2 q_1$ tells us is that it is impossible to reach, by redistribution, a position in which everyone is as well off as he is in the II situation.

'This would seem to be quite acceptable as a definition of increase in real social income. Let us say that the real income of society is higher in Situation II than in Situation I, if it is impossible to make everyone as well off as he is in Situation II by any redistribution of the actual quantities acquired in Situation I. If this definition is accepted, our criteria can be applied to it without change.'[1]

[1] J. R. Hicks, 'The Valuation of the Social Income', *Economica*, May 1940, p. 111.

4   EVALUATION OF REAL NATIONAL INCOME

6. A diagram that we shall place major reliance on in the later discussion can be used to illustrate exactly what is involved in this definition of an 'increase in social real income'. On the axes in Fig. 2 there is laid out the ordinal utility of each of two individuals: the exact scale of U'' or U' is of no consequence, only the north–south and east–west orderings being important. Corresponding to the point A or 2 in Fig. 1, there will actually be some allocation of the total of goods between our individuals, and hence some determined level of well-being for each. Let the point labelled 2 in Fig. 2 represent that actual level of ordinal well-being. Now consider the other situation that was labelled C or 1 in our earlier figure. Behind the

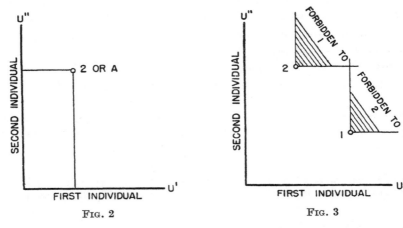

FIG. 2   FIG. 3

scenes, unknown to us from the totals, there is again an actual allocation of the goods to the individuals and again a new point in Fig. 2. If we knew where it was, we could write it in and label it 1. We do not know where this new point will fall: it may be south-west of point 2 so that all individuals are worse off, or south-east so that one individual is better off and the other worse off, and so forth.

Hicks's 1940 definition of an increase in real income from the point 1 to 2 consists of this: if we can be sure that neither point 1 nor any reallocation of its quantities among individuals lies north-east of point 2 (with both individuals better off in 1 than in 2), then point 2 is defined to represent an increase in real income over point 1.

How acceptable is this definition, leaving aside for the moment the question of whether the index-number criteria does permit us to place such a restriction on the admissible position of point 1 ? Upon reflection, we will all agree, I think, that such a definition is not very satisfactory. By means of it a point 1 may be both better and worse than another point 2. This is shown in Fig. 3. Also the definition has small claims on our affections in terms of our common-sense intuitions. Its last disadvantage is a subtle but important one: correctly stated, the new welfare economics is a body of doctrines which attempts to go as far as possible in preparing the way for the final a-scientific step involving ethical judgements; it should never, therefore, prejudice the final step, but only make statements which are uniformly valid for a wide class of ethical systems. Suppose now that we have given to us in Fig. 2 a set of social indifference curves (the contours of a Bergson social welfare function). It is more than possible that a 'point' or 'situation' (they are not quite the same thing) judged by the 1940 criterion to be the superior one may actually be the 'inferior' one in terms of the wider ethical judgements.

7. Instinctively Hicks was reaching out, I believe, for a rather different definition than the one he actually enunciated. The simpler problem of comparing A and B in Fig. 1 will bring this out and at the same time require no intricate index-number reasoning. As before, corresponding to the point A in Fig. 1 there is in Fig. 2 a point 2 representing the ordinal well-being of all individuals. Now with less of *all* goods available to society as shown by B, there will be a new point of individuals' well-being in Fig. 2. Where will the new point lie with respect to the former point 2?

We would have to give the unsatisfactory answer 'anywhere' were it not for one important assumption. We have assumed that behind the scenes of A all individuals are in competitive equilibrium facing the same price ratio. This assures us that all marginal rates of substitution are equal and that there exists no reallocation of the goods of A between them which will permit them both to be better off. (In technical parlance the competitive solution lies somewhere on the *Edgeworth contract locus*.) *A fortiori*, for a point like B, which involves smaller totals for *every* commodity, there is *no* reallocation of goods that could possibly make all individuals better off than they were in A. Without introducing price or index numbers, we know therefore that the point B is forbidden to be northeast of the point A—and we know that B corresponds to a decrease in real income over A according to the old 1940 definition.

But that is not really saying much. It is possible that one individual may be worse off even though the other individual is better off. And we must still entertain the darkest suspicions of a possible contradiction. But this simple case turns out to have at least one surprising feature: if we try to reallocate goods in either of the two situations—always letting the individuals come ultimately into competitive equilibrium—it turns out that we shall *never* find a case where on the 1940 definition the situation B turns out to be 'better' (as well as 'worse') than A. I have not yet proved this in my discussion; but, accepting this fact as true, we find

6   EVALUATION OF REAL NATIONAL INCOME

ourselves on the trail of a better way of defining an increase in real income
—or more accurately, an increase in *potential* real income.

The Crucially Important 'Utility-Possibility Function'

8. Let us consider all possible reallocations between individuals of the
consumption totals corresponding to A or 2. For each way of allocating
the goods there will be a given level of well-being for each and every
individual—as can be indicated by a point on the $U'-U''$ diagram. The
totality of all such possible points obviously cannot go indefinitely far in
the north-east direction; equally obviously there is a frontier curve or
envelope giving, for each amount of one person's utility, the maximum
possible amount of the other person's utility. This frontier is the important
'utility-possibility function' corresponding to A.

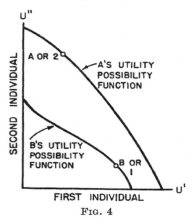

FIG. 4

The point 2 happens to lie on the frontier because at 2 all individuals
are known to be in competitive equilibrium. Corresponding to the smaller
totals of point B, there is also a utility-possibility function. We can now
state the sense in which A or 2 is *potentially* better than B.

The total of all goods being greater in A than in B, the utility-possibility
function of A is uniformly outside and beyond the utility-possibility function of B. (This is shown in Fig. 4.) The reason for this statement is
intuitively obvious and can be expressed in the language of a currently
popular song: A can do everything B can do—(and) better.

9. This, then, is the sense in which we can, without introducing detailed
ethical assumptions, define an 'increase in society's potential real income
in going from point B to point A'. Such an increase means a uniform outward shift in society's utility-possibility function.

Let us now return to the index-number problem. Can we infer that A
is superior to C in terms of our new definition of potential real income?.

P. A. SAMUELSON

If we can, then with minor modifications the 1940 analysis can be accepted. But, unfortunately for economic theory, we cannot make any such inference about potential superiority from the index-number analysis of aggregate price-quantity data.[1]

Any single counter-example will prove the falsity of the index-number criteria as applied to more than one individual. Perhaps the simplest such example would be one in which the first individual cares only for so-called necessaries. If less of total necessaries are available in A, then A's utility-possibility curve must cut inside of B's when we get in the region of the $U''-U'$ quadrant favouring the necessary-loving individual; and hence A cannot represent an unequivocal increase in potential real income. Simple as this example is, it is open to the objection that it seems to involve the case where the individuals consume nothing of some commodity. Actually this is an irrelevant feature of the example.

But, in any case, greater insight into the nature of the problem can be had if we examine the steps in the reasoning linking up the index-number criterion and the 1940 definition of an increase in real income.

10. If we have between the points A and C, or 2 and 1,

$$\sum p_2(q_2'+q_2''+\ldots) > \sum p_2(q_1'+q_1''+\ldots),$$

then according to the 1940 argument we can find some redistribution of the quantities in C or 1, so that the new quantities of every good going to each individual, which we may call

$$q_3'+q_3''+\ldots = q_1'+q_1''+\ldots,$$

are such as to make the crucial index-number criteria hold for each and every individual; namely,

$$\sum p_2 q_2' > \sum p_2 q_3', \qquad \sum p_2 q_2'' > \sum p_2 q_3'', \ldots.$$

Hence there exists a new situation resulting from the reallocation of the q_1's which is worse for *every* individual than is situation 2.

A missing step in the 1940 logic must be filled in at this point. The fact that we can reallocate the q_1's to get a new point q_3 which makes both individuals worse off than they are in 2 is taken to mean that the utility-possibility curve of 1 must be south-west of the point 2. But nothing has been said to show that q_3 is a frontier point on the utility-possibility function of point 1. Fortunately, it can be easily proved that there does exist at least one (and actually an infinite number) reallocation of the q_2's that

---

[1] Simple logic tells us that this negative answer must be forthcoming in a comparison of A and F since each of two curves cannot both lie uniformly outside of each other; and already we have seen reason to believe that the A and F comparison does not differ materially from that of A and C.

8   EVALUATION OF REAL NATIONAL INCOME

(*a*) lies on the utility-possibility function of 1, and (*b*) causes our index-number criteria to hold for each and every individual.[1]

With the above provision, we may accept the 1940 demonstration that when aggregate data satisfy the index-number criterion, the 1940 definition of superiority is definitely realized.[2] But there is nothing in this demonstration that tells us whether the utility-possibility function of 2 lies above (or below) the point 1;[3] all we know is that 1's utility-possibility function lies somewhere south-west of the point 2.

[1] Fig. 5 shows all this. An Edgeworth–Bowley box has been drawn up with the dimensions of the quantities in the q_1 situation. From the south-west corner of the box we measure off the consumption of the first individual, U'. From the north-east corner we measure downward and to the left the consumption of the U'' individual. Any point in the box represents a possible allocation of the total q_1 quantities, with the point marked q_1 being the one actually observed.

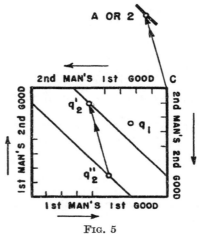

FIG. 5

On this same diagram we may also show the actual quantities consumed by the individuals in the q_2 situation. But now it takes two points in the box, as far apart from each other as C is from A. They are marked q_2' and q_2'' respectively, and the price-lines through their points are drawn in with the slope of the p_2 situation.

As the picture stands q_1 does not satisfy the index-number criteria for the U' individual since q_1 does *not* lie inside the crucial triangle of the point q_2'. Hicks's statement is that there is some reallocation which will move the point q_1 to a new point q_3 which lies between the two parallel lines. For any such point our index-number criteria are satisfied for both individuals. The missing step is to show that there exist points in this strip which are also on the Edgeworth contract curve. Since the contract curve must go from one corner of the box to the other and pass through all levels of U' and U'', it must obviously somewhere pass through the intervening strip between the parallel lines. This supplies the missing step. Readers of Kuznets should note that it is the totals of q_1, not of q_2, that are reallocated so as to lead to Hicks's conclusion.

[2] This is apparently what Little means when he concludes that the 1940 definition is 'immune from Professor Kuznets conditions' (loc. cit., p. 13).

[3] In any case, no one should think that the condition

$$\Sigma\, p_1\, q_2 > \Sigma\, p_1\, q_1$$

which is satisfied in C (but not in F) helps to rule out a contradiction.

11. Our final conclusions may be summarized briefly. The index-number criterion

$$\sum p_2(q'_2+q''_2+...) > \sum p_2(q'_1+q''_1+...)$$

tells us that the utility-possibility function of 2 does lie outside of that of 1 *in the neighbourhood* of the actual observed point 2—but that is all it tells us. The curve may intersect and cross elsewhere—as shown in the later Fig. 6.

The Hicks–Kaldor–Scitovsky Version of New Welfare Economics

12. Having failed to relate the stronger definition of potential superiority to index-number criteria, we must reconsider whether, after all, the 1940 definition of superiority may not be tolerably acceptable. If we examine this definition, we find that it is in all essentials the same one as that earlier suggested by N. Kaldor and by Hicks in his earlier article on the 'Foundations of Welfare Economics'.[1] It will be recalled that these two writers had ruled that situation X is better than situation Y if there exists a reallocation of the goods in X which makes everybody better off than he was in Y. Except that the 1940 definition applied to a *decrease* in well-being between 2 and 1, this is identical with the earlier 1939 definition.

Dissatisfaction early developed over the 1939 definition. In particular T. Scitovsky[2] came forward with the objection that it seemed to assume that there was something right (ethically) about the distribution of income in the *status quo ante* of the Y situation. To get around this he suggested (in effect) that a *double* test be applied.

To say that 'X is better than Y' we must be sure that (*a*) there exists a reallocation of the X goods that could make everybody better off than he actually was in Y; and (*b*) we must make sure there exists a reallocation of the goods in Y that could make everybody worse off than he actually was in X.

Or, in our terminology, the Scitovsky definition of superiority requires the utility-possibility curve of one situation to be beyond that of the other in the neighbourhood of *both* actual observed points.

13. In his criticism of the 1940 definition Kuznets can be generously interpreted to be trying (presumably independently) in effect to reiterate the Scitovsky double criterion. Kuznets says at one point that we must

[1] N. Kaldor, 'Welfare Propositions in Economics', *Economic Journal*, xlix, 1939, pp. 549–52; J. R. Hicks, 'Foundations of Welfare Economics', *Economic Journal*, xlix, 1939, pp. 696–712.

[2] T. Scitovsky, 'A Note on Welfare Propositions in Economics', *Review of Economic Studies*, 1941, pp. 77–88, and 'A Reconsideration of the Theory of Tariffs', *Review of Economic Studies*, 1942, pp. 89–110. To be precise Hicks is in 1940 riding the Scitovsky and Kuznets the Kaldor horse.

10   EVALUATION OF REAL NATIONAL INCOME

supplement the Hicks condition [that there must be a reallocation of the q_1's that makes everyone worse off than he actually was in the q_2 situation] by the further condition that '[it must be] impossible to make *everyone* as well off as he is in situation I by any redistribution of the actual quantities acquired in situation II' (*Economica*, 1948, p. 4).

Kaldor has explicitly accepted the Scitovsky correction, and as far as I know so has Hicks. Therefore they would both presumably have no quarrel with this Kuznets reversibility condition.[1] But both Kuznets and Hicks do not seem to realize that the difficulty is basic and has nothing to do with the question of substitutability of necessaries or luxuries. On the Scitovsky-amended definition, the whole demonstration of superiority of one position over another by aggregate index-number criteria breaks down completely.[2]

14. Our whole theory of arriving at a measure of real income by aggregative price-quantity data has broken down. But the worst is still to come. The Scitovsky conditions are themselves very definitely unsatisfactory. It is not enough to double the 1939 conditions—we must increase them infinitely. Instead of a two-point test we need an infinitely large number of tests—that is to say, we must be sure that one of the utility-possibility functions *everywhere* lies outside the other. Without this test at an infinite number of points, no acceptable definition of an increase in potential real income can be devised at the non-ethical level of the new welfare economics.

Just as Scitovsky has criticized Kaldor and 'compensationists' for assuming the correctness of the *status quo ante*, so we must criticize him for assuming in some sense the correctness of the *status quo ante* and/or the *status quo post*.

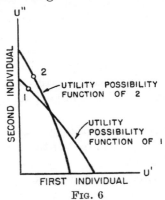

FIG. 6

Suppose, for example, we have *everybody actually* better off in situation 2 than in 1. Kaldor and Hicks will be satisfied to call 2 better than 1. So will Scitovsky. But the utility-possibility curves might very well cross as in Fig. 6, so that according to many ethical welfare functions both Scitovsky and the others would be rendering false statements.

What Scitovsky should have done was to free all of his comparisons from any depend-

---

[1] Little has argued (*Economica*, 1949, pp. 12–16) that there is a confusion in Kuznets on the point of reversibility. Perhaps I am setting down what Kuznets should have meant rather than what he meant to say.

[2] The best that we can say is the following. Imagine the change from point 2 to point 1 to be a continuous one. So long as the two points are sufficiently (!) close together, then the condition $\Sigma p_2 q_2 > \Sigma p_2 q_1$ assures us that 2 is better than 1 in the Scitovsky sense. For changes of any size $\Sigma p_2 q_2 > \Sigma p_2 q_1$ tells us that 1 *cannot* be superior to 2 in Scitovsky or in my sense, and that is all it tells.

ence upon either *actually observed* $U''-U'$ situation. He should, instead, have made the comparison depend upon the totality of all *possible* positions in each situation. This would have led to the definition of potential real income earlier proposed, which seems to be the only satisfactory, self-consistent definition within the sphere of the 'new' (relatively *wert-frei*) welfare economics. Aggregate index numbers can tell us little about this except in a negative way. Even this definition is not—by itself—worth very much of anything for policy purposes, as will be shown.

Inadequacies for Policy of the New Welfare Economics

15. We have seen that the new welfare economics is able to define an increase in potential real income which is unambiguous, consistent, and which will not turn out to contradict a wide class of ethical social welfare functions that must later be introduced into any problem. The new welfare economics does not go all the way in settling the problems of normative policy: taken by itself, and without supplementation, it goes virtually none of the way; but taken in conjunction with later ethical assumptions, it attempts to clear the way of all issues that can be disposed of in a non-controversial (relatively) ethical-free fashion. This is the solid kernel of usefulness in the new approach begun by Pareto, and this should not be lost sight of in the welter of exaggerated claims for the new welfare economics.

The inadequacy for actual policy decisions—even in the most idealized, simplified world—of all of the discussed measures of 'real income' can be illustrated by numerous examples. Consider the very best case where we can establish the fact that situation 2 is *potentially* better than 1 (in the sense of having a uniformly farther-out utility-possibility function). Would a good fairy given the chance to throw a switch from 1 to 2 be able to justify doing so? Upon reflection we must, I am afraid, answer *no*. Potentialities are not actualities—and unless she can give a justification of her act that will satisfy all reasonably defined social welfare functions, she cannot know whether or not to pull the switch.

A few negative remarks are possible: for any ethical system with the property that an increase in one individual's well-being is, others' being equal, a good thing[1]—for all such systems a final optimum position must necessarily be on 2 and not on 1. That we can certainly say. But without going into the realm of (modern, streamlined) 'old' welfare economics, we cannot say more or get conclusive advice on this problem of policy. The attempt to divide the problem into two parts so that one can say 'a change from 1 to 2 is *economically* desirable in the sense of objectively increasing

---

[1] i.e. for all social welfare propositions W, with the property $W = F(u', u'',...)$ and $\dfrac{\partial W}{\partial u'} > 0 < \dfrac{\partial W}{\partial u''}, ...$

12   EVALUATION OF REAL NATIONAL INCOME

production or wealth, whether or not the actual resulting situation will be ethically superior', only gets one into a semantic snarl and glosses over the intrinsic difficulties of the problem.

How much more severe are the policy limitations of some of the modern even weaker 'compensationist' definitions. Following them, the good fairy might do perpetual and irremediable harm. Suppose, for example, that our two *actually observed* points, 1 and 2, both lie above the intersection of the two schedules in Fig. 6, but with the point 1 being south-east of point 2, so as to represent an increase in well-being of one individual and a decrease for the other. The Kaldor condition would be satisfied and so would the Scitovsky condition. Suppose that once the angel has thrown the switch, she can never again reverse it (e.g. capital sunk into a mine may be irrecoverable). Let her now follow the counsel of the compensationists and throw the switch from 1 to 2. According to any ethical view that considers individual U' to be of the elect (or relatively so) and U'' to be relatively undeserving of consideration, the good life lies in a rather easterly direction. For ever and ever 'society' is condemned to 'unhappiness' because of the premature decision based on the Kaldor–Hicks–Scitovsky rules.[1]

Production Possibilities and Group Inferences

16. This completes the problem of making group inferences from simple index-number comparisons. At the non-philosophical level there are still two more grave difficulties to be faced. Up till now I have always spoken of the utility-possibility function of *point A*, not of situation A. But the totals of goods at A or 2 do not fall from heaven in fixed amounts. Obviously other total quantities might instead have been produced. Therefore, the true utility-possibility function corresponding to situation A is really wider and out farther than the one defined for point A. At best, if all markets are perfect and there are no external effects or government distortions, the utility-possibility function for point A may just touch that of situation A at the actual observed point, elsewhere being inside it. The wider schedule is the envelope of a family of schedules corresponding to each *possible* point of total consumption goods. (See Fig. 8.)

Obviously it is the wider possibility function of a 'situation' rather than of a 'point' with which we should be concerned, and before we go throwing

---

[1] If both individuals are better off in the observed 2 point than in the observed 1 point, how reasonable it seems to counsel that the switch be pulled. And if the only alternative were these two situations, almost all old welfare economists might agree. But this need not be our choice of alternatives at all. Realistically, the choice may be between these two points and a third ethically superior point that lies on 1's locus. As a matter of tactics and *realpolitik*, one will sometimes want to follow such simple criteria *and* actually give compensation, or perhaps fail to compensate. But tactics aside, these rules are in principle incomplete.

any switches or making policy decisions we must make sure how alternative production possibilities affect the problem. A few truths continue to remain self-evident, but, generally speaking, this new element makes the problem of definite inference even more difficult—an important but sad fact.

Let us consider an example. Up till now the one unshaken truth that remained was this: If more of every good is observed in point *A* than in point *B*, then *A* represents an increase in potential real national income over *B*. Even this is no longer necessarily valid! Suppose we draw up production-possibility curves showing how much of each good can be produced in total when the total of the other good is specified. Such a chart might look like Fig. 6 except that now the two outputs rather than utilities are on the axes. In Fig. 7 our observed point *A* lies north-east of the observed point *B*, and yet it is obvious that the production-possibility curves can still cross; and it is also obvious, upon reflection, that depend-

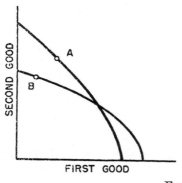 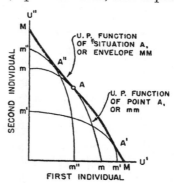

FIGS. 7 and 8

ing upon how much people like one good as compared to another, the *corresponding utility-possibility curve can most definitely cross*—making no unambiguous inference about an increase in potential real income possible.

17. So long as commodities are really economic rather than free goods, this much can be said: *If the production-possibility function of one situation lies uniformly outside that of a second situation, then the utility-possibility function of the one will also be outside that of the other.* In the limiting case where one or both individuals do not care at all for one of the goods, the schedules might just be touching at one or more points. Also it is to be understood that if the total of resources (land, labour, &c.) is not the same in the two situations, these resources are to be treated just like negative commodities, and it is in this sense that one production-possibility function must lie uniformly outside the other.

Hicks attempted in 1940 to explore the relationship between index-number criteria based on price-quantity data and productivity as measured

14   EVALUATION OF REAL NATIONAL INCOME

by the position of the production-possibility function of society. His
treatment was brief and much of it he had abandoned prior to Kuznets's
1948 criticisms. But even after the recent exchange of views I do not feel
the subject is left in its proper state. To analyse the problem in its entirety
would be too lengthy a task, but a number of observations are relevant to
our discussion. In all that follows I shall assume that there are no excise
taxes, so that the irrelevant distinction between income-at-factor-prices
and income-at-market-prices can be disregarded.

Under this last assumption, would the same $\sum pq$ tests relevant to
indicating a (1940-defined) increase in welfare also serve to indicate a shift
in productivity? One is almost tempted to read such a belief into the
following passage:

'If competition were perfect, and if state activities were so designed as not to
disturb the *optimum* organization of production, marginal utilities and prices and
marginal costs would all be proportional, so that the same valuation which would
give us the social income as a measure of economic welfare would also give us the
social income as a measure of productivity.'[1]

Kuznets objected to all this on the grounds that production-possibility
curves, unlike indifference curves, can intersect and can be of variable
curvature. His instinct that something is rotten in Denmark may be a
sound one, but the precise trouble has not really been isolated, nor a worse
difficulty brought to light.

In the first place, there is no need for an individual's indifference curves
always to be concave: he need only be assumed to be in equilibrium at the
observed points. In the second place, it is untrue that collectively defined
indifference curves (*à la* Scitovsky or otherwise) are forbidden to intersect
and cross. Our earlier discussion of the points A and F may be referred to
in this connexion. Neither of these two reasons can serve to isolate the
basic difficulties of making production inferences.[2]

[1] *Economica*, 1940, p. 122. Hicks goes on to say, parenthetically: 'It would not be very
reliable as a measure of productivity, but it might usually satisfy the productivity tests for
small displacements, over which the substitution curves might not differ very much from
straight lines.' To make the only comparisons between different situations that are valid,
this last linearity assumption can be shown to be unnecessary; but it foreshadows Hicks's
later desire for an approximate representation of the production-possibility function in the
neighbourhood of an observed optimal point. A straight line gives, under the assumed
conditions, an upper (rather than a conservative, lower) bound as to what is producible.

[2] Kuznets has a third objection which has little or nothing to do with the problem here
discussed. Working by analogy with the consumption problem, he makes the strange and
unnecessary assumption that a perfect price system is in some sense maximizing 'producers'
surpluses', and he raises the question whether specificity of some resources may not make
it impossible for every producer to be as well off as previously. Both Hicks and I would
consider producers and consumers to be the same units, who buy goods and also sell services;
all such services can be treated as negative goods and all ordinal disutilities treated along
with ordinal utilities. Firms (corporations) provide the place where producers work but
themselves have no welfare feelings, although their owners' welfare is important. The problem at hand is what we can or cannot say about the production-possibility functions *of
society* in two situations.

P. A. SAMUELSON 15

In the production or firm field we have an institutional difficulty absent from the household markets: few families act like monopsonists, but many, if not most, firms sell in markets which are less than perfectly competitive. Let us waive this difficulty for the moment and assume that technological and market conditions are most suitable to perfect competition: namely, constant-returns-to-scale prevails and there is 'free entry'. In this case, any observed point of total output—such as A or 2 in Fig. 1—would represent a *maximum* of $\sum p_2 q$ subject to all the production possibilities of the situation. Geometrically the straight line running through A can never be inside the true production-possibility schedule.

Does this mean that the criterion $\sum p_2 q_2 > \sum p_1 q_1$ in Fig. 1 assures us of *both* of the following: that 2 is better than 1 *in welfare*, and 2 is better *in a production-possibility sense* than 1 ? It must *not* be so interpreted. The production problem involves a certain *maximum* condition, the consumption case a related *minimum* condition. The same index-number calculation can never serve as a crucial indicator for the two problems: if it is a reliable criterion for welfare, it tells us nothing about production; if it has unambiguous production implications, then welfare inferences are impossible.

There are essentially only four possible cases that have to be considered: a comparison of A and C in Fig. 1, of A and D, of A and F, and the almost trivial case of A and B. In this last case, where the A situation has more of every good than the B, we know immediately that the production-possibility function of A lies outside that of B in the neighbourhood of both observed points, and we also know that A's utility-possibility function (defined narrowly for the points rather than broadly for the situations) lies everywhere outside of that of B. All this is obvious, so we can concentrate our attention on the three other possible comparisons. To keep the notation simple we can always give the point A the number 2 and give all other compared points the number 1. Our cases, then, are as follows:

	Concerning 1940 def. of welfare	Concerning position of production-possibility function (p.p.f.)
Case A (or 2) and C (or 1):		
$\sum p_2 q_2 > \sum p_2 q_1$ tells us	2 better than 1	nothing
$\sum p_1 q_2 > \sum p_1 q_1$ tells us	nothing	p.p.f. of 1 outside of p.p.f. of 2 near point 2
Case A (or 2) and D (or 1):		
$\sum p_2 q_2 < \sum p_2 q_1$ tells us	nothing	p.p.f. of 1 outside of p.p.f. of 2 near point 1
$\sum p_1 q_2 > \sum p_1 q_1$ tells us	nothing	p.p.f. of 2 outside of p.p.f. of 1 near point 2
Case A (or 2) and F (or 1):		
$\sum p_2 q_2 > \sum p_2 q_1$ tells us	2 better than 1	nothing
$\sum p_1 q_1 > \sum p_1 q_2$ tells us	1 better than 2	nothing

16   EVALUATION OF REAL NATIONAL INCOME

Under the present assumptions we can make inferences about the shifting of production-possibility functions that are no less strong than those
about welfare. We can never hope to infer from index-number tests that
one production-possibility curve has shifted *uniformly* with respect to
another—but then we have earlier seen that we can never hope to make
such welfare inferences either. It will be noted from the table that where
light is thrown on productivity it is withheld from welfare, and vice versa.
This might almost seem to offer comfort: we seem always to be able to
say *something* about any situation. But, alas, this is an illusion.

The Impossibility of Unequivocal Inferences

18. Even that which we have in the field of welfare indicators is to be
taken away from us now that we have enlarged our alternatives to all the
production possibilities of each situation rather than to the single observed
points. *We shall never be able to infer a genuine change in potential real
income as I have earlier defined the term*—no, not even in the simplest
comparison of A which shows more of every good than the point B. (This
was already shown in Fig. 7.) Unsatisfactory as the 1940 definitions of
welfare were, we are tempted to beat a hasty retreat back to them. But to no
good purpose: even these fragile reeds are blown down by the new winds.

Specifically, the observation $\sum p_2 q_2 > \sum p_2 q_1$ no longer implies that
the utility-possibility function of *situation* 1 lies inside that of A even in
the neighbourhood of the point 2, or anywhere at all for that matter!
The whole 1940 proof by Hicks—as supplemented in my earlier lengthy
footnote concerning the box-diagram—breaks down completely. The
demonstration fails, the argument no longer leads logically to the desired
conclusion. By itself this does not show that there may not be found
some different proof. However, the theorem can be proved to be false, so
that no valid alternative proof exists.

A single example provides a decisive exception to the theorem (that we
can infer a local shift in the utility-possibility function). The point F in
Fig. 1 has a utility-possibility curve which may be almost anywhere with
respect to that of A, as far as anything we know. There is no reason why
it could not always lie outside of A's; there is also no reason why the
point F should not lie on C's production-possibility curve; there is also no
reason why the utility-possibility function of the general situation C
should not be close to or identical with the utility-possibility function of
the point F (except possibly at the observed point C itself). It follows that
we can easily imagine the utility-possibility function of the situation C to
lie *above and beyond* the observed point A—which contradicts the Hicks-
like theorem that situation C's curve must lie somewhere south-west of
the A point. This example shows that the Hicks's proof remains no longer

valid when it ceases to be simply a question of reallocating a given fixed total in the 1 situation.

The Interrelation between Production and Utility-Possibility Functions

19. Production possibilities as such have no normative connotations. We are interested in them for the light they throw on utility possibilities. This is why economists have wanted to include such wasteful output as war goods in their calculations of national product; presumably they serve as some kind of an index of the useful things that might be produced in better times. Our last hope to make welfare statements lies in spelling out the welfare implications of any recognizable shifts in production possibilities.

A uniform outward shift in the production-possibility function—such as can never be revealed by index-number comparisons—must certainly shift the utility-possibility schedule outward. The converse is not true. An outward shift in the utility-possibility function may have occurred as the result of a *twist* of the production-possibility curve. This is because people's tastes for different goods may be such that the points on the new production schedule that lie inward may be points that would never be observed in any optimal competitive market. An 'observable' point is one which, as the result of some allocation of initial resources or so-called 'distribution of income', would lead to one of the points on the utility-possibility frontier.

In the typical case where $\sum p_1 q_1 < \sum p_1 q_2$, so that we know that the production-possibility function of 2 is outside of that of 1 somewhere near the observed point 2, we should like to be able to say that 2's utility-possibility function lies outside that of 1 in the neighbourhood of the observed point 2. But we cannot. The utility-possibility functions of situation 2 and of point 2 both lie outside the utility-possibility function of the points which are known to lie south-west of the observed point 2 on the production-possibilities diagram. But all such points might turn out to be non-observable ones. Only if an observable point 2 is known to give more of all goods than an *observable* point of the situation 1 can we even infer that situation 2 is superior to 1 in the weak 1940 sense. Index-number data are never enough to provide us with knowledge of two such observable points except in the trivial case (like A and B) where one point is better in respect to every good, and where index-number calculations are unnecessary to establish the only fact that can be established: namely, the production-possibility function of A must lie outside that of B near the observed points and the same must be true about the related utility-possibility function.

Under the best conditions of the purest of competition very little indeed

18   EVALUATION OF REAL NATIONAL INCOME

of welfare significance can ever be revealed by price-quantity data alone. Needless to say, with the actual statistical problems in a world of imperfect competition and decreasing costs, observed prices have even less significance as indicators of the shape of society's true production-possibility curve.

Political Feasibility as a Crucial Condition in Welfare Economics

20. The last limitation on the applicability to policy of the new welfare economics concepts is in practice one of the most important of all. It hinges around the practical unattainability of the production-possibility and utility-possibility function earlier discussed. It is not simply that imperfections of competitions are so widespread as to keep society from reaching its optimal production frontier; or that government interferences inevitably cause distortions; or that external diseconomies and economies can never be recognized and computed. All these are true enough.[1]

The essential point now to be stressed is that we could move people to different points on the utility-possibility function only *by an ideally perfect and unattainable system of absolutely lump-sum taxes or subsidies.* In point of fact, suppose that, in the simplest case, competitive *laissez-faire* puts us at one point on the utility-possibility function. Then we can only seek to change the distribution of income by a system of *feasible* legislation: e.g. progressive income tax, rationing, &c. All such policies involve a distortion of marginal decisions, some involving great distortions but in every case some distortion. They move us then *inside* the utility-possibility curve. We can pick policies which strive to minimize the harmful effects of redistribution, but in practice we cannot reduce such effects to zero. A 'feasible utility function' can conceptually be drawn up which lies more or less far inside the utility-possibility function, depending upon how Utopian were our assumptions about legislation, public opinion, &c.

All this is shown in Fig. 9. The point *L* represents the imputation resulting from a situation of relatively *laissez-faire*. It is made to lie on the heavy-line utility-possibility function—which it would only do in a very perfect competitive world.

Let us suppose that the tastes and abilities of the two individuals are identical so that we can use similar indicators of their ordinal preferences. But let them differ in their ownership of resources (say land) so that the

---

[1] They can be thought of as forces keeping us from reaching the true possibility frontier; or if we are in a non-perfectionist mood and willing to compromise with evil, they may be thought of as defining a not-so-far-out but pragmatically obtainable frontier. If the latter interpretation is made, we must be careful to realize that the slopes of the defined frontiers need have little correspondence with market prices, marginal costs of production, &c. As I have earlier pointed out (*Foundations*, p. 221), the constraints under which society is conceived as working are arbitrary and must be given by non-economic assumptions. England's production possibilities would be different if the laws of physics could be disregarded or if we could assume that all workers would do their 'best', or . . . or.

income of U'' is much greater than that of U', as indicated by the position of L relative to the 45°-line of 'equal income'. In a Utopia there might be some way of redistributing wealth or income that would move us along the outside curve from L to the point of complete equality, E, or even beyond. But in practice the only feasible path that Congress or Parliament could follow would be along the light-line utility-feasibility curve.[1]

Space does not permit me to work out the far-reaching implications of this point of view. It is enough to point out here that situation A may have a uniformly better production-possibility function than B, and also a uniformly better utility-possibility function.

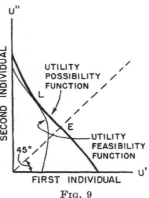

FIG. 9

But a change from B to A might so alter the distribution of market-imputed income away from the 'worthy' and towards the 'unworthy' as to make it an undesirable move from many ethical viewpoints. The *utility-feasibility function* of A may very well cross that of B, so that no statement about potentialities, much less about actualities, can be validly made.

By all means let us pray that feasibilities and possibilities be brought closer and closer. But let us not indulge in the illusion that our prayers have been answered and that we can issue new-welfare-economics prescriptions accordingly.[2]

Final Summary

21. This has been a long and closely reasoned essay. A brief summary may pull the threads together.

1. Certain $\sum pq$ calculations tell us when a single individual has improved himself.

2. The only consistent and ethics-free definition of an increase in potential

---

[1] A strong ethical equalitarian would have to reckon with this fact; and unless his social welfare functions had complete L-shaped corners along the 45° line, or even bent back *à la* Veblen and like the dog-in-the-manger, he would find his feasible optimum at some distance from equality of incomes. All this has a bearing, I believe, on the debate between Meade and Kahn as to whether rationing and food subsidies ought necessarily to be rejected by rational equalitarians in favour of greater reliance on income taxes or other more orthodox devices.

[2] A few comments on the cited Little article on 'Foundations' are perhaps in order. There is much I agree with in this paper, and much I do not yet understand. His semantic jousts with the post-Kaldor school falls under the first heading; his analysis of the meaning of a *social or economic welfare function* under the second. The part of his paper that is most relevant to the present technical discussion is his proposed 'foundations' for a 'system' of welfare economics. In my present understanding of it—still admittedly vague—Little has stated a few theorems of one type. These are understandable in terms of the language of a welfare function, and are more in the nature of one arch or wing of a structure than its foundations. The technical content of the theorems is discussed in the last footnote of the appended Pigou note.

real income of a group is that based upon a uniform shift of the utility-possibility function for the group. $\sum pq$ calculations based on aggregate data never permit us to make such inferences about uniform shifts.

3. The condition $\sum p_2 q_2 > \sum p_2 q_1$ does tell us that the utility-possibility function of the *point* 2 is outside the utility-possibility function of the *point* 1 somewhere near 2. It is not acceptable to define this as an increase in real income for a number of reasons, not the least being that we may end up with 2 defined to be both 'better' and 'worse' than 1.

4. Scitovsky and later Kuznets have suggested a partial strengthening of the earlier definitions of superiority so as to rule out certain revealed inconsistencies. But even these two-sided requirements are not stringent enough; when made infinite-sided, as they must be to avoid inconsistency or implicit ethics, they become equivalent to the definition based upon a uniform shift of the utility-possibility schedule. And even when this rigid definition is realized, we cannot properly prescribe complete policy prescriptions without bringing in ethics.

5. When we come to make inferences about two *situations*, each of which involves a whole *set* of production possibilities rather than about just the observed *points*, even the limited welfare inferences of point 3 break down completely. Under the most perfect conditions suitable for pure competition (where the production-possibility curve can never be concave) a few inferences concerning the local shifts of the production-possibility schedules are possible: e.g. $\sum p_2 q_2 < \sum p_2 q_1$ implies that 1's production-possibility function is outside 2's in the neighbourhood of the observed 2 point.

6. The inferred shifts of production-possibility functions are not enough to permit similar inferences about the utility-possibility functions. This is because that portion of a production-possibility curve which has clearly been revealed to be inside another or 'inferior' may (for all we know) consist entirely of 'unobservable points' that have no correspondence with the truly observable points along the related utility-possibility frontier.

7. The utility-possibility functions defined above are not really possible or available to society; they would be so only in a Utopian world of 'perfect' lump-sum taxes and other ideal conditions. Depending upon how optimistic our assumptions are, we must think of society as being contained within a *utility-feasibility function* which lies inside the *utility-possibility function*. At best these are close together in the neighbourhood of the 'points of relative *laissez-faire*'. Other things being equal, redistribution of income will usually involve 'costs', which have to be weighed against the ethically defined 'advantages' of such policies.

8. All this being true, we come to the paradoxical conclusion that a policy which seems to make possible greater production of all goods and

a uniformly better utility-possibility function for society may result in so great (and ethically undesirable) a change in the imputation of different individuals' incomes, that we may have to judge such a policy 'bad'. Such a judgement sounds as if it necessarily involves ethics, but it may be reworded so as to be relatively free of value judgements by being given the following interpretation: A policy that shifts society's utility-possibility function uniformly outward may not at the same time shift the utility-feasibility function uniformly outward, instead causing it to twist inward in some places. One last warning is in order: to define what is feasible involves many arbitrary assumptions, some of them of an ethical nature.

The above analysis enables us to appraise critically Pigou's important definitions of real income; this has been reserved for a separate appendix, which—except for a few cross-references—is self-contained.

MASSACHUSETTS INSTITUTE
  OF TECHNOLOGY.

A NOTE ON PIGOU'S TREATMENT OF INCOME

1. Despite the vast efforts of government agencies and bureaux in the last 20 years, Pigou's *Economics of Welfare* remains the classic discussion of the definition of real national income. Our previous analysis permits us to make a rapid critique of his masterly analysis. Even if I am right that certain of his formulations need minor amendation, his conclusions for welfare economics remain untouched. Pigou's principal theorem—that each resource should have equal marginal (social) productivity in every use, with price everywhere equal to marginal (social) cost—does not depend for its demonstration upon the elaborate discussion of the national dividend in Part I. In these days, when the national income approach is all the rage as a pedagogic device for coating the pill of elementary economics, it is worth noting that Pigou had seized upon this method of exposition more than a quarter of a century ago. Whether it would have been possible for him to have side-stepped completely the introductory discussion of real national income is irrelevant, since by choosing not to do so Pigou was led to make substantial contributions to the modern theory of economic index numbers (of the Könus, Bowley, Haberler, Staehle type).

2. According to Pigou, economic welfare is 'that part of social welfare that can be brought directly or indirectly into relation with the measuring-rod of money'. The national dividend or real national income is 'the objective counterpart of economic welfare'. Pigou would like to adopt the intuitive position that the dividend should be a function of objective quantities of goods alone, and not depend on 'the state of people's tastes'. But since (a) there is not a single commodity, and (b) all commodities do not move in the same proportion, or (c) even all in the same general direction, Pigou reluctantly considers such an objective definition not feasible, and settles for a more subjective definition according to which *the real income of any person is said to be higher for batch of goods II than for I if II is higher up on his indifference or preference map.*

These are not his words but my interpretation of them, expressed so as to be theoretically independent of any relationship with money or market-price behaviour. Pigou's exact statement for the case of a single individual is as follows:

'Considering a single individual whose tastes are taken as fixed, we say that his

22   EVALUATION OF REAL NATIONAL INCOME

dividend in period II. is greater than in period I. if the items that are added to it
in period II. are items that he wants more than the items that are taken away
from it in period II.' (*Economics of Welfare*, 4th ed., p. 51.)

The wording is cast in a comparative form to pave the way for consideration of
the more complex case of many individuals where it may be especially difficult to
ask people about their wants and desires and theoretically difficult to define what is
meant by the *wants* of the *group*. Pigou extends his definition further:

'Passing to a group of persons (of given numbers), whose tastes are taken as
fixed and among whom the distribution of purchasing power is also taken as
fixed, we say that the dividend in period II. is greater than in period I. if the
items that are added to it in period II. are items *to conserve which they would be
willing to give more money than they would be willing to give to conserve the items
that are taken away from it in period II.*' (Ibid., pp. 51–2.)

For the moment let us accept the assumption of constant tastes and 'distribution
of purchasing power' and the assumption that people know their own minds and
correctly identify *ex ante* desire with *ex post* satisfaction. Pigou then gives another
verbal reformulation of his definition, saying that the dividend is higher in period II
than in I if 'the economic satisfaction (as measured in money) due to the items
added in period II is greater than the economic satisfaction (as measured in money)
due to the items taken away in period II' (p. 54). Under the assumptions stated, Pigou
believes this method of definition to be 'the natural and obvious one to adopt' (p. 52).

3. I wonder. One can sympathize with the attempt to introduce into the definition
something that a statistician might sink his punch-cards into, but has the introduction of money left the problem unambiguous ? I have repeated the definition to myself
aloud again and again ; and yet even in the case of a single consistent individual about
whom unlimited data were available, I would still not be sure how to proceed.

Pigou himself, according to my interpretation of his various writings, is also put
in an ambivalent mood by his definition. In the next chapter he proceeds to work
with index-number expressions of the form $\sum pq$ where the p's and q's are observed
market data. To my mind this is a perfectly valid procedure in the case of a single
individual (and it can be given a measure of validity for the case of a group along
the lines indicated in my present article). But it is not at all clear that Pigou regards
his own procedure as really valid. Again and again he states that the proper procedure is to measure the monetary strength of people's desires not by the marginal
price data observed but rather by some kind of consumers-surplus type of construction indicating how much they could be made to pay rather than do without the
thing altogether.[1]

Pigou's definition has for the moment betrayed him, and I am willing to defend
his practice against his precept. I suspect that what happened is something like the
following: instead of continuing to look for an ordinal indicator of utility, Pigou
suddenly caught a glimpse of the butterfly of cardinal utility and set out in hot

---

[1] Ibid., pp. 57, 59. In his 1945 introductory work, *Income*, p. 13, Pigou still shows a
desire to use some measure of consumers' surplus (or total utility) rather than market values.
In the 1949 *Veil of Money* he is even more explicit in insisting that the relative weight
of goods should in principle depend upon 'how much of their money income people *would
have been willing* to spend . . . [rather than on] how much money they *actually do spend*. . . .
Weighting by reference to this entails, other things being equal, giving a smaller weight to
changes in items of inelastic and a larger weight to changes in items of elastic demand than
"ought" to be assigned to them if our object is, as I have suggested it might be, to measure
importance by reference to impact on economic satisfaction, given that tastes are constant.
Thus at the very basis of any structure we may erect there is an incorrigible flaw. At the
best, we shall have to content ourselves with a makeshift measure, what exactly in the last
resort it is measuring being ill-defined and blurred' (pp. 60–1). Cf. J. R. Hicks, 'Foundation
of Welfare Economics', *Economic Journal*, xlix, 1939, p. 697, for a related criticism of
Pigou's treatment of marginal and intra-marginal concepts.

pursuit. But he realized that the difficulties of this approach were more than statistical, necessarily involving all the familiar difficulties of Marshallian consumers' surplus. Whether or not the butterfly is obtainable or of any use once caught, we must take care not to belittle the solid fruits of index-number theory that are in our grasp.

4. What Pigou does establish—on pp. 62–3—is that

$$\sum p_2 q_2 > \sum p_2 q_1$$

means that II is better than I for any consistent individual. The reasoning is exactly that of the A and C comparison in my Fig. 1. Likewise

$$\sum p_1 q_1 > \sum p_1 q_2$$

would have meant that I was better than II. Pigou prefers to make the comparisons in the more usual Laspeyre and Paasche index-number ratios[1]

$$P = \frac{\sum p_2 q_2}{\sum p_2 q_1} \gtreqless 1 \quad \text{and} \quad L = \frac{\sum p_1 q_2}{\sum p_1 q_1} \gtreqless 1.$$

If we treat work and other efforts as negative commodities, our analysis becomes slightly more general.[2] But our $\sum pq$ expressions may then be zero or negative, so that the method of ratios may be inapplicable even though the proper comparisons can be made in non-ratio form. As we shall see, the use of such ratios has the further disadvantage that it tempts people to attach *cardinal* significance, in an exact or probalistic sense, to the numerical value of the $\sum pq$ ratios.

5. If both P and L are greater than unity, II is clearly better than I. If both are less than unity, then I is better than II. If they are numerically almost equal—and Pigou seems to think they often will be—then the measurement of welfare is thought to be fairly definite. When they differ numerically, Pigou would often measure welfare by some kind of intermediate mean between them: because the geometric mean—which is the Irving Fisher so-called 'Ideal-Index'—has certain convenient properties, Pigou accepts it 'as the measure of change most satisfactory for our purpose' (p. 69).

I cannot persuade myself to follow Pigou's use of the numerical value of the P and L ratios. In the first place, he—along with Kuznets and many others—treats the measures much too symmetrically. When $P > 1$, we already know that II is better than I. If we learn in addition that $L > 1$, we cannot regard this as further corroboration that II is superior to I; at best it serves as corroboration of the fact that we are dealing with a consistent individual.

The case is much different when you tell us that $L > 1$, and nothing else. We have no right to presume that II is definitely better than I. If now you volunteer to us the second bit of information that $P > 1$ also, we cannot regard this as corroboration of an earlier presumption or certainty yielded by the first bit of information. *In its own right* the second fact, that $P > 1$, tells us all we want to know.

With respect to the opposite case, of recognizing when I is better than II, we must attach crucial importance to $L < 1$; and once again the behaviour of P is corroboration of nothing, except of the presence of inconsistency and changed tastes.

---

[1] Pigou lets $x, y, z, \ldots$ stand for q's and $a, b, c, \ldots$ for p's and writes these expressions in the form

$$P = \frac{I_2}{I_1} \frac{x_1 a_1 + y_1 b_1 + \ldots}{x_1 a_2 + y_1 b_2 + \ldots} \quad \text{or} \quad \frac{\sum p_2 q_2}{\sum p_1 q_1} \frac{\sum p_1 q_1}{\sum p_2 q_1} = \frac{\sum p_2 q_2}{\sum p_2 q_1},$$

$$L = \frac{I_2}{I_1} \frac{x_2 a_1 + y_2 b_1 + \ldots}{x_2 a_2 + y_2 b_2 + \ldots} \quad \text{or} \quad \frac{\sum p_2 q_2}{\sum p_1 q_1} \frac{\sum p_1 q_2}{\sum p_2 q_2} = \frac{\sum p_1 q_2}{\sum p_1 q_1}.$$

[2] Pigou's difficulty concerning an increase in the dividend at the expense of leisure, p. 87, n. 1, could then have been avoided.

24   EVALUATION OF REAL NATIONAL INCOME

6. Looking into Pigou's probability argument, we will find one difficulty that stems from his treating of P and L as symmetrical indicators of welfare. Suppose $P = 3 > 1$ and $L = 0.99 < 1$, and these measurements are known to be perfectly accurate, statistically speaking. Then the testimony of the two measures is contradictory, one being greater and the other less than unity. But P exceeds unity by a greater ratio than L falls short of unity, so that $\sqrt{PL}$, the ideal-index, is much greater than unity. Pigou would conclude—according to my interpretation of pp. 65–6—that II is *probably* greater than I.

My conclusion would be different. I would say that either the individual's tastes have definitely changed between the periods or that he was not in equilibrium in both situations. This is because $P > 1$ tells me that II is higher on his indifference curves than is I, and $L < 1$ tells me the exact opposite, and that is the end of it. There is no sense that I can see in believing that, because P is much greater than 1, its testimony is in a loud enough voice to shout down the whisper of $L < 1$.

7. Actually all is not lost as far as exact inference from such a case is concerned. We can validly state: $P > 1$ implies that the batch of goods II is higher *on the indifference curves that prevailed in period II* than *is* the batch of goods I; and $L < 1$ implies that the first batch of goods is higher than batch II *on the indifference curves that prevailed in period I*.

It would be tempting to argue that P always measures welfare from the II period's tastes and L always measures welfare from the I period's tastes. This would be quite wrong, as Pigou is clearly aware. If $P = 0.99$ and $L = 3.0$, we most certainly cannot state the reverse of the previous paragraph's conclusions. We cannot even infer anything about inconsistency. By its nature P can only give definite evidence concerning batch II's superiority over I, and L can only give definite evidence concerning batch I's superiority over II.[1]

8. The case where $P < 1$ and $L > 1$ is the only one to which Pigou explicitly applies his probability reasoning. As in Fig. 1's comparison of A and E, no certain inference is possible. The unknown indifference curve through A could pass above or below the point E. Now the closer is E to the budget-line through A, or what is the same thing the closer is P to 1, then, 'other things being equal', we should expect that the chance of A's indifference curve's passing above E would be increased. The same chance would be increased, the more L is reduced towards unity, 'other things being equal'. This is the basis for Pigou's common-sense view that the degree to which $\sqrt{(PL)} \gtrless 1$ determines the likelihood of II's being better or worse than I. Between 1928 and 1932 Pigou felt compelled to abandon an argument based upon 'the principle of sufficient reason' that attempted to establish this common-sense conclusion. His reason for abandoning it was not because of any impregnation with the modern tendency among statisticians and philosophers to question arguments based on ignorance or on the 'equal-probability of the unknown', but because of technical difficulties previously unnoticed. I think that some of these difficulties could be side-stepped, but since Pigou is content to abandon his old view, and since I am not enamoured of the principle of sufficient reason, I shall confine my attention to the exact inferences possible.

Consider a point A on an individual's indifference map. Consider the region of all alternative points in comparison with A, A being regarded as II and each of these

---

[1] In § 5, chap. vi, p. 58, Pigou leans over backward too far on the issue of the inferences possible when tastes have changed. He believes that the best we can hope for is to devise measures giving the correct results *when tastes have not changed*. This is because he thinks that to make the inference that the batch II is better than the batch I on the basis of the indifference curves of II, we must know what the batch I *would have been* if the indifference curves of II (rather than the actual indifference curves of I) had then prevailed. This is incorrect, as can be noted from the above discussion and from the fact that in my earlier Fig. 1 the inference about A and C was independent of the actual indifference-ratio slope *through C*.

P. A. SAMUELSON   25

points as I. Consider the contour lines of any symmetric mean of P and L, such as $\sqrt{(PL)}$ = constants. Also consider the contour lines of P = constants and L = constants.

Then this much is true: the contour lines $P = 1$, $L = 1$, and $\sqrt{(PL)} = 1$ all go through A and are tangent to the indifference curve through A. Suppose we use any of the three measures $P \gtrless 1$, $L \gtrless 1$, or $\sqrt{(PL)} \gtrless 1$ to decide whether A is better or worse than the other point tested. Then the 'percentage of points' for which we get wrong answers by these methods goes to zero as we confine ourselves to smaller and smaller regions around A. Also the probability will approach one, as we confine ourselves to ever closer regions around A, that all three methods will give the same testimony. In the limit as the region around A shrinks, the use of the P criterion in those rare cases when it disagrees with the L criterion will lead to a biased estimate —in that all points under such conditions of contradiction will in the limit be declared to be worse than A, including those points which are really better than A. Exclusive reliance on L in case of contradiction will result in an opposite bias towards declaring all doubtful points better than A. In the limit as the second point is constrained to lie in ever closer regions to A, the use of $\sqrt{(PL)} \gtrless 1$ criterion will lead to a percentage of wrong decisions that approaches ever closer to zero.[1] These are exact statements about limits.

9. Besides Pigou, other writers such as Kuznets and Little have seen fit to attach significance to the numerical values of the P and L ratios. (Readers not interested in technicalities can skip this section.) Kuznets argues as follows:

> Suppose as we go from I to II, both P and L are greater than they are when we go from I to III. Then II is 'generally' better than III, provided that the shift in prices from II to III has effects on the ratios of certain identical quantity aggregates of an [allegedly] usual sort.[2]

It will be noted that Kuznets is attempting to use certain numerical or cardinal comparisons for the sole purpose of arriving at a purely *ordinal* comparison. There is nothing methodologically objectionable about this; but none the less the Kuznets result is a self-contained truism that does not permit us to make any general inferences of certain validity in any empirical situation.

First an example may illustrate the loopholes in Kuznets's results. Back in my Fig. 1, let us consider the three points A, B, C. Kuznets will find that P and L computed for A and B are *exactly* the same as for A and C. According to his theorem, C and B should be equally satisfactory or approximately so. Actually the indifference curve through C passes above that of B, and if there were any sense in speaking of 'well above' we might use this stronger expression. More than that, by moving C south-west a little or B north-east a little, we could arrive at the even falser presumption that B is better than C.

There is nothing faulty about Kuznets's arithmetic or the truism he derives from his substitution. He would have to say in this connexion: 'My proviso about price-quantity correlation has been violated in the example.' And why should it not be? When Kuznets says that P is 'in general' less than L, he does not mean by the words 'in general' what a mathematician means when he says that the two sides of a triangle are 'generally' greater than the third. Kuznets means, I think it is clear, that *usually* the price-quantity correlation will be such as to make P less than L. (Actually a long line of writers in index-number theory fell into the actual error of thinking that $P \leqslant L$ and between them lies some 'true' value; an almost equally

---

[1] Mathematically, the indifference curve through A is tangential to the $P = 1$ and $L = 1$ contours, lying 'half-way' between them. The contour $\sqrt{(PL)} = 1$ also has their mean curvature and is an osculating tangent to the indifference curve, differing only in its third and higher derivatives. See my *Foundations*, p. 148.

[2] This is my brief transcription of Kuznets's Appendix, *Economica*, 1949, pp. 124–31 and his remarks on p. 5.

long line of writers have pointed out the falsity of this relation.) I venture the conjecture that Kuznets formed his belief concerning the usual or normal numerical dominance of L over P from considering the special case where there are no real income changes and where any increase in the price of a good (or set of goods) is followed by a necessary decrease in its quantity. But it is precisely when we are trying to arrive at an estimate of whether II is better or worse than III that we must not beg the question by assuming that they are on the same indifference locus.

Even in a loose probability sense, it would be dangerous to say that P is usually less than L. If all goods had an income elasticity of exactly one—so that a pure income change resulted in proportionate changes in every item of consumption—then this would be a certainty. But so long as the well-attested Engel's laws and observed budgetary patterns hold, we must *certainly* have a reversal of the $P–L$ relations throughout the area between the income-expenditure curve through A and the straight line joining A to the origin. This shows that my ABC example is not an isolated case, but is typical of what will always be true in some region.[1]

10. So far I have discussed only the single-individual aspects of Pigou's treatment of real income. All these pages of the Appendix were necessary to cover what took scarcely more than a page of my main text. But now I must consider Pigou's analysis of national income in its group-welfare aspects. Because this problem was treated so fully in the main text, my treatment here may be rather brief.

It will be recalled that Pigou regards his inferences as being valid if the members of the group always have 'a fixed distribution of income' (and, of course, unchanging tastes). When we subject his book to microscopic examination, two questions immediately come to mind. (1) Exactly what is meant by 'a fixed distribution of income' between two situations? And (2) even after this by-no-means-simple question has been adequately disposed of, what is it that Pigou thinks is true of the group or of the individuals in the group as we go from one situation to another? Is there a group-mind that registers more utility? Or is it the algebraic sum of utility that has gone up for the group? Or is it that every single member of the group is now better off than before?

11. One must read between the lines to answer these questions—at least, I have not been able to find their explicit answers. I suspect that Pigou does not have any place in his philosophy for any group-mind. But his technical argument seems to come very close to the following Wieser construction:

> 'The theory of the "simple economy" ... begins with the idealizing assumption that the subject is a single person. However, we do not have in mind here the meagre economy of an isolated Robinson Crusoe ... [but] the activities of an entire nation. At the same time millions of people are regarded as a massed unit.'[2]

We may read elements of this general line of reasoning in Pigou's concern with the question of whether market prices can be considered as given to society in the way that they can be assumed to be prescribed for a single small competitive individual. If Fig. 10 applied to a single individual, he could legitimately regard the straight line NN through A as being open to him. But if the chart holds for society, there could be shown on it the true (but possibly unknown) production-possibility or opportunity-cost curve of type MM or of some other shape.

Pigou is uneasy about applying the argument to the group as a whole. 'But, when it is the whole of a group, or, if we prefer it, a representative man who shifts his consumption in this way, it is no longer certain that prices would be unaffected' (p. 61). For a moment, Pigou seems to lapse into the assumption that the representa-

---

[1] Little gives a probability interpretation of the significance of the cardinal size of P on pp. 46–7, *Economica*, 1949. He has in mind a closely related, but distinct, group inference from that discussed in this paper. He also relies on our rough empirical knowledge of preference patterns in evaluating his probabilities.

[2] F. v. Wieser, *Social Economics* (1927), pp. 9–10.

P. A. SAMUELSON   27

tive man knows that he is an image of the group and therefore acts collusively as if a group decision were being made. The group mind knows that the only choice really open to it is along MM; therefore in the initial A situation it does not think that C is obtainable; consequently we cannot infer that A has been revealed to be better than C by a deliberate act of choosing A over C. Something like this Pigou must have believed for the moment, else he would not have felt the need to add a 'certain assumption' of paragraph 8, ruling out the possibility that the production-possibility curve of society is like MM, but instead requiring it to show constant slope like NN. It is fortunate that Pigou's argument can be salvaged without making this extraneous assumption—fortunate because I cannot agree with his appraisal of the *a priori* probabilities: 'In real life, with a large number of commodities, it is reasonable to suppose that the upward price movements caused by shifts of con-

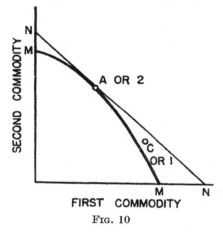

FIG. 10

sumption would roughly balance the downward movements' (p. 62). That is to say, concave or convex curves are equally likely, so we may assume the curve to be a straight line. Rather, I would think that in the conditions most suited to healthy competition—where external economies either balance external diseconomies or both are negligible and where tendencies towards increasing or decreasing returns *to scale* are absent or just balancing—we would still be left with the good old law of diminishing returns in the classical (qualitative and quantitative) senses, so that convex production-possibility schedules are the 'normal' case.

Actually, if Pigou is concerned to make normative statements about points like A and C that hold valid for groups, it does not matter that the true production-possibility curve is something other than NN.[1] We have seen in Hicks's paper and in the text what these valid inferences are. Another way of looking at the problem is by means of the 'collective indifference curves' that Professor Scitovsky has taught us to use in the second of his cited papers.

12. But first we must settle what is meant by Pigou's 'fixed distribution of income'. How tempting to think of money as being concrete and the distribution of income to be fixed if everybody's money income changes proportionally. But money itself means nothing. If two men each have the same money income and if one likes meat and the other cheese and the terms of trade between meat and cheese

---

[1] Pigou does not stand alone. 'Unless the groups considered are small in relation to the whole, market prices cannot be considered as constant, and therefore the condition $\Sigma p_2 q_2 > \Sigma p_2 q_1$ would no longer indicate that goods of situation I were rejected in favour of those of situation II' (*Economica*, 1949, p. 17).

change, then would Pigou consider the distribution of income to have remained fixed ? Probably not. Moreover, if we follow the convenient practice of treating the services of labour and property that people supply as negative commodities, then in the absence of government taxes we might say that everybody has a zero (net) income *always*.

Probably in the beginning Pigou had in mind the simple case of identical individuals, any one of whom is representative, and where they all fare alike. Then when situation II is better than I, it is also true that both individuals are better off. When we leave the case of perfect symmetry, it becomes difficult to say that the extra welfare of one man is always to be some fixed multiple of the increment of welfare of another since this involves ethical inter-personal comparisons that Pigou is trying to avoid in these chapters dealing with the relatively objective aspects of welfare and the national dividend. But for his purposes Pigou needs only to assume that the ordinal well-being of all individuals are required to move always *in the same direction* according to some prescribed relationship. [Some complicated monetary shifts must be assumed to take place to bring this about.]

If I am right in this interpretation, then the comparison of A or 2 and C or 1 in terms of

$$\sum p_2 q_2 > \sum p_2 q_1$$

is immediately obvious and independent of the shape of MM or of any assumptions of group-consciousness. The fortunes of all being linked, any one person reflects the fate of all. Now, obviously, for some one person we must have

$$\sum p_2 q_2 > \sum p_2 q_1,$$

because if the opposite were true for each and every person, how could the totals show this relation ? But if at least one has been made worse off in I than in II, then the 'fixed distribution of income assumption' means that they must all have been made worse off. Q.E.D.

In terms of Scitovsky indifference curves, the story runs as follows : For a prescribed amount of both people's ordinal utility, U' and U'', we can draw up a collective indifference curve. For any prescribed distribution linking U' and U'' in a monotonic fashion we can draw up a family of collective indifference curves. If each person has concave indifference curves, the collective curves will also be concave. But regardless of concavity, the collective curve through A is never permitted to cross below the NN line. This will be obvious to every reader in the case of concave curves ; and the same can be shown to be true in general by simple mathematical argument. It follows that C lies on a lower collective indifference curve than A— *regardless of the true shape of society's production-possibility curve MM.*

13. Pigou's argument has been removed from any dependence on constant (opportunity) cost assumptions. But a worse restriction remains. For him to make any inference, *everybody* in the community must have been made better or worse off. The wind scarcely ever blows that brings good to absolutely everyone. Lucky it is that the remaining fifty-odd chapters of the *Economics of Welfare* do not depend in an essential way upon the results of the early chapters of Part I dealing with the national dividend. Fortunately, too—just as was seen to be true when tastes change —we can make some valid inferences when the distribution of income is known *not* to remain fixed. From our earlier analysis we know that $\sum p_2 q_2 > \sum p_2 q_1$ implies that the II's utility-possibility curve lies outside of I's at least in the neighbourhood of the actual observed situation II.

14. One last case not yet considered by any of the writers. Suppose we have given to us certain well-defined ethical notions concerning inter-personal well-being. In the simplest case they can be summarized in a Bergson social welfare function, $W = W(U', U'', ...)$, with the usual property that anything that helps one man without hurting anyone else will mean an increase in W.

As before, let us observe prices, p, and total quantities for all society, q. And finally, suppose that *the distribution of income is ethically optimal both in situation 1 or C and 2 or A*. What can we now infer from the condition $\sum p_2 q_2 > \sum p_2 q_1$? The answer is that situation A lies higher on the ethical social welfare function than does C.[1]

The logical proof of this result is not so easy as I at first thought it would be. This is because our move from C to the better position A need not represent an improvement for all individuals. U' may go down provided U'' goes up relatively more, as measured, of course, by the W function. Hence, when cost conditions change in such a way as to make it optimal to alter the relative 'distribution of income', our earlier argument cannot apply.

To prove that $W(A) > W(C)$, we can use 'social indifference curves'. But they are not the arbitrary ones of the Scitovsky new-welfare-economics type. They are a unique old-welfare-economics set of curves showing the combinations of total goods capable of giving (when all optimal arrangements have been made) equal levels of W. In the 'normal' case, where playing the game of competition can be depended to follow the invisible hand to bliss, these social indifference curves will be concave. It follows that whenever C lies inside the straight line NN going through A, it must also lie inside the social indifference curve (of equal W) going through A. This proves our result.[2]

[1] This is related to Bergson's interesting interpretation of Pigou in infinitesimal terms. Bergson, 'Reformulation of Certain Aspects of Welfare Economics', *Q.J.E.*, lii (1938), p. 331.

[2] In the last two of his cited papers Little has stated theorems a little bit like the one above. There are two or three different versions, but the typical Little theorem shows that a certain point A is better than another point C because we can imagine going from C to A in two steps: one of these involves an improved distribution of real income (somehow defined) and the other an improvement in each and every person's well-being. I give an abbreviated interpretation of one of the variants discussed in *O.E.P.*, pp. 235–7.

1. Suppose we have a W function as defined above, with $\partial W/\partial U' > 0$, &c., and start at a point C and end up at a point A.
2. The point A is assumed to lie out and beyond the utility-possibility locus of the point C; e.g. there is a point C' on the latter locus that is south-west of the point A in the $U'-U''$ plane. Thus the Scitovsky test is satisfied.
3. Now make the assumption that in terms of W 'the distribution of real income is better' at C' than in C. (Thus, ideally, we should not have been in C in the first place.)
4. Then it follows that A is higher on the assumed welfare function than is C. (This conclusion does not depend upon whether the Hicks–Kaldor test is satisfied.)
5. It does not follow that a little angel, given the choice of throwing a switch that moves society from C to A, ought to throw that switch. There may be an infinity of points on C's locus still better than A. Little's policy conclusion is to be qualified, therefore, by the following statement that he has been kind enough to send to me in private correspondence: 'The shift from C to A ought to be made if the shift does not prejudice any other move which might result in a position still more favourable than A.'

The chain of reasoning involved in 1–4 is simple once we pin down what is meant by 'the distribution of real income being better'. This means $W(C') > W(C)$. Since the Scitovsky test implies $W(A) > W(C')$, the Little result $W(A) > W(C)$ immediately follows. Just as Little talks prose, he can be said to be using a *welfare* function whenever he talks welfare economics. But like the new welfare economists, he wants to see what results he can get with an *incompletely* defined welfare function—a commendable effort, perhaps useful for an important class of policy decisions, but necessarily not complete for all policy situations.

MASSACHUSETTS INSTITUTE

OF TECHNOLOGY.

[7]

WELFARE ASPECTS OF BENEFIT-COST ANALYSIS[1]

JOHN V. KRUTILLA

Resources for the Future, Inc.

I. INTRODUCTION

IN RECENT years there has been substantial interest in developing decision rules for public expenditures under a variety of conditions. To a large extent in the literature dealing with governmental expenditures in the United States the interest has been confined to the field of resource development and the activity known in general as benefit-cost analysis. Benefit-cost analysis can be characterized as the collection and organization of data relevant by some conceptually meaningful criteria to determining the relative preferredness of alternatives (24, Parts II, III). As is typical of much of economic analysis, the objective is to attempt by analysis to indicate how a particular desideratum can be maximized—accomplished by comparing the differences in the relevant costs and benefits associated with alternatives among which choices are to be made. This activity, of course, does not differ in kind from the economic analysis employed in reaching decisions with respect to production or other policies of the firm. Nevertheless, while the analytic activity does not differ in *nature*, the desideratum and the choice variables on which it depends will differ. Essentially, a private cost-gains calculus is employed in deciding private firms' policies; externalities and other divergences between private and social product are neglected. Benefit-cost analysis, on the other hand, seeks to take account of such divergences as a basis for guiding public action either when market prices do not accurately reflect social value or when, by virtue of the indivisible nature of collective goods, no market exists from which to observe directly objective evidence of the community's valuation of the social marginal product. Speaking loosely, while the decision rules of the theory of the firm aim at profit maximization, the decision rules of benefit-cost analysis seek to maximize "public benefits" or "general welfare" within the area of responsibility (29, p. 3).

In this connection the normative nature of the analysis needs to be emphasized. Unlike the assumption of profit maximization, which is a descriptive hypothesis having explanatory value (but cf. 28, 38), benefit-cost analysis is intended to be prescriptive. Underlying the analysis is the value judgment that, if governmental intervention is justified in part[2] by virtue of the market's failure to achieve an efficient allocation of resources (1, 3, 16, 22, 23, 26, 34), public officials ought to apply decision rules which tend to improve the allocation, that is, to improve the *general* welfare

[1] Acknowledgments are due to Robert Dorfman, Otto Eckstein, Francesco Forte, George Hall, Orris Herfindahl, and Vernon Ruttan for helpful comments on an earlier draft of this paper. The substance of this paper was presented as one in a series of lectures given in the training program sponsored by the United Nations Economic Commission for Latin America at the University of Mexico in the summer of 1960.

[2] That part of governmental intervention characterized by Musgrave's "allocation branch" (26).

rather than their personal or specially interested clientele's welfare.[3]

II. INITIAL CONDITIONS AND SIDE EFFECTS

While intervention is required to correct divergences between private and social product and cost, both the initial conditions and the associated side effects of intervention are of relevance in assessing the welfare implications of supramarket allocations of resources. Public intervention to redirect the use of resources involves costs. Assuming that the gross benefit achieved exceeds associated opportunity costs, if, in addition: (a) opportunity costs are borne by beneficiaries in such wise as to retain the initial income distribution, (b) the initial income distribution is in some sense "best," and (c) the marginal social rates of transformation between any two commodities are everywhere equal to their corresponding rates of substitution except for the area(s) justifying the intervention in question, then welfare can be improved by such intervention. And, to the extent that the objective is pursued to the point where the social marginal rates of transformation between commodities in this area and other sectors are likewise equal to the rates of substitution for correspondingly paired commodities, welfare is maximized.

However, since condition (a) is only partially feasible in the majority of cases dealt with by benefit-cost analysis, the likelihood of condition (b) has been subject to considerable question, and in the world of reality condition (c) is improbable, consideration of these stringent conditions is necessary to assess in prag-

matic terms the welfare implications of supramarket allocation of resources suggested by benefit-cost comparisons.

III. IMPLICATION OF REDISTRIBUTIVE EFFECTS FOR THE MEASUREMENT OF WELFARE

Considering condition (a), we may recognize that the practical possibility of multipart pricing or corresponding special assessments is limited; and thus we must retreat to weaker positions. This retreat will require, at best, that the analyst rely on interpersonal comparisons of utility before he can hazard any judgment with respect to welfare, *plus* a degree of faith that the redistributional consequences for the measurement of welfare are of the second order of significance, or (at worst) that the analyst abstain from saying anything about the magnitude or even the direction of the change in either wealth or welfare, that is, about the change in the size of the national real income or its welfare implications.

To claim that welfare has increased, when the *ex ante* distribution is not automatically preserved by the mechanism of intervention, requires that those who gain are able to *and do* compensate those who lose, and still have something remaining. However, if we are uncertain about the "goodness" of the original distribution of income (condition b), we cannot contend that failure to compensate would not result in a greater gain in welfare. Such failure means only that the issue cannot be resolved without making interpersonal comparisons (31).

If we are content to attach no greater normative significance to the result of "maximizing" decision rules, however, than to aver that the national income has been increased, taking the distribution as given, we can envisage a broader applica-

[3] For a positive theory of political behavior, which may more accurately mirror actual rather than "desirable" behavior of public officials, see Downs (4).

tion of benefit-cost decision rules. We are then content to accept the "production-distribution" or the "efficiency-ethics" dichotomy of the Kaldor-Hicks-Scitovsky line of development (9, 10, 15, 36, 37). We say that, if those who benefit by virtue of the increase in production can overcompensate those who suffer losses (but do not actually make the compensating payments), the "aggregate real income" has been increased irrespective of its distribution and, accordingly, of its welfare implications.[4]

Kaldor's production-distribution dichotomy and the resulting test of an increase in real income appear supportable for the more or less marginal adjustments for which benefit-cost criteria were originally developed and typically applied in the United States. This remains true, I believe, despite Samuelson's and De Graaff's criticism of the proposition in general (33, pp. 10–11; 8, p. 90 ff.). At the most fundamental level is De Graaff's criticism, namely, if we wish to base our economics on an individualistic rather than an organic conception of the community and its welfare, and if there is more than one commodity, then the "aggregate real income" cannot be evaluated without weighting components, which in turn is not independent of the income distribution. We may resort to the "size-distribution" dichotomy, but it has no operational significance, for "we do not know the size unless we know the distribution" (8, p. 92).

De Graaff's concern with the distributional implications for aggregate real income corresponds to Scitovsky's concern with the *re*distributional consequences

for measuring the *change* in real income. Consideration of only the latter and lesser question will suffice for our immediate purpose. Scitovsky's critical point can be summarized somewhat as follows: an indicated net increase in real income when valued in terms of prevailing prices may not prove so when valued in terms of prices reflecting the attendant income redistribution. Admittedly, for a structural reorganization of the magnitude implicit in the repeal of the corn laws, the effect of the income redistribution on the constellation of relative prices cannot be ignored. On the other hand, the relative magnitude of the redistribution associated with investment decisions for which benefit-cost expenditure criteria have been traditionally employed will be of the second order of smalls in terms of its implication for measuring the change and, for practical purposes, can be ignored (16, p. 50).[5]

Thus, while the absolute size of the national income may not be independent of its distribution, a relatively small change in its size, for practical purposes, can be considered independently of its *re*distributional consequences in determining the magnitude and direction of the change. The distinction for benefit-cost analysis, of course, is significant, as it provides the theoretical basis for benefit-cost practices. For, if the more simple criteria of Kaldor and Hicks had to be supplemented even by Scitovsky's extension

---

[4] Of course, it is not to be inferred that Hicks ignores the welfare issue, since he attempted a defense of such an interpretation of the rise in social income. Among others, Hotelling (14) preceded and Wantrup (2) followed Hicks in providing a defense of such welfare implications.

[5] This is not necessarily meant to imply that the redistributive implications for welfare (discussed in the following section) can be similarly ignored. Such welfare effects might be important, especially if redistributive effects from expenditures for development of resources were cumulative. But cumulation hardly seems likely in the area of such expenditures. Additional annual expenditures of the Bureau of Reclamation, for example, do not benefit individuals previously favored because such additional expenditures represent predominantly extension of the program to new areas and, accordingly, to different individuals.

alone—not to mention Samuelson's all-possible-distributions test (33)—no *ex ante* judgment with respect to the anticipated change in economic efficiency resulting from a contemplated supramarket allocation could be supported by benefit-cost analysis. This follows because the analyst does not have the power to manipulate the distribution of income experimentally before rendering a judgment; nor does there exist sufficient information regarding individual preference maps to simulate results from hypothetical distributions.

Samuelson's requirement that an improvement in efficiency must be tested not only against the *ex ante* and *ex post* income distributions but against all possible hypothetical distributions stems from two partially distinct considerations. The first involves the degree to which an implicit value judgment has been made in either Kaldor's and Hicks's criterion or Scitovsky's double criterion in spite of the intended preoccupation solely with production or efficiency. That is, to take the *ex ante* distribution (or in the case of Scitovsky the *ex post* as well as the *ex ante*) as a datum confers too significant a normative status on these particular distributions. For, as Fisher has observed:

> The refusal to make a value judgment . . . is in itself a value judgment, not only in the sense that one is saying that one ought to abstain from making value judgments, but also in the sense that the results obtained are those that would result from glorifying the present distribution [7, p. 394].

The second consideration underlying Samuelson's position seems to be concerned with the distinction between the "utility possibility frontier" and the "utility feasibility frontier," that is, between potential and feasible welfare. Here, while the utility-possibility function may be shifted outward uniformly or welfare potentially increased by a policy prescription, the implementation of the policy may cause such distortion of marginal conditions and "undesirable" income redistribution that the utility-feasibility frontier twists inward (33, pp. 18–21).

The first of these observations is related directly to condition (*b*), whereas the second bears obliquely on condition (*c*).

IV. THE WELFARE STATUS
OF THE STATUS QUO

Considering condition (*b*), I believe it fair to say that the redistributive consequences of small changes of the sort encountered in benefit-cost analysis in the United States are negligible. But, as Fisher points out, this does not mean that benefit-cost analysis is free of distributional value judgments. For equating incremental benefits and costs in the designing of projects and "scoping" of programs relies on price data, which in turn are dependent on the prevailing distribution. Accordingly, if for no other reason than this, a judgment is implied regarding the normative status of the existing distribution.

A proper question to raise at this junction, however, is: "Can the prevailing distribution indicate, as a pragmatic approximation, the socially sanctioned one in a democratically organized society?" There are at least three ways in which to answer this question. One can reply with a qualified "yes," following a line of reasoning to be sketched below. One can maintain that it is really not possible to know, but that the answer may not be too important, given the level and distribution of income approached in the United States. Finally one might argue, as does Little, that the prevailing dis-

230   JOHN V. KRUTILLA

tribution of income does not enjoy a social sanction, so that any judgment with
respect to efficiency must be in the nature
of a second-best solution contingent also
on a value judgment that the resulting
income distribution is "good."

It can be argued that the prevailing
distribution of income is approved by the
community, since in a democracy the
community has the means of changing it.
Little discounts this rationale, apparently on the basis of the observed historical tendency toward persistent reduction
of inequalities in income in modern industrial nations (19, p. 114). Yet the degree of income equality sought by a community may not be unrelated to the level
of per capita income, and the reduction
of inequality over time may be only a
function of technological advances and
the increase in efficiency of economic organization.

Differential rewards of income appear
to be compatible with a Jeffersonian conception of democracy which accommo-
dates an aristocracy of ability. Indirect
evidence that the community sanctions
some inequality of income has been reflected perceptively in the writings of
Perlman (27, pp. 164 ff.). Anthony
Downs, in a wholly different fashion,
provides an interesting rationale for the
existence of income inequality in a political democracy (4, pp. 199–200, but also
cf. p. 94).[6] If I interpret Downs correctly,
it seems probable that the income distribution resulting from the explicit redistributive activities of the government
is, assuming that the incidental redistributive consequences of other governmental activities are non-cumulative, a
reasonable approximation to the socially
sanctioned distribution.[7]

[6] For a comprehensive survey of recent thoughts
on egalitarianism which, though exhaustive, is not
conclusive, see Lampman (17).

A second possible argument, related to
the first, is that, although there may be
reasons for rejecting the prevailing distribution as in some sense "best" reflecting a social welfare function, at the present level of income distributional (and
redistributional) questions are not dominant considerations.[8] This does not imply
that all members of society have their
non-frivolous needs met equally amply,
but only that the associated dead-weight
losses of moving toward greater equality
would be judged to exceed the compensating distributional gains.

A third possible argument is that advanced by Little. Little abandons interest in a welfare maximum, regarding such
an aspiration as utopian. Considering the
existing distribution as non-optimal,[9] he
focuses on conditions *sufficient for an improvement* in welfare rather than on conditions *necessary for a welfare maximum*
(19, pp. 115–16). To render an improvement in efficiency desirable, that is, for it

[7] Musgrave, in his discussion of voting methods
(26, chap. vi), observes the numerous difficulties of
implementing an unadulterated social ethic and concludes that perhaps majority voting in a democracy
comes as close to achieving the desired end as the
mechanics of social organization will permit.

[8] Of course, while such an argument can be advanced following, or perhaps interpreting liberally,
Fisher's argument (7, pp. 407–8), at such levels of
income considerations of efficiency may also be of
the second order of significance; that is, freedom
from extension of governmental intervention may be
purchased at the expense of some relative reduction
in potential national income. On the other hand,
maximum efficiency may be viewed as a possible
good in its own right irrespective of the level of opulence if the welfare function depends on the relative
rate of growth vis-à-vis some ideologically competitive society.

[9] Although Little rejects the notion that the prevailing distribution of income is sanctioned, his willingness to rely on prices as indicators of value suggests that its departure from optimality is not sufficient to affect relative prices—or else that individuals' preferences are sufficiently similar that redistributions will not affect the constellation of relative
prices appreciably.

to improve welfare, the attendant redistribution of income must be acceptable. To pursue the matter to its ultimate conclusion, one could accept the frankly ascientific approach suggested by Meade (25, chaps. v, vii) and assign distributional weights based on interpersonal comparisons of welfare in order to incorporate redistributional aspects into a multidimensional objective function. In a similar, if more restricted, sense there is the possibility, consistent with Little's position, of maximizing a one-dimensional benefit function subject to an income-redistribution constraint.[10]

V. WELFARE IMPLICATIONS OF NON-OPTIMAL INITIAL CONDITIONS OF PRODUCTION AND EXCHANGE

The third possibility noted immediately above touches on maximization problems best treated in connection with an evaluation of general condition (*c*), problems associated with the non-existence of the necessary conditions for a Pareto optimum. Here it must be acknowledged that, by reason of market imperfections and distortion of marginal conditions owing to government activities (both explicit redistribution and the financing of supramarket allocations), the Pareto-optimum conditions (*c*) are at best only approximated in practice and at worst are universally breached, so that the slopes of Samuelson's feasibility frontiers have little relation to prices and marginal costs (33, p. 18). The significant problem then remains of evaluating the welfare implications of benefit-maximizing criteria under real world conditions.

Of the major participants in the postwar discussion of welfare economics, only

[10] To implement these suggestions, however, the benefit-cost practitioner would require supplemental legislation suspending the congressional directive in the Flood Control Act of 1936 to the effect that dollar democracy is to prevail.

Little (later joined by Meade) attempts to come to grips with problems of this nature. These problems appear to be at least as great in practical importance as is the issue of interpersonal comparisons and income distribution; and they are, if anything, less susceptible of an intellectually satisfying solution. This is brought home decisively by the pessimistic conclusions of the statement by Lipsey and Lancaster of the general theory of the second best (21). They have demonstrated that, if any one of the conditions for a Pareto optimum is not attainable, it is in general not desirable to achieve any of the remainder (18, pp. 11, 26–27). The following quotation reflects the flavor of their nihilistic conclusions:

> The problem of sufficient conditions for an increase in welfare, as compared to necessary conditions for a welfare maximum, is obviously important if policy recommendations are to be made in the real world. Piecemeal welfare economics is often based on the belief that a study of the *necessary* conditions for a Paretian welfare optimum may lead to the discovery of *sufficient* conditions for an increase in welfare. In his *Critique of Welfare Economics*, I. M. D. Little . . . says, ". . . necessary conditions are not very interesting. It is *sufficient* conditions for improvement that we really want." But the theory of second best leads to the conclusion that there are in general no such sufficient conditions for an increase in welfare. There are necessary conditions for a Paretian optimum. In a simple situation there may exist a condition that is necessary and sufficient. But in a general equilibrium situation, there will be no conditions which in general are sufficient for an increase in welfare without also being necessary for a welfare maximum [18, p. 17].

And, to erode further the faith of the innocent, they conclude that, in general, there is no proof of the existence of a second-best solution (18, pp. 27–28).[11]

[11] Professor Dorfman, in private correspondence, has taken exception to this conclusion. In his opinion, a second-best optimum exists under the same conditions that a Pareto optimum does, but in gen-

Non-existence of a second-best solution in a technical sense, however, does not mean that, if an additional constraint is imposed on the welfare function, there is no actual relative maximum. Intuitively, we perceive that some adjustments in response to the given constraints will be better than others and that there must be an actual peak whether or not we can stipulate what conditions must obtain at the margin for all permutations. But the question remains whether or not supramarket allocations, guided by marginal equalities rather than the unknown appropriate inequalities, will tend to move the economy further away from such an actual relative maximum when similar marginal equalities are absent elsewhere in the economy. While it follows that, in general, supramarket allocations guided by marginal equalities will prevent the economy from achieving the constrained maximum, it does not follow that abstention from intervention would permit the economy to remain closer to the constrained maximum.

The possibility always exists that an observed inefficient situation is dominated by an attainable more efficient situation (12, p. 98; 13, p. 208). An example drawn from the field of resources may illustrate this point. Three alternative plans of development were proposed for the Hell's Canyon reach of the Snake River, the third of which was a privately

advanced plan of development. For the three plans of development the following conditions hold:

$$O_1 > O_2 > O_3$$

and

$$I_1 > I_3 > I_2 ,$$

where O and I refer respectively to physical output and inputs, and the subscripts to the respective plans of development (16, chap. v). As between the second and third alternatives, it is obvious that the efficiency of the former dominates the latter. Hence, we can argue by dominance that, subject to an economic demand for the output, appropriate public intervention is a sufficient condition for an improvement without regard to necessary conditions for a welfare maximum. On the other hand, since the first alternative requires more inputs to achieve the greater output than does either the second or the third, and the value of the difference in output is greater than, equal to, or less than the opportunity costs of the inputs depending on a critical factor price, we cannot make a decision without recourse to prices. Now, if prices are not exact measures of opportunity costs—a condition implicit in the negative theorem of the general theory of the second best—they do not provide an unambiguous criterion.

Three partially distinct positions can be discerned in the approaches adopted by benefit-cost analysts in such cases. McKean takes the following position:

> Those conditions [Pareto optimum] are not completely realized and moving toward the achievement of *one* alone is not necessarily a step in the right direction. However, if a frequency distribution of the possibilities is imagined, it seems likely that increased production where price exceeds cost would usually be a step toward efficiency, even though the other conditions are only partially fulfilled. The conclusion here is that prices and costs show how to "maximize production" [24, pp. 130–31].

---

eral the familiar Pareto-marginal equalities will not hold at a second-best optimum. Therefore, under the second-best conditions, an allocation of resources that satisfies some of the Pareto-marginal equalities is not necessarily preferable to an allocation that satisfies none of them. Nevertheless, there does exist a second-best optimum, that is, an allocation of resources that satisfies the distorting constraints that make "second-besting" necessary and that is socially preferable to any other allocation that satisfies those constraints.

WELFARE ASPECTS OF BENEFIT-COST ANALYSIS   233

Eckstein (5, p. 29), following Little (20, pp. vii–xiv), approaches the problem in the following manner:

[Insofar as there are monopoly elements, prices will exceed marginal costs, but from a quantitative point of view, these deviations are both widely—also perhaps evenly—diffused and relatively small, particularly in the range of markets most relevant to water resource development. Projects in these fields produce outputs which in largest part are producer goods, such as raw materials, electric energy and transportation services. In these areas, advertising, consumer loyalty and asymmetric market power concentrated on the side of the seller are less prevalent than in markets for consumer goods. Thus while prices do not serve their function perfectly, we hold that they are generally adequate for the range of policy decisions with which we are concerned. At the same time, in any application of the methods of this study, we must keep in mind the assumptions which validate the use of prices, and we must not hesitate, in certain situations, to reject them in favor of other measures of social benefit and cost.[12]

A third position supporting the use of prices (adjusted for obvious divergences) as measures of opportunity costs, and of criteria based mainly on the presumption of the existence of marginal equalities is the following (16, p. 73, n. 32). While the benefit-cost analyst must recognize that he does not institute utopian reforms simply by an act of analysis, he must also recognize that his criteria, in the dynamic context of the real world, should be consistent with the higher-level aims which dominate the work of those public servants responsible for policing monopoly, improving market performance, and otherwise monitoring the economy with the objective of increasing the efficiency

of its operation. And, while he must recognize the prevalence of departures from ideal conditions, he should not feed such departures systematically back into the optimizing calculations. For, in contrast to the static situation to which the negative theorem of Lipsey and Lancaster applies, such feedbacks can have a cumulative effect, resulting in progressive divergences from conditions of optimum production and exchange.

The choices in which one alternative clearly dominates another (or all others), while they may be numerous absolutely, must still represent a small proportion of the total of choices which face the economic decision-makers. And the positions advanced above to deal with the more representative situation can neither rest on formal proofs nor claim much by way of an intellectually satisfying status. Also, while the analyst must be sensitive to "higher-level aims," he must by virtue of the nature of his problems and analysis work largely in a suboptimizing or partial-equilibrium context (24, pp. 30 ff.). Conclusions reached by analysis at this level of generality need not hold in more general cases, and may require substantial reconsideration (see, for example, 21, 30, 32). The application of criteria for improving welfare therefore cannot be a mechanical or a compellingly logical activity. Rather, it requires perhaps more intimate knowledge of the economy, experience, and highly developed intuitive sense than analysts commonly possess—which suggests the quality of results and degree of precision to be anticipated.

VI. CONCLUSIONS FOR PRACTICAL
CHOICES "IN THE PUBLIC
INTEREST"

Does the array of positions advanced previously provide an adequate rationale

[12] Consistently with the latter part of the statement, Eckstein has done much original work in developing benefit maximizing criteria subject to a variety of constraints in addition to the resource-technology constraint (5, 6). This effort has been extended and generalized by Steiner (39), Marglin, and other members of the Harvard Water Resources Seminar.

for attempts to evaluate the benefits and costs of resource-development alternatives? Or are the comments herein transparent rationalizations which leave little conviction that analysis of benefits and cost and of their distribution can help significantly to improve welfare through public intervention? One's view, of course, will differ depending on the nature of one's experience, one's temperament, and perhaps also one's personal situation. The academic theorist without responsibility for policy can afford to (and probably should) be puritanical without regard to whether or not this is immediately constructive. On the other hand, the practicing economist in government, charged with responsibility

to act under constraints of time and information, will often be grateful for perhaps even a perforated rationale to justify recommendations "in the public interest." Since the alternative is not to retire to inactivity but, rather, to reach decisions in the absence of analysis, we may take some comfort from the belief that thinking systematically about problems and basing decisions on such analysis are likely to produce consequences superior to those that would result from purely random behavior. Nonetheless, the utility and welfare effects of benefit-cost analysis are likely to be viewed differently, depending on the end of the telescope through which the affected party is privileged to look.

REFERENCES

1. BAUMOL, WILLIAM J. *Welfare Economics and the Theory of the State.* Cambridge, Mass.: Harvard University Press, 1952.
2. CIRIACY-WANTRUP, S. V. "Concepts Used as Economic Criteria for a System of Water Rights," *Journal of Land Economics,* XXXII (November, 1956), 295–312.
3. COLM, GERHARD. "Comments on Samuelson's Theory of Public Finance," *Review of Economics and Statistics,* XXXVIII (November, 1956), 408–12.
4. DOWNS, ANTHONY. *An Economic Theory of Democracy.* New York: Harper & Bros., 1957.
5. ECKSTEIN, OTTO. *Water Resource Development: The Economics of Project Evaluation.* Cambridge, Mass.: Harvard University Press, 1958.
6. ———. "A Survey of the Theory of Public Expenditure Criteria," Paper read at Universities-National Bureau Conference on Public Finance, April, 1959, University of Virginia, Charlottesville.
7. FISHER, FRANKLIN M. "Income Distribution, Value Judgments and Welfare," *Quarterly Journal of Economics,* LXX (August, 1956), 380–424.
8. GRAAFF, J. DE V. *Theoretical Welfare Economics.* Cambridge: Cambridge University Press, 1957.
9. HICKS, J. R. "Foundations of Welfare Economics," *Economic Journal,* XLIX (December, 1939), 696–712.
10. ———. "The Valuation of Social Income," *Economica,* N.S., VII (May, 1940), 105–24.
11. ———. "The Rehabilitation of Consumer's Surplus," *Review of Economic Studies,* VIII (February, 1941), 108–16.
12. HITCH, CHARLES. "Suboptimization in Operations Problems," *Journal of the Operations Research Society of America,* I (May, 1953), 87–99.
13. ———. "Economics and Military Operations Research," pp. 199–209 in "Economics and Operations Research: A Symposium," *Review of Economics and Statistics,* XL (August, 1958).
14. HOTELLING, HAROLD. "The General Welfare in Relation to Problems of Taxation and of Railway Utility Rates," *Econometrica,* VI (July, 1938), 242–69.
15. KALDOR, NICHOLAS. "Welfare Propositions of Economics and Interpersonal Comparisons of Utility," *Economic Journal,* XLIX (September, 1939), 549–52.
16. KRUTILLA, JOHN V., and ECKSTEIN, OTTO.. *Multiple Purpose River Development: Studies in Applied Economic Analysis.* Baltimore: Johns Hopkins Press, 1958.

17. LAMPMAN, ROBERT J. "Recent Thoughts on Egalitarianism," *Quarterly Journal of Economics*, LXXI, No. 2 (May, 1957), 234–66.

18. LIPSEY, R. G., and LANCASTER, KELVIN. "The General Theory of the Second Best," *Review of Economic Studies*, XXIV (1956–57), 11–32.

19. LITTLE, I. M. D. *A Critique of Welfare Economics*. Oxford: Clarendon Press, 1950.

20. ———. *The Price of Fuel*. Oxford: Clarendon Press, 1953.

21. ———. "Direct vs. Indirect Taxes," *Economic Journal*, LXI, No. 243 (September, 1951), 577–84.

22. MARGOLIS, JULIUS. "A Comment on the Pure Theory of Expenditures," *Review of Economics and Statistics*, XXXVII (November, 1955), 347–49.

23. ———. "Secondary Benefits, External Economies and the Justification of Public Investment," *ibid.*, XXXIX (August, 1957), 284–91.

24. McKEAN, ROLAND. *Efficiency in Government through Systems Analysis, with Emphasis on Water Resource Development*. New York: John Wiley & Sons, 1958.

25. MEADE, J. E. *The Theory of International Economic Policy*, Vol. II: *Trade and Welfare*. New York: Oxford University Press, 1954.

26. MUSGRAVE, RICHARD A. *The Theory of Public Finance*. New York: McGraw Hill Book Co., 1959.

27. PERLMAN, SELIG. *A Theory of the Labor Movement*. New York: Macmillan Co., 1928.

28. REDER, M. W. "A Reconsideration of the Marginal Productivity Theory," *Journal of Political Economy*, LV (October, 1947), 450–58.

29. REGAN, MARK, and TIMMONS, JOHN F. "Benefit-Cost Analysis," paper presented before a joint session of the Economics and Engineering Section of the American Association for the Advancement of Science, Berkeley, California, December 27, 1954. Reproduced by the Committee on the Economics of Water Resources Development of the Western Agricultural Economics Research Council.

30. ROLPH, EARL, and BREAK, GEORGE. "The Welfare Aspects of Excise Taxes," *Journal of Political Economy*, LVII (February, 1949), 46–54.

31. RUGGLES, NANCY. "The Welfare Basis of the Marginal Cost Pricing Principle," *Review of Economic Studies*, XVII, No. 2 (1949–50), 29–46.

32. ———. "Recent Developments in the Theory of Marginal Cost Pricing," *Review of Economic Studies*, XVII, No. 3 (1949–50), 107–26.

33. SAMUELSON, P. A. "Evaluation of Real National Income," *Oxford Economic Papers*, N.S., II (January, 1950), 1–29.

34. ———. "The Pure Theory of Public Expenditures," *Review of Economics and Statistics*, XXXVI (November, 1954), 387–89.

35. ———. "Aspects of Public Expenditure Theories," *ibid.*, XL (November, 1958), 332–38.

36. SCITOVSKY, TIBOR. "A Note on Welfare Propositions in Economics," *Review of Economic Studies*, IX (1941), 77–88.

37. ———. "A Reconsideration of the Theory of Tariffs," *ibid.*, IX (1942), 89–110. Reprinted in pp. 358–89 of *Readings in the Theory of International Trade*, ed. Howard S. Ellis and Lloyd A. Metzler. Philadelphia: Blakiston Co., 1949.

38. SIMON, HERBERT. "A Behavioral Model of Rational Choice," *Quarterly Journal of Economics*, LXIX (February, 1955), 99–118.

39. STEINER, PETER O. "Choosing among Alternative Public Investments," *American Economic Review*, XLIX (December, 1959), 893–916.

[8]

Three Basic Postulates for Applied Welfare Economics: An Interpretive Essay

By Arnold C. Harberger

University of Chicago

I would like to extend my thanks to my colleague, Harry G. Johnson, for his helpful comments, to Daniel Wisecarver, for help extending well beyond the normal call of duty for a research assistant, and to Rudiger Dornbusch and Robert Gordon for valuable suggestions given after the first draft of this paper was completed. Needless to add, they do not bear any responsibility for such flaws or deficiencies as may remain in this paper.

THIS PAPER is intended not as a scientific study, nor as a review of the literature, but rather as a tract—an open letter to the profession, as it were—pleading that three basic postulates be accepted as providing a conventional framework for applied welfare economics. The postulates are:

a) the competitive demand price for a given unit measures the value of that unit to the demander;

b) the competitive supply price for a given unit measures the value of that unit to the supplier;

c) when evaluating the net benefits or costs of a given action (project, program, or policy), the costs and benefits accruing to each member of the relevant group (*e.g.*, a nation) should normally be added without regard to the individual(s) to whom they accrue.

In an era when literally thousands of studies involving cost-benefit analysis or other types of applied welfare economics are underway at any given moment, the need for an accepted set of professional standards for this type of study should be obvious. In proffering postulates *a–c* as the basis for such a set of standards, I do not want to overstate their benefits. Just as the road-construction standards that a team of highway engineers must meet can be checked by other highway engineers, so the exercise in applied welfare economics carried out by one team of economists should be subject to check by others. But while the highway engineers can apply professional standards to characteristics such as thickness of base, load-carrying capacity, drainage characteristics, and the like, characteristics such as scenic beauty are beyond their competence as professional engineers. In the same way, any program or project that is subjected to applied-welfare-economic analysis is likely to have characteristics upon which the economist as such is not professionally qualified to pronounce, and about which one economist is not professionally qualified to check the opinion of another. These elements—which surely include the income-distributional and national-defense aspects of any project or program, and probably its natural-beauty aspects as well—may be exceedingly important, perhaps even the dominant factors governing any policy decision, but they are not a part of that package of expertise that distinguishes the professional economist from the rest of humanity. And that is why we cannot expect to reach a professional consensus concerning them. If we are to take a (hopefully justified) professional pride in our work, we also must have the modesty and honesty not to claim for our profession more than we are particularly qualified to deliver. But this does not mean that we need be silent on matters that lie outside the range of our professional expertise; economists should probably participate more rather than less in the public discussion of such matters, but hopefully in a context that recognizes the extra-professional nature of their intervention.

Some readers will undoubtedly recognize that postulates *a-c* underlie most analyses that use the concepts of consumer and producer surplus. That being the case, one might ask, what is the need for a tract on the subject? My answer stems from the fact that, as an inveterate practitioner of applied welfare economics along many different lines, I encounter with considerable regularity colleagues who are skeptical of consumer surplus on one or more of several alleged grounds:

(*i*) Consumer-surplus analysis is valid only when the marginal utility of real income is constant.

(*ii*) Consumer-surplus analysis does not take account of changes in income distribution caused by the action(s) being analyzed.

(*iii*) Consumer-surplus analysis is partial-equilibrium in nature, and does not take account of the general-equilibrium consequences of the actions whose effects are being studied.

(*iv*) Consumer-surplus analysis, though valid for small changes, is not so for large changes.

(*v*) The concept of consumer surplus has been rendered obsolete by revealed-preference analysis.

While I do not have the impression that the skeptics dominate professional opinion in this area, they are sufficiently numerous (and a number of them sufficiently prestigious) that we surely cannot be said to have

achieved a high degree of professional consensus on the subject. Yet I feel, precisely because of the power and wide applicability of the consumer-surplus concept, that a recognizable degree of consensus concerning it would increase, to society's general benefit, the influence on public policy of good economic analysis. Moreover, I think that there is a fair chance of convincing a goodly share of the skeptics that postulates *a* to *c* constitute the most reasonable basis on which to seek professional consensus in the area of applied welfare economics. The merit of attaining something like a consensus, and the possibility of helping to induce some movement toward that end, provide the motivation for this tract.

II

Ordinarily, I would consider it quixotic to expect much to result from any such effort. But in this case my hopes are buoyed by the fact that it is easily possible for many skeptics to join the consensus without really changing their minds on any fundamental issues. How can this happen? Because *i*) we already have a reasonably well-established consensus on the basic methodology of national-income measurement, *ii*) it is easy to show that postulates *a-c* incorporate a greater degree of subtlety of economic analysis than does national-income methodology, and *iii*) most of the "objections" to consumer-surplus analysis hold *a fortiori* with respect to the measurement of national income. If we are prepared to more-or-less agree on national-income methodology (while being mindful of its defects), why should we resist approaching an agreement on a methodology for applied welfare economics (also keeping its defects in mind, but aware at the same time that they are much less serious than those applying to national income)?

Let us consider specifically objections (*i*), (*ii*) and (*v*) above, comparing in each case the force with which the objection applies to consumer-surplus analysis on the one hand, and to the use of national income as an indication of welfare on the other—objections (*iii*) and (*iv*) are dealt with in section III below.

Objection (*i*). I will later show that the assumption of constancy of the marginal utility of real income is not essential for the validity of consumer-surplus measures of welfare. Here, however, I shall only note that the benefits and costs treated in most applications of consumer-surplus analysis (*e.g.*, measures of the efficiency costs of a tax or an agricultural program, cost-benefit analyses of highway or irrigation projects, etc.) involve only a small fraction of a normal year's growth in GNP. Far more vulnerable to the objection that the marginal utility of real income might have changed are observations like "Real GNP doubled between 1950 and 1970," or even "National income will grow by $60 billion next year."

Objection (*ii*). By the same token, the changes in income distribution resulting from a particular measure being subjected to cost-benefit or consumer-surplus analysis are likely to be minimal by comparison with those that occur from decade to decade, or even from year to year, as a consequence of all causes. If, then, it is felt that "distributional weights" should be applied in the former case, before judgments can be made, it is even more important that they should be incorporated in the latter case.

Objection (*v*). Consider the case of the coal miner who, racked with silicosis, voluntarily quits a $7-an-hour job in the mine to take a newly-available $2-an-hour job clerking in a grocery store. National income goes down, but welfare in all likelihood goes up. In this case consumer-surplus analysis accords with revealed preference, while the movement of national income is in the opposite direction from the change in welfare. The same is true for the textbook case of the housekeeper who marries her employer.

Of course, economists do not truly believe that real NNP or national income is a complete measure of welfare. But it is equally true that in most of the contexts in which changes in these magnitudes, or comparisons of them across regions or countries are dealt with, the discussion carries strong welfare connotations, often to the point where it would be meaningless if those connotations were denied. National income and NNP are, in a very real sense, measures of welfare under certain assumptions, but only to a first order of approximation. No one would deny that many other factors are important—the strength of the social fabric, the quality of life, and certainly the issue of to whom the income accrues—but it is not feasible to build these into a national-income measure. Hypothetically, one might contemplate a national income measure incorporating "distributional weights," but two obstacles stand in its way: first, the impossibility of achieving a consensus with regard to the weights, and second, the fact that most of the data from which the national accounts are built are aggregates in the first place, and do not distinguish the individuals or groups whose dollars they represent. Giving equal weight to all dollars of income is mathematically the simplest rule, and our data come that way in any event. In a sense, the second obstacle imposes, rather arbitrarily to be sure, a solution to the perplexing difficulties posed by the first. This solution is obviously a far-from-perfect measure of national welfare—indeed it is surprising how little dissatisfaction has been expressed (until quite recently) with its use as such. But even its firmest detractors would probably not deny the usefulness of the national accounts and the necessity for them to be built on the basis of rules or conventions reflecting some degree of professional consensus.

An easy way to see the relationship between national income and the consumer-surplus concept is to consider the first two terms of the Taylor expansion of a utility function

$$(1) \qquad U = U(X_1, X_2 \cdots X_n)$$

$$\Delta U = \sum_i U_i \Delta X_i$$

(2)

$$+ \frac{1}{2} \sum_i \sum_j U_{ij} \Delta X_i \Delta X_j.$$

Since U_i is a function solely of $(X_1, X_2 \cdots X_n)$, we can write $\sum_j U_{ij} \Delta X_j = \Delta U_i$; with this (2) simplifies to

(3) $\quad \Delta U = \sum_i U_i \Delta X_i + \frac{1}{2} \sum_i \Delta U_i \Delta X_i.$

Now, assuming utility maximization in the face of market prices $(P_1 \cdots P_n)$ we have $U_i = \lambda P_i$, where λ represents the marginal utility of income, and

(4) $\quad \Delta U_i = \lambda^0 \Delta P_i + P_i^0 \Delta \lambda + \Delta P_i \Delta \lambda.$

Substituting from (4) into (3) we obtain

(5)
$$\frac{\Delta U}{\left(\lambda^0 + \frac{1}{2} \Delta \lambda\right)} = \sum P_i^0 \Delta X_i$$
$$+ \frac{1}{2} \sum \Delta P_i \Delta X_i + \frac{1}{4} \frac{\Delta \lambda \sum \Delta P_i \Delta X_i}{\left(\lambda^0 + \frac{1}{2} \Delta \lambda\right)}.$$

Neglecting third order terms, this yields

(5′)
$$\frac{\Delta U}{\lambda^0 + \frac{1}{2} \Delta \lambda} \approx \sum P_i^0 \Delta X_i$$
$$+ \frac{1}{2} \sum \Delta P_i \Delta X_i.$$

The first term on the right-hand side of (5′) measures the first-order change in utility, and can be identified with the change in national income (or, more properly, net national product) expressed in constant prices. The second term measures the second-order change in utility, and can be identified with the change in consumer surplus.[1] The fact

[1] This is strictly true only when the point of departure is one of full, undisturbed equilibrium. When the starting point is one where distortions are already present, some of the change in consumer surplus is incorporated in the first term. This point will be treated in more detail below.

that the consumer-surplus concept is associated with a higher-order term in the Taylor expansion of the utility function is simply the mathematical counterpart of the statement made earlier that "postulates *a–c* incorporate a greater degree of subtlety of economic analysis than does national income methodology."

Note, too, that (5) in effect converts the change in utility into monetary terms by dividing it by the marginal utility of income. There is obviously no problem when the latter is not changing, but when it does change as a consequence of the action(s) being analyzed, the conversion of utility into money is implicitly carried out at the midpoint of the beginning and ending marginal utilities of income. The criticism[2] that consumer-sur-

[2] The origin of this criticism is probably the thought that changes in consumer surplus ought directly to measure changes in utility. That this would be a fruitless pursuit should be obvious—among other things consumer surplus would not be invariant to monotonic transformations of the utility function. However, the measure $\frac{1}{2}\sum \Delta X_i \Delta P_i$ is invariant, with the change in ΔU stemming from a monotonic transformation being offset by the change in $(\lambda + \frac{1}{2}\Delta\lambda)$ in the denominator of the left-hand side of (5). The following way of stating the same argument avoids the approximation implicit in a two-term Taylor expansion: the change in utility stemming from the change in a policy variable from z_0 to z^* is

$$\Delta U = \int_{z_0}^{z^*} \sum_i U_i(z) \frac{\partial X_i}{\partial z} dz.$$

This, being expressed in utils, is not invariant to a monotonic transformation. However, transforming utility into money continuously through the integration process, always at the marginal utility of money prevailing at that point, we have

$$\Delta W = \int_{z_0}^{z^*} \sum_i \frac{U_i(z)}{\lambda(z)} \frac{\partial X_i}{\partial z} dz$$
$$= \int_{z_0}^{z^*} \sum_i P_i(z) \frac{\partial X_i}{\partial z} dz.$$

This obviously is invariant under any transformation of the original utility function which leaves unchanged the relevant behavioral reactions to changes in z.

An issue arises in connection with the comparability of measures of welfare loss, when one is comparing moves on two different paths (say T_1 and T_2) away from the undistorted equilibrium. If the marginal utility of the numeraire (here real income) is constant, there is no issue in this regard. However, comparability does not

plus concepts have validity only when the marginal utility of income is constant must therefore be rejected.

The conversion of utility into money also greatly eases the aggregation problem. Clearly both the first-order and the second-order terms on the right-hand side of (5) can be aggregated over individuals without difficulty.

III

In this section I shall discuss objections (*iii*) and (*iv*), which were left aside in the comparison between consumer surplus and national income methodologies in the preceding section. Objection (*iii*), that consumer-surplus analysis is partial-equilibrium in nature, and fails to take account of general-equilibrium considerations, is totally invalid on a theoretical level, but can fairly be levied against some practical applications.

Taking the theoretical issue first, one need only note that rigorous general-equilibrium formulations of consumer-surplus measurement have long since been a part of the corpus of economic theory. Hotelling [10, 1938], Hicks [7, 1941; 8, 1946; 9, 1956], and Meade [18, 1955, esp. Vol. II] all have derived, in a general-equilibrium framework, measures of welfare change that are consistent with postulates *a-c*, and many others have followed in their train.[3]

The key to understanding the general-equilibrium nature of the consumer-surplus concept is the following simple measure of welfare change:

$$(6) \qquad \Delta W = \int_{z=0}^{z^*} \sum_i D_i(z) \frac{\partial X_i}{\partial z}\, dz.$$

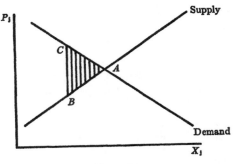

Here D_i represents the excess of marginal social benefit over marginal social cost per unit level of activity i, X_i represents the number of units of activity i, and z is the policy variable, the effects of a change in which we are interested in measuring. The D_i (distortions) can take many forms—about which more will be said below—but here, for simplicity of exposition, I shall assume that all the D_i take the form of taxes. A tax quite obviously drives a wedge between demand price (which under postulate *a* measures the value of the marginal unit to the demander) and supply price (which under postulate *b* measures the value of the marginal unit to the supplier), and this fits most naturally into the framework of this paper.

If a tax is placed on a single good j in the absence of any other distortions, (6) becomes

$$(7) \qquad \Delta W = \int_{T_j=0}^{T_j^*} T_j \frac{\partial X_j}{\partial T_j}\, dT_j,$$

which is equal to the familiar welfare-cost triangle (*ABC* in Figure 1). Though the demand and supply functions of other goods may shift as a consequence of placing a tax on good j, the measure of welfare change is unaffected by such shifts since the distortions D_i in all other markets are, by assumption in this case, zero. However, if taxes on other goods already exist when T_j^* is imposed, the effects of its imposition are given by:

---

require constancy of the marginal utility of real income, but only "well-behavedness." By this I mean that when real income falls by ΔY as a consequence of the imposition of T_2, its marginal utility should change by the same amount as occurs when real income falls by ΔY as a consequence of a tax T_1.

[3] See Corlett and Hague [1, 1953]; Harberger [3, 1964; 4, 1964]; Johnson [11, 1960; 12, 1962]; Lange [14, 1942]; Lipsey and Lancaster [15, 1956–57]; Lipsey [16, 1970]; and McKenzie [17, 1951].

$$(8) \quad \Delta W = \int_{T_j=0}^{T_j^*} T_j \frac{\partial X_j}{\partial T_j} dT_j$$

$$+ \int_{T_j=0}^{T_j^*} \sum_{i \neq j} T_i \frac{\partial X_i}{\partial T_j} dT_j.$$

This is equal to the triangle ABC in Figure 1 (which generates a negative contribution to welfare) plus, with constant T_is, the expression $\sum_{i \neq j} T_i \Delta_i$, where ΔX_i measures the change in the equilibrium quantity of X_i occasioned by the imposition of T_j^*. Any of the terms in this summation, which is what makes the difference between partial- and general-equilibrium approaches when other distortions are present, can be either positive or negative—when the distortion itself is positive (*e.g.*, a tax), a positive contribution is made to the change in welfare if, as a consequence of a new disturbance (in this case the imposition of T_j^*), X_i increases, and a negative contribution if X_i decreases. When the distortion itself is negative (*e.g.*, a subsidy), the contribution to welfare associated with activity i as a consequence of T_j^* is negative if $\partial X_i / \partial T_j > 0$ and positive if $\partial X_i / \partial T_j < 0$. This case is illustrated in Figure 2, where it is assumed that both the demand and supply curves of X_k shift as a consequence of the imposition of T_j^*. If the shift is from the solid demand and supply curves (when $T_j = 0$) to the broken ones (when $T_j = T_j^*$), the area $EFGH$ ($= T_k \Delta X_k$) is an added loss; if the shift is in the other direction it is an added benefit helping to off-

set (and possibly actually outweighing) the triangle ABC in Figure 1.

This is a convenient place to point out the relationship between the general expression (8) for welfare change and the approximation (5′). Define $C_i + T_i = P_i$, and assume constant costs of production C_i, with the resource constraint $\Sigma C_i X_i = Y$, a constant.[4] When a tax is imposed on X_j in the presence of pre-existing taxes on other goods $i \neq j$, we have, substituting $C_i + T_i = P_i^0$ for $i \neq j$, $C_j = P_j^0$ and $T_j^* = \Delta P_j$ into (5′),

$$(5'') \quad \begin{aligned} P_i^0 \Delta X_i + \frac{1}{2} \sum \Delta P_i \Delta X_i &= \sum C_i \Delta X_i \\ &\quad + \sum T_i \Delta X_i + \frac{1}{2} \sum \Delta C_i \Delta X_i \\ &\quad + \frac{1}{2} T_j^* \Delta X_j. \end{aligned}$$

Since $\Sigma C_i \Delta X_i = \Sigma \Delta C_i \Delta X_i = 0$ under our assumptions, we have

$$(5''') \quad \begin{aligned} \sum P_i^0 \Delta X_i + \frac{1}{2} \sum \Delta P_i \Delta X_i \\ = \sum T_i \Delta X_i + \frac{1}{2} T_j^* \Delta X_j \end{aligned}$$

as a measure of the change in welfare stemming from the imposition of T_j^*.[5] This is

[4] These assumptions are consistent with a situation in which the tax revenues received by the government are redistributed to the private sector *via* neutral transfers. For a more detailed treatment see Harberger [3, 1964].

[5] Where no pre-existing distortions are present, and a vector of distortions $T^* = (T_1^*, T_2^* \cdots T_n^*)$ is introduced, (6) becomes, for linear demand and supply curves, $\Delta W = \frac{1}{2} \Sigma T_i \Delta X_i$, where

$$\Delta X_i = \int_{\mu=0}^{1} \left(\frac{\partial X_i}{\partial T} \right)' T^* \mu d\mu.$$

That is to say, if the final set of taxes is (.5, .2, .1), one can imagine the process of integration taking place through steps like (.05, .02, .01), (.10, .04, .02), (.15, .06, .03), etc. The locus of points traced out by this exercise will define the set of triangles $\frac{1}{2} T_i \Delta X_i$. As this exercise can in principle be performed for any set of distortions (not just taxes), it is quite general. One must note, however, that the triangles traced out here are not triangles between stable demand and supply curves but rather triangles defined by the loci of marginal social benefit (demand price) and marginal social cost (supply

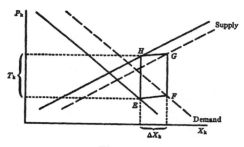

Figure 2.

Harberger: *Postulates for Applied Welfare Economics*

precisely what emerges from (8) in the case where the demand and supply curves for X_j are linear. It also shows how, when there are pre-existing distortions, elements of consumer surplus are present in the expression $\Sigma P_i{}^0 \Delta X_i$, representing the first-order approximation to welfare change.

Let us return to the discussion of objection (*iii*), that consumer-surplus analysis neglects general-equilibrium considerations. While it is clear that no theoretical obstacle stands in the way of taking such considerations into account, it is in fact rarely done in studies involving applied welfare economics. I do not want to appear to defend this neglect—indeed, the sooner it is rectified, the better—but at the same time I want to try to dispel any thoughts that the job of incorporating general-equilibrium aspects is so big as to be effectively hopeless. All that job entails is adding to the standard partial-equilibrium welfare analysis (of the tax $T_j{}^*$ in our example), an expression $\Sigma_{i \neq j} D_i \Delta X_i$. That may look like a formidable task but it need not be. The set of activities with significant distortions is a subset of the set of all activities; the set of activities whose levels are significantly affected by the action under study (*e.g.*, $T_j{}^*$) is another subset of the set of all activities. Only their intersection (see Figure 3) is important for the analysis of the effects of the specific policy action in question, and it is to be hoped that in most cases the number of elements in it will be of manageable size.[6]

Objection (*iv*) can be dealt with on several levels. In the first place, there is the issue

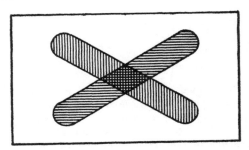

SET OF ALL ACTIVITIES

⦀ Subset with significant D_i

☰ Subset with significant ΔX_i

▦ Intersection of the two subsets

Figure 3.

of the exactness of (5); when the basic utility functions are quadratic, the first two terms of the Taylor expansion are all that are needed to describe the function fully; but when the basic utility functions are not linear or quadratic, (5) will be an approximation. And (5') is vulnerable even when the utility function is quadratic, because of its neglect of the third term of (5). But while (5) and (5') thus may contain errors of approximation which will be smaller, the smaller are the changes being studied, (6) is not subject to the same charge. The integrals set out there can be taken for curved as well as linear demand and supply curves, or, more properly stated, for curved or linear loci of demand prices and supply prices.

At another level entirely, one might interpret the large-versus-small-changes issue as raising up the old consumer-surplus conundrums about the value attaching to the first units of liquid or the first units of food, etc. I prefer to sidestep this issue on the ground that the problems arising in applied welfare economics typically do not involve carrying people to or from the zero point in their demand curves for food or for liquids, and where they do (as, for example in famine relief programs), it appears more appropriate

---

price) as μ goes from zero to one. On this result see Hotelling's equation 19 and the subsequent discussion [10, 1938].

[6] Certain distortions, such as the property tax or the corporation income tax, which apply to a large subset of activities, can be taken into account through the use of shadow prices—*e.g.*, in this case the social opportunity cost of capital. See Harberger [5, 1968 and 6, 1969]. Once the "general" distortions have been dealt with in this way, the remaining ones, it is to be hoped, will be sufficiently small in number so as to keep the problem manageable.

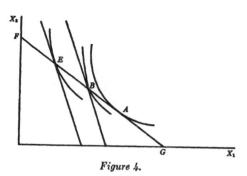

Figure 4.

to approach the problem through assigning a monetary value to the human lives saved or lost, a task which necessarily carries us beyond the narrow confines of consumer-surplus analysis.

At still another level, when large changes are involved, the well-behavedness of functions is less easily guaranteed than when only small changes are present. For example, it is easy to show that the Hicks-Slutsky substitution properties apply to demand functions defined by movements constrained to a locus of the form $\Sigma C_i X_i = Y$, a constant (*FG* in Figure 4) so long as one is concerned with small changes in the neighborhood of the undistorted equilibrium (*e.g.*, in the neighborhood of *A*). However, this cannot be shown to be generally true for large changes. For example, Figure 4 is so constructed that at both B and E the indifference curves intersecting *FG* have the same slope. This means that a demand function constrained to the locus *FG* (with real income being held constant in this sense) will have two quantities associated with the same relative price. Except in the case where the income expansion path at that price coincided with the segment *EB* between these two quantities, there would have to be some range(s) in that quantity interval in which the own-price elasticity of each good was positive, thus violating one of the Hicks-Slutsky conditions.[7]

[7] For a further elaboration of this point see Foster and Sonnenschein [2, 1970].

There are at least two ways in which analyses based on postulates *a* to *c* can be justified in the face of this possible criticism. At the strictly theoretical level, while some results of some exercises in applied welfare economics may derive directly from the Hicks-Slutsky properties, the validity of equation (6) does not depend on the existence of well-behavedness in this sense. Alternatively one may simply take it as a matter of convention that, just as measurements of real national income in a sense are built on a linear approximation of the utility function, so we shall base consumer-surplus and cost-benefit analyses upon a quadratic approximation of that function, incorporating the Hicks-Slutsky properties. This more "pragmatic" approach would presumably be based on the unlikelihood of our encountering cases in which empirical evidence can be mustered showing that such an approximation yields seriously biased numerical estimates of welfare costs and/or benefits.

A final variant of the large-versus-small-changes question concerns the normalization of measures of welfare change to correct for changes in the general price level. Consider the case of a two-good economy with $X_1 C_1 + X_2 C_2 = Y$, a constant. In this context one can analyze the effects of imposing, say, a 100 percent tax on X_1, with no distortion on X_2, or alternatively granting a 50 percent subsidy to X_2 with no distortion in the market for X_1. Assuming that the tax proceeds are returned to the public via neutral transfers and that the money for the subsidy is raised by neutral taxes, we should expect the same real equilibrium to be achieved in both of the alternative situations being compared. We should also, presumably, arrive at the same measure for ΔW. If we set $C_1 = C_2 = 1$, which is simply a question of choice of units and entails no loss of generality, with the 100 percent tax on X_1, the measure of welfare change is $\Delta W = \frac{1}{2} \Sigma \Delta X_1 \Delta P_1 = \frac{1}{2} \Delta X_1$. Alternatively, with a 50 percent subsidy to X_2, the welfare change measure is

$-\frac{1}{4}\Delta X_2$, which is equal to $\frac{1}{4}\Delta X_1$, since under our assumptions $\Delta X_2 = -\Delta X_1$. This ambiguity can readily be resolved through the appropriate choice of a numeraire. When X_1 is the numeraire, the 100 percent tax on it is reflected in the price vector changing from $(1, 1)$ to $(1, \frac{1}{2})$, which is exactly what happens when a 50 percent subsidy to X_2 is introduced, so long as X_1 is the numeraire. Likewise, when X_2 is the numeraire, the 50 percent subsidy to it produces the same price vector $(2, 1)$ as is generated by the 100 percent tax on X_1. My own preference as to a conventional way of correcting for changes in the absolute price level is to normalize on net national product = national income. This entails setting $\Sigma P_i X_i = \Sigma C_i X_i = Y$, a constant, which in turn implies, since $C_i + T_i = P_i$, that $\Sigma T_i X_i = 0$. This normalization automatically calls attention to the fact that most problems of applied welfare economics are "substitution-effect-only" problems, a point to which we shall turn in the next section.

IV

In this section I shall discuss some of the complexities that may arise in applications of the analytical approach represented by postulates *a–c*. Let us first consider in more detail the close relation of the postulates to "revealed preference." Essentially, postulates *a* and *b* state that when demanders (suppliers) pay (get) their demand (supply) price for each marginal unit, the balance of their indifference as between demanding (supplying) that unit and undertaking the relevant available alternative activities has just barely been tipped. In effect, demand and supply prices are measures of the alternative benefits that demanders and suppliers forego when they do what they decide to do.

Equation (6) appears to capture all effects of an exogenous policy change, z, that are relevant to our three postulates—and indeed it does except when the exogenous change z in itself alters the resources available to the

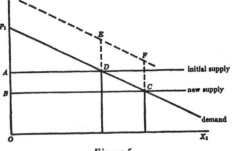

Figure 5.

economy in question, the technological possibilities under which it operates, or the trading conditions that it faces in external markets. So long as the exogenous change does not alter any of these things, all that it entails is the reshuffling of available resources among activities. It is in this sense that "substitution effects only" are involved in expression (6) in such cases.

To see that (6) does not capture the "income effects" of changes in resources, technology, or trading conditions, let us consider them in turn. Suppose, for example, that the exogenous change is that emigrant remittances, which were previously outlawed under foreign countries' exchange controls, are now permitted. The country receiving the remittances clearly gains, even if no distortions whatsoever are present in its economy. Hence (6) fails to capture the direct benefit associated with the remittances, even though in the presence of distortions it would capture the welfare "repercussions" that the receipt of the remittances might engender.

When technological advance occurs, the resources thus freed are enabled to increase total welfare, again even if no distortions are present. In Figure 5, the benefit from a technological advance that reduced unit costs from OA to OB would be given by the area $ABCD$ in the absence of other distortions, and by that area plus expression (6) in their presence. Expression (6) would of course include the area $CDEF$ if a unit tax equal to ED were already in existence on X_1. The exogenous force z in (6) would in this case be the reduction in unit cost (price) of producing X_1 and the terms in $\partial X_i/\partial z$ would include movements due to both the income and the substitution effects of this price change.

An exactly similar analysis applies in the case of an improvement in trading conditions in external markets. Here again a measure of the contribution to welfare that would be entailed in the absence of distortions must be added to (6), and the $\partial X_i/\partial z$ in (6) reinterpreted as above.

I believe that the three cases mentioned—new resources (gifts from outside), new technology (gifts of science and nature), and improved trading terms—or their respective negatives, are the only ones for which estimated first-order income effects must be added to expression (6). It is very important to note that such effects are not generated by price changes taking place within the economy under study in the absence of technical change. In this case, unless there are distortions, the benefits to demanders of a fall in price are cancelled by the costs to suppliers, and *vice versa* in the case of a rise in price. And when distortions are present, (6) captures their effect. Likewise it is important to recognize that no additional term should be added to (6) in cases where production moves from a point on the true (outer) production frontier to some interior point as a consequence of the introduction of a new distortion (such as a tax on the employment of a factor in some lines of industry but not in others).

This brings to mind a second subtlety involved in (6): it is essential to recognize that the X_i refer to activities, not just products. In the case just mentioned the tax would be on the activity of using, *e.g.*, capital in a certain subset of industries—say the corporate sector. D_i would here be the tax per unit of corporate capital, and X_i its amount.

The activities of producing and consuming a given good should be kept analytically separate whenever the distortions affecting them differ;[8] likewise, a given type of activity which is affected by different distortions in different regions should be broken down into as many separate activities as there are different distortions. Perhaps the best guide that can be given in this matter is "identify the relevant distortions and let them define the relevant set of activities."

We now turn to a brief listing of the various types of distortion. (1) Taxes have probably been given sufficient attention already; let me only add that all kinds of taxes (income, excise, property, sales, consumption, production, value-added, etc.) fit easily into the framework presented here. (2) Monopoly profits, in the sense of any return (above the normal earnings of capital) that is obtained as a consequence of artificially restricting sales to a point where price exceeds marginal cost should also clearly be included. Note that for a great many analytical purposes monopoly profits can be treated as a privately-imposed and privately-collected tax. (3) The excess of price over marginal revenue in any external market in which the society in question has monopoly power is another case. This is a negative distortion which can be offset by an optimal export tax or by the implicit tax imposed by a private export monopoly. Categories (4) and (5) are simply the counterparts of (2) and (3) for the case of monopsony, the distortion in (4) stemming from monopsony profits, and that in (5) from the excess of marginal cost over price in any external market in which the society in question has monopsony power. (6) Externalities of all kinds represent distortions, positive or negative. Pollution of air or water is a negative distortion, which could, under postulates *a–c*, be offset by a tax per unit of pollutant equal to what people

[8] Except in the trivial case of a closed economy or of non-traded goods, where production and consumption are necessarily the same.

would be willing to pay not to have it, or what they require as compensation in order to put up with it. The congestion of highways and streets represents another negative distortion, which could in principle be offset by an optimum congestion toll reflecting the extra cost (in terms of time, fuel, wear and tear, etc.) imposed upon others as a consequence of the presence of the marginal driver on the road.

Some readers may be inclined to question my classifying all taxes (and all monopoly profits) as distortions, only to go on to point out cases where they can be used to offset other distortions. Why not make special categories for cases like the optimum tariff, optimum export tax, optimum pollution charge, and optimum congestion toll? My answer is twofold. First, it is overwhelmingly simpler to avoid the special categories, and its cost—if any—is only the acceptance of the idea that distortions can offset each other. But this idea is needed in any event for activities where more than one distortion is present; different distortions applying to a given activity can either reinforce, or wholly or partially offset each other. Second, by avoiding special categories we highlight the fact that we are very unlikely to find optimal taxes and tolls in any real-world context.

V

This brings me back to my main theme: to plead for the "conventionalization" of postulates *a–c*. Arguing in favor of them are the facts that they are both simple and robust and that they underlie a long tradition in applied welfare economics. They are simple both in the sense that their use entails no more than the standard techniques of received economic theory, and in the sense that the data that their use requires are more likely to be available than those required by alternative sets of postulates (in particular any that involve the full-blown use of "distributional weights").

The robustness of the postulates is another attribute of special importance. They can readily be used to define a set of policies that characterizes a full optimum. This entails no more than introducing taxes, subsidies, or other policies to neutralize distortions (*e.g.*, monopoly, pollution) that would otherwise exist, so that the consolidated D_i affecting each activity are all zero, and raising government revenue by taxes that are truly neutral (lump-sum or head taxes),[9] or (cheating only slightly) by almost-neutral taxes such as Kaldor's progressive consumption-expenditure tax [13, 1955]. The postulates can also, in principle, be used to solve second-best problems such as finding the excise tax rates T_i on a subset of commodities X_1, $X_2 \cdots X_k$ that entails the minimum cost of distortions while still raising a given amount of revenue. But these problems, taken from the theoretical literature, are likely to remain textbook problems. The practitioner of applied welfare economics knows full well that his clients do not come to him in search of full optima or elegant suboptima. He is more likely to be asked which of two alternative agricultural programs is better, or what resource-allocation costs a given tax increase involves, or whether a certain bridge is worth its cost. And to be relevant, his answer must recognize the existence of many distortions in the economy, over whose presence neither he nor his client have control. Most applied welfare economics thus answers questions like "Does this action help or hurt, and by approximately how much?" or "Which of two or three alternative actions helps most or hurts least, and by approximately how much?"—all this in a context in which most (if not all) existing distortions have to be taken as given. It is the fact that the three postulates are able to handle these kinds of questions, as well as more elegant optimization problems, that gives them the robustness to which I refer.

[9] The best definition of a head tax is one which must be paid either with money or with the taxpayer's head!

While it is true that there is no complete correspondence between what is traditional and what is right, some weight must be given to the fact that no alternative set of basic assumptions comes nearly as close as postulates *a–c* to distilling the fundamental assumptions of applied welfare economics as we know it. These postulates are reflected not only in the general-equilibrium literature referred to in footnotes 5 and 6, but also in the standard practice of down-to-earth cost-benefit analyses [see, for example: 20, U. S. Inter-Agency Committee on Water Resources, 1958]. And it is here, really, that the need for a consensus is greatest. In the United States, cost-benefit (and its counterpart, "cost-effectiveness") analysis received a major boost when the PPB (Planning-Programming-Budgeting) concept was endorsed by President Lyndon Johnson and decreed as official policy by the Bureau of the Budget. And at the state and local level, investment projects and programs are also being scrutinized with an unprecedented degree of care, largely owing to the increasing concern that people have for environmental issues. Moreover, not just the United States is involved in this movement; the concerns about the environment, the worries about "what we are doing to ourselves," the recognition that our resources are too scarce to be wasted on bad programs, have no national limits. There is, indeed, a worldwide trend in which, country by country, an increasing fraction of the key decision-making posts are occupied by economists, and in which increasing efforts are applied to provide a sound economic justification for the projects that governments undertake. Finally, we have seen in the last decade a growing involvement of international organizations in the issues to which this paper is addressed: three regional development banks newly formed for Africa, Asia, and Latin America; increasing resources are devoted by the United Nations Development Programme to project identification and development, and by the World Bank to project financing. The OECD [19, 1968, 1969] has also shown increasing concern in this area.

The developments described above simply highlight the need for a set of standards, of "rules of the game" by which our professional work in applied welfare economics can be guided and judged. The three basic postulates that have been the subject of this essay provide a *de minimis* answer to this need: their simplicity, their robustness, and the long tradition that they represent all argue for them as the most probable common denominator on which a professional consensus on procedures for applied welfare economics can be based.

And so, having made my plea, let me salute the profession with what might well have been the title of this paper, with what is certainly the key that points to the solution of most problems in applied welfare economics, with what surely should be the motto of any society that we applied welfare economists might form, and what probably, if only we could learn to pronounce it, should be our password:

$$\text{``} \int_{z=0}^{z^*} \sum_i D_i(z) \frac{\partial X_i}{\partial z} \, dz. \text{''}$$

References

1. CORLETT, W. J. and HAGUE, D. C. "Complementarity and the Excess Burden of Taxation," *Rev. Econ. Stud.*, 1953, *21*(1), pp. 21–30.

2. FOSTER, E. and SONNENSCHEIN, H. "Price Distortion and Economic Welfare," *Econometrica*, March 1970, *38*(2), pp. 281–97.

3. HARBERGER, A. C. "Taxation, Resource Allocation and Welfare" in NATIONAL BUREAU OF ECONOMIC RESEARCH AND THE BROOKINGS INSTITUTION, *The role of direct and indirect taxes in the federal revenue system*. Princeton: Princeton

University Press, 1964, pp. 25–75. See esp. pp. 30–33.

4. ———, "The Measurement of Waste," *Amer. Econ. Assoc. Pap. and Proc.*, May 1964, *54*, pp. 58–76.

5. ———, "On Measuring the Social Opportunity Cost of Public Funds" in *The discount rate in public investment evaluation* (Conference Proceedings of the Committee on the Economics of Water Resources Development, Western Agricultural Economics Research Council, Report No. 17, Denver, Colorado, Dec. 17–18, 1968). Pp. 1–24.

6. ———, "Professor Arrow on the Social Discount Rate" in *Cost-benefit analysis of manpower policies*, edited by G. G. SOMERS and W. D. WOOD. Kingston, Ontario: Industrial Relations Centre, Queen's University, 1969, pp. 76–88.

7. HICKS, J. R. "The Rehabilitation of Consumers' Surplus," *Rev. Econ. Stud.*, Feb. 1941, pp. 108–16. Reprinted in AMERICAN ECONOMIC ASSOCIATION, *Readings in welfare economics*. Homewood, Ill.: Richard D. Irwin, Inc., 1969, pp. 325–35.

8. HICKS, J. R. *Value and capital*. Second Edition. Oxford: The Clarendon Press, 1946.

9. ———, *A revision of demand theory*. London: Oxford University Press, 1956. Chapters X and XVIII.

10. HOTELLING, H. "The General Welfare in Relation to Problems of Railway and Utility Rates," *Econometrica*, July 1938, *6*(3). Reprinted in AMERICAN ECONOMIC ASSOCIATION, *Readings in welfare economics*. Homewood, Ill.: Richard D. Irwin, Inc., 1969.

11. JOHNSON, H. G. "The Cost of Protection and the Scientific Tariff," *J. Polit. Econ.*, August 1960, *68*(4), pp. 327–45.

12. ———, "The Economic Theory of Customs Unions" in *Money, trade and economic growth*. London: George Allen and Unwin, 1962, pp. 48 ff.

13. KALDOR, N. *An expenditure tax*. London: George Allen and Unwin, 1955.

14. LANGE, O. "The Foundations of Welfare Economics," *Econometrica*, July–Oct. 1942, *10*, pp. 215–28. Reprinted in AMERICAN ECONOMIC ASSOCIATION, *Readings in welfare economics*. Homewood, Ill.: Richard D. Irwin, Inc., 1969, pp. 26–38.

15. LIPSEY, R. G. and LANCASTER, K. "The General Theory of Second Best," *Rev. Econ. Stud.*, 1956–57, *25*(63), pp. 11–32.

16. LIPSEY, R. G. *The theory of customs unions: A general equilibrium analysis*. London: Weidenfeld and Nicholson, 1970.

17. McKENZIE, L. W. "Ideal Output and the Interdependence of Firms," *Econ. J.*, Dec. 1951, *61*, pp. 785–803.

18. MEADE, J. E. *Trade and welfare*, Vol. II, Mathematical Supplement. London: Oxford University Press, 1955.

19. ORGANIZATION FOR ECONOMIC COOPERATION AND DEVELOPMENT. *Manual of industrial project analysis in developing countries*. Paris, Vol. I, 1968; Vol. II (by I. M. D. LITTLE and J. A. MIRRLEES), 1969.

20. UNITED STATES INTER-AGENCY COMMITTEE ON WATER RESOURCES. *Proposed practices for economic analysis of river basin projects*. Washington: Government Printing Office, 1958.

[9]

THE WELFARE FOUNDATIONS OF COST-BENEFIT ANALYSIS[1]

I. INTRODUCTION

WITH few exceptions, cost-benefit analyses have proceeded by simply adding up total money costs and benefits regardless of who receives them. Indeed, Harberger (1971) has argued that this be considered one of the "three basic postulates" of applied welfare economics. There can be many justifications for this, but the one that seems to hold the most appeal for the "objective" economist is that aggregate money gains and losses measure the efficiency gains of a project in the following sense. If the aggregate is positive, this is taken to indicate that the gainers could compensate the losers and still be better off after the project is undertaken. If negative, the compensation test fails. That net monetary gains measure the efficiency effects of government projects (or policy changes) in this sense seems to be widely accepted in the literature. Statements to that effect may be found in a wide variety of sources besides Harberger, including most recent textbooks on cost-benefit analysis.[2] Mishan fairly well summarises what is being said in the following passage:

> "Since, in general, some people lose and some people gain following any economic change...the CVs [compensating variations] of the gainers...may be added algebraically to the CVs of the losers...If the resulting algebraic sum is positive, gainers can more than compensate losers, and the change will realize a potential Pareto improvement. If, on the other hand, this algebraic sum is zero or negative, the economic change contemplated does not realize a potential Pareto improvement" (Mishan, 1972, p. 317).

We shall not be concerned with the appropriateness of compensation tests as a criterion for welfare change. The disputes over this are well known in the literature. The purpose of this paper will be to argue that, even if we accept compensation tests as welfare criteria, the summation of total money gains and losses (including surpluses) does not in general indicate satisfaction of these tests. In fact, positive net money gains may be observed even when compensation is not possible and vice versa. Furthermore, when comparing alternative projects or policies, the one with the largest net gain is not necessarily the "best" one in the compensation test sense. Since we cannot

[1] The author has benefited from discussions of this paper with Frank Flatters of Queen's University.

[2] See, for example, Mishan (1972, p. 317), Dasgupta and Pearce (1972, p. 57), Pearce (1972, p. 21), Winch (1971, p. 151), Layard (1972, pp. 14–16), Burns (1973, p. 340), Silberberg (1972, p. 951) and Bradford (1971, p. 649). This is not to say that these authors all advocate the use of compensation tests as welfare criteria. For example, Pearce, and Dasgupta and Pearce, point out at length how distributional effects might be integrated into cost-benefit analysis.

rely on money surplus measures to determine the best course of action, there may be no alternative but to incorporate interpersonal comparisons regarding the marginal social utility of incomes to different groups into the cost-benefit analysis. We shall see that once we do this Harberger's "simple measure of welfare change" becomes much more complicated.

We proceed by first briefly summarising the measure of total gains and losses, or total surplus, from a government policy change in a general equilibrium setting. We then show diagrammatically why the total surplus does not coincide in all cases with satisfaction of the compensation test. Throughout, the term "cost-benefit analysis" is being used in the most general sense to include the measurement of benefits and costs of both single projects and other policy changes such as taxes or tariffs.

II. COST-BENEFIT ANALYSIS IN GENERAL EQUILIBRIUM

It has long been advocated that when a project is undertaken which affects output or factor prices one must use consumers' or producers' surpluses to measure the money benefits or losses. Little (1957) objected to the use of consumers' surplus ("a useless theoretical toy") on several grounds, including lack of measurability and its alleged inapplicability in a general equilibrium setting when distortions exist elsewhere or surpluses elsewhere change. Although the measurability problem is seemingly intractable, the work of Harberger (1964, 1971), and, more recently, of Silberberg (1972), Mohring (1971) and Burns (1973) has shown that the concept of consumers' surplus can easily be extended to general equilibrium settings when several prices change and distortions exist.[1] Their measure of aggregate net surplus can be derived for a single person economy as follows. Suppose there are n commodities, X_i, with consumer prices, p_i. Write the consumer's ordinal utility function as follows:

$$U = U(X_1, \ldots, X_i, \ldots, X_n) \qquad \cdot \qquad \cdot \qquad \cdot \qquad (1)$$

Totally differentiating (1) we obtain

$$dU = \Sigma U_i dX_i$$

Assuming the consumer maximises utility we can substitute $U_i = \lambda p_i$, where λ = marginal utility of income:

$$dU/\lambda = \Sigma p_i dX_i$$

A government policy change causing a discrete change in the X_i will generate the following measure of utility change in monetary terms:[2]

$$\int dU/\lambda = \int \Sigma p_i dX_i \qquad \cdot \qquad \cdot \qquad \cdot \qquad (2)$$

[1] Actually, Hotelling (1938) appears to have been the first to make this generalisation. See also Meade (1955).

[2] In a non-monetary economy a numeraire will be chosen and the measure of utility change will be in terms of units of the numeraire good. This is equivalent to setting $\lambda = U_o$ (where X_o is the numeraire), so the measure of welfare change becomes $dU/U_o = \Sigma p_i dX_i$ where $p_i = U_i/U_o$.

Equation (2) may be rewritten in two alternative forms, both of which are interesting for us. The first, due to Harberger, utilises a transformation constraint. Suppose, for simplicity, that it is linear and may be written

$$\Sigma \, p_i' X_i = C \text{ (constant)} . \quad . \quad . \quad . \quad (3)$$

where $p_i' = p_i - D_i$ and D_i is the distortion between consumer and producer prices due to monopoly, taxes, etc. Substituting for p_i in (2) and using $\Sigma \, p_i' dX_i = 0$, (2) reduces to:[1]

$$\int dU/\lambda = \int \Sigma \, D_i \, dX_i \quad . \quad . \quad . \quad . \quad (4)$$

This is Harberger's simple measure of welfare change (*e.g.* Harberger, 1971, p. 789). According to (4) we need only take into consideration changes in output of the distorted goods when evaluating changes in welfare.

The alternative way to proceed (*e.g.* Silberberg, Burns) is to differentiate the consumer's money income as follows:

$$dY = d(\Sigma \, p_i X_i) = \Sigma \, X_i \, dp_i + \Sigma \, p_i \, dX_i$$

Substituting into (2) yields:

$$\int dU/\lambda = \Delta Y - \int \Sigma \, X_i \, dp_i \quad . \quad . \quad . \quad (5)$$

The money measure of utility change is thus the change in income less some aggregate index of price change. Equation (5) constitutes a generalisation of the notion of consumer's surplus since the second term measures areas to the left of demand curves. Note, however, that some of these areas will be due to shifts as well as movements along curves.[2]

Notice that (5) may also be simplified if the change in question is a change in distortions (say, tax rates) and the transformation constraint is linear. Then,

$$\Sigma \, X_i \, dp_i = \Sigma \, X_i (dp_i' + dD_i)$$

From (3), we find that

$$\Sigma \, X_i \, dp_i' = -\Sigma \, p_i' \, dX_i = 0$$

Therefore, (5) reduces to

$$\int dU/\lambda = \Delta Y - \int \Sigma \, X_i \, dD_i \quad . \quad . \quad . \quad (5a)$$

The term in (5a) involving the change in distortions can be interpreted as the changes in consumer's and producer's surplus from a change in distortions. It may be depicted geometrically in the usual way.

The problem with both (4) and (5) is that the right-hand sides involve

[1] We use a linear transformation constraint simply because Harberger does. However, it is not required. If production efficiency is assumed, we can write the transformation constraint as $F(X_1, \ldots, X_n) = 0$. Total differentiation yields: $\Sigma F_i \, dX_i = 0$. This implies that, when we normalise for producer prices p_i', $\Sigma p_i' \, dX_i = 0$.

[2] Burns provides a neat diagrammatic example of the areas involved.

line integrals the valuation of which depends upon the path of integration. This problem is fully discussed in Silberberg, Mohring, and Burns, and we have nothing to add to that discussion. What is clear is that there can be no measure of welfare change in monetary terms which is independent of the path of integration. We therefore must choose a particular path, and the one chosen is that which converts (5) into a compensating variation (CV). This is done by evaluating the integral along a constant utility (indifference) surface. Thus, it is ΔY_c, where

$$\int dU/\lambda = \Delta Y - \int_{\overline{U}} \Sigma\, X_i\, dp_i = -\Delta Y_c$$

Conversely, it is defined as that income change which holds the individual at the same utility level following a change in relative prices and/or income. From the above equation

$$\int dU/\lambda = \Delta Y_c + \Delta Y - \int_{\overline{U}} \Sigma\, X_i\, dp_i = 0 \qquad . \qquad . \qquad (6)$$

ΔY_c is a generalisation of the partial concept of a compensating variation as being the area beneath a compensated demand curve. Thus, if only one price changes and income remains constant, (6) reduces to

$$\Delta Y_c = \int_{\overline{U}} X_i\, dp_i = 0$$

The reason why cost-benefit theorists choose this particular measure of welfare change (path of integration) is presumably because it seems to bear an intuitive relation to the compensation principle. That is, the compensating variation is the maximum amount of income that could be taken away from the gainer after a change without leaving him worse off (at the new set of prices) and the minimum amount that must be given to the losers to make them at least as well off as before the change (at the new set of prices).

We are interested in evaluating the effects of policy changes in which several persons are affected. The above analysis is extended to the case of m individuals ($j = 1, \ldots, m$) using the following social welfare function:

$$W = W(U^1, \ldots, U^j, \ldots, U^m) . \qquad . \qquad . \qquad (7)$$

Proceeding as above, we obtain the analogue to (2):

$$\int dW = \int \sum_j \sum_i \beta_j p_i\, dX_{ij} \qquad . \qquad . \qquad . \qquad (8)$$

where X_{ij} is the consumption of good i by individual j and $\beta_j = \lambda^j \partial W/\partial U^j$ is the marginal *social* utility of income of individual j.

The existence of β_j in (8) complicates things considerably. For one thing, we can no longer reduce it to a simple formula like (4) involving only distortions. The changes in output of all goods must be considered whether distortions exist or not. The necessity for this is most obviously seen by imagining a lump-sum redistributive movement in an undistorted economy.

The more important problem is that the determination of the β_js involves making interpersonal utility comparisons. It was to avoid making these comparisons that the compensation test was devised. If one is willing to accept as a welfare criterion that the gainers *could* compensate the losers, then no evaluation of β_j is required. As noted above, cost-benefit analysis attempts to circumvent interpersonal comparisons in the same sort of way; that is, by aggregating the CVs of different individuals and assuming the resultant sum gives an indication of net compensation payable. Using

$$dY_j = \sum_i p_i dX_{ij} + \sum_i X_{ij} dp_i$$

(8) becomes

$$dW = \int \sum_j \beta_j (dY_j - \sum_i X_{ij} dp_i)$$

The aggregate compensating variation is then the sum of the CVs of the individuals defined so that

$$\int dW = 0 = \sum_j \beta_j \left(\Delta Y_{cj} + \Delta Y_j - \int_{U'} \sum_i X_{ij} dp_i \right) . \qquad (9)$$

where β_j is constant since U^j is constant. The aggregate CV is then

$$\Delta Y_c = \sum \Delta Y_{cj}.$$

Nothing that has been said so far has indicated why the aggregate CV so defined should indicate satisfaction or otherwise of the compensation test. Nor have any of the above-mentioned authors provided any reasons why it should. It seems to have been taken as intuitively obvious. The next section is concerned with showing how unreliable is the ΣCV as a proxy for the compensation test.

III. Compensating Variations and Compensation Tests

The argument will be presented in diagrammatic terms using two-good two-person models. The CV for a person from a combined price and income change is easily depicted as follows. Fig. 1 shows a pair of indifference curves for an individual choosing between two goods X_1 and X_2. The individual starts at the point A with income Y_1 (in terms of good X_1). He chooses B after a rise in income from Y_1 to Y_2 and an increase in the relative price of X_2. Applying (6), his CV is[1]

$$\Delta Y_c = -Y_2 Y_1 + \int \sum X_i dp_i$$

$$= -Y_2 Y_1 + Y_0 Y_1$$

$$= -Y_2 Y_0$$

[1] For a geometric proof that

$$Y_0 Y_1 = \int_{\bar{U}} \sum X_i dp_i \quad \left(= \int X_2 dp_2 \text{ since } dp_1 = 0 \text{ as the numeraire} \right)$$

see Patinkin (1963). This is the well-known result that the Hicksian compensating variation equals the area to the left of the compensated demand curve. Here, $Y_0 Y_1$ is the CV of a price change with Y held constant, and $\int X_2 dp_2$ is the area to the left of the compensated demand curve between the initial and final prices.

The CV is simply the vertical distance between indifference curves taken at the new relative prices. Of course, if we had chosen X_2 as the numeraire, it would be the horizontal distance. Our results are independent of the numeraire chosen.

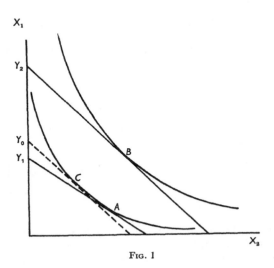

Fig. 1

Our procedure will involve summing these compensating variations for two individuals when one has gained and the other has lost. To compare the resultant ΣCV with compensation criteria, we must be more explicit about what is meant by compensation tests being fulfilled. Two extreme definitions might be cited. The more restrictive one is that used originally by Kaldor (1939), Hicks (1940) and Scitovsky (1941), and more recently by Chipman and Moore (1973). It involves a comparison between two given batches of goods corresponding to the initial and final situations. The gainers can be said to be able to compensate the losers if the final batch could be redistributed lump-sum in such a way as to make both persons better off as compared with the initial batch.[1] This notion of compensation is extremely restrictive since it does not allow the payment of compensation to affect output bundles. This means that the process of compensation is very inefficient indeed, and of the sort particularly prone to either indecisive outcomes or the "Scitovsky Paradox".[2]

Whereas batch comparisons involve movements along utility possibility

---

[1] Actually, Hicks used the reverse test, as de v. Graaff has pointed out. That is, the initial situation is better than the final if the gainers from the latter could not compensate the losers and still be as well off as in the initial situation. We will abide by the Kaldor version of the test.

[2] This is because the utility possibility curves constructed from redistributions of given batches are more likely to intersect than those discussed below.

curves defined by fixed batches (and therefore satisfying only exchange efficiency conditions generally), a more likely interpretation of compensation would involve purchasing power transfers which then cause relative demands and therefore batches to change. In the most extreme form, the transfers may be lump-sum in which case the process of compensation would involve movements along an efficiency locus.[1]

If lump-sum transfers are not considered possible (even hypothetically), the compensation must be considered to move the economy along some sort of feasibility locus of utility combinations intermediate to the batch locus and efficiency locus. The meaning of compensation tests is therefore quite ambiguous and we must endeavour to show how the ΣCV fares against each of the sorts of compensation tests outlined above. In all of what follows, we assume exchange efficiency.

(i) *Single batch; pure redistribution*

We take the simplest possible case to illustrate the contradiction between ΣCV and compensation tests. Consider a pure exchange economy with two goods and two persons. The contract curve is constructed as shown in Fig. 2. A purely redistributive move takes us from I to II along the contract curve. The gainer A could not compensate the loser B for the move and still be better off. Yet, ΣCV is $ac - bc$, which is positive. Furthermore, this sum is always positive for any move along the contract curve. The reader can easily construct an example in which a move is made from a point on the contract curve to a point off it such that $\Sigma CV > 0$; yet clearly, gainers cannot compensate losers for the move. This example of ours is of course not realistic but it is constructed for illustrative purposes only. In fact, this single batch case is but a special case of the batch comparison case outlined below in which the initial and final batches are different. The theorem given there also applies here.

(ii) *Kaldor–Hicks–Scitovsky batch compensation tests*

Let us now consider a comparison between alternative batches of two goods such that one has increased and the other decreased,[2] and one person gains and the other loses. The compensation test involved here is that of determining whether, by lump-sum redistribution of the given batch of goods, one can make both parties better off with one batch rather than the other.

We employ the diagram originally used by Scitovsky (1941, fig. 2, diag. 2). The following theorem will be shown to be evident from the geometric construction:

---

[1] See de V. Graaff, chapter v, for a description of the meaning of efficiency and feasibility loci.

[2] The same sort of results could be derived if both goods increase.

$\Sigma CV > 0$ is a necessary but not a sufficient condition for the satisfaction of a Kaldor–Hicks compensation test involving batch comparisons of commodities.

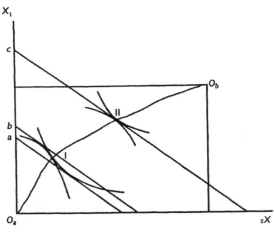

Fig. 2

In Fig. 3 two alternative batches are represented by the boxes with origins O_a and O_b, and O_a and O'_b. The contract curve for the latter is drawn in and labelled PP. The dotted lines to the south-west of p_o represent the locus of intersections of those pairs of indifference curves of A and B which are tangential along the contract curve of the box O_aO_b (not drawn). Thus, any point along the contract curve PP is potentially superior (in the compensation test sense) to all those points on the contract curve of O_aO_b corresponding to the dotted lines. To the north-east of p_o the opposite holds. All points along this portion of the contract curve PP lie off the contract curve of O_aO_b. This means that all points along the latter are potentially superior to all points north-east of p_o along PP. For example, indifference curves a_4 and b_3 might lie on the contract curve of O_aO_b but are not attainable in $O_aO'_b$.

Consider now a move from any point along the dotted line to any point along PP. Such a move always satisfies the compensation test since lump-sum transfers can always move us along PP to a point at which both A and B are better off than at a point on the dotted lines. (To be more precise, it satisfies the simple Kaldor–Hicks compensation test but not necessarily the Scitovsky reversal test. The latter is also satisfied for moves to the contract curve to the south-west of p_o.) For example, consider a move from a_1b_1 to a_2b_2 indifference curves. The CV of the gainer is RT and that of the loser is ST giving a net ΣCV of $RS > 0$. Furthermore, no matter what pair of points we choose along the dotted line and PP, a move to PP will always result in $\Sigma CV > 0$. This is the necessary part of the theorem.

Consider now a move from PP to an inferior position, say from $a_2 b_2$ in $O_a O_b'$ to $a_1 b_1$ in $O_a O_b$.[1] We choose both points to be to the left of p_o to avoid the Scitovsky paradox. If we had chosen a point to the right of p_o on PP, the

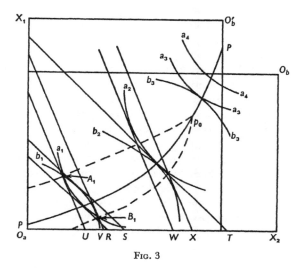

Fɪɢ. 3

dotted line would have been superior. Using a price ratio corresponding to the point $a_1 b_1$ on the $O_a O_b$ contract curve, we find the CV of the gainer and loser to be VX and UW respectively. Clearly, it is possible for $\Sigma CV > 0$ ($VX > UW$) even though the compensation test could not be fulfilled. Therefore, $\Sigma CV > 0$ is not a sufficient condition for the satisfaction of the batch compensation test. It is a relatively easy thing to show that $\Sigma CV > 0$ will be a sufficient condition if both individuals have identical and homothetic indifference curves.[2] But this is a fairly severe restriction on tastes, and unlikely to be true in practice.

(iii) *Samuelson–de v. Graaff compensation tests*

One might argue that for most applications ΣCV provides an accurate indication of the Kaldor–Hicks–Scitovsky batch compensation test. Large

[1] Note that we are moving from the bundle represented by the box $O_a O_b'$ to the bundle $O_a O_b$. The latter bundle is so divided as to leave A and B on indifference curves a_1 and b_1; that is, at points A_1 and B_1. Points A_1 and B_1 are tangential on the contract curve of $O_a O_b$ (not shown).

[2] The proof of this is as follows. When individuals are identical we can draw the indifference curves a_1, a_2, b_1, b_2 on the same map as shown in Fig. F. We know that at the price ratio corresponding to $a_2 b_2$ in Fig. 3, $A_1 A_2 > B_2 B_1$ (these correspond to $RT > ST$). When these indifference curves are homothetic, we can show that at any price ratio this horizontal distance between a_1 and a_2 always exceeds that between b_1 and b_2. With homotheticity, along any ray from the origin, the slopes of indifference curves are the same and the proportionate distance between any two indifference curves is the same. Therefore

$$a_1 a_2 / O a_1 = a_1' a_2' / O a_1' \quad \text{and} \quad b_2 b_1 / O a_1 = b_2' b_1' / O a_1'.$$

changes in relative prices would seem to be required for the test to fail.[1] However, this type of compensation test in which compensation is in the form of a redistribution of a fixed bundle of goods is unduly restrictive. Changes which we would regard as being potential welfare improvements may well fail the Scitovsky test. This may be illustrated using the utility possibility curves (UPCs) of Fig. 4. Consider a policy change which causes the UPC for the economy to shift from UU to $U'U'$. One might think of a move to free trade for example. In the initial situation, the point I is reached. With I is associated the utility curve SS representing the points attainable from a lump-sum redistribution of the bundle of I. Similarly, the final position is II with the utility curve $S'S'$ for its bundle. According to the Hicks–Kaldor–Scitovsky compensation test, it is not possible to judge either I or II to be superior since a redistribution of neither bundle will make both better off with one bundle rather than the other.

Suppose, however, that the hypothetical compensations were assumed to be of lump-sum transfers of income or purchasing power. Such transfers would allow the movement along the curve $U'U'$, causing appropriate changes in the bundles of goods. Situation I could be judged inferior to II by this criterion since lump-sum income transfers could take the economy

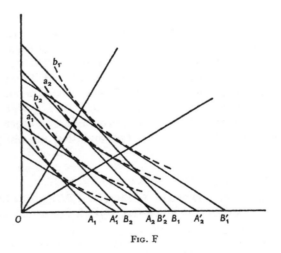

FIG. F

Therefore $a_1 a_2 / b_2 b_1 = a'_1 a'_2 / b'_2 b'_1$

Therefore, if $a_1 a_2 > b_2 b_1$, then $a'_1 a'_2 > b'_2 b'_1$. This implies that if $\Sigma CV > 0$ in going from $a_2 b_2$ to $a_1 b_1$ using the price ratio of $a_2 b_2$, then $\Sigma CV < 0$ when going from $a_1 b_1$ to $a_2 b_2$ using any price ratio. This proves that $\Sigma CV > 0$ is a sufficient condition for satisfaction of the batch compensation test when individuals have identical and homothetic tastes.

[1] ΣCV may also fail when one is trying to decide amongst several courses of action. This is because the magnitude of ΣCV is not an accurate estimate of the "gains from trade" for each alternative.

north-east of **I** to a point such as **III**. Thus, even though the batch compensation test failed, this one would pass.

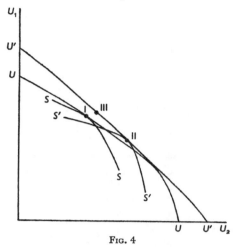

Fig. 4

If lump-sum transfers are considered infeasible, an intermediate form of compensation is appropriate—one that is less restrictive than the batch test, but more restrictive than the above. The transfers introduce some distortions into the economy since they are not lump-sum, but at the same time the bundles of goods do change as the transfer is made. In Fig. 4, the curve $U'U'$ would then be interpreted as a "feasibility locus" rather than an efficiency locus. In this case, it is still possible that the batch test fails even though compensation could be paid using feasible distortionary transfers.

Once it is recognised that the Kaldor–Hicks–Scitovsky batch compensation test is the most restrictive, it is apparent that $\Sigma CV > 0$ is not even a necessary condition for satisfaction of the compensation test. Consider Fig. 5. Suppose we start at position **I** in the Edgeworth box $O_a O_b$. A policy move favouring B and disfavouring A moves the economy to **II** in the box $O_a O'_b$. The two indifference curves labelled $b_1 b_1$ represent the same level of indifference drawn from the origins O_b and O'_b. To find ΣCV, we measure the distance between the old and new indifference curves at the new price ratio. As it is drawn, the CV of the loser exceeds the CV of the gainer by bc, so cost-benefit analysis would advise against making the move. However, the advice would be on slim foundations unless one adhered to the restrictive batch-type comparisons for compensation criteria. For example, the point O'_b may well lie on a production possibility surface passing outside the point O_b. One could contrive any number of examples for which such is the case. The sad truth is that we simply do not know from the market data available whether or not O'_b is "potentially superior" to O_b in any but the most restrictive sense. Cost-benefit analysis can therefore never tell us whether or not a move satisfies the less restrictive compensation tests.

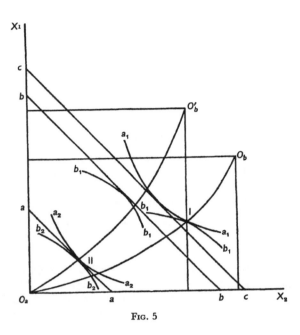

Fig. 5

IV. Conclusions

The measurement of welfare or efficiency gains from government actions has long interested both applied and theoretical economists. There is ample evidence in the literature of attempts to measure the gains (or losses) from taxes, tariffs, customs unions, or government projects. (See the survey article by Currie, Murphy and Schmitz (1971) for a discussion of some of these applications.) Basically, such studies involve estimating changes in consumers' and producers' surpluses arising from the policy change by looking at the appropriate areas bounded by demand and supply curves. More recently, theoretical studies of the measurement of welfare change have extended the concepts of consumers' and producers' surplus to general equilibrium settings so that the change in surplus from a policy change involves not only areas between given demand and supply curves but also changes in areas due to induced shifts in the curves. Moreover, the analytical tools for measuring welfare changes in a general equilibrium framework are now available due to the development of mathematical algorithms for computing general equilibrium solutions. (See Shoven and Whalley (1972, 1973) for a description of one such algorithm and its application to corporate tax changes.)

All of these discussions neglect the distributional effects of the policy change. That is, changes in aggregate consumer and producer surpluses are simply summed up in monetary units regardless of to whom they accrue (either positively or negatively). The justification usually given for this is that a positive value for the aggregate surplus change indicates that the gainers could compensate the losers for the policy change and still be better off. The analysis of this paper has shown that this rationale for ignoring distributional effects is not generally valid. That is, obtaining a positive change in aggregate consumers' and producers' surplus is neither a necessary nor a sufficient condition for the satisfaction of a compensation test which involves the hypothetical payment of monetary compensation from the gainers to the losers.

Suppose, for example, we wish to measure the welfare effects of changing one or more tax rates in a particular tax-distorted economy. Following Harberger (1964, 1971) we evaluate the changes in consumers' and producers' surpluses by looking at the changes in output of all goods (or factors) sold on distorted markets (according to equation (4) above). The aggregate of these changes in surplus may be positive or negative. The point of this paper is that, if some persons gain and others lose, we cannot interpret a positive surplus as an indication that the gainers could compensate the losers and a negative surplus that they could not. The magnitude and sign of the surplus are not related to the ability to compensate losers (except in special cases as, for example, when all persons have identical and homothetic preferences and compensation payments are lump sum as in footnote 2, p. 934). The surplus is evaluated at a set of relative prices corresponding to the new situation, and the process of compensation would change relative prices in a way not predictable from the known data.

This being so, the justification for ignoring the distribution of gains and losses cannot be based on hypothetical compensation as a welfare criterion. Or conversely, the acceptance of compensation tests does not imply using aggregate surplus changes as an indicator of welfare. The fact is that not enough information is available to tell us whether or not a compensation criterion could be satisfied in any particular application. This is over and above the problem of defining what sort of compensation test should be used—compensation by reallocation of a fixed bundle of goods, compensation by transfers of purchasing power allowing the output of goods to change, etc. Compensation tests are simply inoperable.

The only circumstance in which aggregate surplus changes are valid indicators of welfare change would be the fortuitous one in which the marginal social utility of income is identical for all ($\beta_i = \beta_j$, all i, j in equation (9)). However, to assume this is to make a particular interpersonal welfare comparison which has no *a priori* economic justification. The fact is that one cannot escape making such a comparison by appealing to a compensation criterion as a rationale for aggregating money gains. Some distributive weights must be chosen to apply to the gains and losses of surplus of each distinguishable group before they are added up, and that choice must be made on non-economic grounds, say, by political decision-makers. The economist may apply alternative sets of distributive weights to a particular problem and present the alternative evaluations to the politician for ultimate choice. Whatever the mechanism, the ultimate requirement of choosing distributive weights cannot be avoided. As pointed out earlier, once this is done, Harberger's measure is no longer very simple.

ROBIN W. BOADWAY

Queen's University, Kingston, Canada.

Date of receipt of final typescript: March 1974.

REFERENCES

Bradford, D. F. (1971). "Constraints on Public Action and Rules for Social Decision," *American Economic Review*, Vol. 60, Sept., pp. 642–54.

Burns, M. E. (1973). "A Note on the Concept and Measure of Consumer's Surplus," *American Economic Review*, Vol. 63, June, pp. 335–44.

Chipman, J. S. and Moore, J. C. (1973). "Aggregate Demand, Real National Income, and the Compensation Principle," *International Economic Review*, Vol. 14, Feb., pp. 153–81.

Currie, J. M., Murphy, J. A. and Schmitz, A. (1971). "The Concept of Economic Surplus and its Use in Economic Analysis," ECONOMIC JOURNAL, Vol. 81, Dec., pp. 741–99.

Dasgupta, A. K. and Pearce, D. W. (1972). *Cost-Benefit Analysis*, Macmillan, London.

de V. Graaff, J. (1957). *Theoretical Welfare Economics*, Cambridge University Press.

Harberger, A. C. (1964). "Taxation, Resource Allocation and Welfare," in National Bureau of Economic Research and the Brookings Institution, *The Role of Direct and Indirect Taxes in the Federal Revenue System*, Princeton University Press, pp. 25–75.

—— (1971). "Three Basic Postulates for Applied Welfare Economics: An Interpretive Essay," *Journal of Economic Literature*, Vol. 9, Sept., pp. 785–97.

Hicks, J. R. (1940). "The Valuation of Social Income," *Economica*, Vol. 7, May, pp. 105–24.

Hotelling, H. (1938). "The General Welfare in Relation to Problems of Railway and Utility Rates," *Econometrica*, Vol. 6, July, pp. 242–69.

Kaldor, N. (1939). "Welfare Propositions and Interpersonal Comparisons of Utility," ECONOMIC JOURNAL, Vol. 49, Sept., pp. 549–52.

Layard, R. (ed.) (1972). *Cost-Benefit Analysis*, Penguin Books, Middlesex.

Little, I. M. D. (1957). *A Critique of Welfare Economics*, second edition, Oxford University Press.

Meade, J. E. (1955). *Trade and Welfare: Mathematical Supplement*, Oxford University Press.

Mishan, E. J. (1972). *Cost-Benefit Analysis*, George Allen and Unwin, London.

Mohring, H. (1971). "Alternative Measures of Welfare Gains and Losses," *Western Economic Journal*, Dec., pp. 349–69.

Patinkin, D. (1963). "Demand Curves and Consumer's Surplus," in Carl Christ *et al.*, *Measurement in Economics*, Stanford.

Pearce, D. W. (1971). *Cost-Benefit Analysis*, Macmillan, London.

Samuelson, P. A. (1950). "Evaluation of Real National Income," *Oxford Economic Papers*, N.S., Vol. 2, Jan., pp. 1–29.

Scitovsky, T. (1941). "A Note on Welfare Propositions in Economics," *Review of Economic Studies*, Vol. 9, Nov., pp. 77–88.

Silberberg, E. (1972). "Duality and the Many Consumer's Surpluses," *American Economic Review*, Vol. 62, Dec., pp. 942–52.

Shoven, J. B. and Whalley, J. (1972). "A General Equilibrium Calculation of the Effects of Differential Taxation of Income from Capital in the U.S.," *Journal of Public Economics*, Vol. 1, Nov., pp. 281–321.

—— (1973). "General Equilibrium with Taxes: A Computational Procedure and an Existence Proof," *Review of Economic Studies*, Vol. XL, No. 124, Oct., pp. 475–90.

Winch, D. M. (1971). *Analytical Welfare Economics*, Penguin, Harmondsworth.

JeI *JOURNAL OF ECONOMIC ISSUES*
Vol. XVI   No. 1   March 1982

The New Controversy about the Rationale of Economic Evaluation

E. J. Mishan

In an age obsessed with quantification, in which the technology of the computer has begun to spread like an all-devouring fungus, insatiable in its craving for fresh data, it is not surprising that economic calculation, in particular the methods of cost-benefit analysis, should grow in popularity. The purpose of a cost-benefit analysis hardly requires explanation: It is self-describing. Yet, to be explicit, such a technique not only purports to measure the respective magnitudes of aggregate costs and aggregate benefits of a specific project, but also implies a criterion that aggregate benefits exceed aggregate costs. So much is beyond dispute. It remains only to observe that the singularity of the economic method, at least as conventionally understood, resides in the fact that the "objective" data of the economist is, in the final reckoning, nothing other than the subjective valuations of all the individuals affected by the change in question. More specifically, the value of the aggregate benefits of a project is measured ideally by the largest sum of money that the individuals favorably affected are together willing to pay for it, whereas the aggregate costs of that project are equal to the losses suffered by those who are unfavorably affected by it, such losses being ideally measured by the sum of the minimal payments acceptable to them.

As the informed layman is aware, the difficulty economists face in making such calculations is that of estimating the magnitude of the relevant

The author is Professor of Economics, The City University, London, England.

30   E. J. Mishan

effects on people's welfare over time—the operative words being *relevant* and *over time*. With respect to relevance, the scope of the economic calculation is virtually unlimited since, in principle, the reaction of every person in the community to every facet of the project is to count; in fact, every consequence associated with the introduction of the project that can be "brought into relation with the measuring rod of money." In actual studies, however, an indefinite number of so-called intangible effects, which ought indeed to be measured (for example, popular reaction about the geographical consequences of the project, the feeling among minority or majority groups that it will mar the landscape or townscape, or that it will threaten a traditional way of life) tend, not surprisingly, to be omitted from the calculation. And no reasonable economist will gainsay, either, that such intangibles may well be much more important than the tangible effects whose magnitudes are derivable from the market data which are more accessible to economists.

With respect to the passage of time, there is first the problem of how to deal at a given point with the uncertainty of economic estimates that grows greater as one peers farther into the future. There is, moreover, the problem of calculating an appropriate rate of discount if, indeed, this can be justified.[1]

The Revisionists

So much for the scope of, and the common problems associated with, the application of conventional cost-benefit methods.

What has now begun to worry economists within this field is nothing less than the rationale itself of a cost-benefit analysis or, more generally, of all economic calculation. Over the last few years a schism has emerged between, on the one hand, the conventional method of economic calculation as described above and, on the other, what we might call—in order to impart some ideological piquancy to the debate—the revisionist method of economic calculation.

The revisionists do not form a tight school of thought. Rather, they are a loose unself-conscious federation having one or more proposals for departing from the conventional method. Thus revisionism of a popular kind (as found in the UNIDO manual of 1971[2]) proposes, among other things, that the discount rate to be used in project evaluation be determined, not by economic calculation, but as a political datum. Revisionism often goes much farther than this, however, and proposes that the value of goods to which social approval is attached (so-called merit goods) be revised upward by reference to arbitrary or political authority. More generally, revisionism can be associated with proposals for employing a system of weights by which conventionally calculated benefits and costs have their magnitudes altered for one reason or another.

Before going farther, let me briefly illustrate the use of weights in economic calculation with the example of a project that affects the welfare of only three groups in the community, these being A, B, and C. Groups A and B are estimated to gain $5 million each from the project. Group C is estimated to lose $8 million from it. The net social value of the project on the conventional calculation is, therefore, $5 million plus $5 million less $8 million, which is equal to plus $2 million, a positive net benefit that clearly tells in favor of the project.

Of the variety of reasons offered for the employment of weights, let us choose the most common one, that a dollar of gain or loss has greater effect on the satisfaction of a poor man than on that of a rich man. Supposing that group C is that having, on average, the lowest income of the three groups, each dollar of gain or loss to that group, it is urged, should carry a greater weight than is carried by the other two groups. To choose figures arbitrarily, one could attribute a weight of 8 to the money gains or losses of the C group, a weight of 5 to those of the B group, and a weight of 2 to those of the richest group, A. Such a system of weights would be called *distributional* weights inasmuch as they vary inversely with the average income of the three groups, and it represents an attempt to translate from a calculation in terms of money to one in terms of "real" satisfaction.

In practical applications, however, the custom is to choose a weight for the poorest group—group C in our example—equal to unity, the weight being assigned to the gains and losses of the other groups being a fraction of unity. Let us suppose, then, that the weight assigned to the B group is 0.5, and the weight assigned to the A group is 0.3.

Accepting this system of weights, which, as indicated, is designed to yield a "real" measure of the net worth of the project to society, the calculation now takes the form of (5m. $\times$ 0.3) plus (5m. $\times$ 0.5) less (8m. $\times$ 1), or a net social *loss* of 4 million "real" units, a result that obviously tells against the project.

Formally, any revisionist proposal can be expressed as a system of such weights. If, for any reason, a particular kind of good is to be left out of the calculation, a weight of zero is implied. In a like manner, the gains or losses of a particular group of people can be entirely ignored simply by assigning to them a weight of zero. In substituting a politically chosen value for a conventionally calculated economic one, however, it is more straightforward to register the fact as it is than to translate it into a weight.

In this connection, however, it is as well to mention in passing the often repeated allegation of revisionists that the conventional (unweighted) method of calculation cannot be acquitted of the charge of using weights. A moment's reflection makes it evident that a seemingly unweighted calculation is formally equivalent to using a weight of unity for every dollar gained or lost from the change in question, irrespective of the income of the gainer or loser. This interpretation is, of course, admissible, although it is not necessary. An alternative interpretation of the conventional economic calculation is also possible, one we broach later when we examine the ethical implications of the conventional approach.

It must be confessed that, at first glance, the difference between the conventional and the revisionist approach does not look very alarming. Perhaps a compromise solution, or an agreement to differ, would be a satisfactory way of dealing with it. Certainly, all the economists concerned would agree with the view (as expressed recently by R. Sugden and A. Williams[3]) that a cost-benefit analysis is, after all, a technique or way of organized thought for comparing alternative projects or courses of action. Looked at in this way, a cost-benefit analysis is to be judged by reference to its consistency of method and by reference to its explicitness.

This is all very well so far as it goes. But if we are also interested, as we must be, in the social significance of a cost-benefit analysis; if, that is, we are concerned with the claim that a cost-benefit calculation ought indeed to be included among the factors to be seriously considered in any social decision about whether to adopt a project or program, we have to go farther than that. We have also to resolve issues that escape explicit contention only because economists are too prone to circumvent them. More specifically, we have to make up our minds whether the foundation on which economic calculation rests is positive or normative, and whether in the last resort it is essentially political or ethical.

Thus, although economists are loath to recognize the fact, this seemingly innocuous methodological schism between the conventionalists and the revisionists is indicative of a serious fissure in the bedrock in which is imbedded the impressive structure of economic calculation. Unless such a defect is explicitly acknowledged, and unless the problems to which it gives rise are resolved, economic calculation cannot continue to retain its credibility. Their successful resolution will determine the actual nature of economic expertise and thus the rationale, if any, of the advice based on economic calculation that is tendered to governments—more generally, economic advice about the shifting of economic resources from one use to another guided by the familiar rules of resource allocation.

Economic Evaluation 33

Politico-Weights

There are expositional advantages in uncovering first the implications of revisionist proposals that have gathered momentum over the last decade or so. We shall begin, somewhat arbitrarily perhaps, with the publication of the much-trumpeted OECD *Manual* of 1969,[4] to be followed in succession by the UNIDO *Guidelines* of 1972 and the World Bank *Project Analysis* of 1975,[5] to mention only the best known among the officially sponsored texts directing their expertise in the main to the problems of "Third World" countries.

Since repeated reference to that elusive and rather sinister personage, the "policy maker" or "decision maker," is common to the above texts, their revisionism can be expressed by the statement that it employs a system of *politico-weights* inasmuch as the weights are assumed to be determined at some level in the political or administrative hierarchy. I shall leave to later some brief observations on the revisionism that, in contrast, is to be associated with the use of *ethico-weights*, which weights are deemed compatible with the ethics of the particular society for which the resulting economic prescription is intended.

For the present, however, we may take note that a pure case of the use of politico-weights would follow from taking literally the dictum of Sugden and Williams (on p. 236) that "it is no part of the [cost-benefit] analyst's job to judge whether the decision maker's objectives are ethically right, nor whether they are acceptable to the community as a whole." A cost-benefit analysis so conceived may also be regarded as politically based, even though its authority is found at the autocratic end of the political spectrum. As such, it would be a sensible enough instrument for promoting the ambitions of Genghis Khan, who may be said to embody the full authority of the community within his own despotic personality.

We may thus imagine the dialogue between Genghis Khan and his favorite analyst beginning with the former's vehement declaration that four Christian fortified cities, A, B, C, and D, must be razed to the ground this year, and preferably in that order from a score or more tempting alternatives. Our analyst, after being permitted to confer at length with the generals about the relevant probabilities of death and destruction on both sides under a variety of conditions, ends up with the following system of weights which, he assures his sovereign, are wholly consistent with his desires: the death of a Khan warrior -1, the death of a Khan general -20, the death of an adult male Christian $+3.5$, the destruction of a large Christian church $+28.5, \ldots$, and so on.

The four chosen enterprises of Khan, having been scientifically approved and the relative weights made explicit (and, indeed, toasted at each subsequent banquet), the cities A, B, C, and D are razed in the order scheduled. Following these successes, however, recourse to the same set of weights happens to reveal that the greatest social net benefit accrues to the Khan empire if during the next year Christian strongholds F, G, and H are similarly demolished. Alas, our belligerent "policy maker" now proclaims his adamant resolve to put to the sword instead strongholds J, K, L, and M; after all, there is nothing in this revisionist approach that precludes a possible transformation of "broad national objectives." The favorite analyst sighs to himself but, being prudent, he goes quietly to work and eventually comes up with a revised set of weights altogether fitting to the latest policy objectives as unambiguously expressed by his policy maker.

This conception of a cost-benefit analysis illustrated in the stirring example above has the undoubted advantage that no difficulty arises in discovering the locus of political authority. The expertise of the analyst is directed entirely to producing numerical affirmations of the policy maker's objectives, possibly modified to enable a consistent set of weights to be used.

Within a more contemporary context, however, we should be inclined to think of the policy maker as a bureaucrat, one who may or may not be answerable to the community at large. For example, the OECD and UNIDO manuals, both deferring as they do to the broad planning objectives of these sovereign policy makers, do not assign to them the same rank in the political-administrative hierarchy. The authors of the former manual envisage their policy makers as economic supremos in control of a centralized "Project Evaluation Office" that issues directives to all and sundry. In contrast, the authors of the UNIDO manual adopt what they playfully call a "bottoms up" approach, in which the burden of political authority is spread among the lower echelons of civil servants, who in any case are habituated to making local decisions. And although much has been made of this difference in subsequent conferences, in view of our purpose it need not detain us here.

Common to such a revisionist approach is a conception of national or planning objectives as if they were components of a consistent policy or economic philosophy—or, at least, as if, after dialogue between analyst and policy maker, a consistent economic policy or philosophy would emerge. Yet, the reader of these manuals is not, as it happens, referred to the judgments of policy makers whenever a proposed calculation has to be explained and justified. When it comes to the price of labor, the price of capital, the price of imports, the formulas the authors offer are, although often cumbersome, derived only from conventional methods of economic calculations. At the same time, the authors suggest that politico-weights be employed to give adequate expression to distributional, regional, or merit considerations which they believe are included in those national objectives as conceived by policy makers. In particular, the social rate of discount, one of the critical parameters in any cost-benefit calculation, is indeed to be chosen as to be consistent with the policy makers' own ideas of an "optimal" level of investment and, therefore, to their ideas also of a desirable rate of economic growth.

At any rate, the politico-revisionist conception of a cost-benefit calculation has the apparent virtue of removing all the difficulties of principle—and sometimes the difficulties of estimation also—from the path of the economist, who simply assumes the role of devoted analyst wholly absorbed in elaborating techniques that make use of, or issue in, a set of weights consistent with the national objectives as revealed by the political process, whether democratic or autocratic. The fruit of the analyst's labor will then take the form of a quantitative assessment of any project, the actual magnitude of which will depend upon the set of weights—distributional, regional, merit, and so forth—that are thought to reflect the priorities of the multiple objectives being pursued by the relevant political authority. It goes without saying, moreover, that no dimension of a proposed project need lack for an explicit politico-weight (or politically determined value), be it natural beauty, nostalgic sentiment, religious ferment, or insufferable tedium.

Revisionist Flaws

Be that as it may, there are several implications of this politico-revisionist approach which, on reflection, might reduce the composure of its advocates.

The first and the most fundamental is this: The economist who adopts a politico-revisionist approach cannot, with any pretense at consistency, also make reference to an independent economic criterion in judging the alternative projects or policies. A statement, therefore, that policy or project II is *economically* more efficient than I is no longer admissible. For what is presented as an economic calculation has, in fact, no meaning or sanction independent of the will of the relevant political authority.

It is a revealing comment on the myopia that comes with absorption in technicalities that the repeated attempts by economists to extend the reach and the authority of their cost-benefit calculations by recourse to politico-weights will, should it succeed, render them impotent as economists. They may explicate inconsistencies in the objectives or proposed weights of policy makers, but this done, there is no independent source of economic expertise to draw upon.

The second implication follows from the first. Supposing that, for the present, a set of politico-weights were somehow explicitly established—an unlikely event—it would be sure to be vulnerable even to minor political changes that occur so frequently in Western-type democracies at least. Consistency, then, in the methods of project evaluation can scarcely hope to endure beyond a year or two. Worse, the public itself will hardly be impressed by the discovery that these seemingly sophisticated evaluation techniques are no more than political window dressing—mere quantitative rationalizations for whatever policies or projects are favored by the bureaucrats or by the political party in office. (After all, there is always some set of weights that can be invented to produce a positive net benefit for any but the most ridiculous project.)

A third defect, although less important than the two above, is interesting. The employment of distributional politico-weights, despite their undoubted popularity, cannot, alas, be counted upon to exclude projects having manifestly undesirable effects on the distribution of income. The dollar gained by the rich may carry a much smaller weight than the dollar lost by the poor. Yet, it is clearly possible for a project that, on balance, harms the poor to yield a net social benefit on this system of weights if the money gains from the project to the rich are disproportionately large.

I might add in passing, however, that the expected and proper reaction to such a finding would be to exclude it anyway on grounds of inequity. But if this is the case, the use of distributional weights is superfluous. Projects believed to have undesirable effects on income distribution can and generally will be excluded by the political decision-making process without recourse to a prior charade of distributional weights.

To these three implications I append an observation about the fact that, in each of the three official manuals mentioned, the national objectives of these benign policy makers are believed, as a matter of course, to include some significant increase in the country's existing rate of economic growth. To ardent proponents of economic growth, this component of a national plan must appear eminently reasonable, bearing in mind the extent of poverty in Third World countries. Presumably, they believe that if a grand debate of the whole nation were somehow to be contrived on this subject of economic growth, this objective, at least, of the country's rulers would meet with unanimous approval.

Yet, if this were true insofar as economic growth were understood as involving no more than a rise in living standards, it might not be true at all if the full social implications of the sort of modernization entailed by economic growth were also made explicit. In some countries, these would include a diminution of the influence of religion, a weakening of the power of traditional institutions, a disruption of a settled way of life, and, in general, the transformation of an accepted hierarchical society, within which each person has a role to play and within which the mass of people is resigned to material hardship, into a more secular, anonymous, mobile, and restless society.

The transitional phases in any modernization program for such countries, moreover, can hardly avoid the mass exodus from agricultural small holdings clustered about village communities to the huge overcrowded cities which are unable to cope with the mounting unemployment, cities increasingly vulnerable to disease, crime, civic disorder, and breakdown.

For economists who believe that decision makers should defer ultimately, in their choice of multiple objectives, to the desires of society at large, the assumption by them that economic growth (regarded as in fact it is: as a modernization process involving Western technology and enterprise) is sure to be a priority among these objectives, is something of a presumption.

Ethico-Weights

If we turn now to the employment, instead, of a system of what I have called ethico-weights in economic calculation, we can hardly avoid taking a position on the methods proposed by the so-called Cambridge School, which in this connection is to be associated with the great names of Alfred Marshall and A. C. Pigou.[6] A calculation in terms of money was viewed by the Cambridge economists as only a preliminary to a socially acceptable calculation in terms of units of "real" satisfaction, or "utility." And it was regarded as a self-evident maxim of policy that society's objective was to use its economic resources so as to maximize aggregate utility.

Now in order to achieve this grandiose objective, it was not enough merely to "shuffle" resources about with the aim of maximizing the *money* value of society's net income. It was necessary also to shuffle people's money incomes about, always transferring income to people for whom the marginal utility of money was greater than for those from whom it was taken. By accepting two plausible judgments of facts, that people are basically the same in their capacity to enjoy goods, and that the utility enjoyed per additional dollar of income always diminishes, it is simple to deduce that a necessary condition for maximizing society's aggregate utility, or real satisfaction, is a redistribution of income to the point of complete equality.

But even if we accept as a valid ethical goal the maximizing of aggregate utility, and even if we do not demur at the two factual generalizations stated above—which goal and generalizations together produce a conclusion gratifying to those who equate egalitarianism with social justice— there is still no acceptable way of deriving a numerical set of weights, which is essential if we are to compare in utility terms alternative projects for a society in which incomes are not yet equalized.

If, for example, we assign a weight of unity to the marginal dollar of a man having a net income of $5,000 a year, is the weight to be assigned to the marginal dollar of a man earning $10,000 a year 0.8, 0.5, or 0.1? In the event, the economist who favors the use of distributional weights has recourse either to some purely arbitrary scheme—some neat mathematical expression relating the marginal utility of money income inversely to the level of income is common enough[7]—or else to the income tax structure on the fiction that governments are intent on equalizing the real marginal burden of taxation as between the various income groups. In the former scheme, the weights have no social sanction whatever. In the latter —and even if we are so imaginative as to believe that, in continually altering the tax structure, governments are actuated solely by this elusive objective of equalizing real tax burdens—we can hardly escape the conclusion that the distributional weights are no more than politico-weights and, accordingly, will alter not only from one year to the next but from one government to another.

Obviously, neither of the above sets of distributional weights are ethico-weights. In order to qualify as ethical, the set of weights has to be enshrined in the constitution or else conform with a virtual constitution, one that effectively represents an ethical consensus. Could such a system of ethico-weights be established, consistency as well as propriety would require it be employed in all economic calculation; employed, that is, not only in the economic calculation of alternative government projects or programs but also in the economic calculations of every unit in the private sector of the economy. Overall consistency in resource allocation within the economy would be achieved only if all measures, whether of net social benefit or of private profit, be expressed not in dollars but in ethico-weighted dollars.

It would be an interesting academic exercise to rework the calculations of some existing cost-benefit studies employing not only a system of ethico-weights believed appropriate to our existing society, but also systems of weights appropriate to hypothetical societies that may be imagined to have embraced distributional and other aspects of familiar philosophies.

A liberal translation of the Rawlsian conception of social justice,[8] for example, would suggest that the money gains or losses of those with incomes above the average all be weighted by zero, which is effectively to ignore such gains and losses completely. A fanatic egalitarian would have to go farther than that. He would have to attach a *negative* weight to money gains and losses by persons enjoying incomes above the average, in this way translating their gains into a social loss, and vice versa. At the other end of the philosophical spectrum we can place a Nietzchean society in which exclusive importance is attached to the activity and well-being of an elite. The zero weights would now be applied to the money gains and losses of the mass of the nonelite members of society.

Fascinating although such an exercise might be, it would be academic in the pejorative sense of the word.[9] For it would offer no guidance whatever to a satisfactory ethical foundation for current methods of economic calculation.

The Traditional Method

It is high time to return to the currently conventional and, indeed, the traditional method of economic calculation in order to discover what may be said in its favor. No novelty is implied by the focal statement that a movement from economic organization I to an alternative organization II that increases the money value (at constant purchasing power) of society's collection of goods is conventionally *defined* as being economically efficient—irrespective, that is, of which groups lose and which groups gain by the movement from I to II. Put otherwise, if the aggregate money value of the change is positive, the change is said to confer a net social benefit, and the criterion of economic efficiency is met.[10]

On the one hand, such a definition of economic efficiency may be said to be *normative*, or prescriptive, if people believe that it *ought* to be used as a criterion for one or several reasons. It may be said to be operational as well as normative if it would also command an ethical consensus within the society for which it is intended. If, on the other hand, this definition or criterion is *not* assumed to be normative, it has to be regarded as descriptive only: A statement that situation II is economically more efficient than I becomes no more than a shorthand for saying that the algebraic sum of all the money gains and losses in moving from I to II is positive.

It is, of course, entirely possible to conceive the term *economic efficiency* as no more than a descriptive term carrying the above meaning.

And so conceived, the economic calculation of a proposed change that shows the resulting gains to exceed the resulting losses by a specific magnitude can be no more than a numerical datum, one that may be requested by a government agency as being thought relevant to the prospective political debate about the wisdom of making the change. On this view, the economist is no more than the servant of the political authority, one commissioned to prepare a calculation according to the standard format, which is, presumably, approved by that authority. It follows that in the decision-making process the economic calculation itself can always be dismissed as having no social significance whatever.

But, it may be observed, the findings of the economist may be, and sometimes are, disregarded by the political decision-making process even if they are, or were to be, conceived as normative and operational. No matter how unanimous and imperative are the opinions of the economists, their recommendations can constitutionally be overruled by the body politic.

Does it matter, then, whether the conventional economic calculation carries normative significance, or whether the term economic efficiency is normative or descriptive? Before suggesting an answer to so pertinent a question, let us first consider the opinion that conventional economic calculation and the criterion of economic efficiency are indeed founded on an ethical basis.

An economic calculation that shows a particular change to confer a net money gain on society can always be interpreted as a change by which —if this net gain could somehow be costlessly redistributed among all affected by the change in question—every person could be made better off. This manifest tautology can claim two merits. First, it offers a conception of the conventional economic calculation that is different from the one which holds that such calculation implies a set of distributional weights all equal to unity. No such implication need be inferred. Second, the hypothetical transactions conjured by this interpretation provoke one to think why the criterion of economic efficiency which is met by such a calculation might well qualify for society's seal of approval at the ethical level.

In fact, any one or more of the following beliefs about the workings of the economy could, if widely held, produce an ethical consensus favoring the conventional economic criterion. (1) Economic changes that are efficient as defined do not usually have untoward effects on the distribution of income. (2) The existing tax structure offers adequate safeguards against any marked distributional injustice resulting from the application of the conventional economic criterion. (3) Over time, a succession of changes countenanced by the conventional economic criterion is unlikely to make the poorest section of society any worse off. (4) Over time, a succession of such changes has a better chance of raising the living standards of the mass of the population than a succession of changes sanctioned by any other criterion.

So much, at least, may be offered in confirmation of the belief that the economic criterion is backed by an ethical consensus. If the belief is true, the economist will certainly exert a legitimate influence on the formation of economic policy in the small and in the large. The economist is no longer merely the creature of government agencies serving them in the way they wish to be served. And although there is nothing in the Constitution to prevent a government furnishing itself with patently inadequate data and bizzare forms of economic calculations, the economist is effectively authorized by an ethical consensus to reject them as being at variance with the norms of economic expertise. It follows, also, that an economic contribution to a social decision is one that is wholly distinct from and independent of current political objective, no matter how popular.

True, political power will continue to prevail in the last resort. But once the normative nature of economic calculation is acknowledged, there can be no excuse, at least, to succumbing to a professionally degrading state of affairs in which the economist is treated as a mere "numbers man" hired to contrive a set of weights for the express purpose of providing numerical rationalization for the pet projects of incumbent governments.[11]

Finally, two consequences flowing from treating the conventional economic method of calculation as carrying normative, or prescriptive, force can bear some emphasis. First, if the sanction for the conventional criterion of economic efficiency derives from an ethical consensus, it follows that it is not the *fact* of an increase in society's welfare—assuming that such can be satisfactorily defined and detected—that is warrant for the use of this economic criterion. Rather, it is society's fundamental beliefs about what *ought* to count as a contribution to social welfare. Hence, the prescribing economist does not, as popularly supposed (even within the profession), seek to determine in some objective way a measure of the actual change in society's welfare. Insofar as the economist is to prescribe for a particular society, his criterion has to affirm that the project confers an increase in social welfare—measured in the conventional way as a net social benefit expressed in money terms—when, and only when, this society itself would, in its ethical capacity, conceive the project as one conferring an increase in its welfare. And there can be no presumption that this relevant "subjective" assessment of, say, an increase in social welfare—that which society, in its ethical capacity, would agree to call an increase

42   E. J. Mishan

in social welfare—generally coincides with any "objective" assessment of the change in welfare experienced by members of society.

Second, allowing that he justifies the conventional economic calculation by reference to an ethical consensus, the prescribing economist cannot ignore the claims arising from other features of that consensus. This recognition, however, may have the incidental effect of simplifying the calculations. If, for example, it could be shown that the welfare of a group of people would decline simply from its envy of the improved material prospects offered to any other group by a particular program, a measure of this "intangible" spillover effect need not be entered into the conventional calculation if society itself, in its ethical capacity, would reject such a response as unworthy of consideration. Clearly, such a consequence opens a vista of fascinating possibilities for the reflective economist.

Conclusion

Let us summarize and conclude. A charitable, and probably true, interpretation of the motives that inspire the revisionists' proposals is that they reflect the laudable desire to make economic calculation more attractive to society by giving quantitative expression, through the use of weights and of politically determined valuations, to people's legitimate concern with income distribution, quality, economic growth, and other factors. But this desire has led competent economists, especially those addressing their expertise to the problems of Third World countries, to misconceive cost-benefit analysis as a technique designed to realize politically determined objectives, whether these are declared publicly as part of a national plan for the economy or whether they partake, instead, of *ad hoc* decisions taken by local officials.

Had these economists been modest enough to conceive of economic calculation instead as no more than a contribution to a political decision, one in which other social factors such as income distribution, economic growth, ethnic and geographical repercussions, and so on, are also brought to the fore in the ensuing debate, they might have been content to continue refining and expounding the methods of conventional economic calculation and, as a result, to remain in occupation of a clearly marked and defensible territory.

In the event, however, the ambitions of the revisionists to revamp cost-benefit analysis, so as to make it both more comprehensive and more faithful to current political aspirations, have had the effect, ironically, of undermining the claims of the economic expertise they were eager to extend. As indicated earlier, once they had undertaken to shape their quantitative techniques so as to promote consistency and effectiveness in the realization of the economic objectives chosen by "policy makers," they had unwittingly but nonetheless necessarily repudiated their claim to any independent norms of economic expertise. For a change of political office or a change of political objectives must, in general, produce a change in the appropriate system of weights and politically assigned valuations. In consequence, projects and programs that were once calculated by economists to be economically efficient could well become recalculated to become economically inefficient, and vice versa.

If we rule out as impracticable the constitutional establishment of a set of ethico-weights, the economist who would escape the ignominious fate to which revisionism would consign him—that of being swallowed whole by the politician—had best return forthwith to the conventional method of economic calculation.

Insofar as it is founded upon an ethical consensus, his economic expertise is clearly defined and carries with it an authority that the politician and, indeed, the community at large must take seriously. Yet, even if it should transpire that his economic expertise is not sanctioned by an ethical consensus—even, that is, if the term economic efficiency loses its normative significance and becomes no more than a descriptive shorthand —the economist remains his own man. However his contribution is valued, and however his calculations are assessed, his conception at least is clear, and his methods are independent of political fashions.

Epilogue

Although it is hardly possible to guard oneself completely against some misconstruction of the argument and conclusion in so touchy a subject, a few additional remarks designed to maintain perspective should make it harder to misconstrue them.

Assertions that economics cannot be value free, that economists cannot be politically neutral, that they are necessarily involved in the existing reality, and that their theorizing necessarily reflects prevailing belief-systems are not being challenged here. For that matter, I doubt whether such assertions would be challenged by many "mainstream" economists either, since much the same may be said of the physical sciences and scientists, notwithstanding which their theories generally assume a form that renders them amenable, in principle, to tests of validity.

In this article, however, we are concerned largely with normative or prescriptive economics rather than positive economics. And the propositions of normative economics or calculations of net social benefit—*if* they are to have any validity independent of the political process—must turn on an ethical consensus about the components that enter into such propositions or calculations. I have myself suggested in an earlier paper [1979] that at least one of the components of the traditional Pareto criterion, as I understand it, may no longer command a consensus in the West; that, in relevant respects, the necessary consensus may be fragmenting.

For this reason, my conclusions are deliberately tentative. All that we can now say is that if, but only if, the economist's much-cherished Pareto criterion does indeed command an ethical consensus, then his prescriptive allocative propositions and his economic calculations may be regarded as ethically acceptable within the society to which they are addressed. Provisionally assuming this to be the case, the introduction of weights to be attached to the subjective valuations of the individuals concerned can itself be vindicated only if the weights to be adopted also command an ethical consensus.

At present, however, they either are arbitrary or are implicitly or explicitly (as in the manuals referred to) *political*, and, to the extent that they are politically determined, cost-benefit calculations must reflect the outcome of the political process. In consequence, normative economics, instead of being independent of the political mechanisms, partakes of their decisions; instead of normative economics being a counterweight to political power, it acts to reinforce that power.

If, however, there is no longer an ethical consensus to which the normative economists can refer his basic criterion the $\Sigma \Delta v$ calculations carry no ethical sanction. Such calculations might yet be demanded by the politician or decision maker in the conventional format as being in the nature of economic information pertinent to the decision in hand—it being understood, or assumed, that the politician or decision maker knows that such calculations (allowing they are accurate) represent no more than the algebraic sum of the subjective valuations of the economic change in question.

Of course, whether or not there is an ethical consensus for the economist's criterion, the final decision with respect to a project or a program is, in any case, going to be political. There is all the more reason, then, to impel politicians to persuade the public of the wisdom of the economic measures they seek to enact, rather than to allow them to deceive the public by flaunting bogus economic calculations, in particular those making use of a set of weights contrived to yield a net "utility" benefit for whatever measures they happen to favor.

Only the economist ambitious for political patronage will knowingly lend himself to such disingenuousness and, as in the manuals mentioned, cooperate in producing those political weights and political valuations necessary to yield "economic" calculations that, being consistent with the "national objectives" chosen by the political party or regime in power, also rationalize them.

Ethical consensus or no, the economist can indeed remain neutral with respect to the political power game—to the extent, that is, of refusing to have any truck with political weights which, in the last resort, serve only to confer quantitative rationalization on schemes desired by decision makers.

Notes

1. The argument that application of a discount rate to costs and benefits falling on future generations implies a criterion different from that conventionally used by the economist is developed in my paper, "A Difficulty in the Evaluation of Long-Lived Projects," *Zeitschrift für National-ökonomie*, 1979.

2. P. Dasgupta, S. Marglin, and A. Sen, *Guidelines for Project Evaluation* (New York: UNIDO, 1972).

3. R. Sugden and A. Williams, *The Principles of Practical Cost-Benefit Analysis* (Oxford: the University Press, 1978).

4. I. M. D. Little and J. A. Mirrlees, *Manual of Industrial Project Analysis in Developing Countries* (Paris: OECD, 1969). Although no less revisionist in spirit, a technically much revised edition of the former appeared in 1974 under the title *Project Appraisal and Planning for Developing Countries* (New York: Basic Books). The unabated ardor of these authors to improve the economic plight of the poorer countries is seen to be reconciled with their revisionist philosophy at many points in their new book, although it comes to the fore with characteristic emphasis in a remarkable phrase (following their suggestion that distributional weights should be concealed from the public): "It may sometimes be politically expedient to do good by stealth" (p. 55).

5. L. Squire and H. G. Van der Tak, *Economic Analysis of Projects* (Baltimore: Johns Hopkins University Press, 1975).

6. Although the basic notion of diminishing marginal utility in the writings of Marshall, Pigou, and other members of the Cambridge School addressing themselves to a theory of economic welfare began to be superseded about 40 years ago by the simpler money-measure methods advocated by the "New Welfare Economics," the appeal of (diminishing) marginal utility has never been eradicated from the mind of the economist. Much of the recent literature on the economics of intergeneration equity has fallen back on marginal utility, as I point out in a recent survey, "Economic Criteria for Intergenerational Comparisons," *Zeitschrift für Nationalökonomie*, 1977.

7. An elasticity of marginal utility of money with respect to money income that is exactly equal to unity is sometimes assumed.

8. See John Rawls, *A Theory of Justice* (Oxford: the University Press, 1972).

46   E. J. Mishan

9. Just such an exercise was carried out recently as a serious piece of research in the United States, the results being reported in a monograph, *A
   Study of the Ethical Foundations of Benefit Cost Analysis*, a working
   paper of the Research Economics Group of the University of New Mexico, dated August 1979. (It would be mischievous, however, to construe
   this information as serving to confirm the above remark.)

10. It is generally understood by economists that in contemplating the change
    in question, all expenditures associated with gathering the necessary in-
    formation, and with implementation and maintenance of the new situation
    II, are to be included in the costs.

11. This seems as good a place as any to remark that A. C. Harberger's [1978]
    paper, despite what its title may suggest, has little affinity with the broad
    argument of the present essay. Although his paper has intrinsic interest, it
    does not perceive the use of weights in project evaluation as a develop-
    ment which, if continued, must eventually emasculate the economist re-
    garded as an expert offering an independent economic contribution to the
    decision-making process. Nor will his mildly deprecatory comments about
    distributional weights in cost-benefit analysis go far in dissuading the pro-
    ponents of this art from continuing their practice. Indeed, his experimen-
    tal calculations with a range of distributional weights—which form the
    bulk of his paper—could be taken to imply a belief that the radical use of
    distributional weights acts to prevent approval of projects that would
    otherwise generate regressive distributional effects (contrary to my obser-
    vation in my 1974 paper).

    Moreover, in his penultimate section, Harberger concedes—unwar-
    rantably in my view—the treatment of distributional gains as commen-
    surable with efficiency gains. He concludes with the brief observation that
    if the distributional weights are small, their use will not make much differ-
    ence to the results reached by the traditional (unweighted) cost-benefit
    methods, whereas if they are large, "considerations of distribution [could]
    swamp those of efficiency altogether," which would be "unacceptable to
    the vast majority of economists."

    In his final section, Harberger tentatively proposes (1) that policies
    meet a criterion based on the use both of weighted and unweighted valua-
    tions, (2) that the unweighted procedure be vindicated wherever the ex-
    cess gains are large enough actually to effect transfers that would correct
    any regressive distributional change associated with the project, and (3)
    that we ought not perhaps to concern ourselves in the traditional efficiency
    calculus with distributional weights, or with correcting undesirable distri-
    butional effects through cash transfers, in a society in which transfers in
    kind are an accepted means of meeting minimal standards of food, cloth-
    ing, shelter, health care, and education.

    One response to all this by the proponents of distributional weights
    would surely be that Harberger is using the term *efficiency* as being co-
    terminous with the use of "unweighted" valuations, and juxtaposing gains
    in efficiency so defined with possible distributional losses. In contrast, the
    proponents of distributional weights require the use of weights in the en-
    deavor to establish a concept of efficiency in "real" or "util" terms, a leg-
    acy of the neoclassical approach.

Economic Evaluation   **47**

In the present article, I start with an awareness of their commendable ambitions to infuse more realism into the economist's criterion of efficiency and go on to explore the consequences of such ambitions, if successful, for the survival of an independent criterion of economic efficiency and, therefore, for the status of the economist.

References

Chase, S. D., ed. 1969. *Problems in Public Expenditure Analysis.* Washington, D.C.: Brookings.

Dasgupta, A. K., and Pearce, D. W. 1971. *Cost-Benefit Analysis: Theory and Practice.* London: Macmillan.

Dasgupta, P.; S. Marglin; and A. K. Sen. 1972. *Guidelines for Project Evaluation.* New York: UNIDO.

Hicks, J. R. 1939a. "The Foundations of Welfare Economics." *Economic Journal* 49 (December).

Hicks, J. R. 1939b. *Value and Capital.* Oxford: Clarendon Press.

Kaldor, Nicholas. 1939. "Welfare Propositions in Economics and Interpersonal Comparisons of Utility." *Economic Journal* 49 (September).

Harberger, A. C. 1978. "On the Use of Distributional Weights in Social Cost-Benefit Analysis." *Journal of Political Economics* (April).

Irvin, George. 1978. *Modern Cost-Benefit Methods.* London: Macmillan.

Little, I. M. D., and J. A. Mirrlees. 1969. *Manual of Industrial Project Analysis in Developing Countries.* Paris: OECD.

————. 1974. *Project Appraisal and Planning for Developing Countries.* New York: Basic Books.

Pearce, David W. 1971. *Cost-Benefit Analysis.* London: Macmillan.

Maass, A., et al. 1962. *Design of Water Resource Systems.* Cambridge, Mass.: Harvard University Press.

McKean, R. N. 1958. *Efficiency of Government through Systems Analysis.* New York: Wiley.

Mishan, E. J. 1974. "Flexibility and Consistency in Project Evaluation." *Economica.*

————. 1980. "How Valid Are Economic Evaluations of Allocative Changes?" *Journal of Economic Issues* 14 (March).

————. 1969. *Welfare Economics: An Assessment.* Amsterdam: North-Holland.

Pearce, D. W., ed. 1978. *The Valuation of Social Cost.* London: Allen and Unwin.

Pigou, A. C. 1924. *The Economics of Welfare.* London: Macmillan.

Schwartz, H., and R. Berney, eds. 1977. *Social and Economic Dimensions of Project Evaluation.* Washington, D.C.: I.A.D. Bank.

Squire, L., and H. G. Van der Tak. 1975. *Economic Analysis of Projects.* Baltimore: Johns Hopkins University Press.

Sugden, R., and A. Williams. 1978. *The Principles of Practical Cost-Benefit Analysis.* Oxford: the University Press.

Tinbergen, Jan. 1966. *Economic Policy, Principles, and Design.* Amsterdam: North-Holland.

Part II
History of Use

[11]

U.S. Army Engineers and the Rise of Cost-Benefit Analysis

*What modern Pythagoras, what Einstein of our own age, can
determine with unquestioned accuracy the proportionate
share of the benefits to be derived from the
construction of reservoirs in distant lands?*
(Theodore Bilbo, senator from Mississippi, 1936)

THE ARMY CORPS of Engineers was permanently established in 1802,
on the model of the Corps des Ponts et Chaussées. Its officers were recruited from among the top graduates of the military academy at West
Point, the American Ecole Polytechnique. The French emigré L'Enfant,
designer of the great geometric capital of Washington, had a hand also
in its planning. At its creation, much of its technical library was in
French. Like its predecessor, the Corps of Engineers stood for administrative unification. This, and the proud elitism of its officers, made them
politically suspect in nineteenth-century America.[1] Its enemies sustained
this critique into the twentieth century. Harold Ickes, Franklin Roosevelt's secretary of the interior, could have forgiven their centralizing ambitions had they not blocked his, but he was happy to play the populist
against them. He called them "the most powerful and ambitious lobby
in Washington. The aristocrats who constitute it are our highest ruling
class. They are not only the political elite of the army, they are the perfect flower of bureaucracy."[2]

This is engaging hyperbole, but nobody ever quite believed it. Perhaps the Corps of Engineers has been a kind of elite, but its pretensions
as a ruling class have never extended beyond the bounds of its administrative domain. The same could not be said of the Corps des Ponts et
Chaussées, which for two centuries has been intertwined with a real, relatively unified elite. The history of Polytechnique has been most interesting to the French as an exemplar of an educational system that has
perpetuated hierarchy in their society since the Revolution. That of the
Corps des Ponts is, in addition, a story of bureaucratic autonomy, the
triumph of administration over politics. The Army Corps of Engineers,
to American historians, has less to do with social hierarchies than natural
ones—the control of nature. In political terms, it is synonymous with

interest groups, lobbying, "logrolling," and above all "pork barrel." Finally, and most revealingly, the historian of bureaucracy does not portray the Army Corps at the center of an administrative ruling class, but in a scene of utter disunity and savage infighting. This, I argue, is the appropriate context for understanding the pursuit of uniform cost-benefit methods. That form of economic quantification grew up not as the natural language of a technical elite, but as an attempt to create a basis for mutual accommodation in a context of suspicion and disagreement. The regime of calculation was imposed not by all-powerful experts, but by relatively weak and divided ones.

This chapter gives a history of cost-benefit analysis in the United States bureaucracy from the 1920s until about 1960. It is not a story of academic research, but of political pressure and administrative conflict. Cost-benefit methods were introduced to promote procedural regularity and to give public evidence of fairness in the selection of water projects. Early in the century, numbers produced by the Corps of Engineers were usually accepted on its authority alone, and there was correspondingly little need for standardization of methods. About 1940, however, economic numbers became objects of bitter controversy, as the Corps was challenged by such powerful interests as utility companies and railroads. The really crucial development in this story was the outbreak of intense bureaucratic conflict between the Corps and other government agencies, especially the Department of Agriculture and the Bureau of Reclamation. The agencies tried to settle their feuds by harmonizing their economic analyses. When negotiation failed as a strategy for achieving uniformity, they were compelled to try to ground their makeshift techniques in economic rationality. On this account, cost-benefit analysis had to be transformed from a collection of local bureaucratic practices into a set of rationalized economic principles. In the American political context of systematic distrust, though, its weakness became strength. Since the 1960s, its champions have claimed for it almost universal validity.

THE BEGINNINGS OF ECONOMIC QUANTIFICATION IN AMERICAN ENGINEERING

As in France, so in America, academic training for engineers was not the spontaneous creation of the marketplace—of entrepreneurs seizing every opportunity for competitive advantage. Peter Lundgreen shows that "school culture" in engineering had more to do with bureaucracy than with industrialization. Formal engineering study first arose in countries where state engineers provided the model for the profession.

150 CHAPTER SEVEN

In Sweden and several German states, mining academies defined the role of the educated engineer as rational bureaucrat. The French Corps des Mines was modeled mainly on the Saxon Mining Academy in Freiberg, while its Corps des Ponts et Chaussées was itself at the forefront of scientific civil engineering. The Army Corps of Engineers was never powerful enough to shape a national profession, as was the Corps des Ponts in France. Still, it was from the outset an important presence on the American scene.[3]

None of the engineers on the Erie Canal had formal training before the project was undertaken. When the Corps of Engineers surveyed the route of the Chesapeake and Ohio Canal in the 1820s and estimated the cost at $22 million—three times that of the Erie Canal—the Congress rebelled and brought in some practical men, who duly reduced the figure by half. The project then failed utterly. The Corps was limited mainly to river and harbor work after 1838.[4] Although it surveyed a number of routes to the Pacific, it lacked administrative authority over the vast net of railroads that spread across the North American continent in the nineteenth century. Military engineers were nevertheless mainly responsible for the forms of accounting and administration through which railroad companies became prototypes of the modern, managed corporation in America.[5]

Military engineering also had something to do with the application of mathematics to such problems as bridge design. But the sources were more French than American. Charles Ellet Jr. worked his way up the ranks on the Erie and the Chesapeake and Ohio canals, then traveled to Paris in 1830 to study as an external student at the Ecole des Ponts. The calculation of stresses on suspension bridges unfortunately proved a bit more complicated than he had imagined, and he suffered some disastrous failures. Ellet introduced a new variety of economic thinking about public works to the United States, advocating that monopolistic canal charges be based on utility rather than on allocation of costs. Here the stresses that defeated him were of a more political character.[6] Railway rate experts, who tried to settle disputes among cities or between farmers and companies, did not depend on any tradition so organized as in France. Expertise was fashioned as needed by engineers and lawyers in response to political and judicial pressures.[7]

Still, the growing legal and regulatory apparatus in the United States did give some continuity to their efforts. In contrast, American efforts to provide economic evaluations of public investments before the Corps of Engineers entered this domain were almost completely ad hoc.[8] To be effective, cost-benefit analysis had to be institutionalized and routinized. This was the distinctive achievement of twentieth-century army engineers.

Samuel Hays has argued that the growth of governmental expertise and rationality in America depended on the breakdown of small communities in the face of increasingly centralized power. The penetration of the local by the national now provides a major theme of the political and intellectual history of the United States in the period called progressive.[9] The Corps of Engineers, famously, worked on both sides of this divide, exploiting its ability to mobilize intense local interest to gain support for a nationwide program of projects. The idiom of cost-benefit analysis, though, was clearly adapted for the audience in the capital, and not, for example, in Oologah, Oklahoma. When Herb McSpadden came to town to complain that a proposed reservoir on the Verdigris River would cover up the birthplace of his late relative Will Rogers, he ventured to convert its tourist value to money terms. In total the project would cause damages of $70 million, he claimed, "so it is, to use your words, not 'economically feasible.' That is a mighty big word for us out there, but I have got to use your words back here." To which the Mississippi chairman of the Flood Control Committee, Will Whittington, replied: "If when you boys come to Washington, you don't get some big words to take back, it is a loss of time."[10]

In Europe, technical agencies like the Corps des Ponts were often at the forefront of bureaucratic rationalization. In the United States, decisions about public works began to be systematized only near the end of the nineteenth century, as Congress moved away from particularistic legislation toward some conception of its role in terms of enacting general policies. This required, in turn, a stable bureaucracy, and provided room for increased influence by experts. The professionalization of the civil service was advanced by the ending of the spoils system in 1883. Americans were inspired in part by the British model. But the British created space for Oxbridge-educated generalists atop their civil service, whereas in America only politics and money were superior to specialized expertise. And good politics sometimes required deferring to experts. Theodore Roosevelt even appointed a Committee on Scientific Methods.

Expertise did not stand naked. The discipline of science—of facts— was to be a forge of morality and character. Carroll Wright, head of the very influential and effective Massachusetts Bureau of Statistics, said of government statisticians in 1904:

> No matter for what reasons they were appointed, no matter how inexperienced in the work of investigation and of compilation and presentation of statistical material, no matter from what party they came and whether in sympathy with capital or labor, and even if holding fairly radical socialistic views; the men have, almost without exception, at once comprehended the

152 CHAPTER SEVEN

sacredness of the duty assigned to them, and served the public faithfully and honestly, being content to collect and publish facts without regard to individual bias or individual political sentiments.[11]

For practical and moral reasons alike, efficient democratic government seemed to require improved methods of accounting, statistics, and other forms of quantification.[12]

Could quantification settle important issues of public policy? Experience was often disappointing, but hope sprang eternal. The best American engineers, like their French counterparts, understood by the 1880s that railroad pricing could never be fully rationalized by economic calculation. Yet in 1913 Congress required the Interstate Commerce Commission (ICC) to fix the value of all railroad, telegraph, and telephone property, including that of franchises and goodwill. The ICC, though capable of heroic feats of accounting standardization in the interest of systematic regulation, argued that this was impossible. It identified an insurmountable problem of circularity: property, and especially "goodwill," didn't even have a fixed value until after the prices of service were known.[13] The Supreme Court refused to let it off the hook. This appraisal was necessary, the court held, in order to calculate just rates based on cost of service. The result was 50,000 pages of hearings, which still did not suffice to reach a conclusion. Morton Keller calls this "an emblematic Progressive attempt to find fixed grounds for regulating an enterprise whose prime reality was flux," and refers to the investigation of public utilities as "the same black hole into which the railroads had plunged." Courts and Congress learned nothing from the experience. In the 1920s, they were at it again.[14]

Behind this frenzy of quantification, inevitably, was a lack of trust in bureaucratic elites. Another possible strategy for regulating railroads and public utilities was bruited at various times. The Interstate Commerce Commission, as conceived in the 1880s, was to be made up of experts who would be allowed to exercise judgment in the settling of disputes. This conception was even put into law. Soon, "five wise men" on the ICC moved aggressively to change the railroad rate structure. The Supreme Court promptly struck their initiatives down, with the revealing exception of their drive to gather better statistics. In most years Congress was similarly disposed. For legal and political reasons alike, administrative discretion was highly suspect, so the regulators had little alternative but to search relentlessly for facts and to reduce them, if at all possible, to a few decisive numbers.[15]

Such constraints applied less forcefully to the navigation projects that, until early in this century, constituted virtually the entire mission of the Corps of Engineers. Congress could be persuaded to systematize the regulation of railroads but was not at all inclined to give up its power to choose federal water projects. There was no great demand for efficiency; protective tariffs brought in more revenue than the government knew how to invest usefully. It was expended instead on pensions for civil war veterans and river and harbor work. Opponents of this spending worked with modest success to reduce opportunities for purely political choices. After 1902, a Board of Engineers for Rivers and Harbors, within the Corps, had to certify projects as beneficial before they could be recommended to Congress. One secretary of war, Henry L. Stimson, tried in the early 1910s to require the Board to rank projects in order of merit. The Corps resisted this, recognizing, it seems, that congressional choice was the key to congressional favor.[16]

Still, the Corps was anything but a rubber stamp for every proposal that reached it. Since any project could at least bring construction money into a community, and since navigation was a nonreimbursable federal service, there was no shortage of local requests to study the feasibility of waterway improvements. More than half were turned down. Economics was the usual basis for decisions, or at least for their explanation. For example, in 1910 the Board of Engineers recommended a narrower channel than originally proposed near Corpus Christi, Texas, on the ground "that resulting benefits to general commerce and navigation would not at this time be sufficient to justify the cost" of the larger one.[17]

In the 1920s, something more nearly approaching an economic routine began to appear even in favorable reports. It involved estimating project cost, and then itemizing benefits until they exceeded this cost, or fixing potential benefits as a cap on expenditures. In 1925 the Board of Engineers adopted an unfavorable report on Port Angeles Harbor, Washington, "on account of the large expense involved in proportion to the possible benefits."[18] A preliminary report on flood control on the Skagit River, Washington, set mean annual flood damages at $125,000 or $150,000, and added: "These figures will give an approximate basis for considering the feasibility of plans for flood control."[19] None other than U. S. Grant 3d, then district engineer in Sacramento, explained how a $2,670,998 dam and locks on the Sacramento River would save $25,000 in maintenance per year on existing projects, $45,000 per year on costs that would otherwise be needed to maintain a uniform flow on one part of the river, $260,000 capital expenditure plus $80,000 annual maintenance that would otherwise be required to insure a six-foot river depth on another part, and so on. Assuming an interest rate of 4 percent, these converted into capital values of $625,000, $1,125,000, and $2,260,000, respectively. One more benefit of $1,828,000 on the Feather River made the economic justification of the project crystal

154 CHAPTER SEVEN

clear, or so it seemed to the former president's grandson. Unfortunately, powerful shipping interests disagreed, fearing that a lock on the lower river would retard traffic—and so did Grant's immediate superior, the division engineer in San Francisco. The Board of Engineers concurred with the opponents, and recommended instead some channel work.[20]

A district engineer in West Virginia had better luck with a report of 1933 recommending navigation improvements on the Kanawha River. The annual cost of $173,000 exceeded his estimate of annual benefits of $150,000, though it was far surpassed by the $1 million of annual benefits claimed by local navigation interests. Still, an increase of only 300,000 tons per year in coal transport would justify the improvement, and such a prospect in fact did, at least to the relevant authorities in the Corps.[21] One last example is a report by district engineer M. C. Tyler on three sections of channel proposed for Bayou Lafourche, Louisiana. Tyler in every case recommended the largest possible channel dimensions whose cost would not exceed the potential benefits. The Board of Engineers approved smaller ones, thereby increasing the surplus of estimated benefits over costs, though it did not explain the decision in terms of any policy of maximizing net benefits. It simply noted that the smaller channels would be adequate for handling anticipated traffic.[22]

There was not much pretense of rigor in these reports. Still, they show that by sometime in the 1920s, the Board of Engineers expected its recommended projects to promise benefits in excess of costs. Economic calculation was encouraged by legislation in the early 1920s,[23] including new standards for cost allocation. But a strict cost-benefit hurdle was not written into law until 1936. It has sometimes been supposed that the Corps took up cost-benefit analysis only in response to the 1936 act. This clearly is wrong, and indeed it is difficult (though not quite impossible) to imagine that Congress would have required the Corps to base project planning on a form of analysis that scarcely existed, or was entirely foreign to the Corps.

The growth of cost-benefit quantification at the Corps of Engineers was not simply a response to legal mandates. The Hoover era, even before the Hoover presidency, was an exceptionally favorable one for economists. They argued for the neutralization of partisan influence on public works spending.[24] Growing budgets due to flood control acts of 1917 and 1928, the latter in response to the exceptional Mississippi River floods of 1927, created pressure for greater accountability. In 1927, Congress directed the Corps to study all the major river basins of the United States with an eye to improved navigation, water power, flood control, and irrigation. In response, over the next decade the

Corps produced a mass of documents and proposals, called "308 reports" after a House of Representatives document that listed them. As the Corps began to acquire a huge civilian labor force, it relied increasingly on quantification to impose discipline. Hence it was not caught unprepared by the Flood Control Act of 1936, with its famous requirement that no flood control project could receive federal funds unless its benefits, "to whomsoever they may accrue," were projected to exceed its costs.

NUMBERS JUSTIFIED BY AGENCY AUTHORITY

The cost-benefit provision of the 1936 Flood Control Act was one of the heroic efforts of the United States Congress to control its own bad habits. The act was precipitated, as usual, by floods, but also by the continuing depression, for which public works seemed an appropriate remedy. Edward Markham, chief of engineers, explained that the House Flood Control Committee had put together its bill in 1935 by going over the 1,600 projects contained in the "308" reports and choosing those with the best ratio of benefits to cost. We can be sure that regional balance was also a consideration.[25] The bill made it all the way to the full House and Senate, but then, in a last-minute display of animal spirits, it got loaded by floor amendments with a huge collection of projects that the Corps had viewed unfavorably, or even had never studied. The display was so unwholesome that it defeated the bill. No major flood-control legislation was passed in 1935. The language requiring benefits to exceed costs was part of an effort to avoid such an unsavory spectacle in 1936.[26]

The particular hurdle was probably less important than the institutional regularity it implied. Hereafter Congress could only authorize works that had been studied and approved by the Corps. A preliminary examination and then a full survey, each running through several levels of Corps bureaucracy, required months or years, and could not be completed to satisfy the sudden whim of a legislator. When, now more rarely, really disgraceful projects were authorized, a modest standard of decorum was maintained. Official economic analyses helped to cut off debate and bargaining in Congress.[27] Flood control chairmen in the House and Senate routinely invoked the cost-benefit rule in floor debate to block amendments proposing new projects. The rule was construed as a dam, holding back a flood of legislation. The Senate, explained John H. Overton in 1944, cannot make exceptions. "If we did, we would soon be at sea." Whittington's metaphor in the House warned

156 CHAPTER SEVEN

against this and other disasters: "Mr. Chairman, if we propose to make an exception in one case, you let the bars down and you crucify the sound, fundamental principles of flood control."[28]

The Corps did not thereby become all-powerful. After authorization came appropriation, which left ample room for Congress to make political choices. Still, this regularization of the planning process could not but enhance the standing of the Corps. Except when it was challenged by powerful opponents, its numbers were generally accepted on no more authority than its own reputation. That authority was enough. As Overton of Louisiana told the Senate in 1938: "In order to determine whether a project is of value as a flood-control measure, it should be submitted first to the judgment of experts, and the chosen and recognized experts upon this question are the Army engineers."[29]

The expression of this judgment in quantitative form invited Congress to advertise its rationality and objectivity. The cost-benefit standard was an instant cliché. "All of these projects have been studied by my department and on all of them favorable reports have been made and their construction recommended," reported chief of engineers Julian Schley at the beginning of the 1940 House Flood Committee hearings. "We never report a project to Congress," announced Whittington in 1943, "until it has been recommended by the Board of Engineers and the Chief of Engineers stating that . . . the benefits of the project will exceed the cost." He added that "the ability of this committee to secure annual flood-control authorizations up to the war and the invasion of Poland by Hitler, we believe, is due largely to the fact that this yardstick has been adhered to."[30]

Especially on quantitative matters, the responsible congressional committees could be dazzlingly uninquisitive. They asked many factual questions, but it rarely mattered what the answer was. Often the record was left blank for a time, and the response to a statistical query would be inserted afterwards. If a benefit-cost ratio proved to be 1.03, this never provoked comment or alarm, unless perchance there had been recent flooding on the endangered river, when committee members might wonder aloud what miscalculations had generated a number so low. In 1948, local interests in Texas proposed to modify a project on the Neches-Angelina River system to stabilize the local water supply. The Corps didn't mind, though it would, as Colonel Wayne S. Moore explained, "slightly reduce the theoretical ratio of general benefits to costs but not materially." Someone asked how much. "The cost benefit ratio is estimated in the report as 1.08, and as modified by the proposed legislation it will be 1.035, or possibly somewhat greater, a difference which is within the limit of error in the estimates." Nowhere else have I seen margins of error mentioned in these hearings. Nobody noticed or cared that a probable error of .05 might not redound to the credit of the proposed project. The numbers were almost never questioned. In 1954, Prescott Bush of the Senate Flood Control Subcommittee learned that the local contribution for a project in California was "estimated at $22,500, sir. It is calculated according to a rather complex formula. I won't worry you with the details of that formula." "All right," replied the senator.[31]

On what basis did Congress place such implicit faith in these economic numbers? Perhaps its members were frightened by talk of complex formulas. But fear itself was superfluous. In these cozy committees, inquisitiveness was a deadly vice. The congressmen did not leave their faith in the Corps unspoken. It was the better part of valor not to challenge this powerful agency except privately, where factual claims didn't matter so much, and always to praise it publicly. Senator Royal Copeland of New York, who inserted the cost-benefit provision into the 1936 Flood Control Act, told the Senate that Corps engineers are incorruptible, calling them "honorable, straightforward, patriotic men." Whittington proclaimed to the House that "the chief of engineers is impartial and represents Congress and the country." Vandenberg of Michigan explained in 1936 that the new system requires "an independent, nonpolitical, unprejudiced decision as to priorities," adding disingenuously that "no one has ever heard a suspicion or a remote challenge" regarding the integrity and competence of the Board of Engineers."[32]

If anyone did, it was in their interest to suppress it. Senator Robert S. Kerr of Oklahoma, who received not only the customary political benefit, but also a good deal more than the usual measure of personal economic benefit from the projects he sponsored as chairman of the Senate Committee on Rivers and Harbors, reacted with righteous indignation when some Corps numbers were criticized in 1962. These are the finest graduates of West Point, he thundered, and it would be "presumptuous" to challenge their calculations.[33] The Corps studiously avoided any involvement with politics, in public. The record is clear that it was possible to be chief of engineers without even knowing what politics is. When the distinctly friendly Homer Angell of Oregon asked General Lewis Pick, during an uncharacteristically unfriendly congressional investigation in 1952, if his bureaucratic enemies in the Bureau of the Budget might sometimes "put in a dash of politics," Pick was at a loss. "Sir?" he replied. Angell explained: "Sometimes they give it a dash of politics, too, do they not, in determining what projects should go along?" Pick remained shamelessly disingenuous: "I do not know, sir. If they do I do not see it." Such blindness was politically farsighted. In the same hear-

158 CHAPTER SEVEN

ings, George A. Dondero of Michigan remarked that "I can only recall one or two occasions in 20 years where the committee ever doubted the wisdom of the Corps of Army Engineers in sending a project to us."[34]

Sometimes a conspiracy theory is tempting—that the whole enterprise of congressional hearings was a masquerade, to disguise a system of mutual patronage. But this is certainly inadequate. Patronage alone did not make the Corps. It derived prestige from its military connection in a century of frequent war. It had the advantage of military discipline. It was the government's most effective emergency relief agency. It built up considerable expertise on dikes and levees, and whatever the economic justification of its dams, at least they didn't fall down. Its engineers earned a reputation for technical competence. Still, politics seems the best explanation for the failure of Congress to require the Corps to follow rigid rules in its economic analyses. "Do you think there is any agency in this Government anywhere that operates in a more scientific way in arriving at their conclusions than the Army Engineers?" asked Orville Zimmerman of Missouri, thereby disabling a critic. William M. Corry mobilized the advertising expertise of the Zanesville, Ohio, Chamber of Commerce to make the same point:

> I want to say in the beginning that I am no engineer. If I had a stomach ache, I would go to the doctor. If something were wrong with my automobile I would take it to a garage mechanic. By the same token, when I want flood control, I go to the best source possible, to the group of people trained and who through the years have earned the distinction of being the most capable exponents of proper flood control in the world, namely, the Corps of Engineers, United States Army.[35]

Dependence on the Corps is nowhere more complete than along the lower Mississippi. There it has struggled mightily to satisfy the contradictory interests of chemical plants and crayfish packers, barge companies and flood-plain residents, New Orleans and Morgan City. Many suppose that the Corps is already too optimistic about the possibilities of managing this huge river, but the interests always demand still more. Even while protesting, though, they remain assiduous in their deference to an agency whose discretionary power they understand all too clearly.[36]

One of the few real issues engaged by the House Flood Control Committee in the 1930s and 1940s concerned the plan for a Mississippi floodway, to carry off excess flow in times when it is next to impossible to contain the river with levees. The Corps proposed to buy up rights to send this water down what would become the Eudora Floodway, across a corner of Arkansas and a good deal of Louisiana. Louisiana representatives like Leonard Allen complained bitterly, but were almost unfailingly gracious to the agency that drew up the plans. "I know there is not a group of men in Washington I have more confidence in than I have in the Corps of Engineers," he proclaimed in 1938. Whittington, the committee chairman, identified their decisions with engineering and economic necessity. "We have given them the yardstick, have we not, when we say that we ask the Chief of Engineers in the most economical way and at the most advantageous place to provide for 3,000,000 cubic feet per second."[37]

By chance, Whittington's district was in Mississippi. Some of the testimonies from his state were even more deferential to the Corps. Of course they could afford to be. W. T. Wynn, representing a Mississippi flood control district, explained: "The problem, I think, has gotten beyond our local engineers. It is a national problem, and we are the patients, and we think it should be turned over to the Army engineers. Now, how we can tell those engineers how to operate or what kind of medicine to give us, I do not know." But would you just let the army engineers run the water over your state, if the situation were reversed? Allen asked another witness. "Yes, sir," replied Mr. Rhea Blake, "we are saying that right now. We are saying we should turn the whole matter over to the Corps of Engineers."[38]

Three years later, with nothing solved, the rhetoric had reached full flower. Leonard Allen asked again why "every plan that has been proposed and that Mississippi has endorsed has been a plan to run the water over Louisiana?" J. S. Allen, chief engineer of the Mississippi Levee commissioners, replied that "God almighty fixed that; we didn't." He continued: "We recognized the geography of this situation and we respected the opinion of the Army engineers." And finally, God descended to earth: "The ranking engineers in the United States decided on that point."[39] In a subsequent exchange during the same hearings, a witness referred to political pressure on the Corps, and Representative Norrell of Arkansas reacted in horror: "Do you mean to tell this committee that the Army engineers are susceptible to political pressure and influence." The witness denied implying any such thing. Norrell continued: "I just want to get it clear in the record that you didn't mean that public or political influence could be brought to bear upon the Army engineers and further that they are always guided solely by the technical field in which they operate."[40]

Of course the congressmen knew that technical considerations did not abolish choice. In more relaxed moments they happily admitted as much in public discussion. A 1948 proposal to improve the harbor in Half Moon Bay, California, showing a benefit-cost ratio of 1.83, included a dazzling assortment of benefits: "[I]ncreased catch of fish and savings in production and transportation costs, elimination of lost fish-

160 CHAPTER SEVEN

ing time, decrease in damage to fishing craft and in loss of gear, reduction in marine insurance premiums, availability of local marine repair facilities, increased recreational activities and associated business, and from change in land use attributable to harbor improvements." To this list developed by the district engineer, an inspired division engineer added the benefits to a local rock quarry. Congressman Jack Anderson could not contain his enthusiasm: "Mr. Chairman, I think that the Army engineers should be highly commended for having exhausted every possible public benefit and for having surveyed every one that might accrue in the event this is constructed."[41]

A more striking case involved the Savage River, a tributary of the Potomac, in western Maryland. A dam was begun during the late 1930s by the Works Progress Administration, after the Corps of Engineers, in 1935, declared the project "unjustified economically" since benefits, even "at their most liberal evaluation," were only 0.37 of costs. The work was interrupted by war, and in 1945 this embarrassing, half-finished dam was thrown back into the lap of the Corps. By adding hydroelectric facilities to the project, it managed, barely, to rationalize the economics of completing it. Unfortunately, this power generation was so vigorously contested in a public hearing before the Board of Engineers that it was dropped. Now, as General Crawford of the Corps explained with revealing redundancy, "[T]he over-all economic justification of the project was not sufficient to justify the project." The local congressman, J. Glenn Beall of Maryland, professed alarm that his constituents would remain vulnerable to floods. Pressure came also from Senator Jennings Randolph of West Virginia. And indeed the Corps hated to leave standing such a monument to waste and futility.

A few days later, Crawford returned to the hearings, to vent his eloquence on the results of a "further investigation." "We have asked the district engineer to consider the Savage River Dam again, as an individual project separate from the main report. In doing that he has developed other benefits that he did not find it necessary to develop when he wrote his main report. The result is that he finds greater benefit, on further investigation, than he had in his report." Now, it turned out, annual flood-control benefits of a mere $2,700 were augmented by $5,000 for power benefits downstream owing to a better-regulated stream flow, $45,000 for pollution abatement, and $130,000 for improved water supply. The benefit-cost ratio for completing the dam was now 1.5, so "it would be perfectly proper to add this Savage River Dam project" to the report.[42]

This multiplication of benefits provided a helpful general strategy for getting projects over the cost-benefit hurdle. Some classes of benefits were long recognized by the Corps as important, but considered unquantifiable. Occasionally in the 1940s the Corps cited such intangibles to justify projects whose tangible benefits could not be made to exceed costs. A river channel in Michigan with a calculated ratio of 0.82 was "considered meritorious and necessary for the general welfare of the communities affected," on account of pervasive local anxiety. Improvement of the port of Skagway, in the territory of Alaska, was justified despite its ratio of 0.53 "in view of the importance of the port in encouragement of future development in the area." Flood control on the Lackawaxen River in Pennsylvania showed a ratio of only 0.8. But a 1942 flood had cost twenty-four lives, and the intangible benefit of avoiding such loss of life in the future was sufficient for the Corps to recommend the project.[43]

The Corps, however, never relied much on exceptions to the regime of calculation. It was better to systematize them. As the best harbors were developed, levees erected, and dam sites used up, more and more of these so-called intangible benefits were made tangible, and quantified. In consequence, many projects that were turned down, some decisively, in the 1940s or 1950s were eventually approved and built. Boosters recognized this general shift and urged it forward, though the Corps was often hesitant. A private report calling for development of the Red River for the benefit of Arkansas, Oklahoma, Texas, and Louisiana noted that while various individual dams and waterways had failed the cost-benefit test, an integrated project could easily pass it. The Corps of Engineers, it optimistically supposed, recognizes "the pernicious effects of trying to measure national concerns in terms of dime-store economics." How were such losses on each project to be made up in volume? "Present-day procedure was used in computing the ratio of costs to benefits." "Present-day procedure" turned out to permit multiplying unit recreation and water supply benefits by the entire population of the area, and unit irrigation and drainage benefits by all potential agricultural acres, among other extravagances.[44] This was too much for the Corps, even in its most expansive moments, and it refused to endorse this report.

CORPS OPPONENTS AND THE PUSH TO STANDARDIZE

The examples given above demonstrate that Corps economic methods could not, by themselves, determine the outcome of an investigation. This will come as no surprise to most readers. But it is important to understand that these are not typical instances of the quantification of costs and benefits. The Corps transgressed its customary standards most egregiously when the political forces were overwhelming, and when they were all arrayed on one side. In routine matters its prestige sufficed to contain the politics. Generally, congressional investigation was so perfunctory that the Corps was not bound to observe any particular rules of quantification. To the extent there were checks on discretion, they were mainly internal. As will appear later, the top officers of the Corps made real efforts to impose some uniformity on the economic analyses reaching them from the districts and divisions, but this never amounted to a campaign to neutralize personal judgment.

The most powerful force for standardized methods, and in this sense for objectivity, was supplied by opponents of the Corps. Of course there was unhappiness whenever a hoped-for navigation or flood-control project was turned down. The Board of Engineers might be obliged to travel from Washington and conduct a special hearing.[45] Disappointed local interests might complain to a congressional committee.[46] But local interests were generally weak, and were rarely in a position to contest official numbers. Only powerful interests, interests that systematically opposed a whole class of Corps projects, could exert much pressure toward the rigorous standardization of its cost-benefit methods. The most effective of these opponents were the utilities, the railroads, and two rival agencies within the federal government: the Soil Conservation Service of the Department of Agriculture, and the Bureau of Reclamation, in the Department of Interior.

Electric Utilities

Although electric power generation was not part of the Corps' official mission, it was routinely considered as a possible secondary benefit, and occasionally it far outweighed the nominal primary benefit. The Corps was more open to multiple-use river development than the prevailing historiography allows.[47] Bureau of Reclamation dams, especially on the Columbia River, were even more important as sources of power. Private utility companies objected to this government-sponsored competition. Their spokesmen hinted that the Corps was an agency of creeping socialism, and that big dams were in any case unwise.[48] They also pursued the more mundane strategy of scrutinizing economic analyses, often cogently, though it seems they won few victories.

In 1946, both the House Flood Control Committee and the Senate Commerce Committee heard testimony on the Rappahannock River, which runs through and occasionally floods Fredricksburg, Virginia. The opposition was led by the Virginia Electric and Power Company, represented by Frederick W. Scheidenhelm, a hydraulic engineer from New York City. He told the committees that the power benefits for the main dam in question, at Salem Church, had been exaggerated because the Corps had not considered such essential technicalities as load factors. He argued that their cost estimates were outdated, since they had been made before the war. He also pointed out that power production was not an authorized Corps mission, so that here they were building a dog to wag the tail. Only 9 percent of the claimed benefits were for flood control. But even this 9 percent was an exaggeration, for about a third of them pertained to land that would be protected from floods only because it would be underwater, in the reservoir basin. "I think the bottom of the barrel was scraped a little hard . . . in this case."

Scheidenhelm's point commands our respect. On the other hand, the project provides modest evidence that the Corps' economic standards were not infinitely flexible. Its engineers wanted to distribute projects over every region of the country. The people of Fredricksburg didn't want levees, which would reduce property values. Colonel P. A. Feringa of the Corps explained that its engineers had been unable to make a single-purpose pure flood-control dam meet the cost-benefit standard. So they tried various options until they found something whose economics could at least be defended, even at the cost of arousing the ire of electric utilities. It no doubt helped that this opposition generally failed, as it did here. The flood-control committees disagreed with Scheidenhelm, preferring the testimony of one D. C. Moomaw. He pointed out that the Corps had found many projects not to be economically feasible, so "when they state they are, I think we are entirely justified in accepting their statements."[49]

Railroads

The railroad companies had no objection to flood control, but were bitterly opposed to the government-subsidized competition created by expensive canals and channel dredging. Objections on principle got them nowhere, especially since many in Congress regarded them as greedy monopolists. So they argued instead that canal projects were economically unjustifiable. Here, too, the obstacles were very great.

The railroads opposed for decades that most famous of Corps boondoggles, on the Arkansas River, which made Oklahoma a maritime state. The Corps, under great pressure, planned a "truly multiple-purpose project," because only with many different kinds of benefits was there any prospect of getting them up to the level of costs. Colonel Feringa proudly reported to the House Committee on Rivers and Harbors in 1946 a benefit-cost ratio of 1.08, without relying on intangible benefits. "The Corps of Engineers once presented a project to this committee

164 CHAPTER SEVEN

which we thought was very good, but in which we tried to evaluate benefits which are not readily evaluated in dollars and cents." R. P. Hart of the Association of American Railroads objected that for the cost of $435 million the government could build a good double railroad line and haul everything for free. Perhaps he was found to be convincing. The project was not approved in 1946, or indeed for the next fifteen years. But in 1946 Robert S. Kerr was merely governor of Oklahoma. By 1962 he was a senator and chairman of the Senate Committee on Rivers and Harbors. Kerr-McGee Oil Industries had a huge financial stake in the waterway. In 1946 he had testified: "Let us not confine this hearing to the minor subject of comparative water-rail freight costs. Rather let us think about building a greater nation." The line evokes speeches written by Theodore Sorenson. At least, it resonated with the Kennedy administration, which wanted to get the country moving again. In the interim, Congress had decreed that increased employment in undeveloped areas should be recognized as a social benefit of water projects. Kerr sponsored legislation to solidify and increase the valuation of recreation benefits. Such procedures made it easier for projects like this one with powerful political support to clear the formal economic hurdle. Freight to Tulsa now passes through the Robert S. Kerr lock and dam and over the Robert S. Kerr reservoir.[50]

On a few rare occasions the railroads were able to disturb the tranquility of congressional hearings on public works and force the legislators to consider in detail the economic merits of a water project. A nice discussion was generated in some Senate hearings on rivers and harbors in 1946 over a canal in Louisiana and Arkansas. It was proposed by local boosters as part of their ceaseless efforts to develop the Arkansas-White-Red river system after the fashion of the Tennessee Valley Authority, but with the Corps of Engineers firmly in charge. The Association of American Railroads, represented by Henry M. Roberts, found itself at a disadvantage. The project description, sent over by the House of Representatives, hinted at doom: "Red River below Fulton, Arkansas, in accordance with the report of the Chief of Engineers dated April 19, 1946; *Provided*, That the improvement herein authorized between Shreveport and the mouth shall, when completed, be named the 'Overton-Red River Waterway' in honor of Senator John H. Overton, of Louisiana." Overton was chairman of the subcommittee conducting the hearings.

He set their tone by challenging Roberts's credentials. He thought he had settled with the railroads privately, and was not happy to be confronted with their opposition. But the informal settlement hadn't held, as he at last understood. Roberts argued against spending public money to favor one kind of transportation over another. Without massive subsidies, he explained, inland waterway transportation is not cheap. We know, and "we are not amateurs" in these matters. The benefits of this proposed canal, he continued, had been greatly exaggerated. In estimating freight volume by sampling, the Corps seemed to have forgotten that railroad offices are closed on Sundays and holidays. Their tonnage estimates were high in relation to comparable projects. So also was the figure for savings per ton-mile. Besides, the Corps had ignored the cost of getting freight to the river or canal from wherever it originated. Faced with all these defects, the railroads had hired their own experts to recalculate. Roberts proposed a much lower estimate of benefits.

Overton tried to discredit these attacks on the official numbers, and on the experts who made them believable.

> OVERTON: Let me ask you, is it true, or not, that the Board of Engineers have rate experts in their employ?
>
> ROBERTS: Well, that word 'expert,' sir, takes in a lot of territory. I have met two or three men up there I thought were pretty good rate men. Whether they had anything to do with this, or not, I don't know.
>
> OVERTON: They do have them in their employ. Does the Interstate Commerce Commission have some pretty good rate experts?
>
> ROBERTS: They are supposed to be.

It seems the "government experts" were parties to an oxymoron. The difference between railroad rate men and the Corps is that "we are realistic in getting facts. Two and two is four with us." "And not so with the board?" interjected Overton. "Well, we don't reach up in the air and get figures and say they represent actual facts." That is, he disapproved of sampling. "Private enterprise could not survive under such a system. It is like taking your street number and dividing it by your telephone number and getting your age."[51]

Feringa countered Roberts in the most general terms possible: the Corps pursues a just mean in its economic analyses, and it must be succeeding, since it generates antagonism on both sides. "We steer a middle course. We try to be neither proponents nor opponents, but merely the consultants of Congress with no axes to grind, trying to give you the figures as best we know how." The state of Louisiana, in the spirit of boosterism, calculated a benefit-cost ratio of 1.92; Roberts's figures implied one of 0.80. The Corps reported 1.28. Overton inserted that the Corps was too conservative; that real benefits are almost always higher than their estimates. "Still it is a commendable conservatism because it creates confidence by the public and the Congress in the recommendations of the Board of Engineers." This was the favorite posture of the

166 CHAPTER SEVEN

Corps: beset by enthusiasts on both sides, they had learned to take the claims of boosters and opponents alike with a grain of salt. Feringa explained that rate work demands a special kind of expertise. "It is a science in itself, and a man has to be trained for it." He confirmed the special nature of the expertise by presenting it incoherently to the Senate committee.[52]

There followed a revealing exchange. Roberts requested that one of these so-called rate experts be brought in to testify before the committee. Overton demurred: "Oh we have got too much to do now." Roberts: "I thought so." Overton read from the report of the chief of engineers, which he proclaimed to be both thorough and fair. Roberts said he knew the Interstate Commerce Commission had not put correct rates on the bills, because his own crew of seven real experts had gone over them. Overton reacted with horror: "That is quite a reflection on the Interstate Commerce Commission, and on the Board of Engineers." If his committee had to call in witnesses and compare rates in detail, they would require two or three weeks for every project. They had no choice but to trust the report of the Board of Engineers. But then, at last, somebody supported Roberts. Guy Cordon of Oregon inserted that "this is the first time I have had experience with opponents coming in and controverting facts and making their allegations specific." If the committee refused to call in the experts and set the record straight, he couldn't understand why they have hearings at all. It's all wasted time if they just get embalmed in the record.

At last, Overton relented. In came Eric E. Bottoms of the Economics Division, under the Board of Engineers. Roberts was not allowed to challenge Bottoms item by item, so the Corps was given the benefit of the doubt. But Bottoms made clear that economic analysis was a serious business. It involved an immense amount of filing and counting by people who had in fact thought through their methods. The Corps researchers had censused freight movement on the rail lines, then sorted all bills for one day each month according to their judgment of whether the load in question would be more advantageously transported by water. Either for internal reasons, or as a defense against external challenges, the Corps was careful in observing formalities. It had consulted other agencies, such as the Interstate Commerce Commission, for judgments falling within their special competence. If its numbers were too generous, this was accomplished mainly at the level of minute details, which of course could not easily be challenged.[53]

Another waterway that the railroads vigorously challenged, again unsuccessfully, was the Tennessee-Tombigbee. This was a huge project, arousing political forces far too powerful for the cost-benefit analysis to remain innocent. Still, the numbers were not simply fabricated. In 1939, the Board of Engineers managed to raise the benefit-cost ratio above 1.0 only by attaching numbers to certain benefits that had always been regarded as intangible, including $600,000 for national defense and $100,000 for recreation. The chief of engineers, Julian Schley, doubted the propriety of these and some other values, and refused to make an official recommendation. He concluded that the economic analysis was not straightforwardly valid, but fell "within the realm of statesmanship to which the Congress can best assign the proper values." The railroad spokesman, J. Carter Fort, argued that the waterway was merely a huge subsidy for a few special interests, and complained that it depended on the most extreme economic inventiveness. In particular: "That figure for national defense is a figure that must, in its very nature, have been pulled out of the air. No one could possibly put a value on it in money."[54]

After the war, inevitably, the project came up again. Perhaps it was also inevitable that it would now appear economically justified without the intangibles. But it was by the slimmest of margins, a ratio of 1.05. Unquantifiable items make the project rather better, explained chief of engineers R. A. Wheeler; "some day we are going to have to have some sort of a formula" to evaluate them. For now, the Corps had relied on 2,500 questionnaires sent to shippers, of which 1,338 were returned, to estimate potential traffic volume and savings. The railroads again doubted the analysis. But they could do almost nothing. The forms contained privileged business information, which could not be released to private parties.[55]

Six years later, though, this project fell afoul of the powerful House Appropriations Committee. It had been authorized in 1946, and the Corps promptly began preparation of a detailed "definite project report." But before this was finished, it requested a relatively small appropriation to build the first leg of the project. This, its enemies charged, was a scheme to commit Congress to the whole thing. John J. Donnelly of the committee staff subjected chief of engineers Lewis Pick to a withering interrogation. As usual, what mattered most was in the details. Could operators haul eight barges in one tow across Mississippi Sound from Mobile to New Orleans? The Corps assumed they could, but the committee staff had been told they could not, in which case a whole class of purported advantages of the waterway would vanish. Should the costs include the added expense of rebuilding locks on the Mobile River for long barges? The Corps argued that they needed to be rebuilt anyway. There were also doubts about the true time savings for waterway traffic in comparison to Mississippi River traffic? The committee concluded that the most recent benefit-cost ratio of 1.13 was based on serious mistakes for both costs and benefits, and offered its own ratio of 0.27.

168   CHAPTER SEVEN

Pick obviously suffered some moments of acute discomfort, but in the end he was undaunted. He did not attempt to refute the committee staff in detail, but simply claimed greater expertise.

> Without doubt some of the opinions gleaned by the investigative staff from informed sources as to the feasibility of the project have been in sharp conflict with observations and testimony from similar sources found acceptable by the Corps of Engineers' analysts as determinative. In such a situation, the comparative competence and familiarity of the respective staffs with the practical problems of water transportation and their respective experience in canvassing the field, and weighing the information offered by those with special interests to serve, would seem to afford the most reliable test of credibility. The ability to make sound appraisals of the sometimes overenthusiastic claims of waterway advocates is highly important, but it is equally essential to discount the natural hostility of intrenched carrier enterprises which want to forestall troublesome competition and which are dependent upon the good will of existing regulatory agencies. . . . Experience of the Corps of Engineers in the development of successful waterways would seem to furnish the most reliable guide in estimating the future performance of such projects as the Tennessee-Tombigbee improvement.[56]

The experience of the Corps carried the day. It was evidently impossible for private interests opposing particular projects to discredit its officially sanctioned numbers.

Upstream-Downstream: The Agriculture Department

Industries and interest groups were able to enforce some standards of care in the preparation of cost-benefit analyses by the Corps of Engineers. But effective pressure to spell out, and sometimes even to change, cost-benefit practices came mainly from other branches of the federal government. There were dozens of agencies involved in what was called water resources development. Many had a well-defined role that did not threaten the Corps. A few did not. The most bitter rivalry in this field, by all odds, involved the Corps and the Bureau of Reclamation. Second place among the antagonists was held by the Department of Agriculture, and particularly its Soil Conservation Service.

The missions of the Corps and Agriculture were not obviously in conflict. The 1936 Flood Control Act divided their jobs between downstream and upstream. Downstream meant bigger dams. Almost immediately after the Corps began building dams regularly for flood control, it was faced by opposition tinged with populism. This was not simply a matter of ideology. No matter where a dam was to be located, those upstream from it faced the double indignity of being deprived of flood control themselves and, for some, of being flooded out of their homes and off their farms by the reservoir. Many came to believe that big dams were unnecessary for flood control—that floods were artifacts of poor land management and could be avoided through reforestation, contour plowing, and small dams near the headwaters of streams. For such reasons, opposition to the Corps was very often attended by a strong preference for the policies of the Soil Conservation Service.[57] The Corps complained of this, and Congress tried to neutralize it, but with scant success.[58]

Congress considered that upstream people, like everyone else, had something approaching a constitutional right to a cost-benefit analysis for their proposed flood-control measures.[59] The Department of Agriculture had its own approved cost-benefit methods. These treated big downstream structures less generously than the Corps, but they could often justify a network of small, cheap dams as part of a systematic program of soil conservation and small-scale irrigation. The Corps viewed many of these as uneconomical. Such divergent outcomes of economic analysis, of course, fed the controversy. Still worse, from the standpoint of the Corps, a network of small dams protected towns and cities downstream only from small floods. This might be sufficient to tip the benefit-cost ratio against a large dam on the main river without reducing at all the impact of catastrophic major floods.[60] So far as the Corps was concerned, suspect economic practices sanctioned by the Department of Agriculture were undermining its effort to provide real flood protection. This was one of its main incentives in seeking a single, standardized method of cost-benefit analysis throughout the federal government.

The Bureau of Reclamation and the Kings River Controversy

"Hitler could not have selected better people to sabotage the American interests than those who have done that in the San Joaquin Valley," complained Congressman Alfred Elliott of California in 1944.[61] What had these traitors done? They had performed a cost-benefit analysis showing irrigation benefits in excess of flood control benefits for a proposed reservoir on the Kings River. In this case, evidently, the politics of quantification had gotten out of hand. But perhaps this should not have been unexpected, in a time of war. In the files of the Bureau of Reclamation for the Kings River we find the following:

> Repeatedly since 1939 I have written and spoken to Commissioner [John] Page and later to you about my growing apprehension concerning the 'institutional ambitions of the Corps of Engineers.' The battles over the Missouri River and Kings River are the present highlights in a campaign, long-

planned and thoroughly planned by the Corps, which is intended to cover the entire West. On the Missouri the Corps is using its navigation divisions; on Kings River, its flood-control battalions. It is trying to carry out a huge pincers movement. . . . We are making the fight on an unfavorable terrain, from the standpoint of irrigation possibilities. The Corps, not the Bureau, picked the battlefield. If the Corps wins the battle decisively, the whole war may be lost to us; there may remain no secure and important sphere of action for the Bureau on other western rivers. A defeat for the Corps could not be similarly crucial, not with flood control pork barrels in every valley.[62]

The inevitability of war was often denied in early 1939. The Commissioner of Reclamation thought he could negotiate with the Corps. Appeasement seemed at first to work, for on March 28 he issued a triumphant memorandum announcing that "the California district is an outstanding example of cooperation between representatives of the Army and the Bureau of Reclamation."[63] But, as Ickes recognized in a communication to the president, it is dangerous to negotiate from weakness. "It has been alleged that a contest is developing between the Corps of Engineers and the Bureau of Reclamation to see which agency should build the big dams in the west. . . . If such a contest should develop, obviously the Bureau would lose, because it operates under the Reclamation Law which requires that all or most of the money expended be repaid to the Federal Government."[64]

These differences in law governing the Corps of Engineers and the Bureau of Reclamation were poisonous. The Bureau of Reclamation was created in 1902 to provide irrigation water for (what soon became) the seventeen states west of the 97th meridian. It was required to charge farmers for the cost of supplying water, though without interest. This might seem generous, but the Corps required no local contributions at all for navigation projects, and rather little for flood control. The really crucial advantage of the Corps of Engineers in California, though, was that the Bureau was governed by an ethic of homesteading, and was not allowed to provide water to holdings over 160 acres. By 1940 it had found ways of compromising this standard, but not to the extent that it could provide satisfaction in the agricultural plutocracy that was California's Central Valley. In the Kings River valley, big farmers were already pumping great quantities of water out of the river and the ground for irrigation. They were in fact pumping too much, and needed governmental help to be saved from themselves. But they were not about to invite in some federal agency to build expensive water works if it would require them to divest of all but 160 acres each.[65]

By 1939, the Bureau of Reclamation had been involved in California's ambitious water program, the Central Valley Project, for about a decade. So it was natural that when planning began to dam up the Kings River, the Bureau was contacted first. In February 1939, the local congressman introduced legislation for the Bureau to construct a dam at Pine Flat, as compensation to his constituents for a bill to create Kings Canyon National Park.[66] Evidently he was out of touch. In March, under pressure, he withdrew both bills. Not only did local people oppose the park, but many wanted the Corps of Engineers to build this dam. Local water interests had already been negotiating with the Corps for some months, and had even proposed to finance privately the project survey in hopes of getting congressional approval within a year. The district engineer replied that the complexity of procedures made this unlikely. The Corps began drawing up plans early in 1939.[67]

Urged from higher up, local officers of the Corps and the Bureau worked almost from the beginning to harmonize their projects. This would help keep the politics under control. S. P. McCasland, who designed the dam for the Bureau, reported back to headquarters that "the interests" were being kept in the dark about negotiations. Initial plans called for a reservoir at Pine Flat with a capacity of about 800,000 acre-feet, and this was recommended in McCasland's report, dated June 1939.[68] A capacity of 780,000 was proposed to the Corps by L. B. Chambers, district engineer in Sacramento. As justification he sent along to Washington a graph of benefits and costs, and of their ratio, as a function of reservoir capacity. This was sufficiently standard, at least in Sacramento, that such information could be communicated easily by telephone.[69] But the office of the chief of engineers was worried that this would not control the "maximum possible flood," and wondered if a one million acre-foot reservoir might not be better, especially if flood control were to lead to further development in the valley below. The principal engineer on the project, B. W. Steele, explained that the smaller reservoir was based on the flood of 1906, and that a larger one might be justified if the huge 1884 flood was considered as a basis for planning. The district engineer, in contrast, argued simply that the last 200,000 acre-feet were "not economic," and that the downstream valley was already fully developed. But in Washington they wanted to control the maximum possible flood. So Chambers's boss at the division office in San Francisco, Warren T. Hannum, redrew the plans. While the increased capacity was not economically justified (at the margin), there was a sufficient surplus of benefits over costs in the smaller dam to cover the deficit in the last 220,000 acre-feet and still leave a benefit-cost ratio of 1.4.[70] This became the Corps plan. The Bureau of Reclamation immediately acceded to the larger reservoir, not wanting to contest the judgment of the Corps about the requirements of proper flood control.[71]

172   CHAPTER SEVEN

But Page extracted a quid pro quo. The Corps had estimated a much lower cost for their dam. Page thought they were too optimistic about foundation conditions, for which they lacked detailed data. Bureau engineers also pointed out that the army added only 10.1 percent for contingencies, in contrast to their 16 percent. Page persuaded the Board of Engineers to raise its estimate by $1 million to $19 million, and tried to get them up to $20 million.[72] Finally the agencies compromised on $19.5 million. They also compromised on the all-important allocation of benefits. The Corps considered that nearly 75 percent of the reservoir was needed for flood control, so only about a quarter of the costs should be charged to irrigation.[73] This percentage, as everybody recognized, was in fact almost arbitrary, because flood levels could be predicted rather well from the winter snow pack, making it possible to have most of the reservoir available for flood control without much compromising its capacity to hold irrigation water. Normally the Bureau was happy to assign the maximum of costs to flood control, thereby reducing charges to water users for irrigation. In this case, though, Page did not want to see the storage capacity of the reservoir allocated overwhelmingly to the business of the Corps of Engineers. A Solomonic compromise was reached. Half the costs would be allocated to flood control, and half to irrigation.[74]

This is how replication worked in politically charged economic analyses. The two agencies, under pressure from higher authorities, negotiated a settlement. The project reports, both issued as House documents in February 1940, proposed the same structure with the same costs allocated in equal proportions to the same functions. They also agreed on the annual benefits of flood control ($1,185,000) and water "conservation" ($995,000). The reports were never fully harmonized, though, because the Corps released its report to Congress before the negotiations were complete, to the dismay of the Bureau. The Corps claimed that 54 percent of benefits were for flood control, making the dam predominantly a flood-control project. The Bureau of Reclamation included a hydroelectric power facility, with a cost of $2.6 million and annual benefits of $260,000. This power would be used to pump water, and hence counted as conservation. So the Bureau report claimed a total benefit of $1,255,000 for irrigation, giving it the advantage in both costs and benefits. Its report contained a few additional quantitative tricks, subtle but admirable. By counting reduced evaporation from Tulare Lake, into which the Kings River flows, the Bureau managed to increase the available irrigation water annually by 277,000 acre feet, as opposed to only 195,000 acre feet according to the army engineers. It calculated an annual cost for flood control, based on repayment in forty years of capital plus 3½ percent interest, at $486,000. Irrigation, al-

THE RISE OF COST-BENEFIT ANALYSIS 173

though allocated the same costs, was exempt by law from interest charges, so the annual cost was figured at $263,750. Accordingly, the benefit-cost ratio for the flood control portion of the project was a mere 2.4, while the functions of the Bureau could boast a superb ratio of 4.8.[75]

There were a few other differences. The report by the Bureau of Reclamation had an attachment, written five months later. It was a letter signed by the president, Franklin D. Roosevelt, who momentarily forgot that the Corps had any business but navigation. Ickes exploited the lapse: "Again we find the armed forces of the United States are massing to protect farming communities from the floods of an unruly river in the interior of California." On the basis of the Bureau's numbers, the president concluded "that the project is dominantly an irrigation undertaking, and is suited to operation and maintenance under reclamation law. It follows, therefore, that it should be constructed by the Bureau of Reclamation."[76] He elevated the point to a general principle: these jurisdictional conflicts should hereafter be settled by the numbers.

Since both Corps and Bureau were agencies under the executive, the president's letter could scarcely be ignored. Ultimately, though, it proved less important than the other difference between the two reports. The Corps proposed to collect the present value of all future water payments in a lump sum at the outset, and to let local interests take charge of the distribution of the water. The Bureau considered water distribution as part of its mission, and refused to turn it over to local interests. It promised to respect existing water rights, but it also set about renegotiating water contracts. Secretary of Interior Ickes later gave a speech vowing to use the conserved water to create small California farms for returning soldiers. In 1943 a new commissioner of reclamation, Harry Bashore, announced his intention to enforce reclamation law, and not to supply water from Bureau projects to big holdings.[77] It was not clear the Kings River would be exempt.

Already in 1939, water interests near the Kings River had been inclined to favor the Corps. In the 1940s they refused to negotiate water contracts with the Bureau of Reclamation, holding out for the almost complete autonomy offered them by the Corps. In some 1941 Congressional hearings on the Kings River, engineers representing the main water companies—and hence the biggest landholders—testified in favor of construction by the Corps of Engineers. In 1943 this was still more decisive, and by 1944 had become almost hysterical: Hitler himself couldn't have subverted American agriculture more effectively than the economic analysts who assigned a majority of benefits from this project to irrigation. A parade of farmers and engineers traveled to Washington to testify solemnly that they were not much interested in irrigation, but

174 CHAPTER SEVEN

desperately needed flood control. Engineers and lawyers for the water companies recalculated the benefits, and determined that at least three-fourths pertained to flood control. Their testimony was convincing to the congressional flood control committees.[78]

Although the Pine Flat Dam was eventually built by the Corps, the disposition of the water had to be negotiated between users and the Bureau. Predictably, the negotiations were bitter. They lasted from 1953 until 1963. The Kings River Water Association now insisted that irrigation should have priority over all other uses; it even rejected a draft contract giving priority to irrigation "subject only to flood control requirements."[79] Bashore had repeatedly pointed out that all agriculture in the Central Valley of California depended on irrigation. So it might seem that the testimonies of the big water interests and the Corps itself to Congress in the early 1940s about the paramount need for flood control were simply mendacious. This is not quite right. Without irrigation the land was worth practically nothing for agriculture, but given the existing irrigation development in 1940, most of the measured benefits of a dam at Pine Flat could reasonably be attributed to flood control. Tulare Lake, into which the Kings River flows, had no outlet in most years; it expanded and receded with the seasons. It was the scene of extremely large-scale agriculture. The big growers planted in the late spring as the lake receded, and hastened the retreat of the waters by pumping from the lake to irrigate higher ground. This worked adequately in normal years, but in flood years much of the land remained underwater too long to grow crops. Ignoring, as all analyses did, the value of this huge expanse of wetlands to migrating waterfowl, the chief benefit of the proposed works was indeed to contain and stabilize the lake. It accrued almost exclusively to big investors, the only ones who commanded the resources to manage the fluctuations of water level and earn a profit on the intermittent lake bed.

These were the growers whose interests were most effectively represented at the hearings in faraway Washington. Some small farmers, especially members of the Pomona Grange, sent eloquently ungrammatical letters, and even gathered a petition, in favor of the Bureau of Reclamation. They did not call for the breakup of the big holdings, though a few did testify in 1944 at some hearings in Sacramento in favor of enforcing the acreage restrictions of Reclamation law in the Central Valley. The main appeal to them of the Bureau's plan for the Kings River was the cheap power it would provide to help them move water onto their crops. When representatives of the big water interests, especially Charles Kaupke of the Kings River Water Association, told the House committee that his people would prefer no project to one subject to the rules governing the Bureau of Reclamation, the *Fresno Bee* editorialized against him. It anticipated, wrongly as it turned out, that Roosevelt's opposition to the Corps on this issue would prove decisive. It warned that selfish interests might block a federally supported dam promising great local benefit.[80]

There is no indication that any of this mattered much in Washington. The local congressional delegation, and the relevant committees, were firmly allied to the big owners in favor of construction by the Corps. The White House was no less firmly behind the Bureau of Reclamation. Quantitative analysis, to which both sides looked for a resolution, was too loose to provide one. If anything, it obstructed negotiation, as both sides claimed to be conclusively vindicated by a preponderance of benefits. Discrepancies in forms of calculation had contributed to an embarrassing standoff and a political quagmire. Bureaucratic battles like the one over Kings River seemed to reveal a compelling need for the standardization of cost-benefit analysis throughout the federal government.

DISCREPANT ECONOMIC PRACTICES
IN FEDERAL AGENCIES

Any effort to reconcile diverse cost-benefit practices faced the most severe obstacles. Cost-benefit analysis was not merely a strategy for choosing projects. It structured relations within bureaucracies and helped define the form of their interactions with clients and competitors. The Bureau of Reclamation, the odd man out in most interagency discussions of cost-benefit analysis, could least afford to give up its distinctive procedures for measuring benefits. Not just in retrospect, but even at the time, some of its practices were regarded as indefensible, bordering on ludicrous. Be that as it may, they were explicitly codified. The Bureau accepted the methods of other agencies, including the Corps and the Federal Power Commission, for evaluating benefits such as flood control and power generation that were collateral to its primary mission. But it was the specialist on irrigation, and in deference to an economic test written into the Reclamation Act of 1939 it created a set of distinctive, Depression-era methods for quantifying that class of benefits.

The Bureau's analysis of direct irrigation benefits began with the agricultural production made possible by a new supply of water. These products were assumed to provide an irreplaceable livelihood for a set of farmers. To the revenues they receive must be added the "extended benefits radiating outward." First, the new production provided raw materials for processing and sale by others. This embraced five classes of activities: merchandising, direct processing, other stages of processing, wholesale trade, and retail trade. Economic analysts for the Bureau as-

176 CHAPTER SEVEN

signed percentages to each of these activities for each of ten crop groups. For grain, these were, respectively, 8, 12, 23, 10, 30, a total of 83 percent. Increased production imputed to irrigation was multiplied by .83 to measure this class of indirect benefits. Different factors applied to other crop groups. This was not the only multiplier. Farmers who benefit from irrigation water spend most of their income in the local community. The Bureau defined nineteen classes of enterprises to which farmers extend their custom, and, once again, assigned percentage factors to each. These factors were then multiplied by the increased revenue of the enterprises in question. Some 12 percent of increased retail trade purchases, for example, were credited to new irrigation works. So also were 29 percent of increased expenditures on auto repair and, most famously, 39 percent of the new revenues of motion picture theaters. Finally, at least in principle, the grand total was to be reduced by applying a "federal cost-adjustment factor," the ratio of net to gross farm income.[81]

This was by no means the outer limit of accounting inventiveness at the Bureau. It was required to charge farmers for expenses allocated to irrigation. It considered itself at a disadvantage in this respect compared to flood control and navigation, which required no reimbursement at all. As a task force of the first Hoover Commission observed in 1949: "Interagency rivalry has fostered a sort of Gresham's law with respect to Federal financial policies, the tendency being for higher standards of repayment by State, local, and private beneficiaries to be replaced by lower."[82] The Bureau undertook, with dazzling effectiveness, to minimize this disadvantage. By law the farmers were exempted from paying any interest. The period of amortization stretched gradually from ten to forty and then fifty years. By 1952 it had reached the lesser of one hundred years or "the life of the project." A hundred years without interest was a nice subsidy. But irrigators were never charged even this much. The Bureau calculated benefits for flood control, hydroelectric power, pollution abatement, recreation, and fish and wildlife, among others. Its announced policy was to allocate costs to nonreimbursable functions first, up to the entire cost of the project.

During the debates about the Kings River, Harry Bashore happily explained that "the larger the flood-control benefits are the better it suits us, in a way, for the reason that the burden then becomes lighter on the irrigators who have to pay for irrigation benefits." If not all costs could be allocated to nonreimbursable functions, what remained were assigned preferentially to power production. If this power might be used to pump irrigation water, it could (like the irrigation water itself) be exempted from interest on the cost side, but credited with interest on the payment side, so that even less of the initial investment would remain for irrigators to pay off. And still the farmers often defaulted, partly because they became aware that the Bureau had no teeth, but partly also because these "conservation" projects generally brought them such modest increases of income. The Bureau of Reclamation needed its extravagant measures of the benefits of irrigation to keep its mission from drying up.[83] It was much criticized, and in 1952 a panel of academic consultants was enlisted by Commissioner Michael W. Straus to "make an objective appraisal" of its disagreements with other federal agencies. The panel was sympathetic to the concept of secondary benefits, but still concluded that "the applications actually made by the Bureau go far beyond what can be soundly identified as quantitatively measurable secondary benefits . . . attributable to public water-use projects."[84]

Apart from disappointed interest groups, few have thought the Corps of Engineers too strict in its economic analysis. But it always had more requests for projects than there was any hope of building in the immediate future. In the mid-1940s it recommended and received authorization for a great backlog of works, which in the early 1950s became a source of embarrassment on account of delays and the inevitable cost overruns. The backlog would have been worse had the Corps not rejected more than half the requests that reached it.[85] Critics have generally cited those cases in which the Corps departed most flagrantly from its own economic standards as evidence of the political pressures it faced. On this account, many have supposed that its economic analyses were just for show, honored only in the breach. But conspicuous creativity was not the norm. The engineers were embarrassed whenever they had to put a money value on "intangibles"—which in practice meant any act of quantification (even involving uncontroversial values like the saving of life) not yet formulated in terms of rules. In the ordinary run of business, the Corps had to decide about a host of small and intermediate projects, all with some political support. The credibility required to approve some and reject others depended on its reputation for following the rules. Huge and exceptional cases sometimes overwhelmed them. For ordinary decisions it was politically expedient not to play tricks, but to establish and maintain routines.

This was not easy. Since World War II, the Corps has had about forty-six district offices grouped into eleven divisions. After 1936 the number of civilian engineers grew hugely. In 1949 the Corps was made up of 200 army engineers, 9,000 civilian engineers, and 41,000 other civilian employees. The top officers in Washington tried to use cost-benefit analysis to impose some coherence on planning within this unwieldy bureaucracy. District engineers used the economic results to defend their decisions against disappointed supplicants, who might even be supported by higher authorities within the Corps. Boosters were endlessly imaginative in finding economic arguments for projects. They might, for example, calculate the number of seagulls that would reside on a new reservoir, then multiply by their rate of grasshopper consumption and by

178 CHAPTER SEVEN

the value of grain eaten by each grasshopper.[86] If such extravagances were permitted, project planning would be reduced to naked politics, and flood control would lose credibility.

The office of chief of engineers sent out a series of circular letters in the late 1930s and early 1940s specifying the appropriate categories of benefits, and how they were to be quantified. The rules were restated in the army's "Orders and Regulations," section 283.18. By the late 1950s, the Corps was printing, revising, and reprinting whole volumes on the quantification of various classes of benefits. The tone, as befitted a military bureaucracy, was always strict and serious. The first of the circular letters, dated June 9, 1936, urged that the economic analysis should discount "the natural optimism of the engineer" as well as the exaggerations of industrial companies.[87] "Orders and Regulations" declared it appropriate to consider as a benefit the "higher use" of land protected by flood control, but if the flood plain was being developed anyway, the correct measure of benefit was the anticipated reduction in flood damages. The engineer must never use both measures: this is double counting, the cardinal sin. "Indirect damage" estimates must in each case be confirmed on their own merits. Simply adding a percentage to direct damages is not permissible, "except in cases when such relations have been established for certain selected areas and are applied where comparable conditions exist."[88]

To be sure, the rules were not overwhelmingly restrictive. It was permissible to measure "collateral" benefits, such as pollution abatement, as the alternative cost of achieving the same effect, even if nobody intended to do so. Some navigation projects showed as the principal benefit a saving of time, which fishermen and shippers were notably unwilling to subsidize. A Mr. McCoach, who took economic questions for the chief of engineers in some hearings on flood control in 1937, participated in the following exchange:

> Mr. [Charles R.] Clason [Mass.]: Is not the important factor the increase in property value, does not that go up into the millions, while others are floating around in the thousands?
>
> Mr. McCoach: That is correct, but, of course, that is one of the most-controversial items of benefit that you can find.
>
> Mr. Clason: In the absence of an increase in the value of the lands, no dike or levy would ever be considered beneficial?
>
> Mr. McCoach: That is correct.

McCoach went on to explain that Corps measures were actually conservative, because "there are so many indirect and intangible things that you cannot evaluate by what I call the invoice methods." He also acknowledged that "no two men in this room" would agree on how to value property, and that while assessed valuation is taken into account, it is not decisive. Clason was troubled: "If voters write in to me to ask me on what basis they build a dike, I would like to be able to tell them something more definite than guess at the increase in the value of the property." "I would not say it is a guess," McCoach replied, "it is an estimate."[89]

After 1940, though, the Corps moved away from such heavy reliance on changes in property value to justify flood control works. In some districts, they began to be called intangible. Increased property values should, after all, reflect potential or historical flood damages. This was the most formalized of all benefit categories. It was still rather tricky. Even if flood records were good, and went back for many decades, an average of recorded damages was an inadequate measure. Since there had almost always been population growth, an equivalent flood could be expected to cause greater damages in the future than in the past. Moreover, the mean annual level of flood damages was extremely sensitive to the size of the largest probable flood, the project flood, which remained hypothetical. To estimate this, the engineers used probability techniques as well as weather records to plot a flood frequency curve, then drew maps showing the expected extent of the water, depth contours, and the duration of flooding. Average damages calculated from historical records might be only a third of those estimated when a hypothetical maximum flood was factored in. It is only fair to add that on a number of embarrassing occasions the hypothetical flood was promptly exceeded by a real one.[90]

Clearly there was much room for judgment in economic estimation. There was also a perpetual effort to define the terms within which it would operate, and to mark its permissible bounds. Engineers were warned not to take on faith the damage claims of those actually flooded, since they were prone to exaggerate. Quantification of "intangibles" was strongly discouraged. A 1940 report by a district engineer that relied too much on intangibles to get benefit-cost ratios of 1.01 and 1.06 was rejected at the divisional level. The division engineer had no doubt that these benefits were real, but since they were "not susceptible of exact evaluation," they should only have been relied upon to justify projects that at least appeared as marginal based on proper, tangible costs.[91]

There is ample evidence that the Corps took its cost-benefit calculations seriously, even in the face of political pressure. A big flood near the headwaters of the Republican River, in Colorado and Nebraska, caused considerable damage to small towns and farms, and even killed 105 people. A study was promptly requested. The Corps found that a big dam could be justified, but only because of its contribution to flood control on the main stem of the Missouri and Mississippi—that is, it had to be downstream, meaning that it wouldn't help those who had suffered in the 1935 flood. All potential upstream reservoirs showed very low bene-

180 CHAPTER SEVEN

fit-cost ratios, averaging 0.46. The downstream reservoir, though, had a comfortable surplus of benefits over costs—a ratio of 2.35. When this became known, the state engineers of Colorado, Kansas, and Nebraska joined in a petition demanding that this excess be used to cover the cost-benefit deficits of several upstream dams. "We believe it to be the intent of Congress that either the plan should be a complete plan for flood protection on that stream system, or that it should provide as much protection within the Basin as can be provided, and keep the benefits, to whomsoever they may accrue, in excess of the estimated cost of the project." They prepared an integrated package of flood control on the Republican River showing a collective benefit-cost ratio of 1.6. The district engineer resisted this. Such a policy "would conceivably lead to demands by local interests for construction of the maximum number of economically unjustified reservoirs . . . that could be included in a multiple reservoir project." He had to concede that there was precedent for this kind of packaging, though.[92]

An engaging memorandum from the division engineer in Kansas City to the chief of engineers remarks that Senator Norris of Nebraska had come into his office to inquire about plans for the Republican River and to explain the "distress of farmers." It turns out that they wanted to use the flood damage as an excuse to build a big irrigation project, and in fact that they were likely to refuse flood control without it. The division engineer told the senator that the best reservoirs showed benefit-cost ratios of about 0.16 for flood control alone, so they were working on dual-purpose reservoirs.

> It was explained to Senator Norris . . . that the cost of these reservoirs would be between 40 and 60 million dollars; and that the cost-benefit ratio will not be better than 2:1, and will probably be nearer to 3:1 even with very liberal assumptions as to benefits. He was told that we were making every effort to improve the showing of the project, . . . that we have not yet found a justifiable project for him, have scant hope of doing so, but are exhausting our ingenuity to make the report convincing to all concerned.[93]

The balance of politics and objectivity in this letter seems about right. Norris, evidently, accepted the division engineer's reasoning. Perhaps the rejection would have stood for a while, had not the Bureau of Reclamation and Corps of Engineers decided in 1944 to divide up the whole Missouri River watershed, to avoid another bloody war and to block plans for an independent Missouri Valley Authority. Survey reports in the next few years managed to justify a number of projects on the Republican River, most with benefit-cost ratios in the range of 1.0 to 1.2. A huge flood in the lower basin in 1951 settled the matter, and a current map shows reservoirs everywhere.[94]

THE RISE OF COST-BENEFIT ANALYSIS **181**

But this perhaps only exemplified the unfortunate effects of competition from an agency whose cost-benefit standards permitted almost anything. On every possible occasion, the Corps of Engineers favored the establishment of firm standards for cost-benefit analysis, made uniform for all agencies of government. This did not mean discouragingly stringent standards. When an investigative committee asked chief of engineers Lewis Pick whether the number of projects might be reduced by requiring a benefit-cost ratio of at least 1.5, or by demanding large local contributions, he responded with characteristic affability and eloquence: "That is true. I think it is very easy to stop it, sir. If you wanted to stop conservation programs in the United States it would be very easy to stop."[95]

Rather, the Corps was engaged in a perpetual effort to push back the frontiers of cost-benefit analysis so that there would always be a manageable supply of economically approved projects. Occasionally, Corps officers complained of the excessive narrowness of sanctioned benefits, and spoke of "the need for new methods of economic analysis which, by improving the benefit-to-cost ratios, would justify the construction of projects currently judged unfeasible."[96] Such talk suggests that cost-benefit analysis was, to a degree, constraining, at least at any given time. But new methods were indeed forthcoming. The flood-control construction boom of the 1960s, for example, was promoted by new, liberal methods for assessing recreation benefits.

Remarkably, Congress sometimes displayed more commitment to fixed standards than the Corps itself. Through the 1950s, recreation was only made "tangible" by treating it as a source of profits for tourist establishments on or near reservoirs and waterways. But the benefits to tourists themselves are important, announced Pick's successor, R. A. Wheeler, in 1954, and "some day we are going to have to have some sort of a formula" to evaluate them. The National Park Service provided aggressively generous measures in its efforts to justify extensive recreational facilities at reservoirs, after the decision to build them had already been made. The Isabella reservoir on the Kern River was assigned recreation benefits in 1948 by summing travel costs by anticipated tourists, per diem living costs for overnight visitors, a "recreational value" of 12½ cents per visitor-day, benefits to local businesses, and summer-home tract values. This was a Chinese encyclopedia, and Corps engineers would have readily perceived the double counting. The National Park Service, wanting to do better, consulted ten expert economists in the late 1940s, in hopes that they would agree on a correct formula. They did not.[97]

Finally the Congress itself took the bull by the horns. It did not give the Corps a blank check, but attempted to create a rigid, though not

182 CHAPTER SEVEN

especially parsimonious, yardstick. An act was considered in 1957 to credit all projects with $1 per visitor-day as recreational benefit. The Corps considered this rather foolish. The value per day must depend on what use people are making of a reservoir, and on whether there are other equally attractive bodies of water in the immediate vicinity. It would be better, testified assistant chief of engineers John Person in a Senate hearing, to substitute "reasonable value" for this inflexible measure.

Immediately Senator Roman Hruska of Nebraska expressed alarm that "the word 'reasonable' might mean a different thing to different people at different times." Francis Case of South Dakota replied: "Of course that wouldn't be any greater discretion than is accorded the Engineers of the Bureau of Reclamation in evaluating other criteria. We don't spell out the measure of flood damages, nor do we spell out the measure of irrigation values." "Yes, yes, I think we do," interjected Robert Kerr, the chairman, who of all people should have known better. "Not in terms of precise dollars," said Case. "I think we do," repeated Kerr. "We don't tell them what the specifications are, but we tell them to advise us and fix the value in terms of dollars as to what the benefits will be from flood control or flood prevention and they arrive at it." After some more discussion, somebody thought to ask their expert engineer.

> KERR: How do you fix it, General?
> PERSON: Well, the flood damages prevented we determine by a study of the flood frequency curve, records of each flood, the actual damages experienced, and other related matters.
> KERR: It is a fixed specification that guides you then rather than a reasonable estimate?
> PERSON: It is fixed to the extent that we have to have something concrete on which to base it, yes.[98]

The railroads and the Bureau of the Budget opposed this whole initiative to put values on recreation as a loosening of requirements. Congress didn't mind such a relaxation, of course, but it did insist on "objectivity."[99]

THE PUSH FOR UNIFORMITY

In 1943, an interdepartmental dinner group of officials from federal water agencies formed in Washington. The organizer was R. C. Price, from the Bureau of Reclamation, who presented a memoir, complete with graphs, showing how "incremental analysis" could be used to design dams of optimum size.[100] The dinner group was soon formalized as the Federal Inter-Agency River Basin Committee. The records of early gatherings show little sign of personal hostility. At the first formal meeting, "it was stressed by all members that the most fundamental reasons for variations in reports and divergence of views originated in the field" and that a "spirit of cooperation" prevailed among the top officials in Washington. There followed a discussion "at considerable length" of "the status of the Bureau of Reclamation and War Department proposals for the construction of Pine Flat Reservoir on Kings River, California." This, they agreed, was already beyond rescue, but they hoped that other conflicts might somehow be forestalled.[101]

The next meeting was about economic analysis. "The discussion . . . centered around the possibility of setting up principles for determining cost and benefit factors and the necessity of freely admitting that certain items cannot be solved by standardization of the method of approach between the different agencies." Someone suggested a subcommittee on cost allocation. In June one was appointed, under Frank L. Weaver of the Federal Power Commission. Its members chose to work through a case study, a project on the Rogue River in Oregon. In October, they announced their intention to report back at the next meeting. But in November, Weaver had to concede that the subcommittee "had not as yet prepared in final form their memorandum report," though G. L. Beard, of the Corps of Engineers, had written up a draft report. When the report did come in, there was substantial disagreement about its recommendations. This could not easily be resolved. After a year of further meetings, a consensus was reached that the mandate of the subcommittee should be broadened to embrace in full generality the measurement of benefits. It was not only to review existing practices, but also "to consider the possibilities of formulating entirely new principles and methods based on a purely rational approach and unencumbered by present practices and administrative limitations." For this it needed a staff. In April 1946 a new "subcommittee on costs and benefits" was appointed.[102]

That subcommittee's members were high-level administrators from each of four central agencies: the Corps of Engineers, Bureau of Reclamation, Department of Agriculture, and Federal Power Commission. "Also present" were some staff people, who attended far more meetings than their superiors, and who did most of the work. Immediately their assignment was subdivided. A working group from the Department of Agriculture was charged with the modest task of preparing "an objective analysis of the problem, including what constitutes a benefit and what constitutes a cost. . . . [T]he analysis must be purely rational and not influenced by present practices or administrative limitations." Mean-

184 CHAPTER SEVEN

while, members from each of the main agencies would report on their current practices, and the subcommittee would seek to identify the most important similarities and differences.[103] Both jobs proved more difficult than anybody had expected, but the objective analysis took longest.

In April 1947 and December 1948 the subcommittee printed "progress reports" for use of the larger committee, which aimed to describe existing agency practices. Summaries of those reports were eventually published as appendices in the subcommittee's 1950 publication.[104] They did not contribute much to the main report. Having clarified their points of difference, there was no way to resolve them. Neither the interagency committee nor its subcommittee had any authority to bargain away customary procedures. The subcommittee didn't even try. After completing the descriptive sections, it almost stopped meeting. The only hope for agreement was the objective analysis. Its authors had a relevant academic identity as well as their bureaucratic one: they were economists with the Bureau of Agricultural Economics. But there was no precedent for the work that had been requested of them, and since nobody was assigned full-time to the subcommittee, it took them three years to complete a draft. Finally it was distributed in mimeograph form on June 13, 1949, under the title "Objective Analysis."[105]

This formed the heart of the eventual report. The changes made by the full subcommittee were more than trivial, but they did not depart from the basic form of the original statement. It called for maximizing the excess of benefits over costs, meaning that each separable portion of a project should show a surplus of benefits. It mentioned the possibility of discounting according to "social time preference" rather than government interest rates, which in the published version was discarded as a needless complication. Neither the mimeograph nor the published report worked through the problems of quantifying benefits of flood control, navigation, irrigation, recreation, or habitat for fish and wildlife in sufficient detail to serve as a manual, but both offered advice about difficult points and warned against neglecting various classes of side effects. They acknowledged that flooding a wild river valley might well involve scenic or recreational losses as well as gains, a possibility the Corps had generally ignored. On issues of controversy between the Bureau of Reclamation and other agencies, the reports took gentle but unmistakable stands against the Bureau. The assumption of a fifty-year project life seemed quite long enough for an economic analysis. "Secondary benefits"—grinding the grain and baking the bread from wheat grown on newly irrigated land—should only be considered in unusual circumstances.[106]

The printed report, especially, was more ambitious than customary bureaucratic practice in calling for the quantification of intangibles.

Since there is no available framework but market values for evaluating project effects in common terms, it held, these should be assigned whenever possible. It argued firmly that recreation benefits must reflect value to the user, not revenue to concessionaires, and should be assigned a price, though it didn't explain how. Improved health should also be given a price. The published volume, but not the draft, considered that it might be useful to assign some "generally accepted judgment value" to human life, based on consideration of the economic factors involved." It added that lives saved or lost should also be listed as a separate entry on the accounts.[107] Among the most ambitious, and least explicable, moves in the draft and published report was to call for projections of future relative prices. Nobody seems to have had any idea how to accomplish this.

The completed volume came to be known affectionately among water analysts and cost-benefit economists as the Green Book, on account of its cover. Its influence was considerable. But it failed utterly to reconcile the cost-benefit practices of the participating agencies. It was most seriously considered by some interagency water development committees, particularly those concerned with the Columbia River and the Arkansas-White-Red river system. But requests from the former came in too early for the subcommittee to be of much use, and the latter found much of the advice too abstract. It was particularly vexed by the insoluble problem of projecting prices, and the subcommittee was not able to provide much help.[108]

The early 1950s was a difficult time for the Corps of Engineers. Its battles with the Bureau of Reclamation had alienated it from the executive branch. It was accused, especially by friends of the Bureau, of being a pork-barrel agency, more interested in transient political advantage than in systematic water management. The huge cost overruns resulting from the construction in 1950 of projects that had been planned in 1940 and authorized in 1946 led to some severe scrutiny by its customary ally, Congress. The chief of engineers, Lewis Pick, displayed signs of paranoia, though his enemies were real enough. He told one committee that all these inquiries "reflect adversely on the wisdom and ability of Congress."[109] For whatever reason, there was a rash of efforts in the late 1940s and early 1950s to rein in spending on water projects by imposing stricter standards of quantification.

The agency best situated to watch over government spending was the Bureau of the Budget. Beginning in 1943, all project authorizations were sent to the Bureau before going on to Congress. Congress, almost without fail, ignored its advice. In 1952 it attempted to strengthen its hand by issuing cost-benefit instructions in a budget circular, A-47. These were in many respects similar to the recommendations of the

Green Book, though they placed greater emphasis on local cost-sharing. Still, the Bureau of the Budget lacked the personnel to enforce these standards, except superficially. This generally meant refusing to recognize new classes of benefits, and opposing projects that depended for their justification on unquantified intangibles.[110]

The failures of the Budget Bureau, and the evident weakness of the Federal Inter-Agency River Basin Committee, inspired various champions of rationality in water planning to propose that projects be submitted to a panel of independent experts. The first Hoover Commission, in 1949, called for a "Board of Impartial Analysis." It proposed to eliminate interagency rivalry and duplication of effort by consolidating all water planning within the Interior Department. Lewis Pick, always gracious, responded for the Corps: "Those in government who would in all likelihood be charged with centralized authority and responsibility are presently engaged in spearheading the movement to set up in this country, through unbridled exploitation of our natural resources, a totalitarian form of government by regions."[111] Congress was not about to approve the annihilation of its favorite agency, and the Corps argued successfully that a new board of impartial analysis would be redundant in its case. The second Hoover Commission did not try again to eliminate agencies, but recommended that project beneficiaries be required to pay almost all costs. It also called, with no more success, for "objective review" by a special panel, and issued its own "principles to be applied in determining economic justification of water resources and power projects and programs." While admitting that cost-benefit analysis is "easily corrupted," it considered this the fault of incompetent or biased practitioners, not a weakness of the method. People make mistakes in arithmetic too, it noted.[112]

TAKEOVER BY THE ECONOMISTS

In the early 1950s, the Corps of Engineers began what was to become a huge expansion in its employment of economists and other social scientists. Soon, every district office had a section devoted to economic analysis. Some of the early economic specialists were failed engineers, shunted off to a domain where they were likely to do less harm. But the combination of criticism from disgruntled interests, pressure from other agencies of government, and an expanding range of authorized benefits upon which numbers had to be fixed created a need for economic expertise that could not be ignored. The environmental legislation of the 1960s and thereafter, and the increasing likelihood of being subjected to judicial review, further intensified this pressure.[113]

Economic expertise relevant to cost-benefit analysis, however, was almost nonexistent in the early 1950s, outside the bureaucracy itself. When professional economists wrote on the benefits of public works, this was likely to be more closely related to a bureaucratic discourse than an academic one.[114] In the 1950s, there was a convergence. The bureaucracy was looking to quantify an ever more diverse and recalcitrant array of benefits. The new welfare economics presupposed that all pleasures and pains in life were commensurable under a single, coherent, quantifiable utility function. It seemed both intellectually serious and practically useful to try to work this out for such difficult issues as recreation, health, and the saving or loss of life.

Richard J. Hammond, whose early critiques of cost-benefit analysis have never been surpassed, considered that the entry of fancy economics brought its downfall. As a handy bureaucratic convention, the comparison of readily quantifiable benefits with investment costs was perhaps not to be sneered at, but now, he believed, this form of analysis had become a license to concoct imaginary data. Hammond was aware, though, that Adam and Eve felt temptation even before the economic serpent presented them with this apple. Implicit already in its bureaucratic uses, especially in the United States, were pressures to reify its terms, to deny the validity of human judgment, to lust after the impersonality of purely mechanical objectivity. To some economists, this sounded like a definition of science. Cost-benefit analysis first became a respectable economic specialty in the late 1950s.[115]

The analysis of water projects was not its only inspiration, although I believe it was the most important. Transportation studies, especially of highways, provided a largely independent source, though a readily commensurable one.[116] There is also a more distant connection to military uses of operations research, where a form of cost-benefit analysis was developed by the RAND corporation as a strategy of optimization. Operations research itself, in turn, was continuous with Taylorism.[117] Words like optimization and Taylorism, though, should warn us that we are dealing with broad trends of twentieth-century American bureaucratic history and history of science. RAND's form of cost-benefit analysis points toward the wider context of militant quantification. It was also of decisive importance for efforts by Robert McNamara and Charles Hitch during the Johnson administration to reformulate government accounts in a way that would permit comparison of the costs and benefits of various government programs. But economic analysis of defense was accomplished informally, not as public knowledge. Military economics never became a research specialty, and it was not a crucial point of reference for the economists who around 1960 began measuring the benefits and costs of almost every form of government activity.[118] The analysis of water projects was.[119]

From this standpoint, the expansion of terms and the importation of the language of welfare economics in the Green Book appears particularly significant. This was mainly the work of economists, though bureaucratic rather than academic ones. The role of economists at the Bureau of Agricultural Economics deserves closer investigation, but before about 1950 they seem to have preferred a language of rational, systematic planning to the evaluation of projects, one at a time. When they finally took up cost-benefit analysis, they did so with specific reference to water projects.[120] This does not explain where they learned to apply welfare economics to public investment analysis. Citations by Mark M. Regan, the most important author of the "Objective Analysis" that provided a template for the Green Book, do not suggest a direct translation from high theory.[121]

The effort to redefine cost-benefit research according to the standards of economists began in earnest in the mid-1950s. Most authors of the first generation wrote on water projects, often in the guise of a case study.[122] In general, economists agreed with budget officials and with the champions of private industry who dominated the Hoover commissions that the cost-benefit test for water projects had not been strict enough. The most favored vehicle for eliminating marginal projects was the imposition of a uniform discount rate, higher than the rate of interest on government bonds. At the same time, economists did not recoil at the idea of placing money values on the previous generation's intangibles, and in this way they may even have contributed to the construction boom of the 1960s. Only in the 1980s was the quantification of intangibles mobilized as a strategy for discouraging the development of wild places, as researchers began using surveys of citizen preferences to place monetary values on scenic landscapes.[123]

A still more important consequence of this pursuit of unbounded quantification was the spread of cost-benefit techniques to all kinds of government expenditures, and later even to regulatory activities. An early, seemingly unpromising, topic was the economics of public health, which required placing a value on days of sickness and even on lives saved and lost. The economist Burton Weisbrod did not flinch, but used lost productivity as the measure of both, and concluded that even polio vaccination was of doubtful net benefit. Education was another. Gross returns from the labor market permitted an endorsement of high school and college, and, inevitably, of MBA programs, but not of graduate study in science or engineering. The authors duly recommended a shift of educational resources to where salaries were highest.[124] By 1965, economists had used cost-benefit methods to evaluate research, recreation, highways, aviation, and urban renewal. Perhaps the available data were less than ideal for some measures. But as Fritz Machlup commented: "The economic valuation of benefits and costs of an institution,

THE RISE OF COST-BENEFIT ANALYSIS   **189**

plan, or activity must attempt to take account of values of any sort and to apply reasoned argument and rational weighting to problems commonly approached only by visceral emoting."[125]

Cost-benefit analysis is often criticized for preferring easy answers based on what can be measured to complex, balanced investigations.[126] Economists have by no means been immune to this. Although they routinely concede by way of preface that calculation can never replace political judgment, cost-benefit and risk analysts clearly want to rein it in as much as possible. So, typically, they insist that a decision can never be left to the judicious consideration of complex details, but must always be reduced to a sensible, unbiased, decision rule. An effective method should not be a mere language, focusing discussion on central issues, but must be constraining. The great danger, announced the authors of a major study of risk, is that "combatants may learn to conduct their debates in, say, the nomenclature of cost-benefit analysis, transforming the technique into a rhetorical device and voiding its impact."[127]

Cost-benefit analysis was intended from the beginning as a strategy for limiting the play of politics in public investment decisions. In 1936, though, army engineers did not envision that this method would have to be grounded in economic principles, or that it would require volumes of regulations to establish how to do it, or that such regulations might have to be standardized throughout the government and applied to almost every category of public action. The transformation of cost-benefit analysis into a universal standard of rationality, backed up by thousands of pages of rules, cannot be attributed to the megalomania of experts, but rather to bureaucratic conflict in a context of overwhelming public distrust. Though tools like this one can scarcely provide more than a guide to analysis and a language of debate, there has been strong pressure to make them into something more. The ideal of mechanical objectivity has by now been internalized by many practitioners of the method, who would like to see decisions made according to "a routine that, once set in motion by appropriate value judgments on the part of those politically responsible and accountable, would—like the universe of the deists—run its course without further interference from the top."[128] This, the ideal of economists, originated as a form of political and bureaucratic culture. That culture has helped to shape other sciences as well.

Chapter Seven
U.S. Army Engineers and the Rise of Cost-Benefit Analysis

Epigraph from *Congressional Record*, 80 (1936), 7685. Need I stipulate here that my use of this bit of grandiloquence implies no fondness for the notorious racist who uttered it?

1. Shallat, "Engineering Policy"; Calhoun, *American Civil Engineer*, 141–181.

2. Harold L. Ickes, "Foreword," to Maass, *Muddy Waters*, ix.

3. Lundgreen, "Engineering Education"; Porter, "Chemical Revolution of Mineralogy."

4. Lewis, *Charles Ellet*, 11; Shallat, "Engineering Policy," 12–14.

5. Chandler, *Visible Hand*; Hoskin and Macve, "Accounting and the Examination."

6. Lewis, *Charles Ellet*, 17–20, 54; Calhoun, *Intelligence of a People*, 301–304.

7. E.g., Fink, *Argument* (1882).

8. Pingle, "Early Development." On American developments, beginning with the Gallatin report of 1808 on the value of western lands, see Hines, "Precursors to Benefit-Cost Analysis."

9. Hays, "Preface, 1969," in *Conservation*; Wiebe, *Search for Order*; Haskell, *Emergence of Professional Social Science*.

10. House of Representatives, Committee on Flood Control, *Flood Control Plans and New Projects: Hearings . . .* , April 20 to May 14, 1941, 495. To be sure, McSpadden was playing to the crowd, and in fact used economic quantification rather effectively in his testimony. It didn't hurt that he was supported by Oklahoma oil interests. For once, a dam was moved—far enough to save the house.

11. Wright, "The Value and Influences of Labor Statistics" (1904), quoted in Brock, *Investigation and Responsibility*, 154.

12. W. Nelson, *Roots of American Bureaucracy*, chap. 4; Schiesl, *Politics of Efficiency*.

13. Glaeser, *Public Utility Economics*, chap. 6. Glaeser agreed with the ICC that an objective valuation of utility capital was impossible, and called instead for reliance on the judgment of expert professionals (438, 500, 638–639, 696).

14. Keller, *Regulating a New Economy*, 50, 63; also Brock, *Investigation and Responsibility*, 192–200.

15. M. Keller, *Affairs of State*, 428; Skowronek, *Building a New American State*, 144–151.

16. M. Keller, *Affairs of State*, 381–382; Hays, *Conservation*, 93, 213; Reuss and Walker, *Financing Water Resources Development*, 14.

17. 61st Cong., 2d sess., 1910, H.D. 678 [5732], Channel from Aransas Pass Harbor through Turtle Cove to Corpus Christi, Texas. For another example, see R. Gray, *National Waterway*, 222–223.

18. N.A. 77/496/3, Board of Engineers for Rivers and Harbors, Administrative Files, 91, 125.

19. 69th Cong., 1st sess. (1925), H.D. 125, Skagit River, Washington, 21. Or the calculation might be reversed: the capitalized value of expected flood damages defined the limit of permissible expenditure. This method was criticized by G. White, "Limit of Economic Justification."

20. 69th Cong., 1st sess. (1925), H.D. 123.

21. 73d Cong., 1st sess. (1933), H.D. 31 [9758], Kanawha River, West Virginia.

22. 73d Cong., 1st sess. (1933), H.D. 45, Bayou Lafourche, Louisiana.

23. Hammond, "Convention and Limitation."

24. Barber, *New Era to New Deal*, 21.

25. The mean calculated benefit-cost ratio for flood-control projects varied enormously by region. In most places (according to an optimistic accounting) it was between 1.6 and 3.0 or 4.0, but in the lower Mississippi it was 4.8, and in

the upper Mississippi 13.7. The need to spread its largesse more evenly explains why the Corps refused to assign priority to projects according to their benefit-cost ratios. See H.R., Committee on Public Works, *Costs and Benefits of the Flood Control Program*, 85th Cong., 1st sess., House Committee Print no. 1, April 17, 1957.

26. Arnold, *1936 Flood Control Act.*

27. Lowi, "State in Political Science," 5.

28. *Congressional Record*, 90 (1944), 8241, 4221.

29. John Overton in *Congressional Record*, 83 (1938), 8603.

30. H.R., Committee on Flood Control, *Comprehensive Flood Control Plans: Hearings*, 76th Cong., 3d sess., 1940, 13; idem, *Flood Control Plans and New Projects: 1943 and 1944 Hearings*, 78th Cong., 1st and 2d sess., 20.

31. The 1.03 ratio refers to a project on the Lehigh River, Pennsylvania: H.R., Committee on Flood Control, *Flood Control Bill of 1946*, 79th Cong., 2d sess., April–May 1946, 23–36. On the Neches-Angelina: H.R., Committee on Public Works, Subcommittee on Rivers and Harbors, *Rivers and Harbors Bill of 1948*, 80th Cong., 2d sess., February–April 1948, 189. On Prescott Bush: Senate, Committee on Public Works, Subcommittee on Flood Control—Rivers and Harbors, *Hearings: Rivers and Harbors—Flood Control, 1954*, 83d Cong., 2d sess., July 1954, 20.

32. All from *Congressional Record*, 80 (1936), 8641, 7758, 7576.

33. Cited in Ferejohn, *Pork Barrel Politics*, 21.

34. H.R., Committee on Public Works, Subcommittee to Study Civil Works, *Study of Civil Works: Hearings*, 82d Cong., 2d sess., March–May 1952, 3 vols., part 1, at 31, 11.

35. H.R., Committee on Flood Control, *Hearings: Comprehensive Flood Control Plans*, 75th Cong., 1st sess., March–April 1938, 306–307; H.R., Committee on Public Works, Subcommittee on Flood Control, *Hearings: Deauthorize Project for Dillon Dam, Licking River, Ohio*, 80th Cong., 1st sess., June 1947,.81. Of those who opposed the dam, Corry hinted darkly: "Frankly, we question their motives. We do not know what their motives are. We do not believe that they have been brought out at this hearing." The opponents were, in fact, the unfortunates upstream, who were about to find their houses and farms under a hundred feet of water.

36. On the current politics of Mississippi River control, see McPhee, *Control of Nature*, part 1, "Atchafalaya."

37. H.R., Committee on Flood Control, *Hearings*, 1938, at 914, 927–928.

38. Ibid., 927, 912.

39. H.R., Committee on Flood Control, *Flood Control Plans and New Projects: Hearings . . .*, April–May 1941, at 728–729, 732.

40. Ibid., 824, 825. Whittington, who was less inclined to grandstanding, finally became impatient with this exchange: "I don't believe the Army engineers are any freer from political pressure than we are here; but I don't think there is any unrighteous or crooked pressure."

41. H.R., Committee on Public Works, Subcommittee on Rivers and Harbors, *Rivers and Harbors Bill, 1948: Hearings . . .*, 80th Cong., 2d sess., February–April 1948, at 198–199, 201.

42. N.A. 77/111/1552/7249, "Outline of Review. Project Application," dated August 31, 1935; H.R., Committee on Flood Control, *1946 Hearings*, 119–122.

43. H.R., Committee on Flood Control, *1946 Hearings*, 392, 675; Senate, Committee on Public Works, Subcommittee on Flood Control and River and Harbor Improvements, *Hearings: Rivers and Harbors—Flood Control Emergency Act*, 80th Cong., 2d sess., May–June 1948, at 77–82. Such language may also be found in project reports: for example, 76th Cong., 2d sess., H.D. 655 [10504], *Fall River and Beaver Creek, S. Dak.* Once, at least, the Senate even recommended a new dam without a Corps report. This came at the end of years of disagreement between Massachusetts and Connecticut, which wanted flood control on the Connecticut River, and Vermont, which would get most of the submerged land and very little of the benefit. Overton took great care to mark this compromise as exceptional, so it would not be a precedent. See *Congressional Record*, 90 (1944), 8557.

44. H.R., Committee on Flood Control, *1943 and 1944 Hearings*, vol. 1, 1943, 190–233, quotes at 196, 225.

45. H.R., Committee on Flood Control, *Hearings, 1941*, 512–521, excerpted from some exceptional hearings of the Board of Engineers on a flood control project for the Little Missouri River. Meeting in Washington, the Board had turned it down. The new round of hearings in Arkansas, explained board chairman Thomas M. Robins, was "due to the very strenuous efforts of your very able senator from Arkansas, Senator Miller." Those efforts had evidently been exerted throughout the process, for the official Corps report of 1940 had already adopted "irregular" methods in order to quantify recreational benefits and to predict generous increases in farm income, and hence to get the benefit-cost ratio even as high as 0.92. See 76th Cong., 2d sess., H.D. 837 [10505], *Little Missouri River, Ark.*, 50.

46. See H.R., Committee on Flood Control, *Hearings, 1938*, 270–275, in which a representative of the Chamber of Commerce of Chicopee, Massachusetts, complained that a levee on the Connecticut River in the town really was economically justified, and that the Corps' negative report resulted from an inadequate appreciation of the indirect damages due to the closing of factories and consequent unemployment.

47. The Corps is routinely charged with fierce resistance to multiple-use water management until sometime in the 1950s. That interpretation seems to have originated in attacks on the Corps by supporters of the Bureau of Reclamation, particularly Maass, *Muddy Waters*. He made the Bureau stand for rational, systematic management within the executive branch, the Corps for narrowminded pork barrel politics under the patronage of Congress. I find that the Corps was remarkably bold during the 1940s and even 1930s in pursuing new goals of river control (if only to improve its benefit-cost ratios), especially given that its mandate limited it to navigation and flood control. In the late 1950s, the Corps enlisted Maass as a consultant. The charge that he was bought off is unfair, but professional involvement with the Corps certainly improved his opinion of the agency. He claimed that it at last embraced multiple-use river planning in those years. See Reuss, *Interview with Arthur Maass*, 6.

254 NOTES TO PAGES 162–170

48. Testimony of E. W. Opie, H.R., Committee on Flood Control, *1946 Hearings*, 86–90.

49. See ibid. Quotes are from Senate, Committee on Commerce, *Hearings: Flood Control*, 79th Cong., 2d sess., June 1946, at 157, 228. Upstream interests were slightly more effective. A request from the governor of Virginia at least convinced the Senate to lower the dam by 20 feet, at some cost to the calculated benefit-cost ratio. See *Congressional Record*, 92 (1946), 7087. In 1934, a Corps report called flooding on the Rappahannock "inconsequential." N.A. 77/111/1418/7249.

50. The 1946 hearings are H.R., Committee on Rivers and Harbors, *Hearings . . . on . . . the Improvement of the Arkansas River and Tributaries . . .*, 79th Cong., 2d sess., May 8–9, 1946, quotes at 3, 113; see also Moore and Moore, *The Army Corps*, 31–33.

51. Senate, Committee on Commerce, *Hearings: Rivers and Harbors*, 79th Cong., 2d sess., June 1946, at 2, 39–45.

52. Ibid., 61, 75, 86, 142–143.

53. Ibid., 121–122, 125–126, 131. The Corps rebuttal report is printed at 143–153.

54. Senate, Committee on Commerce, Subcommittee on Rivers and Harbors, *Hearings: Construction of Certain Public Works on Rivers and Harbors*, 66th Cong., 1st sess., June 1939, at 6, 10.

55. H.R., Committee on Rivers and Harbors, *Hearings . . . on the Improvement of Waterway Connecting the Tombigbee and Tennessee Rivers, Ala. and Miss.*, 79th Cong., 2d sess., May 1–2, 1946. Pp. 3–117 contain the 1939 report; 119–178 the 1946 revision; 179ff. the hearings; quote at 185.

56. H.R., Committee on Appropriations, *Investigation of Corps of Engineers Civil Works Programs: Hearings before the Subcommittee on Deficiencies and Army Civil Functions*, 82d Cong., 1st sess., 1951; 2 vols., vol. 2, quote at 154–155. Later there was a struggle over how to put environmental values into the analysis; see Stine, "Environmental Politics."

57. See, among many possible examples, H.R., Committee on Public Works, Subcommittee on Flood Control, *Deauthorize Dillon Dam* (1947), 8–11; Senate, Committee on Public Works, Subcommittee on Flood Control, *1948 Hearings*, 100–112; E. Peterson, *Big Dam Foolishness*; Leuchtenberg, *Flood Control Politics*, 49.

58. H.R., Committee on Public Works, Subcommittee to Study Civil Works, *Study of Civil Works: Hearings* (1952), part 2; idem, *The Flood Control Program of the Department of Agriculture; Report*, 82d Cong., 2d sess., December 5, 1952.

59. See H.R., Committee on Flood Control, *1946 Hearings*, 114.

60. Leopold and Maddock, *Flood Control Controversy*.

61. H.R., Committee on Flood Control, *1943 and 1944 Hearings*, vol. 2 (1944), 621.

62. "Memorandum from Harlan H. Barrows, Director CVPS to Commissioner [Harry Bashore], March 15, 1944," in N.A. 115/7/639/131.5.

63. Memorandum from John Page to Secretary of Interior Harold Ickes,

dated March 28, 1939, N.A. 115/7/639/131.5. His instances of cooperation included planning for both the Pine Flat (Kings River) and Friant dams.

64. Memorandum, Ickes to Roosevelt, July 19, 1939, N.A. 115/7/639/131.5.

65. Worster, *Rivers of Empire*, chap. 5; Reisner, *Cadillac Desert*.

66. The files of the Bureau of Reclamation begin with a letter from W. P. Boone of the Kings River Water Association, dated January 2, 1936 (N.A. 115/7/1643/301). The possibilities of government dams on the Kings had already been noticed by the Federal Power Commission: see Ralph R. Randell, *Report to the Federal Power Commission on the Storage Resources of the South and Middle Forks of Kings River, California* (Washington, D.C.: Federal Power Commission, June 5, 1930), a copy of which is in N.A. 115/7/1643/ B. W. Gearhart's bill was H.R. 1972, dated February 7, 1939.

67. "Kings Park and Pine Flat Tie Up Fails," *San Francisco Chronicle*, March 30, 1939, 12; letter, L. B. Chambers to Harry L. Haehl, August 18, 1938, N.A., San Bruno, Calif., R.G. 77, uncatalogued general administrative files (1913–1942) of main office, South Pacific Division, Corps of Engineers, Box 17, FC 501. For further correspondence between water companies and the Corps, see N.A. (Suitland) 77/111/678/7402/1.

68. See memorandum from McCasland to unnamed "Hydraulic Engineer," dated July 22, 1939; S. P. McCasland, *Kings River, California. Project Report No. 29*, dated June 1939; both in N.A. 115/7/642/301.

69. See penciled memorandum of telephone call "by R. A. Sterzik" dated February 25, 1939, which the unnamed recipient of the call recorded as a chart giving annual benefits, annual cost, and "degree of protection" (measured inversely as frequency of floods exceeding capacity) for three reservoir volumes. This pertained to the Kern River, which soon afterward was swept up in the same controversy that surrounded the Kings. N.A., San Bruno, R.G. 77, accession no. 9NS-77-91–033, Box 3, folder labeled "Kern River Survey."

70. Memorandum, May 6, 1939, by B. W. Steele (principal engineer) to the Board of Engineers, recommending a reservoir with capacity of 780,000 acre feet; letter, May 16, 1939, M. C. Tyler, assistant chief of engineers, to Warren T. Hannum, division engineer; "Comment" (on this letter), May 29, 1939, by L. B. Chambers, district engineer, to chief of engineers via division engineer; letter, June 1939?, Hannum to Board of Engineers; all in N.A. 77/111/678/7402/1; memorandum, May 18, 1939, Chambers to Hannum, in N.A. (San Bruno), general administrative files, main office of South Pacific Division of Corps, Box 17, FC 501. The location of the (undated) graphs in the files suggests they were prepared by, or under, Steele. Since they supported the smaller dam, it is significant and perhaps surprising that the files of the Bureau of Reclamation also contain a copy, along with the district engineer's original report.

71. See letter, December 11, 1939, R. A. Wheeler (chief of engineers) to John Page (commissioner of reclamation). Page recommended the change on the same day in a memorandum to the chief engineer in Denver. See N.A. 115/7/642/301.

72. See Page memorandum in previous note; also a letter, October 28, 1939, Denver chief engineer to Page, which I found in the files of the Corps, N.A. 77/111/678/7402.

73. In California they wanted to credit only half of this quarter to irrigation; see memoranda, June 15, 1939, district engineer Chambers to division engineer Hannum; and June 16, 1939, Hannum to Board of Engineers, in N.A. (San Bruno), R.G. 77, general administrative files of main office, South Pacific Division, Box 17, FC 501.

74. This equal division of benefits was proposed in McCasland's *Kings River Project* (note 68); see especially the report summary in the files of the Corps of Engineers. It is attached there to some critical comments by division engineer Hannum, and an equally critical letter (dated January 16, 1940) to the assistant chief of engineers, Thomas M. Robins. Hannum argued that the benefits of flood control far exceeded those of irrigation for the project. But the Corps engineers in Washington were by then feeling pressure from the president, and were eager to advise him that an agreement had been reached; see letter, January 16, 1940, Robins to Page, all in N.A. 77/111/678/7402/1.

75. 76th Cong., 3d sess., H.D. 630 [10503], *Kings River and Tulare Lake, California . . .: Preliminary Examination and Survey* [by Corps of Engineers], February 2, 1940; idem, H.D. 631 [10501], *Kings River Project in California. . .: Report of the Bureau of Reclamation*, February 12, 1940. On the premature release of the Corps report, see memoranda by Ickes and Frederic Delano (of the National Resources Planning Board) to Roosevelt, and the explanation by Harry Woodring, secretary of war, in N.A. (San Bruno), general administrative files of main office, South Pacific Division of Corps, Box 17, FC 501.

76. Roosevelt's decision is printed in the Bureau's report (H.D. 631). On his understanding of the mission of the Corps, and for the Ickes remark, see memoranda by Roosevelt to Woodring, June 6, 1940, and Ickes to Roosevelt, received in the White House the same day; copies of both in N.A. (San Bruno), general administrative files, main office, South Pacific Division of Corps, Box 17, FC 501.

77. Maass and Anderson, *Desert Shall Rejoice*, 264–265; Hundley, *Great Thirst*, 261.

78. H.R., Committee on Flood Control, *Hearings, 1941*, 97ff.; idem, *1943 and 1944 Hearings*, vol. 1, 249ff.; vol. 2, 588ff.; *Congressional Record*, 90 (1944), 4123–4124.

79. Maass and Anderson, *Desert Shall Rejoice*, 260. The Corps changed its allocation of benefits in the Kings River from time to time, evidently for reasons of political convenience: see Maass, *Muddy Waters*, chap. 5. But these changes also reflected genuine uncertainty, as evidenced by the appearance of abstract discussions of allocation methods in internal documents, such as "Summary of Cost Allocation Studies on Authorized Pine Flat Reservoir and Related Facilities, Kings River, California," a report by the Sacramento District, Corps of Engineers, dated October 28, 1946. I thank Allen Louie of the Sacramento District Planning Division for providing me with a copy of this document.

80. Senate, Committee on Irrigation and Reclamation, Subcommittee on Senate Resolution 295, *Hearings: Central Valley Project, California*, 78th

Cong., 2d sess., July 1944; *Fresno Bee*, issues of April 25, 26, 29, May 29, September 27, 30, October 5, 23, all 1941; also several papers in June 1943. A particularly early expression of opposition to the big water interests is a leaflet, the *Pine Flat News*, dated April 15, 1940, in N.A. 115/7/639/023.

81. H.R., Committee on Public Works, Subcommittee to Study Civil Works, *Economic Evaluation of Federal Water Resource Development Projects: Report . . . by Mr. [Robert] Jones of Alabama*, 82d Cong., 2d sess., House Committee Print no. 24, December 5, 1952, at 14–18. Sometimes the Bureau didn't even convert from gross to net agricultural revenue: see A. B. Roberts, *Task Force Report on Water Resources Projects: Certain Aspects of Power, Irrigation and Flood Control Projects*, prepared for the Commission on Organization of the Executive Branch of the Government, Appendix K (Washington, D.C.: USGPO, January 1949), 21.

82. Leslie A. Miller et al., *Task Force Report on Natural Resources: Organization and Policy in the Field of Natural Resources*, prepared for the Commission on Organization of the Executive Branch of Government, Appendix K (Washington, D.C.: USGPO, January 1949), 23.

83. H.R., Committee on Public Works, Subcommittee to Study Civil Works, *Economic Evaluation*, 7; idem., *Hearings*, 489–490; H.R., Committee on Flood Control, *1943 and 1944 Hearings*, vol. 2 (1944), 640, 633. The Bureau even applied this form of accounting to whole river basins, so that better projects could cover for the worst ones: Reisner, *Cadillac Desert*, 140–141. Elizabeth Drew, "Dam Outrage," 56, cited a remark that cost-benefit "measurements are pliant enough to prove the feasibility of growing bananas on Pike's Peak." This remark could only have been inspired by the Bureau of Reclamation, which indeed had to be particularly inventive in the mountains and high plains of Colorado.

84. John M. Clark, Eugene L. Grant, Maurice M. Kelso, *Report of Panel of Consultants on Secondary or Indirect Benefits of Water-Use Projects*, dated June 26, 1952, 3, 12. The occasion for the manual was the Bureau's refusal to endorse the F.I.A.R.B.C. *Proposed Practices*, discussed below. There is a copy of this report in N.A. 315/6/4.

85. H.R., Committee on Public Works, Subcommittee to Study Civil Works, *The Civil Functions Program of the Corps of Engineers, United States Army. Report . . . by Mr. Jones of Alabama*, 82d Cong., 2d sess., December 5, 1952, at 6, reported that since 1930, the Board of Engineers had decided unfavorably on 55.2 percent of surveys and preliminary reports. Many rejected projects were later approved, as benefits came to be defined more expansively. Even so, the Corps used its cost-benefit yardstick to delay the more doubtful projects.

86. In 1938, Sacramento district engineer L. B. Chambers decided against a project on the Humboldt River in Nevada. The interests protested to Warren T. Hannum, the division engineer in San Francisco, complaining that their water had been valued at only $1 per acre-foot, while the city folk in southern California were being credited with values twenty or more times higher. Hannum, seemingly convinced, asked Chambers to justify the analysis, which he then did in some detail. N.A. (San Bruno), general administrative files, main office, South Pacific Division of Corps, Box 17, FC 501. The grasshopper calculation is men-

tioned in an unpublished autobiography by William Whipple, Jr., dated 1987, held by the archives of the Office of History, Army Corps of Engineers. For the number of engineers, see U.S. Commission on Organization of the Executive Branch of Government, *The Hoover Commission Report* (New York: McGraw-Hill, 1949; reprinted, Westport, Conn.: Greenwood Press, 1970), 279.

87. From River and Harbor Circular Letter no. 39, June 9, 1936, in N.A. 77/142/11. Other early circulars on economic analysis include R&H 43 (June 22, 1936); R&H 46 (August 12, 1938); R&H 49 (August 23, 1938); R&H 42 (August 11, 1939); R&H 43 (August 14, 1939); R&H 62 (December 27, 1939); R&H 29 (June 1, 1940); R&H 43 (August 30, 1940). These may be found in N.A. 77/142/11–16. Many of the circulars of 1939 and 1940 are concerned with interagency harmonization of economic procedures. Some manuals from the late 1950s and early 1960s may be found in Office of History, Army Corps of Engineers, XIII–2, 1956–62 Manuals.

88. Quoted in a mimeographed pamphlet by J. R. Brennan, written for the War Department, Corps of Engineers, Los Angeles Engineer District, *Benefits from Flood Control. Procedure to be followed in the Los Angeles Engineer District in appraising benefits from flood control improvements*, December 1, 1943 (earlier editions, October 1, 1939, April 15, 1940), N.A., Pacific Southwest Region (Laguna Niguel, California), 77/800.5. The Chief of Engineers approved this pamphlet for circulation to other districts without sanctioning it as generally binding.

89. H.R., Committee on Flood Control, *Hearings on Levees and Flood Walls, Ohio River Basin*, 75th Cong., 1st sess., June 1937, at 140–141.

90. An example of historical damages ($13,888) averaging much less than "potential damages" ($43,000) is in H.R., 76th Cong., 3d sess. (1940), H.D. 719 [10505], *Walla Walla River and Tributaries, Oregon and Washington*, 17. For a formal discussion of these methods, see Corps of Engineers, Los Angeles Engineer District, *Benefits from Flood Control*, chaps. 1–2. These general methods were often cited in project reports, and occasionally even in congressional hearings, e.g., H.R., Committee on Flood Control, *Hearings, 1938*, 207.

91. 76th Cong., 2d sess., 1940, H.D. 479 [10503], *Chattanooga, Tenn. and Rossville, Ga.*, 29–30, 33.

92. "Memorandum of the States of Colorado, Kansas, and Nebraska with Reference to a Flood Control Plan for the Republican River Basin," July 13, 1942; Memorandum from Kansas City district engineer A. M. Neilson to division engineer, April 11, 1941, both in N.A. 77/111/1448/7402.

93. Letter, C. L. Sturdevant, division engineer, to Thomas M. Robins, office of chief of engineers, December 11, 1939, N.A., 77/111/1448/7402; also H.R., 76th Cong., 3d sess. (1940), H.D. 842 [10505], *Republican River, Nebr. and Kans.* (Preliminary Examination and Survey).

94. The agreement consisted mainly of heaping together most projects that either agency had ever considered. There is extensive discussion in *Congressional Record*, 90 (1944), e.g., at 4132, on the Republican River. For project surveys see 81st Cong., 2d sess. (1949–50), H.D. 642 [11429a], *Kansas River and Tributaries, Colorado, Nebraska, and Kansas*; also Wolman et al., *Report*.

95. H.R., Committee on Public Works, Subcommittee to Study Civil Works, *Study of Civil Works*, 25; idem, *Civil Functions of Corps*, 34 (both 1952).

96. J. L. Peterson of the Ohio River Division of the Corps, 1954, cited in Moore and Moore, *Army Corps*, 37–39.

97. For Wheeler, see H.R., Committee on Rivers and Harbors, *Hearings on Tombigbee and Tennessee*, 185. On Isabella reservoir: *Definite Project Report. Isabella Project. Kern River, California. Part VII—Recreational Facilities* (August 27, 1948), Appendix A. "Preliminary Report of Recreational Facilities by National Park Service," in N.A. (San Bruno), R.G. 77, accession no. 9NS-77-91-033, Box 2. On the survey of experts: U.S. Department of the Interior, National Park Service, *The Economics of Public Recreation: An Economic Study of the Monetary Value of Recreation in the National Parks* (Washington, D.C.: Land and Recreational Planning Division, National Park Service, 1949). The Congress had authorized the Corps to support waterway traffic by yachts, houseboats, etc., in legislation of 1932; see Turhollow, *Los Angeles District*.

98. Senate, Committee on Public Works, Subcommittee on Flood Control—Rivers and Harbors, *Hearings: Evaluation of Recreational Benefits from Reservoirs*, 85th Cong., 1st sess., March 1957, at 33.

99. The need for "objectivity" was invoked by Edmund Muskie of Maine after Elmer Staats of the Bureau of the Budget spoke of the element of judgment: Senate, Committee on Public Works, Subcommittee on Flood Control—Rivers and Harbors, *Hearings: Land Acquisition Policies and Evaluation of Recreation Benefits*, 86th Cong., 2d sess., May 1960, 151; see also U.S. Water Resources Council, *Evaluation Standards for Primary Outdoor Recreation Benefits* (Washington, D.C.: USGPO, June 4, 1964).

100. N.A. 315/2/1, first file, called "Interdepartmental Group," 1943–1945. Price's paper concerned a proposed dam on the Alabama-Coosa river system.

101. N.A. 315/2/1, 1st meeting, January 26, 1944.

102. N.A. 315/2/1, meetings 12 (January 25, 1945), 23 (December 27, 1945), 24 (January 31, 1946), 27 (April 25, 1946).

103. N.A. 315/6/1, 1st meeting, April 24, 1946. The members were G. L. Beard, chief of flood control division, Corps of Engineers; J. W. Dixon, director of project planning, Bureau of Reclamation; F. L. Weaver, chief of river basin division, Federal Power Commission; E. H. Wiecking, office of the secretary of agriculture. Two members of the staff were identified as economists: N. A. Back of Agriculture and G. E. McLaughlin of the Bureau of Reclamation. To them should be added M. M. Regan of Agriculture, who appeared at the second meeting. R. C. Price was also on the staff.

104. The first progress report on "Qualitative Aspects of Benefit-Cost Practices" used by the four agencies is attached to the minutes of the 29th meeting of the subcommittee; the second progress report on "Measurement Aspects of Benefit-Cost Practices" was distributed for the 50th meeting, in N.A. 315/6/1 and 315/6/3. See Federal Inter-Agency River Basin Committee, Subcommittee on Benefits and Costs, *Proposed Practices for Economic Analysis of River Basin Projects* (Washington, D.C.: USGPO, 1950), 58–70, 71–85.

105. A copy is in N.A. 315/6/3, 55th meeting. The principal authors, identified in an almost illegible carbon copy of assignments of tasks in 315/6/5, were evidently M. M. Regan and E. H. Wiecking, with assistance from E. C. Weitsell and N. A. Back.

106. The second edition of *Proposed Practices* (1958) took an even stronger line and denied their legitimacy altogether.

107. FIARBC, *Proposed Practices*, 7, 27. The book retreated some in the 1958 edition, deleting the quoted sentence and listing the value of life with scenic values among "intangibles." But it added a footnote declaring that "it may be desirable in some cases to provide uniform allowances of justifiable expenditure values for certain intangibles" (p. 7) On this topic, see Porter "Objectivity as Standardization."

108. See "First Progress Report of the Work Group on Benefits and Costs: Arkansas-White-Red Report" (by a subcommittee of an interagency committee on the Arkansas-White-Red rivers), in N.A. 315/6/5; also Wallace R. Vawter, "Case Study of the Arkansas-White-Red Basin Inter-Agency Committee," in U.S. Commission on Organization of the Executive Branch of Government [second Hoover Commission], Task Force on Water Resources and Power, *Report on Water Resources and Power* (n.p. June 1955), 3 vols., vol. 3, 1395–1472. Asked for its advice, the F.I.A.R.B.C. subcommittee first recommended an index of 150 for prices received and 175 for prices paid by farmers, then decided to set both at 215, so that the ratios remained constant and the projection was without effect.

The agencies were driven to cooperate in these river basin committees by fear that independent bureaucracies comparable to the Tennessee Valley Authority might be created; see Goodwin, "Valley Authority Idea."

109. H.R., Committee on Public Works, Subcommittee to Study Civil Works, *Study of Civil Works* (1952), 7. Pick dismissed Arthur Maass's severe criticism of the Corps in *Muddy Waters* as an attempt to build up "his philosophy of government, which is a greater centralized authority in the executive branch." Among Maass's crimes was to use the National Archives: "Criticism of the Corps of Engineers is the vehicle selected through which to peddle the philosophy of Government of a small and effective group who have been able to gain access to the archives of this great Government of ours to select and use to their advantage any information which can be found in the writings and sayings of the leaders of those various sections of Government, that is not generally available to all of the people of the United States." In response to a critical article by the governor of Wyoming, he wrote: "Apparently Mr. Miller would have one believe that the corps can influence the vote of the United States Senate. This is, of course, an absurd position." Ibid., 84, 107.

110. See Bureau of Budget files held by Office of History, Corps of Engineers, file labeled "Bureau Projects with Issues. 1947–1960. Corps Projects with Issues. 1948–1960," e.g., a report critical of recreation benefits dated May 31, 1960, and another opposing a project with a calculated benefit-cost ratio of 0.93: this number should be decisive except in the case of "unusual and major intangible benefits" such as loss of life. On the fruitless efforts of the Budget Bureau to rein in the Corps, see Ferejohn, *Pork Barrel Politics*, 79–86. The Budget Bureau's successor agency, the Office of Management and Budget, has become the most outspoken advocate of cost-benefit analysis in the federal government. Its power, on paper at least, reached a peak under Ronald Reagan, who required all new regulations to be supported by cost-benefit analyses. This dis-

couraged new regulations, as intended, but was too unwieldy for O.M.B. to enforce in detail. See Smith, *Environmental Policy*.

111. From a draft manuscript, dated December 15, 1949, in Office of History, Army Corps of Engineers, files on Civil Works Reorganization, 1943–49, First Hoover Commission, III 3–13, "corresp: fragments, MG Pick. 1949." U.S. Commission On Organization of the Executive Branch of Government, *The, [first] Hoover Commission Report on Organization of the Executive Branch of Government* (New York: McGraw-Hill, 1949), chap. 12. For Corps rebuttal by C. H. Chorpening, see H.R., Committee on Public Works, Subcommittee to Study Civil Works, *Study of Civil Works* (1952), 61.

112. U.S. Commission [2d Hoover Commission], *Report on Water Resources* (1955), vol. 1, 24, 104–110; vol. 2, 630, 652–653. The call for an objective panel to evaluate projects was echoed by Engineers Joint Council, *Principles of a Sound Water Policy* (1951 and) *1957 Restatement*, Report No. 105, May 1957, and later by Carter, "Water Projects." On the Hoover commissions and the effort to streamline American bureaucracy, see Crenson and Rourke, "American Bureaucracy."

113. Moore and Moore, *Army Corps*; Reuss, "Coping with Uncertainty."

114. E.g., Clark, *Economics of Public Works*, a work prepared during the Depression under the National Planning Board and the National Resources Board of the Public Works Administration. George Stigler, who wrote an influential paper on the "new welfare economics" in 1943, cut this set of teeth while apportioning benefits for the National Resources Planning Board; see his *Unregulated Economist*, 52.

115. Hammond, *Benefit-Cost Analysis*; idem, "Convention and Limitation."

116. The highway officials developed a "Red Book" to match the water analysts' green one: American Association of State Highway Officials (AASHO), Committee on Planning and Design Policies, *Road User Benefit Analysis for Highway Improvements* (Washington, D.C.: AASHO, 1952); see also Kuhn, *Public Enterprise Economics*.

117. Fortun and Schweber, "Scientists and the Legacy."

118. Leonard, "War as Economic Problem"; Orlans, "Academic Social Scientists."

119. Some economists have wanted to deny that their specialty could have been born impure, and have proposed instead that it was a natural outgrowth of welfare economics, specifically the Kaldor-Hicks reading of Pareto optimality. But histories of cost-benefit analysis by practitioners often recognize its bureaucratic origins; this applies not only to Hammond's critical history, but also Prest and Turvey, "Cost-Benefit Analysis"; Dorfman, "Forty Years." Although the former is a British paper, both identify the origins of cost-benefit analysis specifically with the Army Corps of Engineers.

120. U.S. Bureau of Agricultural Economics, "Value and Price of Irrigation Water," typescript, marked for administrative use only, by the California Regional Office (Berkeley), dated October 1943, no authors named, University of California, Berkeley, Water Resources Library Archives, G4316 G3-1. My impression that most BAE planning was not based on cost-benefit considerations is informed by a cursory inspection of its archives, which suggest that even with respect to water projects it did not habitually undertake to quantify benefits be-

fore the late 1940s. See, for example, U.S. Department of Agriculture, *Water Facilities Area Planning Handbook*, January 1, 1941, in N.A. 83/179/5. After 1950, agricultural economists began publishing regularly on the costs and benefits of water projects, later expanding to the analysis of other programs; for example: Regan and Greenshields, "Benefit-Cost Analysis"; Gertel, "Cost Allocation"; Ciriacy-Wantrup, "Cost Allocation"; Griliches, "Research Costs." On the BAE's history, see Hawley, "Economic Inquiry," 293–299.

121. Regan and Greenshields, "Benefit-Cost," relies on sources like Clark, *Public Works*, and Grant, *Engineering Economy*.

122. Margolis, "Secondary Benefits"; Eckstein, *Water-Resource Development*; Krutilla and Eckstein, *Multiple-Purpose River Development*; McKean, *Efficiency in Government*; Margolis, "Economic Evaluation"; U.S. Bureau of the Budget, Panel of Consultants [Maynard M. Hufschmidt, chairman, Krutilla, Margolis, Stephen Marglin], *Standards and Criteria for Formulating and Evaluating Federal Water Resource Developments* (Washington, D.C.: Bureau of the Budget, June 30, 1961); Haveman, *Water Resource Investment*.

123. See Sagoff, *Economy of the Earth*, 76.

124. Weisbrod, *Economics of Public Health*; Weisbrod, "Costs and Benefits of Medical Research"; Hansen, "Investment in Schooling"; Dodge and Stager, "Economic Returns to Graduate Study."

125. Topics covered in Dorfman, *Measuring Benefits*. Quote from Fritz Machlup, "Comment," on Burton Weisbrod, "Preventing High School Dropouts," at 155. His intention was to disparage Weisbrod's neglect of "noneconomic" values (Machlup's scare quotes).

126. A detailed and well-argued example, the attempt to control pollution in the Delaware River basin, is presented by Ackerman, *Uncertain Search*. His criticism is by no means limited to economic quantification.

127. Fischhoff, *Acceptable Risk*, xii, 55–57, quote at 57. While resisting the use of risk analysis by interested parties, they regard more favorably the implicit codes of professional judgment. "Narrow solutions are to be expected when professionals have a limited perspective on their own and little influence on higher-level policymaking" (p. 64).

128. Written by Partha Dasgupta, Amartya Sen, and Stephen Marglin. They called this ambition unrealizable, but aimed to pursue it as far as possible: United Nations Industrial Development Organization, *Guidelines for Project Evaluation* (Project Formulation and Evaluation Series, no. 2; New York: United Nations, 1972), 172.

References

Ackerman, Bruce, and William T. Hassler, *Clean Coal, Dirty Air*. (New Haven, Conn.: Yale University Press, 1981).

Arnold, Joseph L., *The Evolution of the 1936 Flood Control Act* (Fort Belvoir, Va.: Office of History, U.S. Army Corps of Engineers, 1988).

Barber, William J., *From New Era to New Deal: Herbert Hoover, the Economists, and American Economic Policy, 1921–1933* (Cambridge, U.K.: Cambridge University Press, 1985).

Brock, William, *Investigation and Responsibility: Public Responsibility in the United States, 1865–1900* (Cambridge, U.K.: Cambridge University Press, 1984).

Calhoun, Daniel, *The American Civil Engineer: Origins and Conflict* (Cambridge, Mass.: MIT Press, 1960).

Carter, Luther J., "Water Projects: How to Erase the 'Pork Barrel' Image," *Science*, 182, October 19, 1973, 267–269, 316.

Chandler, Alfred, Jr., *The Visible Hand: The Managerial Revolution in American Business* (Cambridge, Mass.: Harvard University Press, 1977).

Ciriacy-Wantrup, S. V., "Cost Allocation in Relation to Western Water Policies," *Journal of Farm Economics*, 36 (1954), 108–129.

Clark, John M., *Economics of Planning Public Works* (1935; reprinted New York: Augustus M. Kelley, 1965).

Crenson, Matthew A., and Francis E. Rourke, "By Way of Conclusion: American Bureaucracy since World War II," in Galambos, *New American State*, 137–177.

Dorfman, Robert, "Forty Years of Cost-Benefit Analysis," in Richard Stone and William Peterson, eds., *Econometric Contributions to Public Policy* (London: Macmillan, 1978), 268–288.

———, ed., *Measuring Benefits of Government Investments* (Washington, D.C.: Brookings Institution, 1965).

Drew, Elizabeth, "Dam Outrage: The Story of the Army Engineers," *Atlantic*, 225, April 1970, 51–62.

Eckstein, Otto, *Water-Resource Development: The Economics of Project Evaluation* (Cambridge, Mass.: Harvard University Press, 1958).

Federal Inter-Agency River Basin Committee, Subcommittee on Benefits and Costs, *Proposed Practices for Economic Analysis of River Basin Projects* (Washington, D.C.: USGPO, 1950; revised ed., 1958).

Ferejohn, John A., *Pork Barrel Politics: Rivers and Harbors Legislation, 1947–1968* (Stanford, Calif.: Stanford University Press, 1974).

Fink, Albert, *Argument ... before the Committee on Commerce of the United States House of Representatives*, March 17–18, 1882 (Washington, D.C.: USGPO, 1882).

Fortun, M., and S. S. Schweber, "Scientists and the Legacy of World War II: The Case of Operations Research," *Social Studies of Science*, 23 (1993), 595–642.

Glaeser, Martin G., *Outlines of Public Utility Economics* (New York: Macmillan, 1927).

Grant, Eugene L., *Principles of Engineering Economy* (New York: Ronald Press, 1930).

Gray, Ralph D., *The National Waterway: A History of the Chesapeake and Delaware Canal, 1769–1985*, 2d ed. (Urbana: University of Illinois Press, 1989).

Hammond, Richard J., "Convention and Limitation in Benefit-Cost Analysis," *Natural Resources Journal*, 6 (1966), 195–222.

Hansen, W. Lee, "Total and Private Rates of Return to Investment in Schooling," *Journal of Political Economy*, 71 (1963), 128–140.

Haveman, Robert, *Water Resource Investment and the Public Interest* (Nashville: Vanderbilt University Press, 1965).

Hays, Samuel P., *Conservation and the Gospel of Efficiency: The Progressive Conservation Movement, 1890–1920*, 2d ed. (Cambridge, Mass.: Harvard University Press, 1969).

Hines, Lawrence G., "Precursors to Benefit-Cost Analysis in Early United States Public Investment Projects," *Land Economics*, 49 (1973), 310–317.

Keller, Morton, *Affairs of State: Public Life in Late Nineteenth Century America* (Cambridge, Mass.: Harvard University Press, 1977).

————, *Regulating a New Economy: Public Policy and Economic Change in America, 1900–1933* (Cambridge, Mass.: Harvard University Press, 1990).

Krutilla, John, and Otto Eckstein, *Multiple-Purpose River Development* (Baltimore: Johns Hopkins University Press, 1958).

Leonard, Robert, "War as a 'Simple Economic Problem': The Rise of an Economics of Defense," in Craufurd D. Goodwin, ed., *Economics and National Security: A History of Their Interactions* (Durham, N.C.: Duke University Press, 1991), 261–283.

Leopold, Luna B., and Thomas Maddock, Jr., *The Flood Control Controversy: Big Dams, Little Dams, and Land Management* (New York: Ronald Press, 1954).

Leuchtenberg, William, *Flood Control Politics: The Connecticut River Valley Problem, 1927–1950* (Cambridge, Mass.: Harvard University Press, 1953).

Lewis, Gene D., *Charles Ellet, Jr.: The Engineer as Individualist* (Urbana: University of Illinois Press, 1968).

Lowi, Theodore J., "The State in Political Science: How We Become What We Study," *American Political Science Review*, 86 (1992), 1–7.

Lundgreen, Peter, "Engineering Education in Europe and the U.S.A., 1750–1930: The Rise to Dominance of School Culture and the Engineering Profession," *Annals of Science*, 47 (1990), 37–75.

Maass, Arthur, *Muddy Waters: The Army Engineers and the Nation's Rivers* (Cambridge, Mass.: Harvard University Press, 1951).

Maass, Arthur, and Raymond L. Anderson, *... And the Desert Shall Rejoice: Conflict, Growth, and Justice in Arid Environments* (Cambridge, Mass.: MIT Press, 1978).

McKean, Roland N., *Efficiency in Government through Systems Analysis, with Emphasis on Water Resource Development: A RAND Corporation Study* (New York: John Wiley & Sons, 1958).

McPhee, John, *The Control of Nature* (New York: Farrar, Straus & Giroux, 1989).

Margolis, Julius, "Secondary Benefits, External Economies, and the Justification of Public Investment," *Review of Economics and Statistics*, 39 (1957), 284–291.

Moore, Jamie W., and Dorothy P. Moore, *The Army Corps of Engineers and the Evolution of Federal Flood Plain Management Policy* (Boulder: Institute of Behavioral Science, University of Colorado, 1989).

Nelson, William E., *The Roots of American Bureaucracy, 1830–1900* (Cambridge, Mass.: Harvard University Press, 1987).

Peterson, Elmer T., *Big Dam Foolishness: The Problem of Modern Flood Control and Water Storage* (New York: Devin-Adair Co., 1954).

Pingle, Gautam, "The Early Development of Cost-Benefit Analysis," *Journal of Agricultural Economics*, 29 (1978), 63–71.

Prest, A. R., and R. Turvey, "Cost-Benefit Analysis: A Survey," *Economic Journal*, 75 (1965), 683–735.

Regan, Mark M., and E. L. Greenshields, "Benefit-Cost Analysis of Resource Development Programs," *Journal of Farm Economics*, 33 (1951), 866–878.

Reuss, Martin, *Water Resources, People and Issues: Interview with Arthur Maass* (Fort Belvoir, Va.: Office of History, U.S. Army Corps of Engineers, 1989).

———, "Coping with Uncertainty: Social Scientists, Engineers, and Federal Water Resource Planning," *Natural Resources Journal*, 32 (1992), 101–135.

Reuss, Martin, and Paul K. Walker, *Financing Water Resources Development: A Brief History* (Fort Belvoir, Va.: Historical Division, Office of the Chief of Engineers, 1983).

Sagoff, Mark, *The Economy of the Earth: Philosophy, Law, and the Environment* (Cambridge, U.K.: Cambridge University Press, 1988).

Schiesl, Martin J., *The Politics of Efficiency: Municipal Administration and Reform in America* (Berkeley: University of California Press, 1977).

Shallat, Todd, "Engineering Policy: The U.S. Army Corps of Engineers and the Historical Foundation of Power," *The Public Historian*, 11 (1989), 7–27.

Skrowonek, Stephen, *Building a New American State: The Expansion of National Administrative Capacities, 1877–1920* (Cambridge, U.K.: Cambridge University Press, 1982).

Smith, V. Kerry, ed., *Environmental Policy under Reagan's Executive Order; The Role of Benefit-Cost Analysis* (Chapel Hill: University of North Carolina Press, 1984).

Stigler, George, *Memoirs of an Unregulated Economist* (New York: Basic Books, 1988).

Turhollow, Anthony F., *A History of the Los Angeles District, U.S. Army Corps of Engineers* (Los Angeles: Los Angeles District, Corps of Engineers, 1975).

Weisbrod, Burton A., *Economics of Public Health: Measuring the Economic Impact of Diseases* (Philadelphia: University of Pennsylvania Press, 1961).

———, "Costs and Benefits of Medical Research: A Case Study of Poliomyelitis," in *Benefit-Cost Analysis: An Aldine Annual, 1971* (Chicago: Aldine-Atherton, 1972), 142–160.

White, Gilbert F., "The Limit of Economic Justification for Flood Protection," *Journal of Land and Public Utility Economics*, 12 (1936), 133–148.

Worster, Donald, *Rivers of Empire: Water, Aridity, and the Growth of the American West* (New York: Pantheon, 1985).

[12]

The Legal and Institutional Setting for Economic Analysis at EPA

Richard D. Morgenstern

Americans have complicated and sometimes paradoxical attitudes toward the environment. More than ninety percent identify themselves as pro-environment and, in response to surveys, routinely express strong support for clean air, clean water, and generally stringent environmental goals. Yet surveys also find that individuals often resist specific policies, particularly when these policies entail direct financial or inconvenience costs. For instance, stringent automobile inspection and maintenance programs are opposed by almost as many people as favor clean air, even though the former help ensure the latter.

Not surprisingly, the laws and institutions that shape environmental policies in the United States—cutting across all branches of government—reflect some of these same paradoxes. Congress enacts the laws and, through the oversight process, influences their implementation. The courts interpret ambiguous legislative language and, sometimes, force agencies to meet specific statutory or court-ordered deadlines. Implementation responsibilities rest exclusively with the executive branch although, increasingly, these responsibilities are being delegated to the states. The U.S. Environmental Protection Agency (EPA) is primarily responsible for administering the major environmental statutes, with some duties also carried out by other departments of government. (Some environmental laws are not implemented by EPA. For instance, the Endangered Species Act is administered by the Fish and Wildlife Service, and various federal wetlands policies are administered by a number of agencies, including the Department of Agriculture and the Army Corps of Engineers).

This chapter focuses on the uneven and sometimes inconsistent manner in which economic considerations enter into environmental decisionmaking. The focus is on the laws, the executive orders issued by Presidents over the past quarter century, and the culture of EPA, the

6   MORGENSTERN

principal implementing institution. A short section of this chapter reviews the recent substantive and procedural provisions enacted in 1995 and 1996.

THE LAWS

Unlike most other agencies (such as the National Highway Traffic Safety Administration), EPA does not administer a single, organic statute. Instead, the EPA administrator implements nine major laws and more than a dozen minor statutes. Among the major statutes, six of them form the basis for the rules examined in this volume. Three of the laws—the Clean Air Act (CAA), Clean Water Act (CWA) and Safe Drinking Water Act (SDWA)—are based on the environmental medium in which pollution occurs; the Resource Conservation and Recovery Act (RCRA) focuses primarily on a single medium (land) but deals with other matters as well; the Federal Insecticide, Fungicide and Rodenticide Act (FIFRA) deals with a particular set of products; and the Toxic Substances Control Act (TSCA) deals with chemicals in general. While all these laws share a common theme of "protection of human health and the environment," they differ in many respects, including the way economic considerations enter into the design and implementation of environmental policies.

Many of the environmental statutes set goals that, if interpreted literally, would virtually eliminate pollution or any harms therefrom. The Clean Air Act, for instance, directs the EPA administrator to set primary ambient air quality standards that, "...allowing an adequate margin of safety...protect the public health." [Clean Air Act, Section 109 (b) (1)]. Economic considerations are not mentioned in the section dealing with setting these standards. The Clean Water Act states that "... it is the national goal that the discharge of pollutants into navigable waters... and...the discharge of toxic pollutants in toxic amounts be eliminated" [Clean Water Act, Section 101 (a)]. Yet, stated so broadly, these goals beg the question: how much protection is required? Since environmental protection almost always requires some effort, how much effort is enough? How much is too much? How much degradation can be allowed until the environment is no longer considered "protected"? Interestingly, it has been argued that this statutory commitment to perfection is an impediment to the functioning of the agency.[1]

Most statutes leave it up to EPA to determine what specific requirements or limitations should be placed on the conduct of regulated entities. Typically, statutory language is general in nature, granting broad discretion to agency decisionmakers. These decisionmakers, in turn, are empowered to write rules and standards, to issue permits, and to develop

LEGAL AND INSTITUTIONAL SETTING FOR ECONOMIC ANALYSIS AT EPA   7

and oversee requirements to help achieve environmental goals. Current methods of addressing environmental problems include:

- Ambient media standards, used as benchmarks for subsequent, more narrowly defined requirements (for instance, ambient air or water quality standards)
- Emission/effluent standards, which focus on pollution at the point of release into the environment and can themselves be defined in a variety of ways including:
  - limits on total amounts released
  - limits on concentrations discharged to effluent streams
  - percentage reduction from uncontrolled levels
  - rate of emission per unit of output (such as CWA effluent limits)
- Controls on the sale and use of products that have environmental effects when used or disposed of (for instance, mobile source regulations under Clean Air Act, controls on materials affecting stratospheric ozone, and pesticide regulation under FIFRA)
- Controls on contaminants in products directly consumed (such as the SDWA)
- Controls on operations of activities that manage or use hazardous materials (RCRA requirements for management, disposal, transportation of hazardous waste)
- Targets for remediation of past releases (such as RCRA corrective action)
- Controls to prevent degradation of targeted areas or resources (such as prevention of significant deterioration requirements under the Clean Air Act or nondegradation requirements under the Clean Water Act)
- Requirements for public reporting of information (such as the SWDA and EPCRA)
- Protection of workers from exposure during employment (such as FIFRA worker protection standards)
- Decision processes, procedures and certification training requirements for private abatement of hazards (such as the TSCA lead abatement program)

Much as the implementing mechanisms vary across statutes, so do the requirements for considering costs when a regulation is being developed. Sometimes the agency is granted broad discretionary authority to consider the economic impacts of its decisions. At times it is specifically required to consider economic factors. At other times it is explicitly prohibited from considering costs. Several court decisions have held that benefit-cost studies cannot be considered by agencies unless expressly authorized by statute.

8   MORGENSTERN

Table 1 reviews the oportunities to use economic analysis under the six major statutes considered in this volume. TSCA and FIFRA contain explicit mandates for economic analysis. Under the statutes, EPA is required to balance costs and benefits in the screening and regulation of chemicals and pesticides. Apart from TSCA and FIFRA, several statutory provisions require that "costs must be reasonable." However, a 1989 court decision does not interpret this to require a formal benefit-cost analysis or even a precise calculation of costs [F.2d 177, 226 (5th Cir. 1989), modified 885 F.2d 253 (5th Cir. 1989)]. Several other provisions mandate that costs be balanced with benefits but fall short of the formal procedures used in a benefit-cost analysis. The courts generally interpret such statutes to require the agency to consider benefits in light of costs and to avoid setting limits with costs wholly disproportionate to the benefits [*Association of Pacific Fisheries v. EPA*, 615 F.2d 794, 805 (9th Cir. 1980)]. In a 1989 Clean Water Act case, the court held that the cost-balancing test precluded EPA from giving costs primary importance [*Chemical Mfrs. Association v. EPA*, 870F.2d 177, 201 (5th Cir. 1989), *modified* 885 F.2d 253 (5th Cir. 1989), *American Iron and Steel Institute v. EPA*, 526 F.2d 1027, 1051 (3rd Cir. 1977)]. A number of provisions require the agency to consider costs, among other factors, when developing regulations, typically without specifying what weight cost should be given (Downing 1995, 56).

Unlike most major statutes governing environmental regulation, the Regulatory Flexibility Act (RFA) specifically requires agencies to determine whether a regulation has significant economic impact, at least on small businesses and other small entities. When such a finding is made, agencies must identify alternative regulatory approaches for such entities that still meet the statutory objectives, albeit in a less burdensome manner. The RFA has been hailed by the Small Business Administration (SBA) as "small business' most significant mechanism for influencing Federal regulations (SBA 1996, 1)." Yet, implementation of this statute is generally recognized as spotty. Perhaps this can be traced to the fact that, at least prior to 1996, the RFA was not subject to judicial review.

Finally, it is worth noting the Administrative Procedures Act (APA), which establishes the ground rules for public involvement in the regulatory development process. Key APA provisions require that specific procedures are to be followed in proposing and promulgating regulations and that potentially impacted parties have an opportunity to comment on proposed actions. Like EPA's major implementing statutes (and unlike the RFA), failure to adhere to the APA is judicially reviewable. Not surprisingly, procedural issues are given great weight in EPA decisionmaking.

Overall, there is no simple formula by which cost considerations enter into environmental statutes. Key provisions of the various statutes differ markedly, although cost is rarely the pivotal factor determining

Table 1. Analysis Allowable under the Environmental Statutes.

	Benefit-related factors			Cost-related factors			
	Pollution reduction	Health	Welfare	Technical feasibility	Affordability	Cost-effectiveness	Benefit/cost
Clean Air Act (CAA)							
NAAQS/primary		X					
NAAQS/secondary			X				?
Hazardous air pollution		a	a	b	b	b	b
Automobile engines	c	c	c	c	c	c	c
Fuel standards	c	c	c			c	c
New source standards	X			X	X	X	X
Clean Water Act (CWA)							
Effluent guidelines, industrial sources	X	X	X	X	X	X	?
Safe Drinking Water Act (SDWA)							
Maximum contaminant levels		X	X	X	X	X	X
Toxic Substances Control Act (TSCA)		X	X	X	X	X	X
Resource Conservation and Recovery Act (RCRA)		X	X	X	?	?	?
Federal Insecticide, Fungicide and Rodenticide Act (FIFRA)		X	X		X	X	X

?: Uncertain if allowable under this statute.

a: Only marginally relevant in the initial MACT (maximum available control technology) phase; principally relevant for residual risk phase.

b: Affordability, etc. are relevant only within a narrow framework for MACT determinations.

c : Statute contains many specific directives limiting considerations of costs, health, and welfare.

Sources and notes: This table builds off one created by Hahn (1994, 331). The only modifications made to Hahn's table incorporate the 1996 Amendments to the Safe Drinking Water Act. (These recent changes do not apply to the cases in this volume.) Hahn's table in turn was derived from Fraas (1991) and Blake (1991).

program design or the stringency of emission limits. Unless precluded by statute, administrative discretion is accorded a significant weight in establishing most environmental standards. Former EPA Deputy Administrator Alvin Alm was on target when he likened the legislation implemented by EPA to an archeological dig. "Each layer," he wrote, "represents a set of political and technical judgments that do not bear any relationship to other layers (U.S. EPA 1990)."

EXECUTIVE ORDERS: EXPLICIT CALLS FOR ECONOMICS

In the late 1960s and early 1970s a variety of regulatory policies were established in the areas of health, safety, and the environment. These were soon followed by presidential attempts to exert greater executive-branch influence over the regulatory process. Central to this executive branch interest, economic analysis was often seen as a way of influencing the substantive content of federal rules. During the 1970s, under the labels "Quality of Life Reviews" and "Inflation Alerts," Presidents Nixon, Ford and Carter all issued executive orders calling for limited economic analyses of major rules. Further, they sought interagency review of major rules and the accompanying economic analyses as a means of assuring that broad public policy concerns, as opposed to the more compartmentalized issues of the individual agencies, were considered. In effect, the Office of Management and Budget (OMB), representing the executive office of the president, became, in the words of economist Charles Schultze, "the lobby for economic efficiency (Schultze 1977)."

Within a month of taking office, President Ronald Reagan issued Executive Order 12291, which substantially strengthened the requirements for both economic analysis and executive branch review. Described by some scholars as possibly the foremost development in administrative law of the 1980s, E.O. 12291 (46 *Federal Register* 13193; 3 CFR, February 17, 1981) required regulatory agencies to prepare *regulatory impact analyses* (RIAs) on all major regulations and to submit them to OMB for review before taking regulatory action (Pildes and Sunstein 1995, 3). In effect, by requiring agencies to consider the gains from regulation on an equivalent footing with the costs, it attempted to change the "yardstick" used to evaluate environmental regulations for which such considerations are not specifically precluded by law. Most importantly, E.O. 12291 required that "the potential benefits outweigh the costs," and that "of all the alternative approaches to tne given regulatory objective, the proposed action will maximize net benefits to society."

Mandating such an economic yardstick, of course, was not entirely consistent with the spirit of most environmental statutes. As noted, these statutes have, for the most part, focused on noneconomic criteria such as protection of human health "with an adequate margin of safety" or on specific environmental goals like "fishable and swimmable" waters rather than economic efficiency. Further, by requiring that agencies obtain prior approval from OMB before placing either proposals or final rules in the *Federal Register*, E.O. 12291 gave OMB a clear mechanism by which to enforce the provisions of the Order.

President Bill Clinton issued E.O. 12866 in September 1993. It superceded the Reagan executive order and replaced the stipulation that benefits "outweigh" costs with "...a reasoned determination that the benefits of the intended regulation justify its costs [E.O. 12866 1(a), 3 CFR at 638–39 (1995)]". By it, agencies are to "...include both quantifiable measures (to the fullest extent that these can be usefully estimated) and qualitative measures of costs and benefits that are difficult to quantify," and to "select those approaches that maximize net benefits (including potential economic, environmental, public health and safety, and other advantages; distributive impacts; and equity) unless a statute requires another regulatory approach." This formulation endorses benefit-cost analysis as a tool for helping choose among alternative regulatory (and nonregulatory) options while not requiring that benefits quantitatively "exceed" costs. Under President Clinton's executive order, agencies are required to make the implications of various policies explicit but are not forced to adhere to any rigid decisionmaking formula.

Legal scholars have praised this executive order as "a dramatic step:"

> First,...it maintains the basic process...that major regulations be submitted to OMB for general review and oversight.... [It] also maintains the... emphasis on cost-benefit analysis as the basic foundation of decision. President Clinton thus rejected the view that an assessment of costs and benefits is an unhelpful or unduly sectarian conception of the basis of regulation.... Executive Order 12866 includes a set of innovations.... [It] addresses unnecessary conflicts between agencies and OMB, and the appearance (or perhaps the reality) of factional influence (Pildes and Sunstein 1995, 6–7).

Perhaps the most significant change of E.O. 12866 is that it effectively distinguishes between two aspects of benefit-cost analysis: an "accounting framework" for tracking and exploring social decisions versus an "optimizing tool" for attaining maximum social welfare (Lave 1996, 129–30). By dropping the decision rule developed in E.O. 12291 that benefits must "outweigh" costs in favor of the more flexible term, E.O. 12866 clearly endorses the notion of an accounting framework for exploring

12   MORGENSTERN

social decisions. The Clinton rule places much greater emphasis on non-quantifiable benefits including "...public health, and safety, and other advantages; distributive impacts; and equity." By embracing social welfare considerations that may not be easily quantified, such as public health and distribution impacts, E.O. 12866 effectively rejects the idea of using solely quantified benefit-cost analysis as an optimizing tool in favor of a more general approach, relying less on quantitative analysis.

As the Reagan administration did in 1982, Clinton's OMB issued guidelines in early 1996 that lay out the key steps agencies should take in performing economic analyses pursuant to E.O. 12866. The specifics of these guidelines are discussed in the next chapter.

EPA'S CULTURE AND
INCENTIVES FOR POLICY ANALYSES

Unlike OMB, which operates on what might be thought of as traditional utilitarian principles, EPA is a mission-oriented agency with the overall goal of protecting human health and the environment through administration of a complex set of statutes. Even apart from any legal restrictions, EPA's broad scope often works against a consistent use of economics in agency decisionmaking. The agency culture is probably best described as a legal culture, buttressed, in large part, by scientific considerations and, to a far lesser extent, by economic factors. The culture is also significantly shaped by the large number of both congressional and court-ordered deadlines. Most outsiders do not realize the burdens these deadlines place on the agency's ability to function and, particularly, on its ability to use state of the art science and economics in rulemaking. Former Administrator William Ruckelshaus has suggested that EPA suffers from "battered agency syndrome...not sufficiently empowered by Congress to set and pursue meaningful priorities, deluged in paper and lawsuits, and pulled on a dozen different vectors by an ill-assorted and antiquated set of statutes (Ruckelshaus 1995, 3)."

The founding of EPA in 1970 reflected a sea change in thinking about the environment. Broadly stated, it valued esthetics and biology above economic efficiency and commerce. An EPA pamphlet reflects the spirit of that time:

> The subtle metaphor of a "web of life," in which all creatures depended upon one another for their mutual perpetuation, gained currency. Hence, the powerful reaction to Rachel Carson's 1962 classic *Silent Spring* (U.S. EPA 1992, 6).

The notion of "Spaceship Earth" that R. Buckminster Fuller and other "wholistic" thinkers and social critics devised was powerfully reinforced in the public's mind by the first photographs of the "whole Earth." Taken by the Apollo astronauts and widely displayed at the first Earth Day celebration in 1970, these images provided a haunting reminder of the planet's fragility.

In setting up EPA, Congress established an agency that differed from "old line" regulatory agencies like the Federal Deposit Insurance Corporation, the Securities and Exchange Commission, and others in at least three significant ways (Eads and Fix 1984, 12–15; Portney 1990, 7–25). First, many older agencies were set up to control a perceived failure of the market, typically related to monopoly power, fraud in advertising, or unsound financial practices. In contrast, EPA was founded to deal with what economists refer to as externalities and/or the problems associated with highly imperfect information regarding the nature and consequences of environmental discharges. Second, EPA differs from the older agencies in the breadth of its mandate. Whereas most of the older agencies focus on a single industry, EPA is expected to cover a vast territory including virtually every economic sector. Third, at the older regulatory agencies recent legislation and administrative actions have generally curtailed intervention in the markets they regulate—witness the demise of the Civil Aeronautics Board in 1985. In contrast, Congress has repeatedly expanded the scope of responsibility and authority of EPA, at least up until the early 1990s. All of these differences are significant because they impose special problems for effectively managing the agency.

In creating this new agency with its broad mandate, personnel were recruited from the Departments of Interior, Agriculture, and Health, Education and Welfare. As Thomas McGarity describes it, "...President Nixon assembled a loose amalgam of bureaucrats with widely varying institutional backgrounds from several existing regulatory programs and called it the EPA (McGarity 1991, 57)." The new agency also attracted a number of activists from the early environmental movement. The importance of these activists in shaping the agency culture is widely disputed. Some scholars believe they were a dominant influence, others do not.[2] McGarity, for example, argues that "While some of the new hires at EPA joined the agency out of strong ideological desire to protect the environment, most of the original employees that came from existing departments were anything but environmental zealots (McGarity 1991, 57)."[3]

While it is difficult to convey the essence of the early agency staff, former EPA Administrator Ruckelshaus has noted that "I've never worked anywhere where I could find (the great interest, excitement, challenge or fulfillment) to quite the extent as at EPA.... At EPA, you

14   MORGENSTERN

work for a cause that is beyond self-interest and larger than the goals people normally pursue (U.S. EPA 1993, 36)." In a similar vein, former EPA Administrator William Reilly has referred to "the quality of the people who work at EPA, their zeal, their commitment, the fact that for them it's not just a job, they really believe in what they're doing (U.S. EPA 1995, 79)."

The Educational Backgrounds of EPA Employees

The EPA workforce is one of the most highly educated, technically sophisticated, and decidedly interdisciplinary in government. More than two-thirds of the staff hold a college degree; more than half of those college graduates also hold one or more advanced degrees. Table 2 shows a distribution of EPA employees with graduate degrees, according to twenty-seven separate academic disciplines, as recorded in the EPA personnel records as of November 1996. The most popular disciplines, in descending order, are law (18%), biological or life sciences (16%), engineering (16%), physical science (14%), business management and administrative services (7%), public administration including public policy (7%), social science other than economics (5%), health sciences (3%), conservation and natural resources (3%), and economics (2%).

Despite their relative minority status, the agency does employ a considerable number of economists. In fact, there are probably more economists working on environmental issues employed at the EPA than at any other single institution in the world. Perhaps the most relevant question, however, is what influence economists and economic reasoning have on the EPA culture and, specifically, on regulatory decisionmaking.

It is certainly true that being trained in economics does not necessarily make you a strong advocate of economic reasoning. Conversely, you don't have to be an economist to think like one. Nonetheless, as a proxy for their influence, it is useful to consider the number of economists working where individual regulations are written, or in senior management positions within the agency. Table 3 indicates that while more than half of the economists are in the program offices, they constitute only about 3–5% of staff with graduate training in those offices. In contrast, about one-third of the agency's economists are in the Office of Policy, Planning and Evaluation (OPPE) that, historically, has assisted in rule development, but has never had responsibility for issuing rules. In OPPE, about one in seven individuals with a graduate degree specializes in economics. In terms of senior management positions, EPA had 255 members of the Senior Executive Service (SES) as of November 1996. Of the 196 SES members with a graduate degree, almost one-third held a law degree,

Table 2. Profile of EPA Employees with Graduate Degrees.

Discipline	Doctorate	Master's or J.D.	Total number	Total percent*
Law	50	1,201	1,251	18.1
Biological science/life science	500	624	1124	16.2
Engineering	104	992	1,096	15.8
Physical science	323	613	936	13.5
Business management and administrative services	6	463	469	6.8
Public administration	9	442	451	6.5
Social sciences and history/not including economics	52	294	346	5.0
Health professional and related sciences	31	157	188	2.7
Conservation/renewable natural resources	23	154	177	2.6
Economics	31	85	116	1.7
Agriculture	34	76	110	1.6
Architecture	2	101	103	1.5
Education	5	91	96	1.4
Multi/interdisciplinary studies	11	76	87	1.3
Psychology	25	28	53	0.8
Computer/information science	4	45	49	0.7
English language and literature	5	40	45	0.7
Communications	2	34	36	0.5
Library science	0	30	30	0.4
Philosophy and religion	21	9	30	0.4
Liberal arts and sciences, general studies and humanities	0	23	23	0.3
Foreign language/literature	2	11	13	0.2
Visual and performing arts	0	10	10	0.1
Home economics	5	4	9	0.1
Ethnic/cultural studies	1	7	8	0.1
Theological studies/religious vocations	2	6	8	0.1
Other	25	86	111	1.6
Total**	1,248	5,674	6,922	100*

* As percent of total employees at EPA with graduate degrees
** Totals may not add due to double-counting of employees with more than one graduate degree.

Source: EPA Personnel Office, November 1996.

twenty percent held a science degree, and four individuals held their graduate degree in economics.

Not surprisingly, different disciplines rely on distinct approaches to problem definitions and solutions. These differences have been cogently characterized:

Lawyers, having read hundreds of cases in law school, learn there are two sides to every argument. Since defendant and

16   MORGENSTERN

Table 3. EPA Employees with Graduate Degrees in Economics.

EPA office	Doctorate	Master's	Total graduate degrees	SES** graduate degrees
Program offices				
OAR	4 / 68	24 / 457	28 / 525	0 / 13
OPPTS	11 / 239	10 / 370	21 / 609	1 / 19
OSWER	1 / 30	11 / 262	12 / 292	0 / 7
OW	1 / 43	10 / 226	11 / 269	0 / 12
Multimedia offices				
OPPE	13 / 41	21 / 152	34 / 193	3 / 6
OARM	0 / 21	2 / 259	2 / 280	0 / 14
OE	0 / 21	1 / 334	1 / 355	0 / 20
ORD	1 / 531	2 / 441	3 / 972	0 / 29
Regional offices	0 / 238	1 / 2665	1 / 3024	0 / 44
All offices***	31 / 1,250	82 / 5,491	113 / 6,931	4 / 193

*Notes:*The figures in the four rightmost columns are numbers of degrees in economics in comparison to the total number of degrees for each column's category
*Doctorates of law included **SES: EPA's Senior Executive Service ***Includes offices without any economists.
OAR—Office for Air and Radiation; OPPTS—Office of Prevention, Pesticides, and Toxics Substances; OSWER—Office of Solid Waste and Emergency Response; OW—Office of Water; OPPE—Office of Policy, Planning and Evaluation; OARM—Office of Administration and Resources Management; OE—Office of Enforcement (now OECA, Office of Enforcement and Compliance Assurance); ORD—Office of Research and Development.

Source: EPA Personnel Office, November 1996.

plaintiff alike present cogent theories and precedents, lawyers learn that disagreements cannot be resolved by appealing to shared ideas. Hence, fair procedures (such as bargaining) may be the only way to resolve conflicts.

Engineers, on the other hand, are trained to solve problems, not resolve them. The formulae and rules on which they base their calculations are often arbitrary....They come to believe that there are right answers to problems and that those can be arrived at by manipulating data according to a unique "best practice."

Unlike either lawyers or engineers, economists are trained to view all variables as continuous. Regardless of whether price, production, or consumption is at issue, choices are not "yes" or "no" but matters of amount or degree. Thus, economists instinctively see all issues as arenas for trade-offs, and outcomes that produce "a little of this and a little of that" are often judged desirable. (Landy, Roberts, and Thomas 1994, 10)

Simply put, the aversion to "yes" and "no" choices, and the mentality of seeking trade-offs rather than bright lines rests at the core of much economic analysis. Yet, this outlook world view contrasts with that of the professions that dominate the EPA culture. And the fact remains that despite their absolute numbers, as a proportion of the EPA workforce, there are relatively few economists employed at EPA, particularly in program offices and in the ranks of senior managment. One study on the attitudes and beliefs of EPA employees concludes that "educational background, rather than office or job responsibilities of EPA officials, appears to play the dominant role in shaping perspectives about the utility of risk assessment and benefit-cost analysis, the valuation of life, and the distribution of risk (Rycroft, Regan, and Dietz 1989, 419)."

Recent Agency History: Economics Under Seige?

By the late 1980's *Time* magazine proclaimed that "we're all environmentalists now." Concurrent with this "mainstreaming of the environment," and perhaps, in part, because of it, naive notions that economic analysis itself is invariably bad for the environment have found ready adherents. In fact, a series of interviews conducted for this book reveals an unmistakable view within the agency that, within recent years, economics has had to fight harder for its place at the table.

No single factor explains the de-emphasis of economics, but two competing explanations are generally offered. First of all, noneconomists tend to fault the discipline of economics itself, claiming that it is no longer relevant (if it ever was) to environmental issues. In place of neo-classical economics they cite the emerging field of "ecological economics" or the "no-cost" views of environmental protection often associated with Professor Michael Porter of the Harvard Business School. (For further discussion of this perspective, see Porter and van der Linde 1995. For a counter view, see Palmer, Oates, and Portney 1995.)

The idea that government can develop policies that systematically enable us to have a cleaner environment without sacrificing anything else seems improbable to most economists. Economists approach their discipline from the perspective that in a world of limited resources, it is important to try to figure out how to make the most of such resources. Since environmental problems generally derive from "market failures," some form of government intervention is often warranted. Yet, economists emphasize the need for credible estimates of potential damage to human health or the environment as a basis for action.

Secondly, and in contrast to the first view, economists generally see the decline in their influence as part of a larger trend in public affairs to focus on "good news" and to avoid tough choices. They point to the

18   MORGENSTERN

downgrading of economists and of policy offices all around government—not just at EPA. As Phil Lee, a former assistant secretary of health in both the Johnson and Clinton administrations, put it, "nowadays, decisionmakers consult their PR people and interest groups more often than the experts."[4]

Managerial Considerations of Economic Analysis

Albert Nichols observes, in Chapter 4, that economic analysis at EPA "is likely to have more influence when it identifies previously unrecognized opportunities for cost-effective health/environmental gains, than when it concludes that a proposed action fails to yield benefits commensurate with costs." Yet, even when they do make a case for strong regulation, economic analyses can create headaches for agency management by pointing out some contrary information or by making transparent certain costs that, even if clearly outweighed by benefits, are still seen as burdens to some group in the society. Such "on the one hand and on the other hand" sorts of statements provide ammunition for the policy's opponents to use in court or in the media, particularly when taken out of context.

Such barriers are not entirely insurmountable. Before the Congressional Budget Office (CBO) came into existence, few Congress watchers would have predicted that an analytic office within the Congress would acquire the prestige and influence that now attaches to it. It succeeded because it developed a reputation for analytic excellence and fairness and it actively worked to build constituencies appreciative of its product. Unlike EPA, of course, CBO does not carry the burdens of a regulatory agency. Nonetheless, the CBO example suggests that it is possible to develop at least some constituencies for economic efficiency.

Finally, as is well known, EPA managers are very often under significant political pressures from both Congress and the Courts. The famed "Prune Book," which lists the toughest jobs in government, quotes a former EPA administrator who referred to the pressures of his job: "...(it's) like beating a train across a grade crossing—if you make it, it's a great rush. If you don't, you're dead (Trattner 1988, 250)."

A recent report of the National Academy of Public Administration (NAPA), addressing some of the pressures and problems faced at EPA, placed much of the blame on Congress:

> The EPA lacks focus, in part, because Congress has passed more than a dozen environmental statutes that drive the agency in a dozen directions, discouraging rational priority-setting or a coherent approach to environmental management. EPA is sometimes ineffective because, in part, Congress has set impossible

deadlines and unrealistic expectations, given the agency's budget. The EPA can be inefficient, in part, because Congress has
attempted to micro-manage the agency through prescriptive legislation, earmarked appropriations, and direct pressure (NAPA
1995, 8).

Again, Ruckelshaus' comment is on point: "The people who run EPA
are not so much executives as prisoners of the stringent legislative mandates and court decisions that have been laid down... for the past quarter
century (Ruckelshaus 1995, 4)."

Notwithstanding the view that some of the disinterest in economic
efficiency within EPA may stem from congressional actions that "...dis-
courag[e] rational priority setting or a coherent approach to environmental management (NAPA 1995, 8)," the responsibility for the disaffection
regarding economic analysis is, undoubtedly, much broader. Certainly it
is fair to say that economists themselves bear some of the blame, as do
those who have undermined the overall legitimacy of economic considerations and the ability to carry out competent and timely analyses. The
next section of this chapter addresses some changing congressional winds
that may presage new directions for the agency.

NEW LEGISLATIVE DEVELOPMENTS

The 1970s, when most environmental statutes were first enacted, is considered the "environmental decade." In contrast, the 1990s have been a
time of reevaluation, when the complexity of environmental management has proved especially challenging. All the individual regulations
examined in this volume were issued under statutory authorities that
were in place prior to 1995. Both the 103d and 104th Congresses have
considered risk assessment and benefit-cost isssues in some depth.
Although none of the more sweeping proposals were adopted,[5] enacte-
ment of both the Safe Drinking Water Act (SDWA) Amendments of 1996
and the Small Business Regulatory Enforcement Fairness Act of 1996
(SBREFA) can be read as clear signs of congressional concerns about the
absence of economic considerations in environmental management.

In what is undoubtedly the most far-reaching requirement for economic analysis in any environmental law, the SWDA Amendments mandate the use of benefit-cost analysis for all major drinking water rules.
They specifically require the use marginal (as opposed to average) analysis, consideration of risk-risk trade-offs, and the analysis of a rule's
impacts on the broader population, not just its effect on so-called maxi-
mally exposed individuals. The statute also calls for explicit consideration

of nonquantifiable effects, uncertainties, and the degree and nature of the risk being controlled.[6]

It is no coincidence that the drinking water statute is the first substantive law to include such explicit use of economic analysis. Concerns about drinking water are widely shared in our society. The drinking water industry consists primarily of urban and rural water systems, many of which are municipally operated. In contrast to other pollution issues, there are few large industrial polluters of drinking water, and treatment costs are generally passed along directly to customers.

SBREFA is a procedural statute that modifies the requirements for economic impact analysis under the Regulatory Flexibility Act (RFA). SBREFA responds to claims from the small business community that some agencies have failed to comply with RFA. It mandates more rigorous regulatory flexibility analyses and, in cases involving either EPA or the Occupational Safety and Health Adminstration, establishes a small entity stakeholder process including the Small Business Administration. SBREFA also empowers Congress to review and potentially disapprove all individual regulations whether or not they have significant small business impacts.

These provisions present a small but significant change in thinking about the environment. In addition to mandating additional analyses and congressional review, both the SDWA Amendments and SBREFA specifically allow judicial review of any agency's conduct and use of economic analysis carried out pursuant to those statutes. Whether the courts or Congress will prove capable of implementing these mandates in a consistent and balanced manner remains to be seen. In theory, these new provisions are intended to introduce greater rigor into the conduct and use of economic analysis. In practice, neither Congress nor the courts are likely to muster the necessary expertise or resources required to undertake such reviews. Thus, it is questionable whether these solutions will prove fully successful. With these changes, however, Congress is clearly expressing concerns about the need for greater consideration of economic factors in environmental management.

CONCLUSION

The U.S. public has struggled with contradictory desires to protect the environment and avoid the inevitable burdens associated with doing so. As a consequence, the laws and institutions in the United States have evolved somewhat inconsistently. Various statutes forbid, inhibit, tolerate, allow, invite, or require the use of economic analysis in environmental decisionmaking. Most environmental laws place limits on the consideration of economic factors but do not preclude them entirely. For almost three decades, various executive orders had required that economic analyses be conducted. Later chapters of this book show that these Presidential directives have so far failed to produce consistently high quality and relevant economic assessments. The EPA culture has, at best, tolerated the goal of economic efficiency. Recent congressional actions such as the amended Safe Drinking Water Act have expanded the role of economic considerations. Whether this will ultimately provide a more reasoned approach to agency decisionmaking remains to be determined.

ENDNOTES

[1]For example, William D. Ruckelshaus, former administrator of EPA has stated that "the nation was committed to a sort of pie in the sky at some future date.... Each time a new generation of clean technologies came into use, the response from EPA had to be: 'That's great—now do some more,'" whether that 'more' made any sense as an environmental priority or not." (From a speech at the Environmental Law Institute, October 18, 1995, p. 7.)

[2]For an example of those who believe it was dominant, see Harris and Miklis (1989, 231).

[3]See also Marcus (1980, 35–43). In a similar vein, Mark Landy, Marc Roberts, and Stephen Thomas argue: "The agency...was initially staffed primarily by bureaucrats transferred from other federal departments. Mostly scientists and engineers, they had long labored in the bowels of large departments....(T)hey brought with them the concepts, attitudes, and skills that had served their former agencies....By both training and conviction, they were not prepared to shift from being aid and advice givers to aggressive violation hunters (Landy, Roberts, and Thomas 1994, 34)."

[4]Interview, October 23, 1996.

[5]Both the Johnston Amendment, introduced by former Senator J. Bennett Johnston (D-La.) in 1993 and then again in 1994, as well as provisions of the 104th Congress' legislative "Contract with America," introduced by the newly empowered Republican majority in early 1995, would have made benefit-cost analysis a more central element—some might argue *the* central element—in decisionmaking on major environmental rules. By some interpretations, the analysis itself would have been subject to judicial review, thereby establishing the courts as the arbiters of quality. Other provisions of the "Contract" would have increased procedural hurdles, thereby raising significantly the cost and complexity of rulemaking.

[6]Specifically, the statute calls for EPA to consider the following: the quantifiable and unquantifiable benefits of the health risk reduction associated with the contaminants being controlled; the quantifiable and unquantifiable benefits of the health risk reductions of the co-occuring contaminants likely to also be controlled; the quantifiable and unquantifiable costs of compliance; the incremental costs and

22 MORGENSTERN

benefits of each level being considered; the effects of the contaminant on the general population and any vulnerable subpopulations; any increased health risks that may be introduced as a result of compliance and other factors, like the quality of the data, the uncertainties in the analyses, and the degree and nature of the risk being controlled. (Safe Drinking Water Act Amendments of 1996, section 103)

REFERENCES

Blake, F. 1991. The Politics of the Environment: Does Washington Know Best? *American Enterprise* 6(1).

Downing, Donna Marie. 1995. *Cost Benefit Analysis and the 104th Congress: Regulatory Reform, "Reg-icide" or Business as Usual?* Master's thesis. Washington, D.C.: George Washington University, National Law Center.

Eads, George C. and Michael Fix. 1984. *Relief or Reform? Reagan's Regulatory Dilemma.* Washington, D.C.: Urban Institute Press.

Fraas, A. 1991. The Role of Economic Analysis in Shaping Environmental Policy. *Law and Contemporary Problems* 113(54).

Hahn, Robert W. 1994. United States Environmental Policy: Past, Present and Future. *Natural Resources Journal* 34(1).

Harris, Richard A. and Signey M. Miklis. 1989. *The Politics of Regulatory Change: A Tale of Two Agencies.* New York: Oxford University Press.

Landy, Mark K., Marc J. Roberts, and Stephen R. Thomas. 1994. *The Environmental Protection Agency: Asking the Wrong Questions from Nixon to Clinton.* New York: Oxford University Press.

Lave, Lester. 1996. Benefit-Cost Analysis: Do the Benefits Exceed the Costs? In Robert W. Hahn (ed.). *Risks, Costs, and Lives Saved.* Washington, D.C.: American Enterprise Institute.

Marcus, Alfred A. 1980. *Promise and Performance: Choosing and Implementing an Environmental Policy.* Greenwood Press.

McGarity, Thomas O. 1991. The Internal Structure of EPA Rulemaking. *Law and Contemporary Problems* 54(4).

NAPA (National Academy of Public Administration). 1995. *Setting Priorities, Getting Results: A New Direction for the Environmental Protection Agency.* Washington, D.C.: NAPA.

Palmer, Karen, Wallace E. Oates, and Paul R. Portney. 1995. Tightening Environmental Standards: The Benefit-Cost or the No-Cost Paradigm. *Journal of Economic Perspectives* 9(4):119–32.

Pildes, Richard H. and Cass R. Sunstein. 1995. Reinventing the Regulatory State. *The University of Chicago Law Review* 62(1).

Porter, Michael E. and Claas van der Linde. 1995. Towards a New Conception of the Environment-Competitiveness Relationship. *Journal of Economic Perspectives* 9(4): 97–118.

LEGAL AND INSTITUTIONAL SETTING FOR ECONOMIC ANALYSIS AT EPA   23

Portney, Paul R. 1990. EPA and the Evolution of Federal Regulation. In Paul R. Portney (ed.) *Public Policies for Environmental Protection*. Washington, D.C.: Resources for the Future.

Ruckleshaus, William D. 1995. Speech at the Environmental Law Institute, October 18.

Rycroft, Robert W., James L. Regan, and Thomas Dietz. 1989. Incorporating Risk Assessment and Benefit-Cost Analysis into Environmental Management. *Risk Analysis* 8(3).

Schultze, Charles L. 1977. *The Public Use of Private Interest*. Washington, D.C.: The Brookings Institution.

SBA (Small Business Administration) 1996. Highlights of Small Business Regulatory Enforcement Fairness Act of 1996. Fact sheet, March 29. Washington, D.C.: SBA. Office of Chief Counsel for Advocacy.

Trattner, John H. 1988. *The Prune Book: The 100 Toughest Management and Policy-Making Jobs in Washington*. Lanham, Maryland: Madison Books.

U.S. EPA (Environmental Protection Agency). 1990. *EPA Journal* 13 (September/October). Washington, D.C.: U.S. EPA.

———. 1992. *The Guardian: Origins of the EPA*. EPA Historical Publication 1. Spring. Washington, D.C.: U.S. EPA.

———. 1993. *William D. Ruckelshaus Oral History Interview*. Interview 1. January. (202-K-92-0003). Washington, D.C.: U.S. EPA.

———. 1995. *William K. Reilly Oral History Interview*. Interview 4. September. Washington, D.C.: U.S. EPA.

Part III
Philosophy and Foundation

[13]

Cost-Benefit Analysis
An Ethical Critique

Steven Kelman

A T THE BROADEST and vaguest level, cost-benefit analysis may be regarded simply as systematic thinking about decision-making. Who can oppose, economists sometimes ask, efforts to think in a systematic way about the consequences of different courses of action? The alternative, it would appear, is unexamined decision-making. But defining cost-benefit analysis so simply leaves it with few implications for actual regulatory decision-making. Presumably, therefore, those who urge regulators to make greater use of the technique have a more extensive prescription in mind. I assume here that their prescription includes the following views:

(1) There exists a strong presumption that an act should not be undertaken unless its benefits outweigh its costs.

(2) In order to determine whether benefits outweigh costs, it is desirable to attempt to express all benefits and costs in a common scale or denominator, so that they can be compared with each other, even when some benefits and costs are not traded on markets and hence have no established dollar values.

(3) Getting decision-makers to make more use of cost-benefit techniques is important enough to warrant both the expense required to gather the data for improved cost-benefit esti-

mation and the political efforts needed to give the activity higher priority compared to other activities, also valuable in and of themselves.

My focus is on cost-benefit analysis as applied to environmental, safety, and health regulation. In that context, I examine each of the above propositions from the perspective of formal ethical theory, that is, the study of what actions it is morally right to undertake. My conclusions are:

(1) In areas of environmental, safety, and health regulation, there may be many instances where a certain decision might be right even though its benefits do not outweigh its costs.

(2) There are good reasons to oppose efforts to put dollar values on non-marketed benefits and costs.

(3) Given the relative frequency of occasions in the areas of environmental, safety, and health regulation where one would not wish to use a benefits-outweigh-costs test as a decision rule, and given the reasons to oppose the monetizing of non-marketed benefits or costs that is a prerequisite for cost-benefit analysis, it is not justifiable to devote major resources to the generation of data for cost-benefit calculations or to undertake efforts to "spread the gospel" of cost-benefit analysis further.

Steven Kelman, on leave from the Kennedy School of Government at Harvard, is associate director for management planning, Federal Trade Commission. A version of this article was delivered at a Conservation Foundation — Illinois Institute of Natural Resources Conference. The views are the author's.

I

How do we decide whether a given action is morally right or wrong and hence, assuming the desire to act morally, why it should be undertaken or refrained from? Like the Molière character who spoke prose without knowing it, economists who advocate use of cost-benefit analysis for public decisions are philosophers without knowing it: the answer given by cost-benefit analysis, that actions should be undertaken so as to maximize net benefits, represents one of the classic answers given by moral philosophers—that given by utilitarians. To determine whether an action is right or wrong, utilitarians tote up all the positive consequences of the action in terms of human satisfaction. The act that maximizes attainment of satisfaction under the circumstances is the right act. That the economists' answer is also the answer of one school of philosophers should not be surprising. Early on, economics was a branch of moral philosophy, and only later did it become an independent discipline.

Before proceeding further, the subtlety of the utilitarian position should be noted. The positive and negative consequences of an act for satisfaction may go beyond the act's immediate consequences. A facile version of utilitarianism would give moral sanction to a lie, for instance, if the satisfaction of an individual attained by telling the lie was greater than the suffering imposed on the lie's victim. Few utilitarians would agree. Most of them would add to the list of negative consequences the effect of the one lie on the tendency of the person who lies to tell other lies, even in instances when the lying produced less satisfaction for him than dissatisfaction for others. They would also add the negative effects of the lie on the general level of social regard for truth-telling, which has many consequences for future utility. A further consequence may be added as well. It is sometimes said that we should include in a utilitarian calculation the feeling of dissatisfaction produced in the liar (and perhaps in others) because, by telling a lie, one has "done the wrong thing." Correspondingly, in this view, among the positive consequences to be weighed into a utilitarian calculation of truth-telling is satisfaction arising from "doing the right thing." This view rests on an error, however, because it *assumes* what it is the purpose of the calculation to *determine*—that telling the truth in the instance in question is indeed the right thing to do. Economists are likely to object to this point, arguing that no feeling ought "arbitrarily" to be excluded from a complete cost-benefit calculation, including a feeling of dis-

satisfaction at doing the wrong thing. Indeed, the economists' cost-benefit calculations would, at least ideally, include such feelings. Note the difference between the economist's and the philosopher's cost-benefit calculations, however. The economist may choose to include feelings of dissatisfaction in his cost-benefit calculation, but what happens if somebody asks the economist, "Why is it right to evaluate an action on the basis of a cost-benefit test?" If an answer is to be given to that question (which does not normally preoccupy economists but which does concern both philosophers and the rest of us who need to be persuaded that cost-benefit analysis is right), then the circularity problem reemerges. And there is also another difficulty with counting feelings of dissatisfaction at doing the wrong thing in a cost-benefit calculation. It leads to the perverse result that under certain circumstances a lie, for example, might be morally right if the individual contemplating the lie felt no compunction about lying and morally wrong only if the individual felt such a compunction!

This error is revealing, however, because it begins to suggest a critique of utilitarianism. Utilitarianism is an important and powerful moral doctrine. But it is probably a minority position among contemporary moral philosophers. It is amazing that economists can proceed in unanimous endorsement of cost-benefit analysis as if unaware that their conceptual framework is highly controversial in the discipline from which it arose—moral philosophy.

It is amazing that economists can proceed in unanimous endorsement of cost-benefit analysis as if unaware that their conceptual framework is highly controversial in the discipline from which it arose—moral philosophy.

Let us explore the critique of utilitarianism. The logical error discussed before appears to suggest that we have a notion of certain things being right or wrong that *predates* our calculation of costs and benefits. Imagine the case of an old man in Nazi Germany who is hostile to the regime. He is wondering whether he should speak out against Hitler. If he speaks out, he will lose his pension. And his action will have done nothing to increase the chances that the Nazi regime will be overthrown: he is regarded as somewhat eccentric by those around him, and nobody has ever consulted his views on political questions. Recall that one cannot add to the benefits of speaking out any satisfaction from doing "the right thing," because the purpose of the exercise is to determine whether speaking out *is* the right thing. How would the utilitarian calculation go? The benefits of the old man's speaking out would, as the example is presented, be nil, while the costs would be his loss of his pension. So the costs of the action would outweigh the benefits. By the utilitarians' cost-benefit calculation, it would be *morally wrong* for the man to speak out.

Another example: two very close friends are on an Arctic expedition together. One of them falls very sick in the snow and bitter cold, and sinks quickly before anything can be done to help him. As he is dying, he asks his friend one thing, "Please, make me a solemn promise that ten years from today you will come back to this spot and place a lighted candle here to remember me." The friend solemnly promises to do so, but does not tell a soul. Now, ten years later, the friend must decide whether to keep his promise. It would be inconvenient for him to make the long trip. Since he told nobody, his failure to go will not affect the general social faith in promise-keeping. And the incident was unique enough so that it is safe to assume that his failure to go will not encourage him to break other promises. Again, the costs of the act outweigh the benefits. A utilitarian would need to believe that it would be *morally wrong* to travel to the Arctic to light the candle.

A third example: a wave of thefts has hit a city and the police are having trouble finding any of the thieves. But they believe, correctly, that punishing someone for theft will have some deterrent effect and will decrease the number of crimes. Unable to arrest any actual perpetrator, the police chief and the prosecutor arrest a person whom they know to be innocent and, in cahoots with each other, fabricate a convincing case against him. The police chief and the prosecutor are about to retire, so the act has no effect on any future actions of theirs. The fabrication is perfectly executed, so nobody finds out about it. Is the *only* question involved in judging the act of framing the innocent man that of

whether his suffering from conviction and imprisonment will be greater than the suffering avoided among potential crime victims when some crimes are deterred? A utilitarian would need to believe that it is *morally right to punish the innocent man* as long as it can be demonstrated that the suffering prevented outweighs his suffering.

And a final example: imagine two worlds, each containing the same sum total of happiness. In the first world, this total of happiness came about from a series of acts that included a number of lies and injustices (that is, the total consisted of the immediate gross sum of happiness created by certain acts, minus any long-term unhappiness occasioned by the lies and injustices). In the second world the same amount of happiness was produced by a different series of acts, none of which involved lies or injustices. Do we have any reason to prefer the one world to the other? A utilitarian would need to believe that the choice between the two worlds is a *matter of indifference.*

To those who believe that it would not be morally wrong for the old man to speak out in Nazi Germany or for the explorer to return to the Arctic to light a candle for his deceased friend, that it would not be morally right to convict the innocent man, or that the choice between the two worlds is not a matter of indifference—to those of us who believe these things, utilitarianism is insufficient as a moral view. We believe that some acts whose costs are greater than their benefits may be morally right and, contrariwise, some acts whose benefits are greater than their costs may be morally wrong.

This does not mean that the question whether benefits are greater than costs is morally irrelevant. Few would claim such. Indeed, for a broad range of individual and social decisions, whether an act's benefits outweigh its costs is a sufficient question to ask. But not for all such decisions. These may involve situations where certain duties—duties not to lie, break promises, or kill, for example—make an act wrong, even if it would result in an excess of benefits over costs. Or they may involve instances where people's rights are at stake. We would not permit rape even if it could be demonstrated that the rapist derived enormous happiness from his act, while the victim experienced only minor displeasure. We do not do cost-benefit analyses of freedom of speech or trial by jury. The Bill of Rights was not RARGed. As the United Steelworkers noted in a comment on the Occupational Safety and Health Administration's economic analysis of its proposed rule to reduce worker exposure

---

We would not permit rape even if it could be demonstrated that the rapist derived enormous happiness from his act, while the victim experienced only minor displeasure.

---

to carcinogenic coke-oven emissions, the Emancipation Proclamation was not subjected to an inflationary impact statement. The notion of human rights involves the idea that people may make certain claims to be allowed to act in certain ways or to be treated in certain ways, even if the sum of benefits achieved thereby does not outweigh the sum of costs. It is this view that underlies the statement that "workers have a right to a safe and healthy work place" and the expectation that OSHA's decisions will reflect that judgment.

In the most convincing versions of non-utilitarian ethics, various duties or rights are not absolute. But each has a *prima facie* moral validity so that, if duties or rights do not conflict, the morally right act is the act that reflects a duty or respects a right. If duties or rights do conflict, a moral judgment, based on conscious deliberation, must be made. Since one of the duties non-utilitarian philosophers enumerate is the duty of beneficence (the duty to maximize happiness), which in effect incorporates all of utilitarianism by reference, a non-utilitarian who is faced with conflicts between the results of cost-benefit analysis and non-utility-based considerations will need to undertake such deliberation. But in that deliberation, additional elements, which cannot be reduced to a question of whether benefits outweigh costs, have been introduced. Indeed, depending on the moral importance we attach to the right or duty involved, cost-benefit questions may, within wide ranges, become irrelevant to the outcome of the moral judgment.

In addition to questions involving duties and rights, there is a final sort of question where, in my view, the issue of whether benefits outweigh costs should not govern moral

judgment. I noted earlier that, for the common run of questions facing individuals and societies, it is possible to begin and end our judgment simply by finding out if the benefits of the contemplated act outweigh the costs. This very fact means that one way to show the great importance, or value, attached to an area is to say that decisions involving the area should not be determined by cost-benefit calculations. This applies, I think, to the view many environmentalists have of decisions involving our natural environment. When officials are deciding what level of pollution will harm certain vulnerable people—such as asthmatics or the elderly—while not harming others, one issue involved may be the right of those people not to be sacrificed on the altar of somewhat higher living standards for the rest of us. But more broadly than this, many environmentalists fear that subjecting decisions about clean air or water to the cost-benefit tests that determine the general run of decisions removes those matters from the realm of specially valued things.

II

In order for cost-benefit calculations to be performed the way they are supposed to be, all costs and benefits must be expressed in a common measure, typically dollars, including things not normally bought and sold on markets, and to which dollar prices are therefore not attached. The most dramatic example of such things is human life itself; but many of the other benefits achieved or preserved by environmental policy—such as peace and quiet, fresh-smelling air, swimmable rivers, spectacular vistas—are not traded on markets either.

Economists who do cost-benefit analysis regard the quest after dollar values for non-market things as a difficult challenge—but one to be met with relish. They have tried to develop methods for imputing a person's "willingness to pay" for such things, their approach generally involving a search for bundled goods that *are* traded on markets and that vary as to whether they include a feature that is, *by itself*, not marketed. Thus, fresh air is not marketed, but houses in different parts of Los Angeles that are similar except for the degree of smog are. Peace and quiet is not marketed, but similar houses inside and outside airport flight paths are. The risk of death is not marketed, but similar jobs that have different levels of risk are. Economists have produced many often ingenious efforts to impute dollar prices to non-marketed things by observing the premiums accorded homes in clean air areas over similar homes in dirty areas or the premiums paid for risky jobs over similar nonrisky jobs.

These ingenious efforts are subject to criticism on a number of technical grounds. It may be difficult to control for all the dimensions of quality other than the presence or absence of the non-marketed thing. More important, in a world where people have different preferences and are subject to different constraints as they make their choices, the dollar value imputed to the non-market things that most people would wish to avoid will be lower than otherwise, because people with unusually weak aversion to those things or unusually strong constraints on their choices will be willing to take the bundled good in question at less of a discount than the average person. Thus, to use the property value discount of homes near airports as a measure of people's willingness to pay for quiet means to accept as a proxy for the rest of us the behavior of those least sensitive to noise, of airport employees (who value the convenience of a near-airport location) or of others who are susceptible to an agent's assurances that "it's not so bad." To use the wage premiums accorded hazardous work as a measure of the value of life means to accept as proxies for the rest of us the choices of people who do not have many choices or who are exceptional risk-seekers.

A second problem is that the attempts of economists to measure people's willingness to pay for non-marketed things assume that there is no difference between the price a person would require for *giving up* something to which he has a preexisting right and the price he would pay to *gain* something to which he enjoys no right. Thus, the analysis assumes no difference between how much a homeowner would need to be paid in order to give up an unobstructed mountain view that he already enjoys and how much he would be willing to pay to get an obstruction moved once it is already in place. Available evidence suggests that most people would insist on being paid far more to assent to a worsening of their situation than they would be willing to pay to improve their situation. The difference arises from such factors as being accustomed to and psychologically attached to that which one believes one enjoys by right. But this creates a circularity problem for any attempt to use cost-benefit analysis to determine *whether* to assign to, say, the homeowner the right to an unobstructed mountain view. For willingness to pay will be different depending on whether the right is assigned initially or not. The value judgment about whether to assign the right must thus be made first. (In order to set an upper bound on the value of the benefit, one might hypothetically assign the right to the person and determine how much he would need to be paid to give it up.)

Third, the efforts of economists to impute willingess to pay invariably involve bundled goods exchanged in *private* transactions. Those who use figures garnered from such analysis to provide guidance for *public* decisions assume no difference between how people value certain things in private individual transactions and how they would wish those same things to be valued in public collective decisions. In making such assumptions, economists insidiously slip into their analysis an important and controversial value judgment, growing naturally out of the highly individualistic microeconomic tradition—namely, the view that there should be no difference between private behavior and the behavior we display in public social life. An alternative view—one that enjoys, I would suggest, wide resonance among citizens—would be that public, social decisions provide an opportunity to give certain things a higher valuation than we choose, for one reason or another, to give them in our private activities.

Thus, opponents of stricter regulation of health risks often argue that we show by our daily risk-taking behavior that we do not value life infinitely, and therefore our public decisions should not reflect the high value of life that proponents of strict regulation propose. However, an alternative view is equally plausible. Precisely because we fail, for whatever reasons, to give life-saving the value in everyday personal decisions that we in some general terms believe we should give it, we may wish our social decisions to provide us the occasion to display the reverence for life that we espouse but do not always show. By this view, people do

not have fixed unambiguous "preferences" to which they give expression through private activities and which therefore should be given expression in public decisions. Rather, they

> **Precisely because we fail . . . to give life-saving the value in everyday personal decisions that we in some general terms believe we should give it, we may wish our social decisions to provide us the occasion to display the reverence for life that we espouse but do not always show.**

may have what they themselves regard as "higher" and "lower" preferences. The latter may come to the fore in private decisions, but people may want the former to come to the fore in public decisions. They may sometimes display racial prejudice, but support antidiscrimination laws. They may buy a certain product after seeing a seductive ad, but be skeptical enough of advertising to want the government to keep a close eye on it. In such cases, the use of private behavior to impute the values that should be entered for public decisions, as is done by using willingness to pay in private transactions, commits grievous offense against a view of the behavior of the citizen that is deeply engrained in our democratic tradition. It is a view that denudes politics of any independent role in society, reducing it to a mechanistic, mimicking recalculation based on private behavior.

Finally, one may oppose the effort to place prices on a non-market thing and hence in effect incorporate it into the market system out of a fear that the very act of doing so will reduce the thing's perceived value. To place a price on the benefit may, in other words, reduce the value of that benefit. Cost-benefit analysis thus may be like the thermometer that, when placed in a liquid to be measured, itself changes the liquid's temperature.

Examples of the perceived cheapening of a thing's value by the very act of buying and selling it abound in everyday life and language. The disgust that accompanies the idea of buying and selling human beings is based on the sense that this would dramatically diminish human worth. Epithets such as "he prostituted himself," applied as linguistic analogies to people who have sold something, reflect the view that certain things should not be sold because doing so diminishes their value. Praise that is bought is worth little, even to the person buying it. A true anecdote is told of an economist who retired to another university community and complained that he was having difficulty making friends. The laconic response of a critical colleague—"If you want a friend why don't you buy yourself one"—illustrates in a pithy way the intuition that, for some things, the very act of placing a price on them reduces their perceived value.

The first reason that pricing something decreases its perceived value is that, in many circumstances, non-market exchange is associated with the production of certain values not associated with market exchange. These may include spontaneity and various other feelings that come from personal relationships. If a good becomes less associated with the production of positively valued feelings because of market exchange, the perceived value of the good declines to the extent that those feelings are valued. This can be seen clearly in instances where a thing may be transferred both by market and by non-market mechanisms. The willingness to pay for sex bought from a prostitute is less than the perceived value of the sex consummating love. (Imagine the reaction if a practitioner of cost-benefit analysis computed the benefits of sex based on the price of prostitute services.)

Furthermore, if one values in a general sense the existence of a non-market sector because of its connection with the production of certain valued feelings, then one ascribes added value to any non-marketed good simply as a repository of values represented by the non-market sector one wishes to preserve. This seems certainly to be the case for things in nature, such as pristine streams or undisturbed forests: for many people who value them, part of their value comes from their position as repositories of values the non-market sector represents.

The second way in which placing a market price on a thing decreases its perceived value is by removing the possibility of proclaiming that the thing is "not for sale," since things on the market by definition are for sale. The very statement that something is not for sale affirms,

enhances, and protects a thing's value in a number of ways. To begin with, the statement is a way of showing that a thing is valued for its own sake, whereas selling a thing for money demonstrates that it was valued only instrumentally. Furthermore, to say that something cannot be transferred in that way places it in the exceptional category—which requires the person interested in obtaining that thing to be able to offer something else that is exceptional, rather than allowing him the easier alternative of obtaining the thing for money that could have been obtained in an infinity of ways. This enhances its value. If I am willing to say "You're a really kind person" to whoever pays me to do so, my praise loses the value that attaches to it from being exchangeable only for an act of kindness.

In addition, if we have already decided we value something highly, one way of stamping it with a cachet affirming its high value is to announce that it is "not for sale." Such an announcement does more, however, than just reflect a preexisting high valuation. It signals a thing's distinctive value to others and helps us persuade them to value the thing more highly than they otherwise might. It also expresses our resolution to safeguard that distinctive value. To state that something is not for sale is thus also a source of value for that thing, since if a thing's value is easy to affirm or protect, it will be worth more than an otherwise similar thing without such attributes.

If we proclaim that something is not for sale, we make a once-and-for-all judgment of its special value. When something is priced, the issue of its perceived value is constantly coming up, as a standing invitation to reconsider that original judgment. Were people constantly faced with questions such as "how much money could get you to give up your freedom of speech?" or "how much would you sell your vote for if you could?", the perceived value of the freedom to speak or the right to vote would soon become devastated as, in moments of weakness, people started saying "maybe it's not worth *so much* after all." Better not to be faced with the constant questioning in the first place. Something similar did in fact occur when the slogan "better red than dead" was launched by some pacifists during the Cold War. Critics pointed out that the very posing of this stark choice—in effect, "would you *really* be willing to give up your life in exchange for not living under communism?"—reduced the value people attached to freedom and thus diminished resistance to attacks on freedom.

Finally, of some things valued very highly it is stated that they are "priceless" or that they have "infinite value." Such expressions are reserved for a subset of things not for sale, such as life or health. Economists tend to scoff at talk of pricelessness. For them, saying that something is priceless is to state a willingness to trade off an infinite quantity of all other goods for one unit of the priceless good, a situation that empirically appears highly unlikely. For most people, however, the word priceless is pregnant with meaning. Its value-affirming and value-protecting functions cannot be bestowed on expressions that merely denote a determinate, albeit high, valuation. John Kennedy in his inaugural address proclaimed that the nation was ready to "pay any price [and] bear any burden . . . to assure the survival and the success of liberty." Had he said instead that we were willing to "pay a high price" or "bear a large burden" for liberty, the statement would have rung hollow.

III

An objection that advocates of cost-benefit analysis might well make to the preceding argument should be considered. I noted earlier that, in cases where various non-utility-based duties or rights conflict with the maximization of utility, it is necessary to make a deliberative judgment about what act is finally right. I also argued earlier that the search for commensurability might not always be a desirable one, that the attempt to go beyond expressing benefits in terms of (say) lives saved and costs in terms of dollars is not something devoutly to be wished.

In situations involving things that are not expressed in a common measure, advocates of cost-benefit analysis argue that people making judgments "in effect" perform cost-benefit calculations anyway. If government regulators promulgate a regulation that saves 100 lives at a cost of $1 billion, they are "in effect" valuing a life at (a minimum of) $10 million, whether or not they say that they are willing to place a dollar value on a human life. Since, in this view,

cost-benefit analysis "in effect" is inevitable, it might as well be made specific.

This argument misconstrues the real difference in the reasoning processes involved. In cost-benefit analysis, equivalencies are established *in advance* as one of the raw materials for the calculation. One determines costs and benefits, one determines equivalencies (to be able to put various costs and benefits into a common measure), and then one sets to toting things up—waiting, as it were, with bated breath for the results of the calculation to come out. The outcome is determined by the arithmetic; if the outcome is a close call or if one is not good at long division, one does not know how it will turn out until the calculation is finished. In the kind of deliberative judgment that is performed without a common measure, no establishment of equivalencies occurs in advance. Equivalencies are not aids to the decision process. In fact, the decision-maker might not even be aware of what the "in effect" equivalencies were, at least before they are revealed to him afterwards by someone pointing out what he had "in effect" done. The decision-maker would see himself as simply having made a deliberative judgment; the "in effect" equivalency number did not play a causal role in the decision but at most merely reflects it. Given this, the argument against making the process explicit is the one discussed earlier in the discussion of problems with putting specific quantified values on things that are not normally quantified—that the very act of doing so may serve to reduce the value of those things.

My OWN JUDGMENT is that modest efforts to assess levels of benefits and costs are justified, although I do not believe that government agencies ought to sponsor efforts to put dollar prices on non-market things. I also do not believe that the cry for more cost-benefit analysis in regulation is, on the whole, justified. If regulatory officials were so insensitive about regulatory costs that they did not provide acceptable raw material for deliberative judgments (even if not of a strictly cost-benefit nature), my conclusion might be different. But a good deal of research into costs and benefits already occurs—actually, far more in the U.S. regulatory process than in that of any other industrial society. The danger now would seem to come more from the other side. ■

[14]

Defending
Cost-Benefit Analysis
Replies to Steven Kelman

*In our last issue, Steven Kelman of Harvard's Kennedy School of Government
criticized cost-benefit analysis from the perspective not of economics but of
ethical theory. He concluded that in health, safety, and environmental
regulation, (1) certain actions are morally right even where costs exceed
benefits, (2) "efforts to put dollar values on non-marketed things" should not
be supported, and (3) by and large, regulators are already paying enough
attention to cost-benefit analysis.*
*As might be expected, this attack on one of the generally accepted pillars of
regulatory reform provoked a record number of replies from our readership.
A sampling is presented below.*

GERARD BUTTERS, JOHN CALFEE, PAULINE IPPOLITO

IN HIS ARTICLE, Steve Kelman argues against the increased use of cost-benefit analysis for regulatory decisions involving health, safety, and the environment. His basic contention is that these decisions are moral ones, and that cost-benefit analysis is therefore inappropriate because it requires the adoption of an unsatisfactory moral system. He supports his argument with a series of examples, most of which involve private decisions. In these situations, he asserts, cost-benefit advocates must renounce any moral qualms about lies, broken promises, and violations of human rights.

We disagree (and in doing so, we speak for ourselves, not for the Federal Trade Commission or its staff). Cost-benefit analysis is not a means for judging private decisions. It is a guide for decision making involving others, especially when the welfare of many individuals must be balanced. It is designed not to dictate individual values, but to take them into account when decisions must be made collectively. Its use is grounded on the principle that, in a democracy, government must act as an agent of the citizens.

The authors are staff economists with the Bureau of Economics, Federal Trade Commission.

We see no reason to abandon this principle when health and safety are involved. Consider, for example, a proposal to raise the existing federal standards on automobile safety. Higher standards will raise the costs, and hence the price, of cars. From our point of view, the appropriate policy judgment rests on whether customers will value the increased safety sufficiently to warrant the costs. Any violation of a cost-benefit criterion would require that consumers purchase something they would not voluntarily purchase or prevent them from purchasing something they want. One might argue, in the spirit of Kelman's analysis, that many consumers would want the government to impose a more stringent standard than they would choose for themselves. If so, how is the cost-safety trade-off that consumers really want to be determined? Any objective way of doing this would be a natural part of cost-benefit analysis.

Kelman also argues that the process of assigning a dollar value to things not traded in the marketplace is rife with indignities, flaws, and biases. Up to a point, we agree. It *is* difficult to place objective dollar values on certain intangible costs and benefits. Even with regard to intangibles which

DEFENDING COST-BENEFIT ANALYSIS

have been systematically studied, such as the "value of life," we know of no cost-benefit advocate who believes that regulatory staff economists should reduce every consideration to dollar terms and simply supply the decision maker with the bottom line. Our main concerns are twofold: (1) to make the major costs and benefits explicit so that the decision maker makes the trade-offs consciously and with the prospect of being held accountable, and (2) to encourage the move toward a more consistent set of standards.

The gains from adopting consistent regulatory standards can be dramatic. If costs and benefits are not balanced in making decisions, it is likely that the returns per dollar in terms of health and safety will be small for some programs and large for others. Such programs present opportunities for saving lives, and cost-benefit analysis will reveal them. Perhaps, as Kelman argues, there is something repugnant about assigning dollar values to lives. But the alternative can be to sacrifice lives needlessly by failing to carry out the calculations that would have revealed the means for saving them. It should be kept in mind that the avoidance of cost-benefit analysis has its own cost, which can be gauged in lives as well as in dollars.

Nonetheless, we do not dispute that cost-benefit analysis is highly imperfect. We would welcome a better guide to public policy, a guide that would be efficient, morally attractive, and certain to ensure that governments follow the dictates of the governed. Kelman's proposal is to adopt an ethical system that balances conflicts between certain unspecified "duties" and "rights" according to "deliberate reflection." But who is to do the reflecting, and on whose behalf? His guide places no clear limits on the actions of regulatory agencies. Rather than enhancing the connections between individual values and state decisions, such a vague guideline threatens to sever them. Is there a common moral standard that every regulator will magically and independently arrive at through "deliberate reflection"? We doubt it. Far more likely is a system in which bureaucratic decisions reflect the preferences, not of the citizens, but of those in a peculiar position to influence decisions. What concessions to special interests cannot be disguised by claiming that it is degrading to make explicit the trade-offs reflected in the decision? What individual crusade cannot be rationalized by an appeal to "public values" that "rise above" values revealed by individual choices?   ■

[15]

The Issue of Standing in Cost-Benefit Analysis

Dale Whittington
Duncan MacRae, Jr.

Abstract

Insufficient attention has been given in cost-benefit analysis to whose benefits are to be counted. Foreigners, illegal aliens, fetuses, and criminals are problematic cases. Persons or entities may be given "standing" by participation in decision processes; by having their preferences counted, if meaningful preferences exist; by having their welfare counted, if they cannot express their preferences; or by representation by others whom they do not choose. Problems of standing arise in the valuation of life, the consideration of future generations and nonhuman entities, and equity weighting. These problems may be treated by altering the scope of the expert community or by interaction between that community and the political community. They are not always resolvable, but should be treated more explicitly.

INTRODUCTION Despite the extensive literature on cost-benefit analysis, there has been little recognition of the importance of one of its most obvious limitations: a possible lack of agreement on whose benefits are to count in the summation of costs and benefits to individuals affected by a project or policy. The basic criterion of cost-benefit analysis is the Hicks–Kaldor (or potential Pareto improvement) test, which simply states that a project is worthwhile in efficiency terms if the beneficiaries could potentially compensate the losers so that everyone would be at least as well off as before the project and some individuals would be better off. The wisdom of this criterion has been much contested. E. J. Mishan, one of the most widely respected proponents of the use of the potential Pareto improvement rule, argues that the ethical justification for its use rests upon two premises: (1) that each person's welfare is to count and is to count according to his own valuation, and (2) that there is a social

Paper Presented at the Annual Meeting of the Association for Public Policy Analysis and Management, Washington D.C., October 24–26, 1985.

Journal of Policy Analysis and Management, Vol. 5, No. 4, 665–682 (1986)
© 1986 by the Association for Public Policy Analysis and Management
Published by John Wiley & Sons, Inc.   CCC 0276-8739/86/030665-18$04.00

consensus that a change that meets a potential Pareto improvement confers a net benefit on society.[1] The first of these assumptions states that benefits are to be estimated from the preferences of those affected. The second implies that there exists a consensus about whose benefits are to count.

For some classes of problems consensus may indeed exist on both points, but for many types of problems of broad contemporary interest the implied consensus on standing resulting from the second condition does not in fact hold. Serious disagreement can arise as to who should have "standing" in the cost-benefit analysis. In this paper, we explore this question of standing and illustrate its significance in some policy problems, leaving aside questions about what sorts of preferences or welfare should count (as well as other questions about the assumptions of cost-benefit analysis and its underlying utilitarian philosophy). We also consider the relationship between equity weighting schemes and the issue of standing and present some approaches for resolving disputes about standing. Ultimately the questions involved cannot be resolved on technical grounds, but depend on the analyst's claims to express the ethical consensus of a society.[2]

In its purest form, cost-benefit analysis attempts to measure the aggregate sum of net compensating variations—or "willingness to pay"—for persons affected by a project or policy:

$$NB(x) = \sum_{i=1}^{n} [B_i(x) - C_i(x)] \qquad (1)$$

where $B_i(x) - C_i(x)$ = willingness of individual i to pay for project x, that is, his willingness both to pay for the beneficial aspects of the project, $B_i(x)$, and to be paid for the detrimental aspects $C_i(x)$; n = number of individuals affected by project x; $NB(x)$ = net benefits to n individuals from project x. Precisely which individuals should be accounted for in this calculation is obviously a crucial assumption, but in practice it is rarely explicitly addressed. The usual assumption in cost-benefit analysis is that all persons within a country's national boundaries are to be counted in the summation, provided that they have at least some rights of citizenship. For example, there is a clear consensus that children should be counted, even though they do not have the right to vote. On the other hand, though the effects of some policies (such as regulations designed to reduce acid rain) have dramatic consequences outside a country's borders, economists have rarely argued in favor of a universalist utilitarianism that would count affected foreigners equally with citizens. If applied to international questions of income equity or the welfare of the poor, a universalist policy could diverge widely from views of justice held by most citizens of rich countries.

The practice of equating standing with citizenship worked reasonably well in most early applications of cost-benefit analysis. For instance, in the appraisal of water resources development projects, it served to broaden the focus of the analysis from the immediate beneficiaries of a project (often limited to a small district or region) to include other citizens who would have to pay the costs of what typically turned out to be porkbarrel projects. Neither the costs nor the benefits commonly spilled over national boundaries. Though the techniques of cost-benefit analysis were often misused, the thrust of the analysis should theoretically have detected narrowly conceived projects that were designed to serve only a few who would gain something at the expense of the majority, who would lose more.[3]

The issue of standing may also have been neglected in the literature because economists felt they had little expertise that could be brought to bear on the question. Thus, following Mishan, they attempted to calculate the willingness to pay for "each person in the defined community," leaving the determination of the "defined community" to the political process.[4]

PROBLEMATIC EXAMPLES Today, however, President Reagan's Executive Order 12291 has expanded the use of the cost-benefit criterion to include all "major" regulations and cost-benefit analysts are increasingly confronting situations in which the issue of standing is both important and controversial.[5] To illustrate the nature of the problem, we offer three examples.

First, suppose that a proposed federal regulation would increase the eligibility of AFDC recipients to receive subsidized abortions. A cost-benefit analysis would theoretically require a comparison of the beneficiaries' willingness to pay and the costs to the public that the service would involve. But what about the costs to the fetuses? Should the fetuses have standing in the cost-benefit calculation? Clearly, on this question there is no ethical consensus in our society to which a cost-benefit analyst can appeal.

Lest we be accused of having chosen a uniquely intractable example, consider the case of illegal aliens. Estimates of the number of illegal aliens currently in the United States run as high as 20 million. Should the benefits their children receive from public education be included in a social cost-benefit analysis of educational policies? More broadly speaking, almost any estimate of consumer surplus associated with public or private goods in the United States, if derived from market observations of prices and quantities, will reflect illegal aliens' willingness to pay. Should the cost-benefit analyst attempt to deduct their willingness to pay from such aggregate measures of benefits? Again, there is no consensus on this question.[6]

As a third example, consider the cost-benefit analysis of the Job Corps program prepared by David Long, Charles Mallar, and Craig Thornton.[7] The Job Corps is a federally funded program that provides a variety of services to disadvantaged youths, primarily vocational training, basic education, and health care. In their evaluation Long, Mallar, and Thornton divided society into two groups: Corpsmembers and everybody else (the rest of society). Both groups were accorded standing in the analysis. One type of benefit identified and estimated was the reduction of crime that would result because Corpsmembers would be occupied and therefore have fewer opportunities, and needs, to resort to crime. One component of these benefits would be a reduction in property crimes such as robbery, burglary, larceny, and theft of motor vehicles. The authors put the cost to the rest of society of a burglary arrest at $9,996, of which $5,895 was attributed to criminal justice system costs. But the criminals were estimated to benefit from a burglary by $1,247 on average (assuming they net 35 percent of the value of stolen property); thus the net cost to society would be $8,749 per arrest. In a sense, this is a rigorous application of utilitarian principles of analysis. But should the gains of the criminal from the crime be granted standing—and if so, to what extent? After all, as a society we prohibit an individual convicted of a felony from voting while incarcerated; if the vote is a criterion for citizenship, political "standing" is presumably withheld from convicted burglars. This is not to say, however, that convicted criminals lose all their rights, or that someone who violates the law on one occasion should have all his or her preferences in other spheres of life ignored.

Society places moral bounds on the application of cost-benefit calculations by not granting standing to certain individuals or to the preferences of certain individuals in specific situations. Cost-benefit analysis also typically takes for granted the existing system of property rights in the sense that illegal transfers of property are not permitted, even if on occasion they should produce a net economic benefit. It is thus conceivable that the majority of society would disagree with Long, Mallar, and Thornton that the gains of criminals should be included in the summation of costs and benefits of the Job Corps—even conceding the legitimacy of criminals' desires to avoid "cruel and unusual punishment." Our invocation of society's values here illustrates that notions of standing, like all the valuative postulates of cost-benefit analysis, depend on support from "society." There are, of course, continuing arguments within society and the polity (as well as within the professions) as to what the prevailing or legitimate values are and whether they should be changed. We return to this issue, and the problems it poses for an expert group claiming to express a social consensus, in the final part of this discussion. We aim here, first, to raise the issue of standing as one that can often be treated more explicitly and systematically by cost-benefit analysts—perhaps as a form of sensitivity analysis. This may require the statement of more than one possible view available for analysis of a given problem. Second, we hope to show that in some cases means of resolution of such diverse views may be sought.

TYPES OF STANDING To explore the issues implicit in the examples presented above, we need to examine the concept of standing in more detail. Suppose the preferences of an individual i are described by a utility function $U_i(.)$, the arguments of which are quantities of a collection of goods $X_1, \ldots, X_m$. One's utility may, of course, depend on the utility of others, so that

$$U_i = U_i(X_1, \ldots, X_m, U_j). \tag{2}$$

This causes no conceptual problems in measuring changes in the utility of individual i that would result from changes in the availability of goods. But individual j is not considered to have "standing" merely because his preferences are taken into account by individual i. In cost-benefit analysis, standing is typically taken to mean the "right" to be included in the set of individuals whose changes in utility (however measured) are aggregated (in the set of individuals $i = 1, \ldots, n$).

In policy analyses, however, standing has multiple meanings. All appear to fall along a continuum of political involvement by the individual. At the point of greatest involvement, standing is defined as the right to represent one's own preferences—to be a decision-maker. Thus in democracies one has standing if one is enfranchised to vote, though actual systems of representation can also allow various degrees of participation or influence. Similarly, in our legal system one has standing if one is among the parties whose interests can be considered in the case.

A second and more inclusive concept of standing is the right to have one's preferences included in a utilitarian aggregation of welfare. These preferences may be inferred from demand data or from surveys of representative samples, as well as by questioning each affected person. This notion of standing, commonly used in cost-benefit analysis, assumes that the individual, now living, has preferences that can be evaluated numerically, but need not participate personally in expressing them. In this concept, standing can again be not only present or absent, but also fractional: equity weights allow this.

A third and still more inclusive notion of standing permits the analyst's estimation of the welfare of persons who may at present be incapable of expressing preferences. It is in this sense that certain classes of citizens, such as infants, can also be granted standing. Though in practice it may be difficult to determine infants' preferences (and foolish to assume that they are fixed), efforts are sometimes made to estimate infants' welfare and to count it along with that of adults. Similar reasoning, as we shall see, might be applied to future generations. In this third type of standing, the person or entity experiencing "well-being" is counted as such but need not even be capable of expressing preferences at present.

The ethical bases for the second and third notions of standing are somewhat different and relate to two versions of utilitarianism. The third and most inclusive notion of standing is founded in a utilitarian approach that attempts to measure an individual's "well-being" independently of his preferences. The second, or intermediate, notion of standing rests in part upon a utilitarian approach that defines welfare as satisfaction of preferences. In cost-benefit analysis, for example, each person is assumed to be the best judge of his or her own preferences for consumption. Human beings may thus be viewed as producers of welfare through their consumption. The planner or cost-benefit analyst seeks to maximize a sum of welfare, but not necessarily by giving the persons affected free choice of policies or political participation (even though their preferences are taken as the best measure of their welfare). If a public project is to be built, for example, the preferences of those affected for specific outcomes are estimated, but the persons themselves are not necessarily encouraged to vote as citizens on the building of the project.

This perspective was satirized in Aldous Huxley's *Brave New World* (first published in 1932). In that novel those whose happiness is counted are accorded standing of a sort, but they are not necessarily participants either in the political process or in the estimation of their welfare.[8] Their "citizenship" entitles them to be counted, but nothing more. If this view is taken literally and extended to living adult citizens, it can be both paternalistic and undemocratic.

A fourth notion of standing is the right to have one's preferences represented by others, even though the person represented does not participate in choosing those others; this extends the notion of having one's preferences counted by an analyst. A common example is the inclusion of children's demand in parents' willingness to pay for a good or service. In a recent paper, Fred Frohock has examined decisions on therapy in a neonatal setting, decisions that are always representational because infants are too young to make decisions for themselves.[9] How could one go about representing another who did not choose him to do so? Frohock suggests three approaches. One would be for the representative authority to act on the basis of what the individual being represented would choose for himself. But evidence such as a will or past declarations of an individual's prior wishes is not present in the neonatal setting. A second approach—which has been challenged in court, often successfully—would be to invest some representative with the authority to make decisions on behalf of another when there is no indication what the affected individual would have chosen. A third would be to represent the "best interests" of the individual, whether or not the individual can express those interests. This last approach is analogous to procedures we consider below for valuing lives of future generations and nonhuman entities. In practice, hospitals that deliver such neonatal services have developed all sorts of complex advisory committees to deal with such issues.

STANDING AND THE VALUATION OF HUMAN LIFE The ambiguities involved in the application of a concept of standing within a neonatal nursery bear upon the widely discussed problem of valuing human life within a cost-benefit framework. There are two basic approaches to the valuation of human life in cost-benefit analysis: human capital, and willingness to pay. The fundamental difference between them hinges on the concept of standing. The human capital approach is similar to the procedure a farmer might use to place a dollar value on an animal; Mark Thompson likens it to the way in which a machine is valued.[10] As Mishan points out, this "so-called net output method" for evaluating a life calculates "what matters to the rest of society": "the resulting loss, or gain, to it following the death of one of its members."[11] For a dairy cow, for example, the profit-maximizing farmer would consider the discounted value of the time stream of revenues from the sale of the following: (1) the milk, (2) the carcass after the cow was slaughtered, and (3) any calves produced. Counted against these benefits would be the costs of feeding and sheltering the cow and other routine expenses.

How would the farmer value the life of a newborn calf? The calf would have the same potential of producing a stream of benefits (somewhat differentiated by sex), but there would be a delay in receiving them because of a costly and unproductive period of early growth. Similarly, a human capital approach to valuing human life would place a lower value on the life of a child lost to illness or an accident than on the life of a young adult, because substantial investments in education and training would already have been made in the latter and benefits would be expected from them sooner.

Suppose now that the calf is sick and the farmer is considering veterinary treatment. Here the farmer's calculation goes farther than the human capital approach in denying standing to the organism that embodies the capital; the calf's life or well-being is not considered to be of value in itself. The farmer has the option of letting the calf die and breeding another. The value to be assigned to the calf's life (in terms of the cost that would be worth paying to preserve it) would then be the greater of (1) the discounted stream of expected net benefits minus veterinary expenses for restoring the calf to good health, or (2) a slightly postponed discounted stream of benefits minus the comparable "replacement cost" of producing another calf and rearing it up to the same age. Like the farmer with his calf, the analyst who chooses the human capital approach does not consider the preferences of the organism at risk, but unlike the the farmer, the analyst does grant the individual standing to the extent that the individual's life is not valued at the opportunity cost of raising another person.

The way in which replacement costs are handled in the human capital approach is fundamentally related to the question of standing. Though today there seems to be a clear consensus that healthy infants have standing within the community, that has not always been the case. In the year 1152 an English nobleman, John Marshal, gave his young son as a hostage in order to avert a threatened siege against his castle. But this was merely a tactic of delay: he soon abandoned his son to the enemy, telling the besieger's messenger that "he had the anvils and hammers with which to forge still better sons."[12] Infanticide has been practiced in a wide variety of cultures throughout history. Deformed or retarded infants, for example, have had a lesser claim on a community's hearts and resources than others. In some American Indian tribes it was the father's duty to kill deformed newborns.

The willingness-to-pay approach to valuing life gives the person affected a higher level of standing by considering his or her prefer-

672 | **Standing in Cost-Benefit Analysis**

ences, which can be measured either by observing an individual's behavior or by asking direct questions. If an analyst asks a person what sum (compensating variation) would be acceptable as compensation for that person's certain death, presumably the answer is an infinite sum—which implies the action cannot be justified on the Paretian criterion.[13] Nevertheless, the fact that the individual has standing is taken to mean that his or her preferences on the matter cannot be excluded from the analysis.

As Mishan points out, a more realistic and interesting question would be how much a person would accept in compensation for an additional risk of death (that is, for a specified increase in probability).[14] We are still faced, however, with the unsettling result that the willingness-to-pay procedure would place different values on the lives of the sick and the healthy. These differences do not result simply from differences in wealth and ability to pay. When medical treatment is involved, as Richard Thaler and William Gould have demonstrated, the willingness-to-pay approach gives more weight to the stronger preferences of the sick than to the weaker preferences of the healthy.[15] This could lead to suboptimal investments in terms of saving lives, placing resources in remediation rather than in prevention where they might be more effective.

We are also faced with the problem of choosing between policies dealing with infant mortality. Infants cannot themselves place values on their future lives because they are too young to make such judgments and do not themselves possess the resources to pay. Thus their interests must be represented in some form by others. We suspect that there would be a societal consensus that any value assigned to the life of an infant must not be based on a concept of willingness to pay. The analyst would ultimately confront two different approaches for valuing life, both with ethical sanction: one for infants and children (who are represented), and another for adults (who choose).

THE STANDING OF FUTURE GENERATIONS The policy issues posed by this continuum of meanings of standing are nowhere better illustrated than in the area of environmental policy affecting future generations. Indeed, concepts of standing are at the heart of much of environmental ethics and value systems. The problem of projecting long-term environmental damages and the welfare of future generations occurs in a variety of environmental regulatory situations.

For example, consider the question of what to do about uranium mill tailings at mining sites. As a society we must decide how much money to spend today to reduce deaths and illnesses from long-term exposure to low levels of hazardous substances, such as radon gas, that escape from these sources. As required by Executive Order 12291, the Environmental Protection Agency prepared a regulatory impact analysis that attempted to compare the costs of control with the health benefits that would result from the control of radioactive emissions.[16] Because mill tailings remain hazardous for very long periods (hundreds of thousands of years), a crucial question in the cost-benefit analysis is whether future generations have standing in the calculation. In most past cost-benefit studies this has not been a major issue, either because the costs and benefits were presented on an annualized basis, or because analysts assumed a 25- to 50-year planning horizon. EPA's analytical approach was to limit the benefits considered from reducing this hazard to those occurring only over the next hundred years, without discounting them. But arbitrarily assigning standing only to that limited group of present and near-future generations merely served to muddy the waters further.

There are, in fact, two basic approaches to the problem of standing of future generations. The first is to assume that they have no standing. In that case, the welfare of future generations would still enter the reckoning, but only as an argument in the utility functions of individuals alive today. Thus, following Amartya Sen, my utility could be hypothesized as dependent on my own consumption, the consumption of others, the consumption of my heirs, and the consumption of others' heirs, as in Equ. (2) on p. 5.[17] If I were asked how much I would be willing to pay to clean up radioactive uranium mill tailings, my answer would reflect the depth of my feelings and preferences for future generations.

Though it is common practice in cost-benefit analyses to exclude future generations, economists have long recognized that there is no ethical basis for such a practice. Starting as early as Frank Ramsey's seminal paper, the welfare of future generations has been included directly in economic growth models (not indirectly through the utility functions of existing individuals).[18] Indeed, Ramsey himself rejected the notion of discounting the utility of future generations, an approach he considered both unimaginative and unethical.[19] The approach presented by Partha Dasgupta, Stephen Marglin, and Amartya Sen in the UNIDO project appraisal manual is consistent with Ramsey's position. They do not advocate placing less value on the welfare of future generations, but rather justify discounting on equity grounds: that since incomes are increasing and thus the marginal utility of income is declining, less weight should be placed on providing income to future generations than to the relatively poorer current generation.[20] Current practice in cost-benefit analysis may thus reflect a lack of explicit attention to the problem of whether to grant standing to future generations, rather than any clear ethical consensus on the matter.[21]

THE STANDING OF NON-HUMAN ENTITIES In his now classic essay, *Should Trees Have Standing?*, Christopher Stone presents a legal brief for allowing suits to be brought to court on behalf of nonhuman species, ecosystems, and environmental entities.[22] This ethical contention cannot be dismissed out of hand, particularly in a society with strong religious beliefs in the sanctity of nature. In cultures throughout the world, notions of murder and sacredness extend beyond the human species. In Buddhist traditions, consciousness is thought to extend to all sentient beings, and man himself may be reincarnated in various species. In Western culture, accusations of "murder" are often made in connection with debates over whaling and scientific experimentation with higher animals such as dogs and monkeys. The higher the level of consciousness of the nonhuman species, the more people seem inclined to grant it some rights or standing.

Whatever one's personal assessment of Stone's argument, it clearly strikes at a key assumption of cost-benefit analysis: that only the preferences of members of the human species are to count in aggregate measures of social welfare. Stone's position is an ethic widely accepted among members of the environmental movement. If cost-benefit analysis is viewed as a form of argumentation, it is *a priori* unlikely to convince, or even interest, someone who believes the "preferences" of trees should be included in the calculation.[23]

EQUITY WEIGHTS The question of who has standing is closely related to a long-standing controversy over the wisdom of considering income distribution consequences in cost-benefit analyses—that is, of using equity weights in calculations of a project's gains and losses. The arguments of a social welfare function are the utility levels of the individuals with standing, and the partial derivative of the social welfare function with respect to an individual's utility measures the social value of an increase in his utility: in effect, his equity weight. But because utility is unobservable, for practical policy purposes changes in individual welfare are measured in terms of income, and equity weights are expressed in terms of the social value of an extra unit of income accruing to various individuals or income classes. In practice, economists have typically proposed equity weighting schemes based on a function relating an individual's utility (U) to his income (Y), assuming that all individuals in the community have the same utility function. For example, two commonly used functional forms are[24]

$$(d\underline{U}/d\underline{Y}) = Y^a, \quad \text{with } a < 0 \tag{3}$$

and

$$(d\underline{U}/d\underline{Y}) = e^{-(Y/Y_0)}. \tag{4}$$

The derivative of the function evaluated at a particular income level is termed the equity weight. Then to determine the social value of the change resulting from a proposed project, the willingness to pay of the individuals in each income class is multiplied by the corresponding weight. In effect, gains to the poor are weighted more heavily than gains to the rich, so that a premium is placed on projects that benefit the poor at the expense of the rich. The product of the equity weight and the aggregate willingness to pay is still measured in money terms.

As critics of equity weighting have pointed out, such schemes revive notions from the "old welfare economics" of comparing the utilities of different persons on a cardinal scale.[25] The "new welfare economists" have gone to great lengths to avoid such "unscientific" comparisons and have sought to develop the Paretian approach as an alternative. In the context of decisions as to who has standing, however, the Paretian approach is not immune to similarly "unscientific" interpersonal comparisons. It is simply another system of assigning weights to individuals, in which all weights are either 0 or 1. All individuals granted standing in the analysis are weighted equally as regards their monetary benefits and costs; everyone outside this "defined community" is ignored. To be sure, complex interpersonal utility calculations may be avoided for comparisons among individuals assigned a weight of 1, provided an ethical consensus exists on the use of the Paretian criterion. But interpersonal comparisons of some characteristics of individuals are unavoidable in the decision as to who receives a weight of 0.

For example; in its environmental impact statement on uranium milling, the United States Nuclear Regulatory Commission concluded that the adverse health effects of radon gas emissions from uranium mill tailings would extend far beyond the borders of the United States.[26] Adverse effects on citizens of Canada and Mexico were estimated to be 10 percent of the total forecast for the North American continent; exposure in Continental Europe and Asia would add 25 percent more to that total. Thus roughly one-third of the benefits of controlling radon gas emissions were expected to accrue to individuals outside the United States. In its final analysis, the Nuclear Regulatory Commission included the effects on Canadians and Mexicans, effectively assigning them full standing. Individuals in Europe, Asia, and the rest of the world were not counted. In the public comments on the environmental impact statement, representatives of the uranium industry objected to the equal treatment granted to Canadians and Mexicans; in the subsequent Regulatory Impact Analysis on uranium mill tailings (mentioned previously) the Environmental Protection Agency assigned 0 weight to everyone outside the borders of the United States. Obviously, the results of such analyses can be heavily influenced by ethically questionable and typically obscure judgments on who has standing.

WAYS TO DEAL WITH STANDING Any attempt to resolve these issues of standing must reconcile two sometimes incompatible goals of cost-benefit analysis: to make expert judgments and to reflect values that are in keeping with those of "society." Whatever its theoretical elegance, cost-benefit analysis is essentially an ethical procedure for comparing elementary values, including intrapersonal comparisons among valuations of various goods; interpersonal comparisons; comparisons over time; and comparisons of the values of various alternative uncertain events. For social support of these valuations, analysts look to clients, to segments of society, to authoritative public decisions, or to argumentative claims that their assessments are consistent with societal values. They also claim support from the respect accorded to economics and to technical expertise generally; but in so doing, they may have to deemphasize aspects of cost-benefit analysis that are less precise or command less consensual support within and outside economics.[27]

Cost-benefit analysts can seek to reconcile their expertise with their need for support from society or the political community in four general ways:

(1) By assuming certain "social" values without interaction with the political community, and simply postulating these values within the expert community.

(2) By relinquishing certain valuative decisions to "politics" and deliberately narrowing the scope of analysts' judgments to matters in which they can claim expertise.

(3) By interacting with the existing political community in the development of postulates, or parameter estimates, acceptable to both.

(4) By seeking out, or taking part in building, alternative institutions for decision-making within the political community. Each of these approaches is applicable to the full range of valuative and methodological postulates of cost-benefit analysis or policy analysis. Let us consider them here, however, primarily with regard to the question of standing.

Postulation of Values Within the Expert Community Mishan effectively assumes that he (or his expert community) knows the values of society better than do political officials; and he proposes a relation of economics to society (albeit through the pages of a technical publication read primarily by persons trained in economics) with this claim:

> Economists are not alone in being unimpressed by the workaday wisdom of majority rule in modern societies. Notwithstanding conventional safeguards, a majority in power is capable of irresponsible and even tyrannical behaviour toward individuals and minorities. . . The consequences of these deficiencies in the working of democracy can be limited by decentralized institutions, and by constitutional restrictions that rest upon a broad consensus. The acceptance of either, that is, depends on near-unanimous acceptance of a number of ethical premises. . . In addition there may be a number of ethical premises which, though they appear to command widespread assent, are not written into a constitution. . . . They can be then said to form part of a virtual constitution. And if, among these ethical propositions that comprise a virtual constitution, there are several on which a welfare economics can be raised then—provided always that the logical structure is flawless—its guiding rules can truthfully claim to rest on a widely accepted ethical base. Such rules, on any ethical ranking, would therefore transcend economic decisions reached by political processes. . . .[28]

This reasoning leads Mishan to what is commonly termed the Paretian approach to the practice of cost-benefit analysis.[29]

From this perspective, it would seem that economists or philosophers could set forth valuative postulates that they judged to command wide support, and on them build procedures for policy choice. They would then have to decide at the start what political community should be the reference for this consensus. Mishan has said that the economist who undertakes a cost-benefit analysis asks whether "society as a whole will be better off by undertaking this project rather than not undertaking it."[30] Similarly, Dasgupta, Marglin, and Sen have remarked that in developing countries the cost-benefit analyst is dealing with a "government" that has the responsibility to pursue policies that are in the "national interest."[31] In both these statements the economists seem to be assuming that the membership of a society or nation can be delimited without troublesome ambiguities and that this membership is so much a matter of consensus that it need not be examined. To attempt such an examination would indeed take them beyond their realm of expertise. The self-contained logical structure of the argument is most easily preserved by ignoring such questions.

Relinquishing Certain Valuations to Politics Robert Sugden and Alan Williams suggest that this stance, which they call the "decision-making" approach, is a conceivable alternative to the Paretian approach.[32] In the decision-making approach, the task of the analyst is "to assist the decision-maker in making choices that are consistent with his (that is, the decision-maker's) objectives." If one claims to serve a political community, one can adopt a particular version of this approach by assuming that the decisions made by legitimate organs of government embody the political community's objectives. This approach then spares the analyst the task of making ethical judgments and protects the claimed sphere of expertise by not mixing into it controversial nonexpert judgments. Members of expert groups often urge their colleagues to refrain from dealing with problems for which they lack expertise.[33]

As for the issue of standing, this approach makes no effort to resolve the question but rather defines it as outside the competence of the expert group. The analyst's choice of the governmental organs for which he will work implicitly announces that he delegates the definition of standing to them. Note that both of the first two approaches maintain the customary isolation of the expert community's discourse from interference by laymen. The first unilaterally claims to resolve valuative issues; the second unilaterally abandons them to others to decide.

Interactive Approaches It is also possible for the analyst to interact with political authorities, or even with the public, in ways that preserve to varying degrees the claim of expertise in a delimited area. One way to achieve this is through limiting the analyst's claim to expertise to that of encouraging logical consistency.[34]

The form of this approach best known to cost-benefit analysts is that proposed by Dasgupta, Sen, and Marglin.[35] They assume that the local project evaluators (analysts) in a developing country are dealing with a Central Planning Office, which in turn deals with policy-makers. The Central Planning Office can tell the policy-makers, or national political leadership, the implications that projected decisions will have for national parameters—such as the social rate of discount (which implicitly assigns weights to the welfare of future generations), the social opportunity cost of capital, and the shadow value of labor—and ask that these implications be consistent from one policy choice to another. In the resulting dialogue, the political leaders can conceivably be educated in the meaning of the parameters and the need for consistency.

Consistency is, however, a weak value premise from which to approach the question of standing. Any set of persons or organisms may be consistently defined as those who "count," whether by elitists, racists, proponents of the local or national interest, universal utilitarians who claim to represent the entire world population and its future members, or advocates of the well-being of other species. A broader role for the analyst, but one that exceeds the usual claims of expertise, would then involve espousal of substantive views on who shall count. Such ethical arguments may transcend even social scientists' most ambitious claims of expertise, but they have been pursued in the philosophical literature on public policy.[36]

Creating New Institutions for Decision-making In the previous approach, it was assumed that the existing governmental structure was the analyst's client and that no changes were to be made in it except for the linking of analysts or planners to the existing decision-making process. But proposals have also been made for changing the structures of decision-making themselves to accommodate analysis or to facilitate adjudication of problems between members of previously separate units. With respect to standing, what is at stake is the possible creation of new decision mechanisms that give standing, or increased weight, to participants who had insufficient influence before. We assume here that influence corresponds to the capacity to count one's own welfare more heavily. Such influence may lead to a "counting" of welfares directly through voting processes rather than by cost-benefit analysis; or if cost-benefit analysis is undertaken for such a newly created institution, it may incorporate new weights.

The community mediation procedures that have been adopted to facilitate dispute resolution are an apt example.[37] Some communities that have failed to reach agreement on policies for economic development have invited mediators in to help resolve their disputes. One strategy that such mediators have used has been to devise a temporary alternative governmental organ in which representatives of the city government are put together with newly chosen representatives of neighborhoods and business. The deliberations of this new group extend over a period of months and consensus is sought. The effect has been to give a greater weight to interests that have been judged to be underrepresented.

Other decision-making structures that have given standing to previously unconnected groups involve the creation of new decision units that embrace formerly separate subunits. For example, as in the *Genossenschaften* in Germany, decision units that com-

bine upstream polluters and downstream users of water, have fa-
cilitated deliberation about conflicts of interest. Similarly, by creating an international authority for the protection of water quality
and fisheries, the Organization of African Unity could potentially
play a key role in ensuring sound management practices for the
East African Lakes.

CONCLUSION Perhaps controversies among nations represent the types of questions about standing that are hardest to resolve in cost-benefit
analysis. The treatment of future generations within one nation, or
of resident aliens, may involve some greater degree of fellow feeling for these other persons by present citizens than matters concerning other nations. When such feeling exists, it may become
easier either for decision-making bodies to incorporate representatives of the groups in question, or for arguments among present
members to be couched in terms that extend beyond sheer present
member interests to principles concerning present outsiders.

In recent years, the United States has become less willing to
share its sovereignty with other nations through international
bodies. Yet for Americans perhaps one of the most puzzling and
frustrating aspects of the present famine in Africa has been the
callousness and lack of concern of African national governments,
such as those in Ethiopia and Sudan, for the plight of the victims.
Nevertheless, this is actually analogous to some of the problems
inherent in our government's decisions about the ethical treatment of extranationals: for example, with the disposal of uranium
mill tailings, whether to grant standing—at least to Mexicans and
Canadians!—when projecting adverse worldwide health effects
from long-term exposure to radon gas. The famine victims are
seemingly not even accorded standing by the governments of the
countries in which they are citizens. We expect the ruling oligar-
chies in these governments to operate on the principle that all
citizens of a nation-state somehow have equal standing, but in fact
nothing could be further from the truth. Leaders in these countries
typically view individuals in the famine areas, often from different
tribes and hundreds of miles away, as being about as remote as
they seem to Americans themselves. The concept of a nation state
is still frail. Our notions of standing are not easily transferable.

Questions of standing, then, are among the most difficult value
questions for analysts (or citizens) to resolve. It is not surprising
that they have been neglected in professional discussion. Yet it
seems to us that issues of standing lie at the heart of many public
policy debates. If advocates of cost-benefit analysis continue to
claim—as they often do—to possess a powerful, broadly applicable methodology for analyzing policy alternatives, they must explicitly address these issues of standing rather than treat them as a
matter of secondary or even less importance. If we believe such
problems should be discussed by analysts, we must recognize that
some are more amenable to discussion than others, owing to
greater support by the sentiments of "society." We can always,

Standing in Cost-Benefit Analysis

however, discuss them in terms of philosophical principles, and not merely calculate the valuations that present "members" hold for "outsiders'" welfare.

For helpful suggestions we are indebted to Peter G. Brown, Philip J. Cook, William Drummond, James J. Gallagher, Susan Hadden, Eric Hyman, Gerald J. Postema, E. J. Mishan, A. K. Sen, V. Kerry Smith, David Warner, and two anonymous referees.

DALE WHITTINGTON is Associate Professor of City and Regional Planning at the University of North Carolina at Chapel Hill.

DUNCAN MACRAE, JR., is William Rand Kenan, Jr., Professor of Political Science and Sociology at the University of North Carolina at Chapel Hill.

NOTES   1. Ezra J. Mishan, "The Nature of Economic Expertise Reconsidered," in *Economic Efficiency and Social Welfare: Selected Essays on Fundamental Aspects of the Economic Theory of Social Welfare* (London: George Allen & Unwin, 1981), p. 182.

2. Ezra J. Mishan, *Introduction to Normative Economics* (Oxford: Oxford University Press, 1981), p. 17. Conceivably an analyst might engage in the debates that shape society's ethical views, but such engagement might run counter to the claim of factual expertise.

3. See Steve H. Hanke and Richard A. Walker, "Benefit-Cost Analysis Reconsidered: An Evaluation of the Mid-State Project," *Water Resources Research*, 10 (5) (October 1974): 898–908; and W. Norton Grubb, Dale Whittington, and Michael Humphries, "The Ambiguities of Benefit-Cost Analysis: An Evaluation of Regulatory Impact Analyses Under Executive Order 12291," in V. Kerry Smith, ed., *Environmental Policy Under Reagan's Executive Order: The Role of Benefit-Cost Analysis* (Chapel Hill: University of North Carolina Press, 1984). Many project appraisals continue to count only state or local effects, but this practice is not usually discussed in cost-benefit textbooks.

4. Mishan, *Introduction to Normative Economics.*

5. V. Kerry Smith, ed., *Environmental Policy under Reagan's Executive Order: The Role of Benefit-Cost Analysis* (Chapel Hill: University of North Carolina Press, 1984).

6. Using an argument based on human rights rather than aggregate welfare, James W. Nickel contends that "the minimal requirements of survival and a decent life . . . are possessed whether or not one is a native or an alien." See his "Human Rights and the Rights of Aliens," in Peter G. Brown and Henry Shue, eds., *The Border that Joins: Mexican Migrants and U.S. Responsibility* (Totowa, N.J.: Rowman and Littlefield, 1983, p. 40.)

7. David A. Long, Charles D. Mallar, and Craig V. D. Thornton, "Evaluating the Benefits and Costs of the Job Corps," *Journal of Policy Analysis and Management*, 1 (1) (Fall 1981): 55-56.

8. Duncan MacRae, Jr., *Policy Indicators* (Chapel Hill: University of North Carolina Press, 1985), Chapter 6.

9. Fred Frohock, "Representational Rationality: A Case Study of Therapy Decisions in a Neonatal Nursery." Center for the Study of Citizenship, Syracuse University, Occasional Paper, 1985.

10. Mark S. Thompson, *Benefit-Cost Analysis for Program Evaluation* (Beverly Hills, Calif.: Sage, 1980), p. 196.

11. Ezra J. Mishan, *Cost-Benefit Analysis*, 3rd ed. (London: George Allen & Unwin, 1982), p. 323.

12. Sidney Painter, *William Marshal* (Baltimore: Johns Hopkins University Press, 1933), p. 14.

13. Mishan, *Cost-Benefit Analysis*, p. 327. The example in our text assumes that the compensating variation is the appropriate measure of welfare change, as opposed to the equivalent variation.

14. *Ibid.* p. 328.

15. Richard Thaler and William Gould, "Public Policy toward Life Saving: Should Consumer Preferences Rule?" *Journal of Policy Analysis and Management*, 1 (2) (Winter 1982): 223-42.

16. U.S. Environmental Protection Agency (USEPA), *Regulatory Impact Analysis of Environmental Standards for Uranium Mill Tailings at Active Sites* (Washington, D.C.: USEPA, Office of Radiation Programs, 1983). See also, "An Examination of EPA's Regulatory Impact Analysis for Uranium Mill Tailings," by Dale Whittington and William Drummond. Presented at the Annual Meetings of the Allied Social Science Association, Dec. 1984, Dallas, Texas.

17. Amartya K. Sen, "Isolation, Assurance, and the Social Rate of Discount," *Quarterly Journal of Economics* 81 (1967): 112-24.

18. Frank P. Ramsey, "A Mathematical Theory of Saving," *Economic Journal*, 38 (1928): 543-59.

19. "It is assumed that we do not discount later enjoyments in comparison with earlier ones, a practice which is ethically indefensible and arises merely from the weakness of the imagination." Ibid. p. 543.

20. Partha Dasgupta, Amartya Sen, and Stephen Marglin. *Guidelines for Project Evaluation* (New York: United Nations, 1972), pp. 164–166.

21. Parfit, writing more recently, recognizes that there can be some moral justification for considering the claims of persons with whom we have special relations, but he argues that discounting based on this ground should not go on indefinitely weighting later generations less and less. "Energy Policy and the Further Future: The Social Discount Rate," by Derek Parfit, in Douglas MacLean and Peter G. Brown, eds., *Energy and the Future* (Totowa, N.J.: Rowman and Littlefield, 1983).

22. Christopher D. Stone, *Should Trees Have Standing? Toward Legal Rights for Natural Objects* (Los Altos, Calif.: William Kaufmann, 1974).

23. Harvey Goldstein, "Planning as Argumentation," *Environment and Planning B*, vol. 2 (1984): 297-312.

24. A. Myrick Freeman, "Project Design and Evaluation with Multiple Objectives," in Robert H. Haveman and Julius Margolis, eds., *Public Expenditure and Policy Analysis*, 2nd ed. (Chicago: Rand McNally, 1977), p. 253.

25. See Mishan, *Introduction to Normative Economics*, and Arnold C. Harberger, "On the Use of Distributional Weights in Social Cost-Benefit Analysis," *Journal of Political Economy*, 86 (2), (1978): S87–S120.

26. U.S. Nuclear Regulatory Commission, *Final Generic Environmental Impact Statement on Uranium Milling*, NUREG-0706, vols. 1-3 (1980).

27. Arnold C. Harberger, "Three Basic Postulates for Applied Welfare Economics: An Interpretive Essay," *Journal of Economic Literature* 9 (3), (September, 1971): 785-797.

28. Mishan, *Cost-Benefit Analysis*, pp. 156-157.

29. Robert Sugden and Alan Williams, *The Principles of Practical Cost-Benefit Analysis* (Oxford: Oxford University Press, 1978), p. 93.

30. Mishan *Cost-Benefit Analysis*, pp. xxi, xxii.

31. Dasgupta, Sen, and Marglin, *Guidelines.*

32. Sugden and Williams, *The Principles. . .* , p. 92.

33. Harberger, "Three Basic Postulates. . . ," p. 785.

34. Sugden and Williams, *The Principles. . .* , pp. 187-198, 238.

35. Dasgupta, Sen, and Marglin, *Guidelines. . .* , pp. 139-140, Ch. 18.

36. See Duncan MacRae, Jr., *The Social Function of Social Science* (New Haven: Yale University Press, 1976), and Peter G. Brown and Henry Shue, eds., *Food Policy: The Responsibility of the United States in Life and Death Choices* (New York: Free Press, 1977).

37. Lawrence Susskind, "The Role of Negotiation in Planning," Lecture at University of North Carolina at Chapel Hill, Feb. 1, 1984.

[16]

Is Cost-Benefit Analysis Legal? Three Rules

Richard O. Zerbe, Jr.

Abstract

When benefit-cost analysis produces a result that is objectionable does this mean that the technique is objectionable? It means only that the technique cannot rise above the individual and community values on which it rests. That is, values in benefit-cost analysis rest in large measure on law. An understanding of what values count and whose values count and why they count cannot then be separated from law. This understanding of value obviates most criticisms of benefit-cost analysis as a technique. Benefit-cost analysis also contributes to the law so that, for example, when there is a discrepancy between legal and psychological ownership, efficiency suggests that the law change to reflect psychological ownership. The values considered in benefit-cost analysis are very broad and include those associated with income distribution—the most radical proposition in this article—as well as the value of harm even when it is specifically unknown. An appreciation of the broad range of what is meant by value further dislodges criticisms of benefit-cost analysis.

The Book Thief

Derek sues Amartya for stealing his book, and asks for the return of the book and costs. Derek is poor and Amartya is rich. Derek loves the book but Amartya cares only a little for it. Derek would have been willing to pay $10 for the book, or would have sold the book to Amartya for $15. Amartya would pay $20 for it, but would sell it for $22.50. A benefit-cost analyst hired by Amartya testifies at the trial that the value of the book is greater for Amartya than for Derek, in the sense that Amartya's willingness to pay exceeds Derek's willingness to pay. So the benefit-cost analyst suggests that wealth is maximized if the book goes to Amartya. The court finds, however, that because Amartya stole the book, it belongs to Derek, the benefit-cost analysis notwithstanding.[1]

INTRODUCTION

There has been substantial and long-standing confusion about whether benefit-cost analysis, the primary economic tool for the analysis of normative issues, is

Journal of Policy Analysis and Management, Vol. 17, No. 3, 419–456 (1998)
© 1998 by the Association for Public Policy Analysis and Management
Published by John Wiley & Sons, Inc.   CCC 0276-8739/98/03419-38

itself normative.[2] In recent years, the use of economically defined efficiency norms for legal analysis (generally under the rubric of wealth maximization) has subjected benefit-cost analysis to widespread criticism on the basis that it possesses defects in principle.[3] The critics contend that benefit-cost analysis is overused and inappropriate for many kinds of questions. Both criticism and defense have come mainly from nonpractitioners: philosophers and lawyers on one side,[4] and lawyers on the other.[5] Because practitioners have generally ignored the critics, fundamental disagreement about the usefulness of benefit-cost analysis remains. A resolution of this debate lies in a deeper understanding of the context and aims of benefit-cost analysis and particularly in an appreciation of the interrelationship between it, the law, and the psychology of values. In this article and in two companion articles, I examine this debate. This article addresses certain benefit-cost critics. The second considers application of equity in a benefit-cost context to certain important legal cases [Zerbe, 1998]. The third explores examples in the legal literature in which economic efficiency is misused and shows how an expanded concept of efficiency can be usefully applied to law [Zerbe, 1997].

Neither the law nor benefit-cost analysis stand wholly outside each other; they are intertwined. The values used in benefit-cost analysis are shaped by law just as those used in law are shaped by benefit-cost analysis. The common law is influenced by efficiency, yet efficiency is not well defined outside the law.

Efficiency is a matter of psychology as well as law. Economists have tended to believe that economics can be independent of psychological assumptions.[6] Yet, rationality and hence efficiency can be nothing more than a psychological interpretation which we place on behavior [Lewin, 1996]. Costs and benefits are necessarily psychological constructs; they are a matter of subjective emotion.

The confusion about the context of benefit-cost analysis is particularly important with the increased interest in legislation mandating its application.[7]

---

[1] This example is based on a reworking of an example offered by Dworkin [1980, pp. 197–198].

[2] The arguments in this article also can be applied to risk assessment.

[3] This article considers benefit-cost analysis in principle rather than in practice. Critics do not distinguish between the two, but the distinction is important, because the implications are different for criticisms of current technique and criticisms of the whole method of analysis. Criticisms of practice hold out the possibility of changes that can improve the analysis; criticisms of principle, of course, hold out no such promise.

[4] For example, Kennedy [1981] finds that the only role for the notion of economic efficiency is one of "limited heuristic usefulness" (p. 444).

[5] Among those involved in these sorts of discussions are Kennedy [1981], Posner [1980, 1983], Dworkin [1980], Kelman [1981], Anderson [1993], Sagoff [1988], Williams [Smart and Williams, 1973], and Rizzo [1980].

[6] This was not the case, say, before 1914. See, for examples, the essay on economics in the 1911 edition of the *Encyclopaedia Britannica* [Hewins, 1911] and the essay by Medema and Zerbe [1998].

[7] This is reflected in the healthy interest that Congress, a series of presidents, and the states have developed in regulatory reform to increase efficiency and rationality. President Reagan issued two executive orders dealing with benefit-cost analysis: Executive Order 12291 and Executive Order 12498. President Clinton issued Order 12866, which kept intact the basic process initiated by President Reagan. For a delineation of the criticisms of these orders and a discussion, see Pildes and Sunstein [1995]. The State of Washington recently passed a law requiring application of benefit-cost analysis to substantive regulations of nine state agencies, and Virginia recently required economic impact analysis in certain cases [Washington Regulatory Reform Act, Washington Laws, 1995, Chapter 403]. Eight states have statutes incorporating aspects of benefit-cost analysis, according to a personal communication from Jonathan Seib [1995]. In addition, the state of Wisconsin enacted legislation in 1995 that requires economic feasibility to be incorporated into environmental remediation decisions.

In this article I suggest a framework in which benefit-cost analysis can be regarded as a scientific tool (in the sense of meeting consistent standards). I consider the role of benefit-cost analysis in the policy process: whether or not benefit-cost analysis is deficient in values, whose values should count, and when the willingness-to-pay (WTP) measure of value should be used rather than the willingness-to-accept (WTA) measure.

I conclude that benefit-cost analysis is not, in principle, subject to the defects that its critics have alleged.

THREE RULES

Benefit-cost analysis can be seen as a useful scientific tool of analysis if, along with consistent technical procedures, the profession adopts three rules for its application.

1. The role of benefit-cost analysis is to provide information relevant to the decision, not to provide the decision.
2. Benefit-cost analysis in principle rests on all existing values; it is not missing values nor is it a tool to create or develop values.
3. Benefit-cost analysis rests on both the law and the psychological reference point and informs them. (Preferences must be taken as they lie.)

I will expand upon these rules in the following sections. My purpose is to convince my fellow practitioners, as well as other proponents and critics of benefit-cost analysis, that these three rules strengthen its rationale, and that within the context provided by these rules, economists and other practitioners should use it "without apology" [Willig, 1976].

THE ROLE OF BENEFIT-COST ANALYSIS IS TO PROVIDE INFORMATION-RELEVANT TO THE DECISION, NOT TO PROVIDE THE DECISION

Benefit-Cost Analysis and Wealth Maximization

The law is the decision. It awarded the book to Derek and not Amartya regardless of the benefit-cost analysis. Economists appear to give the impression at times that benefit-cost analysis provides not simply a reasonable answer, but the only answer. Sagoff [1988] notes, "Those who favor efficiency as the goal of social policy tend to think of it as a grand value that picks up, incorporates, and balances all other values" (p. 40). This should not be its role. Nor is it the role that it actually plays. If we recognize that the role of benefit-cost analysis is to provide information to the decision process, and not to provide the decision, the burden is lifted that would require that benefit-cost analysis provide the right moral answer. It cannot.

A version of benefit-cost analysis which is sometimes called wealth maximization[8] appears to hold that benefit-cost analysis furnishes the decision, that distributional effects are not to be considered, and that benefit-cost analysis

---

[8] Lesser and Zerbe [1995] and also Tolley [1982] have considered a distinction between benefit-cost analysis and cost-benefit analysis that is similar to the one that I am making here between benefit-cost analysis and wealth maximization.

is a sufficient tool to consider fundamental questions of value such as whether or not slavery or rape should be allowed [Posner, 1980, 1983, 1984].[9] Wealth maximization, then, is a sort of deus ex machina, not well grounded in economic theory, by which decisions are to be made. This an improper view of benefit-cost analysis. Although benefit-cost analysis is most usefully seen as grounded in economic theory,[10] its results are to be understood as part of a nexus with the institutional context on which it must rely, so that both benefit-cost analysis and the law must rely upon established rights and duties in making policy decisions, and each informs the other [Heyne, 1988].[11]

BENEFIT-COST ANALYSIS IN PRINCIPLE RESTS ON ALL EXISTING VALUES; IT IS NOT MISSING VALUES NOR IS IT A TOOL USED TO CREATE OR DEVELOP VALUES

Three widespread criticisms of benefit-cost analysis are that it compares unfavorably with voting and with the political process,[12] that it is missing particular values, and that it does not indicate the "right thing to do" [Anderson, 1993; Kelman, 1981; Sagoff, 1988]. All three objections may be seen as arising from an improper view that benefit-cost analysis is missing values in a general sense. The proper view is contained in an understanding of what a good is.

What is a Good?

The proper view is captured by Page's [1992] description:

You are asked to compare two worlds. The first is the status quo: the world the way it is now. The second is identical with the status quo except for a change brought about by the project. In the comparison, you take into account the ramifications of the project, differences in income to you and others, differences in habitat, and so on; but except for the changes brought on by the project, the two worlds are the same.

Suppose that you value the first world more highly than the second. (You value the status quo more highly than the world with the project.) Then you are asked what is the minimum you need to be compensated so that you would value the change (with the compensation) just as much as the status quo. If you value the world with the project more than the status quo, then you are asked how big a payment you could make in the changed world (with the project) so that you would just value equally the status quo and the world with the project (with its ramifications but less the payment). We ask these questions of everyone affected by the decision, which in principle could be everyone in the world. The economic criterion says that if the sum of all the compensations (to those who would lose by the project) is less than the equilibrating payments (from those who would gain by the project) then the change from the status quo is worth making.

---

[9] Posner [1984], who coined the term "wealth maximization," considers that it is, however, identical to Kaldor-Hicks Efficiency.

[10] For example, W. A. S. Hewins [1911], writing the section on economics in the classic 1911 edition of the *Encyclopaedia Britannica*, notes that "it is doubtful whether the most complete investigation in terms of money (q.v.) would ever enable us to include all the elements of the standard of life in a money estimate" (p. 900).

[11] See Medema and Zerbe [1998]. Zerbe [1997] considers whether or not Kaldor-Hicks Efficiency is just.

[12] See Lesser and Zerbe [1995] for a treatment of this problem.

The compensations measure the costs to the losers; the equilibrating payments measure the benefits to the gainers. (p. 102)[13]

Among the problems with benefit-cost analysis that Page notes are: valuations are income-constrained, people may find it hard to compare two worlds, there are estimation problems, and the value of future generations may not be counted. Where people find it sufficiently difficult to compare two worlds, preferences may not be well formed; thus, the technical requirements for conducting a benefit-cost analysis would be violated.

Voting

Page [1992] addresses the first objection—that benefit-cost analysis compares unfavorably with voting—by showing that it is "surprisingly similar" to voting, and that similar objections apply to each (p. 103). He points out that benefit-cost analysis envisions a sort of voting process with the widest possible participation, in which votes are weighted by both intensity of desire and by income. Page's description also addresses the second objection—that it is missing values—by showing that it allows all viewpoints to be heard [Hildred and Beauvais, 1995] so that it meets the requirement for democratic decisionmaking. The long-standing use of benefit-cost analysis suggests vitality, and an understanding of the context for benefit-cost analysis also suggests its integrity and addresses the third objection—that it does not indicate the "right thing to do."[14]

Particular Values

Although benefit-cost analysis does not ignore particular values, that it does is the most widespread and persistent criticism of it [Anderson, 1993, pp. 194–195; Kelman, 1981; Sagoff, 1988]. For instance, Williams [Smart and Williams, 1973, pp. 97–98] considers the case of George:

George
George, who has taken his Ph.D. in chemistry, finds it extremely difficult to get a job. An older chemist who knows about the situation says that he can get George a decently paid job in a certain laboratory, which pursues research into chemical and biological warfare. George says that he cannot accept this because he is opposed to chemical and biological warfare. The older man replies that George's refusal is not going to make the job or the laboratory go away; what is more, he happens to know that if George refuses to take the job, it will certainly go to a contemporary of George's who is not inhibited by any such scruples and is likely if appointed to push along the research with greater zeal than George would. What should George do? (pp. 97–98)

Williams argues that under a utilitarian analysis George must accept the job, because it improves the position of his family and advances the work more slowly (a desirable aim). Similarly, the objection to the use of benefit-cost analysis

---

[13] This description is consistent with the theoretical economics literature that provides the intellectual underpinnings for benefit-cost analysis. [Broadway and Bruce, 1984; Zerbe and Dively, 1994].
[14] Thus, benefit-cost analysis meets Dewey's criterion for truth [Hildred and Beauvais, 1995].

made by Kelman is essentially that it rests on utilitarianism and that utilitarianism requires a sort of expediency in decisionmaking as in the case of George.

Yet, benefit-cost analysis does not rest on utilitarianism of this sort. Normative economic analysis is concerned with ranking states of the world, so that whether or not integrity is included in a utilitarian analysis is neither here nor there for the conduct of a benefit-cost analysis. In Williams's example, if George (or Williams himself) chooses a world in which George has integrity over one in which he does not, then integrity would have value for a benefit-cost analysis. The description by Page [1992, p. 102] does not contemplate leaving out values, nor does the theoretical work by economists underlying benefit-cost analysis [Boadway and Bruce, 1984; Zerbe and Dively, 1994]. In the opening remarks of their well-known book on welfare economics, Boadway and Bruce [1984] note:[15]

A social ordering permits one to compare all states of the world and rank each one as "better than," "worse than," or "equally good as" every other. Ideally we would like the (social) ordering to be complete (so that all states could be ranked or ordered) and transitive.... The term "state of the world" can be interpreted as a complete description of a possible state of an economy including economic characteristics, political conditions such as freedom of speech and non-discrimination, physical characteristics such as the weather, and so on. (p. 1)

Both Sagoff [1988] and Anderson [1993] devote a good deal of effort to distinguishing between our preferences as consumers and our choices as citizens. They maintain that benefit-cost analysis treats goods like health, safety, and environmental quality as mere commodities, and that cost-benefit analysis assumes:

that the public nature of some instances of these goods is merely a technical fact about them and not itself a valued quality. The possibility that national parks and public safety might be valued as shared goods does not enter into its evaluations ... cost-benefit analysis assumes that the preferences people express in private consumer choices should be normative for public choice, as if the valuations people make as consumers exhaust their concerns. (Anderson, 1993, pp. 193–194)

Both Anderson [1998] and Sagoff [1988] assume that benefit-cost analysis measures people's valuations of noncommodity goods as long as "they are privately appropriated, exclusively enjoyed goods" [Anderson, 1993, p. 193]. For example, Anderson finds that the opportunity to earn a living is "a need and a responsibility" (p. 199). She finds, therefore, that using wage premiums as the basis to estimate the cash values people place on their lives is incorrect, because these premiums also reflect the risks people feel obliged to accept in order to discharge their responsibilities. That is, using wage premium data to measure the cost of risk results is a miscalculation, in that what is being measured also includes the values of responsibility and duty. Sagoff [1988] uses child labor laws as an instance in which narrow market consequentialist ends may differ from our choice as citizens. These views are based on an assumption

---

[15] See also the remarks of W. A. S. Hewins [1911]: "The concept of the standard of life involves also some estimate of the efforts of and sacrifices people are prepared to make to obtain it; of their ideals and character; of the relative strength of the different motives which usually determine their conduct" (p. 900).

about the "commodity fetishism of welfare economics: the assumption that people intrinsically care only about exclusively appropriated goods, and that they care about their relationships with others only for their instrumental value in maximizing private consumption" [Anderson, 1993, p. 203]. These arguments fail as criticisms of benefit-cost analysis *in principle* because they mischaracterize what the use of economics attempts to do as a normative tool.

Sagoff [1988] and Anderson [1993] use the distinction between publicly and privately valued goods to mischaracterize the values contained in benefit-cost analysis as preferences of consumers and not as our choices as citizens. This is incorrect. Benefit-cost analysis deals with choices and their value cognates. The values relevant for a benefit-cost analysis are precisely those associated with choices, whether or not these are public preferences of citizens or mere consumer choices. My choice as a consumer to drive to work may fail to reflect my choice as a citizen to tax automobiles and subsidize bus service. The fact that I do not currently use the bus service may not reflect my willingness to enhance and support it. Similarly, the value I place on preventing child labor need not arise from concern about myself directly or about my own children, but rather from concern for others and from my concept of a good society. Such values are relevant to choice, and therefore to the choice between two worlds that represents the foundation for a benefit-cost framework.[16]

What is Value?

The critics see benefit-cost analysis as concerned only with market values. They see the economist's attempt to supply a price or shadow price for some commodity not provided by the market (such as environmental quality or an increase in safety) as an effort to supply a market price for goods whose value is more than just their market value. However, in the language of benefit-cost analysis, the market is a *metaphor* for a mechanism for determining value. Market values, in the language of the metaphor, need not represent "mere commodities" (to use the language of the critics) but instead represent choices. What is being valued may exist outside a commodity-type market. For instance, the value that I place on a friendship is not one that I wish determined in a commodity market. When I do harm to my friend by canceling a lunch appointment at the last minute in order to attend a lecture of particular interest [Sunstein, 1994],[17] I do not compensate my friend by offering a sum of money. Yet, I might perform other acts, perhaps with a monetary value, consistent with friendship to show its value to me. I might offer to drive him when he needs a lift; I might give him a present; I might agree to participate in an activity he enjoys. So when I talk about the value of friendship and its value in the "market for friendship," I am merely calling attention to the fact that friendship has a

---

[16] Critics say that these values are difficult to quantify (although a benefit-cost framework is not limited to quantification) or capture. This is, however, an empirical matter and the one for which the critics I discuss offer no evidence.

[17] Sunstein [1994] notes that "we may believe that goods are comparable without believing that they are commensurable" (p. 798). I would say further that the use of monetary figures to rank preferences can be done even where the choices are not made with respect to a monetized frame of reference. We do not think of friendships in terms of money but we make trade-offs with respect to them. The problem of future generations and of estimation are endemic to any decision process that uses information.

value, and that this value should be considered in a benefit-cost analysis that affects the quantity or quality of friendship. The value of friendship in principle has been neither missed nor undervalued by benefit-cost analysis.

Is Efficiency Equitable?[18]

Another widespread objection to benefit-cost analysis is that it does not consider distributional consequences [see, for example, Anderson, 1993, p. 191]. In truth, the technical theoretical standard for benefit-cost analysis *requires* that distributional effects be considered. The misunderstanding arises because the Kaldor-Hicks (or potential Pareto) criteria,[19] which are often identified with benefit-cost analysis—although not absolutely necessary to it—require that every dollar be weighted the same (in utility terms) regardless of who receives it, *by the person who receives it.* The criteria also require, however, that the valuations *others* place on a change in income (for someone other than themselves) be included because the distribution itself is one of the goods being valued. (For an explanation, see the Appendix, where I consider the derivation of a social welfare function that meets the Kaldor-Hicks requirement.)

In Page's [1992, p. 102] description of benefit-cost analysis, as long as the income distribution is valued, it will be one of the goods that exists in the two possible worlds, and must be considered in the choice between them (p. 102). A change in income distribution has a value, positive or negative, that can be determined by the willingness to pay (WTP) or the willingness to accept (WTA), and in this respect is like any other good (see the Economic Theory of Value section in this article). To see this, ask yourself if you would pay $1 to live in a world in which income inequality was less by 50 percent than in the present world, without otherwise affecting your own income. If you or others answer yes, there will be a WTP for the change. Thus, the distributional effects of a policy can be treated like any other good for which there is a WTP or WTA, and incorporated into a benefit-cost analysis. Now, suppose that the transfer of the $1 was from the poorest member of society to, say, Bill Gates. The transfer would be seen as a loss by some; and the sum of their WTA not to have this transfer occur may far exceed the WTP for those who see it as a gain. In this case, the transfer fails the benefit-cost test, with distributional effects considered. A benefit-cost analysis that uses only the potential Pareto compensation test counts the value of money equally to the recipients (constant marginal utility of income).[20] Thus, it assumes that extra dollars received by Bill Gates and by the poorest member of society are valued equally by them. (However, it does not assume that others value equally an extra dollar to Bill Gates and the poorest member. Many of us would be willing to pay something—positive or negative—to affect a transfer from Bill Gates to the poorest member.)

---

[18] For an expanded treatment of this, see Zerbe [1997].
[19] A barrage of critical responses to the use of the Kaldor-Hicks criteria has missed this point [see Baker, 1980; Bebchuck, 1980; Coleman, 1980; Dworkin, 1980; Kennedy, 1981; Rizzo, 1980]. These criticisms have led some to argue unwisely for requiring actual compensation of the losers, to turn potential Pareto gains into actual Pareto gains [Coleman, 1980].
[20] The potential Pareto compensation test is met when it would be possible for the winners to fully compensate the losers from their winnings.

Benefit–Cost Analysis I

275

Is Cost-Benefit Analysis Legal? Three Rules / 427

Ignoring Distributional Effects[21]

I will say that wealth maximization is a version of Kaldor-Hicks criteria that ignores income distribution (so that this version drops the right-hand side of equation (A.12) found in the Appendix). Wealth maximization assumes that income is treated equally regardless of who receives it. In practice, benefit-cost analysis very often ignores distributional effects on the basis of expediency. By a benefit-cost test itself this is justified where the costs of attempting to ascertain distributional effects are likely to be greater than the benefits [Zerbe and Dively, 1994, pp. 241–242]. This in turn is most likely to occur where there are other inexpensive mechanisms for affecting redistributions—such as tax policy, where the changes in income are small, and where the changes affect people similarly situated. These conditions seem often to be met.

What Can We Say? Reasonable Propositions

Benefit-cost analysis allows us to make the following reasonable propositions. We can say that:

- Basing a decision on the Kaldor-Hicks criteria of benefit-cost analysis—that net benefits are positive—is likely to yield an improvement in social welfare if distributional effects are counted as part of the good being valued.
- It is reasonable to ignore distributional effects—that is to use the wealth maximization criteria—where the gains from considering these effects are likely to be less than the costs of their determination. One such situation is when the project involves marginal changes, and when the original income distribution is just. If the distribution is just, there are no distributional gains to be made.
- The costs of affecting compensation or of redistribution from projects whose main goal is narrow efficiency (defined without regard to distributional effects) are likely to be greater than the costs of achieving the distributional gains through explicitly redistributional policies. In this situation it may be expedient to ignore redistributional consequences because the costs of considering them when proposing policies of narrow efficiency may be less than their benefits, which are limited to the cost of achieving the same gains through the low-cost explicit redistributional policies.

What We Cannot Say; Limitations and the Right Thing to Do

So we can say a lot. But we cannot say everything. The fundamental criticism of benefit-cost analysis (as with any scheme for aggregating preferences) is that there is no compelling moral logic for aggregating preferences. The valuations in benefit-cost analysis are in part determined by income, and income is surely an incomplete moral basis for determining value across individuals. In the example of Derek and Amartya, we cannot say that the world would be a better place were Amartya to be given the book by a decisionmaker (the tyrant)

---

[21] For an expanded treatment of this, see Zerbe [1997].

on the grounds that Amartya is willing to pay more for it than Derek. Benefit-cost analysis cannot measure aggregate values, because there is no cardinal measure of utility. Its data have validity only to the extent to which they are deemed useful.

The standard, and most prestigious, interval scale for measurement in benefit-cost or benefit-risk analysis is that developed by Von Neumann and Morgenstern (NM) [1944]. The NM axioms imagine that the rational gambler with complete knowledge of the objects of spending calculates the outcomes of every action and selects that which best fulfills the requirement of a fully known, transitive preference function under budget constraints [Hildred and Beauvais, 1995, p. 1087; Machina, 1987]. Schoemaker's [1982] conclusive and rather devastating critique of these axioms shows that the NM approach yields only ordinal preference rankings, as Von Neumann and Margenstern themselves pointed out.

Yet, even if preferences could be aggregated, we cannot determine what is the right thing to do using benefit-cost analysis.[22] This problem would exist, even if we suppose what can never be—that there is a cardinal measure of utility so that measures of benefits and costs can be aggregated to produce an index of aggregate well-being. We should not imagine that measurable utility is a formula for decisionmaking without cavil. Consider the following example modified from Sen [1982]:

Ali and the Bashers
Ali is a successful shopkeeper who has built up a good business in London since emigrating from East Africa. He is hated by a group of racists, and a particular gang of them, the bashers, would like to beat him up.

Suppose that we can measure utility and find the following utilities in the two states of the world, bashing and no bashing. When there are only 4 bashers, the total utility from beating up Ali is less than the total utility from not beating him up. When, however, there are 10 bashers, the total utility from bashing is greater than that from not bashing. In general, the number of bashers can be increased without limit; and we might imagine that there are those who will gain utility from only watching Ali being bashed. As shown in Table 1, total utility is higher when Ali is bashed where there are at least 10 bashers.

Table 1: The utility of bashing.

State of affairs	Ali's utility	Each basher's utility	Total utility (4 bashers)	Total utility (10 bashers)
No Bashing	15	5	35	65
Bashing	10[a]	6	34	70

[a] I assume that Ali has positive utility as long as he is not dead.

[22] The test of Pareto superiority so restricts the choices that can be compared that it is of limited use. This test is met when a move from A to B harms no one and improves the situation of at least one person.

Benefit–Cost Analysis I   277

Is Cost-Benefit Analysis Legal? Three Rules / 429

An objection to this sort of example is that we should also count the utility of those who will be affected by Ali's being bashed; and that because most people will not be in favor of it, a complete accounting would not allow the bashing. Yet, we can imagine a society in which racists are a majority, or in which no other parties will know about the bashing, so that a complete accounting for utility produces a bad result.[23] It is easy to allow "bad utility" (utility arising from bad acts) to increase without limit. Hence, even a decision analysis based on cardinal utility can result in an action or a consequence to which we will object. We cannot, then, argue that benefit-cost analysis should be the sole standard on the basis that it measures values according to some logically compelling principle. It does not.

Moral theory has yet to suggest a simple rule for aggregation of preferences which can be universally applied and accepted. There can be no agreement that benefit-cost analysis, or any other formula for aggregating preferences, should be the sole basis for decisionmaking. The argument that benefit-cost analysis does not tell us the "right thing to do" has been repeatedly well made [Anderson, 1993; Kelman, 1981; Sagoff, 1988]. Critics of benefit-cost analysis are quite right that it is of no aid in the fundamental task by which community values are formed [Kennedy, 1981, p. 388].[24] Nonetheless, the point is almost wholly irrelevant. Who would think that benefit-cost analysis was a tool for these tasks?[25] How could it be? The aforementioned authors, especially Kelman [1981] and Sagoff [1988], go on, however, to argue that because benefit-cost analysis does not tell us the right thing to do, it should not be used, or at least much used. This does not follow. What does follow is rule one—that the law is the decision; the role of benefit-cost analysis is not to provide the decision, but to provide information relevant to the decision. If we recognize this, then the moral burden is lifted that would require benefit-cost analysis to provide the right moral answer. It cannot. If we believe that benefit-cost analysis is not the decision, we can accept that benefit-cost analysis does not give us the answer. Then benefit-cost analysis becomes something both less grandiose and more useful, not least to the law.

Benefit-cost analysis, however, does more than provide information to a decision process; it is necessarily part of the process. Its use affects the shape of and framework for the process. For critics, this is a negative characteristic. Hildred and Beauvais [1995] see cost-utility analysis as "flawed science that deprives citizens of opportunity to participate in democratic processes that bear on resource allocation in health care" (p. 1092). They comment that the use of cost-utility analysis for medical decisionmaking "gives an aura of scientific precision that diverts attention from the social dimension of preference and choice and disguises the actual power behind the allocation of medical system resources" (p. 1092). These are legitimate concerns. Not only the quality and type of data, but also how the data are presented, influence the tenor of the debates. Data presented in one form will tend to focus attention on those issues most amenable to quantification and to drive out discussion of qualitative issues. Hard numbers drive out soft. Yet, presented in another way, data in a benefit-

---

[23] Williams has an interesting example of a prejudiced majority [Smart and Williams, 1973, p. 105].
[24] The notion of generating a complete system of law through the application of benefit-cost analysis is incoherent, as is the concept of economic efficiency itself if applied to a whole system of legal rules.

cost framework can illuminate qualitative discussion, reduce the power of special interests to push inefficient projects, and contribute to the quality of the argument [Weisbrod, 1981].

In benefit-cost analysis, questions about data—which are most relevant, and their quality and mode of presentation—are important and valid. Valid, also, are questions about the effect on the decision process of benefit-cost analysis itself. But the legitimacy of these issues does not justify or inform the conclusion of its critics that it should be little used. Anderson's [1993] declaration, for example, that "facts are best presented qualitatively" is an empirical assertion for which she furnishes no evidence (p. 215).[26] Because the assertions of the critics do not rest on a presentation of empirical data, and are at variance with the experience of many practitioners, we should properly remain agnostic as to whether they can rise to the level of criticisms in principle.

What Can We Gain?

A methodology that holds out the promise of introducing greater rationality into the regulatory process has continuing appeal, as evidenced by recent attempts to pass benefit-cost legislation. In February 1995, the U.S. House of Representatives overwhelmingly passed H.R. 1022, the Risk Assessment and Cost Benefit Act of 1995. The purpose of the legislation is to "reform regulatory agencies and focus national economic resources . . . through scientifically objective and unbiased risk assessments and through the consideration of costs and benefits in major rules" (p. 1).[27] Critics of benefit-cost analysis appear concerned that the political aspects of the decisionmaking process will be circumvented. They worry that worthy projects that do not have positive net benefits will be overlooked [see Graham, 1995, p. 61]. Yet, the bill stipulates only that cost-benefit analysis be used "to the extent feasible," and that deliberations take into account "qualitative benefits." A decision may be supported as long as the rules' benefits are "reasonably related to costs" or "likely to justify" their costs, even if they are not known with certainty [Graham, 1995]. The bill reserves to Congress the power to designate which rules are major rules and therefore subject to benefit-cost analysis. The drafters of the legislation thus left a "way out" of the cost-benefit analysis of proposed regulations by not designating a rule as "major."

Although Kelman [1981], Sagoff [1988], Anderson [1993], and other critics see benefit-cost analysis as playing a dominant role, it is much more common for the results of such an analysis to be overridden by the political process. Several generations of economists have pointed this out [Davis, 1988; Hanke

---

[25] Benefit-cost analysis, says Kelman [1981] is based on utilitarianism, which is not an appropriate moral standard in many cases. How does one decide whether or not lying is appropriate? Kelman notes that the utilitarian analyst uses circular reasoning, in trying to determine whether or not lying is right, by assuming that the individual knows the action is wrong. A good deal of Mark Sagoff's [1988] criticism of economics is aimed at developing this same point. Benefit-cost analysis, in fact, assumes no such thing. Benefit-cost analysis not only assumes existing moral values, but attempts to take all values as they are found.

[26] One state that requires benefit-cost analysis for rulemaking, the state of Washington, demands qualitative as well as quantitative analysis.

[27] The floor debate suggests that an implication of this requirement is that a decision rule would be adopted that only those regulations with a net positive outcome would be promulgated. This is an example of attempting to use the result of the benefit-cost analysis as the decision itself.

Benefit–Cost Analysis I 279

Is Cost-Benefit Analysis Legal? Three Rules / 431

and Walker, 1974].[28] In fact, only the federal government has extensive requirements for benefit-cost analysis for executive agencies. According to Graham [1995], the greater and better use of benefit-cost (and benefit-risk) techniques could reduce some of the nation's $600 billion in annual regulatory costs (if these figures are too high, more conservative estimates are also large) (pp. 62–63). Graham [1995] cites Tengs as suggesting that a reallocation of resources to more cost-effective programs could save 60,000 lives per year at no increased cost to taxpayers or to industry (p. 62). That is, Tengs suggests that the marginal cost-of-life saving in, say, program A is perhaps $1 billion but in program B is only $1 million so that more lives can be saved by moving resources from program B to program A. Yet, there are several statutes that forbid a benefit-cost type of balancing.[29] Only eight states have statutes requiring the application of some cost analysis, economic impact analysis, or benefit-cost analysis.[30] Of these, only the state of Washington requires a benefit-cost analysis.[31] In a survey of municipal governments of over 100,000 in population, which included conversations with the chief financial officers of these governments, less than half either understood the process of discounting (let alone the other aspects of benefit-cost analysis) or used discount rates in project evaluation [Dively and Zerbe, 1993]. The major reason given by municipalities for not using benefit-cost analysis was that its findings could interfere with political considerations. Dively and Zerbe interpreted the results as evidence of the salutary effects of benefit-cost analysis, and are strengthened in this conclusion by the fact that benefit-cost analysis was more likely to be used where the financial officials were independently elected rather than appointed.

In practice, benefit-cost analysis has provided a framework by which a structured discussion can take place that has exposed inefficient projects—and has helped to kill a number of projects that were, in general, also disfavored by environmentalists. For example, benefit-cost analysis has been the basis of the most powerful criticisms of overcutting of timber by the U.S. Forest Service. Benefit-cost analysis provided an avenue by which critics could question an analysis; and these criticisms helped to mobilize and to provide a source of information for environmentalists and others. The outcome is that today the ability of the Army Corps of Engineers or the Bureau of Reclamation to sponsor an inefficient project, or one that is environmentally unsound, has been seriously curtailed.

---

[28] John Graham [1995] laments, in fact, that, "Congress has never passed comprehensive legislation aimed at bringing more scientific rigor and economic efficiency to the regulation of health, safety, and environmental hazards" (p. 61).

[29] For example, see the Delaney Clause, 21 U.S.C. § 348 (C)(3)(A)(1950), which forbids the use of carcinogens in food additives, and the standards for nitrogen dioxide concentrations, 42 U.S.C. § 7409(c) (1988), as well as the standards as given in the *Federal Water Pollution Control Act*, 33 U.S.C. § 1311(b) (1988) and in the *Clean Air Act*, 42 U.S.C. §§ 7475(a)(4), 7503(a)(2) (1988 & Supp. V (1993)).

[30] These are Arizona, California, Colorado, Florida, Illinois, Oregon, Virginia, and Washington. According to George Tolley [1982], since 1995 Wisconsin has required that economic feasibility be incorporated into remediation decisions.

[31] Chapter 403, Washington Law, 1995 (Engrossed Substitute House Bill 1010, partially vetoed, effective July 23, 1995). The Washington law requires nine enumerated agencies to determine that the probable benefits of the rule are greater than its probable costs, taking into account both the qualitative and quantitative benefits and costs and the specific directives of the statute being implemented.

Sagoff [1988] and other critics stress the virtues of the political process by which opinions and interests may be subject to scrutiny, and values may be formed and expressed. Far from quarreling with these virtues, the advocates of benefit-cost analysis realize that its proper role is to enhance them. Evidence suggests it has done so. A recent survey of comparative risk projects by the states concludes that the most effective projects have been the ones that specifically set out to include key representatives of the public, in addition to technical experts. The survey finds that:

> . . . the ordeal of working as a group to rank problems forces group members to clarify their own thinking as they search for points of agreement with their colleagues or sharpen points of disagreement. The ranking process exposes weak argument, poor data, and fuzzy thinking. The process tends to break down preconceptions about the problems. The process also breaks down individuals' prejudices about the other participants. The result: members of ranking committees have discovered they agreed on far more than they had expected. They have come to share a strong conviction that their insights are important, and should be used to influence public policy. In short, the process has frequently built coalitions for change. (Minard, 1996, p. 8)

Sagoff's [1988] treatment of the political model is so flattering and so undiscriminating as to deny common experience, as well as an enormous body of critical literature. Such literature acknowledges that political processes often involve gains to interest groups at the expense of a broader population. It is just this undesirable character of the political process which benefit-cost analysis was developed to combat. In this role, it is a tool that can aid in the political discourse that Sagoff advocates.

BENEFIT-COST ANALYSIS RESTS ON BOTH THE LAW AND THE PSYCHOLOGICAL REFERENCE POINT AND INFORMS THEM (PREFERENCES MUST BE TAKEN AS THEY LIE)

The Dam
In the early 1900s, the free-flowing Elwha River on the Olympic Peninsula in Washington State was blocked by two hydroelectric dams. The dams provided power for a privately owned pulp and paper company. These dams blocked the migration path for several species of salmon and trout. Before the dams, there were 10 runs of salmon and trout, among the most spectacular in the Northwest, which fed more than 22 species of wildlife, and which were the basis of much of the culture of the Lower Elwha S'Klallam Tribe. The possibility of removing the dams on the Elwha arose as part of the applications for relicensing them. An environmental impact statement (EIS) was required. Before the EIS was complete, Congress passed the Elwha River Ecosystem and Fisheries Restoration Act in October 1992. Under that act, the secretary of the Interior was directed to study ways to restore the Elwha ecosystem. As a result, the National Park Service proposes to eliminate the two dams on the Elwha and to fully restore the Elwha River ecosystem.[32]

A benefit-cost analysis has been done for the restoration of the Elwha as part of the Elwha River ecosystem final environmental impact statement (FEIS). The FEIS (1995) sets out benefits and costs, as illustrated in Table 2.

---

[32] Based on U. S. Department of the Interior [1995].

Table 2. Present value of benefits and costs for the restoration of the Elwha (figures are in millions of 1995 dollars).

Present value of market market benefits (willingness to pay)	Present value of nonmarket benefits for United States (willingness to pay)	Present value of costs (willingness to accept)
$164	$30,000[a]	$247-$273

Note: Present value is calculated using a real discount rate of 3, and the life of the project is 100 years.
[a] This is based on a 10-year life, and I have used 3 percent as the discount rate in determining present value.

Without the inclusion of nonmarket benefits for the country, the benefit-cost analysis suggests that the project's benefits fall short of its costs. Should the nonmarket benefits be included? The examples of the Elwha and of Derek and Amartya (the book thief) raise two issues. The first is whose values should be counted, that is, the issue of psychological standing [Whittington and MacRae, 1986]. The second is how values should be counted, that is, the issue of psychological ownership. To address these issues, one must understand the economic theory of value.

The Economic Theory of Value

Benefits and costs are measured by the willingness to pay (WTP) and by the willingness to accept (WTA). The WTP reflects the price that someone who does not have a good would be willing to pay to buy it. The WTP is the maximum amount of money one would give up to buy some good or service or would pay to avoid some harm.[33] The WTA reflects the price that someone who has the good, and therefore has greater wealth than if he did not have the good, would accept to sell it. The WTA is the minimum amount of money one would accept to forego some good or to bear some harm. The WTP and the WTA are based, in turn, on compensating and equivalent variations. These are exact utility indicators for an individual, in the sense that they serve to provide a complete ranking of choices for an individual. Gains and losses are related to the WTP and the WTA as follows.

The benefits from a project may be either gains or losses restored. The costs of a project may be either a gain foregone or a loss. Both the benefits and the costs are the sum of the appropriate WTP and WTA measures. Thus, the relation of benefits and costs to the WTP and the WTA is:

- *Benefits:* The sum of the WTP for changes that are seen as gains and of the WTA for changes that are seen as restoration of losses.
- *Costs:* The sum of the WTA for changes that are seen as losses and of the WTP for changes that are seen as foregone gains.

---

[33] These are nontechnical definitions, and as such are not wholly accurate. See Zerbe and Dively [1994] for complete definitions.

The relationships are summarized in Table 3.[34] The important point here is that benefits and costs are to be measured by both the WTP and the WTA where costs include gains foregone and benefits include losses restored.

Table 3. Benefits and cost related to gains and losses.

	Gain and gain foregone	Loss and loss restored
Benefits	WTP—the sum of CVs for a positive change—is finite	WTA—the sum of EVs for a positive change—could be infinite
Costs	WTP—the sum of CVs for a negative change—is finite	WTA—the sum of EVs for a negative change—could be infinite

Notes: The WTP is the willingness to pay; the WTA is the willingness to accept. Compensating variation is CV; equivalent variation is EV.

The traditional decision to use the WTP for gains and the WTA for losses has previously not been well motivated. The correct motivation lies first in an implicit recognition of psychological and legal ownership or of right. Ownership implies a right to have a loss of what one owns measured by the willingness to sell it, by the WTA. That is, the very choice of the WTP or the WTA is a normative choice whose first justification lies in a concept of ownership. And equally cogent justification relies on the fact that the effects of gains and losses differ psychologically.

Standing

"Standing" concerns who shall have their values counted [Whittington and MacRae, 1990]. In economic theory this issue does not arise, because everyone's values are to be counted, as Page [1992] suggests. There are two main economic criteria for standing. First, individuals must be able to rank choices: They can say that one is better than, equal to, or less than another (completeness). The implication of the completeness assumption is that individuals have sufficient knowledge of the choices to know which makes the greater contribution to their utility. Second, the individuals must be rational (reflective and transitive).[35] In general, the economist would grant standing to all who are rational and who have knowledge to make choices. Consider the following cases.

The Book Thief

Regarding the theft of Derek's book by Amartya, we should ask: Why not count the value of the stolen book to Amartya, since no questions of completeness or rationality were raised? In an earlier article, I [Zerbe, 1991] suggested that goods should count for naught in the hands of the thief, because this is the legal status. I did not explain why. The explanation is that to count the value of the stolen

---

[34] The difference between benefits and costs is simply their sign: positive for benefits and negative for costs.

[35] Preferences are said to be reflective when a choice X is at least as good as itself, and transitive when an ordering such as A>B>C implies A>C (where > means "is preferred to"). See Boadway and Bruce [1984, pp. 34–35]. Other assumptions are sometimes made.

Benefit–Cost Analysis I

283

Is Cost-Benefit Analysis Legal? Three Rules / 435

goods to the thief, or to consider the value of the book to anyone other than Derek, examines only one question when there are instead two to be considered. The first question concerns the value of returning the book; the second question concerns the value of holding theft itself to be illegal—that is, deeming that the goods count for nothing in the hands of the thief. The presence of these different questions may explain explicitly why some studies consider the value of the goods to the thief and others do not.[36]

Every benefit-cost question thus involves two issues: the value of the action being contemplated—for example whether or not to build a dam, or to tear one down—and whose values are to count in addressing the first question. The realization that more than one thing is being valued clarifies the nexus between the legal system and benefit-cost analysis. The question of standing is thus part of the fundamental question of the pattern of rights that are assumed extant in performing a benefit-cost analysis [Zerbe, 1991, pp. 97–98]. It is usually neither feasible nor cost-effective for the analyst testifying in the sort of case represented by *Derek v. Amartya* to perform the metacontingent valuation study required. Instead, the analyst takes the current law against theft as a prior determination that, were such a study to be undertaken to address the issue of whether the value of the goods to the thief should be counted, its answer would be in the negative. The determination of prior rights may then be taken as a reasonable conditional finding about the results, were everyone to be surveyed. This sort of approach is consistent with counting preferences where they lie, but takes into account missing values. For, if the analyst does count the value of the goods to the thief, he or she fails to account for the (negative) value placed on theft by others.

Of course, we may provide a benefit-cost analysis of the law itself. For example, we might wish to consider whether or not drugs should be legalized. In this case standing should be given to illegal drug users.

The rights that establish standing are not different from those that establish the WTP or the WTA themselves [Zerbe, 1991]. The WTP will depend in part on income and wealth, which are sanctioned by the legal system. Whether an action that results in a positive change is felt as a loss restored or as a gain, is in large part a matter of established property rights. Courts and policy analyst assume well-settled rules of property rights to conduct their analysis.

The Foreigner

Benefit-cost analyses are done from a point of view: for a client, as it were. An analysis done for New York City will not often consider the effect on the residents of Yonkers (except as effects on them may affect New York City residents); an analysis for the state of Illinois will not usually consider effects on the residents of Iowa; an analysis done for the U.S. Department of the Interior will not normally consider effects on residents of another nation. Again, there are actually two goods involved. One is the action to be taken; the other is the issue of whether the foreigner should have standing. The existence of these city, state,

---

[36] Among those who have valued goods in the hands of the thief are Becker [1968], Polinsky [1980, 1983], Polinsky and Shavell [1979], and Faith and Tollison [1983]. Among those who have argued or undertaken analyses contrary to this position are Stigler [1970], Shavell [1985], Trumbull [1990], and Zerbe [1991].

436 / *Is Cost-Benefit Analysis Legal? Three Rules*

or national jurisdictions may reasonably be taken as evidence of a prior decision (a benefit-cost decision) about which foreign parties have no legal standing to complain.[37]

The Expert and Happyville

You have a problem. You are Director of Environmental Protection in Happyville, a community of 1,000 adults. The drinking water supply in Happyville is contaminated by a naturally occurring substance that each and every resident believes may be responsible for the above-average cancer rate observed there. So concerned are they, that they insist you put in place a very expensive treatment system to remove the contaminant. Moreover, you know for a fact that each and every resident is truly willing to pay $1,000 each year for the removal of the contaminant.

The problem is this. You have asked the top ten risk assessors in the world to test the contaminant for carcinogenicity. To a person, these risk assessors—including several who work for the activist group, Campaign Against Environmental Cancer—find that the substance tests negative for carcinogenicity, even at much higher doses than those received by the residents of Happyville. These ten risk assessors tell you that while one could never prove that the substance is harmless, they would each stake their professional reputations on the substance being harmless. You have repeatedly and skillfully communicated this to the Happyville citizenry, but because of a deep-seated skepticism of all government officials, they remain completely unconvinced and truly frightened— still willing, that is, to fork over $1000 per person per year for water purification.

First, what are the annual benefits of removing the contaminant from the Happyville drinking water system? Second, suppose that: (1) the contaminant was not naturally occurring, but rather the result of industrial contamination; (2) our estimate of $1,000 per person for annual willingness to pay for purification was based on a state-of-the-art contingent valuation study; and (3) a lawsuit had been brought against the source of contamination. If the answer to your first question was $1,000,000 in annual benefits, would you be willing to support a judgment of $1,000,000 in annual damages against that source?[38]

There is no simple "answer" to the problem of Happyville. The economist's treatment of these issues is more abstract, but is not different in principle from that in legal analysis.[39] The fact that the perception of the Happyville residents differed from expert opinion diminishes the probability of physical harm and thus the probability of liability. We also would wish to know, as do the courts, how widespread was the fear. Even where the fear might rest on an assessment of risk that differs from expert opinion, the courts often recognize damage if that fear is widespread [see 61 Wash. 47, 51, 111 p. 879, 881 (1910)]. They do not give the same status to quirky perception. In *Criscuola v. Power Authority of State of New York*, 621 N.E. 2d, 119 (1993), 602 N.Y.S. 2d, 588 (1993), the Court found that:

personal or quirky fear or perception of danger or of health risks is not proof enough to recover consequential market value damages in eminent domain action, but public's or

---

[37] The benefit-cost analyst Arnold Harberger refuses as a matter of policy, and I suspect of principle, to perform a benefit-cost analysis from any but a national perspective.

[38] This problem was created by Paul Portney [1992, p. 131].

[39] The ninth circuit has noted that psychological stress might be cognizable under the National Environmental Protection Act (NEPA) if it were caused by a direct sensory impact [see *Animal Lovers Volunteers Assoc. (ALVA) v. Weinberger*, 765 F. 2d 937, 938 (9th Cir. 1985)].

Benefit–Cost Analysis I   *285*

Is Cost-Benefit Analysis Legal? Three Rules / 437

market's relatively more prevalent perception should suffice, scientific certitude or reasonableness notwithstanding.[40]

People will care about who pays as well as how much is paid. If our tax money is being spent foolishly we suffer a larger loss because in addition to the taxes we pay, there is a sense of waste.[41] We are, however, unlikely to object if the residents of Happyville spend only their own money. Thus, the benefit-cost analyst could suggest that if nonresidents of Happyville are required to pay for treating the drinking water for Happyville, they are apt to suffer special losses to the extent to which they believe their money is going for an irrational cause. The courts then are liable to refuse to find standing or a nuisance, or to bar recovery of damages, depending upon the extent to which the fear reflects more general community values.[42] This is in fact what they do.

Psychological values count in economics, and are the basis for determining values, as they usually do in law. A decline in property values that rests on a reasonable fear of contaminated drinking water, risk of disease, and the like represents a fairly straightforward case in both law and economics.

Does Harm Occur Where it is Unknown?

The question of standing is extremely important for those who claim nonuse values for environmental goods. Nonuse value arises from the value placed on the very existence of a good (existence value) or from the value one places on passing it on to others (bequest value). Probably it mainly represents the value one places on the existence of the good for others to use whether they are future or existing users.[43] Both court decisions and economic analyses have been inconsistent about who has standing with respect to nonuse value. In the case of the Nestucca oil spill, the populations of Washington and British Columbia were used for estimating damages, while in the case of the Exxon Valdez spill the population of the entire United States was held to be the potentially affected population [Dunford et al., 1997]. In a more recent case, *Montrose Chemical Corp. v. Superior Court*, the Trustees defined the potentially affected population as the English-speaking households in California [Dunford et al., 1996, p. 80].

The potential dam removal on the Elwha illustrates the importance of this issue. By far the largest benefit from removing the dams on the Elwha is found for the general population of the United States. Nevertheless, the majority of

---

[40] See also 45 Wash. 2d 180, 191–192, 273 P. 2d 645, 651 (1954).

[41] This is consistent with the asymmetric value function of Kahneman and Tversky [1979]. Thaler [1981, pp. 11–12] points out that a sense of waste is recorded as a loss.

[42] In the most important United States Supreme Court cases outlining the breadth of effects to be considered under NEPA, *Metropolitan Edison Co. v. People Against Nuclear Energy*, 460 U.S. 766, 75 L Ed.2d 534, 103 S. Ct. 1556 [1983] the Supreme Court stated that psychological health damage caused by the risk of a nuclear accident was beyond the purview of NEPA, 460 U.S. at 775. The Court noted that examining purely psychological effects with no direct physical change in the environment would make NEPA unmanageable: "The scope of the agency's inquiries must remain manageable if NEPA's goal of 'insur(ing) a fully informed and well considered decision' ... is to be accomplished," 460 U.S. at 776. This decision can be considered as the Court's response to a divergence between the expert's perception of risk and the plaintiffs'. That is, that psychological harm will be recognized where it is reasonably attached both to a "legitimate" estimate of the actual physical environmental consequences from an accident and its probability.

[43] In this regard, it represents a type of altruism that is similar to the value one may give to the distributional effects discussed earlier.

that population had never heard of the possibility of dam removal anywhere in the United States to improve fish habitat (71 percent), had never heard of the possibility of dam removal specifically on the Elwha (86 percent), and probably had never heard of the Elwha. The contingent value survey nevertheless found that the best estimate of the WTP value of removing dams on the Elwha for the U.S. population outside of Washington State was about $6.3 billion per year for 10 years. Most of this value is nonuse value.

"(N)on-use values reflect the utility that people obtain from natural resources based solely on the knowledge that they have about the services of those resources . . ." [Dunford et al., 1996, p. 80]. Dunford et al. argue that without specific knowledge of the injury or of the potential gain, there can be no loss. In this regard, use values and nonuse values are thought to be fundamentally different. The reasoning is this: For a use good, one may suffer a loss or at least a gain unrealized even if one is unaware of it. This cannot be true for a nonuse good, because value arises solely from knowledge and not from use. Without knowledge of the good, it has no value. Contingent valuation surveys by their very nature inform a sample of people about a possible event or decision which (having learned about it) they may then value. But, the reasoning continues, it is a mistake then to use their informed value to represent the value of those who are ignorant.

This argument fails, because it ignores the relation of wealth to value. People who care about salmon runs and free-flowing rivers care about environmental wealth. They care about the Elwha as belonging to a class of goods that constitutes this wealth. Those who put a nonuse value on species preservation may not know about a particular species, but may be reasonably said to care about it as part of a genera or class of species they do care about. Even if people never hear about the Elwha, they have a sense of their environmental wealth, and knowledge of what has happened to salmon runs and free-flowing rivers.

Consider the analogy of a rich man with many businesses run by others. We would say that he incurs a loss when one of his businesses suffers as a result of a poor decision, even if he never knows of that loss or decision, and even if he does not spend most of his wealth. He knows the magnitude of his wealth, even if he does not know each project that adds to or subtracts from it. He knows about changes in his wealth. As a result of a decision he knows nothing about, he suffers a psychological loss associated with the decline in wealth. So also does one who regards the environmental wealth of the nation as partly her own suffer a psychological loss from the deterioration of this wealth even when she has no knowledge of the particular event that decreases it.

The benefit-cost analyst would say that insofar as a particular loss leads to a loss of environmental wealth, and insofar as environmental wealth is valued, there is a psychological and therefore an economic loss. The analyst would point out that nonusers who do not know about the particular loss at the time of the contingent valuation survey may know about it later, and suffer a loss in environmental wealth that is linked directly to it. The loss to nonusers from destruction of particular environmental amenities is real and important. The implication is that what nonuse users value is not the specific environmental good, but the benefits for others that flow from this class of good.

Summary

I have said that two things are involved in valuing one good: the value of the item itself, and the value of the law that determines standing. Where the law is

Benefit–Cost Analysis I 287

Is Cost-Benefit Analysis Legal? Three Rules / 439

clear that theft is illegal, the analyst should deny standing to the thief to have his values for the stolen goods count. The value of the goods to the thief, or the utility of the bashers, should be considered in addressing the question of whether or not theft or bashing should be illegal. A benefit-cost standard may be applied to the issue of whether or not standing should be granted. When the value to a defined group from granting them standing is greater than the loss of value to others from granting standing, the economist can argue on benefit-cost grounds for granting standing to the defined group.

When the issue is whether the jurisdiction should have powers to produce a self-regarding analysis, or whether the jurisdiction should exist at all, or whether the foreigner should have standing, the values to the foreigner are liable to be relevant to that discussion. Again, these matters cannot be separated from legal determination of rights granting standing. The Happyville residents should have standing, and then their values should count, if no (implicit) prior decision has been made that they should not.[44] The benefits of treating the drinking water should not alter with the change from contamination by a natural substance to contamination by industrial discharge (of the same substance), unless the legal standing also has changed.

The benefit-cost analyst should not give or take away standing where the courts have not.[45] To do so would make the analysis irrelevant to the real world, and show a misunderstanding of the proper context of benefit-cost analysis as an adjunct to the law. Where the courts have not decided standing, the analyst can show the effects with and without standing being granted.

The whole process of requiring environmental impact statements as part of the relicensing process suggests a public stake in environmental protection. Moreover, the policy process surrounding the issue of dam removal on the Elwha has been directed in part by an act of Congress. Therefore, the FEIS is correct in including estimates of this nonmarket value [Flatt, 1994].

The Choice of the WTA or the WTP As Measures of Value

The Elwha Again

In the previous example of the Elwha, estimates of nonmarket value were taken as reported by Loomis [1995]. Some believe, however, that determination of nonuse benefits through the use of a questionnaire (contingent valuation method or CVM) technique is likely to be subject to aggregation bias. Aggregation bias arises because the value reported as the WTP by respondents varies inversely with the number of items presented for valuation. In fact, the ratio of stated

---

[44] In 11 state jurisdictions all that is required is a showing that fear exists and affects market value. In four others, there is a reluctance to admit unreasonable fear as a basis for damages. See *Criscuola v. Power Authority of State of New York* 81 N.Y. 2D 649, 652 (1993). See also *Willsey v. Kansas City Power & Light Co.* 6 Kan. App. 2D, 599 (1993).

[45] The Comprehensive Environmental Response, Compensation, and Liability Act (CERCLA) excludes certain types of releases from natural resource damage [43 CFR Section 11.24(b) (1980)]. Exempt are damages previously identified in an environmental impact statement as irreversible and irretrievable, damages occurring before the enactment of CERCLA, damages resulting from other federally permitted releases, and releases associated with certain pesticide products. In a similar spirit, the Oil Pollution Act of 1990 (OPA) does not apply to discharges allowed under permits issued under federal, state, or local laws [§ 1002 (c)(1)], or from vessels owned or charted and operated by a federal, state, local, or foreign government agency that is not engaged in commerce [§ 1002 (c)(2)].

WTP when an amenity is considered alone to the stated WTP when the amenity is considered along with others is as large as 142 to 1 [Coursey and Roberts, 1992]. Suppose that when the reported figures for the WTP for nonmarket values are adjusted to account for these problems, and when, in addition, the value of the WTA measure is calculated, the figures in Table 4 are the result. Should the WTP or WTA be used in calculating benefits?

Table 4. Present value of benefits and costs for the restoration of the Elwha (nonmarket values adjusted) (figures are in millions of 1995 dollars).

Present value of market benefits (willingness to pay)	Present value of nonmarket benefits for Pacific Northwest (willingness to pay)	Present value of nonmarket benefits (willingness to accept)	Present value of costs (willingness to accept)
$164	$80[a]	$240[b]	$247-$273

Note: Present value is calculated using a real discount rate of 3, and the life of the project is 100 years.
[a] This figure is adjusted from that of Loomis [1995] by dividing by 142 to eliminate any aggregation bias, and is further adjusted to eliminate existence value. The figure is meant to be hypothetical, in the sense that I am making no judgment about whether Loomis' figures do include aggregation bias or whether existence value should not be counted.
[b] This figure is assumed to be three times the WTP figures as representing a probable lower bound.

The Logic of Choosing the WTA for Losses and the WTP for Gains

The logic of using the WTA to measure loss rests on a normative decision to recognize ownership. The WTA recognizes the initial or reference position as one that incorporates already having the good [Zerbe and Dively, 1994]. The WTP incorporates an initial position in which one does not have the good and asks what the good is worth from this position. Ownership is both legal and psychological. Where psychological and legal ownership correspond, the situation is clear: Ownership establishes a reference point from which losses are to be calculated by the WTA and gains by the WTP. In a sense this has long been noted:

Hume and Adam Smith, for example, both said that expectations arising out of rights of property deserved greater protection than expectations to something which had never been possessed. To deprive somebody of something which he merely expects to receive is a less serious wrong, deserving of less protection, than to deprive somebody of the expectation of continuing to hold something which he already possesses. (Atiyah, 1979, p. 428)[46]

Why the Choice to Use the WTP or the WTA Makes a Difference

Returning to the example of the Elwah, if the WTP figures are used for nonmarket benefits, benefits fall short of costs by about $19 million. If the WTA figures are used, however, the benefits again comfortably exceed the costs.

---

[46] I am indebted to Jack Knetsch for this reference.

The question with respect to the Elwha is whether to use the WTP or the WTA figures for benefits. Until recently it was thought that the choice of WTP or WTA made little difference, aside from exceptional cases, and that the source of the difference was solely income effects [Willig, 1976]. Neither proposition is correct. Researchers have demonstrated repeatedly that WTA questionnaires generate values from 3 to 19 times greater than those elicited by WTP questionnaires, as reported by one source [Levy and Friedman, 1994]. For environmental goods, the ratio of WTA to WTP may be as much as 142 to 1, according to another source [Coursey and Roberts, 1992].[47] There are three reasons for the difference: income effects, substitution possibilities, and loss aversion. The latter two reasons have been appreciated only in recent years.

Income Effects

Consider the value of your book. The price at which you are willing to sell your book is the WTA, and recognizes your psychological (and legal) ownership of the book. Your willingness to buy the same book is measured by the WTP, and assumes you did not already have the book. This difference produced by the income consequences of owning or not owning the book will be small in the case of the (inexpensive) book, because ownership or its lack does not much change your wealth. A house may be a different matter. The more valuable the good, the greater the difference, the greater the effect—hence, the income effect.

Figure 1 shows the operation of income effects in creating a divergence between the WTP and the WTA. U_0 and U_1 are indifference curves that show two goods that are perfect substitutes. Let us call them fame and income. Income is shown on the vertical axis and fame on the horizontal axis. U_1 has a steeper slope than U_0 at every quantity of fame indicating that fame is more valuable at a higher level of income. The initial level of income is at I_0 at point A on indifference curve U_0 so that the initial amount of fame is F_0. The consumer gains more fame in moving to position F_1. To gain fame as presented by position F_1, the consumer is willing to give up income $(I_0\text{-}I_1)$ to arrive at point C which is just as satisfying a position as point A, the initial point. This difference in income $I_0\text{-}I_1$ is the WTP. The WTA is shown by also beginning with income I_0, but at point B on indifference curve U_1 representing a higher level of satisfaction corresponding with having greater fame available. The consumer would be willing to accept less available fame if he gained income sufficient to put him at point D, a point that is equally satisfying as B. This income is $I_2\text{-}I_0$ and is the WTA. The WTA will exceed the WTP because U_1 is steeper than U_0.

Both the WTP and the WTA measure the effect of a change. While doing so, the WTA presumes greater wealth than the WTP does; the greater wealth consists of possessing, in a psychological sense, the very good in question—here the book or the house. This greater wealth means that the money measure of a positive change is larger for a normal good than when the same person has lower wealth. Whether or not the higher measure (which includes the greater wealth) is the better measure depends on whether that person possesses psychological ownership of the good being considered. The WTA measures the change from the perspective of one who claims the good.

---

[47] See the citations in Levy and Friedman [1994, p. 495, n. 6]. See also Coursey, Hovis, and Schulze [1987].

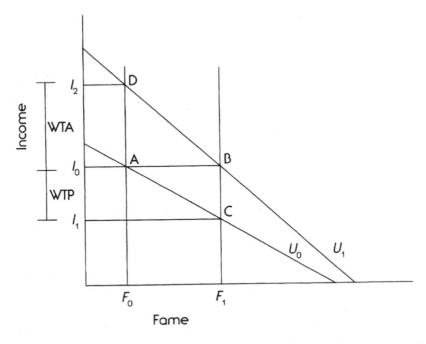

Figure 1. The income effect (WTA is willingness to accept; WTP is willingness to pay).

Substitution Possibilities

Recently, Hanneman [1991] showed that the poorer the substitutes for the good, the greater the divergence between the WTP and the WTA. Put another way, the more unique the good, the greater the divergence. The substantial divergence between the WTP and the WTA for environmental goods arises in part from the fact that many of these goods have no close substitutes. The divergence between the WTP and the WTA is infinite for goods with no substitutability; call them time and money (income). This can be shown by Figure 2. Initial income is I_0. The WTP for a move from position A on U_1 to position C (also on U_1) leaves the consumer with less income but more time. The consumer is willing to give up I_0-I_1 because any income greater than I_1 is worthless to the consumer without more time. This is the WTP. A consumer who begins at position B also with income I_0 but on the higher indifference curve U_2 will be unwilling to accept any amount of money in exchange for giving up time because additional money is of no value without additional time. The WTA is infinite.[48] Because the WTP is finite and the WTA is infinite the difference is also infinite.

---

[48] In order for the WTA not to be infinite, U_2 would need to cross the vertical line extended upward from I_0.

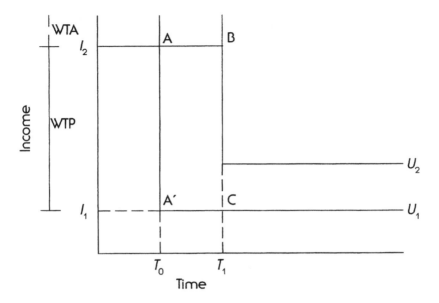

Figure 2. Pure substitution effect: Divergence between willingness to accept (WTA) and willingness to pay (WTP) can be infinite.

Loss Aversion

The standard benefit-cost approach in which losses are valued according to the WTA and gains according to the WTP is consistent with the empirically derived asymmetrical value function of Tversky and Kahneman [1981]. This function reflects a state in which individuals value losses more highly than they value gains. Individuals appear to place a significantly higher value on the units of a good they already have and might lose or have to give up than they place on getting additional units of the same good. This should not affect the way market goods are valued because individuals adjust their subjective marginal evaluations to the market price. Figure 3 shows the value function. Among other things this function shows that losses have a greater value than equivalent gains and that the way in which goods are packaged will affect their value. For example, the value of two smaller goods is greater than the value of one equivalent good so that, as Thaler [1981] notes, one should not put all of one's presents in one package.

Where the Psychological and Legal Measures Differ[49]

But what if the psychological and legal measures differ? The measure of values in economics is ultimately psychological. Loss is a psychological state. The

[49] For an expanded treatment of this, see Zerbe [1997].

444 / *Is Cost-Benefit Analysis Legal? Three Rules*

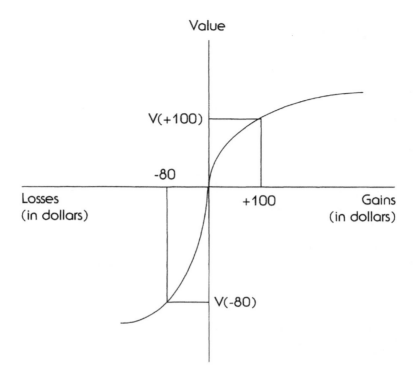

Figure 3. Value function.

common assumption that a choice should be based on assigned legal entitlements is incorrect. Levy and Friedman [1994], for example, assert, "the determination of the conceptually appropriate form of CV [CVM, contingent valuation method] query is a matter of property rights, not economics or psychology" (p. 509). This is not accurate. The law will, of course, be the major determinant of psychological reference points. This is very different from saying, as Levy and Friedman imply, that in the event of a conflict between the law and the psychological reference point, the law ought to govern [Knetsch, 1997, pp. 13–32]. In this respect, benefit-cost analysis informs the law because it is efficient that the law should conform to the psychological reference point. This proposition can be put in the form of a theorem:

- *Theorem:* Efficiency requires that the legal definitions of property and measure of damage correspond to psychological reference points.[50]

---

[50] This is consistent with the rule that efficiency requires that the right should go to whoever values it the most.

Benefit–Cost Analysis I 293

Is Cost-Benefit Analysis Legal? Three Rules / 445

A heuristic proof of this theorem can be made by imagining that the condition for efficiency is not met. Imagine that Amartya believes that he owns a right or a property, let's say a first edition of Dickens's *Great Expectations*, and that Derek also believes that Amartya owns the book. They discover that the law, however, holds that Derek, not Amartya, owns it. Amartya suffers a loss of the first edition psychologically and therefore economically, while Derek gains it. Because losses are, on the average, worth more than equivalent gains (due to income effects, substitution possibilities, and loss aversion), on the average Derek will gain less than what Amartya loses. This is perfectly general. The application of law to affect a legal ownership different from psychological ownership must, on average, impose net losses, as long as Amartya and Derek may be regarded as equivalents (on average one does not have a greater income than the other, or does not differ in some other relevant characteristic). Underlying this proof is the notion that changing preferences to be in accordance with the law cannot be described as efficient. This idea violates the proper context for benefit-cost analysis—which requires that preferences be taken as they lie—and the very concept of efficiency.[51] If, for example, one class of claimants psychologically possesses property so that its removal is felt as a psychological loss, and a rival claimant has a lesser psychological claim or no claim, efficiency requires that the law grant the right to the psychological possessor. The common-law doctrine of adverse possession codifies just such a scenario.

Ellickson [1987] studied a change in the law in Shasta County, California. In one half of the county, ranchers were liable for straying cattle; in the other half, farmers bore any damage under the law. In fact, however, this change did not alter the time-honored custom enforced by social norms by which ranchers were liable for damage caused by their cattle. The psychological reference point was one of liability for straying cattle. Thus, in Shasta County, efficiency suggests a change in the law to place liability on the owners of straying cattle. In a sense, this has long been recognized. This does not mean for certain that the law should be changed so that ranchers are liable, though it suggests it; liability rules are not ownership rules. It is possible that the efficient rule is farmer liability, but the psychological reference point of rancher liability makes this conclusion unlikely because a change imposes a loss properly measured by the WTA on farmers. In considering whether or not to change the liability rule, the calculation of gains and losses of the change should reflect the psychological reference point.

The law attempts to conform with or to recognize the discrepancy between measures of value for benefits and costs.[52] In this respect, law is correct in recognizing the primacy of the psychological basis for valuation. Cohen and Knetsch [1992] point to six classes of legal rules that are consistent with recognizing the valuation disparity between gains and losses.[53] Evidence suggests that restoration of environmental health following an environmental injury is

---

[51] In any event, benefit-cost analysis cannot evaluate the advantages of a change in preferences, because it does not take preferences as they lie.

[52] See Levy and Friedman [1994] for a discussion of the concept of ownership in federal environmental law.

[53] These are the rules of adverse possession, limitations on recovery of lost profits, contract modifications, gratuitous promises, opportunistic behavior, and repossession. To these I would add limitations on recovery of property from theft.

viewed differently (as the restoration of a loss) from monetary compensation
for that injury (which is viewed as a gain). Under the common-law measure of
natural resource damage, as well as some new statute law, there is implicit
recognition of the asymmetry between gains and losses, in the sense that
restoration of environmental health following an environmental harm is given
a different status from market measures of damages. The generally accepted
common-law measure of damages is the lesser of either the cost of restoration
of the natural resource or diminution of market value attributable to the injury
to the resource. This is not an *absolute* rule, however. The law recognizes
restoration as an appropriate measure of damage if the cost of restoration is
reasonable in comparison to the diminution in the value of land.[54] Because
restoration costs may be recognized as reasonable if they are greater by 50
percent or more of the market diminution of value, restoration clearly is afforded
special status. Recently, a number of environmental statutes have been
interpreted by the courts or regulatory agencies to state a preference for
restoration costs—including variation of replacement, rehabilitation, and the
acquisition of equivalent resources—over diminution of economic value.[55]
Regulations first adopted by the U.S. Department of the Interior (DOI) in
response to the Comprehensive Environmental Response, Compensation, and
Liability Act (CERCLA) held that the public trustee was required to select the
lesser of either restoration costs or diminution of value of the resources at issue.
New parallel regulations giving greater weight to restoration were, however,
adopted by both the DOI and the National Oceanographic Atmospheric
Administration (NOAA) in response to *State of Ohio*.
    There are also a number of areas in which some types of public rights to
ownership are recognized in the law. For example, the concept of public rights
in national land remains basic common law today in nonenvironmental cases,
and is not irrelevant in environmental law [Levy and Friedman, 1994, p. 515, n.
88; pp. 517–519].

Dual and Uncertain Ownership

The meat of much of the law concerns cases in which ownership or right in
some form is asserted by more than one party. A psychological sense of
ownership may exist for the same good by different people. Amaryta and Derek
may, for example, both assert ownership to a book. Both may have legitimate
expectations of ownership. In a contest at law one will lose. This will be felt as
a psychological loss. The economic theory is clear. Benefits are to be calculated
using WTP for gains and WTA for losses restored, while costs are to be calculated
using WTA for losses and WTP for gains foregone.[56] Whether a change is a gain
or a loss restored, or a change is a loss or a gain forestalled, is determined by a
psychological reference point. The psychological reference point is the correct

---

[54] See *Heninger v. Dunn*, 101 Cal. App. 3rd 858, 106, 162 Cal. Rptr. 104, 106–107 (1980); *Newsome v. Billips*, 671 S. W. 2d 252, 255 (Ky. App., 1984); *Trinity Church v. John Hancock Mutual Life Ins.*, 399 Mass. 43, 502 N. E. 2d 532 (1987).

[55] *State of Ohio v. U.S. Department of the Interior*, 830 F. 2nd 432 D.C. Cir. (1989).

[56] The use of the WTA to represent the sense of a loss restored is the correct measure even if loss aversion does not exist. Zerbe [1997] shows that when ownership is uncertain, using the Kaldor-Hicks criteria to determine ownership requires a consideration of both the WTP and the divergence between the WTA and the WTP.

one, because benefit-cost analysis rests—and has always been thought to rest—on the preferences of individuals, whether acting as consumers or as citizens. If such sense of ownership exists, the analyst uses the WTA for the calculation of loss to both parties. The analyst values the book for both, using the WTA. The analyst counts values as they lie but does not know how they lie. The sense of ownership may in fact belong to only one so that the other party is lying. Or, the sense of ownership may illegitimately belong to both. Amaryta may believe he owns whatever he steals. But this is not an attitude society may wish to encourage and Amaryta may be denied standing to have his values considered. When rights are indeterminate and important, it is well known that the results of a benefit-cost analysis may be indeterminate.[57] This is just a reflection of the wisdom of rule one.

For many goods, environmental goods for example, the sense of psychological ownership may be diffuse, unformed, or uninformed. Public debate, discussion, and political leadership can help to fix the reference point. This is just the sort of discussion commended by Sagoff [1988], and to which benefit-cost analysis can contribute, remembering that this contribution will be more salient and less resented if in keeping with rule one. Thus, with respect to the problem of the Elwha dams, the discussion here suggests that the restoration of the Elwha may be viewed as the restoration of a previous loss rather than as a gain. As another example, consider the Headwaters Grove in Northern California which is the last major privately owned stand of ancient redwoods. For about 10 years, the Pacific Lumber Company has been trying to cut the trees, filing logging plans with the California Forestry Board. The value of these trees as timber has been estimated at between $100 and $500 million. These efforts have been thwarted by environmental groups [Goldbert, 1996]. This seems like an example in which the WTP of the environmental groups is less than the WTA of the timber company, but in which the WTA of the environmental groups is much higher. The probability that the WTA is a better measure of the psychological effect of the loss of the redwoods to environmental groups and to others, suggests that some recognition of property rights on their behalf is appropriate and that, as shown by their ability to delay the cutting of this timber, the courts have recognized this.

A benefit-cost analysis might reasonably then calculate benefits using both WTP and WTA measures of benefits. From the public discussion itself, an indication of the proper sense of psychological and hence legal ownership might be born. A recognition of public rights to free-flowing water is not unthinkable.

Public opinion may be unreliable and misguided; it may be caused by sensationalism in news accounts or formed on the basis of poor or inaccurate information. Again, the analysis and the analyst can contribute information to the debate, but if there is no debate then there is no basis in benefit-cost analysis to disregard public values. The reliability of psychological reference points is a matter of public process; their unreliability should properly and explicitly increase the uncertainty of the guidance provided by benefit-cost analysis.

---

[57] Baker [1980] uses the discrepancy between WTA and WTP to attack the use of a Kaldor-Hicks or potential Pareto test. He points out correctly that compensation is not possible when starting points are considered, because the sum of expectations of parties in dispute will exceed the total to be gained. This is true but is not, as Baker means it to be, a counterargument for adopting a Pareto or a potential Pareto test where rights are in dispute. See Zerbe [1997].

448 / *Is Cost-Benefit Analysis Legal? Three Rules*

The Existing Practice

In practice, the issue of whether to use the WTP or the WTA rarely arises, except in defining what effects are benefits (use the WTP) and what are costs (use the WTA). The panel of experts on the use of contingent valuation methods to assess natural resource damages notes that "virtually all previous [contingent valuation] studies have described scenarios in which respondents are asked to pay to prevent future occurrences of similar accidents," without regard for the issue of whether the WTP or the WTA is the appropriate measure [Arrow et al., p. 4603]. The panel states that "the willingness to pay format should be used instead of the compensation required because the former is the conservative choice" (p. 4608). This is incorrect as a matter of principle; the choice of a welfare criterion should not be a question of being conservative; it should be a question of selecting the right measure. Perhaps we should adopt a conservative valuation of the right measure, but this is a different matter.

A Suggested Solution

A solution for the issues of standing and the psychological reference point starts with a recognition of their relationship to legal analysis. The questions of standing and whether to use WTP or WTA measures should not be separated from the legal context. Three interrelated questions are being asked: What is the value of the good in question? Who has standing? Where does the psychological sense of ownership lie? The first question cannot be answered separately from the other two.

The second and third questions are already answered where legal rights are clear enough and where they are associated with the psychological sense of ownership. The analyst is free to concentrate on the first question. That is, in most cases the practical rule is to refer to the law, to use legal standing as the guide, and to use ownership itself to determine the reference point. Having determined that Derek owns the book, we need not further ask if Derek would regard its theft as a loss, nor if Amartya's valuation of the book should be counted.[58]

In other cases, standing or ownership will be less clear, or there may be reason to suspect that the decision embodied in the law is inefficient. The analyst must then address a different set of questions. Before answering the first question (what is the value of the good in question?) she must ask: Who should have standing? Where does the psychological reference point lie, if different from the legal one? In addressing these questions, the analyst contributes to the law.

CONCLUSION

Benefit-cost analysis should be seen as the consistent application of a set of procedures by which economics can furnish information useful to the decisionmaking process. These procedures require, most of all, a recognition

---

[58] Carson and Mitchell [1993] note that the difference between WTA and WTP is one of property rights (p. 241, n. 17).

Benefit–Cost Analysis I 297

Is Cost-Benefit Analysis Legal? Three Rules / 449

that the application of benefit-cost analysis cannot proceed without the institutional context in which it is found. This view is consistent with the technique of normative analysis as originally developed by economists, and is grounded in economic theory and in an understanding of the limitations, as well as the strengths, of economics [Lesser and Zerbe, 1995; Tolley, 1982].

The analyst testifying in the trial of *Derek v. Amartya* makes three mistakes. First, she says that the book should go to Amartya, ignoring rule one (the benefit-cost analysis is not the decision). Second, she fails to count the value of the goods as zero in the hands of the thief. In this sense, she fails to incorporate missing values and fails to recognize that benefit-cost analysis rests on law. Society has made a prior decision (that may reasonably be thought to meet the standards of benefit-cost analysis) that this value is zero with respect to this sort of question; the analyst is not facing the question of whether or not book thievery should be legal. That is, with respect to the question of the value of the book, society has denied standing to the thief. Third, she compares the WTP of Amartya with the WTP of Derek without regard to the psychological reference point. Even if Amaryta feels a psychological sense of ownership because he believes that whatever he steals belongs to him, this is not an attitude that society may want to encourage. That is, he may lack standing to have the book treated as a loss in evaluation.

The example of the Elwha raised issues of standing with respect to nonuse value and when to use WTA rather than WTP measures of value. The benefit-cost analyst considering the Elwha must decide who has standing to have their values considered: the citizens only of Clallam County, or of the state of Washington, or of the Pacific Northwest, or of the United States. Where value comes from knowledge about the quantity or level of a general stock of goods, and where this knowledge exists, there is a loss from changes in the stock of goods, even when one does not know of the particular loss or losses. Where there is a divergence between the psychological reference point and the legal one, it is efficient for the law to conform to the psychological reference point. Similarly, where the value in granting standing to a defined group is greater than the loss of value in granting standing to a competing group, the economist can argue on benefit-cost grounds for granting standing to the defined group. Finally, the analyst must consider where the psychological reference point lies in considering questions such as whether the restoration of the free-flowing river is felt as a loss restored or as an environmental gain. Where the analyst cannot answer these questions, the benefit-cost analysis should include information based on alternative assumptions about standing and the psychological reference point. This information should inform the legal processes. Changes in the law may in turn affect the psychological reference point.

The questions of value in benefit-cost analysis should not—and in a real sense cannot—be separated from their legal context [Heyne, 1988]. The objections we have been discussing are those that have been raised by philosophers and lawyers, generally nonpractitioners of benefit-cost analysis. Some of them have seen benefit-cost analysis as a sort of a deus ex machina by which the application of economic theory to the process of valuation is made, and through which proponents of benefit-cost analysis suggest decisions should be made. Unfortunately, they have been encouraged in this view by the wealth maximization school of law and by economists' uncritical use of benefit-cost analysis as "the answer."

450 / *Is Cost-Benefit Analysis Legal? Three Rules*

The advocates of benefit-cost analysis have claimed too much, but its critics would throw out the baby with the bathwater. Neither the extravagant claims nor the trenchant criticisms apply to benefit-cost analysis. What is left, and what was original as benefit-cost analysis, is something both more useful and more defensible than the critics have maintained.

APPENDIX

Consider social welfare as a function of the utilities of all of the individuals in society so that welfare is:

$$W = W(U_1, U_2, \ldots U_N) \tag{A.1}$$

A change in welfare is found by totally differentiating equation (A.1) to give:

$$dW = \sum_i^N \frac{\partial W}{\partial U} dU_i \tag{A.2}$$

Thus, a change in welfare is given by the change in the ith person's utility dU_i multiplied by the social weight given to the ith person's utility. The utility of the ith person is a function of goods and services consumed. That is:

$$U_i = U(X_1, X_2, \ldots, X_m) \tag{A.3}$$

and thus a change in the utility of the ith person is:

$$dU_i = \sum \frac{\partial U_i}{\partial X_{ij}} dX_{ij} \tag{A.4}$$

A well-known result from consumer welfare theory is that the additional utility given to the ith person by a new unit of good X_j is the price (explicit or implicit) times i's marginal utility of income or:

$$\frac{\partial U_i}{\partial X_{ij}} = \frac{\partial U_i^*}{\partial Y_i} P_j \tag{A.5}$$

where Y represents income and P represents the price of good X_j [see Varian, 1996]. The term U_i^* is from the indirect utility function so that it assumes individual choice of the optimal quantity given income and price. The term

$\frac{\partial U_i}{\partial Y_i}$ is i's marginal utility of income, that is, the utility of an additional dollar.

Substituting equations (A.4) and (A.5) into equation (A.2) gives:

Benefit–Cost Analysis I   *299*

Is Cost-Benefit Analysis Legal? Three Rules / 451

$$dW = \sum_i \sum_j \ (\frac{\partial W}{\partial U_i})(\frac{\partial U^*}{\partial Y_i})(P_{jd}X_{ij}) \qquad (A.6)$$

This says that the change in welfare is the sum of all of the income changes

for an individual, $\overset{M}{\underset{j}{\sum}}P_{jd}X_{ij}$, multiplied by that individual's marginal utility of

income, $\frac{\partial U^*}{\partial Y_i}$, times the marginal social weight given to that individual, $\frac{\partial W}{\partial U_i}$,

summed over all individuals. Equation (A.6) can be rearranged to give:

$$dW = \sum_i \sum_j P_{jd}X_{ij} + \sum_i \sum_j (\frac{\partial W}{\partial U_i}\frac{\partial U^*}{\partial Y_i} - 1)P_{jd}X_{ij} \qquad (A.7)$$

That is, dW = efficiency effect + distribution effect. This equation has divided a change in welfare into two parts—an efficiency effect and a distributional effect. The efficiency effect is the first expression on the right-hand side of the equation; the distributional effect is the second expression on the right-hand side. The efficiency effect is the sum of the changes in income. The distributional effect shows the amount which, when added to the income effect, will give the total welfare effect, taking into account the individual's marginal utility of income and the marginal social weight for that individual. The utilitarian proposition is that each person should have the same weight given to his or her utility so

that the term $\frac{\partial W}{\partial U_i}$ may reasonably be regarded as having a weight of one for

all.

The Kaldor-Hicks (KH) assumptions treat everyone's marginal utility of income and the social weight of each person's utility as equal. These assumptions make the last expression on the right-hand side equal to zero so that we are left with:

$$dW = \sum_i \sum_j P_{jd}X_{ij} \qquad (A.8)$$

This is the KH equation, and on this basis it is said that the KH measure does not consider distributional effects. The distributional part of the equation has disappeared because we gave everyone the same marginal utility of income and we assumed that everyone's utility had the same social weight.

The income distribution is just such a good as I have defined and as Page [1992] has described. It is a good that is one of the X_{ij} goods that is included in equation (A.8). A change in the income distribution has a value to some whose income does not directly change and thus an implicit price P_j will give rise to a change in income and in utility for those who place a value on the income distribution. The change in the income distribution will give rise to a change as expressed in a money measure by the sum of the WTPs for those who will gain from the change and the WTAs for those who prefer the status quo. This approach

452 / *Is Cost-Benefit Analysis Legal? Three Rules*

meets the requirement of the KH test that everyone's income by treated the same.[59]

This can be modeled explicitly. Let social welfare, W, be a function of the incomes of the n people in society. Let the utility of each individual depend not only on his own income but also on that of others. Thus:

$$W = W(U^1, U^2, \ldots U^n) \qquad (A.9)$$

$$U^i = U^i(P, Y_1, Y_2 \ldots Y_n) \qquad (A.10)$$

and similarly for each person i.

The KH measures of welfare treat as unobservable the marginal utility of income, and assume that $\frac{\partial U_i}{\partial Y_t} = 1$ for all individuals. Because the criteria treat all utility equally, then $\frac{\partial W}{\partial U_i} = 1$ for all individuals. Adopting these assumptions and differentiating equation (A.9) we obtain:

$$dW = \sum_i Y_i + Y'_1(Z_1) + Y'_2(Z_2) + \ldots Y'_n(Z_n) \qquad (A.11)$$

or

$$dW = \sum_i Y'_t + \sum_i Y'_i Z_i \qquad (A.12)$$

where Y'_t is the change in 1's income and Z_1 is $dY_1 \frac{\partial U_2}{\partial Y_1} + dY_1 \frac{\partial U_3}{\partial Y_1} + \ldots dY_1 \frac{\partial Un}{\partial Y_1}$.

A similar definition holds for W_2, W_3, and the like. The WTP or the WTA for person 1 can be found by differentiating equation (A.9) from 1's perspective and setting the result equal to zero and solving for dY_t, which gives person 1's WTP for person 2 as:

$dY_1 = \dfrac{\frac{\partial U_1}{\partial Y_2}}{\frac{\partial U_1}{\partial Y_1}} dY_2$, and for person 3 as $dY_1 = \dfrac{\frac{\partial U_1}{\partial Y_3}}{\frac{\partial U_1}{\partial Y_1}} dY_3$, and continuing for each person.

---

[59] The difference between the good "income distribution" and other goods is that changes in income distribution are not separable from changes in the allocation of other goods. This is, however, a technical not a philosophical difference. We value goods because of their characteristics and the distribution of goods is a characteristic of who possesses goods.

Benefit–Cost Analysis I   *301*

Is Cost-Benefit Analysis Legal? Three Rules / 453

Because by the KH assumption $\frac{\partial U_1}{\partial Y_1} = 1$, it will be seen that the weight for

person 1 in equation is (A.11) and (A.12) is the sum of the WTP or the WTA of those who care about person i's income. We can call the sum of the Z_i's the *marginal social value of i's income*. Equation (A.12) then says that a change in welfare is the sum of the income changes over individuals, plus the social value (as reflected in the WTP or WTA) of changes in the income distribution. That is, the first term on the right-hand side is the welfare change without considering distributional changes, and the second term is the value of the distributional changes. Equation (A.12) may reasonably be regarded as the fundamental equation of benefit cost-analysis.[60] Thus, a measure that treats the marginal utility of income as 1 for all and that assumes an equal value of all utility changes nevertheless includes a distributional effect.[61] Such measures are the KH measures.

---

[60] For equation (A.12) to be complete, time in the form of discounting future values needs to be introduced. To do this is straightforward.

[61] For example, if Richard receives an income increase of $50 and Ronald an increase of $100, the total money measure of the welfare increase ignoring distributional effects would be $150. If Richard and Ronald care about each other so that Richard weights an increase in Ronald's income by 0.1 and Ronald weights an increase in Richard's income by 0.2, the total money measure of the increase in Kaldor-Hicks welfare is $170. For a way of totally taking into account these interactive effects see Zerbe and Dively [1994].

I wish to thank Tom Mumford for research assistance; Diane Larson for editing and research assistance; members of the University of Chicago workshop in public policy and economics, Cass Sunstein, George Tolley, Alison Cullen, Don Coursey, and Victor Flatt for comments; Robert Lande for suggestions; and Yale Law School for support as an Olin Fellow. I also would like to thank two anonymous referees for their useful and most encouraging comments.

RICHARD O. ZERBE JR. is Professor in the Graduate School of Public Affairs at the University of Washington, and Adjunct Professor at the University of Washington School of Law.

REFERENCES

Anderson, Elizabeth (1993), *Value in Ethics and Economics* (Cambridge, MA: Harvard University Press).

Arrow, Kenneth, Robert Solow, Paul Portney, Edward E. Leamer, Roy Radner, and Howard Schuman (1993), *Report on the National Panel on Contingent Valuation*, 58 Fed. Reg. 10, 4601, 4602-4614 (15 Januray 1993).

Atiyah, P. S. (1979), *The Rise and Fall of Freedom of Contract* (Oxford, England: Oxford University Press).

Baker, Edwin C. (1980), "Starting Points in the Economic Analysis of Law," *Hofstra Law Review* 8(4), pp. 939–972.

Bebchuck, Lucian A. (1980), "The Pursuit of a Bigger Pie: Can Everyone Expect a Bigger Slice?" *Hofstra Law Review* 8(3), pp. 671–710.

Becker, Gary (1968), "Crime and Punishment: An Economic Approach," *Journal of Political Economy* 76(2), pp. 169–217.

Boadway, Robin W. and Neil Bruce (1984), *Welfare Economics* (Oxford, England: Basil Blackwell).

Carson, Richard and Robert Mitchell (1993), "Contingent Valuation in the Legal Arena," in Raymond J. Kopp and V. Kerry Smith (eds.), *Valuing Natural Assets: The Economics of Natural Resource Damage Assessment* (Washington, DC: Resources for the Future).

Cohen, David and Jack L. Knetsch (1992), "Judicial Choice and Disparities between Measures of Economic Values," *Osgoode Hall Law Journal* 30(3), pp. 737–770.

Coleman, Jules L. (1980), "Efficiency, Utility, and Wealth Maximization," *Hofstra Law Review* 8(3), pp. 509–551.

Coursey, Don L., Elizabeth Hoffman, and Matthew L. Spitzer (1987), "Fear and Loathing in the Coase Theorem: Experimental Tests Involving Physical Discomfort," *Journal of Legal Studies* (16)2, pp. 217–248.

Coursey, Don L., John L. Hovis, and William D. Schulze (1987), "The Disparity between Willingness to Accept and Willingness to Pay Measures of Value," *The Quarterly Journal Of Economics*, pp. 679–690.

Coursey, Don L. and Russell D. Roberts (1992), "Aggregation and the Contingent Valuation Method for Evaluating Environmental Amenities," Working Paper, Olin School of Business, Washington University, St. Louis, Mo.

Davis, Robert K. (1988), "Lessons in Politics and Economics from the Snail Darter," in V. Kerry Smith (ed.), *Environmental Resources and Applied Economics: Essays in Honor of John Krutilla* (Washington, DC: Resources for the Future).

Dively, Dwight and Richard O. Zerbe (1993), "A Survey of Municipal Discount Rates Practices," Working Paper, Graduate School of Public Affairs, University of Washington, Seattle, WA.

Dunford, Richard W., F. Reed Johnson, Rob A. Sandefur, and Emily S. West (1997), "Whose Losses Count in Natural Resource Damages?" *Contemporary Economics Policy* 15(4), pp. 77–87.

Dworkin, Ronald M. (1980), "Is Wealth a Value?" *The Journal of Legal Studies* 9(2), pp. 191–226.

Ellickson, Robert C. (1987), "A Critique of Economic and Sociological Theories of Social Control," *Journal of Legal Studies* 16(1), pp. 67–99.

Faith, Roger L. and Robert D. Tollison (1983), "The Pricing of Surrogate Crime and Law Enforcement," *Journal of Legal Studies* 12, pp. 401–411.

Flatt, Victor B. (1994), "The Human Environment of the Mind: Correcting NEPA Implementation by Treating Environmental Philosophy and Environmental Risk Allocation as Environmental Values under NEPA," *Hastings Law Journal* 46(1), pp. 85–123.

Goldbert, Carey (1996), "Glint of Hope for a grove of Returns," *New York Times*, April 21, p. 16.

Graham, John D. (1995), "Edging toward Sanity on Regulatory Risk Reform," *Issues in Science and Technology* 11(4), pp. 61–66.

Hanke, Steve H. and Richard A. Walker (1974), "Benefit Cost Analysis Reconsidered: An Evaluation of the Mid State Project," *Water Resources Journal* 10(5), pp. 898–908.

Hanneman, W. Michael (1991), "Willingness to Pay and Willingness to Accept: How Much Can They Differ?" *American Economic Review* 81(3), pp. 635–647.

Hewins, W. A. S. (1911), writing the section on economics in the classic edition of the *Encyclopaedia Brittanica* (p. 900).

Heyne, Paul (1988), "The Foundations of Law and Economics," *Research in Law and Economics* 11, pp. 53–71.

Hildred, William and Fred Beauvais (1995), "An Instrumentalist Critique of 'Cost-Utility Analysis,'" *Journal of Economic Issues* 29(4), pp. 1083–1096.

Benefit–Cost Analysis I   *303*

Is Cost-Benefit Analysis Legal? Three Rules / 455

Kahneman, Daniel and Amos Tversky (1979), "Prospect Theory: An Analysis of Decision under Risk," *Econometrica* 47, pp. 263-291.

Kelman, Steven (1981), "Cost-Benefit Analysis: An Ethical Critique," *Regulation* 5(1)(January/February), pp. 33–40.

Kennedy, Duncan (1981), "Cost-Benefit Analysis of Entitlement Problems: A Critique," *Stanford Law Review* 33, pp. 387–445.

Knetsch, Jack L. (1997), "Reference States, Fairness, and Choice of Measure to Value Environmental Changes," in Max H. Bazerman (ed.), *Environment, Ethics, and Behavior: The Psychology of Environmental Valuation and Degradation* (San Francisco: The New Lexington Press).

Kopp, Raymond and V. Kerry Smith (1993), "Glossary Terms for Natural Resource Damage Assessment," in Raymond J. Kopp and V. Kerry Smith (eds.), *Valuing Natural Assets: The Economics of Natural Resource Damage Assessment* (Washington, DC: Resources for the Future).

Lesser, Jonathan and Richard O. Zerbe (1995), "What Economics Can Contribute to the Sustainability Debate," *Contemporary Economic Problems* 13(3), pp. 88–100.

Levy, Daniel S. and David Friedman (1994), "The Revenge of the Redwoods? Reconsidering Property Rights and the Economic Allocation of Natural Resources," *The University of Chicago Law Review* 61(2), pp. 493–525.

Lewin, Shira B. (1996), "Economics and Psychology: Lessons for Our Own Day from the Early Twentieth Century," *Journal of Economic Literature* 34, pp. 1293–1323.

Loomis, John (1995), *Measuring the Economic Benefits of Removing Dams and Restoring the Elwha River: Results of a Contingent Valuation Survey.* Working Paper, Department of Agricultural and Resource Economics, Colorado State University, Fort Collins, CO.

Machina, Mark (1987), "Choice under Uncertainty: Problems Solved and Unsolved," *Journal of Economic Perspectives* 1(1), pp. 121–154.

Medema, Steven and Richard Zerbe (1998), "Ronald Coase, the British Tradition and the Future of Economic Method," in Steven Medema (ed.), *Coasian Economics: Law and Economics and the New Institutional Economics* (Boston: Kluwer).

Minard, Richard A. Jr. (1996), "Comparative Risk and the States," *Resources for the Future* 122(Winter), pp. 6–10.

Page, Talbot (1992), "Environmental Existentialism," in Robert Costanza, Bryan G. Norton, and Benjamin D. Haskell (eds.), *Ecosystem Health: New Goals for Environmental Management* (Washington, DC: Island Press).

Pildes, Richard H. and Cass R. Sunstein (1995), "Reinventing the Regulatory State," *University of Chicago Law Review* 62(1), pp. 1–129.

Polinsky, A. Mitchell and Stephen Shavell (1979), "The Optimal Tradeoff between Probability and Magnitude of Fines," *American Economic Review* 69(5), pp. 880–891.

Polinsky, A. Mitchell (1980), "Private versus Public Enforcement of Fines," *Journal of Legal Studies* 9(1), pp. 105–127.

Polinsky, A. Mitchell (1983), *An Introduction to Law and Economics* (Boston: Little Brown).

Portney, Paul R. (1992), "Trouble in Happyville," *Journal of Policy Analysis and Management* 11(1), pp. 131–132.

Posner, Richard A. (1980), "The Ethical and Political Basis of the Efficiency Norm in Common Law Adjudication," *Hofstra Law Review* 8(3), pp. 487–508.

Posner, Richard A. (1983), *The Economics of Justice* (Cambridge, MA: Harvard University Press).

Posner, Richard A. (1984), "Wealth Maximization and Judicial Decision Making," *International Review of Law and Economics* 4(2), pp. 131–135.

Risk Assessment and Cost Benefit Act of 1995, H.R. 1022, 104th Cong., 1st sess., 28 February 1995.

Rizzo, Mario (1980), "The Mirage of Efficiency," *Hofstra Law Review* 8(3), pp. 641–658.

Sagoff, Mark (1988), *The Economy of the Earth* (Cambridge, England: Cambridge University Press).

Schoemaker, P. J. H. (1982), "The Expected Utility Model: Its Variants, Purposes, Evidence, and Limitations," *Journal of Economic Literature* 20(2), pp. 529–563.

Sen, Amartya (1982), "Rights and Agency," *Philosophy and Public Affairs* 11(1), pp. 3–39.

Shavell, Steven (1985), "Criminal Law and the Optimal Use of Nonmonetary Sanctions As a Deterrent," *Columbia Law Review* 85, pp. 1232–1262.

Smart, John J. C. and Bernard Williams (1973), *Utilitarianism—For and Against* (Cambridge, England: Cambridge University Press).

Stigler, George (1970), "The Optimal Enforcement of Law," *Journal of Political Economy* 78(3), pp. 526–536.

Sunstein, Cass R. (1994), "Incommensurability," *Michigan Law Review* 92(4), pp. 779–861.

Thaler, Richard H. (1981), *Quasi Rational Economics* (New York: Russell Sage Foundation).

Tolley, George (1982), "Benefit-Cost Analysis and the Common Sense of Environmental Policy," in Daniel Swartzmann, Robert L. Liroff, and Kevin Croke (eds.), *Cost-Benefit Analysis and Environmental Regulations: Politics, Ethics, and Methods* (Washington, DC: The Conservation Foundation).

Trumbull, William N. (1990), "Who Has Standing in Cost-Benefit Analysis?" *Journal of Policy Analysis and Management* 9(2), pp. 201–218.

Tversky, Amos and Daniel Kahneman (1981), "The Framing of Decisions and the Psychology of Choice," *Science* 211, pp. 453–458.

U. S. Department of the Interior (1995), *Elwha River Ecosystem Restoration: Final Environmental Impact Statement* (National Park Service, Denver Service Center).

Varian, Hal (1996), *Intermediate Microeconomics*, 4th ed. (New York: W. W. Norton).

Von Neumann, John and Oscar Morgenstern (1944), *Theory of Games and Economic Behavior* (Princeton, NJ: Princeton University Press).

Weisbrod, Burton (1981), "Benefit Cost Analysis of a Controlled Experiment: Treating the Mentally Ill," *Journal of Human Resources* 16(4), pp. 494–500.

Whittington, Dale and Duncan MacRae Jr. (1986), "The Issue of Standing in Cost-Benefit Analysis," *Journal of Policy Analysis and Management* 5(4), pp. 665–682.

Whittington, Dale and Duncan MacRae Jr. (1990), "Comment: Judgments about Who Has Standing in Cost-Benefit Analysis," *Journal of Policy Analysis and Management* 9(4), pp. 536–547.

Willig, Robert (1976), "Consumer Surplus without Apology," *American Economic Review* 66(4), pp. 589–597.

Zerbe, Richard O. Jr. (1991), "Comment: Does Benefit-Cost Analysis Stand Alone? Rights and Standing," *Journal of Policy Analysis and Management* 10(1), pp. 96–105.

Zerbe, Richard O. and Dwight Dively (1994), *Benefit Cost Analysis in Theory and Practice* (New York: Harper Collins).

Zerbe, Richard O. Jr. (1997), "The Foundations of Kaldor-Hicks Efficiency: On The Kindness of Strangers," Working Paper, Graduate School of Public Affairs, University of Washington, Seattle, WA.

Zerbe, Richard O. Jr (1998), "An Integration of Equity and Efficiency," *Washington Law Review* 73.

[17]

Available online at www.sciencedirect.com

ECOLOGICAL ECONOMICS

Ecological Economics 58 (2006) 449–461

www.elsevier.com/locate/ecolecon

Analysis

An aggregate measure for benefit–cost analysis

Richard O. Zerbe Jr.[a,1], Yoram Bauman [b,*], Aaron Finkle [c]

[a] *School of Public Affairs, University of Washington, Box 353055, Seattle, WA 98195, United States*
[b] *Department of Economics, Whitman College, 345 Boyer Ave., Walla Walla, WA 99362, United States*
[c] *Department of Economics, Willamette University, 900 State Street, Salem, OR 97301, United States*

Received 12 January 2004; received in revised form 14 June 2005; accepted 5 July 2005
Available online 12 September 2005

Abstract

The Kaldor–Hicks (KH) criterion has long been the standard for benefit–cost analysis, but it has also been widely criticized for ignoring equity and, arguably, moral sentiments in general. We suggest replacing KH with an aggregate measure called KHM, where the M stands for moral sentiments. KHM simply adds to the traditional KH criterion the requirement that any good for which there is a willingness to pay or accept count as an economic good. This suggested expansion of KH, however, must confront objections to counting moral sentiments in general and non-paternalistic altruism in particular. We show that these concerns are unwarranted and suggest that the KHM criterion is superior to KH because it provides better information.
© 2005 Elsevier B.V. All rights reserved.

Keywords: Benefit–cost; Moral sentiments; Potential compensation test

1. Background

The Kaldor–Hicks (KH) criterion arose out of discussions among prominent British economists during the late 1930s.[2] Before that time, it was generally

---

* Corresponding author. Tel.: +1 206 351 5719; fax: +1 509 527 5026.

E-mail addresses: zerbe@u.washington.edu (R.O. Zerbe), yoram@smallparty.org (Y. Bauman), afinkle@u.washington.edu (A. Finkle).

[1] Tel.: +1 206 616 5470; fax: +1 206 685 9044.

[2] These economists were Robbins, Hicks, Kaldor, and Harrod, all writing in the *Economic Journal*.

0921-8009/$ - see front matter © 2005 Elsevier B.V. All rights reserved.
doi:10.1016/j.ecolecon.2005.07.015

assumed that each individual had an "equal capacity for enjoyment" and that gains and losses among different individuals could be directly compared (Mishan, 1981, pp. 120–121; Hammond, 1985, p. 406). Robbins (1932, 1938) disturbed this view by arguing that interpersonal comparisons of utility were unscientific. Kaldor (1939, pp. 549–550) acknowledged Robbins' (1938, p. 640) point about the inability to make interpersonal utility comparisons on any scientific basis, but suggested it could be made irrelevant. He suggested that when a policy led to an increase in aggregate real income,

...the economist's case for the policy is quite unaffected by the question of the comparability of indivi-

450

R.O. Zerbe Jr. et al. / Ecological Economics 58 (2006) 449–461

dual satisfaction, since in all such cases it is possible to make everybody better off than before, or at any rate to make some people better off without making anybody worse off.

Kaldor went on to note (1939, p. 550) that whether such compensation should take place "is a political question on which the economist, qua economist, could hardly pronounce an opinion."[3] Hicks (1939) accepted this approach, which came to be called KH.

Thus, it came to be thought that including considerations of income distribution or of compensation would involve interpersonal utility comparisons, and that such comparisons should be avoided by excluding consideration of actual compensation or of income distribution.[4] It was thought that this exclusion would lead to a measure of efficiency that was more scientific.[5]

KH separates efficiency and equity and proposes to leave the latter to the politicians. Undoubtedly, there is some merit in separate accounting, but it does not follow that economists should refrain from providing information on equity and on moral sentiments. Increasingly, economists have not refrained (e.g., Andreoni, 1995; Palfrey and Prisbey, 1997; Office of Management and Budget, 2003).

The modern version of KH may be reasonably characterized by the following assumptions: (1) every dollar is treated the same regardless of who receives it, i.e., equal marginal utility of income;[6]

(2) a project is efficient if it passes the Potential Compensation Test (PCT), i.e., if the winners could hypothetically compensate the losers (Kaldor, 1939, pp. 549–550);[7] (3) gains are measured by willingness to pay (WTP) and losses by willingness to accept (WTA); and (4) equity effects are to be disregarded. More controversial is whether or not moral sentiments, under which equity effects are a sub-category, are to be excluded in a KH test. To ignore moral sentiments imposes a substantial cost-it amounts, for example, to a dismissal of existence values in those instances in which they arise from moral sentiments. This topic is of interest because analyses that include moral sentiments can differ materially from those that do not (Portney, 1994).

2. An aggregate measure

Insofar as KH excludes moral sentiments, it excludes goods that can in fact be valued in the same manner that KH values other goods. That is, KH excludes some goods for which there is a WTP.[8] A logical extension or clarification of KH requires including all goods for which there is a WTP. Such an extension of KH we call an "aggregate measure" or

---

[3] It was thought that politicians or non-economists should make judgments and decisions about income distribution effects.

[4] As will be seen, economists' commendable but impossible efforts to avoid interpersonal utility comparisons created additional problems.

[5] Many economists have ignored the normative nature of any efficiency criterion. See, for example, the criticisms of economic efficiency and economists' use of it in the Hofstra Law Review (1980, 1981) volumes 8 and 9 and in volume 8 of the Journal of Legal Studies (1979).

[6] There are a number of recommendations that benefit–cost analysis incorporate distributional weights, e.g., Feldstein (1974), who proposes that the weights be inversely proportional to income. Thus, benefit–cost analysis has long entertained practices that imply a declining marginal utility of income.

[7] Subsequently, Tibor de Scitovsky (1941) (who later used the name Scitovsky) suggested an additional potential compensation test, according to which a project is acceptable when the potential losers could not bribe the potential winners to not undertake the project (Zerbe and Dively, 1994, p. 97). The KH criterion takes the status quo as the starting point and the Scitovsky version takes the new situation as the starting point. When KH is applied to both end states it satisfies both versions of the PCT, the Kaldor version and the Scitovsky version. Thus, we shall use the term KH to refer to both versions. It would be more accurate to call the sum of the equivalent variations the Scitovsky criterion, but this is awkward as he suggested that both versions of the PCT need to be satisfied and this double criterion is known as the Scitovsky criterion. For additional information, see Roger McCain's statement on this in http://www.ibiblio.org/pub/academic/economics/sci.econ.research/Monthly.compilations/ser.94.aug.1–114.

[8] We do not deal here with the question of when WTP is a better or worse measure than willingness to accept (WTA). That is, we do not assume that moral sentiments should be measured by WTP rather than WTA. This issue is discussed elsewhere (Zerbe, 2001).

R.O. Zerbe Jr. et al. / Ecological Economics 58 (2006) 449–461 451

KHM.[9] KHM recognizes that there will be a WTP for some of the values reflected in moral sentiments; these WTP measures of moral sentiments receive a weight of one across different individuals, just as is done for other goods under KH. Thus, including compensation or changes in income distribution as economic goods requires no interpersonal utility comparisons beyond the pre-existing requirement to treat all equally (Zerbe, 1998).

We raise the question of whether or not, in principle, KHM is better suited for welfare analysis than KH. We do not consider measurement issues.[10] We suggest that the arguments advanced against including moral sentiments are incorrect or unpersuasive and that there are advantages to KHM over KH.

3. A definition of moral sentiments

By "moral sentiments," we mean those involving concern for other beings or entities. The focus of debate has been moral sentiments that involve concern for humans. These moral sentiments also include immoral sentiments, as might arise when one wishes harm to others. One may care about others as a result of kinship, empathy, envy or hatred, or as a matter of justice. Charity is an expression of moral sentiment. One may care about the utility function of others; this

is called non-paternalistic altruism. One may care about others from one's own perspective, as when a parent requires a child to eat spinach when the child would rather not; this is called paternalistic altruism. One may have an existence value for goods unrelated to their use or for goods based on their use or appreciation by others that can reflect paternalistic altruism, non-paternalistic altruism, or both. According to Johansson (1992), it would not be uncommon for non-use values such as bequest values and benevolence toward friends and relatives to account for 50–75% of the total WTP for an environmental project. In economic terms, we will say that moral sentiments exist when there is a WTP for them.

4. Arguments against the inclusion of moral sentiments in benefit–cost analysis

There are three principal arguments against including moral sentiments in benefit–cost analysis. The first is that doing so produces inconsistencies with the Potential Compensation Test (PCT) that lies at the heart of KH-based benefit–cost analysis (Winter, 1969; Milgrom, 1993). The second is that such inclusion can result in double counting. The third, which we address first, arises from an invariance claim.

4.1. Invariance

The invariance claim is that non-paternalistic altruism is unimportant because such sentiments simply reinforce the conclusions that would be reached otherwise. In particular, as McConnell (1997, p. 27) notes, a project that "fails the original test with beneficiaries...will also fail when it incorporates the willingness to pay of those who are altruistic towards the direct beneficiaries". The idea is that consideration of altruism only adds fuel to the fire if the project fails to generate net benefits for the supposed beneficiaries. Similarly, a project that passes the original benefit–cost test will pass a fortiori when it includes positive altruistic sentiments. (It is recognized that this invariance claim does not hold when it includes negative altruism.) This invariance claim is also derived by Bergstrom (1982), Johansson (1992, 1993), Jones-Lee (1992), Madariaga and McConnell (1987), McConnell (1997), Milgrom (1993), and Quiggin (1997).

---

[9] Zerbe (2001) has called for a more detailed and refined version of KHM under the rubric KHZ. A project will pass the KHZ criterion when (1) the sum of the WTPs for a change exceeds the sum of the absolute value of the WTAs; (2) all values count, or, more precisely and as with KHM, all goods and sentiments for which there is a WTP are regarded as economic goods; (3) gains and losses are measured by WTP and WTA, respectively, and from a psychological reference point that is determined largely by legal rights; and (4) transaction costs of operating within a set of rules (but not the costs of changing rules) are included in determining efficiency. (This latter assumption is necessary to define inefficiency; otherwise, all arrangements are tautologically efficient.) The KHZ measure makes explicit the necessary connection between an efficiency criterion and the legal system. KHZ also views benefit–cost analysis as supplying information relevant to the decision, not as supplying the decision itself. The rationale for these assumptions and their consequences for legal analysis may be found in Zerbe (2001).

[10] Consideration of measurement issues would unduly expand the length of this paper and divert attention from the issues of principle we discuss.

The claim is correct for homogenous groups, but even in this case it fails as a guide to inclusion of moral sentiments. The sign of a project's net benefits may be invariant to inclusion of moral sentiments, but the magnitude of net benefits is not, and the magnitude of net benefits can have policy relevance. This point is not always recognized. For example, McConnell (1997, p. 25) notes, "[I]n the standard case, when the benefits of resource preservation to users exceed the costs, consideration of non-use benefits is superfluous as long as they are not negative." Yet inclusion of altruism may affect the ranking of projects being compared and thus affect which project is chosen. This is true even when the net present value without moral sentiments is already negative—meaning that including moral sentiments would further reduce the net present value—because one may be constrained to make recommendations among projects that all have negative net present values. Including moral sentiments can therefore contribute useful information.

Moreover, the inclusion of non-paternalistic altruism can change the sign of net benefits in cases involving heterogeneous groups. Suppose, for example, that a project benefits a group of users U but fails a benefit–cost test because of negative impacts on a group of taxpayers T. Altruistic feelings for group U (by a group of altruists A, or even by group T) can change the sign of net benefits. Their inclusion will reverse the sign of the project's net benefits as long as the altruistic sentiments are sufficiently large. Similarly, a project that benefits T but imposes net costs on U may pass a standard benefit–cost test but fail a test that includes group A's altruistic feelings for U.[11] In general, inclusion of moral sentiments can reverse the sign of net benefits when the net benefits to those users who are the object of altruism are different in sign from the total of net benefits.

4.2. Double counting

The double counting criticism centers on the argument that altruists could simply make cash transfers to

the targets of their altruism instead of supporting projects that benefit those individuals. The double counting criticism therefore goes further than simple invariance to cover the case when ordinary net benefits to users are positive: Diamond and Hausman (1993, 1994) and McConnell (1997, p. 23) claim that including existence value when it arises as non-paternalistic altruism is double counting.[12] McConnell considers projects in which the benefits to users are less than the costs of the project and states that "the project will never pay, no matter what the sharing arrangement".

Consider, for simplicity, that users bear none of the project's cost. McConnell suggests that even when benefits to users, B_U, are positive, it is unnecessary to count non-paternalistic moral sentiments and that doing so leads to double counting. He compares the project to a direct transfer of cash from the general public (here, the altruists) to users. Since direct transfer to users of some amount less than the cost of the project, C, is cheaper than the project while creating equivalent moral sentiments, counting benefits representing moral sentiments will distort the choice. More precisely, McConnell notes (p. 29) that instead of undertaking the project it would always be better to give the beneficiaries a cash payment equal to $B_U + \Delta$ for any positive transfer Δ such that $B_U + \Delta < C$.

It is possible, however, to expand this result to the more realistic case in which there is a cost to making cash payments. When this is done, it becomes necessary to include moral sentiments. McConnell assumes that cash payments can be made without cost, so that transaction costs and deadweight tax costs are zero. Instead, let ϕ be the loss per dollar of attempted transfer, meaning that $(1 - \phi)$ reaches the user and ϕ is lost in administrative and other costs associated with the transfer. The amount that will have to be paid in cash in order for users to receive the same benefits as the project is $B_U/(1 - \phi)$. This cash payment will be superior to the project only if $B_U/(1 - \phi) < C$. Whether or not direct payment to users is more efficient than the project depends on the cost of transferring money

---

[11] Another possibility is that negative altruism could shift a benefit–cost test from negative to positive if the project fails to generate net benefits for the supposed beneficiaries.

[12] The Diamond and Hausman claim is a bit more general, but McConnell shows that the claim is properly limited to only non-paternalistic altruism.

directly and the amount by which the cost of the project exceeds the benefits to its users. The larger the costs of transferring money, or the smaller the divergence between the cost of the project and its benefits to users, the more likely it is that the project will be superior to a direct cash transfer. In terms of McConnell's argument, providing users with $B_U + \Delta$ in cash requires altruists to pay $(B_U + \Delta)/(1 - \phi)$, and this is necessarily superior to a project with cost C only if $(B_U + \Delta)/(1 - \phi) < C$. The fact that $B_U < C$ does not ensure that this requirement is met unless $\phi = 0$. For example, if $\phi = 0.5$, then the project's benefit to users would need to be less than 50% of the cost of the project for direct payment to be superior. If benefits to users were 90% of costs, the project would be superior for any transfer cost greater than 10% ($\phi = 0.1$).

Furthermore, it will never be the case that counting moral sentiments results in double counting. This is because the WTP for the project depends on the availability of substitutes, a point that has not been recognized by previous commentators. One such substitute is for altruists to provide a direct transfer to users. In order to provide benefits of B_U to users, the altruists need to allocate $B_U/(1 - \phi)$, so the net social cost of the direct transfer is

$$(B_U)(\phi)/(1 - \phi). \tag{1}$$

When ϕ is zero, the price of the direct transfer substitute is zero. As one will not pay more for a good than its cost elsewhere, the WTP for the project will be zero. In this case there is no double counting as the benefits from moral sentiments are zero. For any $\phi > 0$, there will be a benefit from the moral sentiments. As ϕ approaches 1, the price of the direct transfer project in which income is transferred from altruists to users approaches infinity.

There will be, then, an existence value from the project's benefits to users when and only when there are no perfect substitutes available at a lower price. A positive existence value does not violate the invariance result and is entirely consistent with McConnell's model once transaction costs are introduced. To include it in benefit–cost evaluations will not result in double counting; it is a real value that should be included in the benefit–cost calculus.

We conclude that it is necessary to count moral sentiments to know if benefits exceed costs as well as to know the magnitude of net benefits.[13] The technical arguments against its inclusion are unpersuasive.

5. The potential compensation problem with including moral sentiments

Perhaps the strongest argument that economists have against including non-paternalistic moral sentiments is concern that inclusion can lead to acceptance of projects that do not pass the Potential Compensation Test (Milgrom, 1993). The PCT requires that winners from a project are hypothetically able to compensate the losers while retaining some of their gains. No actual compensation is required.

Milgrom (1993) argues that including non-paternalistic moral sentiments in benefit–cost analysis leads to potential violations of the PCT. He considers a project that costs $160 and affects two people. Individual U, the user, gains $100 from the project and bears none of its costs. Individual A, the altruist, has a gross gain of $50 + 0.5$ times U's net surplus, i.e., a gross gain of $100; A also bears the entire $160 cost of the project, for a net loss of $60. The project passes a benefit–cost test if altruism is included but fails if altruism is excluded. (The net benefits are $200 - $160 = $40 and $150 - $160 = -$10, respectively). Less evident is that the project fails the PCT: each dollar that U gives A in compensation provides a net benefit to A of only $0.50, so even transferring U's entire $100 gain cannot overcome A's initial net loss of $60. Milgrom concludes that altruism and other moral sentiments should not be included in benefit–cost analysis.

We argue below that this is the wrong conclusion, but first, we examine the extent to which moral sentiments may lead to inconsistencies with the PCT. Imagine that there is a project with benefits and

---

[13] The issue of double counting is treated elegantly at the level of a social welfare function by Johansson (1992). He shows that altruistic values will already be included in questionnaires to determine the optimum provision of a public good. The difficulty in ignoring altruism means that in a practical sense it is better to include it than to ignore it.

costs distributed between users U and altruists A. Let α be the "warm glow" experienced by the altruists from each \$1 increase in U's net benefits. Aside from altruism, direct net benefits from the project are NB_A and NB_U for A and U, respectively. We assume that the sum of these is negative. A also gets indirect altruistic benefits based on the net benefits to U. These are measured by A's WTP, which is \$$\alpha$ per \$1 net benefit to U. Therefore, the total net benefits including altruism are

$$NB_U + NB_A + \alpha(NB_U). \tag{2}$$

The net benefits (including altruism) to A are

$$NB_A + \alpha(NB_U), \tag{3}$$

which we assume to be negative. To pass the PCT, U must be able to compensate A with some transfer T; the minimum acceptable transfer satisfies

$$NB_A + T + \alpha(NB_U - T) = 0. \tag{4}$$

Solving for T shows that applying this hypothetical transfer to A will result in total net benefits of

$$(NB_U - T) = (NB_A + NB_U)/(1 - \alpha), \tag{5}$$

which will be negative for $0 < \alpha < 1$ since the numerator is assumed to be negative. Thus, it is said that to pass a PCT, benefits should exceed costs without considering moral sentiments.

However, ordinary net benefits need not be positive to pass the PCT when $\alpha > 1$; we can compensate A by having him give money to U. Suppose, for example, that A transfers \$200 to U at a cost of \$210. This does not pass the ordinary benefit–cost test. But if A gains two dollars in satisfaction for every dollar transferred to U, then the gains to A are \$400 − \$210 or \$190; in this case, the project passes a benefit–cost test counting moral sentiments and also the PCT since there are no losers.

It is useful to distinguish between α_i, which represents the altruism of an individual, and α, which is this value summed over all altruists. Since the number of altruists can be very large, α can also be very large, reflecting the fact that moral satisfaction has qualities

similar to public goods.[14] Consider, for example, a situation in which 200 altruists are charged \$1 each to transfer \$200 to users. If the value of α_i is \$0.10 (i.e., each altruist gets a gross benefit of \$0.10 for each dollar transferred), then α will be 20 and the altruistic gain will be \$4000. Values of $\alpha < 1$ are unlikely except in cases where moral sentiments are unimportant, in the sense of being either restricted to a few people, or weak, or both.

More generally, consider the conditions under which a transfer project counting moral sentiments would pass KHM but fail the PCT. If C is the amount of the attempted transfer and ϕ is the cost or waste per dollar of attempted transfer, the gains to the users will be $(C - \phi C)$ and the gains to the altruists will be $\alpha(C - \phi C) - C$. A necessary condition for failing the PCT is that the gains of the altruists be negative, which will be true only if $\alpha < 1/(1 - \phi)$; this in turn implies that $\alpha < 1$ is a necessary condition for failing the PCT. Next, note that the project will pass KHM as long as total net gains, $C(1 - \phi)(1 + \alpha) - C$, are positive, which will be true as long as $\alpha > \phi/(1 - \phi)$. If $\alpha < 1$, then this implies $\phi < 0.5$ (waste less than 50%), so both $\alpha < 1$ and $\phi < 0.5$ are necessary conditions for

---

[14] We have treated α as a constant, following Milgrom (1993). It will not be. Rather, as with any good, the marginal value of moral satisfaction will fall as more is purchased, so that α will be a declining function of the amount transferred from altruists to users. The social optimum requires that transfers take place as long as α is greater than the transfer cost per dollar. That is, welfare is maximized if transfers from altruists to users continue until $\alpha = \phi/(1 - \phi)$, where ϕ is the waste per dollar of attempted transfer. Pure transfer projects, which have ordinary net benefits of zero, will pass the PCT as long as $\bar{\alpha}$, the average value of α, is greater than the average cost of the transfer, even if at the margin α is less than the cost per dollar transfer. The value of $\bar{\alpha}$ may be found by integrating the demand for moral satisfaction from $T = 0$ to the optimal T, T^*, and then dividing the result by the amount transferred, T^*. In this case, both users and altruists gain from the transfer. For projects in which moral sentiments are significant, it will likely be the case that $\bar{\alpha} > \phi/(1 - \phi)$. Thus, transfer projects will pass the PCT. As with the social optimum for any public good, the quantity of transfers is determined where the marginal cost of transfers, $\phi/(1 - \phi)$, intersects the aggregate demand curve. Note that this is a social welfare maximization result, not the result from individual choice by altruists. The price paid and the satisfaction gained will be different for each individual. An individual altruist would transfer an additional dollar to users only as long as that altruist's warm glow, α_i, was greater than $1/(1 - \phi)$.

a project to be accepted under KHM and fail the PCT. This is a narrow range, especially because α will be greater than 1 as long as there are a number of altruists with modest altruistic sentiments. Milgrom (1993) assumes that $\phi = 0$ and that there is only one altruist, with $\alpha_i = \alpha = 0.5$. If instead there are 15 altruists, each with $\alpha_i = 0.1$, then we will have $\alpha = 1.5$ and it will be impossible to replicate Milgrom's example.[15] Thus, projects that include moral sentiments will pass a KHM and fail the PCT only in trivial cases.

6. The PCT: problems with excluding moral sentiments

The previous section showed that including moral sentiments in benefit–cost analysis can lead to inconsistencies with the PCT. This section shows that excluding moral sentiments can also lead to inconsistencies with the PCT. The combination of these results raises fundamental questions about the usefulness of the PCT.

Returning to Milgrom's example of a $160 project that provides users U with $100 in benefits, suppose that altruists bear the entire cost of the project but also have gross benefits of $40 + 1.5$ times U's net surplus. This project would pass a PCT because there is no need for compensation: U has net benefits of $100 and A has net benefits of $40 + (1.5)(\$100) - \$160 = \$30$. Excluding altruism, however, the project still does not pass KH. Thus, KH can reject a project that passes the PCT.

More strikingly, in this example, KH rejects the project even though both A and U gain. Following Milgrom's advice, therefore, leads us afoul of what may be the most fundamental principle of benefit–cost analysis: never pass up an opportunity to make a Pareto improvement.

In addition, we note that failure to pass the PCT can apply also to KH. For over 20 years, it has been known that a positive sum of compensating variations, the standard benefit–cost test, is a necessary but not a sufficient condition for the passage of a compensation test (Boadway and Bruce, 1984). Symmetrically, the sum of equivalent variations is a sufficient but not a necessary condition for passage of such a test. The CV test will lead to the approval of projects that fail the compensation test; the EV test will lead to the rejection of projects that pass the compensation test.

Finally, Baker (1980, p. 939) has pointed out a legally relevant failure of KH to pass a PCT. He notes that when rights are in dispute, the usual case in matters at law, the sum of the expectations of the parties will normally exceed the value of the right so that no potential compensation is possible. For example, suppose a piece of property is worth $120 to Ronald and $100 to Richard. The ownership of this property is in dispute between Richard and Ronald but each believes with 80% probability that he owns the property. The total value of expectations is $176 and the winner could not in principle compensate the loser. If the property is awarded to Ronald, he has a gain of $24, which is not sufficient to compensate Richard, who suffers a loss of $80. As long as the sum of expected values is greater than the actual value, the project cannot pass the PCT. Baker maintains that the inability to determine the efficient allocation is an indictment of benefit–cost analysis generally and of KH in particular.[16]

Altogether, these arguments call into question the value of the PCT. The argument for dropping the PCT is that it does no work for us that is not already done by the KHM criterion that net benefits should be positive. The fact that a project passes the PCT does not mean that losers can actually be compensated. Actual compensation is not costless, so actual compensation can take place only if the net gains are sufficient to cover both the compensation of losers and the cost of making the compensation. Thus, the PCT cannot claim the virtue of providing for actual

---

[15] We have not addressed the issue of the allocation of the costs among users and altruists. As long as $\alpha > 0$ then costs should be shifted to altruists. This is because the cost to them of an additional dollar is less than a dollar as long as $\alpha > 0$. As more of the costs are borne by altruists α will fall and further transfers would be inefficient once $\alpha = 0$. The value of α relevant for the determination of benefits to altruists is its average value. As long as this average value is greater than 1, the PCT is passed.

[16] Baker's criticism doe not, however, apply to KHM. What is important in KHM is whether net benefits are positive, not whether a potential compensation test is satisfied.

compensation when desired. Moreover, this sort of information about compensation is valuable only if we value moral sentiments.

The moral basis of KH, rather, lies in the powerful argument that its use will increase wealth and will likely result in all, or at least most, groups gaining over time from its application so that losers in one period become winners in the next. This justification, however, applies, a fortiori, to KHM. Indeed, one common argument against KH is that it is dependent on income, so that low-income individuals are more likely to lose and, having lost, become ever more likely to lose in subsequent rounds (Richardson, 2000). This is less likely under KHM as long as there are moral sentiments against generating income losses for the poor.

7. Why an aggregate measure is superior to KH

We have shown that the use of KHM can, at least in principle, change both the sign and the magnitude of net benefits calculated under KH. But is KHM superior to KH? As long as one accepts the moral premise of benefit–cost analysis—that it is the WTP that counts—the answer is "yes" for a simple reason: KHM gives a more complete accounting of WTP.

Another way of answering the question is to perform a benefit–cost analysis of the choice between KHM and KH.[17] In other words, we ask if a move from a world that uses KH to one that uses KHM would itself be supported by either KH or KHM. Users will gain from such a move, as KHM will justify altruists bearing more of the costs of projects. Altruists may lose if they bear more of the costs, but by definition, they will lose less than users gain. Thus, such a move to the use of KHM is justified by KHM itself.

The most compelling argument for KHM over KH is simply that KHM reveals more information about actual preferences and is thus more informative. That is, the basic argument is that KHM provides useful information not provided by KH. Consider the nuclear waste example below.

---

[17] For reasons beyond the scope of this paper, Zerbe (2001) finds that KHZ is superior to both KH and KHM.

8. An extended example: the discount rate problem and moral harm

In benefit–cost analysis, future benefits and costs are discounted using an interest rate termed the discount rate. Discounting brings up a number of issues, particularly when the discounting extends beyond the lives of the decision makers (Ahearne, 2000). Here we are concerned with only one—the widespread criticism of the use of discounting in benefit–cost analysis on the grounds that it is unethical to discount future generations' benefits and costs (e.g., Parfit, 1992, 1994; Schultze et al., 1981). Critics argue that the utility of future generations should be on par with the utility of the present generation (Schultze et al., 1981; Pearce et al., 1989). For example, Parfit (1992, p. 86) contends that "the moral importance of future events does not decline at n% per year." Similarly, Brown (1990) notes that "discounting imperils the future by undervaluing it."[18] This sort of criticism has been noted with favor by economists (e.g., Schultze et al., 1981; Pearce et al., 1989), lawyers (Plater et al., 1998, pp. 107–109), and philosophers (Parfit, 1992, 1994). The following is an example of the sort of problem that concerns these critics:

A nuclear project is being considered that produces benefits of about $100 billion at a cost of about $60 billion but, in addition, produces a toxic time bomb that will cause enormous environmental costs sometime in the far future.[19] Suppose that waste-disposal technology will contain this waste for 500 years, after which it will escape its sarcophagus and generate environmental damage of $263 trillion in constant current-year dollars. The present value of these damages discounted at a 3% real social rate of time preference (SRTP) is about $100 million. This amount is not insignificant, but it is far less than the damage that will occur in 500 years and far too small to affect

---

[18] Shrader–Frechette has argued that both the decision and the process by which it is made require informed consent. This is not possible when decisions affect future generations. See Ahearne (2000).

[19] Cases in which this sort of issue have arisen include Baltimore Gas & Electric v. Natural Resources Defense Council, Inc. 462 U.S. 87, (1983); and Pacific Gas and Electric Co et al. v. State Energy Resources Conservation and Development Commission, 461 U.S. 190, (1991). See also 123 U.S. 45 (1999).

the results of the benefit–cost analysis. Discounting these damages then results in the project going forward as the benefits are determined to exceed the costs by almost $40 billion.

It is said that this project would be unfair to future generations and therefore that the use of discounting in benefit–cost analysis is immoral. A commonly proposed solution to the problem of unethical harm to future generations is to use low, or even negative, discount rates (e.g., Schultze et al., 1981) or not to use discount rates at all (Parfit, 1994). This sort of argument is a moral plea about what our sentiments should be towards future generations, but not an effective statement about what or whether discount rates should be used or even about the relevant actual moral sentiments. The proposed solution of using no or low discount rates is ad hoc and, if generally applied, will lead to other ethical problems—for example, the adoption of projects that give less benefit to both present and future generations.[20]

Under KHM, we can give standing to moral sentiments of the present generation about future generations. This provides a solution to the ethical dilemma of the discount rate problem by acknowledging the validity of ethical concerns while also acknowledging the values that commend use of a discount rate. In Table 1 below, a standard KH benefit–cost approach is compared to KHM under three different options.[21] In one option, the current generation allocates enough funds to fully compensate the future generation. (We assume that the costs of such an allocation, including administrative costs, total $10 billion in present value terms.) In a second option, the current generation engages in mitigation efforts (such as creating a more secure holding container or shipping the waste into space) that eliminate the harm to future generations at a cost to current generations of $7.5 billion. The third option involves neither compensation nor mitigation.

The WTP, by the current generation to avoid the moral harm the project would cause to future generations, is $50 billion. In KH, moral harm is ignored so this value is not included. Going ahead with the project and providing neither compensation nor mitigation therefore gives the highest net present value (NPV) under KH. Under KHM, however, the NPV for this option is negative: consideration of moral harm reduces the NPV from $39.9 billion under KH to −$10.1 billion under KHM. The KHM approach shows that the preferred alternative involves either compensation or mitigation, whichever is cheaper. If neither mitigation nor compensation is feasible, the project is rejected by KHM.

One might object and say that moral harm cannot exceed the $100 million present value of the future loss. If the current generation can compensate future generations for $100 million, then would not this represent the maximum willingness to pay? The answer is no, for two reasons. First, the costs of compensating are clearly not $100 million. The administrative costs of providing compensation so far into the future must be included, and these may well be enormous, perhaps even infinite. The ability to provide the required long-lived institutions that would carry out compensation has been found to be improbable (Leschine and McCurdy, 2003).

Second, the parties deciding on compensation may not be the same parties that suffer moral harm. That is, for goods supplied by the public, there is a distinction between those who would purchase moral satisfaction and those who make the decision to purchase it. The transaction costs of actually persuading the decision makers to compensate may be prohibitive, especially since any attempt at agreement may suffer from a free rider problem.[22] If no purchase of moral satisfaction occurs, one must conclude that the transactions cost of purchase is at least as great as the moral harm to the present generations.

KHM provides a solution to the ethical dilemma of the discount rate problem by acknowledging ethical

---

[20] For example, consider two projects with initial costs of $100. Project A has benefits of $150 in the first period. Project B has benefits of $150 in 100 years. With negative or sufficiently low discount rates, project B is preferred. Project A, however, may result in greater wealth in 100 years so that it is superior for both current and future generations.

[21] A similar but not identical table is presented in Zerbe (in press).

---

[22] Critics of benefit–cost analysis suggest that the values individuals hold as private persons differ from those they hold for public decision-making (Anderson, 1993; Sagoff, 1988). This argument, however, works better as a caution to measure the actual values than as a criticism of the methodology of benefit–cost analysis (Zerbe, 2001).

Table 1
Comparison of KH and KHM[a] present values of gains and losses (in Billions)

Benefits and costs	[1]	[2]	[3]
	No compensation or mitigation occurs	Compensation occurs	Mitigation occurs
Ordinary benefits	100	100	100
Ordinary costs to current generation	−60	−60	−60
Harm to future generations	−0.1	−0.1	0
Cost of actual compensation	N/A	−10	N/A
Mitigation costs	N/A	N/A	−7.5
Moral harm to present generation	−50	0	0
KH NPV	39.9	29.9	32.5
KHM NPV	−10.1	29.9	32.5
Conclusion	Project is approved by KH but rejected by KHM because of moral harm	Compensation eliminates moral harm	Mitigation eliminates moral harm

[a] Costs are indicated by a minus sign. Note that not all items are relevant to KH and that mitigation and compensation are substitutes so that one or the other but not both are included in the KHM calculation.

concerns as valid and seeking an ethical solution while also acknowledging the values that commend use of a discount rate. Under KHM, the economic efficiency of the project depends on the sentiments of the present generation. For example, the present generation may find that compensation for environmental harm is unwarranted, given their belief that future generations will be wealthier than the present one, or the present generation may feel that future generations should be free of problems caused by the current generation. Evidence from Kunreuther and Easterling (1992, p. 255) and from Svenson and Karlsson (1989) suggests that, at least as regards nuclear waste disposal, individuals tend to place a high weight on future consequences.

It is not the amount of compensation actually required for those injured that is directly relevant here. Rather, it is the amount of compensation the current generation thinks is correct. This information could be determined, at least in principle, by a contingent valuation survey measuring the WTP or WTA of those who have moral sentiments about the project.

9. Acceptability of KH and KHM

No criticism of KH is more widespread than that it neglects distributional effects and moral sentiments (Zerbe, 1991). A representative view comes from the former Solicitor General of the United States, Charles Fried (1978, p. 93f), who sees the economic analysis of rights as using a concept of efficiency that is removed from distributional questions. He holds that economic analysis does not consider whether the distribution is fair or just, and concludes from this that efficiency does not provide "any privileged claim to our approbation" (1978, p. 94). The view that efficiency is unconcerned with distributional issues or with fairness is widespread in both law and economics (Zerbe, 1998, 2001). Adoption of an aggregate measure such as KHM would obviate this. Economists generally pay little attention to criticisms from outside the profession. Yet if acceptance of our criterion by those outside the profession is important, these criticisms are another reason to include moral sentiments in benefit–cost analysis.

10. Choices

Quiggin (1997, p. 152f) usefully suggests four possible responses to the difficulties he and others raise regarding the inclusion of moral sentiments: (1) discard moral sentiments and non-use values and maintain that benefit–cost analysis furnishes a complete evaluation, (2) adopt an aggregate WTP criteria, replacing the usual distinction between equity and efficiency, (3) consider moral sentiments but only outside of benefit–cost analysis, and (4) ignore concern for others in general, but accept other forms of non-use value. To this choice set we add the possibility that we could (5) adopt an aggregate criterion that maintains the distinction between equity and non-equity goods. This paper has so far suggested dropping choices (1) and (4) and adopting choices (2) or (5). As for choice (3), we assume that it refers to the sentiments of many economists that KH should be used to determine efficiency and that considerations of the income distribution should be relegated to macroeconomics, where they may be more appropriately handled. In this case, choices (2) and (5) are superior to choice (3) for the following reasons:

1. Some equity issues are not just matters of general income distribution and therefore cannot be handled well or at all by macroeconomic policy. For example, moral sentiments can address the effects of particular people being injured, altogether apart from sentiments about income distribution in general.
2. There is no conflict between KHM and choice (3) when it is cheaper to achieve a particular result through macroeconomic policy. In this case, the macro policy is a superior substitute for achieving moral satisfaction, so it eliminates consideration of the equity results of particular projects. As a result, equity effects can be ignored in many (but not all) cases. (If the project can achieve some desirable equity effect more cheaply than any other policy, this advantages would show up in the benefit–cost analysis as part of the gain in moral sentiments.)
3. In practice, the separation proposed in choice (3) means that economists will not address equity issues in the ordinary course of benefit–cost analyses. This means we will give advice that is incorrect by our own standards, e.g., that we will reject projects that pass the Pareto test such as the example we gave earlier.
4. Economics in general, and benefit–cost analysis in particular, has been widely and repeatedly criticized for this omission (Zerbe, 2001). The critical literature in philosophy and law is huge. There are reasons for economists to ignore much of this, but it is a mistake for the profession to not at least listen and make changes where warranted. The change we propose is arguably war-

ranted and would enhance the standing of benefit–cost analysis.[23]

5. There is now a substantial literature (e.g., Andreoni, 1995; Andreoni and Payne, 2003) pointing out the importance of considering the effects of moral sentiments on economic behavior.

No persuasive reason for ignoring moral sentiments in principle has been advanced. We have shown that there are examples in which their inclusion will improve the quality of analysis. We do not know of a single example in which their exclusion produces a superior analysis. The assumption by KH of an equal value for the marginal utility of money for all was made to allow British economists of the 1930s to make normative suggestions about the repeal of the Corn Laws. The decision to abandon the form of KH that ignores moral sentiments is equally justified today for a similar reason: we wish to make normative information available that is as useful as possible. As this paper shows, results in important cases will be better using KHM.

11. Conclusion

This paper has demonstrated that value is added by including moral sentiments in economic analysis and that the objections that have been raised to it are not persuasive. Of course, the ability to include such sentiments in practice is limited by the difficulty of measurement. But this is true of any values, particularly non-market ones, and not just moral ones.

In the long run, it seems likely that an aggregate measure that includes moral sentiments will be adopted either in addition to or as a substitute to KH. As a practical matter, it is neither possible nor efficient for benefit–cost analysis to consider all relevant goods and affected individuals, so any analysis will fail to meet the requirements of theoretical perfection, whether for KH or KHM. Nonetheless, in performing practical analysis it is always desirable to have in mind the best theoretical template so that practical decisions

---

[23] Even Richard Posner (1985) advocates including effects of moral sentiments on grounds that they are part of the market-based approach of benefit–cost analysis.

can be well-considered and not ad hoc. Our purpose has been to contribute to this template.

Acknowledgements

We thank members of the environmental seminar at the University of Washington.

References

Ahearne, John F., 2000. Intergenerational issues regarding nuclear power, nuclear waste, and nuclear weapons. Risk Analysis 20, 763–770.

Anderson, Elizabeth, 1993. Value in Ethics and Economics. Harvard University Press, Cambridge, MA.

Andreoni, James, 1995. Cooperation in public goods experiments: kindness or confusion? American Economic Review 85, 891–904.

Andreoni, James, Payne, Abigail, 2003. Do government grants to private charities crowd out giving or fundraising? American Economic Review 93, 792–812.

Baker, Edwin C., 1980. Starting points in the economic analysis of law. Hofstra Law Review 8, 939–972.

Bergstrom, T.C., 1982. When is a man's life worth more than his human capital? In: Jones-Lee, M.W. (Ed.), The Value of Life and Safety. North Holland, Amsterdam.

Boadway, Robin W., Bruce, Neil, 1984. Welfare Economics. Basil Blackwell, New York.

Brown, Peter, 1990. Greenhouse economics: think before you count. The Report from the Institute for Philosophy & Public Policy 10, 3–4.

Diamond, P.A., Hausman, J., 1993. On contingent valuation measurement of nonuse values. In: Hausman, Jerry A. (Ed.), Contingent Valuation: A Critical Assessment. North-Holland, Amsterdam.

Diamond, P.A., Hausmann, J., 1994. Contingent valuation: is some number better than no number? Journal of Economic Perspectives 8, 45–64.

Feldstein, Martin, 1974. Distributional preferences in public expenditure analysis. In: Hochman, Harold M., Peterson, George E. (Eds.), Redistribution Through Public Choices. Columbia University Press, New York, pp. 136–161.

Fried, Charles, 1978. Right and Wrong. Harvard University Press, Cambridge MA.

Hammond, Peter, 1985. Welfare economics. In: Fiewel, George (Ed.), Issues in Contemporary Microeconomics and Welfare. Macmillan, New York.

Hicks, J.R., 1939. The foundations of welfare economics. Economic Journal 49, 696–712.

Hofstra Law Review, 1980. Volume 8.

Hofstra Law Review, 1981. Volume 9.

Johansson, Per-Olov, 1992. Altruism in cost–benefit analysis. Environmental and Resource Economics 2, 605–613.

Johansson, Per-Olov, 1993. Cost–Benefit Analysis of Environmental Change. Cambridge University Press, Cambridge.

Jones-Lee, M.W., 1992. Paternalistic altruism and the value of statistical lives. Economic Journal 102, 80–90.

Journal of Legal Studies, 1979. Volume 8.

Kaldor, Nicholas, 1939. Welfare propositions in economics and interpersonal comparisons of utility. Economic Journal 49, 549–552.

Kunreuther, Howard, Easterling, Douglas, 1992. Are risk-benefit tradeoffs possible in siting hazardous facilities? American Economic Review 80, 252–256.

Leschine, Thomas, McCurdy, Howard, 2003. The stability of long run institutions. Working Paper. University of Washington.

Madariaga, B., McConnell, K.E., 1987. Exploring existence value. Water Resources Research 23, 936–942.

McConnell, K.E., 1997. Does altruism undermine existence value? Journal of Environmental Economics and Management 32, 22–37.

Milgrom, Paul, 1993. Is sympathy an economic value? Philosophy, economics, and the contingent valuation method. In: Hausman, Jerry A. (Ed.), Contingent valuation: A Critical Assessment. North-Holland, Amsterdam.

Mishan, Ezra J., 1981. Introduction to Normative Economics. Oxford University Press, New York.

Office of Management and Budget, 2003. Informing Regulatory Decisions: 2003 Report to Congress on the Costs and Benefits of Federal Regulations and Unfunded Mandates on State, Local, and Tribal Entities. U.S. Government, Washington, DC (online at whitehouse.gov/omb/inforeg/2003_cost-ben_final_rpt.pdf).

Palfrey, Thomas, Prisbey, Jeffrey, 1997. Anomalous behavior in public goods experiments: how much and why? American Economic Review 87, 829–846.

Parfit, Derek, 1992. An attack on the social discount rate. In: Mills, Claudia (Ed.), Values and Public Policy. Harcourt Brace Javanovich, Fort Worth.

Parfit, Derek, 1994. The social discount rate. In: Goodwin, R.E. (Ed.), Politics of the Environment. Edward Elgar, Aldershot, England.

Pearce, David, Markandya, A., Barbier, E., 1989. Blueprint for a Green Economy. Earthscan Publications, London.

Plater, Zgymunt, Robert, J.B., Abrams, H., Goldfarb, W., Graham, R.L., 1998. Environmental Law and Policy: Nature, Law, and Society. West Publishing Co., St. Paul.

Portney, P., 1994. The contingent valuation debate: why economists should care. Journal of Economic Perspectives 8, 3–17.

Posner, Richard A., 1985. Wealth maximization revisited. Notre Dame Journal of Law, Ethics & Public Policy 2, 85–106.

Quiggin, J., 1997. Altruism and benefit–cost analysis. Australian Economics Papers 36, 144–155.

Richardson, H., 2000. The stupidity of the cost–benefit standard. Journal of Legal Studies 29, 971–1004.

Robbins, Lionel, 1932. An Essay on the Nature and Significance of Economic Science. Macmillan, London.

Robbins, Lionel, 1938. Interpersonal comparisons of utility: a comment. Economic Journal 48, 635–641.

Sagoff, Mark, 1988. The Economy of the Earth. Cambridge University Press, New York.

Schultze, William D., Brookshire, D.S., Sandler, T., 1981. The social rate of discount for nuclear waste storage: economics of ethics. Natural Resources Journal 21, 811–832.

Scitovszky, Tibor de, 1941. A note on welfare propositions in economics. Review of Economics and Statistics 9, 77–88.

Svenson, Ola, Karlsson, G., 1989. Decision making, time horizons, and risk in the very long-term perspective. Risk Analysis 9, 385–398.

Winter, S.G., 1969. A simple remark on the second optimality theorem of welfare economics. Journal of Economic Theory 1, 99–103.

Zerbe Jr., Richard O., 1991. Comment: does benefit–cost analysis stand alone? rights and standing. Journal of Policy Analysis and Management 10, 96–105.

Zerbe Jr., Richard O., 1998. Is cost–benefit analysis legal? Three rules. Journal of Policy Analysis and Management 17, 419–456.

Zerbe Jr., Richard O., 2001. Efficiency in Law and Economics. Edward Elgar, Aldershot, England.

Zerbe Jr., Richard O., in press. Should moral sentiments be incorporated into benefit–cost analysis? An example of long-term discounting, Policy Sciences.

Zerbe, Richard O. Jr., Dively, Dwight, 1994. Benefit–Cost Analysis in Theory and Practice. Harper Collins, New York.

Part IV
Factors Affecting Willingness to Pay and Accept

[18]

Experimental Tests of the Endowment Effect and the Coase Theorem

Daniel Kahneman

University of California, Berkeley

Jack L. Knetsch

Simon Fraser University

Richard H. Thaler

Cornell University

Contrary to theoretical expectations, measures of willingness to accept greatly exceed measures of willingness to pay. This paper reports several experiments that demonstrate that this "endowment effect" persists even in market settings with opportunities to learn. Consumption objects (e.g., coffee mugs) are randomly given to half the subjects in an experiment. Markets for the mugs are then conducted. The Coase theorem predicts that about half the mugs will trade, but observed volume is always significantly less. When markets for "induced-value" tokens are conducted, the predicted volume is observed, suggesting that transactions costs cannot explain the undertrading for consumption goods.

I. Introduction

The standard assumptions of economic theory imply that when income effects are small, differences between an individual's maximum

Financial support was provided by Fisheries and Oceans Canada, the Ontario Ministry of the Environment, and the behavioral economics program of the Alfred P. Sloan Foundation. We wish to thank Vernon Smith for encouraging us to conduct these experiments and for providing extensive comments on earlier drafts. Of course, the usual disclaimer applies.

[*Journal of Political Economy*, 1990, vol. 98, no. 6]

willingness to pay (WTP) for a good and minimum compensation demanded for the same entitlement (willingness to accept [WTA]) should be negligible (Willig 1976). Thus indifference curves are drawn without reference to current endowments; any difference between equivalent and compensating variation assessments of welfare changes is in practice ignored;[1] and there is wide acceptance of the Coase theorem assertion that, subject to income effects, the allocation of resources will be independent of the assignment of property rights when costless trades are possible.

The assumption that entitlements do not affect value contrasts sharply with empirical observations of significantly higher selling than buying prices. For example, Thaler (1980) found that the minimal compensation demanded for accepting a .001 risk of sudden death was higher by one or two orders of magnitude than the amount people were willing to pay to eliminate an identical existing risk. Other examples of similar reported findings are summarized in table 1. The disparities observed in these examples are clearly too large to be explained plausibly by income effects.

Several factors probably contribute to the discrepancies between the evaluations of buyers and sellers that are documented in table 1. The perceived illegitimacy of the transaction may, for example, contribute to the extraordinarily high demand for personal compensation for agreeing to the loss of a public good (e.g., Rowe, d'Arge, and Brookshire 1980). Standard bargaining habits may also contribute to a discrepancy between the stated reservation prices of buyers and sellers. Sellers are often rewarded for overstating their true value, and buyers for understating theirs (Knez, Smith, and Williams 1985). By force of habit they may misrepresent their true valuations even when such misrepresentation confers no advantage, as in answering hypothetical questions or one-shot or single transactions. In such situations the buying-selling discrepancy is simply a strategic mistake, which experienced traders will learn to avoid (Coursey, Hovis, and Schulze 1987; Brookshire and Coursey 1987).

The hypothesis of interest here is that many discrepancies between WTA and WTP, far from being a mistake, reflect a genuine effect of reference positions on preferences. Thaler (1980) labeled the increased value of a good to an individual when the good becomes part of the individual's endowment the "endowment effect." This effect is a manifestation of "loss aversion," the generalization that losses are weighted substantially more than objectively commensurate gains in

---

[1] For example, the conventional prescription for assessing environmental and other losses is that, "practically speaking, it does not appear to make much difference which definition is accepted" (Freeman 1979, p. 3).

TABLE 1

SUMMARY OF PAST TESTS OF EVALUATION DISPARITY

STUDY AND ENTITLEMENT	MEANS			MEDIANS		
	WTP	WTA	Ratio	WTP	WTA	Ratio
Hypothetical surveys:						
Hammack and Brown (1974): marshes	$247	$1,044	4.2			
Sinclair (1978): fishing				35	100	2.9
Banford et al. (1979):						
Fishing pier	43	120	2.8	47	129	2.7
Postal service	22	93	4.2	22	106	4.8
Bishop and Heberlein (1979): goose hunting permits	21	101	4.8			
Rowe et al. (1980): visibility	1.33	3.49	2.6			
Brookshire et al. (1980): elk hunting*	54	143	2.6			
Heberlein and Bishop (1985): deer hunting	31	513	16.5			
Real exchange experiments:						
Knetsch and Sinden (1984): lottery tickets	1.28	5.18	4.0			
Heberlein and Bishop (1985): deer hunting	25	172	6.9			
Coursey et al. (1987): taste of sucrose octa-acetate†	3.45	4.71	1.4	1.33	3.49	2.6
Brookshire and Coursey (1987): park trees††	10.12	56.60	5.6	6.30	12.96	2.1

* Middle-level change of several used in study.
† Final values after multiple iterations.
‡ Average of two levels of tree plantings.

the evaluation of prospects and trades (Kahneman and Tversky 1979; Tversky and Kahneman, in press). An implication of this asymmetry is that if a good is evaluated as a loss when it is given up and as a gain when it is acquired, loss aversion will, on average, induce a higher dollar value for owners than for potential buyers, reducing the set of mutually acceptable trades.

There are some cases in which no endowment effect would be expected, such as when goods are purchased for resale rather than for utilization. A particularly clear case of a good held exclusively for resale is the notional token typically traded in experimental markets commonly used to test the efficiency of market institutions (Plott 1982; Smith 1982). Such experiments employ the induced-value technique in which the objects of trade are tokens to which private redemption values that vary among individual participants have been assigned by the experimenter (Smith 1976). Subjects can obtain the prescribed value assigned for the tokens when redeeming them at the end of the trading period; the tokens are otherwise worthless.

No endowment effect would be expected for such tokens, which are valued only because they can be redeemed for cash. Thus both buyers and sellers should value tokens at the induced value they have been assigned. Markets for induced-value tokens can therefore be used as a control condition to determine whether differences between the values of buyers and sellers in other markets could be attributable to transaction costs, misunderstandings, or habitual strategies of bargaining. Any discrepancy between the buying and selling values can be isolated in an experiment by comparing the outcomes of markets for real goods with those of otherwise identical markets for induced-value tokens. If no differences in values are observed for the induced-value tokens, then economic theory predicts that no differences between buying and selling values will be observed for consumption goods evaluated and traded under the same conditions.

The results from a series of experiments involving real exchanges of tokens and of various consumption goods are reported in this paper. In each case, a random allocation design was used to test for the presence of an endowment effect. Half of the subjects were endowed with a good and became potential sellers in each market; the other half of the subjects were potential buyers. Conventional economic analysis yields the simple prediction that one-half of the goods should be traded in voluntary exchanges. If value is unaffected by ownership, then the distribution of values in the two groups should be the same except for sampling variation. The supply and demand curves should therefore be mirror images of each other, intersecting at their common median. The null hypothesis is, therefore, that half of the goods provided should change hands. Label this predicted volume *V**. If there is an endowment effect, the value of the good will be higher for sellers than for buyers, and observed volume *V* will be less than *V**. The ratio *V/V** provides a unit-free measure of the undertrading that is produced by the effect of ownership on value. To test the hypothesis that market experience eliminates undertrading, the markets were repeated several times.

A test for the possibility that observed undertrading was due to transaction costs was provided by a comparison of the results from a series of induced-value markets with those from the subsequent goods markets carried out with identical trading rules. Notice that this comparison can also be used to eliminate numerous other possible explanations of the observed undertrading. For example, if the instructions to the subjects are confusing or misleading, the effects should show up in both the induced-value markets and the experimental markets for real goods. Section II describes studies of trading volume in induced-value markets and in consumption goods markets. Section III provides a further test for strategic behavior and demonstrates that the disparity findings are not likely caused by this. Section IV investigates the extent to which the undertrading of goods is produced by reluctance to buy and reluctance to sell. Section V examines undertrading in bilateral negotiations and provides a test of the Coase theorem. Section VI describes an experiment that rules out income effects and a trophy effect as explanations of the observed valuation disparity. Implications of the observed effects are discussed in Section VII.

II. Repeated Market Experiments

In experiment 1, 44 students in an advanced undergraduate law and economics class at Cornell University received a packet of general instructions plus 11 forms, one for each of the markets that were conducted in the experiment. (The instructions for all experiments are available from the authors.) The first three markets were conducted for induced-value tokens. Sellers received the following instructions (with differences for buyers in brackets):

> In this market the objects being traded are tokens. You are an owner, so you now own a token [You are a buyer, so you have an opportunity to buy a token] which has a value to you of $*x*. It has this value to you because the experimenter will give you this much money for it. The value of the token is different for different individuals. A price for the tokens will be determined later. For each of the prices listed below, please indicate whether you prefer to: (1) Sell your token at

this price and receive the market price. [Buy a token at this price and cash it in for the sum of money indicated above.] (2) Keep your token and cash it in for the sum of money indicated above. [Not buy a token at this price.] For each price indicate your decision by marking an X in the appropriate column.

Part of the response form for sellers follows:

At a price of $8.75 I will sell _____ I will not sell _____

At a price of $8.25 I will sell _____ I will not sell _____

The same rectangular distribution of values—ranging from $0.25 to $8.75 in steps of $0.50—was prepared for both buyers and sellers. Because not all the forms were actually distributed, however, the induced supply and demand curves were not always precisely symmetrical. Subjects alternated between the buyer and seller role in the three successive markets and were assigned a different individual redemption value in each trial.

Experimenters collected the forms from all participants after each market period and immediately calculated and announced the market-clearing price,[2] the number of trades, and the presence or absence of excess demand or supply at the market-clearing price.[3] Three buyers and three sellers were selected at random after each of the induced markets and were paid off according to the preferences stated on their forms and the market-clearing price for that period.

Immediately after the three induced-value markets, subjects on alternating seats were given Cornell coffee mugs, which sell for $6.00 each at the bookstore. The experimenter asked all participants to examine a mug, either their own or their neighbor's. The experimenter then informed the subjects that four markets for mugs would be conducted using the same procedures as the prior induced markets with two exceptions: (1) One of the four market trials would subsequently be selected at random, and only the trades made on this

---

[2] The instructions stated that "*it is in your best interest to answer these questions truthfully.* For any question, treat the price as fixed. (In economics jargon, you should act as 'price takers'.)" All the subjects were junior and senior economics majors, so they were familiar with the terms used. If subjects asked how the market prices were determined, they were told, truthfully, that the market price was the point at which the elicited supply and demand curves intersected. The uniformity of the results across many different experiments suggests that this information had no discernible effect on behavior. Furthermore, the responses of the subjects in the induced-value portion of the experiments indicate that nearly all understood and accepted their role as price takers. See also experiment 5, in which a random price procedure was used.

[3] When this occurred, a random draw determined which buyers and sellers were accommodated.

trial would be executed. (2) In the binding market trial, *all* trades would be implemented, unlike the subset implemented in the induced-value markets.[4] The initial assignment of buyer and seller roles was maintained for all four trading periods. The clearing price and the number of trades were announced after each period. The market that "counted" was indicated after the fourth period, and transactions were executed immediately. All sellers who had indicated that they would give up their mugs for a sum at the market-clearing price exchanged their mugs for cash, and successful buyers paid this same price and received their mugs. This design was used to permit learning to take place over successive trials and yet make each trial potentially binding. The same procedure was then followed for four more successive markets using boxed ballpoint pens with a visible bookstore price tag of $3.98, which were distributed to the subjects who had been buyers in the mug markets.

For each goods market, subjects completed a form similar to that used for the induced-value tokens, with the following instructions:

> You now own the object in your possession. [You do not own the object that you see in the possession of some of your neighbors.] You have the option of selling it [buying one] if a price, which will be determined later, is acceptable to you. For each of the possible prices below indicate whether you wish to: (1) Sell your object and receive this price [Pay this price and receive an object to take home with you] or (2) Keep your object and take it home with you. [Not buy an object at this price.] For each price indicate your decision by marking an X in the appropriate column.

The buyers and sellers in the consumption goods markets faced the same incentives that they had experienced in the induced-value markets. Buyers maximized their potential gain by agreeing to buy at all prices below the value they ascribed to the good, and sellers maximized their welfare by agreeing to sell at all prices above the good's worth to them. As in the induced-value markets, it was in the best interest of the participants to act as price takers.

As shown in table 2, the markets for induced-value tokens and consumption goods yielded sharply different results. In the induced-value markets, as expected, the median buying and selling prices were identical. The ratio of actual to predicted volume (V/V^*) was 1.0,

---

[4] The experimental design was intended to give the markets for consumption goods every possible chance to be efficient. While in the induced-value markets not everyone was paid, in the consumption goods markets everyone was paid. Also, the consumption goods markets were conducted after the induced-value markets and were repeated four times each, to allow the subjects the maximum opportunity for learning.

TABLE 2

RESULTS OF EXPERIMENT 1

INDUCED-VALUE MARKETS

Trial	Actual Trades	Expected Trades	Price	Expected Price
1	12	11	3.75	3.75
2	11	11	4.75	4.75
3	10	11	4.25	4.25

CONSUMPTION GOODS MARKETS

Trial	Trades	Price	Median Buyer Reservation Price	Median Seller Reservation Price
Mugs (Expected Trades = 11)				
4	4	4.25	2.75	5.25
5	1	4.75	2.25	5.25
6	2	4.50	2.25	5.25
7	2	4.25	2.25	5.25
Pens (Expected Trades = 11)				
8	4	1.25	.75	2.50
9	5	1.25	.75	1.75
10	4	1.25	.75	2.25
11	5	1.25	.75	1.75

aggregating over the three periods. In contrast, the median selling prices in the mug and pen markets were more than twice the median buying prices, and the V/V^* ratio was only .20 for mugs and .41 for pens. Observed volume did not increase over successive periods in either the mug or the pen markets, providing no indication that subjects learned to adopt equal buying and selling prices.

The results of the first and last markets for coffee mugs are also displayed in figure 1. There are five features to notice in this figure: (1) Both buyers and sellers display a wide range of values, indicating that in the absence of an endowment effect there would be enough rents to produce gains from trade. Indeed, the range of values is similar to that used in the induced-value markets, which had near-perfect market efficiency. (2) The distribution of selling prices has a single mode, unlike some recent results in which an evaluation discrepancy could be explained by a bimodal distribution of compensation demanded (Boyce et al. 1990). (3) The payment of a small commission for trading, such as $0.25 per trade, would not significantly alter the results. (4) The mugs were desirable. Every subject assigned a positive value to the mug, and the lowest value assigned by a seller

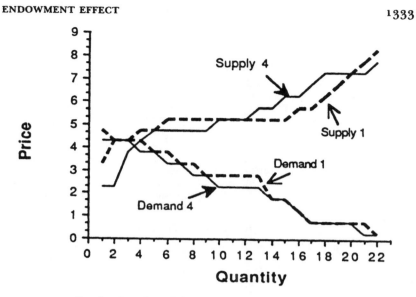

Fɪɢ. 1.—Supply and demand curves, markets 1 and 4

was $2.25. (5) Neither demand nor supply changed much between the first and last markets.

Experiment 2 was conducted in an undergraduate microeconomics class at Cornell ($N = 38$). The procedure was identical to that of experiment 1, except that the second consumption good was a pair of folding binoculars in a cardboard frame, available at the bookstore for $4.00. The results are reported in table 3.

In experiments 3 and 4, conducted in Simon Fraser University undergraduate economics classes, the subjects were asked to provide minimum selling prices or maximum buying prices rather than to answer the series of yes or no questions used in experiments 1 and 2. The induced-value markets were conducted with no monetary payoffs and were followed by four markets for pens in experiment 3 and five markets for mugs in experiment 4. In experiment 3, subjects were told that the first three markets for pens would be used for practice, so only the fourth and final market would be binding. In experiment 4, one of the five markets was selected at random to count, as in experiments 1 and 2. Other procedures were unchanged. The results are shown in table 4.

Experiments 2–4 all yielded results similar to those obtained in experiment 1. Summing over the induced-value markets in all four experiments produced a V/V^* index of .91. This excellent performance was achieved even though the participants did not have the

¹334   JOURNAL OF POLITICAL ECONOMY

TABLE 3

RESULTS OF EXPERIMENT 2

INDUCED-VALUE MARKETS

Trial	Actual Trades	Expected Trades	Price	Expected Price
1	10	10	3.75	4.25
2	9	10	4.75	4.25
3	7	8	4.25	4.75

CONSUMPTION GOODS MARKETS

Trial	Trades	Price	Median Buyer Reservation Price	Median Seller Reservation Price
			Mugs (Expected Trades = 9.5)	
4	3	3.75	1.75	4.75
5	3	3.25	2.25	4.75
6	2	3.25	2.25	4.75
7	2	3.25	2.25	4.25
			Binoculars (Expected Trades = 9.5)	
8	4	1.25	.75	1.25
9	4	.75	.75	1.25
10	3	.75	.75	1.75
11	3	.75	.75	1.75

benefit of experience with the trading rules, there were limited monetary incentives in experiments 1 and 2, and there were no monetary incentives in experiments 3 and 4. In the markets for consumption goods, in which all participants faced monetary incentives and experience with the market rules gained from the induced-value markets, V/V^* averaged .31, and median selling prices were more than double the corresponding buying prices. Trading procedures were precisely identical in markets for goods and for induced-value tokens. The high volume of trade in money tokens therefore eliminates transaction costs (or any other feature that was present in both types of markets) as an explanation of the observed undertrading of consumption goods.

It should be noted that subjects in the position of buyers were not given money to use for purchases, but rather had to make transactions using their own money. (Subjects were told to bring money to class and that credit and change would be available if necessary. Some subjects borrowed from friends to make payments.) The aim was to study transactions in a realistic setting. While the present design makes potential sellers slightly wealthier, at least in the first market, the magnitude of the possible income effect is trivial. In one of the

TABLE 4

RESULTS OF EXPERIMENTS 3 AND 4

Trial	N	Object	Actual Trades	Expected Trades	Ratio of Seller Median Value to Buyer Median Value
Experiment 3					
1	26	Induced	5	6.5	
2	26	Pen	2	6.5	6.0
3	26	Pen	2	6.5	6.0
4	26	Pen	2	6.5	5.0
5	26	Pen	1	6.5	5.0
Experiment 4					
1	74	Induced	15	18.5	
2	74	Induced	16	18.5	
3	74	Mug	6	18.5	3.8
4	74	Mug	4	18.5	2.8
5	72	Mug	4	18	2.2
6	73	Mug	8	18	1.8
7	74	Mug	8	18.5	1.8

markets the equilibrium price was only $0.75, and the prices in other markets were never above a few dollars. Also, as shown in experiments 7 and 8 below, equal undertrading was found in designs that eliminated the possibility of an income effect or cash constraint.

As shown in tables 2–4, subjects showed almost no undertrading even in their first trial in an induced-value market. Evidently neither bargaining habits nor any transaction costs impede trading in money tokens. On the other hand, there is no indication that participants in the markets for goods learned to make valuations independent of their entitlements. The discrepant evaluations of buyers and sellers remained stable over four, and in one case five, successive markets for the same good and did not change systematically over repeated markets for successive goods.

A difference in procedure probably explains the apparent conflict between these results and the conclusion reached in some other studies, that the WTA-WTP discrepancy is greatly reduced by market experience. The studies that reported a disciplinary effect of market experience assessed this effect by comparing the responses of buyers and sellers in preliminary hypothetical questions or nonbinding market trials to their behavior in a subsequent binding trial with real monetary payoffs (Knez et al. 1985; Brookshire and Coursey 1987; Coursey et al. 1987). In the present experiments, the markets for consumption goods were real and potentially binding from the first trial, and the WTA-WTP discrepancy was found to be stable over a series of such binding trials.

It should be stressed that previous research did not actually demonstrate that the discrepancy between buyers and sellers is eliminated in markets. Although the discrepancy between the final selling and buying prices in the sucrose octa-acetate experiment of Coursey et al. (1987) was not statistically significant, the ratio of median prices of sellers and buyers was still 2.6.[5] If the buyers and sellers had been allowed to trade according to their final bids, a total of nine advantageous exchanges would have occurred between the two groups, compared to the theoretical expectation of 16 trades (for details, see Knetsch and Sinden [1987]). This V/V^* ratio of .56 is quite similar to the ratios observed in experiments 1–4. In the study by Brookshire and Coursey (1987), the ratio of mean prices was indeed reduced by experience, from a high of 77 for initial hypothetical survey responses to 6.1 in the first potentially binding auction conducted in a laboratory. However, the ratio remained at 5.6 in the final auction.

III. Testing for Misrepresentation

As previously stated, subjects faced identical incentives in the induced-value and consumption goods phases of experiments 1–4. Therefore, it seems safe to attribute the difference in observed trading to the endowment effect. However, some readers of early drafts of this paper have suggested that because of the way market prices were determined, subjects might have felt that they had an incentive to misstate their true values in order to influence the price, and perhaps this incentive was perceived to be greater in the consumption goods markets. To eliminate this possible interpretation of the previous results, experiment 5 was carried out in a manner similar to the first four experiments, except that subjects were told that the price would be selected at random. As is well known, this is an incentive-compatible procedure for eliciting values (see Becker, DeGroot, and Marschak 1964).

Each participant received the following instructions (with appropriate alternative wording in the buyers' forms):

> After you have finished, one of the prices listed below will be selected at random and any exchanges will take place at that price. If you have indicated you will sell at this price you will receive this amount of money and will give up the mug; if you have indicated that you will keep the mug at this price

[5] The ratio of the mean selling and buying prices is 1.4 if all subjects are included. However, if one buyer and one seller with extreme valuations are excluded, the ratio is 1.9. These numbers were reported in an earlier version of Coursey et al. (1987).

> then no exchange will be made and you can take the mug
> home with you.
>
> . . . Your decision can have no effect on the price actually
> used because the price will be selected at random.

The experiment was conducted in a series of six tutorial groups of a business statistics class at Simon Fraser University. The use of small groups helped assure complete understanding of the instructions, and the exercises were conducted over the course of a single day to minimize opportunities for communication between participants. Each group was divided equally: half of the subjects were designated as sellers by random selection, and the other half became buyers. A total of 59 people took part.

Two induced-value markets for hypothetical payoffs and a subsequent third real exchange market for money and mugs were conducted with identical trading rules used in all three. All participants maintained the same role as either buyers or sellers for the three markets. As in experiments 1 and 2, the prices that individuals chose to buy or to sell were selected from possible prices ranging from $0.00 to $9.50 listed by increments of $0.50.

The results of this experiment were nearly identical to the earlier ones in which the actual exchanges were based on the market-clearing price. Even though possibly less motivating hypothetical values were used in the two induced-value markets, nearly all participants pursued a profit-maximizing selection of prices to buy or sell the assets. Fourteen exchanges at a price of $4.75 were expected in the first induced-value market on the basis of the randomly distributed values written on the forms. Thirteen trades at this price were indicated by the prices actually selected by the participants. The results of the second hypothetical induced-value market were equally convincing, with 16 of the 17 expected exchanges made at the expected price of $5.75. The procedures and incentives were apparently well understood by the participants.

Mugs, comparable to those used in other experiments, were distributed to the potential sellers after the induced-value markets were completed. A mug was also shown to all the potential buyers. The following form with instructions, nearly identical to the ones used in the induced-value markets, was then distributed (with the alternative wording for buyers in brackets):

> You now [do not] have, and own a mug which you can
> keep and take home. You also have the option of selling it
> and receiving [buying one to take home by paying] money
> for it.
>
> For each of the possible prices listed below, please indicate

whether you wish to: (1) Receive [pay] that amount of money and sell your [buy a] mug, or (2) Not sell your [buy a] mug at this price.

After you have finished, one of the prices listed below will be selected at random and any exchanges will take place at that price. If you have indicated you will sell [buy] at this price you will receive this amount of money [a mug] and will give up the mug [pay this amount of money]; if you have indicated that you will keep the [not buy a] mug at this price then no exchange will be made and you can take the mug home with you [do not pay anything].

Notice the following two things: (1) Your decision can have no effect on the price actually used because the price will be selected at random. (2) It is in your interest to indicate your true preferences at each of the possible prices listed below.

For each price indicate your decision by marking an X in the appropriate column.

	I Will Sell [Buy]	I Will Keep [Not Buy] the Mug
If the price is $0	_____	_____
If the price is $0.50	_____	_____
⋮		
If the price is $9.50	_____	_____

After the instructions were read and reviewed by the experimenter and questions were answered, participants completed the forms indicating either their lowest selling price or their highest buying price. A random price, from among the list from $0.00 to $9.50, was then drawn, and exchanges based on this price were completed.

The results again showed a large and significant endowment effect. Given the 29 potential buyers, 30 potential sellers, and the random distribution of the mugs, 14.5 exchanges would be expected if entitlements did not influence valuations. Instead, only six were indicated on the basis of the values actually selected by the potential buyers and sellers ($V/V^* = .41$). The median selling price of $5.75 was over twice the median buying price of $2.25, and the means were $5.78 and $2.21, respectively.

IV. Reluctance to Buy versus Reluctance to Sell

Exchanges of money and a good (or between two goods) offer the possibilities of four comparisons: a choice of gaining either the good or money, a choice of losing one or the other, buying (giving up money for the good), and selling (giving up the good for money) (Tversky and Kahneman, in press). The endowment effect results from a difference between the relative preferences for the good and money. The comparison of buying and selling to simple choices between gains permits an analysis of the discrepancy between WTA and WTP into two components: reluctance to sell (exchanging the good for money) and reluctance to buy (exchanging money for the good).

Experiments 6 and 7 were carried out to assess the weight of reluctance to buy and reluctance to sell in undertrading of a good similar to the goods used in the earlier experiments. The subjects in experiment 6 were 77 Simon Fraser students, randomly assigned to three groups. Members of one group, designated sellers, were given a coffee mug and were asked to indicate whether or not they would sell the mug at a series of prices ranging from $0.00 to $9.25. A group of buyers indicated whether they were willing to buy a mug at each of these prices. Finally, choosers were asked to choose, for each of the possible prices, between a mug and cash.

The results again reveal substantial undertrading: While 12.5 trades were expected between buyers and sellers, only three trades took place ($V/V^* = .24$). The median valuations were $7.12 for sellers, $3.12 for choosers, and $2.87 for buyers. The close similarity of results for buyers and choosers indicates that there was relatively little reluctance to pay for the mug.

Experiment 7 was carried out with 117 students at the University of British Columbia. It used an identical design except that price tags were left on the mugs. The results were consistent with those in experiment 6. Nineteen trades were expected on the basis of valuation equivalence, but only one was concluded on the basis of actual valuations ($V/V^* = .05$). The median valuations were $7.00 for sellers, $3.50 for choosers, and $2.00 for buyers.

It is worth noting that these results eliminate any form of income effect as an explanation of the discrepant valuations since the positions of sellers and choosers were strictly identical. The allocation of a particular mug to each seller evidently induced a sense of endowment that the choosers did not share: the median value of the mug to the sellers was more than double the value indicated by the choosers even though their choices were objectively the same. The results imply that the observed undertrading of consumption goods may be largely due to a reluctance to part with entitlements.

V. Bilateral Bargaining and the Coase Theorem

According to the Coase theorem, the allocation of resources to individuals who can bargain and transact at no cost should be indepen-

dent of initial property rights. However, if the marginal rate of substitution between one good and another is affected by endowment,
then the individual who is assigned the property right to a good will
be more likely to retain it. A bilateral bargaining experiment (experiment 8) was carried out to test this implication of the endowment
effect.

The subjects were 35 pairs of students in seven small tutorials at
Simon Fraser University. The students were enrolled in either a beginning economics course or an English class. Each student was randomly paired with another student in the same tutorial group, with
care taken to assure that students entering the tutorial together were
not assigned as a pair. A game of Nim, a simple game easily explained, was played by each pair of participants. The winners of the
game were each given a 400-gram Swiss chocolate bar and told it was
theirs to keep.

An induced-value bargaining session was then conducted. The
member of each pair who did not win the Nim game, and therefore
did not receive the chocolate bar, was given a ticket and an instruction
sheet that indicated that the ticket was worth $3.00 because it could be
redeemed for that sum. The ticket owners were also told that they
could sell the ticket to their partner if mutually agreeable terms could
be reached. The partners (the chocolate bar owners) received instructions indicating that they could receive $5.00 for the ticket if they
could successfully buy it from the owner. Thus there was a $2.00
surplus available to any pair completing a trade.

The pairs were then given an unlimited amount of time to bargain.
Subjects were told that both credit and change were available from
the experimenter. Results of the bargaining sessions were recorded
on their instruction sheets.

Of the 35 pairs of participants, 29 agreed to an exchange ($V/V^* =
.83$). The average price paid for the 29 tickets was $4.09, with 12 of
the exchange prices being exactly $4.00. Payments of the redemption
values of the tickets were made as soon as the exchanges were completed. These payments were made in single dollar bills to facilitate
trading in the subsequent bargaining session. After the ticket exchanges were completed, owners of the chocolate bars were told that
they could sell them to their partners if a mutually agreeable price
could be determined. The procedures used for the tickets were once
again applied to these bargaining sessions.

An important effect of the preliminary induced-value ticket bargains was to provide the ticket owners with some cash. The average
gain to the ticket owners (including the six who did not sell their
tickets) was $3.90. The average gain to their partners (the chocolate
bar owners) was only $0.76. Thus the potential chocolate bar buyers

were endowed with an average of $3.14 more than the owners, creating a small income effect toward the buyers. Also, to the extent that a windfall gain such as this is spent more casually by subjects than other money (for evidence on such a "house money effect," see Thaler and Johnson [1990]), trading of chocolate bars should be facilitated.

Results of the chocolate bar bargains once again suggest reluctance to trade. Rather than the 17.5 trades expected from the random allocations, only seven were observed ($V/V^* = .4$). The average price paid in those exchanges that did occur was $2.69 (the actual prices were $6.00, $3.10, $3.00, $2.75, $2.00, $1.00, and $1.00). If the six pairs of subjects who did not successfully complete bargains in the first stage are omitted from the sample on the grounds that they did not understand the task or procedures, then six trades are observed where 14.5 would be expected ($V/V^* = .414$). Similarly, if two more pairs are dropped because the prices at which they exchanged tickets were outside the range $3.00–$5.00, then the number of trades falls to four, and V/V^* falls to .296. (No significant differences between the students in the English and economics classes were observed.)[6]

To be sure that the chocolate bars were valued by the subjects and that these valuations would vary enough to yield mutually beneficial trades, the same chocolate bars were distributed to half the members of another class at Simon Fraser. Those who received chocolate bars were asked the minimum price they would accept to sell their bar, while those without the bars were asked the maximum price they would pay to acquire a bar. The valuations of the bars varied from $0.50 to $8.00. The average value ascribed by sellers was $3.98, while the buyers' average valuation was $1.25. (The median values were $3.50 and $1.25.)

VI. The Endowment Effect in Choices between Goods

The previous experiments documented undertrading in exchanges of money and consumption goods. A separate experiment (Knetsch 1989) establishes the same effect in exchanges between two goods. Participants in three classes were offered a choice between the same two goods. All students in one class were given a coffee mug at the

---

[6] We conducted two similar bargaining experiments that yielded comparable results. Twenty-six pairs of subjects negotiated the sale of mugs and then envelopes containing an uncertain amount of money. Buyers had not been given any cash endowment. These sessions yielded six and five trades, respectively, where 13 would be expected. Also, some induced-value bilateral negotiation sessions were conducted in which only $0.50 of surplus was available (the seller's valuation was $1.50 and the buyer's was $2.00). Nevertheless, 21 of a possible 26 trades were completed.

beginning of the session as compensation for completing a short questionnaire. At the completion of the task, the experimenters showed the students a bar of Swiss chocolate that they could immediately receive in exchange for the mug. The students in another class were offered an opportunity to make the opposite exchange after first being given the chocolate bar. The students in a third class were simply offered a choice, at the beginning of the session, between a chocolate bar and a mug. The proportion of students selecting the mug was 89 percent in the class originally endowed with mugs ($N = 76$), 56 percent in the class offered a choice ($N = 55$), and only 10 percent in the class originally endowed with chocolate bars ($N = 87$). For most participants a mug was more valuable than the chocolate when the mug had to be given up but less valuable when the chocolate had to be given up. This experiment confirms that undertrading can occur even when income effects are ruled out. It also demonstrates an endowment effect for a good that was distributed to everyone in the class and therefore did not have the appeal of a prize or trophy.

VII. Discussion

The evidence presented in this paper supports what may be called an instant endowment effect: the value that an individual assigns to such objects as mugs, pens, binoculars, and chocolate bars appears to increase substantially as soon as that individual is given the object.[7] The apparently instantaneous nature of the reference point shift and consequent value change induced by giving a person possession of a good goes beyond previous discussions of the endowment effect, which focused on goods that have been in the individual's possession for some time. While long-term endowment effects could be explained by sentimental attachment or by an improved technology of consumption in the Stigler-Becker (1977) sense, the differences in preference or taste demonstrated by more than 700 participants in the experiments reported in this paper cannot be explained in this fashion.

The endowment effect is one explanation for the systematic differences between buying and selling prices that have been observed so often in past work. One of the objectives of this study was to examine an alternative explanation for this buying-selling discrepancy, namely that it reflects a general bargaining strategy (Knez and Smith 1987) that would be eliminated by experience in the market (Brookshire

---

[7] The impression gained from informal pilot experiments is that the act of giving the participant physical possession of the good results in a more consistent endowment effect. Assigning subjects a chance to receive a good, or a property right to a good to be received at a later time, seemed to produce weaker effects.

and Coursey 1987; Coursey et al. 1987). Our results do not support this alternative view. The trading institution used in experiments 1–7 encouraged participants to be price takers (especially in experiment 5), and the rules provided no incentive to conceal true preferences. Furthermore, the results of the induced-value markets indicate that the subjects understood the demand-revealing nature of the questions they were asked and acted accordingly. Substantial undertrading was nevertheless observed in markets for consumption goods. As for learning and market discipline, there was no indication that buying and selling prices converged over repeated market trials, though full feedback was provided at the end of each trial. The undertrading observed in these experiments appears to reflect a true difference in preferences between the potential buyers and sellers. The robustness of this result reduces the risk that the outcome is produced by an experimental artifact. In short, the present findings indicate that the endowment effect can persist in genuine market settings.

The contrast between the induced-value markets and the consumption goods markets lends support to Heiner's (1985) conjecture that the results of induced-value experiments may not generalize to all market settings. The defining characteristic of the induced-value markets is that the values of the tokens are unequivocally defined by the amount the experimenter will pay for them. Loss aversion is irrelevant with such objects because transactions are evaluated simply on the basis of net gain or loss. (If someone is offered $6.00 for a $5.00 bill, there is no sense of loss associated with the trade.) Some markets may share this feature of induced-value markets, especially when the conditions of pure arbitrage are approached. However, the computation of net gain and loss is not possible in other situations, for example, in markets in which risky prospects are traded for cash or in markets in which people sell goods that they also value for their use. In these conditions, the cancellation of the loss of the object against the dollars received is not possible because the good and money are not strictly commensurate. The valuation ambiguity produced by this lack of commensurability is necessary, although not sufficient, for both loss aversion and a buying-selling discrepancy.

The results of the experimental demonstrations of the endowment effect have direct implications for economic theory and economic predictions. Contrary to the assumptions of standard economic theory that preferences are independent of entitlements,[8] the evidence

---

[8] Although ownership can affect taste in the manner suggested by Stigler and Becker (1977), in the absence of income effects, it is traditional to assume that the indifference curves in an Edgeworth box diagram do not depend on the location of the endowment point.

presented here indicates that people's preferences depend on their reference positions. Consequently, preference orderings are not defined independently of endowments: good A may be preferred to B when A is part of an original endowment, but the reverse may be true when initial reference positions are changed. Indifference curves will have a kink at the endowment or reference point (see Tversky and Kahneman, in press), and an indifference curve tracing acceptable trades in one direction may even cross another indifference curve that plots the acceptable exchanges in the opposite direction (Knetsch 1989).

The existence of endowment effects reduces the gains from trade. In comparison with a world in which preferences are independent of endowment, the existence of loss aversion produces an inertia in the economy because potential traders are more reluctant to trade than is conventionally assumed. This is not to say that Pareto-optimal trades will not take place. Rather, there are simply fewer mutually advantageous exchanges possible, and so the volume of trade is lower than it otherwise would be.

To assess the practical significance of the endowment effect, it is important to consider first some necessary conditions for the effect to be observed. Experiments 6 and 7 suggest that the endowment effect is primarily a problem for sellers; we observed little reluctance to buy but much reluctance to sell. Furthermore, not all sellers are afflicted by an endowment effect. The effect did not appear in the markets for money tokens, and there is no reason in general to expect reluctance to resell goods that are held especially for that purpose. An owner will not be reluctant to sell an item at a given price if a perfect substitute is readily available at a lower price. This reasoning suggests that endowment effects will almost certainly occur when owners are faced with an opportunity to sell an item purchased for use that is not easily replaceable. Examples might include tickets to a sold-out event, hunting licenses in limited supply (Bishop and Heberlein 1979), works of art, or a pleasant view.

While the conditions necessary for an endowment effect to be observed may appear to limit its applicability in economic settings, in fact these conditions are very often satisfied, and especially so in the bargaining contexts to which the Coase theorem is applied. For example, tickets to Wimbledon are allocated by means of a lottery. A standard Coasean analysis would imply that in the presence of an efficient ticket brokerage market, winners of the lottery would be no more likely to attend the matches than other tennis fans who had won a similar cash prize in an unrelated lottery. In contrast, the experimental results presented in this paper predict that many winners of Wimbledon tickets will attend the event, turning down opportunities to sell their tickets that exceed their reservation price for buying them.

Endowment effects can also be observed for firms and other organizations. Endowment effects are predicted for property rights acquired by historic accident or fortuitous circumstances, such as government licenses, landing rights, or transferable pollution permits. Owing to endowment effects, firms will be reluctant to divest themselves of divisions, plants, and product lines even though they would never consider buying the same assets; indeed, stock prices often rise when firms do give them up. Again, the prediction is not an absence of trade, just a reduction in the volume of trade.

Isolating the influence of endowment effects from those of transaction costs as causes of low trading volumes is, of course, difficult in actual market settings. Demonstrations of endowment effects are most persuasive where transaction costs are very small. By design, this was the case in the experimental markets, where the efficiency of the induced-value markets demonstrated the minimal effect of transaction costs, or other impediments, on exchange decisions, leaving the great reluctance to trade mugs and other goods to be attributable to endowment effects.

Endowment effects are not limited to cases involving physical goods or to legal entitlements. The reference position of individuals and firms often includes terms of previous transactions or expectations of continuation of present, often informal, arrangements. There is clear evidence of dramatically asymmetric reactions to improvements and deteriorations of these terms and a willingness to make sacrifices to avoid unfair treatment (Kahneman, Knetsch, and Thaler 1986). The reluctance to sell at a loss, owing to a perceived entitlement to a formerly prevailing price, can explain two observations of apparent undertrading. The first pertains to housing markets. It is often observed that when housing prices fall, volume also falls. When house prices are falling, houses remain on the market longer than when prices are rising. Similarly, the volume for stocks that have declined in price is lower than the volume for stocks that have increased in value (Shefrin and Statman 1985; Ferris, Haugen, and Makhija 1988), although tax considerations would lead to the opposite prediction.

Another manifestation of loss aversion in the context of multiattribute negotiations is what might be termed "concession aversion": a reluctance to accept a loss on any dimension of an agreement. A straightforward and common instance of this is the downward stickiness of wages. A somewhat more subtle implication of concession aversion is that it can produce inefficient contract terms owing to historic precedents. Old firms may have more inefficient arrangements than new ones because new companies can negotiate without the reference positions created by prior agreements. Some airlines, for example, are required to carry three pilots on some planes while others—newer ones—operate with two.

Loss aversion implies a marked asymmetry in the treatment of losses and forgone gains, which plays an essential role in judgments of fairness (Kahneman et al. 1986). Accordingly, disputes in which concessions are viewed as losses are often much less tractable than disputes in which concessions involve forgone gains. Court decisions recognize the asymmetry of losses and forgone gains by favoring possessors of goods over other claimants, by limiting recovery of lost profits relative to compensation for actual expenditures, and by failing to enforce gratuitous promises that are coded as forgone gains to the injured party (Cohen and Knetsch 1989).

To conclude, the evidence reported here offers no support for the contention that observations of loss aversion and the consequential evaluation disparities are artifacts; nor should they be interpreted as mistakes likely to be eliminated by experience, training, or "market discipline." Instead, the findings support an alternative view of endowment effects and loss aversion as fundamental characteristics of preferences.

References

Banford, Nancy D.; Knetsch, Jack L.; and Mauser, Gary A. "Feasibility Judgements and Alternative Measures of Benefits and Costs." *J. Bus. Admin.* 11, nos. 1, 2 (1979): 25–35.

Becker, Gordon M.; DeGroot, Morris H.; and Marschak, Jacob. "Measuring Utility by a Single-Response Sequential Method." *Behavioral Sci.* 9 (July 1964): 226–32.

Bishop, Richard C., and Heberlein, Thomas A. "Measuring Values of Extramarket Goods: Are Indirect Measures Biased?" *American J. Agricultural Econ.* 61 (December 1979): 926–30.

Boyce, Rebecca R.; Brown, Thomas C.; McClelland, Gary D.; Peterson, George L.; and Schulze, William D. "An Experimental Examination of Intrinsic Environmental Values." Working paper. Boulder: Univ. Colorado, 1990.

Brookshire, David S., and Coursey, Don L. "Measuring the Value of a Public Good: An Empirical Comparison of Elicitation Procedures." *A.E.R.* 77 (September 1987): 554–66.

Brookshire, David S.; Randall, Alan; and Stoll, John R. "Valuing Increments and Decrements in Natural Resource Service Flows." *American J. Agricultural Econ.* 62 (August 1980): 478–88.

Cohen, David, and Knetsch, Jack L. "Judicial Choice and Disparities between Measures of Economic Values." Working paper. Burnaby, B.C.: Simon Fraser Univ., 1989.

Coursey, Don L.; Hovis, John L.; and Schulze, William D. "The Disparity between Willingness to Accept and Willingness to Pay Measures of Value." *Q.J.E.* 102 (August 1987): 679–90.

Ferris, Stephen P.; Haugen, Robert A.; and Makhija, Anil K. "Predicting Contemporary Volume with Historic Volume at Differential Price Levels: Evidence Supporting the Disposition Effect." *J. Finance* 43 (July 1988): 677–97.

Freeman, A. Myrick. *The Benefits of Environmental Improvement.* Washington: Resources for the Future, 1979.

Hammack, Judd, and Brown, Gardner Mallard, Jr. *Waterfowl and Wetlands: Toward Bio-economic Analysis.* Baltimore: Johns Hopkins Press (for Resources for the Future), 1974.

Heberlein, Thomas A., and Bishop, Richard C. "Assessing the Validity of Contingent Valuation: Three Field Experiments." Paper presented at the International Conference on Man's Role in Changing the Global Environment, Italy, 1985.

Heiner, Ronald A. "Experimental Economics: Comment." *A.E.R.* 75 (March 1985): 260–63.

Kahneman, Daniel; Knetsch, Jack L.; and Thaler, Richard. "Fairness as a Constraint on Profit Seeking: Entitlements in the Market." *A.E.R.* 76 (September 1986): 728–41.

Kahneman, Daniel, and Tversky, Amos. "Prospect Theory: An Analysis of Decision under Risk." *Econometrica* 47 (March 1979): 263–91.

Knetsch, Jack L. "The Endowment Effect and Evidence of Nonreversible Indifference Curves." *A.E.R.* 79 (December 1989): 1277–84.

Knetsch, Jack L., and Sinden, J. A. "Willingness to Pay and Compensation Demanded: Experimental Evidence of an Unexpected Disparity in Measures of Value." *Q.J.E.* 99 (August 1984): 507–21.

———. "The Persistence of Evaluation Disparities." *Q.J.E.* 102 (August 1987): 691–95.

Knez, Marc, and Smith, Vernon L. "Hypothetical Valuations and Preference Reversals in the Context of Asset Trading." In *Laboratory Experiments in Economics: Six Points of View,* edited by Alvin E. Roth. Cambridge: Cambridge Univ. Press, 1987.

Knez, Peter; Smith, Vernon L.; and Williams, Arlington W. "Individual Rationality, Market Rationality, and Value Estimation." *A.E.R. Papers and Proc.* 75 (May 1985): 397–402.

Plott, Charles R. "Industrial Organization Theory and Experimental Economics." *J. Econ. Literature* 20 (December 1982): 1485–1527.

Rowe, Robert D.; d'Arge, Ralph C.; and Brookshire, David S. "An Experiment on the Economic Value of Visibility." *J. Environmental Econ. and Management* 7 (March 1980): 1–19.

Shefrin, Hersh, and Statman, Meir. "The Disposition to Sell Winners Too Early and Ride Losers Too Long: Theory and Evidence." *J. Finance* 40 (July 1985): 777–90.

Sinclair, William F. *The Economic and Social Impact of Kemano II Hydroelectric Project on British Columbia's Fisheries Resources.* Vancouver: Dept. Fisheries and Oceans, 1978.

Smith, Vernon L. "Experimental Economics: Induced Value Theory." *A.E.R. Papers and Proc.* 66 (May 1976): 274–79.

———. "Macroeconomic Systems as an Experimental Science." *A.E.R.* 72 (December 1982): 923–55.

Stigler, George J., and Becker, Gary S. "De Gustibus Non Est Disputandum." *A.E.R.* 67 (March 1977): 76–90.

Thaler, Richard. "Toward a Positive Theory of Consumer Choice." *J. Econ. Behavior and Organization* 1 (March 1980): 39–60.

Thaler, Richard, and Johnson, Eric J. "Gambling with the House Money and Trying to Break Even: The Effects of Prior Outcomes on Risky Choice." *Management Sci.* 36 (June 1990).

Tversky, Amos, and Kahneman, Daniel. "Reference Theory of Choice and Exchange." *Q.J.E.* (in press).

Willig, Robert D. "Consumer's Surplus without Apology." *A.E.R.* 66 (September 1976): 589–97.

[19]

Willingness To Pay and Willingness To Accept: How Much Can They Differ?

By W. Michael Hanemann*

In many empirical studies, analysts seek to obtain money measures of welfare changes due not to price changes but to changes in the availability of public goods or amenities, changes in the qualities of commodities, or changes in the fixed quantities of rationed goods. The conventional welfare measures for price changes are the compensating (C) and equivalent (E) variations, which correspond to the maximum amount an individual would be willing to pay (WTP) to secure the change or the minimum amount she would be willing to accept (WTA) to forgo it. Karl-Göran Mäler (1974) was perhaps the first to show that the concepts of C and E can readily be extended from conventional price changes to such quantity changes. For price changes, Robert Willig (1976) demonstrated that C and E are likely to be fairly close in value, with the difference depending directly on the size of the income elasticity of demand for the commodity whose price changes. Subsequently, Alan Randall and John Stoll (1980) examined the duality theory associated with fixed quantities in the utility function and showed that, with appropriate modifications, Willig's formulas for bounds on C and E do, indeed, carry over to this setting. Within the environmental-economics literature, Randall and Stoll's results have been widely interpreted as implying that WTP and WTA for changes in environmental amenities should not differ greatly unless there are unusual income effects.[1] However,

recent empirical work using various types of interview procedures has produced some evidence of large disparities between WTP and WTA measures.[2] This has led to something of an impasse: how can the empirical evidence of significant differences between WTP and WTA be reconciled with the theoretical analysis suggesting that such differences are unlikely? Can they be explained entirely by unusual income effects or by peculiarities of the interview process?

In this note, I reexamine Randall and Stoll's analysis and show that, while it is indeed accurate, its implications have been misunderstood. For quantity changes, there is no presumption that WTP and WTA must be close in value and, unlike price changes, the difference between WTP and WTA depends not only on an income effect but also on a substitution effect. By the latter, I mean the ease with which other privately marketed commodities can be substituted for the given public good or fixed commodity, while maintaining the individual at a constant level of utility. I show that, holding income effects constant, the smaller the substitution effect (i.e., the fewer substitutes available for the public good) the *greater* the disparity between WTP and WTA. This surely coincides with common intuition. If there are private goods that are readily substitutable for the public good, there ought to be little difference between an individual's WTP and WTA for a change in the public good. However, if the public good has almost no substitutes (e.g., Yosemite National Park, or in a different context, your own life), there is no reason why WTP and WTA could not differ vastly: in the limit, WTP could equal the individual's entire (finite)

*Department of Agricultural and Resource Economics, University of California, Berkeley, CA 94720.
[1] This view is expressed by, for example, Myrick Freeman (1979 p. 3), Mark A. Thayer (1981 p. 30), Jack L. Knetsch and J. A. Sinden (1984 p. 508), Robin Gregory (1986 p. 326), Don L. Coursey et al. (1987 p. 678), and most of the participants in a recent symposium on valuing amenity resources edited by George L. Peterson et al. (1988 pp. 104, 129, 138, 152, 168, 230, 238, 259).

[2] See the summaries in table 3.2 of Ronald G. Cummings et al. (1986) and table 1 of Ann Fisher et al. (1988).

income, while WTA could be infinite. My argument is developed in the following two sections. Section I deals specifically with the two polar cases of perfect substitution and zero substitution between the public good and available private goods. Section II deals with Randall and Stoll's extension of Willig's formulas and shows that their bounds are, in fact, consistent with substantial divergences between WTP and WTA. Section III presents empirical application of these bounds and relates them to Mäler's concept of weak complementarity.

I. Two Polar Cases

The theoretical setup is as follows. An individual has preferences for various conventional market commodities whose consumption is denoted by the vector $\mathbf{x}$ as well as for another commodity whose consumption is denoted by q.[3] This could represent the supply of a public good or amenity; it could be an index of the quality of one of the private goods; or it could be a private commodity whose consumption is fixed by a public agency.[4] The key point is that the individual's consumption of q is fixed exogenously, while she can freely vary her consumption of the x's. These preferences are represented by a utility function, $u(\mathbf{x}, q)$, which is continuous and nondecreasing in its arguments (I assume that the x's and q are all "goods") and strictly quasiconcave in $\mathbf{x}$. The individual chooses her consumption by solving

$$(1) \quad \max_{\mathbf{x}} u(\mathbf{x}, q) \text{ subject to } \sum p_i x_i = y$$

taking the level of q as given. This yields a set of ordinary demand functions, $x_i = h^i(\mathbf{p}, q, y)$, $i = 1, \ldots, N$, and an indirect utility function, $v(\mathbf{p}, q, y) \equiv u[h(\mathbf{p}, q, y), q]$,

which has the conventional properties with respect to the price and income arguments and also is nondecreasing in q.[5] Now suppose that q rises from q^0 to $q^1 > q^0$ while prices and income remain constant at $(\mathbf{p}, y)$. Accordingly, the individual's utility changes from $u^0 \equiv v(\mathbf{p}, q^0, y)$ to $u^1 \equiv v(\mathbf{p}, q^1, y) \geq u^0$. Following Mäler, the compensating and equivalent variation measures of this change are defined, respectively, by[6]

$$(2) \quad v(\mathbf{p}, q^1, y - C) = v(\mathbf{p}, q^0, y)$$

$$(3) \quad v(\mathbf{p}, q^1, y) = v(\mathbf{p}, q^0, y + E).$$

Dual to the utility maximization in (1) is an expenditure minimization: minimize $\sum p_i x_i$ with respect to $\mathbf{x}$ subject to $u = (\mathbf{x}, q)$, which yields a set of compensated demand functions, $x_i = g^i(\mathbf{p}, q, u)$, $i = 1, \ldots, N$, and an expenditure function, $m(\mathbf{p}, q, u) \equiv \sum p_i g^i(\mathbf{p}, q, u)$, which has the conventional properties with respect to $(\mathbf{p}, u)$ and is nonincreasing in q. In terms of this function, C and E are given by

$$(2') \quad C = m(\mathbf{p}, q^0, u^0) - m(\mathbf{p}, q^1, u^0)$$

$$(3') \quad E = m(\mathbf{p}, q^0, u^1) - m(\mathbf{p}, q^1, u^1).$$

It is evident from (2) and (3) that $0 < C < y$ while $E \geq 0$.[7] The questions at issue are: i) is it true that $E / C \approx 1$? and ii) what factors affect this ratio? As a first cut at an answer, I compare two polar cases. In the first case, at least one private good—say, the first—is a perfect substitute for some

---

[3] I am treating q as a scalar here, but it could be a vector without seriously affecting the analysis in this section. In the next section, however, the analysis would become significantly more complex if q were a vector and more than one element of q changed.

[4] These alternative interpretations are offered, respectively, by Mäler (1974), Hanemann (1982), and Randall and Stoll (1980).

[5] These properties are established in my earlier paper (Hanemann, 1982).

[6] I have taken the liberty of defining C and E as the negative of quantities appearing in Willig (1976) and in Randall and Stoll (1980), so that sign(C) = sign(E) = sign($u^1 - u^0$).

[7] I assume throughout that $q^1 > q^0$ and $u^1 \geq u^0$. The analysis could be repeated for a case in which quality decreases and $u^1 < u^0$. In that case, C and E are both nonpositive and correspond, respectively, to the compensation that the individual would be willing to accept to consent to the change and the amount that she would be willing to pay to avoid the change. This would reverse the inequalities presented in what follows, but it would not affect the substance of my argument.

transformation of q. Thus, the direct utility function assumes the special form

$$(4) \quad u(\mathbf{x}, q) = \bar{u}\big[x_1 + \psi(q), x_2, \dots, x_N \big]$$

where $\psi(\cdot)$ is an increasing function and $\bar{u}(\cdot)$ is a continuous, increasing, strictly quasi-concave function of N variables. As W. M. Gorman (1976) has shown, assuming an interior solution, the resulting indirect utility function is

$$(5) \quad v(\mathbf{p}, q, y)$$
$$= \bar{v}\big[p_1, p_2, \dots, p_N, y + p_1 \cdot \psi(q) \big]$$

where $\bar{v}(\cdot)$ is the indirect utility function corresponding to $\bar{u}(\cdot)$. Substitution of (5) into (2) and (3) yields the following:[8]

PROPOSITION 1: *If at least one private market good is a perfect substitute for q, then $C = E$.*

At the opposite extreme, I assume that there is a zero elasticity of substitution not just between q and x_1 but between q and *all* the x's. Thus, the direct utility function becomes

$$(6) \quad u(\mathbf{x}, q)$$
$$= \bar{u}\left[\min\left(q, \frac{x_1}{\alpha_1} \right), \dots, \min\left(q, \frac{x_N}{\alpha_N} \right) \right]$$

where $\alpha_1, \dots, \alpha_N$ are positive constants and $\bar{u}(\cdot)$ is conventional direct utility function. In this case, the indirect utility function $v(\mathbf{p}, q, y)$ has a rather complex structure and changes its form in different segments of $(\mathbf{p}, q, y)$-space. It will be sufficient for my purposes to focus on just one of these segments. Suppose that $q \le y / \sum p_i \alpha_i$; then, the maximization of (6), subject to the budget constraint, yields demand functions and an indirect utility function of the form $x_i = h^i(\mathbf{p}, q, y) = \alpha_i q$, and $u =$

$v(\mathbf{p}, q, y) = \bar{u}(q, \dots, q) \equiv w(q)$. In this region of $(\mathbf{p}, q, y)$-space, the individual does not exhaust her budget, and her marginal utility of income is therefore zero. Now suppose that $q^0 \le y / \sum p_i \alpha_i$ and $q^1 > q^0$. Since $v(\mathbf{p}, q^1, y) > w(q^0)$, it is evident from (2) that the individual would be willing to pay some positive but limited amount C to secure this change. However, for any positive quantity E, no matter how large, $v(\mathbf{p}, q^0, y + E) = v(\mathbf{p}, q^0, y) = w(q^0)$. This implies the following proposition.

PROPOSITION 2: *If there is zero substitutability between q and each of the private-market goods, it can happen that, while the individual would only be willing to pay a finite amount for an increase in q, there is no finite compensation that she would accept to forgo this increase.*

It should be emphasized that this result obtains only in a portion of $(\mathbf{p}, q, y)$ space; in other regions, even with (6), E would be finite.[9] However, the result in Proposition 2 can also be established for other utility functions that permit some substitutability between q and the x's as long as the indifference curves between q and each of the x's become parallel to the x axis at some point. The implication of these two propositions is that the degree of substitutability between q and private-market goods *does* significantly affect the relation between C and E. In the next section, I show how this observation can be reconciled with the bounds on C and E derived by Randall and Stoll.

II. Randall and Stoll's Bounds

In order to extend Willig's bounds from price to commodity space, Randall and Stoll focus on a set of demand functions different from those considered above. Suppose that the individual could purchase q in a market

---

[8] This result caries over, of course, if *more* than one private good is a perfect substitute for q. In the most general case, $u(\mathbf{x}, q) = \bar{u}[x_1 + \psi_1(q), \dots, x_N + \psi(q)]$ and $C = E = \sum p_i [\psi_i(q^1) - \psi_i(q^0)]$.

[9] Indeed, if $\bar{h}^i(\alpha_1 p_1, \dots, \alpha_N p_N, y) \le q^0$, $i = 1, \dots, N$, it can be shown that $v(\mathbf{p}, q^0, y) = v(\mathbf{p}, q^1, y) = \bar{v}(\alpha_1 p_1, \dots, \alpha_N P_N, y)$ and $C = E = 0$, where $\bar{h}^i(\cdot)$ and $\bar{v}(\cdot)$ are the ordinary demand functions and the indirect utility function associated with $\bar{u}(\cdot)$.

638 THE AMERICAN ECONOMIC REVIEW JUNE 1991

at some given price, π. It must be emphasized that this market is entirely hypothetical since q is actually a public good. Instead of (1), she would now solve[10]

$$(7) \quad \max_{\mathbf{x},q} u(\mathbf{x},q)$$

$$\text{subject to } \sum p_i x_i + \pi q = y.$$

Denote the resulting ordinary demand functions by $x_i = \hat{h}^i(\mathbf{p},\pi,y)$, $i = 1,\ldots,N$ and $q = \hat{h}^q(\mathbf{p},\pi,y)$. The corresponding indirect utility function is $\hat{v}(\mathbf{p},\pi,y) \equiv u[\hat{h}(\mathbf{p},\pi,y),\hat{h}^q(\mathbf{p},\pi,y)]$. The dual to (7) is: minimize $\sum p_i x_i + \pi q$ with respect to $\mathbf{x}$ and q subject to $u = u(\mathbf{x},q)$. This generates a set of compensated demand functions, $x_i = \hat{g}^i(\mathbf{p},\pi,u)$, $i = 1,\ldots,N$ and $q = \hat{g}^q(\mathbf{p},\pi,u)$, and an expenditure function, $\hat{m}(\mathbf{p},\pi,u) \equiv \sum p_i \hat{g}^i(\mathbf{p},\pi,u) + \pi \hat{g}^q(\mathbf{p},\pi,u)$. These functions are hypothetical, since q is really exogenous to the individual, but they are of theoretical interest because they shed light on the relation between C and E.

For any given values of q, $\mathbf{p}$, and u, the equation

$$(8) \quad q = \hat{g}^q(\mathbf{p},\pi,u)$$

may be solved to obtain $\pi = \hat{\pi}(\mathbf{p},q,u)$, the inverse compensated demand (i.e., willingness-to-pay) function for q: $\hat{\pi}(\cdot)$ is the price that would induce the individual to purchase q units of the public good in order to attain a utility level of u, given that she could buy private goods at prices $\mathbf{p}$. Let $\pi^0 \equiv \hat{\pi}(\mathbf{p},q^0,u^0)$ and $\pi^1 \equiv \hat{\pi}(\mathbf{p},q^1,u^1)$ denote the prices that would have supported q^0 and q^1, respectively. The two expenditure functions dual to (1) and (7) are related by

$$(9) \quad m(\mathbf{p},q,u) \equiv \hat{m}[\mathbf{p},\hat{\pi}(\mathbf{p},q,u),u]$$

$$- \hat{\pi}(\mathbf{p},q,u) \cdot q.$$

This implies that[11]

$$(10) \quad m_q(\mathbf{p},q,u) = -\hat{\pi}(\mathbf{p},q,u).$$

Combining (10) with (2') and (3') yields these alternative formulas for C and E, expressed in terms of the willingness-to-pay function:

$$(2'') \quad C = \int_{q^0}^{q^1} \hat{\pi}(\mathbf{p},q,u^0)\,dq$$

$$(3'') \quad E = \int_{q^0}^{q^1} \hat{\pi}(\mathbf{p},q,u^1)\,dq.$$

It can be shown that sign $(\hat{\pi}_u) = \text{sign}(\hat{h}_y^q)$. Therefore, for given $(\mathbf{p},q)$, the graph of $\hat{\pi}(\mathbf{p},q,u^1)$ lies above (below) that of $\hat{\pi}(\mathbf{p},q,u^0)$, and $E > (<) C$, when q is a normal (inferior) good. Figure 1 shows E and C for the case in which q is normal: E corresponds to the area $q^0 \alpha \gamma q^1$, while C corresponds to the area $q^0 \beta \delta q^1$.

Using techniques pioneered by Willig (1976), Randall and Stoll (1980) establish bounds on the difference between each of C and E and the area under an inverse ordinary demand function for q. From this, they derive bounds on the difference between C and E. However, the requisite inverse ordinary demand function is obtained in a rather special manner. Given any level of q, one can ask what market price π would induce the individual to purchase that amount of public good if it were available in a market, while still allowing her to purchase the quantity of the x's that she actually did buy at market prices $\mathbf{p}$ and with income y. In conducting this thought experiment, one needs to supplement the individual's income so that she can afford q as well as the x's. Thus, for given $(\mathbf{p},q,y)$, one seeks the price π that satisfies

$$(11) \quad q = \hat{h}^q(\mathbf{p},\pi,y+\pi q).$$

---

[10]It is now necessary to assume that $u(\cdot)$ is strictly quasi-concave in both $\mathbf{x}$ and q, rather than $\mathbf{x}$ alone. See footnote 22 for an example in which this is a nontrivial restriction.

[11]Using subscripts to denote derivatives, differentiate (9) and note that $q = \hat{g}^q(\mathbf{p},\pi,u) = \hat{m}_\pi(\mathbf{p},\pi,u)$ by Shephard's lemma. Equations similar to (9)–(12) are presented by J. P. Neary and K. W. S. Roberts (1980).

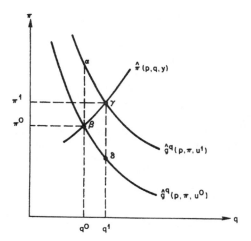

FIGURE 1. WTP AND WTA FOR A CHANGE IN q

The solution will be denoted by $\pi = \hat{\pi}(\mathbf{p}, q, y)$. This inverse function is related to the inverse compensated demand function by the identities[12]

(12a) $\hat{\pi}(\mathbf{p}, q, y)$

$\equiv \hat{\pi}[\mathbf{p}, q, v(\mathbf{p}, q, y)]$

(12b) $\hat{\pi}(\mathbf{p}, q, u)$

$\equiv \hat{\pi}[\mathbf{p}, q, m(\mathbf{p}, q, u)]$.

Both identities play a role in the analysis. From (12a) it follows that $\pi^0 \equiv \hat{\pi}(\mathbf{p}, q^0, u^0) \equiv \hat{\pi}(\mathbf{p}, q^0, y)$ and $\pi^1 \equiv \hat{\pi}(\mathbf{p}, q^1, u^1) = \hat{\pi}(\mathbf{p}, q^1, y)$. Hence, the graph of $\hat{\pi}(\mathbf{p}, q, y)$ as a function of q intersects the graph of $\hat{\pi}(\mathbf{p}, q, u^0)$ at $q = q^0$, and the graph of $\hat{\pi}(\mathbf{p}, q, u^1)$ at $q = q^1$. This is depicted in

Figure 1.[13] From (12b) and (10), one obtains

(13) $m_q(\mathbf{p}, q, u)$

$= -\hat{\pi}[\mathbf{p}, q, m(\mathbf{p}, q, u)]$

which is the fundamental differential equation underlying Randall and Stoll's analysis.[14] Also, by differentiating (12b) and then using (13), it can be shown that the concavity of $\hat{m}(\mathbf{p}, \pi, u)$ in π, which itself follows from the quasi-concavity of $u(\mathbf{x}, q)$ in q, implies the following negativity condition on the Slutsky term associated with $\hat{\pi}(\mathbf{p}, q, y)$: $\hat{\pi}_q - \pi \hat{\pi}_y \leq 0$.[15]

Define the quantity

(14) $A \equiv \int_{q^0}^{q^1} \hat{\pi}(\mathbf{p}, q, y) \, dq$

which corresponds to the area $q^0 \beta \gamma \delta q^1$ in Figure 1. This is a sort of Marshallian consumer's surplus, which is to be compared with C and E.[16] Let

$$\xi \equiv \frac{\partial \ln \hat{\pi}(\mathbf{p}, q, y)}{\partial \ln y}$$

be the income elasticity of $\hat{\pi}(\mathbf{p}, q, y)$; Randall and Stoll call this the "price flexibility of income." Assume that, over the range from $(\mathbf{p}, q^0, y)$ to $(\mathbf{p}, q^1, y)$, this elasticity is bounded from below by ξ^L and from above by ξ^U, with neither bound equal to 1. Using

---

[12] Note that $\hat{\pi}(\mathbf{p}, q, y)$ is *not* an inverse ordinary demand function in the sense of Ronald W. Anderson (1980), because it involves an income adjustment as well as a price effect.

[13] It is commonly supposed the $\hat{\pi}_q < 0$, so that $\pi^0 > \pi^1$ when $q^0 < q^1$ (see e.g., Richard E. Just et al., 1982 fig. 7.12), but this is not correct. It can be shown that $\pi^0 \gtrless \pi^1$ according to whether $\eta \lessgtr 1/\alpha$, where η and α are defined in the text below equation (16'). Since $\Sigma \alpha_i \eta_i + \alpha \eta = 1$ by the Engel aggregation condition, where $\alpha_i \equiv p_i \hat{h}^i(\mathbf{p}, \pi, y + \pi q)/(y + \pi q)$ and $\eta_i \equiv (y + \pi q) \hat{h}_y^i(\mathbf{p}, \pi, y + \pi q)/\hat{h}^i(\mathbf{p}, \pi, y + \pi q)$, it follows that $\pi^0 \lessgtr \pi^1$ if and only if $\Sigma \alpha_i \eta_i \lessgtr 0$.

[14] This corresponds to Randall and Stoll's equation 7.

[15] Also, because $\hat{m}(\cdot)$ is linearly homogeneous in $(\mathbf{p}, \pi)$, it follows that $\hat{\pi}(\mathbf{p}, q, y)$ is linearly homogeneous in $(\mathbf{p}, y)$.

[16] Its relation to the conventional Marshallian consumer's surplus associated with the demand for the x's is analyzed in Proposition 4.

the mean-value theorem, as in Willig's (1976) equation 18, and integrating (13) yields Randall and Stoll's result, namely, the following.

PROPOSITION 3: *Assume* $\xi^L \leq \xi \leq \xi^U$ *where* $\xi^L \neq 1$ *and* $\xi^U \neq 1$. *Then,*

(i) $\quad 0 \leq \left[1 + (1 - \xi^L) \dfrac{A}{y}\right]^{\frac{1}{1-\xi^L}} - 1 \leq \dfrac{E}{y}$

(ii) $\quad 0 \leq 1 - \left[1 - (1 - \xi^U) \dfrac{A}{y}\right]^{\frac{1}{1-\xi^U}} \leq \dfrac{C}{y} \leq 1.$

If $\xi^U < 1$, *or if* $\xi^U > 1$ *and* $1 + (1 - \xi^U) \dfrac{A}{y} > 0$,

(iii) $\quad \dfrac{E}{y} \leq \left[1 + (1 - \xi^U) \dfrac{A}{y}\right]^{\frac{1}{1-\xi^U}} - 1.$

If $\xi^L > 1$, *or if* $\xi^L \leq 1$ *and* $1 - (1 - \xi^L) \dfrac{A}{y} \geq 0$,

(iv) $\quad \dfrac{C}{y} \leq 1 - \left[1 - (1 - \xi^L) \dfrac{A}{y}\right]^{\frac{1}{1-\xi^L}}.$

Applying a Taylor approximation, as in Willig (1976), and assuming that the conditions in (iii) and (iv) are satisfied, one obtains

(15) $\quad \xi^L \dfrac{A^2}{2y} \leq E - C \leq \xi^U \dfrac{A^2}{2y}.$

This is commonly interpreted as implying that C and E are likely to be close in value, but whether or not that is correct clearly depends on the magnitudes of A/y and the bounds ξ^L and ξ^U. The magnitude of A/y depends in part on the size of the change from q^0 to q^1; but what can be said about the likely magnitude of the income elasticity, ξ? Could it happen, for example, that $\xi^L = \infty$? To answer that question, dif-

ferentiate (11) implicitly:

(16) $\quad \dfrac{\partial \hat{\pi}(\mathbf{p}, q, y)}{\partial y}$

$$= - \frac{\hat{h}_y^q(\mathbf{p}, \pi, y + \pi q)}{\hat{h}_\pi^q(\mathbf{p}, \pi, y + \pi q) + q\hat{h}_y^q(\mathbf{p}, \pi, y + \pi q)}.$$

By the Hicks-Slutsky decomposition, the denominator is equal to the own-price derivative of the compensated demand function for q and is nonpositive:

$$\hat{g}_\pi^q[\mathbf{p}, \pi, v(\mathbf{p}, q, y)]$$

$$= \hat{h}_\pi^q(\mathbf{p}, \pi, y + \pi q) + q\hat{h}_y^q(\mathbf{p}, \pi, y + \pi q)$$

$$\leq 0.$$

Converted to elasticity form, (16) becomes

(16′) $\quad \xi = - \dfrac{\eta(1 - \alpha)}{\varepsilon}$

where

$$\eta \equiv \frac{(y + \pi q)\hat{h}_y^q(\mathbf{p}, \pi, y + \pi q)}{\hat{h}^q(\mathbf{p}, \pi, y + \pi q)}$$

is the income elasticity of the *direct* ordinary demand function for q,

$$\alpha \equiv \frac{\pi \hat{h}^q(\mathbf{p}, \pi, y + \pi q)}{y + \pi q}$$

is the budget share of q in relation to "adjusted" income, and

$$\varepsilon \equiv \frac{\pi \hat{g}_\pi^q[\mathbf{p}, \pi, v(\mathbf{p}, q, y)]}{\hat{g}^q[\mathbf{p}, \pi, v(\mathbf{p}, q, y)]}$$

is the own-price elasticity of the compensated demand function for q.

The denominator in (16′) can be related to the overall elasticity of substitution between q and the private market goods $x_1, \ldots, x_N$. Assume that the prices $p_1, \ldots, p_N$ vary in strict proportion (i.e., $p_i = \theta \bar{p}_i$ for some fixed vector $\bar{p}$ and some positive scalar θ). Let the aggregate Allen-Uzawa elasticity of substitution between q and the Hicksian composite commodity $x_0 \equiv \Sigma \bar{p}_i x_i$ be denoted by σ_0. By adapting W. E. Diewert's (1974) analysis, the following formula can be established relating σ_0 to the compensated own-price elasticity for q: $\varepsilon = -\sigma_0(1-\alpha)$.[17] Hence, (16') may be written

$$(17) \qquad \xi = \frac{\eta}{\sigma_0}.$$

This equation is my fundamental result. It explains the findings in the preceding section about the importance of substitution elasticities. It demonstrates that for changes in q, unlike for changes in p, the extent of the difference between C and E depends not only on income effects (i.e., η) but also on substitution effects (i.e., σ_0). If, over the relevant range, either $\eta = 0$ (no income effects) or $\sigma_0 = \infty$ (perfect substitution between q and one or more of the x's), then $\xi^L = \xi^U = 0$ and, from Proposition 3, $C = A = E$. On the other hand, if either the demand function for q is highly income elastic or there are very few substitutes for q among the x's so that σ_0 is close to zero, this could generate very large values of ξ and a substantial divergence between C and E.

---

[17]In deriving this result, one evaluates $\hat{m}(\mathbf{p}, \pi, u)$, $\hat{g}^q(\mathbf{p}, \pi, u)$, and $\hat{g}(\mathbf{p}, \pi, u)$ at $u = v(\mathbf{p}, q, y)$. Hence, the budget shares introduced above satisfy $\alpha \equiv \pi \hat{h}^q(\mathbf{p}, \pi, y + \pi q)/(y + \pi q) = \pi \hat{g}^q(\mathbf{p}, \pi, u)/\hat{m}(\mathbf{p}, \pi, u)$, and $\alpha_j \equiv p_j \hat{h}^j(\mathbf{p}, \pi, y + \pi q)/(y + \pi q) = p_j \hat{g}^j(\mathbf{p}, \pi, u)/\hat{m}(\mathbf{p}, \pi, u)$. In addition to the compensated own-price demand elasticity, ε, I introduce the compensated cross-price demand elasticities $\varepsilon_j \equiv \partial \ln \hat{g}^q(\mathbf{p}, \pi, u)/\partial p_j$. The homogeneity of $\hat{g}^q(\cdot)$ in $(\mathbf{p}, \pi)$ implies that $\varepsilon + \Sigma \varepsilon_j = 0$. Under the assumption that $p_j = \theta \bar{p}_j$, $j = 1, \ldots, N$, the Allen-Uzawa elasticity of substitution between q and the composite good x_0 is given by $\sigma_0 \equiv [(\partial \hat{g}^q/\partial \theta) \cdot \theta/q]/\alpha_0$ where $\alpha_0 \equiv \Sigma \alpha_j = 1 - \alpha$ is the expenditure share of x_0 and θ is treated as its price. Observe that $\partial \hat{g}^q/\partial \theta = \Sigma(\partial \hat{g}^q/\partial p_j) \cdot \bar{p}_j = \Sigma(\partial \hat{g}^q/\partial p_j) \cdot (p_j/\theta) = (q/\theta)\Sigma \varepsilon_j = -(q/\theta)\varepsilon$. Hence, $\sigma_0(1-\alpha) = (\theta/q)(\partial \hat{g}^q/\partial \theta) = -\varepsilon$.

III. Applications

In the first application of (17), the price flexibility of income, ξ, is assumed to be a constant. In that case, as Randall and Stoll note, the bounds in Proposition 3 hold as equalities, and (for simplicity I focus on the case where $\xi \neq 1$):

$$(18a) \qquad \frac{C}{y} = 1 - \left[1 - (1-\xi)\frac{A}{y} \right]^{\frac{1}{1-\xi}}$$

$$(18b) \qquad \frac{E}{y} = \left[1 + (1-\xi)\frac{A}{y} \right]^{\frac{1}{1-\xi}} - 1.$$

However, before these formulas can be used to calculate C and E, one must determine how A varies with ξ.

If the price flexibility of income is to be constant, the inverse ordinary demand function must take the form

$$(18c) \qquad \hat{\pi}(\mathbf{p}, q, y) = \psi(\mathbf{p}, q) y^{\xi}$$

where $\psi \geq 0$. Define $G(\mathbf{p}, q) \equiv \int \psi(\mathbf{p}, q) \, dq$; from (14):[18]

$$(18d) \qquad A = y^{\xi} [G(\mathbf{p}, q^1) - G(\mathbf{p}, q^0)].$$

Substituting (18c) into (13) and integrating yields the indirect utility function that generates (18c):

$$(18e) \qquad v(\mathbf{p}, q, y)$$

$$= T\left(\left[y^{1-\xi} + (1-\xi)G(\mathbf{p}, q) \right]^{\frac{1}{1-\xi}}, \mathbf{p} \right)$$

where $T(\cdot)$ is some function that is homogeneous of degree zero, increasing in its first argument, and nonincreasing in its other arguments.

---

[18]In order to satisfy the negativity and homogeneity conditions, $\psi(\cdot)$ should be increasing in q and homogeneous of degree $1-\xi$ in $\mathbf{p}$. It follows that $G(\cdot)$, too, is homogeneous of degree $1-\xi$ in $\mathbf{p}$.

The corresponding demand function for q, $\hat{h}^q(\mathbf{p}, \pi, y)$ can be derived from (18e) by solving $\max_q[v(\mathbf{p}, q, y - \pi q)]$. In general, a closed-form solution cannot be obtained. However, implicit differentiation of the first-order condition for this maximization yields the following expression for the income elasticity of demand:

$$\eta = \frac{\xi\psi + \xi\psi^2 q y^{\xi-1}}{-q\psi_q + \xi\psi^2 q y^{\xi-1}}.$$

It follows that having a constant ξ is generally *not* consistent with having a constant η or a constant σ_0. An exception occurs when

$$(19a) \qquad \xi\psi \equiv -q\psi_q$$

in which case $\eta \equiv 1$ and, from (17), $\sigma_0 \equiv 1/\xi$ (i.e., the price flexibility of income is merely the reciprocal of the elasticity of substitution between q and the x's). Integrating (19a) yields $\psi(\mathbf{p}, q) = K(\mathbf{p})q^{-\xi}$ for some function $K(\mathbf{p}) \geq 0$ which is homogeneous of degree $1 - \xi$, and $G(\mathbf{p}, q) = K(\mathbf{p})q^{1-\xi}/(1 - \xi)$. Hence,

$$(19b) \quad A/y$$
$$= K(\mathbf{p})y^{\xi-1}\Big[(q^1)^{1-\xi} - (q^0)^{1-\xi}\Big]\Big/(1-\xi)$$

and the formulas for C and E become

$$(19c) \quad C/y$$
$$= 1 - \left\{1 - K(\mathbf{p})y^{\xi-1}\Big[(q^1)^{1-\xi} - (q^0)^{1-\xi}\Big]\right\}^{\frac{1}{1-\xi}}$$

$$(19d) \quad E/y$$
$$= \left\{1 + K(\mathbf{p})y^{\xi-1}\Big[(q^1)^{1-\xi} - (q^0)^{1-\xi}\Big]\right\}^{\frac{1}{1-\xi}} - 1.$$

This model with a unitary income elasticity, η, is the only case in which ξ, η, and σ_0 can all be constant simultaneously. It can be shown to be a generalization of the CES utility model $u(\mathbf{x}, q) =$

$[\phi(\mathbf{x})^{1-\xi} + aq^{1-\xi}]^{1/1-\xi}$ with homogeneous aggregator function, $\phi(\cdot)$.[19]

Equation (19b) makes explicit the dependence of A on ξ. From (19c) and (19d), it follows that the ratio E/C is increasing in both $K(\mathbf{p})$ and ξ. Table 1 tabulates this ratio for several values of K and ξ, for cases where $q^0 = 1$ and $q^1 = 3$. Observe that a low elasticity of substitution ($\sigma_0 \approx 0.07$) can generate a fivefold difference between C and E, even when A/y is very small.[20] A similar divergence between C and E can be obtained with a relatively moderate elasticity of substitution ($\sigma_0 = 0.99$), provided that the change matters a lot, in the sense that C/y is large ($C/y \approx 0.8$). However, C is almost identical to E when moderate or large elasticities of substitution are combined with low values of C/y.

The second application is the case in which the inverse demand function takes the form

$$(20a) \quad \hat{\pi}(\mathbf{p}, q, y) = \psi(\mathbf{p}, q)e^{\gamma(\mathbf{p})y}$$

and the price flexibility of income is $\xi = \gamma(\mathbf{p}) \cdot y$, for some $\gamma(\cdot) \geq 0$ which is homogeneous of degree -1 in $\mathbf{p}$, and some $\psi(\cdot) \geq 0$ which is homogeneous of degree 1 in $\mathbf{p}$. Substituting (20a) into (13) and integrating yields the indirect utility function that generates (20a):

$$(20b) \quad v(\mathbf{p}, q, y)$$
$$= T\left(-\frac{e^{-\gamma(\mathbf{p})y}}{\gamma(\mathbf{p})} + G(\mathbf{p}, q), \mathbf{p}\right)$$

---

[19] The difference is that the CES model generates an indirect utility function of the form

$$\tilde{v}(\mathbf{p}, q, y) \equiv \big[y^{1-\xi} + K(\mathbf{p})q^{1-\xi}\big]^{1/1-\xi}$$

whereas the indirect utility function associated with (19a)–(19c) is

$$v(\mathbf{p}, q, y) = T[\tilde{v}(\mathbf{p}, q, y), \mathbf{p}].$$

[20] This is the order of magnitude by which WTA exceeds WTP in some of the empirical studies summarized in table 3.2 of Cummings et al. (1986).

Table 1—Simulations of WTP and WTA for a Generalized
CES Utility Model

ξ	y	$K(\mathbf{p})$	σ_0	A/y	C/y	E/y	E/C
14	1	0.95	0.0714	0.073	0.05	0.259	5.175
1.01	100	1.4	0.99	1.602	0.796	4.026	5.059
0.677	100	8.1	1.481	2.414	0.991	4.975	5.003
0.677	100	0.1	1.481	0.03	0.029	0.03	1.02

where $G \equiv \int \psi(\mathbf{p}, q)\, dq$, and T is some function that is homogeneous of degree zero, increasing in its first argument, and nonincreasing in the other arguments. The corresponding formula for the elasticity of substitution between q and the x's, expressed as a function of $(\mathbf{p}, q, y)$, can be shown to be

$$(20c) \qquad \sigma_0 = \frac{\psi y + q\psi^2 e^{\gamma y}}{-qy\psi_q + \gamma yq\psi^2 e^{\gamma y}}.$$

From (20a) and (20b) it follows that

$$(20d) \quad A = e^{\gamma(\mathbf{p})y}\left[G(\mathbf{p}, q^1) - G(\mathbf{p}, q^0)\right]$$

$$(20e) \quad C = \gamma(\mathbf{p})^{-1} \cdot \ln\left[1 + \gamma(\mathbf{p})A\right]$$

$$(20f) \quad E = -\gamma(\mathbf{p})^{-1} \cdot \ln\left[1 - \gamma(\mathbf{p})A\right].$$

(note that, when $\gamma A > 1$, $E = \infty$). The ratio E/C is clearly increasing in $\gamma(\mathbf{p})$ and A.

In order to proceed further, it is necessary to take a closer look at A. For this purpose, I focus on the special case of (20) in which $\gamma(\mathbf{p}) = \gamma/p_N$, $\psi(\mathbf{p}, q) = \delta e^{\alpha + \delta q} p_1^{1-\beta} p_N^\beta/(\beta-1)$, and

$$(21a) \quad v(\mathbf{p}, q, y) =$$

$$T\left(-\frac{p_N}{\gamma}e^{-\gamma y/p_N} + \frac{e^{\alpha+\delta q}}{\beta-1}p_1^{1-\beta}p_N^\beta, p_2, p_3, \ldots, p_N\right)$$

with γ and δ as positive constants and with $\beta > 1$. This implies the following log-log demand function for good 1:[21]

$$(21b) \quad \ln x_1 = \ln h^1(\mathbf{p}, q, y)$$
$$= \alpha - \beta \ln(p_1/p_N)$$
$$+ (\gamma y/p_N) + \delta q.$$

Since $\lim_{p_1 \to \infty} \partial v(\mathbf{p}, q, y)/\partial q = 0$, good 1 is weakly complementary with q in the sense of Mäler, and C and E can be expressed in terms of the area between the compensated demand curves $g^1(\mathbf{p}, q^0, u)$ and $g^1(\mathbf{p}, q^1, u)$. Furthermore, in this model the quantity A corresponds to the change in the Marshallian consumer's surplus associated with good 1.

$$(21c) \quad A \equiv \int_{q^0}^{q^1} \hat{\pi}(\mathbf{p}, q, y)\, dq$$

$$= \left(\frac{p_1}{\beta-1}\right)\left[h^1(\mathbf{p}, q^1, y) - h^1(\mathbf{p}, q^0, y)\right]$$

$$= \int_{p_1}^{\infty}\left[h^1(\mathbf{p}, q^1, y) - h^1(\mathbf{p}, q^0, y)\right]dp_1.$$

Hence, the formulas for C and E become

$$(21d) \quad \frac{C}{p_N} = \frac{1}{\gamma}\ln\left\{1 + \left(\frac{\gamma}{\beta-1}\right)\left(\frac{p_1}{p_N}\right)\right.$$
$$\left. \times\left[h^1(\mathbf{p}, q^1, y) - h^1(\mathbf{p}, q^0, y)\right]\right\}$$

$$(21e) \quad \frac{E}{p_N} = \frac{1}{\gamma}\ln\left\{1 - \left(\frac{\gamma}{\beta-1}\right)\left(\frac{p_1}{p_N}\right)\right.$$
$$\left. \times\left[h^1(\mathbf{p}, q^1, y) - h^1(\mathbf{p}, q^0, y)\right]\right\}.$$

[21] It follows that, in this model, the income elasticity of demand for good 1 is equal to γy, the price flexibility of income.

TABLE 2—SIMULATIONS OF WTP AND WTA FOR A LOG-LOG UTILITY MODEL

ξ	α	δ	γ	A/y	C/y	E/y	E/C
14	−13.58	0.2	0.14	0.0695	0.0486	0.259	5.334
1.01	1.42	0.3	0.0101	0.959	0.6704	3.414	5.092
0.677	2.151	0.3	0.00677	1.427	0.9987	5.004	5.011
0.677	2.28	0.13	0.00677	0.039	0.0385	0.0396	1.027

These are tabulated in Table 2 for several values of α, γ, and δ for the case in which $p_N = 1$, $p_1 = 1.5$, $\beta = 1.125$, $y = 100$, $q^0 = 1$, and $q^1 = 3$.[22] The simulations confirm that $\xi = \gamma y$ and A are the key determinants of the ratio E/C. When either ξ or A is large, then $E \gg C$; when ξ and A are both small, then $E \approx C$.

This example is a striking illustration of the power of Proposition 3. From mere inspection of the ordinary demand function for x_1 in (21b) it is hardly obvious that the term $\xi = \gamma y$ should be a key determinant of the relationship between WTP and WTA for a change in q.[23] The example also raises another issue: the possibility that the quantity A, which forms the basis for Proposition 3, may be related to the conventional Marshallian consumer's surplus associated with a private market commodity, x_1. Under what circumstances does this carry over to other utility models? Could it, in fact, apply to the

first example based on a generalization of the CES utility model?

By way of answer to the first question, the following lemma establishes that weak complementarity is but one of two conditions that must be satisfied if A is to be equated with a change in the Marshallian consumer's surplus:

LEMMA 1: *Suppose there is a private market good, say* x_1, *with the properties that* (a) *it is nonessential and weakly complementary with* q, *and* (b)

$$\frac{\partial \hat{\pi}(\mathbf{p}, q, y)}{\partial p_1} = -\frac{\partial h^1(\mathbf{p}, q, y)}{\partial q}.$$

Then,

$$(22) \quad A = \int_{p_1}^{\infty} [h^1(\mathbf{p}, q^1, y) - h^1(\mathbf{p}, q^0, y)] \, dp_1.$$

PROOF:

Weak complementarity implies $\lim_{p_1 \to \infty} m_q(\mathbf{p}, q, u) = 0$. Nonessentiality implies $\lim_{p_1 \to \infty} m(\mathbf{p}, q, u) < \infty$. Hence, by (13), condition (a) implies $\lim_{p_1 \to \infty} \hat{\pi}(\mathbf{p}, q, y) = 0$. Accordingly, one can express $\hat{\pi}(\cdot)$ as

$$\hat{\pi}(\mathbf{p}, q, y) = -\int_{p_1}^{\infty} \frac{\partial \pi(\mathbf{p}, q, y)}{\partial p_1} \, dp_1$$

$$= \int_{p_1}^{\infty} \frac{\partial h^1(\mathbf{p}, q, y)}{\partial q} \, dp_1$$

where the second equality follows from condition (b). Invoking the definition of A in (14) and changing the order of integration yields (22).

---

[22] The parameter values in these simulations are chosen to satisfy the inequalities $(\beta - 1)p_N \leq \gamma p_1 h^1(\mathbf{p}, q, y) \leq \beta p_N$, which ensure that the direct utility function implied by (21) is quasi-concave in $\mathbf{x}$ and q. If $u(\mathbf{x}, q)$ were not quasi-concave in q, the formulas in (21d) and (21e), would still be valid, but the Randall-Stoll bounds in Proposition 3 would not apply. That happens with another special case of (20) in which $\gamma(\mathbf{p}) = \gamma/p_N$ but $\psi(\mathbf{p}, q) = \delta p_N e^{\alpha - \beta(p_1/p_N) + \delta q}/\beta$. This generates an ordinary demand function for good 1 that is identical to (21b), except that $\ln(p_1/p_N)$ is replaced by (p_1/p_N). Also, (21c)–(21e) hold for this model, except that $\beta - 1$ is replaced by β. However, the implicit utility function $u(\mathbf{x}, q)$ can be shown to be quasi-convex *in* q.

[23] Also, it is hardly obvious that from the demand function in (21b) one can recover σ_0, the elasticity of substitution between q and the x's (*all* the x's, not just x_1). This is obtained by substituting $\gamma(\mathbf{p}) \equiv \gamma/p_N$ and $\psi(\mathbf{p}, q) \equiv \delta e^{\alpha + \delta q} p_1^{1-\beta} p_N^{\beta}/(\beta - 1)$ into (20c). The corresponding formula for η can be obtained from $\eta = \sigma_0 \xi = \sigma_0 \gamma y / p_N$.

Application of Lemma 1 yields the answer to the second question:

PROPOSITION 4: *Partition the price vector as* $\mathbf{p} = (p_1, \mathbf{p}_{(1)})$. *Equation (22) holds if and only if* $v(\mathbf{p}, q, y)$ *can be expressed in the form*

$$(23) \quad v(\mathbf{p}, q, y) = T\left[G(\mathbf{p}, q), \mathbf{p}_{(1)} y\right]$$

where $\lim_{p \to \infty} G_q(\mathbf{p}, q) = \lim_{p_1 \to \infty} G_{p_1}(\mathbf{p}, q) = 0$.

PROOF:

Observe that the conditions on the derivatives of $G(\cdot)$ ensure that x_1 is nonessential and weakly complementary with q. The main task is to show that the functional structure in (23) is necessary and sufficient to satisfy condition (b) of Lemma 1. First use (10) and (12a), and then twice differentiate the implicit function $v(\mathbf{p}, q, y) - u = 0$ to obtain

$$\frac{\partial \hat{\pi}(\mathbf{p}, q, y)}{\partial p_1}$$

$$= -m_{qp_1}[\mathbf{p}, q, v(\mathbf{p}, q, y)]$$

$$\quad - m_{qu}[\mathbf{p}, q, v(\mathbf{p}, q, y)] \cdot v_{p_1}(\mathbf{p}, q, y)$$

$$= -(v_q v_{yp_1} - v_y v_{qp_1}) / v_y^2.$$

Comparing this with $\partial h^1(\mathbf{p}, q, y)/\partial q = (v_{p_1} v_{qy} - v_y v_{qp_1})^2 / v_y^2$, it can be seen that condition (b) will be satisfied if and only if $v_q v_{yp_1} = v_{p_1} v_{qy}$. However, this is equivalent to requiring that (v_q / v_{p_1}) be independent of y, which in turn is equivalent to (23).

The log-log utility model in (21a) clearly satisfies the conditions of Proposition 4. The generalized CES utility model in (18) could also meet the conditions of the proposition, provided that p_1 appears only in the first argument of $T(\cdot)$.

Equation (23) expresses a restriction on the marginal rate of substitution between q and the price of a weakly complementary private-market good, p_1 (i.e., that it be independent of income). This condition was first introduced by Willig (1978) in his paper

on hedonic price adjustments for valuing marginal changes in q: his theorem 1 characterized the circumstances under which the marginal value of q equals the derivative with respect to q of the Marshallian consumer's surplus for x_1, averaged over the number of units of the good consumed. Proposition 4 expresses a similar result using a different and more compact proof. Combining Propositions 3 and 4 provides a way to value *nonmarginal* changes in q by employing the change in Marshallian consumer's surplus to compute A and then using A to bound WTP or WTA. These two propositions, in effect, establish a new link between Willig's two seminal papers.[24]

IV. Conclusion

A recent assessment of the state of the art of public-good valuation concludes "Received theory establishes that ... WTP ... should approximately equal ... WTA.... In contrast with theoretical axioms which predict small differences between WTP and WTA, results from contingent valuation method applications wherein such measures are derived almost always demonstrate large differences between average WTP and WTA. To date, researchers have been unable to explain in any definitive way the persistently observed differences between WTP and WTA measures" (Cummings et al., 1986 p. 41.)[25] This paper

---

[24] I am very grateful to a referee for pointing out the connection with Willig's theorem 1. In my notation, Willig's theorem states that (23) is equivalent to the equality $v_q(\mathbf{p}, q, y)/v_{p_1}(\mathbf{p}, q, y) = \hat{\pi}(\mathbf{p}, q, y)/h^1(\mathbf{p}, q, y)$.

[25] Some of the debates on divergences between WTP and WTA have focused on the concept of loss-aversion, introduced in the economics literature by Daniel Kahneman and Amos Tversky (1979). This is a different phenomenon from that involved in the Randall-Stoll bounds: it concerns the disparity between the WTP to obtain a change from q^0 to $q^0 + \Delta$ (for some $\Delta > 0$) and the WTP to avoid a change from q^0 to $q^0 - \Delta$, which is not the same as the disparity between WTP and WTA for the same change from q^0 to $q^1 = q^0 + \Delta$. However, the loss/gain disparity can be analyzed using the tools developed in this paper. In a separate paper, I have identified the conditions under which it will *exceed* the disparity between WTP and WTA studied here.

offers an explanation by showing that the theoretical presumption of approximate equality between WTP and WTA is misconceived. This is because, for public goods, the relation between the two welfare measures depends on a substitution effect as well as an income effect. Given that the substitution elasticity appears in the denominator of (17) and that the Engel aggregation condition places some limit on the plausible magnitude of the income elasticity in the numerator, this suggests that the substitution effects could exert a far greater leverage on the relation between WTP and WTA than the income effects. Thus, large empirical divergences between WTP and WTA may be indicative not of some failure in the survey methodology but of a general perception on the part of the individuals surveyed that the private-market goods available in their choice set are, collectively, a rather imperfect substitute for the public good under consideration.

REFERENCES

Anderson, Ronald W., "Some Theory of Inverse Demand for Applied Demand Analysis," *European Economic Review*, November 1980, *14*, 281–90.

Coursey, Don L., Hovis, John J. and Schulze, William D., "The Disparity Between Willingness to Accept and Willingness to Pay Measures of Value," *Quarterly Journal of Economics*, August 1987, *102*, 679–90.

Cummings, Ronald G., Brookshire, David S. and Schulze, William D., *Valuing Public Goods: An Assessment of the Contingent Valuation Method*, Totowa, NJ: Rowman and Allanheld, 1986.

Diewert, W. E., "A Note on Aggregation and Elasticities of Substitution," *Canadian Journal of Economics*, February 1974, *7*, 12–20.

Fisher, Ann, McClelland, Gary H. and Schulze, William D., "Measures of Willingness to Pay versus Willingness to Accept: Evidence, Explanations and Potential Reconciliation," in George L. Peterson, B. L. Driver, and Robin Gregory, eds., *Amenity*

Resource Valuation: Integrating Economics with Other Disciplines, State College, PA: Venture, 1988, pp. 127–34.

Freeman, A. Myrick, *The Benefits of Environmental Improvement: Theory and Practice*, Baltimore: Johns Hopkins University Press, 1979.

Gorman, W. M., "Tricks With Utility Functions," in M. Artis and R. Nobay, eds., *Essays in Economic Analysis*, New York: Cambridge University Press, 1976, pp. 211–43.

Gregory, Robin, "Interpreting Measures of Economic Loss: Evidence from Contingent Valuation and Experimental Studies," *Journal of Environmental Economics and Management*, December 1986, *13*, 325–37.

Hanemann, W. Michael, "Quality and Demand Analysis," in Gordon C. Rausser, ed., *New Directions in Econometric Modeling and Forecasting in U. S. Agriculture*, Amsterdam: North Holland, 1982, pp. 55–98.

Just, Richard E., Hueth, Darrell L. and Schmitz, Andrew, *Applied Welfare Economics and Public Policy*, Englewood Cliffs, NJ: Prentice-Hall, 1982.

Kahneman, Daniel and Tversky, Amos, "Prospect Theory: An Analysis of Decisions Under Risk," *Econometrica*, March 1979, *47*, 263–91.

Knetsch, Jack L. and Sinden, J. A., "Willingness to Pay and Compensation Demanded: Experimental Disparity in Measures of Value," *Quarterly Journal of Economics*, August 1984, *99*, 507–21.

Mäler, Karl-Göran, *Environmental Economics: A Theoretical Inquiry*, Baltimore: Johns Hopkins University Press, 1974.

Neary, J. P. and Roberts, K. W. S., "Theory of Household Behavior Under Rationing," *European Economic Review*, January 1980, *13*, 25–42.

Peterson, George L., Driver, B. L. and Gregory, Robin, eds., *Amenity Resource Valuation: Integrating Economics with Other Disciplines*, State College, PA: Venture, 1988.

Randall, Alan and Stoll, John R., "Consumer's Surplus in Commodity Space," *American Economic Review*, June 1980, *71*, 449–57.

Thayer, Mark A., "Contingent Valuation Techniques for Assessing Environmental Impacts: Further Evidence," *Journal of Environmental Economics and Management*, March 1981, *8*, 27–44.

Willig, Robert, "Consumer's Surplus Without Apology," *American Economic Review*, September 1976, *66*, 589–97.

_____, "Incremental Consumer's Surplus and Hedonic Price Adjustment," *Journal of Economic Theory*, April 1978, *17*, 227–53.

[20]

Journal of Environmental Economics and Management **44**, 426–447 (2002)
doi:10.1006/jeem.2001.1215

A Review of WTA / WTP Studies

John K. Horowitz and Kenneth E. McConnell

*Department of Agricultural and Resource Economics, University of Maryland,
College Park, Maryland 20742-5535*
E-mail: horowitz@arec.umd.edu

Received February 23, 2000; revised November 1, 2000; published online January 31, 2002

Willingness to accept (WTA) is usually substantially higher than willingness to pay (WTP).
These constructs have been studied for roughly 30 years and with a wide variety of goods.
This paper reviews those studies. We find that the less the good is like an "ordinary market
good," the higher is the ratio. The ratio is highest for non-market goods, next highest for
ordinary private goods, and lowest for experiments involving forms of money. A generalization of this pattern holds even when we account for differences in survey design: ordinary
goods have lower ratios than non-ordinary ones. We also find that ratios in real experiments
are not significantly different from hypothetical experiments and that incentive-compatible
elicitation yields higher ratios. © 2002 Elsevier Science (USA)

1. INTRODUCTION

The difference between willingness to pay (WTP) and willingness to accept
(WTA) has been widely studied through both theory (Hanemann [33, 34], Randall
and Stoll [66], Willig [82]) and experiments. In a typical experiment, a subject is
given some item, like a coffee mug, and offered money to return it to the
experimenter. The dollar amount the subject asks for is his WTA. Another subject
is not given a mug and instead is asked to pay for one. The amount he offers is his
WTP. Previous authors have shown that WTA is usually substantially larger than
WTP, and almost all have remarked that the WTA/WTP ratio is much higher than
their economic intuition would predict (e.g., Kahneman *et al.* [45], hereafter KKT.)

The pervasiveness of high WTA/WTP ratios and the wide variety of goods that
have been used in the experiments have combined to sustain interest in WTA vs.
WTP for roughly 30 years. We analyze those studies here. Although large
WTA/WTP ratios are well documented, the findings do not seem to have had
much of an effect on either economic models or discussions of policy design, as
Knetsch [46] has noted. A wider role for these findings has been hampered, we
believe, by two issues.

First, it has seemed possible that the high observed ratios are due to "weak"
experimental features such as hypothetical payments, student subjects, or elicitation questions that are not incentive-compatible. According to this argument, more
realistic experiments, such as those with real money or incentive-compatible
elicitation, will yield lower and more reasonable ratios. Likewise, we might suspect
that repeating a given experiment with the same group of participants would cause
the ratios to fall to closer-to-expected levels over time, as Coursey *et al.* [20] found
in some of their experiments. These possibilities have not been investigated on a

426

broad-based scale. A finding that design features were playing a major role would almost surely make the literature's WTA/WTP findings of less concern despite their preponderance.

The second issue that has blocked a wider role for the WTA/WTP findings is an absence of a rich set of behavioral patterns that any behavioral model might be expected to cover or explain. For which goods is a high ratio most likely to be found? A few studies have claimed that the ratio is smaller for goods that have close substitutes (Harless [36], Shogren *et al.* [71], hereafter SSHK), but the evidence about this, or other possible trends, has remained diffuse. In addition to providing a guide for future model-building, these patterns should make it easier to understand how the ratio might manifest itself in real-world economic behavior.

This paper uses a collection of WTA/WTP studies to address these issues. We found 45 studies that reported usable data. The studies draw on a remarkable range of goods: chocolates, pens, mugs, movie tickets, hunting licenses, visibility, nuclear waste repositories, nasty-tasting liquids, pathogen-contaminated sandwiches, and many others. This variety allows unique insight into the WTA/WTP ratio. To our knowledge, no other economic issue has been experimentally studied across such a wide variety of goods.

With regard to experiment design, we find that ratios in real experiments are not significantly different from hypothetical experiments, and that incentive-compatible elicitation yields higher ratios, not lower. In other words, survey techniques that would be expected to yield a "truer" picture of preferences lead either to no change or to higher observed ratios. We also found that students tended to have lower, not higher, ratios than the general public, so moving the experiments out of the classroom seems not to lead to lower ratios. The evidence on the effects of repetition is mixed, but there is not strong evidence that the ratio decreases through iteration. Therefore, high WTA/WTP ratios are not the result of experimental design features that would be considered suspect, even apart from their WTA/WTP results.

With regard to patterns in the observed ratios, we find that, on average, the less the good is like an "ordinary market good," the higher is the ratio. The ratio is highest for public and non-market goods, next highest for ordinary private goods, and lowest for experiments involving forms of money. A generalization of this pattern holds even when we account for differences in survey design: ordinary goods have lower ratios than non-ordinary ones. This pattern is the major result we discovered.

This paper does not take up the issue of whether the WTA/WTP findings provide evidence for or against the neoclassical paradigm, even though that potential has been the theme of much of the literature we reviewed. Rather, our goal is to draw broad-based results from this long and rich experimental track record. We are not concerned with whether the observed ratios are consistent with the standard neoclassical model. It is possible to investigate these results without addressing the neoclassical question.

We end this introduction with several examples of the importance of the WTA/WTP ratio. The ratio comes into play in the context of the assignment of property rights, since the difference between a WTA and WTP experiment is a difference in property rights over the item being valued. Therefore the WTA/WTP ratio measures the consequence of assigning a property right one way or the other.

Consider the case of preserving land from development: In our set of studies, the mean WTA/WTP ratio is approximately 7. This number suggests, roughly speaking, that the amount of land that would be preserved if development rights were held by the general public is 7 *times higher* than the amount that would be preserved if the rights were deeded to the landowner and had to be purchased by the public.[1] This difference would substantially alter the balance of environmental preservation and urban development in the United States.

As Knetsch [46] has pointed out, a large difference between WTA and WTP can have other potent effects on environmental policy. These occur when the appropriate welfare measure is willingness to accept (because, in most instances, environmental quality can only deteriorate) but policy analysts use willingness to pay as the measure of benefits. For marketed goods, predictions about volume of trade or gains from trade may be seriously flawed if they are derived without recognizing the frequently large difference between individuals' willingness to pay and their willingness to accept for goods (Borges and Knetsch [10]; see Franciosi *et al.* [26] for the counter-implication). Fischel [24] reviews the arguments about whether the WTA/WTP ratio justifies compensating landowners by more than their property's market value when property is taken by eminent domain.

There seems to be a further lesson implied by these examples. Because holders of some "right" appear to value the right differently from non-holders, one of the most economically consequential decisions will be the *initial* establishment of the property rights, especially for environmental and other public amenities for which property rights are unclear (Knetsch [46]). Such a prediction runs contrary to economists' understanding of the consequences of assigning property rights. It is with this possibility in mind that we undertake this review.

2. THE STUDIES

A list of the studies is given at the end of the paper. A sample of the data is given in Table I. A table with data from all of the studies is available from the authors. We have not re-analyzed the authors' analyses. For example, if the authors chose to remove outliers, we have accepted their decision and used the means and medians they reported. When multiple trials were conducted, we have used the authors' summary of the results. There are 45 studies that are usable for our analysis and five that are not, for reasons explained below.

Let $i = 1 \ldots 45$ index the individual studies we used for the analysis. Let $k = 1 \ldots K_i$ index the experiments within a study, where K_i is the number of experiments reported in study i. The pair ik is the unit of observation; that is, a line in the data table (see Table I), which we call an *experiment*. Let N_{ik} be the number of subjects in experiment k of study i. There are 208 observations in our data set.

There are six experiments in five studies for which the authors did not report the number of subjects. These experiments are excluded from parts of the analysis.

Dependent variable. The variable that is the focus of most of the analysis is mean WTA/mean WTP. This is labeled RATIO_{ik}. The highest RATIO_{ik} is 2858,

---

[1] This case presumes that for developers, willingness to pay for development rights equals willingness to sell.

A REVIEW OF WTA / WTP STUDIES 429

TABLE I

Sample of Data (First 12 Observations)

Study	Med. WTA/med. WTP	Mean WTA/mean WTP	Mean WTP	Private/public good	Hyp./real	Elicitation Technique	Subjects	N
#1. Adamowicz et al.	—	1.95	$4.76	Private (movie ticket)	Hyp.	Open	Students	157
	1.85	1.70	$28.50	Private (hockey ticket w/subst.)	Hyp.	Closed	Students	150
	1.87	1.91	$36.60	Private (hockey tkt w/o subst.)	Hyp.	Closed	Students	150
#2. Banford et al.	2.60	2.78	$43.10	Public (ocean pier)	Hyp.	Closed, iterated	Local public	71
	4.40	4.24	$21.97	Public (home postal deliv.)	Hyp.	Closed, iterated	Local public	71
#3. Bateman et al.	3.95	2.81	£0.78	Private (10 chocolates)	Random real	Open; IC	Students	89, 96
	2.00	2.09	8.7 chocs.	Private (money—£2.00)	Random real	Open; IC	Students	96, 89
	1.30	2.53	£0.60	Private (4 cans of Coke)	Random real	Open; IC	Students	89, 96
	2.00	2.00	2.5 cans	Private (money—£0.80)	Random real	Open; IC	Students	96, 89

(Pounds sterling were converted at £1 = $1.55. To calculate mean WTP for treatments 2 and 4, we used the prices implied by treatments 1 and 3.)

Study	Med. WTA/med. WTP	Mean WTA/mean WTP	Mean WTP	Private/public good	Hyp./real	Elicitation Technique	Subjects	N
#4. Benzion et al.	—	1.76	$4.90	Private ($40 in 0 ⇔ 6 mos.)	Hyp.	Open	Students	204
	—	1.92	$6.80	Private ($40 in 0 ⇔ 1 yr.)	Hyp.	Open	Students	204
	—	1.96	$9.80	Private ($40 in 0 ⇔ 2 yrs.)	Hyp.	Open	Students	204

found by SSHK (Study #38) in the first round of a study of salmonella contamination. We drop this observation because it is 25 times larger than the next highest ratio, 113, found by Brookshire and Coursey (#8). Therefore, there are 201 $(208 - 6 - 1)$ observations in our main sample.

Aggregation: individual means vs. group means. Most studies report only mean WTA/ mean WTP, even when open-ended WTA and WTP values were collected from all individuals. Only two studies reported both the mean of individual WTA/WTP ratios and the ratio of mean WTA/mean WTP (Dubourg *et al.* #13; Eisenberger and Weber, #15). In those two experiments, the result

$$(1) \qquad \sum_i \frac{\text{WTA}_t}{\text{WTP}_i} > \frac{\sum_i \text{WTA}_i}{\sum_t \text{WTP}_i}$$

was obtained, where i represents the individual subject. The right-hand side is our dependent variable. Therefore, the literature's high reported ratios are not due to using aggregated measures.

Kachelmeier and Shehata [44] found a correlation between WTA and WTP of 0.35, and Borges and Knetsch [10] found a correlation of 0.24. These relatively low correlations also suggest that little has been lost by the literature's concentrating on the ratio of means.

Median vs. mean. There are 41 experiments that reported ratios of both means and medians. The ratio involving means was greater than the ratio involving medians in close to 80% of the experiments. An unweighted regression of the former on the latter yielded

$$(2) \qquad \frac{\text{Mean WTA}}{\text{Mean WTP}} = \underset{(0.72)}{2.67} + \underset{(4.15)}{1.58} \frac{\text{Median WTA}}{\text{Median WTP}} \qquad n = 41.$$

T-ratios are in parentheses. Studies #24 and #42 reported only ratios of medians. We predicted their ratio of means with the use of (2) and used those ratios in our regressions. To test sensitivity to using the predicted ratio, we also estimated our main model without studies 24 and 42.

Mean WTP. This is the denominator of RATIO_{ik}. In the regressions, mean WTP is deflated to 1983 dollars, using the Consumer Price Index.

Private/public good. We label as a public good any good for which a collective decision was being made, even if the good might actually be private (e.g., hunting permits) or have both private (access) and public (quality) dimensions (e.g., home postal delivery). The item types are discussed further in Section 3.

Increments and decrements. Most studies ask for willingness to pay to go from A to B and willingness to accept the change from B to A, which is the comparison that has been the subject of most theoretical analysis. A few studies ask about willingness to pay for the change from A to $A + \Delta$ and willingness to accept the change from A to $A - \Delta$ (Brookshire and Coursey, #8; Jones-Lee *et al.* #49; Thaler, #42; Viscusi, Magat, and Huber, #44); see Hanemann [34] for a discussion of the difference between this comparison and the standard one. We did not distinguish between these in our analysis.

Hypothetical, real, and random real. A study is hypothetical if the valuation question was purely hypothetical, and real if it was carried out for real money and real exchange. A study is "random real" if several valuation questions were asked and (only) one of them was chosen at random and carried out for real money and real exchange. Random real experiments are classified as REAL = 1 in the regressions.

Elicitation technique and incentive compatibility. The main techniques are the following: (1) A simple open-ended question such as "What is the maximum you would be willing to pay to obtain X?" These questions do not provide subjects with incentives to reveal their true maximum WTP, but strategic bias was typically considered unimportant when many of these studies were conducted (see Schulze *et al.* [68]). (2) An incentive-compatible (IC) open-ended question. These use Vickrey auctions, Becker–deGroot–Marschak mechanisms, or something similar. (3) Payment card. A payment card has several values printed on it, and the subject then circles his own WTP or WTA. These may be IC (e.g., combined with a Vickrey auction) or not. (4) Single closed-ended, yes–no question. The individual is asked whether he or she would pay or accept some specified amount, call it c. The amount c varies across the sample, but each individual answers only one valuation question. WTA and WTP means must be estimated from the group's responses. We used the authors' estimates unless otherwise noted. Simple closed-ended questions are incentive compatible. (5) Iterated closed-ended question. Each individual answers several closed-ended questions with different values of c. If c is varied a fixed number of times (usually twice), then WTA and WTP means must still be estimated from group responses. If c is varied until the subject is roughly indifferent between yes and no, then each subject's individual value is eventually observed and no estimation is necessary. Iterated closed-ended questions are not incentive compatible.

Because we are interested in the effects of these survey methods, we used the same categorization for hypothetical as for real questions. Incentive compatibility can be important even for hypothetical experiments if responses have at least some probability of affecting a real-world outcome, as Carson *et al.* [17] point out.

Subjects. Many of the subjects were students. When a local issue was being studied with non-students, subjects were the "local public." When an issue without a clear location-specific connection was being studied with non-students, the subjects were the "public." For empirical purposes, we distinguish only between students and the rest of the subjects.

Number of observations. If only a single number of observations is listed, then each of these N_{ik} subjects answered both a WTP and WTA question. If there were missing values for some subjects (but all subjects were asked both questions), we list the smaller number of responses, if available. If two numbers are listed, separate subject groups answered the WTA and WTP questions. The first number is WTA observations, the second is WTP observations.

Rules for including studies. We included every study we could find, including studies we do not have copies of, but whose ratios were reported in other studies. There are seven such studies in data set. Because these are frequently several years old and unpublished, we decided not to try to gather more information about them.

TABLE IIA
Summary Statistics (Weighted)

Statistic	N	Mean	Standard error
RATIO$_{ik}$	201	7.17	0.93
RATIO$_{ik}$ (excludes estimated RATIOs)^a	175	7.18	1.02
RATIO$_{ik}$ (excludes study #4)	169	7.86	1.07
Median WTA/median WTP	66	5.52	1.03
Mean WTP ($1983)	169	$175	22.40
REAL (real = 1, hypothetical = 0)	201	0.22	0.03
IC (incentive-compatible = 1)	201	0.25	0.03
STUDENT (student subjects = 1)	201	0.35	0.03
OPEN-ENDED (open-ended = 1)	201	0.56	0.04

^{a}Excludes 25 experiments in study #24 and 1 experiment in #42 in which only ratios of medians were reported.

We exclude from the analysis three studies that used dichotomous choice but had only one offer price (#46, #47, #48). We estimated WTA and WTP from these studies using the Turnbull estimator, but such estimates are imprecise (Haab and McConnell [31]).

A few studies elicited open-ended WTA values but dropped responses that said "I will not accept this trade under any condition." Therefore, their calculated mean WTA is a lower bound on true mean WTA. Of these, we include Dubourg *et al.* (#13) and Viscusi *et al.* (#44) but drop Jones-Lee *et al.* (#49) because its percentage of "never-accept" responses is quite large (81%). We further exclude one study from 1968 in which the mean WTP was negative but the mean WTA was positive (Slovic and Lichtenstein, #50). All analysis is based on studies #1 through #45.

After completing this research, we learned of several studies that were not included. To facilitate future research, we list them here.[2] They are Bell and Leaworthy [4], Brookshire *et al.* [14], Brown and Mathews [16], Franciosi *et al.* [26], Hartman *et al.* [37], Jones-Lee [42], and McClelland and Schulze [57].

Weights. In calculating summary statistics in Table IIA, we weighted observations by sqrt(N_{ik})/sqrt(K_i). The numerator gives higher weight to experiments with more subjects, but at a decreasing rate. The denominator treats different

---

[2] We thank Richard Carson, Praveen Kujal, Carol Mansfield, and an anonymous referee for these citations.

TABLE IIB
Summary Statistics (Unweighted): Quantiles

Statistic	Minimum	10%	25%	50%	75%	90%	Maximum
RATIO$_{ik}$ ($n = 206$)	0.74	1.16	1.66	2.60	6.12	10.52	112.67
Median WTA/median WTP ($n = 67$)	1.00	1.33	1.67	2.33	3.00	7.28	42.94
Mean WTP ($1983) ($n = 173$)	$0.12	$0.34	$0.91	$3.73	$34.51	$280	$5847

TABLE IIIA
Ratio by Type of Good

Good	Mean RATIO	Standard error	Number of experiments
Public or non-market goods	10.41	2.53	46
Health and safety	10.06	2.28	32
Ordinary private goods	2.92	0.30	59
Lotteries	2.10	0.20	25
Timing	1.95	0.17	39
All goods	7.17	0.93	201
Unknown number of subjects	6.71	Not calculated	6

Public or non-market: studies #2, 5, 6, 8, 9, 12, 17, 18, 20, 26, 31, 35, 36, 37, 39, 43, 45.
Health and safety: studies #13, 16, 32, parts of #38, 44.
Ordinary private goods: studies #1, 3, 7, 24, 29, 30, 34, parts of #38, 41.
Lotteries: studies #11, 15, 19, 23, 25, 27, 40.
Timing: studies #4, 21, 28, 42.
Unknown number of subjects: studies #10, 14, 22, last observation of #24, 33.

experiments within the same study as providing neither completely independent information (in which case the denominator would be 1) nor fully duplicated information (in which case the denominator would be K_i). There are six experiments that have no weights because authors did not report the number of subjects.

3. TYPE OF GOOD

The mean of $RATIO_{ik}$ is 7.17 with standard error 0.93 ($n = 201$). The median is 2.60. The data are summarized in Table II. Statistics are weighted by sqrt(N_{ik})/sqrt(K_i) in Tables IIA and III.

The studies contain a wide variety of goods. We classify them in five broad categories: health and safety, lotteries, ordinary private goods, the time at which a good will be received or given up, and public or non-market goods not included in any of the other categories. We also subdivide the timing and public/non-market categories. Summary statistics for mean RATIO by good type are given in Tables IIIA, IIIB, and IIIC.

The main result is that the farther a good is from being an ordinary private good, the higher the ratio. The pattern is striking (see Table IIIA). Ratios are highest for health/safety and public/non-market goods, next highest for ordinary private

TABLE IIIB
Ratio by Type of Good: Timing Studies

| Type of good | RATIO | | |
	Mean	S.E.	n
Timing of receipt of private goods (study #28)	2.82	0.39	5
Timing of receipt of money (Studies #4, 21, 42)	1.84	0.18	34

TABLE IIIC

Ratio by Type of Good: Public/Non-Market Goods

Type of good	RATIO		
	Mean	S.E.	*n*
Misc. public and non-market goods			
(#2, 6, 8, 18, 31, 39, 43, 45)	27.57	7.50	19
Hunting (#5, 9, 17, 20)	10.47	5.29	8
Visibility (#35, 36)	7.40	2.31	7
Siting (#26, 37)	4.14	1.83	4
Sucrose octa-acetate (#12)	3.99	0.47	8

goods and lotteries, and lowest for surveys that involve the time at which a good is received. The health/safety and public/non-market ratios are almost identical. The latter finding is not surprising since health and safety are themselves public/non-market goods.

The pattern continues: The closer the good comes to being actual money, the smaller the ratio. Lotteries, which were all based on money payments, have lower ratios on average than ordinary private goods. Timing studies that involve money have lower ratios than timing studies that involve goods (Table IIIB). In this regard, it is reassuring (if a little self-evident) to note that no significant difference between WTA and WTP is observed when the good is money, as in experiments using tokens [45, p. 1328].

Timing studies that involve goods behave like ordinary private goods, although the sample size is small. Timing studies that involve money behave like lotteries. This latter finding is particularly striking given the close connection economists recognize between choice over time and choice under uncertainty (Prelec and Loewenstein [63], Quiggin and Horowitz [64]).

In the public and non-market goods category (Table IIIC), the lowest ratio is for tasting of sucrose octa-acetate, a bitter non-hazardous substance that is perhaps more like an ordinary private good than any of the other items in Table IIIC. The elicited ratio is just slightly higher than for the ordinary private goods category. The pattern for other studies in the public and non-market goods category is similar but weaker, although the number of observations in many of the subcategories is low.

There are two anomalies, siting and hunting, that merit discussion because they pertain to issues that have been proposed to be resolved through the issuance of property rights.

Hunting permits are private goods and might therefore be expected to have lower ratios. But if subjects believed that their responses would also be used to make other wildlife policy decisions, then the hunting permit survey is not merely a question about a simple private good, it is implicitly a question about wildlife management, a public good.[3]

For siting studies, the relatively low ratios may be explained by subjects believing that they *did* essentially hold a property right. The fact that often only one suitable

---

[3] A subject's response may affect not just whether he gets a hunting permit but whether he will have to pay for permits in the future or whether hunting opportunities will be expanded/curtailed or may affect other wildlife programs.

waste site is available in a community and that the siting survey may lead subjects to believe that any other siting-type decisions would also be subject to citizen review may make the siting problem more like a private good, i.e., one that subjects had relatively clear control over; and this yields a lower ratio.[4] The sample size for this conclusion is small, however, and the explanation deserves further scrutiny.

The result in Table IIIA is consistent with Hanemann's finding that the lower the substitution elasticity between a bundle of market goods and the rationed good is, the higher the WTA/WTP ratio will be [33]. If non-market goods have lower substitution elasticities than ordinary goods, then our results are consistent with Hanemann's model.

4. REGRESSION ANALYSIS

This section uses a random effects model to look at the effects of type of good, survey design, mean WTP, and year. Three major survey design features are examined through regressions: hypothetical or real payoffs, elicitation technique, and student or non-student subjects. For type of good, we divided the sample into (a) ordinary goods and (b) all others. A more precise disentangling of good type and survey design is desirable, but it is nearly impossible because finer classifications of good types do not contain the full range of survey design features, and so separate effects cannot be discerned.

Econometric Model

The econometric model we use is

(3) $\text{RATIO}_{ik} = \beta x_{ik} + u_i + \varepsilon_{ik},$

where u_i is a study-specific error and x_{ik} is a vector of experiment and study characteristics. We weight observations by $\text{sqrt}(N_{ik})$ to give experiments with more subjects greater weight.

This model has the structure of an unbalanced random effects model. The advantage of the random effects model is that it allows covariance among the experiments in a given study. In some studies, there is only one experiment, so a fixed effects model cannot be estimated.

The model can be estimated as a maximum likelihood model by fixing $\rho = \sigma_u^2/(\sigma_u^2 + \sigma_\varepsilon^2)$, estimating β conditional on ρ, and then iterating on ρ until the likelihood function is maximized (Nerlove [62, Chap. 19]). The value of ρ will be between 0 and 1, with $\rho = 0$ being the ordinary least-squares value.

In the regressions, all values of ρ are less than or equal to 0.12, with two regressions having $\rho = 0$ (#4 and #6). A low value of ρ indicates that between-experiment random variation is large relative to within-study random variation. This is a desirable finding; it suggests that quantifiable survey characteristics are capturing the greater part of the explainable variation.

The results of the weighted random effects model are given in Table IV. The basic regression is the first column (regression 1). We also ran each of the Table IV regressions, using (i) OLS with the observations weighted by $\text{sqrt}(N_{ik})/\text{sqrt}(K_i)$,

[4] One community's responses might affect decisions made for another community. If subjects were concerned only about their own community, this would be sufficient for our explanation.

TABLE IV

Regression Results: Dependent Variable = RATIO

	#1	#2	#3	#4	#5	#6	#7	#8[a]	#9[b]
INTERCEPT	6.08	4.71	2.90	8.01	2.94	4.90	7.44	5.16	18.59
	(1.12)	(1.01)	(0.59)	(1.37)	(0.77)	(1.05)	(1.04)	(0.79)	(1.96)
ORDINARY	−6.12	−6.32	−5.92	−8.14	−5.02	−8.22	−16.44	−6.73	−7.84
(Ordinary = 1)[c]	(1.78)	(1.77)	(1.70)	(1.98)	(1.62)	(1.14)	(2.86)	(1.81)	(2.13)
REAL	−7.09	1.17	−0.27	−6.10	−6.75	−5.54	−6.83	−7.79	−8.02
(Real = 1)	(1.47)	(0.34)	(0.08)	(1.23)	(1.78)	(1.31)	(1.43)	(1.51)	(1.56)
IC	10.59	—	—	11.14	9.34	11.18	11.95	10.87	6.93
(Inc. Comp. = 1)	(2.45)			(2.55)	(2.56)	(2.90)	(2.81)	(2.39)	(1.44)
STUDENT	−13.24	−11.71	−12.50	−14.49	−10.04	−13.44	−15.71	−13.05	−15.28
(Student = 1)	(3.75)	(3.16)	(3.47)	(3.81)	(3.20)	(3.73)	(4.41)	(3.46)	(3.97)
MEAN WTP	−0.005	−0.005	−0.005	−0.005	—	—	−0.005	−0.005	−0.03
(Deflated to $1983)	(1.72)	(1.80)	(1.95)	(1.71)			(1.81)	(1.63)	(3.83)
OPEN-ENDED	—	−0.54	—	—	—	—	—	—	—
(Open-ended = 1)		(0.21)							
CLOSED-ENDED	—	—	−5.17	—	—	—	—	—	—
(Closed-ended = 1)			(1.73)						
MEAN WTP × ORDINARY	—	—	—	0.34	—	—	—	—	—
				(0.89)					
REAL × ORDINARY, β_5	—	—	—	—	—	−0.26	—	—	—
						(0.02)			
IC × ORDINARY, β_6	—	—	—	—	—	−6.99	—	—	—
						(0.55)			
STUDENT × ORDINARY, β_7	—	—	—	—	—	11.53	14.13	—	—
						(1.86)	(2.23)		
YEAR	0.07	0.10	0.15	0.05	0.09	0.07	0.07	0.07	0.02
	(1.06)	(1.60)	(2.11)	(0.65)	(1.65)	(1.06)	(0.82)	(0.98)	(0.19)
ρ	0.08	0.11	0.10	0[d]	0.12	0[d]	0.05	0.07	0.07
R^2	0.20	0.16	0.18	0.20	0.14	0.17	0.23	0.20	0.23
N	169	169	169	169	201	201	169	152	137

T-statistics are in parentheses.
[a] Ordinary goods: #1, 3, 7, 24, 29, 30, 34, parts of 38, and 41.
[b] Excludes most of #24 (KKT) and all of 42, which reported only ratio of medians.
[c] Excludes #4 (BRY).
[d] Equations estimated by OLS.

and (ii) random effects with unweighted observations. The regressions gave the same patterns of sign and significance as appear in Table IV. An unweighted OLS regression yielded different conclusions.

Type of Good

Non-ordinary goods have significantly higher ratios—they are typically 6 to 8 points higher than ordinary goods. This effect occurs even when we take survey design features and mean WTP into account. The pattern that we uncovered in Section 3, that the farther a good is from being an ordinary private good the higher the ratio, remains a prominent and robust feature of the observed WTA/WTP behavior.

Only "ordinary private goods" (see Table IIIA) are counted as ordinary goods in these regressions. Lotteries and timing experiments are counted as non-ordinary goods. We adopt this division even though the previous analysis shows lotteries and timing to be like ordinary private goods in many ways. The reason for our classification is that *ex ante*—before any statistical analysis was conducted—we believe that most economists would have proffered that experiments with lotteries or timing were more unusual than experiments with goods like mugs and pens; that they were more like non-market goods. We did not want the observed differences in the ratios to influence how we classified the goods for our analysis of survey design effects.[5]

Survey Design

We next turn our attention to survey design features. The main question that confronts us is whether there is any evidence that high ratios are an experimental artifact. Much has been written elsewhere about survey design for valuing non-market goods, and our compilation of studies provides some insight into those general survey design issues. Our main focus, however, is whether high WTA/WTP ratios are the result of questionable survey design and easily identifiable influences, or instead truly present a broad-based picture of preferences.

Hypothetical vs. real payoffs. Real experiments do not yield ratios that are significantly different from those of hypothetical experiments. In some instances, such as when we account for whether an experiment uses closed-ended elicitation (regression 3), the effect of realness essentially disappears entirely. Realness has its statistically strongest effect only when the mean WTP is not included. This effect loses its significance when the mean WTP is included.

The high values of the WTA/WTP ratio initially led some researchers to claim that hypothetical surveys were unsuitable for eliciting preferences. Our results show that real experiments do not yield significantly lower ratios. Thus, any claim about the suitability of hypothetical surveys must rest on evidence other than the size of the WTA/WTP ratio.

Elicitation technique. Studies that are incentive compatible (IC) have significantly higher ratios. This result is unexpected. If high ratios were the result of "strategizing" by the subjects rather than a feature of true preferences then we

---

[5] To test the effect of the classification of lottery and timing goods, we also estimated regression 1 with the lottery and timing experiments excluded. The following table shows that the pattern of inferences is not sensitive to their omission. The patterns of sign and size are quite similar to the specification in Table IV.

Intercept	Ordinary	Real	IC	Student	Mean WTP	Year	ρ	R^2	N
18.70	−7.69	−12.83	11.13	−14.89	−0.03	−0.03	0.07	0.22	116
(1.62)	(1.53)	(1.71)	(1.70)	(2.60)	(3.30)	(0.20)			

would expect incentive-compatible experiments to result in lower ratios. They do not.

We also looked at other categorizations of elicitation techniques. Open-ended studies, typically construed as not being incentive compatible, had no statistically significant effect (regression 2). Closed-ended questions, which are considered incentive compatible, do yield lower ratios than non-closed-ended questions (regression 3), although the statistical significance is not strong. Furthermore, the lower ratios of closed-ended questions may be due to functional form and range-of-integration assumptions imposed by the researcher; these assumptions would likely lead to a lower WTA being inferred.

Intuition about the effect of elicitation method is complicated, leading to weak hypotheses about the effect of elicitation on the ratio. Under some approaches, subjects might either overstate WTA or WTP (if they want a good to be provided and feel they will not have to pay full price) or under-report them, if they think they might thereby get the good at a cheaper rate [17]. The overall effect that elicitation will have on the ratio is unknown.

Students vs. non-students. Students exhibit significantly and substantially lower ratios than non-students. This result is unexpected. Its main implication for our research is that high WTA/WTP ratios are exhibited by the general public, not just college undergraduates.

For non-ordinary goods, students exhibit lower ratios than do non-students. For ordinary goods, students exhibit the same ratios as non-students, because in regressions 6 and 7 we cannot reject the hypothesis that $\beta_{STUDENT} + \beta_{STUDENT \times ORDINARY} = 0$ ($F = 0.17$ with a p value of 0.68 for regression 6; and $F = 0.06$ with a p value of 0.79 for regression 7).

Ordinary goods and survey features. We also checked whether these survey design features had the same effect on both ordinary and non-ordinary goods. The hypothesis that coefficients on the three survey features crossed with ORDINARY are jointly zero cannot be rejected in regression 6 ($F = 1.96$). In other words, with respect to realness, elicitation approach, and student subjects, the responses are the same for both ordinary and non-ordinary goods.

If we look at these effects individually, however, students do appear to behave differently for ordinary and non-ordinary goods. For ordinary goods, students have the same ratios as non-students, since the coefficients on STUDENT and STUDENT × ORDINARY sum to approximately zero (as discussed above). For non-ordinary goods, students have lower ratios.

Likewise, the hypothesis that MEAN × ORDINARY is zero cannot be rejected (regression 4). In words, we find that the relationship between mean WTP and WTA/WTP is the same for ordinary and non-ordinary goods.

Other Findings

We next take up other survey design patterns and possible influences on the ratio. These yield less direct evidence about the "reliability" of the ratio but are useful because they help form a broad picture of WTA/WTP behavior.

Mean WTP. This variable requires us to exclude 32 experiments that do not report the mean WTP. We find that the higher the WTP is, the lower the

WTA/WTP ratio is. On average, a $200 increase in mean WTP causes the ratio to decrease by 1 point. The relationship between RATIO and mean WTP is the same for both ordinary goods and other goods (regression 4).

It is possible that mean WTP is endogenous. We performed a Hausman test for endogeneity of the right-hand-side mean WTP, both in an OLS model ($\rho = 0$) and for the model with the optimal value of ρ , for regressions 1–3 and 7–9. In all cases, the test statistic does not rise to a level that would lead to rejection of the null hypothesis of no endogeneity.

Year. There has been a slight increase in the ratio over the 30 years that it has been studied. This result does not have an obvious behavioral explanation. One possible explanation is that as the existence of a disparity has been established over the years, researchers have tended to study situations where it might arise.

When Benzion *et al.* (#4, hereafter BRY) is excluded, YEAR has a small and statistically insignificant coefficient (regression 9). However, in the analog to regression 5 with BRY excluded (not shown), the YEAR coefficient is larger and statistically significant. In other words, the increase in the ratio over the years is a relatively robust finding that is only mildly sensitive to inclusion of BRY.

Income. Only a few studies have looked at the relationship between WTA/WTP and income. Therefore, we do not include income as an explanatory variable in the regressions. Adamowicz *et al.* [1] found that WTA-WTP is decreasing in income, but the coefficient is not significant. Horowitz [39] found no significant relationship between WTA/WTP and subjects' wealth.

Individual studies. In regressions 8 and 9, we re-ran regression 1 without KKT and Thaler (#24 and #42) and BRY (#4), respectively. Neither exclusion affects the results much. KKT (#24) and Thaler (#42) reported only ratios of medians, but their techniques were similar to the other studies, so it is not surprising that their results are consonant with the overall findings. BRY (#4), however, differed substantially from the other studies. In BRY, each student subject was given a 64-question survey that asked the subject, for example, to "state an amount of money x so that he or she would be indifferent between paying yt time periods from now or paying x immediately" [5, p. 275]. The sheer number of questions (i.e., experiments) makes this study stand out. Also, for some responses it was necessary for us to convert a future WTA or WTP to its present value; we used the discount rate implicit in the question. Dropping this study has almost no effect on the coefficients but does slightly increase the standard errors of some estimates, as might be expected. We also ran the other regressions without BRY (not shown). There was little change. Regressions 1–7 therefore include all of the studies.

Sample selection. The studies in Table I are not a random sample. They must be selected by editors or, for unpublished studies, by the other researchers that cite them and, at a minimum, by the authors themselves, who felt the experiment worth conducting and the results worth writing up. We see three ways in which sample selection might affect our results. First, experiments in which the elicited WTAs were extremely high are less likely to enter our sample. The main consequence is that our observed mean RATIO is below the population mean. We suspect that this will be more of a problem for the types of goods that tend to exhibit high

RATIOS.[6] Therefore, the coefficient on ORDINARY is probably biased upward, and the difference between ordinary and non-ordinary goods may be greater than our regressions indicate.

Studies using non-incentive-compatible techniques also likely have a lower probability of being published. Even in our own analysis, for example, we have in places excluded the BRY study because of the suspicious incentive structure. However, the fact that some elicitation methods are not included in the empirical analysis does not necessarily bias the coefficient on IC as long as the relationship between the ratio and the elicitation method is consistent and the exclusion does not remove all variation in IC.

5. DO PRACTICE AND FAMILIARITY LOWER THE WTA/WTP RATIO?

Several authors have suggested that repeating an experiment for the same subjects might lower the ratio, primarily because WTA would be reduced as subjects realized they would be content to take home a smaller amount of real money than they first thought. KKT refer to the "conclusion reached in some other studies that the WTA-WTP discrepancy is greatly reduced by market experience" [45, p. 1335]. We list the relevant studies in Tables VA and VB.

The evidence is mixed. Brookshire and Coursey (#8) found that the ratio decreased. Their study design is not readily generalizable because they informed their subjects of the compensation fund that was available and then elicited WTA bids until either the total WTA was less than the fund or five trials had been conducted; in their WTP experiments, they told subjects the cost of the item and elicited bids until they covered that cost or reached a maximum of five trials.

Coursey *et al.* (#12, hereafter CHS) also showed a decrease in WTA, but their sample size was small, and, like Brookshire and Coursey (#8), they repeated their experiment with an explicit goal, namely until a consensus was reached, with a

---

[6] An example is study #49, a health and safety study in which at least 80% of subjects implicitly claimed an infinite WTA. Another example is our own censoring of the largest SSHK observation, also a health and safety study.

TABLE VA

Studies in Which Hypothetical Elicitation(s) Preceded Real Elicitation(s)

Study	Procedure	Sequence of mean WTA/mean WTP
#7. Boyce *et al.*	Ten practice rounds[a]	Not reported
	One binding round	1.66 (no-kill), 2.36 (kill)
#12. CHS	One practice round[a]	3.79
	Iterated practice rounds[a]—first and final bids	5.26, 3.80
	Four practice rounds[b]	3.95, 6.13, 3.90, 3.49
	Maximum of six rounds until no subject objected[b]	1.59
#24. KKT	Three practice rounds[c] (pens)	6.00, 6.00, 5.00
	One binding round	5.00

[a] No information on other bids was announced after a round.
[b] Other subjects' bids were announced after each round.
[c] The market-clearing bid was announced after each round.

A REVIEW OF WTA / WTP STUDIES 441

TABLE VB

Studies with Repeated, Random-Real Elicitations

Study	Repetitions	Information revealed after each round	Sequence of mean WTA/mean WTP
#24. KKT	4 (mug)	Market-clearing bid announced	1.91, 2.33, 2.33, 2.33
	4 (pen)	Market-clearing bid announced	3.33, 2.33, 3.00, 2.33
	4 (mug)	Market-clearing bid announced	2.71, 2.11, 2.11, 1.89
	4 (binocs.)	Market-clearing bid announced	1.67, 1.67, 2.33, 2.33
	5 (mug)	Market-clearing bid announced	3.8, 2.8, 2.2, 1.8, 1.8
#34. Morrison	5 (chocolates)	No information on others' bids announced	0.99, 1.09, 1.09, 1.13, 1.13
	5 (mug)	No information on others' bids announced	2.01, 2.22, 2.42, 2.29, 2.19
#38. SSHK	5 (candy)	High bidder and reigning price announced	1.28, 1.16, 0.98, 0.93, 0.93
	20 (sandwich) (rounds 1, 7–10, and 17–20)	High bidder and reigning price announced (?)	8.74, 2.11, 2.60 (pathogen 1) 2858, 3.39, 2.20 (pathogen 2) 4.00, 3.22, 2.20 (pathogen 3) 16.09, 6.42, 6.61 (pathogen 4) 34.04, 3.05, 4.65 (pathogen 5)
	10 (mug)	High bidder and reigning price announced (?)	2.76, 1.74, 1.10, 1.05, 1.07, 1.45, 1.29, 1.24, 1.16, 0.74[a] 2.74, 1.98, 1.27, 1.03, 1.21, 1.31, 0.97, 1.19, 1.23, 0.80[a]
#8. Brookshire and Coursey	Repeated until WTP covered cost or WTA did not exceed fund. Max. of 5 trials	Sum of WTP or WTA announced	3.92, 3.63, 2.90, 2.28 (25 tree) 8.08, 8.19, 11.16, 8.28, 7.39 (50 tree)

[a] WTA was elicited in two ways, but only one set of WTPs was elicited. Thus, the denominators are the same in the two sequences. In the first WTA set, an identical mug was for sale just outside the experiment. In the second set, no mug was available. See SSHK [71] for details.

maximum of 10 trials. In a reassessment, Gregory and Furby [30] emphasized the smallness of CHS's samples and claimed that the paper's reported convergence "depends upon inclusion of... suspicious outlying groups" (p. 285). There appears to be no convergence in CHS's initial repeated hypothetical rounds; there was convergence only in the final real rounds.

Knez *et al.* [48] looked at the number of instances in which an individual subject's WTP exceeded his WTA and concluded that this number fell when the experiment was repeated. Under this result, the WTA/WTP ratio would likely have been *rising* with repetition. They did not report any ratios, so actual results are unknown.

The strongest evidence of a falling ratio comes from SSHK, who showed a significant decrease in the ratio between their first and middle rounds, for both contaminated sandwiches and mugs. This was observed in five separate experiments with a total of roughly 60 subjects. In a subsequent experiment, Shogren *et al.* ([72], cited in Shogren and Hayes [70]) showed that the ratio fell in a Vickrey auction but not in a Becker–DeGroot–Marschak auction, and argue that the former is more like a market.

Studies that explicitly claim that WTA/WTP did not fall include KKT (#24) and Morrison (#34).

In summary, the idea that the ratio will fall as subjects become familiar with an experiment may be intuitively compelling, but the evidence is weak. Some experimental techniques appear to aid convergence, such as repeating the experiment to aim for a goal and having an outside market for the good, as KKT did for their last mug experiment. In many cases, even when the ratio does fall, it falls to levels that still seem high.

Last, we should note that even if the ratio were to fall with practice, the implications would be limited because the ratio has its most important economic role in environmental and public policy decisions for which familiarity and practice are likely to be absent.

6. CONCLUDING COMMENTS

Our research investigates a body of empirical work that has appeared to challenge both the neoclassical model of the consumer and a belief in the "neutrality" of property rights. Before this challenge can stand it has been necessary to establish two related points: (i) The high observed WTA/WTP ratios do not appear to be experimental artifacts. Our claim is based on the findings that hypothetical or non-incentive-compatible experiments do not yield statistically significantly higher ratios; that high ratios are exhibited by a broad-based (i.e., non-student) population; and that familiarity with the experiments does not uniformly lead to lower ratios.

(ii) A robust and economically useful response pattern exists. We find that the farther a good is from being an "ordinary private good," the higher the ratio. The pattern prevails even when we account for possible differences in survey designs. The extensive literature on the WTA/WTP ratio provides sturdy evidence for these claims.

We leave for future papers the two major unanswered questions that this research raises. First, and we believe most important: To what extent can a disparity between WTA and WTP, or anticipation of it, be observed in real-world economic choices? Are there "remedies," and, if so, are they desirable? Second, does the WTA/WTP disparity provide sufficiently broad and deep evidence against the neoclassical model? Does that evidence warrant substantially modifying that model, at least in some situations for which economists' expertise might be called upon?

LIST OF STUDIES

See references for full citation.

#1. Adamowicz *et al.* [1].
#2. Banford *et al.* [2].
#3. Bateman *et al.* [3].
#4. Benzion *et al.* [5].

#5. Bishop *et al.* [9]. Further details appear in Bishop and Heberlein [7].

#6. Bowker and MacDonald [11].

#7. Boyce *et al.* [12].

#8. Brookshire and Coursey [13].

#9. Brookshire *et al.* [15].

#10. Casey [18], cited in Eisenberger and Weber [23].

#11. Coombs *et al.* [19].

#12. Coursey *et al.* [20].

#13. DuBourg *et al.* [21].

#14. Eby [22], cited in Meyer [56].

#15. Eisenberger and Weber [23].

#16. Gerking *et al.* [27].

#17. Hammack and Brown [32].

#18. Hanemann *et al.* [35]. Further details appear in Hoehn and Loomis [38] and Mansfield [54].

#19. Harless [36].

#20. Bishop and Heberlein [8]. See also Welsh [81], cited in Mansfield [54].

#21. Horowitz [39].

#22. Hueth *et al.* [40], cited in Bergstrom [6].

#23. Kachelmeier and Shehata [44].

#24. Kahneman *et al.* [45].

#25. Knetsch and Sinden [47].

#26. Kunreuther and Easterling [49].

#27. Lichtenstein and Slovic [50].

#28. Loewenstein [51].

#29. Loewenstein and Adler [52].

#30. Loomis *et al.* [53].

#31. Mantymaa [55].

#32. McDaniels [58].

#33. Meyer [59], cited in Hyman and Stiftel [41]. Further details appear in Meyer [60].

#34. Morrison [61].

#35. Rae *et al.* [65].

#36. Rowe *et al.* [67].

#37. Schulze *et al.* [69], cited in Fisher *et al.* [25].

#38. Shogren *et al.* [71].

#39. Sinclair [73], cited in Banford *et al.* [2] and Gordon and Knetsch [28].

#40. Singh [74].

#41. Smith [76].

#42. Thaler [77].

#43. Van Kooten and Schmitz [78].

#44. Viscusi *et al.* [79].

#45. Welle [80], cited in Mansfield [54].

#46. Gregory [29].

#47. Marshall *et al.* [56].

#48. McDaniels [58].

#49. Jones-Lee *et al.* [43].

#50. Slovic and Lichtenstein [75].

REFERENCES

1. W. L. Adamowicz, V. Bhardwaj, and B. Macnab, Experiments on the difference between willingness to pay and willingness to accept, *Land Econom.* **69**, 416–427 (1993).

2. N. D. Banford, J. Knetsch, and G. Mauser, Feasibility judgments and alternative measures of benefits and costs, *J. Bus. Admin.* **11**(1 & 2), 25–35 (1979/1980).

3. I. Bateman, A. Munro, B. Rhodes, C. Starmer, and R. Sugden, A test of the theory of reference-dependent preferences, *Q. J. Econom.* **CXII**, 479–505 (1997).

4. F. W. Bell and V. R. Leaworthy, "An Economic Analysis of the Importance of Saltwater Beaches in Florida," Department of Economics, Florida State University (1985).

5. U. Benzion, A. Rapoport, and J. Yagil, Discount rates inferred from decisions: An experimental study, *Management Sci.* **35**, 270–284 (1989).

6. J. Bergstrom, Concepts and measures of the economic value of environmental quality: A review, *J. Environ. Management* **31**, 215–228 (1990).

7. R. C. Bishop and T. Heberlein, Measuring values of extramarket goods: Are indirect measures biased? *Amer. J. Agric. Econom.* **61**, 926–930 (1979).

8. R. C. Bishop and T. Heberlein, Does contingent valuation work, *in* "Valuing Environmental Goods" (R. Cummings, D. Brookshire, and W. Schulze, Eds.) Rowman and Allanheld, Totowa, NJ (1986).

9. R. C. Bishop, T. A. Heberlein, and M. J. Kealy, Contingent valuation of environmental assets: Comparisons with a simulated market, *Nat. Resour. J.* **23**, 619–633 (1983).

10. B. Borges and J. Knetsch, Tests of market outcomes with asymmetric valuations of gains and losses: Smaller gains, fewer trades, and less value, *J. Econom. Behavior Organ.* **33**, 185–193 (1998).

11. J. M. Bowker and H. F. MacDonald, An economic analysis of localized pollution: Rendering emissions in a residential setting, *Can. J. Agric. Econom.* **41**, 45–59 (1993).

12. R. R. Boyce, T. C. Brown, G. H. McClelland, G. L. Peterson, and W. D. Schulze, An experimental examination of intrinsic values as a source of the WTA-WTP disparity, *Amer. Econom. Rev.* **82**, 1366–1373 (1992).

13. D. S. Brookshire and D. L. Coursey, Measuring the value of a public good: An empirical comparison of elicitation procedures, *Amer. Econom. Rev.* **77**, 554–566 (1987).

14. D. Brookshire, D. Coursey, and W. Schulze, Experiments in the solicitation of private and public values: an overview, *in* "Advances in Behavioral Economics" (L. Green and J. Kagel, Eds.), Vol. III, Ablex, Norwood, NJ (1990).

15. D. S. Brookshire, A. Randall, and J. Stoll, Valuing increments and decrements in natural resource service flows, *Amer. J. Agric. Econom.* **62**, 478–488 (1980).

16. G. Brown and S. Mathews, Economic valuation of the 1967 sport salmon fishery of Washington, Washington Department of Fisheries Bulletin, Technical Report 2 (1970).

17. R. Carson, T. Groves, and M. Machina, Incentive and informational properties of preference questions, unpublished manuscript, Department of Economics, University of California, San Diego (2000).

18. J. T. Casey, Predicting buyer-seller gaps for risky and riskless options, working paper, State University of New York at Stony Brook (1990).

19. C. H. Coombs, T. G. Bezembinder, and F. M. Goode, Testing expectation theories of decision making without measuring utility or subjective probability, *J. Math. Psych.* **4**, 72–103 (1967).

20. D. L. Coursey, J. L. Hovis, and W. D. Schulze, The disparity between willingness to accept and willingness to pay measures of value, *Q. J. Econom.* **102**, 679–690 (1987).

21. W. R. DuBourg, M. Jones-Lee, and G. Loomes, Imprecise preferences and the WTP-WTA disparity, *J. Risk Uncertainty* **9**, 115–133 (1994).

22. P. A. Eby, "The Value of Outdoor Recreation: A Case Study," Master's thesis, University of British Columbia (1975).

23. R. Eisenberger and M. Weber, WTP and WTA for risky and ambiguous lotteries, *J. Risk Uncertainty* **10**, 223–233 (1995).

24. W. Fischel, The offer/ask disparity and just compensation for takings: A constitutional choice perspective, *Internat. Rev. Law Econom.* **15**, 187–203 (1995).

25. A. Fisher, G. McClelland, and W. Schulze, Measures of WTP versus WTA: Evidence, explanations and potential reconciliation, *in* "Amenity Resource Valuation: Integrating Economics with Other Disciplines" (G. Peterson, B. Driver, and R. Gregory, Eds.), Venture Publishing, State College, PA (1989).

26. R. Franciosi, P. Kujal, R. Michelitsch, V. L. Smith, and G. Deng, Experimental tests of the endowment effect, *J. Econom. Behavior Organ.* **30**, 213–226 (1996).

27. S. Gerking, M. De Haan, and W. D. Schulze, The marginal value of job safety: A contingent value study, *J. Risk Uncertainty* **1**, 185–199 (1988).

28. I. M. Gordon and J. Knetsch, Consumers surplus and the evaluation of resources, *Land Econom.* **55**, 1–10 (1979).

29. R. Gregory, Interpreting measures of economic loss: evidence from contingent valuation and experimental studies, *J. Environ. Econom. Management* **13**, 325–337 (1986).

30. R. Gregory and L. Furby, Auctions, experiments, and contingent valuation, *Public Choice* **55**, 273–289 (1987).

31. T. Haab and K. E. McConnell, Referendum models and negative willingness to pay: Alternative solutions, *J. Environ. Econom. Management* **32**, 251–270 (1997).

32. J. Hammack and G. M. Brown, "Waterfowl and Wetlands: Toward Bioeconomic Analysis," Johns Hopkins University Press for Resources for the Future, Baltimore, MD (1974).

33. M. Hanemann, Willingness to pay and willingness to accept: How much can they differ? *Amer. Econom. Rev.* **81**, 635–647 (1991).

34. M. Hanemann, The economic theory of WTP and WTA, *in* "Valuing Environmental Preferences: Theory and Practice of the Contingent Valuation Method in the US, EU, and Developing Countries" (I. Bateman and K. G. Willis, Eds.), Oxford Univ. Press, London (1999).

35. M. Hanemann, J. B. Loomis, and B. Kanninen, Statistical efficiency of double-bounded dichotomous choice contingent valuation, *Amer. J. Agric. Econom.* **73**, 1255–1263 (1991).

36. D. W. Harless, More laboratory evidence on the disparity between willingness to pay and compensation demanded, *J. Econom. Behavior Organ.* **11**, 359–379 (1989).

37. R. S. Hartman, M. J. Doane, and C. K. Woo, Consumer rationality and the status quo, *Q. J. Econom.* **106**, 141–162 (1991).

38. J. P. Hoehn and J. B. Loomis, Substitution effects in the valuation of multiple environmental programs, *J. Environ. Econom. Management* **25**, 56–75 (1993).

39. J. K. Horowitz, Discounting money payoffs: An experimental analysis, *in* "Handbook of Behavioral Economics" (S. Kaish and B. Gilad, Eds.), Vol. 2B, JAI Press, Greenwich, CT (1991).

40. D. Hueth, S. Voorhies, and R. Cosagrande, Estimating benefits from controlling nuisance pests: An application of the interactive bidding technique, Paper presented at the Annual Meeting of the American Agricultural Economics Association, Clemson (1981).

41. E. L. Hyman and B. Stiftel, "Combining Facts and Values in Environmental Impact Assessment," Westview, Boulder, CO (1988).

42. M. W. Jones-Lee, "The Value of Life: An Economic Analysis," Univ. of Chicago Press (1976).

43. M. W. Jones-Lee, M. Hammerton, and P. Philips, The value of safety: results of a national sample survey, *Econom. J.* **95**, 49–72 (1985).

44. S. Kachelmeier and M. Shehata, Examining risk preferences under high monetary incentives: Experimental evidence from the People's Republic of China, *Amer. Econom. Rev.* **82**, 1120–1141 (1992).

45. D. Kahneman, J. L. Knetsch, and R. H. Thaler, Experimental tests of the endowment effect and the Coase theorem, *J. Polit. Econom.* **98**, 1325–1348 (1990).

46. J. Knetsch, Environmental policy implications of disparities between willingness to pay and compensation demanded measures of values, *J. Environ. Econom. Management* **18**, 227–237 (1990).

47. J. L. Knetsch and J. A. Sinden, Willingness to pay and compensation demanded: Experimental evidence of an unexpected disparity in measures of value, *Q. J. Econom.* **99**, 507–521 (1984).

48. P. Knez, V. Smith, and A. Williams, Individual rationality, market rationality, and value estimation, *Amer. Econom. Rev.* **75**, 397–402 (1985).

49. H. Kunreuther and D. Easterling, Gaining acceptance for noxious facilities with economic incentives, *in* "The Social Response to Environmental Risk" (D. Bromley and K. Segerson, Eds.), pp. 151–186, Kluwer Academic, Dordrecht (1992).

50. S. Lichtenstein and P. Slovic, Reversals of preference between bids and choices in gambling decisions, *J. Exp. Psych.* **89**, 46–55 (1971).

51. G. F. Loewenstein, Frames of mind in intertemporal choice, *Management Sci.* **34**, 200–214 (1988).

52. G. Loewenstein and D. Adler, A bias in the prediction of tastes, *Econom. J.* **105**, 929–937 (1995).

446   HOROWITZ AND McCONNELL

53. J. Loomis, G. Peterson, T. Brown, P. Champ, and B. Lucero, Estimating WTA using the method of paired comparison and its relationship to WTP estimated using dichotomous choice CVM, unpublished manuscript (1996).

54. C. Mansfield, "Despairing over Disparities: An Empirical Analysis of the Difference Between Willingness to Pay and Willingness to Accept," Ph.D. dissertation, Department of Economics, University of Maryland (1994).

55. E. Mantymaa, Willingness to pay and willingness to accept: An empirical test of differences with environmental commodities in a CVM field study, unpublished manuscript (1997).

56. J. Marshall, J. Knetsch, and J. Sinden, Agents' evaluations and the disparity in measures of economic loss, *J. Econom. Behavior Organ.* **7**, 115–127 (1986).

57. G. McClelland and W. Schulze, The disparity between willingness to pay and willingness to accept as a framing effect, *in* "Frontiers in Mathematical Psychology" (D. R. Brown and J. E. K. Smith, Eds.), Springer-Verlag, Berlin/New York (1991).

58. T. McDaniels, Reference points, loss aversion, and contingent values for auto safety, *J. Risk Uncertainty* **5**, 187–200 (1992).

59. P. Meyer, "A Comparison of Direct Questioning Methods for Obtaining Dollar Values for Public Recreation and Preservation," Environment Canada, Vancouver, BC (1976).

60. P. Meyer, Publicly vested values for fish and wildlife: Criteria in economic welfare and interface with the law, *Land Econom.* **55**, 223–235 (1979).

61. G. Morrison, Willingness to pay and willingness to accept: Some evidence of an endowment effect, *Appl. Econom.* **29**, 411–417 (1997).

62. M. Nerlove, Likelihood inference in econometrics, unpublished manuscript (1999).

63. D. Prelec and G. Loewenstein, Decision-making over time and under uncertainty: A common approach, *Management Sci.* **37**, 770–786 (1991).

64. J. Quiggin and J. K. Horowitz, Time and risk, *J. Risk Uncertainty* **10**, 37–55 (1995).

65. D. A. Rae, J. Hausman, and J. Wickham, Benefits of visual air quality in Cincinnati: Results of a contingent ranking survey, Charles River Associates, Research Project 1742 for Electric Power Research Institute (1982).

66. A. Randall and J. Stoll, Consumer surplus in commodity space, *Amer. Econom. Rev.* **70**, 449–455 (1980).

67. R. Rowe, R. d'Arge, and D. Brookshire, An experiment on the economic value of visibility, *J. Environ. Econom. Management* **7**, 1–19 (1980).

68. W. Schulze, R. d'Arge, and D. Brookshire, Valuing environmental commodities: Some recent experiments, *Land Econom.* **57**, 151–172 (1981).

69. W. D. Schulze, G. McClelland, B. Hurd, and J. Smith, Estimating benefits for toxic waste management: An application of the property value method, Draft Report, U.S. Environmental Protection Agency, Washington, DC (1985).

70. J. Shogren and D. Hayes, Resolving differences in willingness to pay and willingness to accept: Reply, *Amer. Econom. Rev.* **87**, 241–244 (1997).

71. J. F. Shogren, S. Y. Shin, D. J. Hayes, and J. R. Kliebenstein, Resolving differences in willingness to pay and willingness to accept, *Amer. Econom. Rev.* **84**, 255–270 (1994).

72. J. Shogren, R. Wilhelmi, C. Koo, S. Cho, C. Park, and P. Polo, Auction institutions and the measurement of WTP and WTA, unpublished manuscript (1996).

73. W. F. Sinclair, "The Economic and Social Impact of the Kemano II Hydroelectric Project on British Columbia's Fisheries Resources," Federal Department of the Environment, Fisheries, and Marine Services, Vancouver, BC (1976).

74. H. Singh, The disparity between willingness to pay and compensation demanded: Another look at laboratory evidence, *Econom. Lett.* **35**, 263–266 (1991).

75. P. Slovic and S. Lichtenstein, Relative importance of probabilities and payoffs in risk taking, *J. Exp. Psych. Monogr.* **78**, 1–18 (1968).

76. V. L. Smith, Comments, *in* "Valuing Environmental Goods: An Assessment of the Contingent Valuation Method" (R. G. Cummings, D. S. Brookshire, and W. D. Schulze, Eds.), Rowman & Allanheld, Totowa, NJ (1986).

77. R. Thaler, Some empirical evidence on dynamic inconsistency, *Econom. Lett.* **8**, 201–207 (1981).

78. G. C. Van Kooten and A. Schmitz, Preserving waterfowl habitat on the Canadian prairies: Economic incentives versus moral suasion, *Amer. J. Agric. Econom.* **74**, 79–89 (1992).

79. W. K. Viscusi, W. Magat, and J. Huber, An investigation of the rationality of consumer valuations of multiple health risks, *RAND J. Econom.* **18**, 465–479 (1987).

80. P. Welle, "Potential Economic Impacts of Acid Deposition: A Contingent Valuation Study of Minnesota," Ph.D. dissertation, Department of Agricultural Economics, University of Wisconsin–Madison (1986).

81. M. Welsh, "Exploring the Accuracy of the Contingent Valuation Method: Comparisons with Simulated Markets," Ph.D. dissertation, Department of Agricultural Economics, University of Wisconsin–Madison (1986).

82. R. Willig, Consumer's surplus without apology, *Amer. Econom. Rev.* **66**, 589–597 (1976).

[21]

WILLINGNESS TO PAY, COMPENSATING VARIATION, AND THE COST OF COMMITMENT

JINHUA ZHAO and CATHERINE L. KLING*

Hicksian welfare theory is static in nature, but many decisions are made in a dynamic environment. We present a dynamic model of an agent's decision to purchase or sell a good under the realistic conditions of uncertainty, irreversibility, and learning over time. Her willingness to pay (WTP) contains both the intrinsic value of the good as in Hicksian theory plus a commitment cost associated with delaying to obtain more information. The Hicksian equivalence between WTP/Willingness to accept (WTA) and compensating and equivalent variations no longer holds. The WTP and WTA divergence may arise and observed WTP values are not always appropriate for welfare analysis. (JEL D60, D83)

I. INTRODUCTION

Hicksian welfare theory, which is static in nature, forms the basis of modern welfare analysis. This theory has provided a wealth of compelling principles with direct applicability for empirical welfare analysis (see, for example, Hoehn and Randall 1987; Bockstael and McConnell 1983; Randall and Stoll 1980). The equivalence of the maximum willingness to pay (WTP) for a good with the Hicksian concept of compensating (or equivalent) variation (CV or EV) is a central precept of this theory. This specific principle has provided the necessary theoretical basis for substantial literature in several areas of applied economics, including work on valuing public goods, experimental economics, and price discriminating monopoly, to name only a few.

Thus, researchers in search of the value of a public good have designed surveys eliciting consumers' maximum WTP to obtain the public good. If the assumptions of the static Hicksian theory hold, this measure can be

* We thank Subir Bose, Dermot Hayes, David Hennessy, Brent Hueth, Lise Vesterlund, David Zilberman, seminar participants at UC Berkeley, UC Davis, UC Santa Barbara, and the AERE 1999 Summer Meeting, and three anonymous referees for their helpful comments. The usual disclaimer applies.

Zhao: Associate Professor, Department of Economics, Heady Hall, Iowa State University, Ames, IA 50011. Phone 1-515-294-5857, Fax 1-515-294-0221, E-mail jzhao@iastate.edu

Kling: Professor, Department of Economics, Heady Hall, Iowa State University, Ames, IA 50011. Phone 1-515-294-5767, Fax 1-515-294-0221, E-mail ckling@iastate.edu

readily interpreted as the compensating variation, a theoretically defensible welfare measure that can be directly applied to cost-benefit analysis using stated preference methods (Mitchell and Carson 1989; Carson 1997; Smith 2000). Likewise, experimental economists elicit WTP or willingness to accept (WTA) based on actual transactions to test a variety of consumer theory hypotheses, including the empirical disparity between WTP and WTA (Horowitz and McConnell 2002; Horowitz et al. 1999; List forthcoming) and the equivalence between revealed and stated preference values (Cummings and Taylor 1999; List 2001).

However, many decisions in the real world are made in dynamic settings: Purchase decisions may be delayed while information is gathered, purchase "mistakes" can be reversed by return policies, and there are often costs associated with these transactions. In this article we explore the Hicksian concepts of compensating and equivalent variation as well as WTP (and WTA) in explicitly dynamic situations; specifically, where the agent is uncertain about the value of the good under consideration but can latter

ABBREVIATIONS	
CV:	Compensating Variation
CVM:	Contingent Valuation Method
EV:	Equivalent Variation
QOV:	Quasi-Option Value
WTA:	Willingness to Accept
WTP:	Willingness to Pay

obtain more information about it. We find that, although CV and EV have natural expected value counterparts that are conceptually akin to the static CV and EV, their relationship to the WTP and WTA concepts becomes much more complicated. Specifically, in addition to CV/EV, WTP and WTA will also depend critically on a variety of factors related to the timing of the formation of these values. Even if expected CV and EV are unchanging with the acquisition of new information, WTP and WTA will generally not be. Thus, at any point in time, WTP or WTA will not be equivalent to the expected CV or EV.

The intuition behind the breakdown of the equivalence between CV/EV and WTP/WTA in an intertemporal setting has to do with the nature of the measures themselves. The Hicksian concepts of CV and EV can be thought of as measuring the intrinsic value of a good. Specifically, CV measures the amount of compensation necessary after a change in price or other attribute that holds the consumer's utility constant. Consequently, this measure depends only on the utility function itself, not on the timing of a transaction or any other characteristics of the exchange environment.

In contrast, the consumer's WTP (or WTA) for a good is a fundamentally behavioral concept. The behavior in question is that of buying (or selling) a good. How much one is willing to pay (or accept) for a good at a particular point in time will depend on a variety of factors, including, of course, the expected intrinsic value. However, also included will be the consumer's rate of time preference, the ability to reduce the risk of a bad purchase or sale by gathering more information, and the ease of later reversing the transaction if so desired. Note that all of these features are related in some way to the timing of the behavioral decision. Thus, in a static model, the behavioral concepts collapse to the intrinsic Hicksian measures. However, in an explicitly dynamic setting, the equivalence between Hicksian values and the behavioral WTP/WTA values will not necessarily hold.

In practice, in many markets timing of the transaction is an integral part of the decision. For example, an art collector considering selling a painting may want to gather information about the painting's market value before deciding to offer it for sale. Likewise, a consumer considering the purchase of a new style of blue jeans might want to learn more about current styles and substitutes before actually making the purchase, especially if the store has a limited

return policy.[1] Thus, timing may play a key role in market transactions by allowing agents to acquire information about the good, such as the prevailing market prices (including prices of substitutes) and to solidify their own preferences for the good. The information helps the agent reduce the likelihood of having to reverse a trade (thus incurring the associated transaction cost) later on. Thus, to make a purchase on the first day that the new styles are in the stores, the jeans shopper will be willing to pay less than he or she might if he or she waited and gathered further information. Alternatively, for the art collector to sell the painting to the first bidder and forgo further learning, he or she will demand a higher price in compensation for the quick action. In both cases, the price at which the buyer or seller is willing to purchase or sell the good (WTP or WTA) is determined both by the intrinsic value of the good (CV or EV) and how quickly the decision has to be made (or the amount of information available).

In this article we present a model that explicitly demonstrates the effect that timing of an action can have on WTP and WTA. Specifically, by *committing* to a purchase or sale decision, the agent has to abandon learning opportunities and thus demands appropriate "compensation." Consequently, the WTP for a commodity will be reduced by a commitment cost, and the agent's WTA will be increased by another commitment cost. Readers familiar with the real options literature in investment theory will recognize that these commitment cost concepts are related to option values arising in investment decisions. As Arrow and Fisher (1974), Henry (1974), Epstein (1980), Kolstad (1996), and Dixit and Pindyck (1994) have demonstrated, this role of future information means that there is a benefit, called quasi-option value (QOV),[2] associated with waiting to make a decision. Later, we demonstrate how the commitment costs are related to and distinct from QOV. More important, this article develops a systematic framework for

1. In fact, the literature on herd behavior focuses explicitly on information and the timing of decisions by a group of agents (Banerjee 1992; Bikhchandani et al. 1992).

2. QOV is distinct from the option value concept in the option price literature (Ready 1995). It measures a conditional value of information and exists even for risk neutral agents. See Hanemann (1989) for additional discussion of QOV. Dixit (1992), reviewed in Hubbard (1994), provides a nice review of the QOV literature, and Fisher (2000) establishes the equivalence between the Arrow-Fisher-Henry model and the Dixit and Pindyck (1994) framework.

studying the effects of uncertainty, irreversibility and new information in consumer welfare analysis. Because commitment costs, in addition to the intrinsic value of the good (i.e., CV or EV), enter the WTP/WTA measurement, the standard relationship in Hicksian welfare theory between the WTP/WTA and CV/EV fails to hold.

The article is organized as follows. Section II constructs a model of an agent's decision to buy or sell a good, under conditions of uncertainty and irreversibility. WTP and WTA are seen to contain commitment costs and variables that affect the magnitude of these commitment costs are examined. In section III, we investigate the relationship between WTP/WTA and CV/EV. In Section IV, we discuss some of the implications of these theoretical results for applied welfare analysis.

II. A MODEL OF WTP/WTA FORMATION

In this section, we model a situation typical of real-world welfare economic problems, namely, an agent's decision to purchase or sell a good when the good has uncertain value to the agent. However, unlike the Hicksian framework, we assume that information becomes available over time that reduces this uncertainty, and the agent can purchase the good either now or later when more information arrives. We consider only two goods, a composite good (or money) and the specific good being traded, with perfect substitution between them. In particular, the agent's utility function is given by

(1) $U(m, n) = m + nG,$

where m is money, n is the amount of the traded good, and G is its unit value. This utility function implies that the agent is risk-neutral, with constant elasticity of substitution between the two goods. For simplicity, we impose the condition that $n \in \{0, 1\}$, that is, the agent can only trade *one unit* of the specific good.[3]

Suppose the agent can trade in either period 1 (current) or 2 (future). She is uncertain about the value G, and her current belief is described by distribution $F_0(\cdot)$, or density function $f_0(\cdot)$,

both defined on $[0, G_H]$.[4] She knows that more information about G will be available in period 2, and specifically, the information comes in the form of a *signal* about G, denoted by $s \in S \subset \mathcal{R}$, where S is the set of all possible signals. There is no cost associated with acquiring the signal. However, the agent must wait until period 2 to obtain the information. Conditional on the true value of G, the possible signals are described by the conditional density function $h_{s|G}(\cdot)$, defined on S. Let $h(\cdot)$ be the unconditional density function of signal s, that is, $h(s) = \int_0^{G_H} h_{s|G}(s) dF_0(G)$, and let $H(\cdot)$ be the corresponding distribution function. Observing s, the agent updates her belief about G according to Bayes's rule, $f_{G|s}(G) = h_{s|G}(s) f_0(G)/h(s)$. The associated conditional distribution function is denoted as $F_{G|s}(\cdot)$.

To fix ideas, suppose an agent is considering purchasing a particular painting.[5] She has some idea (described by her prior F_0) about its value to her, but before making an offer, she wishes to consult a friend who is an art dealer. Her dealer friend agrees but can only inspect the painting two weeks later. In this example, the signal is her friend's opinion that she will rely on to update her own belief about the painting's value. Thus, our potential art patron can either make an offer now with her current level of knowledge and associated uncertainty, or wait for two weeks when she can make an offer based on a better estimate of the painting's value.

For simplicity, we assume that the agent observes the true value of G *immediately* after she finishes the trade.[6] After G is realized, the agent can reverse the trade, that is, return the good that she purchased or buy back the good that she sold, at a certain cost. Let $c_P > 0$ denote the cost of returning and $c_A > 0$ the cost of repurchasing the good. Ex post, it may be

---

3. This assumption allows us to work with the constant marginal utility function in (1) without imposing a budget constraint. Otherwise, we need to work with a more general utility function with decreasing marginal utility. The assumption greatly simplifies our analysis and does not affect our major results.

4. Without loss of generality, we let the lowest possible value of G be zero. We could use a more general representation, such as $G_L (< G_H)$, and the results would remain the same.

5. This example is based on the painting experiments performed by Neill et al. (1994), where paintings were offered for sale to subjects who used their own money to (or not to) purchase paintings that were exhibited in the experiments.

6. Usually a buyer learns the true value of a good after using it, implying that she observes G after purchasing the good. Similarly, a seller often learns the true market value of a good after other people have bought, used, and possibly resold it. We assume away the time lag between trading and the realization of G, without affecting the major results of our model.

desirable to return the good and incur c_P if G turns out to be quite low and repurchase the good and incur c_A if G is quite high. In our example, if the art patron purchases the painting but later finds it less appealing, she may wish to resell it. However, this may involve significant transaction costs if the secondary market is not well established, say, if she has to auction the painting off on her own.

The agent may be anxious to use the good or the proceeds from selling the good and is therefore less willing to wait for the signal. To capture this *impatience* factor, we assume that she discounts the second period benefit at rate $\beta \in [0, 1]$. Note that β may equal 1 (no discounting) if the agent currently does not need the good or the proceeds from selling it. Again in our example, the art patron may be very impatient (i.e., have a low β) if, say, she needs the painting for a party the next day. But her β would be much higher if the painting is needed for a party next month. In the latter case, she will be more likely to wait for her dealer friend's opinion before making an offer.

In traditional static welfare measurement where the opportunity of future learning is not considered, WTP is defined to be the maximum price the agent is willing to pay for the good, and WTA is the minimum price she requires for giving up the good. We denote these concepts as WTP_S and WTA_S, respectively. However, when the possibility of future learning is considered, we have instead:

DEFINITION 1. *WTP is the maximum price at which an agent is willing to buy the good **in the current period**, and WTA is the minimum price at which she is willing to sell the good **in the current period**.*

To determine WTP and WTA, we set an arbitrary price p for the good and consider whether the agent would want to trade now or wait for the signal. Intuition suggests that if the price is sufficiently low, the agent will want to buy now because the signal will not be very useful. Similarly, she will sell now if the price is sufficiently high. Indeed, we will show that there exists a unique critical price, p_P, at which she is indifferent between buying now and waiting (i.e., below which she would buy now and above which she would want to wait), and a unique critical price, p_A, at which she is indifferent between selling now and waiting (i.e., below which she would want

to wait and above which she would sell now). Then $WTP = p_P$ and $WTA = p_A$.

The Determination of WTP

Define $V(p, s)$ to be the expected net surplus of the agent if she purchases one unit of the good at price p after observing signal s. That is,

$$(2) \quad V(p,s) = \int_0^{G_H} \max\{p - c_P, G\} dF_{G|s}(G) - p$$
$$= \int_0^{G_H} \max\{-c_P, G - p\} dF_{G|s}(G).$$

The integrand, $\max\{p - c_P, G\}$, represents the agent's ex post payoff from either keeping the good (thus getting G) or returning it (thus getting her money p back, minus the transaction cost, c_P). To reduce clutter, we let $V(p, 0)$ be the expected net surplus based on the prior information F_0 (i.e., without observing any signals).[7] That is, $V(p, 0) = \int_0^{G_H} \max\{-c_P, G - p\} dF_0(G)$.

Because $\max(\cdot)$ is a convex operator, we know $V(p, s)$ is decreasing and convex in p. If $p \leq c_P$, $\max\{-c_P, G - p\} = G - p$ for all $G \in [0, G_H]$ (i.e., the agent will never return the good). In this case $V(p, s) = \bar{G}(s) - p$ where $\bar{G}(s) = \int_0^{G_H} G dF_{G|s}(G)$ is the expected value of G if signal s is observed. If $p = G_H$, $\max\{-c_P, G - p\} \leq 0$ for all $G \in [0, G_H]$. Continuity of $V(p, s)$ in p then implies that $V(p, s) < 0$ for p sufficiently close to G_H. Note that as long as $f_{G|s}(\cdot)$ is strictly positive, almost surely on $[0, G_H]$, $V(p, s)$ is strictly decreasing in p for $p < G_H$. Even when p is close to G_H, there is always a positive probability that $G - p > -c_P$ (e.g., when G is close to G_H), causing $V(p, s)$ to be decreasing in p. For technical clarity, we assume throughout that $f_{G|s}(\cdot)$ is bounded away from zero on $[0, G_H]$ for all $s \in S$.

Figure 1 graphs $V(p, 0)$, where $\bar{G}$ stands for $\bar{G}(0)$. Because $V(p, 0) = 0$ at the unique $p = \tilde{p}_P$, we know $\tilde{p}_P$ is the static measure of the agent's WTP, or WTP_S. Note that $\tilde{p}_P > \bar{G}$, the expected value of the good, due to the existence of the return option.[8] It is

---

7. To make this statement strictly true, we have to require that $0 \in S$, and signal 0 does not contain any information about G.

8. The difference $\tilde{p}_P - \bar{G}$ is the value of the "money-back guarantee" under which the agent can return the good at cost c_P. This value has been modeled in a greater detail in Heiman et al. (forthcoming).

FIGURE 1

Static Welfare Measurement: *WTP*

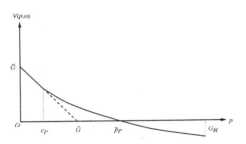

FIGURE 2

Dynamic Welfare Measurement: *WTP*

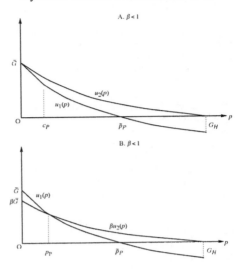

obvious from Figure 1 that $\bar{p}_P = \bar{G}$ if c_P is sufficiently high. That is, the static WTP_S equals the intrinsic value of the good $\bar{G}$ when returning the good becomes too costly. We consider this special case in greater detail later in this section.

Let $u_1(p)$ be the agent's expected net surplus if she buys the good at price p in period 1 (without any signal). Then

$$(3) \quad u_1(p) = V(p,0) = \int_S V(p,s)dH(s).$$

Let $u_2(p)$ be her expected net surplus if at price p, she does not buy in period 1 but instead makes her decision in period 2. Observing s, the agent will buy the good only if her expected surplus conditional on s is nonnegative, yielding expected payoff $\max\{0, V(p,s)\}$. Thus ex ante, before the signal is realized, her expected surplus of not buying in period 1 is

$$(4) \quad u_2(p) = \int_S \max\{0, V(p,s)\}dH(s)$$
$$= \int_{S_{P1}(p)} V(p,s)dH(s),$$

where $S_{P1}(p) = \{s \in S : V(p,s) \geq 0\}$. Because $V(p,s)$ is decreasing and convex in p, so are $u_1(p)$ and $u_2(p)$. [$u_2(\cdot)$ is convex because $\max\{\cdot,\cdot\}$ is a convex operator.] Comparing (3) and (4), we know $u_1(p) \leq u_2(p)$ for all $p \in [0, G_H]$, and the inequality is strict if $S_{P1}(p)$ has a probability measure of less than one. The appendix shows that this condition is satisfied if for any $p > 0$ there are always some signals that would predict that the good's value is below p with at least a certain strictly positive probability. We assume that this condition is

true. The expression $u_2(p) - u_1(p)$ then measures the gain (without discounting) from waiting: New information enables the agent to avoid "bad" purchases for which signal s falls in the "no-purchase" set, $S_{P2}(p) = S/S_{P1}(p) = \{s \in S : V(p,s) < 0\}$.

Figure 2A graphs both $u_1(p)$ and $u_2(p)$. Note that $u_2(0) = u_1(0) = \bar{G}$ because when $p = 0$, $V(0,s) \geq 0$ for all $s \in S$, or $S_{P1}(0) = S$. That is, when the price is zero, the agent will buy the product whose value is nonnegative regardless of the signal, so waiting becomes pointless. Further, $u_2(G_H) = 0$ because if $p = G_H$, the expected net payoff $V(G_H,s)$ is negative regardless of the signal. Then the agent will not buy the good for any signal, and the net benefit is zero.

In fact, Figure 2A illustrates the optimal decision when there is no discounting. Because $u_2(p) > u_1(p)$ for $p > 0$, the agent always waits for the signal if $p > 0$. This result is obvious: Because waiting incurs no cost but can prevent possible "bad purchases" [the case of $V(p,s) < 0$] when $p > 0$, she will not buy in the current period. Thus, the agent's WTP in the current period is zero, the lowest possible value of G.

The effect of discounting is illustrated in Figure 2B. The discount factor is $\beta < 1$, and the WTP is p_P at which $u_1(p_P) = \beta u_2(p_P)$. If the agent is asked to buy the good at a price p, and she has to answer *now*, then her answer will be "no" if $p > p_P$ and "yes" if $p \leq p_P$. Thus $WTP = p_P$. The appendix shows that p_P exists and is unique.

WTP is closely related to the Arrow-Fisher-Henry QOV given by $QOV(p) = \max\{0, \beta u_2(p) - u_1(p)\}$. For a given price p, QOV measures the additional benefit of being able to wait for the new information, conditional on the fact that waiting is optimal (Hanemann 1989). Then the *WTP* is the maximum price at which *QOV* is zero.[9] In the current period, the agent will not pay a higher price than p_P because at that price she will simply wait instead of making the purchase.

In this article, we define a distinct concept of "commitment cost" that measures the difference between the static and dynamic *WTP*: $CC_P = \tilde{p}_P - p_P \geq 0$, or written differently,

$$(5) \qquad WTP = WTP_S - CC_P.$$

This commitment cost measures the compensation, in terms of a lower price (for both periods), that the agent demands to give up the opportunity of waiting by buying the good now. It represents the minimum amount of money needed, in terms of an overall price reduction, to induce the agent to buy in this period. Conceptually, it is similar to $QOV(\tilde{p}_P)$: given price $\tilde{p}_P$, both QOV and CC_P measure how much is needed to induce the agent to buy in the current period. The difference is that QOV is expressed in terms of a direct income transfer, whereas CC_P is expressed in terms of a price cut for both periods, thus allowing application to modeling consumer welfare measurement. Zhao and Kling (2002) establish a monotonic functional relationship between the two measures.

Consider again the painting example. Suppose the listed price of the painting is $\tilde{p}_P$. Without the opportunity of her friend's help, the patron is indifferent between buying and not buying. However, given the possibility of information from her friend, she will wait at this price. The seller could induce her to buy *now* in one of two ways: by offering the patron a *one-time discount* (equivalent to a direct income transfer) of at least $QOV(\tilde{p}_P)$, or by permanently lowering the price by at least

CC_P. The permanently lower price may induce a current purchase because it lowers the value of the future information. The one-time discount is offered only if the agent buys now, so that she will have to pay $\tilde{p}_P$ if she buys two weeks later, whereas the price change in determining CC_P lasts for at least two weeks. Thus, QOV is measured in direct income transfer, and CC_P is measured in (permanent) price discounts.

The reason for the monotonic relationship between CC_P and QOV is that the two measures are derived from the same decision problem, that is, making a purchase facing uncertainty, irreversibility, and future learning. To decide when to purchase the good, the QOV literature takes as given the cost (or price), and looks for the *signals s* that will lead to the purchase. In our model, we study the same problem but flip the question: Given the possible signals, at what cost (or price) should the agent purchase the good. Both CC_P and QOV require the same conditions to arise, namely, uncertainty, costly reversibility, future learning, and the ability to delay the decision. Although the QOV literature emphasizes the investment decision rules, by asking the flip side of the QOV question, we focus on the welfare measure in the dynamic purchase decision, rather than on the decision rule itself.[10]

WTP and CC_P depend on the incentive of the agent to wait for new information. Intuition suggests that this incentive rises as the agent becomes more patient (has a lower discount rate), as the future signal becomes more informative about the good, or as the cost of returning the good (or the penalty

---

9. Strictly, $WTP = \inf\{p \in [0, G_H] \cdot QOV(p) > 0\} = \inf\{p \in [0, G_H] : \beta u_2(p) > u_1(p)\}$.

10. This relationship between CC_P and QOV is established for the case where the quantity traded is exogenously fixed. When the agent can freely choose how much to buy, the optimal quantity is one at which the associated QOV is just zero (see, e.g., Dixit and Pindyck 1994). Similarly, we can show that the commitment cost at this quantity is also just zero. The intuition is that when quantity purchased is small, the possible loss from committing without further information is small relative to the gain from acting early. The agent then needs no compensation for buying now. However, compensation is needed for large quantities, either in the form of a QOV or a CC_P. Therefore, CC_P and QOV are different forms of the compensation needed for early actions both for fixed and for endogenous quantities. Here we model a fixed quantity mainly to be consistent with the majority of lab experiments and CVM surveys: Subjects routinely are required to buy/sell fixed quantities of goods in experiments, and CVM surveys are often used to estimate the welfare effects of exogenously given quantity changes.

for making a bad purchase) increases. Proposition 1 (proved in the appendix) shows that this intuition is correct, where the informativeness of the signal is defined in the sense of Blackwell (1951, 1953): S' is more informative than S if $h_{S'|G}$ is sufficient for $h_{S|G}$.

PROPOSITION 1. *WTP is decreasing in β, the informativeness of signal S, and the return cost c_P. CC_P is increasing in β and the informativeness of S.*

Special Case: Absolute Irreversibility

Now we consider the special case where $c_P \geq G_H$ so that the agent will never return the good and the purchase is absolutely irreversible. This case is interesting not only because it generates an analytical solution for WTP and CC_P but also because it represents interesting real-world situations. For instance, destruction of an old-growth forest or significant erosion of fragile coastline habitat are extremely costly to reverse.

From (2), we know that with $c_P \geq G_H$, $V(p, s) = \int_0^{G_H}(G - p)dF_{G|s}(G) = \bar{G}(s) - p$. Thus $WTP_S = \bar{G}$. The appendix shows that

(6) $CC_P = [\text{Prob}(S_{P2})/([1/\beta] - \text{Prob}[S_{P1}])]$
$\times [\bar{G} - E(G|S_{P2})]$,   and

(7) $WTP = \bar{G} - CC_P = WTP_S - CC_P$,

where $E(G \mid S_{P2}) = [1/\text{Prob}(S_{P2})] \int_{S_{P2}} \bar{G}(s)$ $dH(s) < \bar{G}$ is the expected value of G conditional on $s \in S_{P2}$ being realized. Note that $E(G|s) < \bar{G}$ for all $s \in S_{P2}$, because S_{P2} is the set in which realized signals predict low G values (thus no purchase is made). Thus, $CC_P > 0$. Further, CC_P increases in β; the size of the regret set, S_{P2}, which can be avoided by waiting; and the expected penalty for making a mistake, $\bar{G} - E(G \mid S_{P2})$.

The Determination of WTA

The derivation of WTA, shown in the appendix, is parallel to that of WTP. $W(p,s)$, the net gain of selling one unit of the good at p when the signal is s, is increasing and convex in p. Figure 3 graphs the expected net benefit of selling in the first period (i.e., without waiting for the signal), $W(p, 0)$. $\tilde{p}_A$ is the minimum price the agent requires to give up the good and is thus the

FIGURE 3
Static Welfare Measurement: WTA

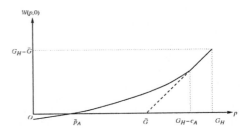

FIGURE 4
Dynamic Welfare Measurement: WTA

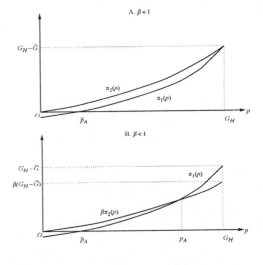

static WTA measure, WTA_S. Again $\tilde{p}_A < \bar{G}$ due to the "goods-back guarantee". Because she can buy it back if the good turns out to be highly valuable, she is willing to sell the good at a lower price than she otherwise would.

Let $\pi_1(p)$ and $\pi_2(p)$ be the agent's expected net surplus if she decides to sell the good in period 1 and to wait one more period, respectively. Figure 4 graphs $\pi_1(p)$ and $\beta\pi_2(p)$ for both $\beta = 1$ and $\beta < 1$. Without discounting, $WTA = G_H$, and with discounting, $WTA = p_A > \tilde{p}_A = WTA_S$.

Defining the commitment cost of selling now as $CC_A = p_A - \tilde{p}_A \geq 0$, we know

(8) $WTA = WTA_S + CC_A.$

Similar to Proposition 1, we have

PROPOSITION 2. *WTA is increasing in β, the informativeness of signal S, and the repurchase cost c_A. CC_A is increasing in β and the informativeness of S.*

The special case of absolute irreversibility is also derived in the appendix. In particular,

$$(9) \quad WTA = \bar{G} + CC_A = WTA_S + CC_A.$$

III. WTP/WTA AND THE HICKSIAN MEASURES

We now relate the dynamic measures WTP and WTA to the Hicksian welfare measures CV and EV. Because our model deals with giving up or obtaining *one* unit of the traded good, CV and EV are implicitly defined as

$$(10) \quad EU(m - \tilde{CV}, 1) = EU(m, 0)$$
$$EU(m + \tilde{EV}, 0) = EU(m, 1),$$

where $\tilde{CV}$ and $\tilde{EV}$ are the CV and EV associated with one unit change in the traded good.[11] With perfect substitution in the utility function (1), our model yields

$$(11) \quad \tilde{CV} = \tilde{EV} = \bar{G}.$$

Equations (7) and (9) make clear that the correspondences that hold between $\tilde{EV}$ and $\tilde{CV}$ and WTP_S/WTA_S do not hold between $\tilde{EV}/\tilde{CV}$ and WTP/WTA.[12] Neither WTP nor WTA correctly measures the intrinsic value of the good, $\bar{G}$: They miss by their associated commitment costs. Because only WTP and WTA are observable in empirical welfare measurement (not CV or EV), the commitment costs make it difficult to infer CV/EV from WTP/WTA. That is, unlike the static case, going from "behavioral observations" to "preferences" is not direct anymore: Actions depend not only on intrinsic values but also

11. Because we are measuring the welfare effects of a quantity change, $\tilde{CV}$ and $\tilde{EV}$ are in fact *compensating surplus* and *equivalent surplus*, respectively (Randall and Stoll 1980). Because they are conceptually similar to CV and EV, we follow standard usage (Hanemann 1991) and continue to use the terms CV and EV.

12. When a trade can be reversed, we observed that even WTP_S/WTA_S do not measure CV/EV correctly due to the return and repurchase options.

on commitment, information, and the prospect of learning.

The existence of commitment costs indicates that some of the properties of CV and EV cannot be carried over to WTP and WTA. For example, WTP and WTA will not necessarily share the symmetry that CV and EV exhibit related to a reverse welfare change. The CV for a change from bundles A to B exactly equals the EV for a change from B to A. However, different directions of irreversibility and thus differences in CC_A and CC_P imply that the WTP for a change from A to B will not necessarily equal the WTA for a change from B to A. It is therefore important in applied welfare analysis to find out whether commitment costs exist and, if so, their magnitudes. Next, we discuss several cases where new insights can be obtained from applying our dynamic welfare measurement framework.

IV. IMPLICATIONS

Based on our model, commitment costs arise when the following conditions are met: the agent (1) is uncertain about the value of the good, (2) expects that she can learn more about the value in the future, (3) has some willingness to wait (i.e., her discount factor β is strictly positive), (4) expects a cost associated with reversing the action of buying or selling, and (5) is forced to make a trading decision now even though she might prefer to delay the decision. Commitment costs and the difference between WTP/WTA and CV/EV are larger as each of these factors become stronger.

In this section, we highlight a few of the implications these results have for welfare analysis. We discuss situations in which commitment costs may arise and be relevant. Although separate analysis would be needed to formally explore the applications in each area, we focus on intuitive descriptions of why commitment costs may be important in that particular application.

Before beginning, we note that although we only modeled uncertainty about the marginal utility of the traded good, our model applies to cases where the agent is uncertain about the prices of the good in other stores and the prices of complement and substitute goods. Similarly, her future learning may be about the utility and relevant price information. The following discussion will be based on this more general interpretation of uncertainty.

WTP/WTA Divergence in Experiments and Surveys

A well-known and considered puzzle in applied welfare economics is that WTP and WTA measures obtained from experimental and contingent valuation studies are typically widely divergent and these divergences cannot reasonably be explained by the magnitude of the income effects.[13] These findings have seriously challenged Hicksian welfare theory: Using a meta-analysis of over 200 WTA and WTP observations from 45 experiments and surveys, Horowitz and McConnell (forthcoming) found *no* preference structure in the Hicksian framework that is consistent with the observed WTA and WTP ratio. The WTP/WTA divergence identified in contingent valuation surveys has been implicitly viewed as evidence of the failure of the survey methods—because it conflicts with the Hicksian theory! The divergence has prompted the NOAA panel to recommend using WTP as the welfare measure regardless of the property rights involved (Arrow et al. 1993).

There have been several attempts to explain this WTP/WTA divergence. One theory that has been forwarded and gained considerable following is reference-dependent preferences, also variously referred to as loss aversion or endowment effects (Kahneman and Tversky 1979; Tversky and Kahneman 1991). This approach is inconsistent with Hicksian theory and posits that the structure of the utility function depends on the endowment of the consumer: She values goods more highly once she owns them. Her indifference curves for different endowments will cross. Numerous experiments have been conducted, and their results interpreted as supporting this theory over neoclassical preferences (Harbaugh et al. 2001; Horowitz and McConnell 2002).

Another explanation is due to Hanemann (1991), who builds on Randall and Stoll (1980) and demonstrates that large divergences between CV and EV (and thus WTP and WTA) can occur when there are no good substitutes for the good being valued. Others have suggested that it may be the process of preference formation (Hoehn and Randall 1987) or the auction mechanisms used in laboratory experiments that induce these divergences (Kolstad and Guzman 1999). These explanations operate within the Hicksian framework but are limited in their applications.[14]

All of these explanations implicitly assume that WTP/WTA obtained based on agents' behaviors accurately measures the intrinsic welfare CV/EV and interpret any difference between WTP and WTA as that of CV and EV. Our results provide a different, and in some sense complementary explanation for the WTP/WTA disparity. When either CC_A or CC_P exists, the divergence may arise even without endowment effects or the lack of substitution possibilities. That is, even if $CV = EV$, we may still have the following relationship:

$$(12) \qquad WTP \leq CV = EV \leq WTA.$$

Because both the endowment and substitution effect arguments implicitly accept the fundamental interpretation of CV and EV as WTP or WTA, if indeed a divergence exists between CV and EV due to these effects, our results imply that the observed divergence between WTP and WTA would be even bigger, over and above that between CV and EV. In this sense, our explanation is complementary to the existing ones.[15]

Therefore, for our model to explain (at least partially) the WTP/WTA divergence, we only need to investigate whether the experimental and survey settings give rise to at least one of the commitment costs CC_A and CC_P. In a companion paper (Zhao and Kling 2001), we argue that experiments and surveys in general satisfy conditions (1)–(5) (specified at the beginning of this section) needed for commitment costs to arise. Specifically, they require a subject to make a decision (buying/selling in experiments and a particular answer in surveys) within a certain time frame (within the experiment or survey session), forgoing future learning opportunities. The decision is typically irreversible, and the subject is willing to postpone the

---

13. See Horowitz and McConnell (2002) for a nice review of the literature on these divergences and Hammack and Brown (1974) for one of the first contingent valuation illustrations.

14. For example, Hanemann's theory cannot explain the divergence in experiments where the traded good, usually a coffee mug, a pen, and so on, has many good substitutes. Kolstad and Guzman (1999) does not apply to experiments where the auction mechanism is not used.

15. Our model can be expanded to incorporate these considerations. A formulation based on Hanemann's specification would change the utility function in (1) to one with a lower elasticity of substitution. Endowment effects can be accommodated by changing the distribution function of G: An agent who owns the traded good tends to have a prior of G, $F_0(\cdot)$, with a higher mean.

decision. Together, these conditions can lead to commitment costs in these settings. In fact, we showed that in some special cases, the commitment costs can generate divergences twice the total intrinsic value of the good. The essence of this explanation is that the WTP/WTA divergence may have been induced by the limited information and learning opportunities in experiments and survey settings and is not necessarily inconsistent with neoclassical preferences or Hicksian welfare theory.

Zhao and Kling (2001) discussed in detail published experimental results that are consistent with our hypothesis. Here we focus on contingent valuation method (CVM) surveys and briefly discuss how commitment costs can arise and lead to inaccurate welfare measurement.

CVM surveys are mainly used to measure *values* of certain environmental goods or improvements, but the survey questions are often in the form of *decisions* for the subjects to make. For example, the researcher may be interested in the value of clean water or the welfare gains from improved water quality in a polluted lake. The survey question may be "are you willing to pay $X for a project that will improve the water quality to a certain level?" with X varied across surveys. The researcher's interest is not in the subject's decision itself but the implied welfare measures of the decision. (Later we will discuss cases in which the interest is exactly in the decisions rather than in the values.)

Once a subject is faced with this *decision*, he will consider factors that will affect his optimal choice but are not directly related to the expected value of the project. He may be uncertain about the value of improved water quality, depending on how often he will visit the lake, the exact future water quality, his future income, how many others will be visiting the lake, and the water quality in other lakes (substitutes). He may expect that more (likely not perfect) information about these factors will be available in the future, enabling him to make a better judgment about his decision. He may foresee that (at least with a positive probability) the project (or a substitute project) may be proposed in the future even if the proposed CVM 'referenda' were not to pass at this time. That is, he may believe that the "purchase" of better water quality can be delayed even if that means undertaking the transaction outside of the CVM instrument. Thus, he may be unwilling to commit payment now. However, the subject has to answer the survey question within a set time frame, forgoing learning opportunities. As a result, commitment cost will arise and affect his decision/response.

If the researcher is interested in the subject's valuation of improved water quality given the current information, this commitment cost should not be part of the valuation and is policy-irrelevant. Thus, if the welfare measure computed by the analyst from a set of such responses is used in a benefit-cost analysis determining whether to undertake the project now, the welfare measure will understate the true benefits, by the amount of the commitment cost. By posing a decision and inadvertently forcing a time limit on making the decision, CVM surveys may lead to inaccurate welfare measurement.

Furthermore, in many CVM surveys, the effects of a proposed project are typically described in terms of the *expected* improvements, without specifying the ranges or distributions of the improvements. To the extent that the subjects have less information about these improvements than the policy maker or researcher, failure to accurately describe the uncertainties in surveys may not prevent the subjects from perceiving improvements that are more uncertain than the true distributions. Because higher uncertainties lead to higher commitment costs, more accurate description of the distributions will help reduce the commitment costs.

Although an empirical question, this type of policy-irrelevant commitment cost may be particularly high in a WTA question for unique environmental goods or personal health, situations in which WTA has been found to diverge significantly from WTP (Horowitz and McConnell forth-coming). For significant commitment costs to arise, the respondent must feel that it will be difficult to reverse the transaction if it is undertaken. Once a subject's health has been compromised (increased exposure to a carcinogen or unhealthy food), respondents may feel it will be very difficult to reverse the transaction (reverse the effects of exposure to a carcinogen). Thus, there may be high commitment costs due to the high cost of reversal. In contrast, once having purchased better health, respondents may feel it is easy to reverse the transaction (by engaging in unhealthy practices in the future), reducing the commitment cost in WTP.

These considerations require the researcher to design surveys that accurately reflect information about the good to be valued, as well as the ability to delay. In a CVM study to evaluate residents' WTP for cleaning up a local lake, Corrigan et al. (2002) found that when the respondents are explicitly told they will receive a second chance in the future to vote on the cleanup, WTP drops significantly, and the associated CC_P accounts for 25% to 57% of the intrinsic value. This result suggests that respondents' beliefs about delay possibilities can lead to significantly different WTP values, the difference being a commitment cost.

Real Markets and Policy Relevant Commitment Costs

A related issue is whether commitment costs exist in real market transactions. Unlike experiments and surveys, a key feature of a market transaction is that a consumer is not *forced* to make a decision in any time period. Rather, one can gather information up to the point where the benefit of further waiting does not compensate for the cost anymore. This can happen if one has already gathered enough information or if the cost of waiting is too high. For example, a shopper can obtain price information from all local stores by visiting them or by checking their advertisements, and then decide on the best deal. For goods that are part of daily consumption, she may already have enough information about these goods. In both cases, her level of uncertainty is low at the transaction time, and the commitment costs are likely to be small if they exist at all. In other circumstances, a consumer may be highly impatient if she happens to need the good urgently, again reducing the commitment costs. In the extreme, commitment costs completely vanish if she is sufficiently impatient (with $\beta = 0$)—the case for desperate last-minute shoppers, hungry tourists, or a variety of other common situations.

Of course, there are also situations where market transactions may not remove commitment costs. If a consumer is *induced* (i.e., given incentives) to make a transaction (by, for example, limited-time price discounts), the transaction price may contain commitment costs. As we discussed in section II, the price discounts are similar to QOVs and imply the existence of commitment costs that drive the difference between WTP and CV/EV.

In summary, if there is always the opportunity to gather at least a little more information, and if the cost of doing so is not too high, a consumer may never *completely* exhaust his or her learning opportunities before making a trade. Thus, the difference between *WTP/WTA* and *EV/CV* may be persistent in market transactions. But the difference will decline as the consumer becomes more efficient in information gathering and as the cost of waiting eventually becomes sufficiently high. The magnitude of persistent commitment costs requires empirical study.

Even in CVM surveys, it is important to distinguish between commitment costs that arise as a real part of the problem being studied and those that are induced via the format of the survey. The former will be policy-relevant commitment costs, where the value of interest is WTP or WTA inclusive of the relevant commitment costs. Some decisions are inherently characterized by uncertainty and irreversibility and therefore contain commitment costs that are not survey-induced, but rather are characteristics of the real situation. For example, a graduate student who is given one week to decide on a job offer has to consider the associated commitment costs in making her decision. Additionally, a decision to build an elementary school or local hospital this year will likely have policy-relevant commitment costs.[16] In these cases, a survey that accurately replicates the real market features will elicit WTA and WTP measures that contain the commitment costs. But these commitment costs represent real uncertainty and should enter the welfare calculations, thus WTA or WTP are in fact appropriate welfare measures. Public good examples with uncertainty, irreversibility and future learning abound and, in fact, prompted the Arrow and Fisher (1974) inquiry into real options.

Furthermore, if the survey is intended to gauge the subjects' responses to a *decision* that the society faces, rather than to infer their *valuation*, commitment costs should again be part of the decision and is policy-relevant. Such a survey is similar to a referendum or a vote, reflecting the result of a collective decision. For example, polls are regularly conducted to measure the public's opinions on certain issues.

If the WTP/WTA divergence in surveys is due to policy-relevant option values, the

16. Note again the similarity to the real options theory of investment where option values are important components of an investment decision.

NOAA panel's recommendation to use WTP will be inapt when property rights would suggest that WTA is the more appropriate measure. However, if the divergence arises due to policy-irrelevant commitment costs that affect WTA more significantly than WTP (as it was argued may well be the case for health and unique environmental goods), then the NOAA panel recommendation is well founded.

Marketing Strategies

A central message of our model is that the WTP and WTA values are time-dependent, or more accurately, information-dependent. Because commitment cost CC_P reduces WTP from a consumer's valuation of a product, firms should have incentive to develop strategies that reduce or remove this commitment cost. We will show that many commonly used marketing strategies do have the potential of reducing the commitment costs or at least reacting to their existence.

A major conclusion of the introductory pricing literature (Shapiro 1983; Vettas 1997) is that prices of new products are typically low at initial introduction and gradually increase afterward. Shapiro (1983) argued that this price path may be caused by repeat purchases because early buyers, after using the product and thus knowing its (high) quality, will come back and buy the product again, raising the demand. Vettas (1997) showed that in the case of durable goods, if the consumers can communicate with each other and if high demand signals high product quality, a monopolist will have an incentive to reduce the price early to increase the quantity sold.

Even without repeat purchases or consumer communication, our model would predict an increasing price path for durable and other goods as long as consumers can gather information about the product as time goes by (such as consulting publications, like *Consumer Reports*). Given the limited information consumers may have about the new product, an initially lower price is a sensible response to the lower WTP (or a lower demand curve). Furthermore, the "limited time offer" of introductory prices reduces the ability of the consumers to delay (and still face the same low price) and raises the consumer's WTP. Of course, if early users of the product can spread information about the product to others, firms will have even higher incentive to subsidize

early users (by reducing their prices further) to raise the WTP of potential buyers. In fact, firms may provide information about the new product themselves: New product promotion quite often is accompanied by heavy advertising and sometimes by demonstrations in stores (Heiman et al. 2001).

The advertising literature argues that informative advertising can increase demand by providing consumers with more information about the product, such as its features, price, and location of stores (Nelson 1970; 1974). Presumably if the consumers are risk-averse, more information about the product quality will increase their demand. Further, more information reduces a consumer's search cost for a preferred product, thereby increasing the demand. Our hypothesis provides an additional explanation: More information reduces the commitment cost and raises a consumer's WTP and consequently the overall demand for the product.

Firms regularly adopt measures that reduce irreversibility in consumers' purchasing decisions, effectively reducing or even eliminating the commitment cost in WTP. Examples include money-back guarantees for consumption goods, trial periods (say, 30 days) for services, and so on. These offerings also provide incentives for consumers to learn about the product before finally committing to purchase it. Using option value arguments, Heiman et al. (forthcoming) showed that money-back guarantees significantly increase the demand for the underlying product.

V. FINAL REMARKS

Hicksian welfare theory is static in nature, but decisions in reality are often dynamic. In this article, we presented a model of an agent's choice to purchase or sell a good under conditions of uncertainty, irreversibility, and learning over time. We examined the implications of such a model for welfare measurement with particular attention to the commonly used measures, WTP and WTA. These two measures, which infer value from observing actions, contain both the intrinsic value of the good, measured by CV or EV, and the commitment cost of forgoing the opportunity of better information. Thus, the Hicksian equivalence between WTP/WTA and CV/EV breaks down.

We also discussed the implications of our finding for a range of issues in welfare analysis, including the WTP/WTA disparity in experiments and surveys, survey design, welfare measurement using market data, and firms' marketing strategies. Future work is needed to carefully study each of these implications by developing models tailored to each situation. In particular, empirical research, experiments, and surveys are needed to test the importance of commitment costs in these cases.

Our dynamic decision model is similar to that found in the QOV literature. But our study is not about QOV per se. We study an application of a variation of QOV models to consumer decision making, in particular its implications for welfare analysis. Although investment theory has recognized the value of being flexible in dynamic investment decisions under uncertainty and irreversibility, the theory of consumer behavior and welfare measurement has only begun to incorporate the joint effects of uncertainty and irreversibility and the value of being flexible. Although there exist individual studies on various aspects of dynamic consumer behavior, there has not been a systematic theoretical framework that unites these aspects (as the QOV literature has done in dynamic investment analysis). Our article constitutes a first step toward such a framework. In the process, we found that even such a step yields significant implications for the fundamental welfare constructs of Hicksian welfare theory.

APPENDIX: MODEL DETAILS

This appendix contains the details of the WTP/WTA model. We assume that the density function of G, $f(\cdot)$, is continuous and bounded away from zero. This guarantees that $V(p,s)$, $u_1(p)$ and $u_2(p)$ are continuous and strictly decreasing in p.

Sufficient Condition for $u_2(p) > u_1(p)$

Now we describe a sufficient condition for $u_2(p) > u_1(p)$ when $p > 0$. For $p \in (0, G_H)$ and $\delta < 1$, let $S(p,\delta) = \{s \in S : \text{Prob}_{G|s}(G \in [0,p] \mid s) > \delta\}$ be the set of signals that predict that the good's value will be below price p with a probability higher than δ.

Assumption 1. For any $p \in (0, G_H]$, there exists $0 \le \delta < 1$ such that the set $S(p,\delta)$ has a positive probability measure.

This assumption essentially ensures that for any price $p > 0$, there are always some signals that would predict that the good's value will be below the price with probability higher than a certain δ. The agent should not buy the good if these signals are realized. Because these signals will realize with a positive probability, delaying will always be beneficial without discounting, that is, $u_2(p) > u_1(p)$ for $p > 0$. Proposition 3 shows that this intuition is correct.

PROPOSITION 3. *Assumption 1 implies that $u_2(p) > u_1(p)$ for $p \in (0, G_H]$.*

Proof. Choose any $p^* \in (0, G_H]$ and set the corresponding

$$\delta^* = 1 + \left[\int_0^{p^*} \max\{-c_P, G - p^*\} dF_{G|s}(G) \right] \Big/ (G_H - p^*) < 1.$$

We only need to show that $V(p^*, s) < 0$ for $s \in S(p^*, \delta^*)$. This is true because

$$
\begin{aligned}
(A\text{-}1) \quad V(p^*, s) &= \int_0^{p^*} \max\{-c_P, G - p^*\} dF_{G|s}(G) \\
&\quad + \int_{p^*}^{G_H} \max\{-c_P, G - p^*\} dF_{G|s}(G) \\
&< \int_0^{p^*} \max\{-c_P, G - p^*\} dF_{G|s}(G) \\
&\quad + (G_H - p^*)\text{Prob}_{G|S}(G \in [p^*, G_H] \mid s) \\
&< \int_0^{p^*} \max\{-c_P, G - p^*\} dF_{G|s}(G) \\
&\quad + (G_H - p^*)(1 - \delta^*) < 0.
\end{aligned}
$$

The first inequality follows because

$$
\begin{aligned}
\int_{p^*}^{G_H} \max\{-c_P, G - p^*\} dF_{G|s}(G) \\
= \int_{p^*}^{G_H} (G - p^*) dF_{G|s}(G) \\
= (G_H - p^*) F_{G|s}(G_H) - \int_{p^*}^{G_H} F_{G|s}(G) dG \\
< (G_H - p^*) F_{G|s}(G_H) - (G_H - p^*) F_{G|s}(p^*) \\
= (G_H - p^*)\text{Prob}_{G|s}(G \in [p^*, G_H] \mid s),
\end{aligned}
$$

where the second equality is from integration by parts and the inequality follows because $F_{G|s}(G)$ is strictly increasing in G. The second inequality in (A-1) follows from the fact that for $s \in S(p^*, \delta^*)$, $\text{Prob}_{G|s}(G \in [p^*, G_H] \mid s) < 1 - \delta^*$. The third inequality in (13) follows from the definition of δ^*. ∎

Existence and Uniqueness of p_P

Let $d(p) = \beta u_2(p) - u_1(p)$, where $\beta < 1$. To show the existence and uniqueness of p_P, we only need to show $d(p) = 0$ has a unique solution on the interval $[0, G_H]$. We know $d(0) < 0$ because $u_2(0) = u_1(0) > 0$, and $d(G_H) > 0$ because $u_2(G_H) = 0$ and $u_1(G_H) < 0$. Thus, a sufficient condition for existence is that $d(\cdot)$ is continuous on $[0, G_H]$, and a sufficient condition for uniqueness is that $d(\cdot)$ is strictly increasing in $[0, G_H]$.

Note that $V(\cdot, s)$ is continuous for all $s \in S$. Then (3) implies that $u_1(\cdot)$ is continuous. Because $\max(\cdot)$ is a continuous operator, (4) implies that $u_2(\cdot)$ is continuous. Therefore, $d(\cdot)$ is continuous and p_P exists.

To show the strict monotonicity of $d(\cdot)$, we first demonstrate that $u_2(p) - u_1(p) = -\int_{S_{P2}(p)} V(p,s) dH(s)$ is increasing in p. Suppose $p_2 > p_1$. Because $V(p,s)$ is strictly decreasing in p, we know $V(p_2,s) < V(p_1,s)$ and $S_{P2}(p_2) \supset S_{P2}(p_1)$. Because $V(p,s) < 0$ for $s \in S_{P2}(p)$, we get $u_2(p_2) - u_1(p_2) > u_2(p_1) - u_1(p_1)$, or $u_2(p_2) - u_1(p_2) = (1-\beta)u_2(p_2) + d(p_2) > u_2(p_1) - u_1(p_1) = (1-\beta)u_2(p_1) + d(p_1)$. Because $u_2(p)$ is strictly decreasing in p, we know $u_2(p_2) < u_2(p_1)$. Thus, $d(p_2) > d(p_1)$: $d(p)$ is strictly increasing in p and p_P is unique.

Proof of Proposition 1. Because $d(\cdot)$ is strictly increasing on $[0, G_H]$, we know p_P, thus WTP, decreases when the curve $d(\cdot)$ is shifted up. Thus, WTP is decreasing in β. Because WTP_S is independent of β, $CC_P = WTP_S - WTP$ is increasing in β.

Kihlstrom (1984) shows that $u_2(p)$ increases as the signal service S becomes more informative about G in the sense of Blackwell (1951, 1953). Thus WTP is decreasing and CC_P is increasing in the informativeness of S.

To show the effect of c_P, note that $u_2(p) - u_1(p) = -\int_{S_{P2}(p)} V(p,s)dH(s)$ is strictly increasing in c_P, because $V(p,s)$ is strictly decreasing in c_P. However, $u_2(p) - u_1(p) = (1-\beta)u_2(p) + d(p)$, and $u_2(p)$ is strictly decreasing in c_p. Thus, $d(p)$ is strictly increasing in c_p. That is, WTP is decreasing in c_P. ∎

The Special Case of Absolute Irreversibility

To derive (6) and (7), we substitute $u_1(p) = \bar{G} - p$ and $u_2(p) = u_1(p) - \int_{S_{P2}}(\bar{G}(s) - p)dH(s)$ into $u_1(p) = \beta u_2(p)$ and solve for p. We then get

$$p_P = [(1-\beta)\bar{G} + \beta\text{Prob}(S_{P2})E(G|S_{P2})] / [1 - \beta + \beta\text{Prob}(S_{P2})].$$

Equations (6) and (7) then directly follow.

Derivation of WTA

The net benefit of selling, $W(p,s)$ is defined as

$$(A\text{-}2) \quad W(p,s) = \int_0^{G_H} (\max\{G - c_A, p\} - G)dF_{G|s}(G)$$
$$= \int_0^{G_H} \max\{-c_A, p - G\}dF_{G|s}(G).$$

Note that for $p > G_H - c_A$, $W(p,s) = p - \bar{G}(s)$.
The definition of $\pi_i(p)$, $i = 1, 2$ is given by

$$(A\text{-}3) \quad \pi_1(p) = W(p, 0) = \int_S W(p,s)dH(s)$$

$$(A\text{-}4) \quad \pi_2(p) = \int_S \max\{0, W(p,s)\}dH(s)$$
$$= \int_{S_{A2}(p)} W(p,s)dH(s),$$

where $S_{A2}(p) = \{s \in S : W(p,s) \geq 0\}$ is the set where the realized signals indicate that selling is desired. We define $S_{A1}(p) = S/S_{A2}(p) = \{s \in S : W(p,s) < 0\}$. $\pi_1(p) < \pi_2(p)$ as long as $S_{A1}(p)$ has a positive probability measure. We make necessary assumptions parallel to Assumption 1 to guarantee that this is true.

The proof of Proposition 2 is similar to that of Proposition 1.

The special case of absolute irreversibility occurs if $c_A \geq G_H$. Similar to the case of WTA, we can get

$$(A\text{-}5) \quad WTA_S = \bar{G}$$

$$(A\text{-}6) \quad CC_A = [\text{Prob}(S_{A1})/([1/\beta] - \text{Prob}[S_{A2}])] \times [E(G|S_{A1}) - \bar{G}],$$

and (9). Note that $E(G|s) > \bar{G}$ for all $s \in S_{A1}$, because S_{A1} is the set in which realized signals predict high G values (thus, no sale is made). Consequently, $CC_A > 0$.

REFERENCES

Arrow, Kenneth J., and Anthony C. Fisher. "Environmental Preservation, Uncertainty, and Irreversibility." *Quarterly Journal of Economics*, 88, 1974, 312–19.

Arrow, Kenneth, Robert Solow, Paul R. Portney, E. E. Leamer, R. Radner, and E. H. Schuman. "Report of the NOAA Panel on Contingent Valuation." *Federal Register*, 58, 1993, 4601–14.

Banerjee, Abhijit V. "A Simple Model of Herd Behavior." *Quarterly Journal of Economics*, 107(3), 1992, 797–817.

Bikhchandani, Sushil, David Hirshleifer, and Ivo Welch. "A Theory of Fads, Fashion, Custom, and Cultural Change as Information Cascades." *Journal of Political Economy*, 100(5), 1992, 992–1026.

Blackwell, D. "The Comparison of Experiments," in *Proceedings of the Second Berkeley Symposium on Mathematical Statistics and Probability*. Berkeley: University of California Press, 1951, 93–102.

———. "Equivalent Comparisons of Experiments." *Annals of Mathematical Statistics*, 24, 1953, 265–72.

Bockstael, Nancy E., and Kenneth E. McConnell. "Welfare Measurement in the Household Production Framework." *American Economic Review*, 73, 1983, 806–14.

Carson, Richard. "Contingent Valuation: Theoretical Advances and Empirical Tests since the NOAA Panel." *American Journal of Agricultural Economics*, 79, 1997, 1501–07.

Corrigan, Jay R., Catherine L. Kling, and Jinhua Zhao. "The Dynamic Formation of Willingness to Pay: An Empirical Specification and Test." Working Paper, Iowa State University, 2002.

Cummings, Ronald G., and Laura O. Taylor. "Unbiased Value Estimates for Environmental Goods: A Cheap Talk Design for the Contingent Valuation Method." *American Economic Review*, 89, 1999, 649–65.

Dixit, Avinash K. "Investment and Hysteresis." *Journal of Economic Perspectives*, 6, 1992, 107–32.

Dixit, Avinash K., and Robert S. Pindyck. *Investment under Uncertainty*. Princeton, NJ: Princeton University Press, 1994.

Epstein, Larry G. "Decision Making and the Temporal Resolution of Uncertainty." *International Economic Review*, 21, 1980, 269–83.

Fisher, Anthony C. "Investment under Uncertainty and Option Value in Environmental Economics." *Resource and Energy Economics*, 22, 2000, 197–204.

Hammack, Judd, and Gardner Brown. *Waterfowl and Wetlands: Towards Bioeconomic Analysis.* Baltimore, MD: Johns Hopkins University Press, 1974.

Hanemann, W. Michael. "Information and the Concept of Option Value." *Journal of Environmental Economics and Management,* 16, 1989, 23–37.

———. "Willingness to Pay and Willingness to Accept: How Much Can They Differ?" *American Economic Review,* 81, 1991, 635–47.

Harbaugh, William, Kate Krause, and Lise Vesterlund. "Are Adults Better Behaved than Children? Age, Experience, and the Endowment Effect." *Economics Letters,* 70, 2001, 175–81.

Heiman, Amir, Bruce McWilliams, and David Zilberman. "Demonstrations and Money-Back Guarantees: Market Mechanisms to Reduce Uncertainty." *Journal of Business Research,* 54, 2001, 71–84.

Heiman, Amir, Bruce McWilliams, Jinhua Zhao, and David Zilberman. "Valuation and Management of Money-Back Guarantee Options." *Journal of Retailing,* forthcoming.

Henry, Claude. "Investment Decisions under Uncertainty: The Irreversibility Effect." *American Economic Review,* 64, 1974, 1006–12.

Hoehn, John P., and Alan Randall. "A Satisfactory Benefit Cost Indicator from Contingent Valuation." *Journal of Environmental Economics and Management,* 14, 1987, 226–47.

Horowitz, John K., and K. E. McConnell. "A Review of WTA/WTP Studies." *Journal of Environmental Economics and Management,* 44, 2002, 426–47.

———. "Willingness to Accept, Willingness to Pay and the Income Effect." *Journal of Economic Behavior and Organization,* forthcoming.

Horowitz, John K., K. E. McConnell, and John Quiggin. "A Test of Competing Explanations of Compensation Demanded." *Economic Inquiry,* 37, 1999, 637–46.

Hubbard, Glenn R. "Investment under Uncertainty: Keeping One's Options Open." *Journal of Economic Literature,* 32, 1994, 1816–31.

Kahneman, Daniel, and Amos Tversky. "Prospect Theory: An Analysis of Decision under Risk." *Econometrica,* 47 (2), 1979, 263–91.

Kihlstrom, Richard E. "A 'Bayesian' Exposition of Blackwell's Theorem on the Comparison of Experiments," in *Bayesian Models in Economic Theory,* edited by Marcel Boyer and Richard Kihlstrom. North-Holland, 1984, 13–31.

Kolstad, Charles D. "Fundamental Irreversibilities in Stock Externalities." *Journal of Public Economics,* 60, 1996, 221–33.

Kolstad, Charles D., and Rolando M. Guzman. "Information and the Divergence between Willingness-to-Accept and Wilingness-to-Pay." *Journal of Environmental Economics and Management,* 38, 1999, 66–80.

List, John A. "Do Explicit Warnings Eliminate the Hypothetical Bias in Elicitation Procedures? Evidence from Field Auctions for Sportscards." *American Economic Review,* 91, 2001, 1498–507.

———. "Does Market Experience Eliminate Market Anomalies?" *Quarterly Journal of Economics,* forthcoming.

Mitchell, Robert, and Richard Carson. *Using Surveys to Value Public Goods: The Contingent Valuation Method.* Washington D.C.: Resources for the Future, 1989.

Neill, Helen R., Ronald G. Cummings, Philip T. Ganderton, Glenn W. Harrison, and Thomas McGuckin. "Hypothetical Surveys and Real Economic Commitments." *Land Economics,* 70, 1994, 145–54.

Nelson, P. "Information and Consumer Behavior." *Journal of Political Economy,* 78, 1970, 311–29.

———. "Advertising as Information." *Journal of Political Economy,* 82, 1974, 729–54.

Randall, Alan, and John R. Stoll. "Consumer's Surplus in Commodity Space." *American Economic Review,* 70, 1980, 449–55.

Ready, Richard C. "Environmental Valuation under Uncertainty," in *The Handbook of Environmental Economics,* edited by Daniel W. Bromley. Blackwell, 1995, 569–93.

Shapiro, Carl. "Optimal Pricing of Experience Goods." *Bell Journal of Economics,* 14, 1983, 497–507.

Smith, V. Kerry. "JEEM and Non-market Valuation: 1974–1998." *Journal of Environmental Economics and Management,* 2000, 39, 351–74.

Tversky, A., and D. Kahneman, "Loss Aversion in Riskless Choice: A Reference-Dependent Model." *Quarterly Journal of Economics,* 106, 1991, 1039–61.

Vettas, Nikolaos. "On the Informational Role of Quantities: Durable Goods and Consumers' Word-of-Mouth Communication." *International Economic Review,* 38, 1997, 915–44.

Zhao, Jinhua, and Catherine L. Kling. "A New Explanation for the WTP/WTA Disparity." *Economics Letters,* 73, 2001, 293–300.

———. "Environmental Valuation under Dynamic Consumer Behavior." Working Paper, Iowa State University, 2002.

[22]

BIASED VALUATIONS, DAMAGE ASSESSMENTS, AND POLICY CHOICES: THE CHOICE OF MEASURE MATTERS ☆

Jack L. Knetsch

Should the monetary value of the damages caused by an oil spill be measured by how much people are willing to pay to avoid it or by the minimum compensation they demand to accept it? Should a decision to clean up the spill turn on how much people are willing to pay to have it done or by the compensation necessary for them to agree not to have it done? Should efforts to reduce global climate change be economically justified by how much people would pay to avoid it or by the compensation required not to deal with it?

The conventional view that underlies nearly all official and unofficial recommendations and studies of such issues, is that it does not matter which metric is chosen to value environmental (or other) changes, because it is assumed that all such measures will result in essentially the same estimates of value. The intuition of most people, or at least of most non-economists, is very different. It seems quite obvious to them that different estimates will result

☆This is an expansion of a presentation at the "2006 Benefit-Cost Conference: What Can We Do to Improve the Use of Benefit Cost Analysis?", University of Washington, May 2006, and has benefited from comments by participants at this conference. Another version is scheduled to appear in Ecological Economics.

Research in Law and Economics, Volume 23, 345–358
Copyright © 2007 by Elsevier Ltd.
All rights of reproduction in any form reserved
ISSN: 0193-5895/doi:10.1016/S0193-5895(07)23018-0

from use of different measures of the value of a positive or a negative change of the sort that is often the subject of such assessments. If this is correct – and the empirical evidence seems to be clear that it is – then the choice of measure does indeed matter. Changes that impose losses or result in mitigation, or reductions, of losses are, for example, likely to be seriously undervalued with the willingness-to-pay measure commonly used to assess them.

Inappropriate choices of measures will likely distort benefit-cost analyses, damage assessments, regulatory design, and expenditure decisions. They are also likely to undermine the more informal ways of thinking about the severity of problems and ways of dealing with them – the habits of mind that influence judgments and policy proposals.

THE MEASURES AND DIFFERENT VALUATIONS RESULTING FROM THEM

As commonly pointed out in most instructional and operational manuals, and the benefit–cost and valuation texts on which they are largely based, there is general agreement among economic analysts that the economic values of gains and losses are correctly assessed by two different measures. The value of a gain is appropriately measured by the maximum sum people are willing to pay for it (the so-called WTP measure) – the amount that would leave them indifferent between paying to obtain the improvement and refusing the exchange. The value of a loss is accurately measured by the minimum compensation people demand to accept it (the so-called willingness-to-accept, or WTA, measure) – the sum that would leave them indifferent between being paid to bear the impairment and remaining whole without it.

It is in practice routinely assumed, consistent with conventional views of standard theory, that while the two measures of a change may differ slightly due to the presence of an income effect the measures will yield, for all practical purposes, equivalent estimates of value – "we shall normally expect the results to be so close together that it would not matter which we choose" (Henderson, 1941, p. 121); "... there is no basis consistent with economic assumptions and empirical income effects for WTP and WTA to exhibit sizable differences" (Diamond, Hausman, Leonard, & Denning, 1993, p. 66); "... economists expect that the difference between them will be small in most cases" (U.S. EPA, 2000, p. 60). This assumption of equivalence between the measures is rarely questioned or challenged – especially not by those demanding numbers and those supplying them. Consequently, estimates of environmental values are in practice made with little worry over the choice of measure used to assess these values. While the WTA measure is widely acknowledged to be the appropriate metric for assessing the value of losses, and reductions in losses, the WTP measure is normally used instead on grounds that it does not matter which is used, and it is usually more convenient to come up with WTP estimates – "... because it is often easier to measure and estimate", (U.S. EPA, 2000, p. 61).

The equivalence assumption is, however, little more than an assertion. In spite of how deeply it is entrenched in justifying how valuations are carried out, empirical evidence that has been accumulating for over two decades strongly suggests that it is not a particularly good assertion, and it is an especially poor one to use as a basis for assessing environmental, and similar, changes. The findings from numerous replicated studies suggest that the value of losses assessed with the WTA measure are commonly from two to four or more times greater than the value of otherwise commensurate gains assessed with the WTP measure (reviewed in, for example, Samuelson & Zeckhauser, 1988; Kahneman, Knetsch, & Thaler, 1991; Rabin, 1998; and, with a focus on environmental values, Horowitz & McConnell, 2002).

The findings of the pervasive difference between people's valuations of gains and losses are from a broad array of widely reported hypothetical survey studies, controlled experiments involving real exchanges, and an increasing number of studies of people's real-life decisions in uncontrolled natural experiments. For example, in perhaps the earliest report of a large disparity between the measures, bird hunters said they would be willing to pay an average of $247 to preserve a marsh area that contributed to the propagation of ducks, but would demand an average of $1044 to agree to its destruction (Hammack & Brown, 1974). In a simple experimental test – typical of many others – individuals were found willing to pay $5.60, on average, for a 50 percent chance to win $20, but these same people demanded an average of $10.87 to give up the identical chance to win the same prize (Kachelmeier & Shehata, 1992). Similar greater weightings of losses than of gains have been reported in people's investment and consumption choices, as in the example of their reluctance to realize a loss to their investment portfolio and continuing to disproportionately hold shares which have declined in value from their purchase price – a practice that results in substantially lower overall returns (Odean, 1998); in the example of people responding differently to price increases than to price decreases, giving rise to a price elasticity of –1.10 for increases in the price of eggs and –0.45 for decreases (Putler, 1992); and in the example of employees increasing payments to their retirement schemes from 3.5 percent of their wages to 11.6 percent when the choice of contribution was changed from the more aversive loss from current income to the much less aversive foregoing of a portion of their future wage increases (Thaler & Benartzi, 2004). Many other studies have demonstrated that the valuation disparity is pervasive, usually large (though variable depending on the entitlements at issue and the further particulars of the context of the valuation), and not merely the result of income effects, wealth constraints, or transaction costs (for example, Kahneman, Knetsch, & Thaler, 1990; Camerer, 2000; Knetsch, Tang, & Thaler, 2001).

Hanemann (1991) has correctly pointed out that large differences in gain and loss values for an identical entitlement can be consistent with standard theory under particular conditions that include a positive income effect and a lack of substitutes for the good. However, large differences have been observed under conditions that violate those required for this standard theory explanation, and are more likely the result of an endowment effect which is, as Hanemann notes, "a different phenomenon" (1991, p. 645n) not taken into account by standard theory.

Some other reports have suggested that the difference between valuations of gains and losses diminishes, or even disappears, with repeated trials. However, the evidence demonstrating this elimination has come from experiments using a second price Vickrey auction in which the highest bidder buys at the second highest bid, and the lowest seller sells at the second lowest offer. Further tests have shown that the reduction in the difference between the valuations is likely an artifact of this particular experimental design and that the valuation disparity does not generally go away (Knetsch et al., 2001). Other reports that people in the business of trading are less likely to exhibit endowment effects, at least with respect to buying and selling goods (for example, List, 2003), is not an unexpected result as trading is the point of their enterprise – "There are some cases in which no endowment effect would be expected, such as when goods are purchased for resale rather than for utilization" (Kahneman et al., 1990, p. 1328). This recognition says little, however, about the many other instances of an endowment effect on other types of valuations, and has even less to offer for environmental valuations. Plott and Zeiler (2005) also reported a decrease and elimination of the valuation disparity under particular experimental conditions, but here too the reason seems to have more to do with particulars of the test design and less to do with the absence of an endowment effect under conditions that more realistically reflect the usual circumstances of actual environmental valuations.

Although differences in people's evaluation of gains and losses may not be universal, current evidence strongly suggests that it is pervasive, and

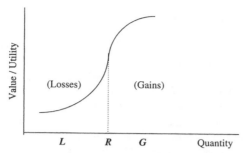

Fig. 1. Value of Gains and Losses from Reference State.

especially so for changes that are likely to be the subject of environmental damage assessments and benefit–cost or other forms of policy analyses involving environmental values.

Rather than the conventional value function used to justify the choice of measure now used to assess environmental values, a long line of decision studies, together with the valuation disparity evidence, suggest that people: (1) value changes from a reference state, and commonly not as comparisons between two end points as assumed in standard economic theory; (2) value losses from the reference far more than gains beyond it; and (3) experience diminishing marginal effects of both gains and losses (Kahneman & Tversky, 1979). These characteristics of people's valuations are illustrated in a value function much like that of Fig. 1. Changes in the quantity of a good or entitlement between the reference state, *R*, and *L*, are in the domain of losses and have a much larger impact on the welfare of an individual, or value, than changes between *R* and *G* that are in the domain of gains.

THE CHOICE OF MEASURE

The different valuations of gains and losses, as illustrated in Fig. 1,[1] give rise to very different valuations of both positive and negative changes depending on whether they are changes in the domain of losses below or short of the reference state or in the domain of gains above or beyond the reference. A change in either direction in the domain of losses can be expected to have a greater impact on welfare – have greater value – than an otherwise commensurate change in the domain of gains.

JACK L. KNETSCH

Further, the measure that is appropriate to assess the value of positive changes and to assess the value of negative changes will also vary – and "… the choice between a WTP and a WTA framing of valuation questions will matter" (Brown & Gregory, 1999, p. 333). The WTP measure will be correct for valuing some positive changes, and the WTA measure will be called for in others. Similarly, the WTP measure will be appropriate for assessing the value of some negative changes and the WTA measure will be for others. While the choice of measure of the values of negative and positive changes are likely to have substantial practical importance, little attention has been paid to criteria for making them – a situation likely not helped by the lack of attention to the implications of the endowment effects by economists and the absence of interest on the part of public and private agencies and organizations.[2]

While further refinements might be expected to provide more definitive criteria, present evidence suggests that the most appropriate choice of measure largely turns on what people regard as the reference state that forms the basis of particular valuations, and their characterization of the change at issue relative to that reference. In large part, the criterion for determining which measure best reflects, or is more consistent with, real welfare changes, appears to be akin to the distinction between compensating variation (CV) and equivalent variation (EV) measures of the welfare gains and losses associated with a change (usually portrayed in texts as a change in the price of a commodity, but can be a change in a risk to health, a change in environmental amenity, or whatever).

The CV measures of a change in welfare are based on the initial state as the reference for valuing the change in welfare caused by the change – "The change in income necessary to restore the consumer to his original indifference curve is called the compensating variation" (Varian, 1990, p. 248). This would be, for example, the state or position before a change involving the gain or the loss of an entitlement, or before an environmental improvement or deterioration has occurred. The EV measures the welfare change on the basis of the reference state being the position after the change – "… it is the income change that is equivalent to the price [or entitlement] change in terms of the change in utility" (Varian, 1990, p. 249).

The Value of a Positive Change

A positive change in environmental quality is appropriately assessed in terms of the WTP measure if it is in the *domain of gains* beyond the reference state, for example, a move from R to G in Fig. 1. It is the CV measure as it takes the present state as the reference, and is therefore the payment that would leave the individual indifferent between gaining the improvement and remaining at the present reference position. This is the usual case to which the time honoured "WTP-for-a-gain" rule aptly applies.

A positive change in the *domain of losses* starts from a position inferior to the reference state and moves to the reference, a move from *L* to *R* in Fig. 1. The reference that is the basis for measuring the value of such a change is the position after the change. This is then an EV measure of the compensation that would leave the individual indifferent between attaining, or returning to, the reference state and remaining at the inferior present position. It is the appropriate measure of the value of actions that involve mitigation of losses in which people's reference is the absence of the harm – containing or cleaning up after an oil spill, for example. The benefits of such actions will likely be seriously understated when estimated using the WTP measure, as is now common practice in, for example, contingent valuation surveys that ask people for their maximum willingness to pay to clean up a spill or similar environmental disruption.

The Value of a Negative Change

The value of a negative change in the *domain of losses* is a move from the reference to a position inferior to the reference, a move from *R* to *L* in Fig. 1. The reference serving as the basis for the valuation of the change is therefore the position before the change, calling for the CV measure of the compensation necessary for the individual to be indifferent between avoiding the loss and accepting it. This is the case to which the well accepted "WTA-for-a-loss" rule correctly applies, but which is so often now ignored in practice as the damages due to, for example, an oil spill continue to be assessed in terms of how much people are presumed to be willing to pay to avoid such a loss.

The value of a negative change in the domain of *gains*, a move from *G* to *R* in Fig. 1, takes the post move position as the reference and is, therefore, an EV measure. This is the sum the individual would be willing to pay to avoid moving to the reference state, which is inferior to the present position.

Valuations and Reference States

The relationship between the reference state and the alternative measures of the value of positive and negative changes can be summarized in the following array:

Reference State	Basis of Valuation Measures		
	Measure	Positive change	Negative change
Present	Compensating variation	WTP to improve	WTA to accept loss
After change	Equivalent variation	WTA to forego reference	WTP to avoid reference

Both positive changes and negative changes in the domain of losses call for the WTA measure. The value of a negative change of a loss from the reference (R to L in Fig. 1) is correctly valued by the minimum sum an individual requires to accept it. The value of a positive change in the domain of losses from a present inferior position to, or return to, a superior state that the individual regards as the reference state (L to R in Fig. 1), is correctly measured by the sum demanded to forego such a move.

Both positive and negative changes in the domain of gains call for the WTP measure. The value of a negative change (from G to R in Fig. 1) is properly measured by the willingness to pay to avoid a move to a reference state that the individual finds inferior to the present position. The value of a positive change (from R to G in Fig. 1) is appropriately measured by the amount the individual is willing to pay to move to a superior position beyond the reference point.

The discrimination between the measures depends on what is regarded as the reference state and the nature of the change relative to that reference.

One prominent suggestion, especially from economists, is that any reference state is given by extant legal entitlements – "WTP and WTA can also be identified with what they imply about property rights" (U.S. EPA, 2000, p. 60). The value of controlling waste discharges would then, for example, be measured by people's WTA to accept them if discharges are legally prohibited, but by their WTP to reduce pollution levels if discharges are not regulated.

However, the presence or absence of legal prohibitions seems an unlikely general determinant of the reference people use to value a change. Assignments of legal entitlements, such as whether or not a person has a cause of action against a neighbour or other party for some offence, turn not only on efficiency, equity, fairness, and other justice goals, but also asymmetries in avoidance costs and costs of enforcement, compliance, and transfer of original entitlements. The choice of a valuation measure is not about possible compatibilities with assignments of entitlements, it is about choosing a metric that best reflects actual changes in economic welfare resulting from particular changes. While the correlation between reference states and extant legal entitlements may be high in most jurisdictions – likely in part due to the strong tendency of legal regimes to evolve in ways that offer greater protection to more important values – there are many cases in which the two diverge.

Discriminating between the CV and EV measures of gains and losses, and consequently the appropriate choice of measure of the value of positive and negative changes, may more usefully be determined by what Zerbe (2001) refers to as "psychological ownership" (p. 20), what Bromley (1995) suggests are people's "legitimate expectations" (p. 132), or what people feel is deserving or "right". The reference state may be one reflected in what most people in the community regard as the expected or normal state (Kahneman & Miller, 1986). Such a distinction would be similar to ones used, for example, in tests of what is acceptable and unacceptable neighbourly behaviour (Ellickson, 1973), and the harm/benefit test for legal liability whereas actions preventing harms are treated differently from ones that are undertaken to provide benefits (Fischel, 1995). As Kahneman and Miller (1986) suggest, normal conditions do not raise the questions or comments that deviations from the norm do. For example, an oil spill would prompt comment and questions of how it happened, whereas another day without such a spill would not give rise to any similar questions of why that happened – no spills would be the reference of expected normality, a spill would be a departure from the reference.

The predictability of an adverse consequence also does not seem to make it likely that such events will necessarily be incorporated into what people regard as the reference state. Spills, for example, are a fairly predictable result of tanker traffic and the transfer of oil and other potentially harmful materials. Yet the absence of spills seems likely to be the reference state for most people, suggesting that the compensation required to forego a reduction in spills (the WTA measure) might be the better measure to use in deciding whether or not to implement programs or projects designed to reduce such occurrences.

Determining the appropriate reference state appears to be largely an empirical matter of which state is likely to best describe people's feeling about particular changes. Although the reference state will often be the status quo, in important cases it may not be the determining factor. For example, polluted air and water may accompany some industrial activities or the growth of urban areas, but most people in the area might still regard unspoiled environments as the norm, and this would then be the reference for their subjective reactions and valuations of both losses caused by these developments and the benefit of cleanup activities – the WTA to accept pollution, and the WTA to forego controls.[3]

Legal entitlements would, of course, determine if an injured party is or is not entitled to relief from environmental harms. However, just as actual payments are not required for use of the potential Pareto criterion for selection of socially efficient projects, legal entitlements implying payments are in this sense also not as useful a determinant of which measure more accurately reflect changes in welfare that accompany environmental changes. What people regard as the reference state for such changes appears to have the greater claim on usefully serving that purpose.

DISCOUNTING THE VALUE OF FUTURE GAINS AND FUTURE LOSSES

The amount that an individual is willing to pay now to secure a future benefit is what that person regards as the present value of the future gain. Similarly, the sum demanded now to accept a future loss is a person's present value of this future outcome. Just as people are willing to pay less for a gain than they demand to accept a loss, they can also be expected to be willing to pay less now for a future gain than the sum they would accept to agree to a future loss.

The relatively smaller WTP sum, and consequent smaller present valuation of a future gain, implies that individuals use a higher rate to discount future gains; and the relatively larger WTA sum, and consequent larger present valuation of a future loss, similarly implies that they use a lower rate to discount future losses. While reports of empirical evidence of this distinction are not yet plentiful, those that are available appear to be consistent with this expectation (for example, Loewenstein, 1988).

If benefit–cost valuations are to reflect people's preferred tradeoffs of present and future outcomes, the evidence suggests that different rates for discounting future gains and future losses are called for, rather than the single invariant rate prescribed by texts and manuals, and used in practice.

The disparity between the valuations of future gains and future losses also requires the choice of appropriate measures to value these future outcomes. These choices, and the criteria for choosing between them are analogous to the problem of choosing appropriate measures for valuing present or near term positive and negative changes.

The use of different rates that more accurately reflect people's preferences would, for example, likely give more weight to future environmental and other losses – as they are discounted at lower rates – and consequently justify greater present sacrifices to deal with them than would be the case following the usual practice of invariant rates. It would also likely call for more actions that reduce risks of future losses relative to ones that provide future gains, as the latter would be discounted at higher rates.

CONCLUDING COMMENTS

The evidence that people commonly value losses, and reductions of losses, more, and often far more, than gains, suggests that otherwise commensurate changes will have different values and that appropriate choices of assessment measures need to be made. Conventional benefit–cost, and other, analyses as currently advocated and practiced, have largely ignored this evidence and its implications for the choice of measure to assess the values of gains and losses.

An indication of the significance of the lack of attention to the valuation disparity is suggested by considering a hypothetical choice between two equally costly projects serving the same numbers of people: **A** would shorten the distance between two points and reduce travel time by 10 min on this route; **B** would replace a bridge and eliminate the need for a detour that increased travel time by 10 min when a bridge failed. Traditional analyses of the benefits and costs of transit projects would lead to the conclusion that there is nothing on these facts to choose between the two projects. As they cost the same, and as the conventional measure of how much people are presumed to be willing to pay for a 10-min reduction in travel time would yield identical estimates of the benefits of the two projects, analysts would be indifferent between them. People other than analysts – transportation users and taxpayers among them – would, of course, be very unlikely to be indifferent. As a series of surveys of students, senior Singapore public servants, and international transportation experts revealed, only a small proportion of people would consider the two of equal worth, while the vast majority would favour project **B** that reduces a loss, over project **A** that provides a less-valued gain (Chin & Knetsch, 2007). The reason for this preference is, presumably, that, contrary to conventional economic analyses and traditional assessments of costs and benefits, projects that prevent or reduce losses are valued more highly than ones that provide gains.

The distinction between what people perceive as a gain and what they think of as preventing or mitigating a deterioration in environmental quality has considerable practical importance. The common practice of estimating the "value of damages to health (both morbidity and mortality) due to air pollution" on measures of people's "willingness to pay to avoid such effects" (Alberini & Krupnick, 2000, p. 37), would, for example, seem to be justified only on a showing that people regard suffering ill health due to pollution as being the normal or reference state and that relief (the change at issue) is therefore in the domain of gains. It seems more likely that in such cases there would be more agreement that "the benefits derived from pollution control are the damages prevented" (Tietenberg, 1996, p. 71), and that a WTA measure is therefore called for. This appears even more certain to be the case with interventions to preserve wildlife habitats, historic buildings, cultural sites, and scenic attractions – justifications to establish national parks, for example, turn largely, not on gaining a new park, but on preserving the amenities or artifacts of the area.

While more realistic valuations using more appropriate measures of gains and losses can be implemented on current evidence, further improvement in the guidance provided by cost–benefit and other such assessment studies would likely follow from better information, particularly in two areas. The first is the extent to which there are differences between WTP and WTA valuations of different kinds of environmental changes. The second is the extent to which people regard various types of changes as gains or as reductions of losses – the conditions or causal factors that determine the reference state they use in judging their value.

NOTES

1. There may well be other differences depending on other valuation contexts, but only those related to the differing valuations of gains and losses are considered here.

2. Some perhaps perverse incentives, having to do with career downsides of seeming to depart from accepted conventions, may help explain the otherwise curious widespread ignoring of the valuation disparity evidence and the choice of measure issue, by, for example, public environmental "protection" agencies, environmental advocacy groups, consultants and others providing damage estimates to litigants, research organizations, organizers of professional forums, private and public sources of research funding, and textbook writers (Knetsch, 2000).

3. Further examples are provided in Knetsch (2005).

REFERENCES

Alberini, A., & Krupnick, A. (2000). Cost-of-illness and willingness-to-pay estimates of the benefits of improved air quality: Evidence from Taiwan. *Land Economics, 76,* 37–53.

Bromley, D. (1995). Property rights and natural resource damage assessments. *Ecological Economics, 14,* 129–135.

Brown, T., & Gregory, R. (1999). Why the WTA–WTP disparity matters. *Ecological Economics, 28,* 323–335.

Camerer, C. (2000). Prospect theory in the wild. In: D. Kahneman & A. Tversky (Eds), *Choices, values, and frames.* Cambridge, UK: Cambridge University Press.

Chin, A., & Knetsch, J. (2007). Values depend on the measures: Are many transport projects valuations seriously biased?

Diamond, P., Hausman, J., Leonard, G., & Denning, M. (1993). Does contingent valuation measure preferences? Experimental evidence. In: X. Hausman (Ed.), *Contingent valuation: A critical assessment.* Amsterdam: Elsevier.

Ellickson, R. (1973). Alternatives to zoning: Covenants, nuisance rules, and fines as land use controls. *University of Chicago Law Review, 40,* 581–781.

Fischel, W. (1995). *Regulatory takings: Law, economics, and politics.* Cambridge, MA: Harvard University Press.

Hammack, J., & Brown, G. (1974). *Waterfowl and wetlands: Toward bioeconomic analysis.* Washington, DC: The Johns Hopkins Press for Resources for the future.

Hanemann, M. (1991). Willingness to pay and willingness to accept: how much can they differ? *The American Economic Review, 81,* 635–647.

Henderson, A. (1941). Consumer's surplus and the compensation variation. *Review of Economic Studies, 8,* 117.

Horowitz, J., & McConnell, K. (2002). A review of WTA/WTP studies. *Journal of Environmental Economics and Management, 44,* 426–447.

Kachelmeier, S., & Shehata, M. (1992). Examining risk preferences under high monetary incentives: Experimental evidence from the People's Republic of China. *The American Economic Review, 82,* 1120–1140.

Kahneman, D., Knetsch, J., & Thaler, R. (1990). Experimental tests of the endowment effect and the Coase theorem. *Journal of Political Economy, 98,* 1325–1348.

Kahneman, D., Knetsch, J., & Thaler, R. (1991). The endowment effect, loss aversion, and status quo bias. *Journal of Economic Perspectives, 5,* 193–206.

Kahneman, D., & Miller, D. (1986). Norm theory: Comparing reality to its alternatives. *Psychological Review, 93,* 136–153.

Kahneman, D., & Tversky, A. (1979). Prospect theory: An analysis of decisions under risk. *Econometrica, 47,* 263–291.

Knetsch, J. (2000). Environmental valuations and standard theory: Behavioral findings, context dependence, and implications. In: T. Tietenberg & H. Folmer (Eds), *The international yearbook of environmental and resource economics 2000/2001* (pp. 267–299). Cheltenham, UK: Edward Elgar.

Knetsch, J., Tang, F., & Thaler, R. (2001). The endowment effect and repeated market trials: Is the Vickrey auction demand revealing? *Experimental Economics, 4,* 257–269.

Knetsch, J. L. (2005). The appropriate choice of valuation measure in usual cases of losses valued more than gains. *Singapore Economic Review, 50,* 393–406.

List, J. (2003). Does market experience eliminate market anomalies? *Quarterly Journal of Economics, 118*, 47–71.

Loewenstein, G. (1988). Frames of mind in intertemporal choice. *Management Science, 34*, 200–214.

Odean, T. (1998). Are investors reluctant to realize their losses? *The Journal of Finance, 53*, 1775–1798.

Plott, C., & Zeiler, K. (2005). The willingness to pay – Willingness to accept gap, the 'endowment effect,' subject misconceptions, and experimental procedures for eliciting valuations. *The American Economic Review, 95*, 530–545.

Putler, D. (1992). Incorporating reference price effects into a theory of consumer choice. *Marketing Science, 11*, 287–309.

Rabin, M. (1998). Psychology and economics. *Journal of Economic Literature, 36*, 11–46.

Samuelson, W., & Zeckhauser, R. (1988). Status quo bias in decision making. *Journal of Risk and Uncertainty, 1*, 7–59.

Thaler, R., & Benartzi, S. (2004). Save more tomorrow: Using behavioral economics to increase employee saving. *Journal of Political Economy, 112*, S164–S182.

Tietenberg, T. (1996). *Environmental and natural resource economics* (4th ed.). New York: HarperCollins.

U.S. Environmental Protection Agency. (2000). *Guidelines for preparing economic analyses*. Washington, DC: Environmental Protection Agency.

Varian, H. (1990). *Intermediate microeconomics: A modern approach*. New York: W.W. Norton.

Zerbe, R. (2001). *Economic efficiency in law and Economics*. Cheltenham, UK: Edward Elgar.

Part V
Contingent Valuation

[23]

JOURNAL OF ENVIRONMENTAL ECONOMICS AND MANAGEMENT 22, 57–70 (1992)

Valuing Public Goods: The Purchase of Moral Satisfaction*

Daniel Kahneman[†] and Jack L. Knetsch[‡]

[†] Department of Psychology, University of California, Berkeley, Berkeley, California 94720; and
[‡] School of Resource and Enviromental Management, Simon Fraser University, Burnaby, British Columbia, Canada V5A 1S6

Received March 2, 1990; revised December 14, 1990

Contingent valuation surveys in which respondents state their willingness to pay (WTP) for public goods are coming into use in cost–benefit analyses and in litigation over environmental losses. The validity of the method is brought into question by several experimental observations. An embedding effect is demonstrated, in which WTP for a good varies depending on whether it is evaluated on its own or as part of a more inclusive category. The ordering of various public issues by WTP is predicted with significant accuracy by independent ratings of the moral satisfaction associated with contributions to these causes. Contingent valuation responses reflect the willingness to pay for the moral satisfaction of contributing to public goods, not the economic value of these goods. © 1992 Academic Press, Inc.

There is substantial demand for a practical technique for measuring the value of non-market goods. Measures of value are required for cost–benefit assessments of public goods, for the analysis of policies that affect the environment, and for realistic estimates of environmental damages resulting from human action, such as oil spills. In recent years the contingent valuation method (CVM) has gained prominence as the major technique for the assessment of the value of environmental amenities. This paper is concerned with a critique of CVM.

The idea of CVM is quite simple: respondents are asked to indicate their value for a public good, usually by specifying the maximum amount they would be willing to pay to obtain or to retain it. The total value of the good is estimated by multiplying the average willingness to pay (WTP) observed in the sample by the number of households in the relevant population. This value is sometimes divided into *use value* and *non-use value* by comparing the WTP of respondents who expect to enjoy the public good personally (e.g., benefit from improved visibility or from the increased number of fish in a cleaned up stream) to the WTP of respondents who have no such expectations. Specific questions are sometimes added to partition non-use value further into the value of retaining an option for future use, a bequest value, and a pure existence value [15].

The accuracy of the CVM is a matter of substantial practical import, not only in cost–benefit assessments but also in litigation over liability and damages. The validity of the technique is take as a rebuttable presumption in environmental cases brought in the United States under the Comprehensive Environmental Response, Compensation and Liability Act of 1980 (CERCLA). The research on the method has been reviewed in two authoritative volumes, which offer detailed

*This research was supported by Fisheries and Oceans Canada, the Ontario Ministry of the Environment, and the Sloan Foundation. Interviews and preliminary statistical analyses were performed by Campbell–Goodell Consultants, Vancouver, British Columbia. We benefited from conversations with George Akerlof, James Bieke, Brian Binger, Ralph d'Arge, Elizabeth Hoffman, Richard Thaler, and Frances van Loo, from a commentary by Glenn Harrison, and from the statistical expertise of Carol Nickerson.

guidelines for its use ([8, 17]; see also [11]). Some assessments of CVM have been very favorable, as illustrated by the claims that "the necessary structure for constructing a hypothetical market for the direct determination of economic values within the Hicksian consumers' surplus framework has been developed" [6, p. 173] and that contingent valuation "is potentially capable of directly measuring a broad range of economic benefits for a wide range of goods, including those not yet supplied, in a manner consistent with economic theory" [17, p. 295]. Acceptance of the technique is not universal, however, and some strong reservations about the adequacy of CVM to support specific compensation claims have recently been expressed [7, 9, 19].

The present article reports an experimental investigation of what is perhaps the most serious shortcoming of CVM: that the assessed value of a public good is demonstrably arbitrary, because willingness to pay for the same good can vary over a wide range depending on whether the good is assessed on its own or embedded as part of a more inclusive package. We next provide evidence for a similar difficulty in the response to payment schedules: WTP estimates can be much larger when the payment is described as a long-term commitment rather than as a one-time outlay. Another study suggests that WTP for public goods is best interpreted as the purchase of moral satisfaction, rather than as a measure of the value associated with a particular public good. Lastly, we examine the categories of expenditures from which contributions to public goods are drawn.

PART I. THE EMBEDDING EFFECT

The standard interpretation of CVM results is that the WTP for a good is a measure of the economic value associated with that good, which is fully comparable to values derived from market exchanges and on the basis of which allocative efficiency judgments can be made. However, two related observations that cast doubt on this interpretation have been discussed in the CVM literature. The first is an order effect in WTP responses when the values of several goods are elicited in succession: the same good elicits a higher WTP if it is first in the list rather than valued after others. For example, Tolley and Randall [22] found that estimates of the value of improved visibility in the Grand Canyon differed by a factor of three depending on whether this item appeared first or third in a survey. Because the order in which goods are mentioned in a survey is purely arbitrary, any effect of this variable raises questions about the validity of responses.

Another problem for CVM is an effect that we call *embedding*, also variously labeled as a part–whole effect, symbolic effect, or disaggregation effect [8, 17]: the same good is assigned a lower value if WTP for it is inferred from WTP for a more inclusive good rather than if the particular good is evaluated on its own. A finding that we obtained some time ago illustrates the embedding effect: the expressed willingness of Toronto residents to pay increased taxes to prevent the drop in fish populations in all Ontario lakes was only slightly higher than the willingness to pay to preserve the fish stocks in only a small area of the province (reported in [14]). It is quite unlikely that the respondents in Toronto viewed saving fish in the Muskoka area as a fully adequate substitute for saving fish in the whole province. The similar WTP observed for separate regions and for the whole of Ontario therefore appears anomalous. Further, the result raises a question about the proper assessment of WTP for a particular region: should this be estimated by the WTP assessment for that region in isolation, or by allocating to it a share of the sum offered for the cleanup of lakes in the entire province?

The embedding problem was noted long ago by investigators who were concerned with the appropriateness of aggregating WTP for several commodities obtained from different samples into an estimate of WTP for the package ([13], as summarized in [17, pp. 44–46]). Schulze *et al.* stated that "*no* researcher would be willing to defend the summation of CV values that have been obtained in various studies for *many* types of environmental effects; indeed the summation of average CV values for public goods thus far available in the literature would *exhaust* the budget of the average individual" [21, p. 6; emphases in the original].

The effects of order and embedding observed in assessments of value for public goods are difficult to reconcile with standard value theory. To appreciate why this is so, it is useful to consider the conditions under which assessments of the value of private goods would exhibit these effects. Two generic cases can be identified. The first involves goods which are perfect substitutes for one another and for which satiation is attained by the consumption of one unit. Thus, in the absence of opportunities for storage, resale, or altruistic giving, most adults will have zero WTP for a second large ice cream cone offered immediately after the consumption of the first. This is an order effect—the positive value of consuming an initial ice cream cone could be associated with any of those potentially available, but the value of any cone considered immediately thereafter would be zero. The value of ice cream cones under these circumstances also exhibits an embedding effect: WTP for 100 ice cream cones will not be higher than WTP for 1, much as WTP for improved fishing in all of Ontario was little more than WTP for fishing in a small area of that province. Although the notions of substitution and satiation may apply to some environmental goods, they do not readily extend to existence values for beautiful sites, historical landmarks, or endangered species. If it is found that WTP to save all threatened historical landmarks in a region is not much higher than WTP to save any single landmark, this can hardly be because each individual landmark provides as much utility as the whole set. Indeed, the uniqueness of the valued goods is the essence of existence value, as this notion has been discussed since Krutilla [15].

Effects of order and embedding are also expected in another extreme case: goods for which people are willing to pay a large part of their wealth. For example, the sum that an individual will pay to avoid the loss of both an arm and a leg is likely to be much less than the sum of WTP to save each limb separately, because the amount the person is willing to pay to save one limb is almost certain to be high in relation to available wealth, leaving little to prevent the second loss. In this case, order and embedding effects are produced by limited wealth. However, median WTP in CVM studies commonly falls in the range of $40–100 [9], far too small to be severely restrained by wealth.

The problem for the interpretation of CVM results is the following: if the value of a given landmark is much larger when it is evaluated on its own that when it is evaluated as part of a more inclusive package of public goods, which measure is the correct one? The discussions of the problem in the literature provide no agreed principles that would define the proper level of aggregation for the evaluation of a specific good. In the absence of such principles, the results of CVM become arbitrary. This criticism could be fatal. No measuring instrument can be taken seriously if its permitted range of applications yields drastically different measures of the same object.

Embedding a Public Good

Our first study was conducted to document the embedding effect in a controlled experimental design, focusing on the valuation of a public good that is of personal relevance to respondents: the increased availability of equipment and trained personnel for rescue operations in disasters. Coincidentally, the study was conducted within weeks of the San Francisco earthquake of 1989, a fact that certainly enhanced the relevance of the topic.

Three samples of adults living in the greater Vancouver region in Canada were interviewed by telephone. Samples were evenly split by gender. All calls were made in evening hours. The interviewers introduced themselves as being from a professional polling firm "conducting interviews on behalf of researchers at Simon Fraser University." All respondents were initially told:

> The federal and provincial governments provide a wide range of public services that include education, health, police protection, roads, and environmental services.

Respondents in one sample were then told to focus on environmental services, which were described as including "preserving wilderness areas, protecting wildlife, providing parks, preparing for disasters, controlling air pollution, insuring water quality, and routine treatment and disposal of industrial wastes." They were then asked the following question:

> If you could be sure that extra money collected would lead to significant improvements, what is the most you would be willing to pay each year through higher taxes, prices, or user fees, to go into a special fund to improve environmental services?

The evaluation questions were concluded at this point if the respondent's answer was zero. Other respondents were then asked:

> Keeping in mind the services just mentioned, including those related to providing parks, pollution control, preservation of wilderness and wildlife, and disposal of industrial wastes, I would like to ask you in particular about improved preparedness for disasters. What part of the total amount that you just mentioned for all environmental services do you think should go specifically to improve preparedness for disasters?

Subjects were allowed to answer by stating a dollar amount, a fraction, or a percentage. Where necessary, the interviewer immediately computed the dollar amount of the offered contribution and recorded that value. A third question was asked after some aspects of preparedness for disasters were listed (emergency services in hospitals; maintenance of large stocks of medical supplies, food, fuel, and communication equipment; ensuring the availability of equipment and trained personnel for rescue operations; and preparing for cleanup of oil, toxic chemicals, or radioactive materials):

> Keeping in mind all aspects of preparedness for disasters, what part of the total amount you allocated to improving preparedness do you think should go specifically to improve the availability of equipment and trained personnel for rescue operations?

TABLE I

Willingness to Pay for Selected Classes of Goods and Allocations of Totals to Less Inclusive Groups

		Sub-sample		
Public good		Group 1 (N = 66) ($)	Group 2 (N = 78) ($)	Group 3 (N = 74) ($)
Environmental	Mean	135.91		
services	Median	50.00		
Improve disaster	Mean	29.06	151.60	
preparedness	Median	10.00	50.00	
Improve rescue	Mean	14.12*	74.65**	122.64
equipment, personnel	Median	1.00	16.00	25.00

*Two respondents did not answer this question, reducing N to 64.

**Four respondents did not answer this question, reducing N to 74.

The same procedure was followed with the second sample, except that the initial question they answered referred to "a special fund to improve preparedness for disasters," with a subsequent allocation to "go specifically to improve the availability of equipment and trained personnel for rescue operations." Respondents in the third sample were told to focus on preparedness for disasters and were asked to state their willingness to pay "into a special fund to improve availability of equipment and trained personnel for rescue operations."

Table I presents the medians and means of the willingness to pay responses for each of the questions in the three surveys. Zero responses are included in the calculations; respondents who stated a zero response to the initial question were assigned zero responses to subsequent allocation questions.[1] As in other applications of CVM, the data included extremely high responses, in some cases up to 25% of reported household incomes, which probably reflect a misunderstanding of instructions. These responses have considerable effect on the means of WTP, but there is no agreed way to draw a line beyond which responses will be rejected. To avoid this problem, our analyses of WTP results are based on medians, using all responses. The qualitative conclusions are unaffected by this choice of statistics.

The WTP for the public good mentioned in the first question posed to respondents was hardly affected by the inclusiveness of this good. The percentages of positive contributions were 61% for improvements in "the availability of equipment and trained personnel for rescue operations," 63% for "preparedness for disasters," and 65% for "all environmental services." The median WTP was $25 at the lowest level of inclusiveness and $50 at the two higher levels, but the difference

[1]Glenn Harrison has suggested that this procedure could bias the results, because of the theoretical possibility that a respondent might be willing to pay for a good but not for a bundle that includes it. Note that this objection can be eliminated by informing respondents in advance that they will have an opportunity to allocate each contribution to an inclusive good among its separate constituents. It seems highly implausible that this minor procedural change would significantly alter results. The reasons for refusals to contribute in CVM surveys are commonly quite general (rejection of responsibility, opposition to extra taxes, etc.) and therefore likely to apply to the constituents as well as to more inclusive goods.

was not significant in a Mann–Whitney test in which the two higher levels were combined. The means of WTP across levels of embedding were also very close, and the differences among them did not approach statistical significance by F test. The pattern is the same as that which we observed in our previous study, in which WTP to preserve fish in all Ontario lakes was only slightly higher than WTP to maintain but a particular few.

The bottom rows of Table I display the effect of position in the embedding structure on stated WTP for a particular good. The median amounts allocated to "equipment and trained personnel" vary from $25 when that good is evaluated on its own to $1.50 when the initial question concerns WTP for "environmental services." The three values shown in the last row of the table differ markedly from each other in the predicted direction. Group 1 differs significantly from Groups 2 and 3, by both parametric and nonparametric tests. The difference between Groups 2 and 3 only approaches significance.[2]

As in other studies, WTP values were small relative to reported incomes. Pooling over the three samples, the median WTP stated in response to the first question was $37.50 for respondents stating a family income under $20,000 (23% of total sample), $50 for income between $20,000 and $40,000 (39% of total), and $100 for families with incomes in excess of $40,000 (38% of total). The corresponding means were $97, $131, and $230. Clearly, these values are not in the range in which the embedding effect could be explained by constraints of wealth or income.

The results of this study demonstrate a large embedding effect. The key finding is that WTP is approximately constant for public goods that differ greatly in inclusiveness. The inevitable consequence of the insensitivity of WTP to inclusiveness is that estimates of WTP for the same particular good differ—by a factor of 16 for medians or 8 for means—depending on the scope of the initial question. An even larger embedding effect could probably be obtained by asking respondents to make explicit allocations to all the sub-categories at each level of embedding: the procedure of the present study, in which respondents make an allocation to a single subordinate good, appears likely to enhance its importance.

The specific good evaluated in the present study is fairly well defined, and the answer is interpretable as a quantity choice: how much extra equipment and personnel would you be willing to pay for? The good also has personal use value for most respondents, because improved availability of equipment and personnel for rescue operations would contribute to their safety and that of their families. The findings therefore extend the evidence for embedding: unlike demonstrations of embedding for existence value, the present results cannot be explained by invoking a concept of symbolic response [14; 17, p. 250].

Temporal Embedding of Payments

The embedding effects discussed so far apply to the specification of the good that is to be acquired. A related effect can arise in the specification of the schedule of payments. The question is whether respondents in a CVM survey are likely to make the appropriate discriminations between a one-time payment and a long-term commitment to a series of payments for a good. The issue is of some importance to the practical implementation of CVM. For example, willingness to pay was assessed in one study by asking people to state the amount that they would be willing to pay annually for 10 years in order to acquire a good, and conventional discount factors were applied to obtain an estimate of the present value of WTP [20].

---

[2] An earlier draft mistakenly stated that all three groups differed significantly from one another.

The issue of whether the participants in a CVM survey actually perform the discount calculations that are imputed to them has not been systematically examined, to our knowledge. The observations of embedding effects in which respondents did not discriminate between goods that vary in inclusiveness suggested the hypothesis that a similar failure of discrimination could be found between payments that vary in temporal inclusiveness. A small study was carried out to examine this hypothesis.

After completion of the main part of the interview, participants in the three groups of the first study were asked one of two versions of the following question. The version presented to each individual was selected at random:

> Now we would like to ask you how much you would be willing to pay (as a one-time payment/every year for a period of five years) to a fund to be used exclusively for a toxic waste treatment facility that would safely take care of all chemical and other toxic wastes in British Columbia.

Median WTP was $20, both in the group that considered a one-time payment ($N = 106$) and in the group that considered a five-year commitment ($N = 100$). The corresponding means were $141 and $81. The difference between the means was produced almost entirely by a few extremely high responses in the one-year group. There were five responses stating WTP of $1000 or more in that group, averaging $1800. There were only two such responses in the five-year group, averaging $1300. These extreme responses contribute approximately $54 to the difference of $60 between the means of the two groups. The results provide no reliable indication that the respondents discriminated between payment schedules that differed greatly in total present value.

The Significance of Embedding

What can be learned from these demonstrations of embedding? It may be useful to state the obvious qualification, that the present results have not established that insensitivity to inclusiveness is a *universal* characteristic of the valuations elicited in CVM studies. No single study could do so. The conservative conclusion from our findings is that future applications of CVM should incorporate an experimental control: the contingent valuation of any public good should routinely be supported by adequate evidence that the estimate is robust to manipulations of embedding, both in the definition of the good and in the specification of the number of payments. Whether this challenge can be met by appropriate CVM techniques is a question that will likely be the subject of further research.

Another defense of CVM against the embedding problem should be mentioned: the observation that different embeddings lead to different valuations of the same good would not be as troubling if there were a way of selecting one of these valuations as the correct one. As noted earlier, however, we were unable to identify in the existing CVM literature any compelling principles that could guide the choice of the appropriate embedding level for the good to be valued, or of a duration for the schedule of payments. Indeed, it is far from obvious that such principles can be found. Should the value of the damaged Alaska shoreline be assessed by WTP to clean up the damage done to it, by aggregating separate estimates of WTP to clean up parts of it, or by allocating to the cleanup a fraction of total WTP for environmental improvements? In the absence of agreed answers to such questions, our results suggest that current standards for the use of CVM may allow estimates of the value of a good that differ by more than an order of magnitude, all with an a priori equal claim to validity. As illustrated by the two examples reported here, the designer of a contingent valuation survey may be able to determine the estimated value of any good by the choice of a level of embedding. This potential for manipulation severely undermines the contingent valuation method.

PART II. THE PURCHASE OF MORAL SATISFACTION

The results presented in Part I do not support the interpretation of WTP for a public good as a measure of the economic value of this good. It remains a fact, however, that respondents express a willingness to contribute for the acquisition of many public goods, and there is no reason to doubt their sincerity or seriousness. Indeed, some elegant experiments have confirmed the willingness of people to pay for existence value—subjects actually paid to prevent a plant from being destroyed [5]. What is the good that respondents are willing to pay to acquire in such experiments or in CVM surveys? We offer the general hypothesis that responses to the CVM question express a willingness to acquire a sense of moral satisfaction (also known as a "warm glow of giving"; see [1, 2]) by a voluntary contribution to the provision of a public good. In attaining this satisfaction, the public good is a means to an end—the consumption is the sense of moral satisfaction associated with the contribution. An interesting feature of the warm glow of moral satisfaction is that it increases with the size of the contribution; for this unusual good, the expenditure is an essential aspect of consumption [18]. The interpretation of the responses to the hypothetical questions used in CVM in terms of moral satisfaction is consistent with Andreoni's economic analyses of actual donations to public goods, both in the field [1, 2] and in experimental situations [3], which distinguish the utility derived from increasing the total supply of the good from the utility gained in the act of giving.

Public goods differ in the degree of moral satisfaction that they provide to the individual making a contribution. Saving the panda may well be more satisfying for most people than saving an endangered insect and cancer research may be a better cause than research on gum disease. The quality of causes as sources of moral satisfaction will reflect individual tastes and community values. Our first hypothesis is that differences in WTP for various causes can be predicted from independent assessments of the moral satisfaction associated with these causes.

The results of Part I can be explained by invoking the additional hypothesis that moral satisfaction exhibits an embedding effect: the moral satisfaction associated with contributions to an inclusive cause extends with little loss to any significant subset of that cause. A closely related idea is that people may be willing to "dump their good cause account" on any valued cause [7]. Thus, contributing to the provision of rescue equipment may be as satisfying as contributing to the more inclusive cause of disaster preparedness. Indeed, a narrowly defined cause can be even more satisfying than a cause that includes it: it could be the case, for example, that saving the panda is more appealing than saving endangered species. Different subsets of a cause may vary in their appeal. In general, however, moral satisfaction could be expected to be about the same for an inclusive cause and for representative subsets of it.

An experiment was conducted to test these hypotheses. For the purpose of the experiment, a set of 14 pairs of public goods was constructed (see Table II). Each pair consisted of two causes, one of which was embedded in the other. The items were chosen to include two types of embedding: geographical embedding (e.g.,

TABLE II

Maximum Willingness to Pay for Various Causes and Ratings of Satisfaction from Making Contributions

Cause	Satisfaction Mean	WTP ($)	
		Median	Mean
Reduce acid rain damage in Muskoka, Ont.	7.18	20	40.91
Reduce acid rain damage in eastern Canada	7.25	50	214.55
Restore rural B.C. museums	4.67	10	32.78
Restore rural Canada museums and heritage buildings	5.79	20	113.47
Improve sport fish stocks in B.C. fresh water	5.25	10	41.89
Improve sport fish stocks in Canada fresh water	6.61	10	147.16
Protection for marmot, a small animal in B.C.	5.48	1.5	33.27
Protection for small animals in B.C.	6.42	10	141.75
Research on dengue fever, a tropical disease	4.57	0	52.42
Research on tropical diseases	4.97	4	17.83
Protection Peregrine falcon, an endangered bird	6.46	25	125.00
Protect endangered birds	6.98	20	59.07
Improve sport facilities in small communities in B.C.	6.22	10	209.75
Improve sport facilities in small communities in Canada	5.42	10	55.96
Rehabilitate recently released young offenders	5.78	50	233.16
Rehabilitate all recently released criminals	4.97	0	25.04
Habitat for muskrats, wild N. American rodent	4.70	0	51.60
Habitat for muskrats, squirrels, and other wild N. American rodents	4.59	4	52.28
Improve literacy of recent adult B.C. immigrants	6.30	10	190.53
Improve literacy of adults in B.C.	7.10	10	56.61
Replant trees in cutover areas in B.C.	7.80	20	151.70
Replant trees in cutover areas in western Canada	7.53	20	54.74
Increase research on toxic waste disposal	7.87	50	234.12
Increase research on environmental protection	7.44	50	98.77
Famine relief in Ethiopia	6.38	20	157.67
Famine relief in Africa	5.57	25	72.68
Research on breast cancer	8.12	50	243.14
Research on all forms of cancer	8.38	50	162.09

famine relief in Ethiopia or in Africa) and categorical embedding (e.g., research on breast cancer or research on all forms of cancer). The 14 issues were arbitrarily divided into two sets, labeled A and B, respectively, including the first 4 and the last 10 issues in Table II.

A special telephone survey of adult residents of the Vancouver region was conducted, with respondents randomly assigned into four groups. Respondents in groups 1 ($N = 60$) and 2 ($N = 61$) judged the moral satisfaction associated with the various causes (group 1 judged the inclusive items of set A and the embedded items of set B; group 2 judged the remaining items). After an introduction similar to that used in the surveys described in Part I and an indication that the questions were about "various causes to which people might be willing to make voluntary contributions," the instructions given to these two groups were:

> Please consider each of the causes separately and independently; that is, assume you are only being asked about the one cause. Indicate the degree of satisfaction you would receive from contributing to each cause on a scale from 0 to 10, with 0 indicating no satisfaction at all and 10 indicating a great deal of personal satisfaction.

Groups 3 ($N = 61$) and 4 ($N = 60$) were matched respectively to groups 1 and 2, but they provided measures of WTP for the same sets of causes. After the same introduction and indication of what the questions were about, these respondents received the following instructions:

> Please consider each of the causes separately and independently; that is, assume you are only being asked about the one cause. Indicate the most that you would be willing to pay for each.

The order in which the causes were presented was randomly determined separately for each respondent.

Table II presents the mean ratings of moral satisfaction and the medians and means of WTP for the 28 public goods included in the study, arranged in pairs. In each case, the embedded good is the first member of the pair. There is as usual a large discrepancy between mean and median WTP, due to extremely large WTP reported by a few individuals in each group. As before, we chose to focus on medians, without discarding any responses. The moral satisfaction ratings, which were made on a bounded scale, are not susceptible to large effects of a few aberrant responses, and the means of the satisfaction ratings were accordingly used in the analysis.

The hypothesis that WTP is predictable from assessments of moral satisfaction was tested by ranking the 14 issues evaluated by each group and by comparing the ranking of these issues by WTP and by moral satisfaction. The rank correlations between the means of satisfaction ratings made by group 1 and the median WTP of group 3 was 0.78 ($p < 0.01$). The corresponding correlation between the responses of groups 2 and 4 was 0.62 ($p < 0.02$). The general hypothesis that WTP can be predicted by ratings of moral satisfaction is strongly supported. As may be seen in Table II, there was only one striking discrepancy in the rankings of issues by WTP and by moral satisfaction: the rehabilitation of young offenders was one of the four causes eliciting the largest monetary contributions, but it ranked very low as a source of moral satisfaction. The discrepancy was not predicted, and any account of it must be speculative. One hypothesis is that the illegitimate context in which the need for public contributions arises makes it difficult to describe these contributions as yielding any kind of satisfaction—including moral satisfaction.

The data of Table II also allow a test of the effects of inclusiveness (embedding) on both moral satisfaction and WTP. The more inclusive causes have a very slight advantage on both dimensions overall, but the effect is weak and inconsistent: the more inclusive cause is associated with a higher rating of moral satisfaction for 8 of the 14 pairs of causes and with a lower rating for the other 6. Median WTP is higher for the inclusive than for the embedded cause in 6 pairs, identical in 6 others, and inferior in the remaining 2 pairs. On the other hand, mean WTP is higher for the embedded cause in 9 of the 14 pairs.

The results of this experiment support the proposed interpretation of willingness to pay for public goods as an expression of willingness to pay to acquire moral satisfaction. With only one salient exception, causes that were judged to provide little moral satisfaction also elicited relatively low WTP. Overall, there was a close correspondence between the rankings of issues by the two measures. Furthermore, the interpretation of WTP as an index of moral satisfaction helps explain the embedding effect: if the inclusiveness of the cause does little to enhance moral satisfaction, increasing inclusiveness should have little effect on WTP, as was indeed observed both in this study and in Part I.

The Sources of Contributions to Public Goods

The question posed to respondents in a CVM survey is an unusual one, which has some features of a market survey, an opinion poll, and an appeal on behalf of a new charity. Respondents who follow instructions consider the possibility of a significant financial commitment to the provision of a public good. If they are serious about it, such a commitment to a new expenditure entails a corresponding reduction in other categories of spending. To understand the decisions of respondents in CVM surveys it is useful to identify the categories of spending from which they would expect to draw their contributions.

In the budget of most households there already exists a category of spending that is dedicated to obtaining moral satisfaction—voluntary contributions to charity. Spending on charity is far from negligible. For example, in fiscal 1988 donations by individuals in the United States totaled $86 billion, approximately $350 per capita. The respondent in a CVM study is likely to consider a new contribution in the context of the existing pattern of voluntary donations by the household. It is of interest to find out whether respondents view the proposed payment as a substitute to current charitable giving or as an addition to the moral satisfaction budget, requiring a reduction in other categories of spending. To test these possibilities, participants in the survey of Part I who had stated a positive WTP for the cause presented to them were asked a series of questions in the following format:

> Suppose you were actually called on to make the contribution to environmental services you indicated earlier. Which expenditure categories do you think this money would mainly come from? Would you spend less on _____ ?

The expenditure categories mentioned in the questions included food, charities, holidays (vacations), entertainment, savings, and "other things." After answering this series of questions, respondents who had listed more than one category were asked: "From which category do you think most of the money would come?" and the relevant list of categories was repeated to them. Table III presents the results.

TABLE III

Percentage of Respondents Indicating Reduced Spending in Various Expenditure Categories ($N = 137$)

Category	"Reduction"	"Greatest reduction"
Food	19.1	2.3
Charities	34.6	9.3
Holidays	64.2	15.5
Entertainment	76.1	41.1
Savings	46.2	22.5
Other things	65.9	9.3

The results indicate that added spending on environmental and disaster services would be drawn from discretionary spending, and especially from entertainment. Respondents would not expect to alter their eating habits. More important, they would not withdraw the contribution from current charitable giving. Most respondents apparently viewed the contribution as an addition to the "good cause" budget, not as a substitute for existing items in that spending category. The observed pattern of responses is the same as would be expected in answers to the question: "If you made an *extra* contribution to charity, where would it come from?" In the terms of the present analysis, the respondents appear to have considered the contingent valuation question as an opportunity to acquire additional moral satisfaction. Note that if households contribute only to causes that yield high moral satisfaction, the only way to increase the consumption of this good is by increasing contributions—to the currently favored causes or to equally satisfying causes.

CONCLUDING REMARKS

The research reported here had two objectives: to examine the proposition that CVM results are susceptible to an embedding effect that could render them largely arbitrary and consequently useless for practical purposes and to advance the interpretation of what people do in answering CVM questions.

The central result of the first study was that willingness to pay was almost the same for a narrowly defined good (rescue equipment and personnel) and for vastly more inclusive categories (all disaster preparedness, or even all environmental services). Correspondingly, the value assigned to the more specific good varied by an order of magnitude depending on the depth of its embedding in the category for which WTP was initially assessed. This result appears to invalidate a basic assumption of CVM: that standard value theory applies to the measures obtained by this method. As the choice of embedding structure is arbitrary, the estimates of value obtained from CVM surveys will be correspondingly arbitrary.

Our assessment of the validity of the CVM is in marked contrast to that reached by Mitchell and Carson [17] in their comprehensive review of the literature on this method. Mitchell and Carson recognized the potential severity of the embedding effect, but sounded a hopeful note in their discussion of it (p. 250), arguing that such an effect is not inevitable. The evidence cited for this conclusion was the observation that WTP to improve water quality nationwide, assessed in a national survey [16], was approximately twice as high as an estimate of WTP to raise the quality of water in the Monongahela River system in Pennsylvania, assessed in a local survey conducted by other investigators using a similar instrument [10]. Given the uncertainties of comparisons across studies and sampling areas, this evidence against embedding is not persuasive.

There was some prior reason to hope that the embedding effect might be restricted to non-use values, but the present results show that estimates of use value are not generally immune to embedding effects: an essentially complete embedding effect was obtained for disaster preparedness, a public good for which respondents have use value. Our tentative conclusion is that the factor that controls the magnitude of the embedding effect is not the distinction between public goods that have use value and those that only have non-use value. A more important distinction could be between public goods for which private purchase is conceivable and other goods for which it is not. Access to clean air and the right to fish in a stream could be privately purchased in a market, and sometimes are. The respondents in contingent valuation surveys have some experience in the purchase of such goods and could rely on this experience to determine their willingness to pay [6]. On the other hand, few respondents have experience in individual purchases of improvements in disaster preparedness, air traffic control, maintenance of species, or expansion of parks. The only way to procure such goods is by concerted public action, and the decision to make a voluntary contribution to such action has more in common with charity than with the purchase of consumption goods. Note that we do not assert that the CVM is necessarily valid for public goods that could be purchased by individuals. Our point is that the purchase of moral satisfaction is especially plausible as an interpretation of WTP for goods that could not be so purchased, even when these goods have use value.[3]

Students of CVM have long known that the respondents' answers to questions about their willingness to accept compensation for the loss of public goods (WTA) are strongly affected by moral considerations. Participants are prone to respond with indignation to questions about the compensation they would require to accept pollution of the Grand Canyon National Park, or of an unspoiled beach in a remote region. The indignation is expressed by the rejection of the offered transaction as illegitimate, or by absurdly high bids. The practitioners of contingent valuation hoped to avoid the difficulties of assessing WTA by substituting WTP even where WTA is the theoretically appropriate [8, 12]. The present results suggest that the adoption of the WTP measure does not really avoid moral concerns because the voluntary contribution to the provision of such goods can be morally satisfying. A treatment that interprets contributions to public goods as equivalent to purchases of consumption goods is inadequate when moral satisfaction is an important part of the welfare gain from the contribution [2]. The amount that individuals are willing to pay to acquire moral satisfaction should not be mistaken for a measure of the economic value of public goods.

---

[3]The application of CVM to goods such as hunting licenses in limited supply [4] is perhaps best viewed as a special case of market research, because these goods are in all essential respects conventional private goods.

REFERENCES

1. J. Andreoni, Giving with impure altruism: Applications to charity and ricardian equivalence, *J. Polit. Econom.* **97**, 1447–1458 (1989).

2. J. Andreoni, Impure altruism and donations to public goods: A theory of warm-glow giving, *Econom. J.*, 100 (June 1990).

3. J. Andreoni, "An experimental test of the public goods crowding-out hypothesis," Working paper, University of Wisconsin (1990).

4. R. C. Bishop and T. A. Heberlein, Measuring values of extramarket goods: Are indirect measures biased? *Amer. J. Agr. Econom.* **61**, 926–930 (1979).

5. R. R. Boyce, T. C. Brown, G. D. McClelland, G. L. Peterson, and W. D. Schulze, "An Experimental Examination of Intrinsic Environmental Values," Working Paper, University of Colorado (1990).

6. D. S. Brookshire, M. A. Thayer, W. D. Schulze, and R. C. d'Arge, Valuing public goods: A comparison of survey and hedonic approaches, *Amer. Econom. Rev.* **72**, 165–176 (1982).

7. R. G. Cummings, Letter to Office of Environmental Project Review, Department of the Interior, November 10, 1989.

8. R. G. Cummings, D. S. Brookshire, and W. D. Schulze (Eds.), "Valuing Environmental Goods: An Assessment of the Contingent Valuation Method," Rowman and Allanheld, Totawa, NJ (1986).

9. R. C. d'Arge, A practical guide to economic valuation of the environment, *in* "Thirty-fourth Annual Rocky Mountain Mineral Law Institute Proceedings," Matthew Bendier and Co., New York (1989).

10. W. H. Desvousges, V. K. Smith, and M. P. McGivney, "A Comparison of Alternative Approaches for Estimating Recreation and Related Benefits of Water Quality Improvements," Report to the U.S. Environmental Protection Agency, Washington, DC (1983).

11. B. Fischhoff and L. Furby, Measuring values: A conceptual framework for interpreting transactions with special reference to contingent valuation of visibility, *J. Risk Uncertainty* **1**, 147–184 (1988).

12. A. M. Freeman, "The Benefits of Environmental Improvement: Theory and Practice," Johns Hopkins Press, Baltimore (1979).

13. J. P. Hoehn and A. Randall, "Aggregation and Disaggregation of Program Benefits in a Complex Policy Environment: A Theoretical Framework and Critique of Estimation Methods," Paper presented at the American Agricultural Economics Association Meetings, Logan, UT (1982).

14. D. Kahneman, Comments on the contingent valuation method, *in* "Valuing Environmental Goods" (R. G. Cummings, D. S. Brookshire, and W. D. Schulze, Eds.), Rowman and Allanheld, Totawa, NJ (1986).

15. J. V. Krutilla, Conservation reconsidered, *Amer. Econom. Rev.* **57**, 787–796 (1967).

16. R. C. Mitchell and R. T. Carson, "A Contingent Valuation Estimate of National Freshwater Benefits," Report to the U.S. Environmental Protection Agency, Washington, DC (1984).

17. R. C. Mitchell and R. T. Carson, "Using Surveys to Value Public Goods: The Contingent Valuation Method," Resources For the Future, Washington, DC (1989).

18. H. Margolis, "Selfishness, Altruism and Rationality," Cambridge Univ. Press, New York (1982).

19. C. V. Phillips and R. J. Zeckhauser, Contingent valuation of damage to natural resources: How accurate? How appropriate? *Toxics Law Reporter*, 520–529 (1989).

20. R. D. Rowe, W. D. Schulze, and D. Hurd, "A Survey of Colorado Residents' Attitudes about Cleaning Up Hazardous Waste-Site Problems in Colorado," Report for the Colorado Attorney General's Office, Denver (1986).

21. W. D. Schulze, R. G. Cummings, and D. S. Brookshire, "Methods Development in Measuring Benefits of Environmental Improvements," Vol. II, Report to the U.S. Environmental Protection Agency, Washington, DC (1983).

22. George S. Tolley and A. Randall, "Establishing and Valuing the Effects of Improved Visibility in the Eastern United States," Report to the U.S. Environmental Protection Agency, Washington DC (1983).

[24]

JOURNAL OF ENVIRONMENTAL ECONOMICS AND MANAGEMENT 22, 71–89 (1992)

Arbitrary Values, Good Causes, and Premature Verdicts*

V. KERRY SMITH

*Resource and Environmental Economics Program, Department of Economics,
North Carolina State University, Raleigh, North Carolina, 27695-8110;
and Resources for the Future, Washington, D.C. 20038*

Received August 31, 1990; revised March 4, 1991

This paper offers an alternative interpretation of the conclusions Kahneman and Knetsch propose based on two contingent valuation (CVM) surveys. The evaluation argues that while framing is important to CVM estimates, the design, implementation, and empirical findings reported from these surveys do not support their judgments. Moreover, with the exception of temporal embedding, conventional economic descriptions of individual behavior can explain the response patterns that they suggest are at variance with standard value theory. © 1992 Academic Press, Inc.

1. INTRODUCTION

Nearly 50 years ago, Hotelling [25] and Ciriacy-Wantrup [14] proposed different methods for measuring people's values for services available outside conventional markets. While their respective methods (i.e., the travel cost–demand model for recreation sites and the contingent valuation methodology) developed quite differently, several hundred applications of each have been completed to date.

Approaches for measuring the values of nonmarket commodities are usually classified into two groups: (a) indirect or revealed preference methods that rely on observable choices together with a maintained model of the motivations for those choices and (b) direct or stated preference methods that use survey techniques to ask people how they would value or respond to hypothetical changes in the good of interest. As the set of resources to be valued has expanded, analysts increasingly have relied on surveys and contingent valuation methods (CVM). Often data for applying the indirect methods in these cases do not exist, and even if data could be collected, isolating the behavioral choices that are likely to be associated with the good to be valued often has been infeasible.

Because many economists distrust people's reports of their behavioral intentions, considerable attention has focused on the accuracy and reliability of CVM.[1]

---

*This paper has benefited from the comments of anonymous referees and a number of readers, including Richard Bishop, Ron Cummings, Bill Desvousges, Ann Fisher, Rick Freeman, John Payne, Alan Randall, and Bill Schulze. None of them are responsible for errors or misinterpretations in the revised paper. Partial support of this research was provided by National Science Foundation Grant SES-8911372. Thanks are also due to Barbara Scott for constructive editing that improved several earlier drafts of the paper.

[1]Often these concerns are attributed to Samuelson's classic discussion of strategic incentives with public goods. However, in later writing on the implications of this theory, he was more optimistic about

71

Based on two limited surveys, Kahneman and Knetsch have concluded that CVM-based valuation estimates are "largely arbitrary and consequently useless for practical purposes." Their findings are derived from what they describe as controlled experiments designed to document an embedding effect depending on how people's values for one commodity are elicited in relation to a more inclusive package of goods that includes it.

This paper provides an alternative view of Kahneman and Knetsch's analysis and conclusions. Basically I argue that *none* of their conclusions are correct. Four factors contributed to this judgement:

• The questions used to evaluate embedding are flawed. Their framing does not satisfy the criteria that Kahneman (see Kahneman and Tversky [29]) helped to develop in his earlier research on how people interpret valuation questions.

• The implementation of their contingent valuation surveys does not adhere to generally accepted practices for designing and analyzing CVM survey results.

• The properties they attribute to standard value theory in suggesting that their CVM findings are not consistent with expectations are themselves incorrect. Moreover, because they do not describe the commodities offered to respondents adequately, several different explanations can be offered using conventional economic theory.

• The interpretation of their results and what CVM-based willingness-to-pay estimates may be measuring does not appear to be consistent with their question or their own findings.

Kahneman and Knetsch's paper was written to stimulate responses from CVM practitioners and critics. My paper is not intended to defend CVM. It evaluates the design and methodology of Kahneman and Knetsch's two telephone surveys and then turns to the substance of the conclusions they draw from their evidence. While I found all aspects of this work to be incompatible with their conclusions, it is important to acknowledge that the Kahneman/Knetsch paper discusses a central issue in designing and implementing CVM research. The framing of the commodity to be valued using CVM must reflect an understanding of how people perceive it, what people consider related goods (either complements or substitutes), and how people understand the processes involved in altering their consumption patterns as part of adjusting to an exogenously imposed change in the good of interest.

These are not new issues. They have been discussed in a number of earlier papers describing embedding, the part–whole problem, or superadditivity.[2] Nonetheless, because Kahneman and Knetsch have stated their conclusions provocatively, their discussion is likely to stimulate multiple responses and as such may well enhance our understanding of framing issues.

---

the prospects for eliciting people's values than the subsequent literature has implied. In one paper [45], he offers examples of ways to deal with allocation decisions involving public goods. In one of these, he seems to endorse a form of CVM with attention to the possibility of strategic incentives by proposing that analysts "interrogate people for their tastes with respect to public goods in such large homogeneous groups as to give each respondent the feeling that his answer can be a 'true' one without costing him anything extra" (p. 1235).

[2]See Cummings, *et al.* [18], Mitchell and Carson [42], and McClelland *et al.* [41] for discussion of these issues.

ARBITRARY VALUES   73

STEPS IN THE COMMONDITY EMBEDDING

I   II   III

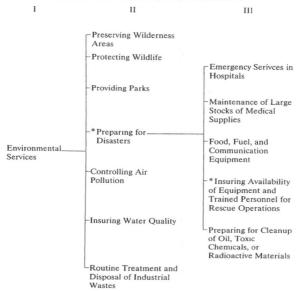

2. THREE QUESTIONS ABOUT KK'S RESEARCH DESIGN AND IMPLEMENTATION

Kahneman and Knetsch (hereafter KK) conducted two telephone surveys of adult residents in Vancouver to investigate the effects of: (a) the commodity description, payment terms, and question sequence used when respondents were asked to value increments to environmental services; (b) the motivations for the valuations reported for a wide array of public goods; and (c) the sources from existing expenditures for the stated payments in CVM questions in the survey about (a). Three questions about their surveys should be asked.

Did respondents understand the inclusive commodities as KK intended? Figure 1 illustrates the pattern of inclusion implied by KK's questions and describes the commodities used in the survey that provide the central data for their overall conclusion. One-third of their initial survey's respondents were first asked how much they would pay annually for "significant improvements" in environmental services. This same group was asked progressively about the items in Fig. 1 marked with asterisks under Steps II and III, each as a portion of the immediately preceding valuation response. The second group of respondents entered the question sequence at Step II. This group was asked about preparing for disasters as their first question with a follow-up question to value the same good (as for the first third of the sample) in Step III. The last group was asked only about payments to ensure the availability of equipment and trained personnel for rescue operations. KK's embedding conclusion is based on the observation that the values for the initial payments are not significantly different according to the step (i.e., I, II, or III) that starts the valuation. Further, the value of the Step III commodity depends on whether earlier steps preceded it.

While this pattern *can* be explained by conventional economic models, one question logically prefaces any interpretation of the findings: Did the respondents understand the questions as the analysts intended? Fischhoff and Furby's [20] critique of earlier CVM studies for valuing visibility changes offers some of the best general guidance. They observed:

> Transactions are complex social and psychological phenomena. Each has many features that participants may consider in deciding whether to accept it. Knowing how people have interpreted these features is essential in order to know what transaction people thought they were facing. Specifying all relevant features, and ensuring that they have been understood, is essential to staging transactions. *Unless a feature is specified explicitly (and comprehensively), evaluators must guess its value and, hence, what the offer really means. If they guess wrong, then they risk misrepresenting their values.* [20, pp. 179–180; emphasis added].

Table I applies Fischhoff and Furby's categorization of the issues to be considered in evaluating CVM questions to KK's embedding questions. Their first set of questions about progressive degrees of "inclusiveness" of the commodity definition do not adequately define the change or its extent and timing. The context and initial conditions are also left to each respondent. On these grounds alone, their results would be difficult to interpret. With deliberate sequencing of effects, Mitchell and Carson [42, p. 302] recommend completely informing respondents of what is to come *before* they are asked to value the first improvement. They also suggest that respondents be given the opportunity to revise their responses.[3]

Indeed, Kahneman's own earlier research (see Kahneman and Tversky [29]) anticipated the very issues raised by Fischhoff and Furby on the importance of clearly defining both aspects (price and commodity) of a transaction:

> The basic example of a transaction is the purchase of goods after which one has more goods and less money than before. A transaction must be evaluated according to the balance of costs and benefits in a mental account.
>
> The framing of a transaction can alter its attractiveness by controlling the costs and benefits that are assigned to its account.... *Framing effects in consumer behavior may be particularly pronounced in situations that have a single dimension of cost (usually money) and several dimensions of benefit*...The attractiveness of a course of action may thus change if its cost or benefit is placed in a larger account.
>
> If a decision is influenced by the reference point with which possible outcomes are compared, what determines the reference point? *The dependence of impressions, judgments and responses on a point of reference is a ubiquitous psychological phenomenon.* [29, p. 168; emphasis added]

Thus, if we accept these observations, we must conclude that KK's failure to completely describe the reference and target levels for the changes that they posed very likely led to disparities in respondents' perceptions of what was to be obtained from the transaction. Equally important, there is no reason to believe that respondents perceived the components of environmental services as KK presented

---

[3]It is not possible to judge whether the latter was offered from KK's description of the survey process. Also, telephone interviews impose definite limitations on the survey process. While the length of a question alone does not seem to influence its performance in eliciting nonfactual information (see Kalton and Schuman [30]), its complexity does.

ARBITRARY VALUES   75

TABLE I

Applying the Fischhoff–Furby Criteria to Kahneman and Knetsch

Components in defining transactions	Commodity embedding	Temporal embedding
The good		
Substantive definition		
Context	Poorly defined	Poorly defined
Source of change	Not clear	Not clear
Formal definition		
Reference and target levels	Not identified	Not identified
Extent of change	Vaguely defined	Not clear
Timing of change	Not identified	Not clear
Certainty of provision	Assured	Assured
The value measure		
Substantive definition		
Attributes	Clear	Not clear
Context	Clear	Not clear
Constituency	Individual[a]	Individual[a]
Formal definition		
Reference and target levels	Direct question CV[b]	Direct question CV[b]
Extent	Clear	Clear
Timing of payment	Clear	Clear
Certainty of payment	Clear	Clear
The social context		
Other people involved	Unclear	Unclear
Resolution mechanism	Unclear	Unclear
Other stakes	Unclear	Unclear

[a]Because the sample was screened to correspond to adults, it is not clear how household heads will respond to the question in comparison with adults who live in a household but are not the household head.

[b]A direct payment CVM question means that the WTP was asked directly. Fischhoff and Furby [20] criticize this approach. Mitchell and Carson's [42] discussion seems to imply that there are situations where it can provide acceptable results.

them. All of the health services, supplies, and rescue-related personnel and equipment services could have been treated equally well as part of an inclusive definition of a commodity described as "health services." Without initially discussing the topic with people in focus groups or other informal pretests before designing and implementing their survey, analysts do not know how to structure commodities consistent with people's perceptions.

This issue is crucial to KK's assumption that respondents who were not willing to pay for significant increases in the commodities identified with levels I and II would *automatically* have zero values for those at lower levels in the embedding structure. If respondents' perceptions about the components of each embedded commodity differ from KK's views, they may have positive values for KK's embedded goods and fail to recognize that the authors intended them as part of the aggregates presented as environmental services or preparedness for disasters.

The bias created by treating the values as zero is potentially serious, *not* small as Kahneman and Knetsch contend.[4]

The temporal embedding question fares worse than the commodity embedding question using the Fischhoff–Furby criteria. Different sets of respondents were asked to consider payments as one-time expenditures versus as five annual disbursements to "a fund to be used exclusively for a toxic waste treatment facility." This question does not completely describe how decisions are made about the facility's construction, its continued operation once built, and how the costs of those operations would be recovered. It is certainly conceivable that respondents would interpret the payments as being part of the capital costs for the facility and that the operating costs of providing the "public good" treatment services that the facility produces would be handled under future undisclosed terms. While KK's respondents may have considered the temporal and embedding questions as interrelated, this seems unlikely because the commodity was different and the question was asked after completion of the main part of the interview. Nonetheless, it is unclear from KK's description whether respondents were to "connect" the two valuation tasks or treat them independently.

Based on these problems, it is not clear that respondents understood the inclusive commodities—whether as components of an aggregate or as a time sequence of payments—as KK intended. Thus, the framing of the commodities does not correspond to what would be required to clearly test the embedding issue.

Does KK's sampling design and survey methodology conform to accepted CVM practice? Unfortunately, the sampling design portion of this question cannot be answered because KK do not describe how they selected their samples. They report that calls were made in the evening hours to adults and samples were evenly split among "experiments" by gender. No information was given on response rates or the details of the survey procedures. Based on Mitchell and Carson's [42] proposed six-point checklist for evaluating contingent valuation studies (i.e., Background, Sampling and Aggregation Procedures, Scenario, Survey Procedures, Data Analysis, and Evidence of Reliability), I find it very hard to evaluate several crucial questions:

(a) How was the questionnaire developed? Was it pretested?

(b) How do the samples of completed interviews versus those with reported WTP responses compare in size and characteristics?

(c) Was an analysis of protest responses to the WTP questions conducted?

(d) Were statistical models relating the WTP responses to the economic and demographic characteristics of respondents estimated?[5] Thus, KK's sampling

---

[4]See footnote 1 in Kahneman and Knetsch [28]. Their explanation of the reasons for small bias from imputing a zero to progressively embedded components when a respondent reports zero for the highest level is not correct. Based on their description, respondents do not know the components of lower levels in the embedded structure until *after* they provide a positive value for the aggregate that includes them.

[5]KK do report summary information across the questions used in the commodity embedding by family income. However, it is impossible to judge whether reported WTPs would have been significantly affected by income. Moreover, their comparison is with family income, and the questions are posed as the individual's WTP. Because the description of survey methodology did not indicate whether attempts were made to identify household decision makers, it is difficult to judge whether family income is the appropriate measure for income in analyzing the reported WTPs.

design and survey methodology cannot be evaluated for conformity with accepted CVM practice based on what their paper reports.

Is KK's statistical analysis appropriate to the hypotheses tested? Although statistical methods alone cannot compensate for the failure to meet Fischhoff and Furby's criteria for defining the transaction components, the practices used can be evaluated on their own merits. The authors confine their analysis to medians and testing of hypotheses with nonparametric statistics. These types of tests are consistent with most recommendations in the literature. However, it appears that no attempt was made to examine the influence of economic and demographic variables or variables that might be linked to prospective use of or past experience with the commodities for the WTP responses. Equally important, recent advances in the use of selection effects models (see Heckman [24]) to take account of protest, zero, and/or outlying responses were apparently not considered as part of KK's hypotheses testing. (See Smith and Desvousges [48] and Irwin *et al.* [26].) It is difficult to judge how much any of these refinements would influence KK's overall conclusions. Nonetheless, when we argue that CVM data result from the same behavioral decision process as actual choices, we must expect these responses to be influenced by the factors (real or stated) that constrain those choices, such as people's income levels, the availability of substitutes, and perhaps demographic variables (as proxy measures for differences in tastes). This expectation is not markedly different from what we would expect as part of understanding a household's purchases of food or any other marketed commodity. As Mitchell and Carson suggest, these types of analyses provide one opportunity to gauge the validity of the CVM measures.

Analysis of selection effects can serve multiple purposes—identifying elements in the context used for the commodity or value concept as part of the framing that have not been adequately addressed, assisting in specifying the economic and demographic factors that distinguish people who "demand" the commodity from those who do not, and gauging the apparent level of understanding of the questions asked.

Because their assignment of zero WTP for all lower or embedded commodities with respondents reporting zero value for "significant improvements" in one of the higher levels of these commodities is a maintained assumption that accepts KK's specification of the aggregate structure for the commodity, the analysis should have been conducted with and without these observations. About one-third of the samples of commodity inclusiveness at Steps I and II would be affected by this decision. Thus, this decision could easily affect the differences in means or medians reported for each commodity across the embedding order used to elicit values.

A growing set of results suggests that when people's risk perceptions are important to interpreting the experimentally controlled preferences of subjects, even at the level of simple summary statistics, comparisons that permit within-subject evaluations rather than relying exclusively on between-subject medians or means can be more sensitive indicators of subjects' responses. People's experience both within and outside the laboratory can be important to observed behavior. Because many of the same types of perception issues can arise with environmental amenities, we might expect the same types of qualifications to be relevant for them as well. For example, comparing the median value for the ratio of reported WTPs for the Step II to the Step III commodities across respondents in each of samples 1 and 2 might have narrowed the range of differences that seem to be present in KK's Table I. Harless's [22] recent analysis of individual specific ratios of WTA (willingness to accept) to WTP in experimental markets involving lotteries found that they were *not* significantly different from unity—a contradiction of earlier experimental evidence that partially motivated their surveys (see [28]). Within-subject comparisons represent one way to control for the effects of individuals' characteristics and constraints on their responses or behavior. In the context of surveys, this type of control has been recognized as essential to analyzing the responses. Researchers traditionally assume that laboratory experiments with people as subjects could exercise sufficient control over what motivates their actions to treat responses as arising from a common structure, except for random error. When perceptions are formed as part of people's behavioral responses to experimental situations, it is not clear that the results of these experiments can be analyzed as if they were produced by independent replications of the *same* controlled process across subjects.

3. ECONOMIC INTERPRETATIONS OF KK'S RESULTS

Kahneman and Knetsch's broad interpretation of their finding relies on the premise that the valuation responses observed cannot be explained by standard value theory. This premise is not correct. After devoting several pages to a detailed critique of the design, implementation, and interpretation of their survey and arguing that it is seriously flawed, why pursue their conclusions further? The answer lies in the questions they pose, not in their methodology. The embedding issue is widely acknowledged as a fundamental aspect of implementing the Fischhoff–Furby approach to framing CVM questions. Decisions on the commodity definition must be based on what is to be valued and how people interpret that commodity. Economic theory is not limited to the role that Kahneman and Knetsch suggest. Theory can provide a method for understanding what to expect from CVM responses. Because this role has often been ignored in designing and interpreting many CVM studies, I propose to illustrate how most of KK's findings can be explained using conventional economics. I have divided my discussion into three areas: commodity embedding, temporal embedding, and good causes (or moral satisfaction).

Commodity embedding. The incomplete definition of both the commodities and the increments to them involved in KK's CVM transactions provide the basis for multiple interpretations of their first finding: "...WTP [that] is approximately constant for public goods that differ greatly in inclusiveness." This conclusion follows from comparing the diagonal elements in their Table I. Before the problems with their interpretation of these results are discussed, consider their premise that standard value theory would not be consistent with their findings. There are several aspects of any answer to this premise, including respondent's perceptions of the changes to the commodities in each question and the specification of what is "held constant" in forming a value. The second aspect provokes two interrelated questions: would the degree of inclusiveness of a commodity definition influence how WTP responds to changes in that commodity, and would the amount of responsiveness depend on what was held constant?

To address these issues, consider the properties of price flexibility (i.e., percentage change in price with a percentage change in the quantity of a good) as the definition of the commodity changes.

To keep the discussion simple, I have used a two-commodity example—the good of interest and a Hicksian composite of everything else. Using Anderson's [1] duality result for price flexibilities and price elasticities together with the Hicks–Allen equations linking price, income, and substitution elasticities, the price flexibility for the commodity of interest, Q, is designated as θ,

$$\theta = -\left[\frac{1 - k_Q N_Q}{\sigma} + k_Q\right],\tag{1}$$

where

N_Q = income elasticity of demand for Q

k_Q = share of the budget "spent" on Q[6]

σ = Allen elasticity of substitution between Q and the composite of all other goods.

From Eq. (1) we can see that narrowing the definition of Q so that more substitutes are included in the composite good will increase σ and therefore *ceteris paribus* reduce WTP's degree of responsiveness to increments in Q. We would expect the reverse pattern to arise from expanding the definition of Q because this would leave few substitutes in the composite good and little ability to substitute that composite for Q.

However, this is not the complete story. The derivation of Eq. (1) makes an important limiting assumption. All quantities are treated as parametric, so θ measures how WTP responds to changes in Q *when the amount of the other commodity is fixed*. If we modify this assumption, treat Q as rationed, and specify that all other goods are available at fixed prices, then the price flexibility for this situation θ^*, is given by Eq. (2) (for another alternative, in terms of a mixed demand framework, see Chavas [13])

$$\theta^* = -\left[\frac{1 - k_Q N_Q}{(1 - k_Q)\sigma}\right].\tag{2}$$

θ^* can imply greater responsiveness of WTP to the definition of Q. Thus, we can anticipate how the framing of the commodity *together with an understanding of how people perceive their ability to adjust to changes in Q* (i.e., modify other goods' consumption at a fixed price or not) will affect the size of the WTP response to those incremental changes in Q. Describing Q as a reduction in the capacity (or quality) available to someone for one specific skiing area in a location with many alternative areas should imply a willingness to pay to avoid it different from that when Q is defined to include all of the alternative areas. Moreover, the response also depends on whether these other sites are constrained in availability or freely accessible at fixed prices.

---

[6]This share is treated symmetrically in the two definitions of the price flexibility—as expenditures at the shadow price in comparison to income plus all such expenditures for rationed commodities. The analysis parallels Hanemann's [21] recent explanation of disparities between willingness-to-pay and willingness-to-accept measures of Hicksian surpluses.

There are a number of potential explanations for the relative constancy of the three sample's WTPs for *significant improvements* in their first-step commodities—environmental services, preparedness for disasters, or availability of equipment and trained personnel for rescue operations. Three aspects of the process are important:

 (i) This was the first question posed to each respondent.

 (ii) Remaining valuation questions in the sequence apparently were not identified (in contrast to Mitchell and Carsons's recommended protocol).

 (iii) Respondents were not given the opportunity to revise.

Taken together, one does not know how respondents in each sample interpreted the quantity change corresponding to "significant improvements" in each of the three services that KK compare to develop their conclusions. We could, for example, hypothesize that they envision different changes so that it all works out correctly as I illustrate below. Alternatively, we could simply say that no prior expectation is warranted given the problems in commodity framing. Only when the nesting illustrated in my Fig. 1 is explained to respondents can they be expected to initiate an allocation process. Moreover, even in this case, we would need to know what they perceived as the levels of the other elements in each aggregate to understand the WTP changes across the embedded commodities.

 More formally, if my Fig. 1 is treated as a guide to a commodity aggregation for environmental services, Q, as a public good with the determinants specified as nested components, the following equations define an aggregation structure consistent with the figure,

$$Q = F(Z_1, Z_2, Z_3, Z_4, Z_5, Z_6, Z_7) \tag{3a}$$
$$Z_4 = G(X_1, X_2, X_3, X_4, X_5), \tag{3b}$$

where Z_j, $j = 1, 2, \ldots, 7$, identify the seven components of environmental services named in Fig. 1 (in the same order) and X_i, $i = 1, 2, \ldots, 5$, identify the five components of preparing for disasters.

 KK's question amounts to asking values for a vaguely specified dQ, dZ_4, and dX_4. Thus, we can define the interpretation given to the changes in Q's components so that they yield an equivalent change in the aggregate Q. This is what the following equations do for this example. dZ_4 and dX_4 correspond to the changes in each required to yield $\overline{dQ}$, with all other elements in $F(\cdot)$ and $G(\cdot)$ held constant[7]:

$$dZ_4 = \frac{1}{F_4} \overline{dQ} \tag{4}$$

$$dX_4 = \frac{1}{F_4 \cdot G_4} \overline{dQ}, \tag{5}$$

where $F_j = \partial F / \partial Z_j$ and $G_i = \partial G / \partial X_i$.

---

[7]A more general expression for this first interpretation is to recognize that, as in the case of defining Hicksian consumer surplus measures for sets of price changes, there is a comparable requirement to define the path of integration for quantity (or quality) changes consistently (see Bockstael and Kling [11]). To the extent that the questions defining KK's inclusive commodities are vague in specifying the commodity changes as well as the beginning and ending points of the change, they are unlikely to be consistently perceived across respondents and to describe the analytical equivalent of a consistent path of integration for any of them.

The moral of this demonstration is that asking questions is not simple (as KK imply in the beginning of their paper). It is exceptionally difficult, time consuming, and often costly to develop a CVM survey that responds to the criteria enumerated by Fischhoff and Furby [20] in defining the value and commodity elements in CVM transactions. Because questions can be asked does not assure that they will be understood and answered as intended. KK's judgment of their commodity specification is quite different from mine. For example, they observe:

> The specific good evaluated in the present study is fairly well defined, and the answer is interpretable as a quantity choice: how much extra equipment and personnel would you be willing to pay for? *The good also has personal use value for most respondents, because improved availability of equipment and personnel for rescue operations would contribute to their safety . . . .*

Without the emergency, no commodity is transferred, so an entirely different interpretation seems more appropriate to this good. Increases in personnel and equipment provide increased safety (or equivalently risk reductions) rather than increments to a public good available with certainty. Emergency preparedness could be treated as public averting behavior that respondents could perceive as reducing the probabilities of the most severe outcomes possible from disasters. Under this interpretation, even if we defined the dZ_4 to be perceived as comparable to a certain change in Q, if respondents' values are derived from some type of surplus measure based on the expected utility model, then we would expect their values for dZ_4 to be less than those for an equally sized dQ available with certainty (see Johansson [27, pp. 40–42]).

KK also express concern that the WTP for equipment and trained personnel varies depending upon where it is elicited in the embedded structure. This is not counterintuitive, but rather is reassuring given their design. Respondents receiving all three steps (in Fig. 1) are asked to allocate at each step the value that they provided for the preceding step. Thus, not only are the changes in commodities different, the levels of the other elements in the $F(\cdot)$ and $G(\cdot)$ functions are as well. (See Randall and Hoehn [44] for a general discussion of these types of issues.)

Thus, there are multiple problems in moving down the nested structure. Some commodities (at the higher levels) may well be interpreted as quantity changes (as KK intended). However, the commodities selected for the embedded alternatives could easily be interpreted as changing probabilities (KK describe them as increasing the quantity of safety). In these situations we combine two issues—comparisons across *ex ante* and *ex post* values and nested allocations of value. We can explain the results that might be expected with each task separately. In combination, the survey's questions present an unnecessarily complex task to both respondents and analysts.

Temporal Embedding. KK's temporal embedding conclusion requires that respondents perceive the question as they intended for both the time sequence of payments *and* the temporal availability of the commodity. I believe that it is equally possible, based on the question they present, that respondents did not perceive this question as KK intended. Nonetheless, this qualification does not explain their results. Rather it is a cautionary note to interpreting any findings from vaguely structured questions.

82   V. KERRY SMITH

Additional evidence on people's responses to continuing versus one-time payments in a CVM context can be reported. As part of evaluating CVM versus indirect methods for valuing public efforts to provide drinking water in rural areas of Pakistan, I recently participated in research comparing a random utility model (RUM) with contingent valuation surveys. In contrast to past comparisons, this study examined an actual decision situation involving households' connection decisions to public water systems versus CVM surveys in areas where water connections were not available. The RUM framework was used to describe people's actual connection decisions. The pricing schemes included fixed and continuing charges (but independent of the amount of water consumed). Analyses were conducted in areas with quite different alternative sources (to public systems) for drinking water. The pattern of connections indicated that prices (both the continuing and the fixed components) were important to connection; decisions (see Altaf *et al.* [4]).

Parallel contingent valuation surveys were conducted in areas with the same types of substitute water supplies but without opportunities to connect to public water systems. The questions identified varying terms for the fixed components of the price and asked a maximum monthly tariff. We compared the consistency between behavior underlying the WTP for connections implied by the RUM models and the CVM responses in two ways. First, the RUM estimates by area were used to predict the tariff each household in the samples involved in the contingent valuation surveys "should have bid," given the levels of fixed charges and the relative contribution of each household's economic and demographic factors in explaining connection decisions. Second, multivariate statistical models based on the CVM responses (i.e., models with the stated WTP as a function of the question terms as well as the household's economic and demographic characteristics) were used to forecast connection decisions that households in villages with access to public water systems "should have made." Both the predicted WTP/stated tariff and the predicted/actual frequency comparisons indicated a strong association between the RUM estimates and the CVM responses (see Smith *et al.* [51]).

By comparing the influence of fixed and continuing tariffs on connection decisions, it was possible to infer discount rates. As with other studies of this type (see Hausman [23] and Brookshire *et al.* [9]), the implicit discount rates based on actual choices were quite variable. Responses to the CVM questions did appear to consider the difference between the fixed charge and the monthly tariffs, but not necessarily in a way consistent with the discounting rule KK propose to use in evaluating the importance of temporal embedding.

Such findings have been observed in numerous studies of consumers' purchasing decisions for durables where an implicit trade-off exists between one-time charges (the initial price) and continuing costs (i.e., associated with efficiency of operation). For the most part, these studies derive a test of discounting by comparing within-subject responses and not the across-subject format used by KK. Thus, they can be assumed to exercise some control for differences in individuals' characteristics and constraints. KK's results ignore the effects such differences might have on responses to one-time versus continuing costs. Nonetheless, it is important to acknowledge that KK's findings are qualitatively comparable with a number of studies relying on actual choices. As such, there is no reason to conclude that they result from CVM. Instead, they may imply that a conventional model's characterization of how people make decisions over time is too simple.

Good Causes. KK's second survey is described as motivated by two hypotheses:

(i) "...differences in [CVM elicited] WTP for various causes can be predicted from independent assessments of the moral satisfaction associated with these causes" [bracketed term added].

(ii) "...the moral satisfaction associated with contributions to an inclusive cause extends with little loss to any significant subset of that cause."

To develop their test of these questions, KK conducted a second survey, and this sample was divided into four groups. Each of 14 potential causes (see KK's Table II) was described in a specific and an inclusive mode. Two of the groups were asked to rate different subsets of these 14 (part described in specific and part in inclusive terms) using an index of *personal* satisfaction (ranging from 0 to 10), and two groups were asked their willingness to pay for corresponding groupings of the causes. Based on the description given, the questions again seem to violate most of Fischhoff and Furby's criteria for CVM transactions.

There are several problems with KK's interpretation of these results. First, their question did not distinguish collective from individual satisfaction. At best, the request for a rating of personal satisfaction yields a utility index. The issue posed by Andreoni [2, 3] concerns whether donations (or private efforts to supply some public good) lead to two types of contributions to an individuals' utility. One of them is associated with the amount personally given and a second from the overall level *for the same cause* (*or public good*) across all people involved, including the individual's contribution. Nothing in the wording or design of KK's questions allows these two to be distinguished. Moreover, Andreoni does *not* argue that the contributions would be aggregated across all causes. His models assume only one cause.

Because these analyses have focused on *one* mixed good with private and public components (or *one* type of donation that has warm glow and altruistic effects), the models involved do *not* rationalize the Cummings [17] conjecture that people's response to CVM questions represent a "dumping of the contents of their good cause account" on the first valued cause posed to them in a CVM question. The only questions that can be answered with the KK experiment concern how the elicited WTPs relate to respondent's personal satisfaction index.

KK conclude (again based on simple nonparametric tests using medians) that WTP for public goods is an expression of WTP to acquire moral satisfaction and that the inclusiveness of cause does little to enhance moral satisfaction. However, all their results suggest is that CVM elicited WTP is related to an index of utility. This is what we would expect. For the "good cause"/moral satisfaction argument to be demonstrated, we would have to have (among other things) a constant relationship between WTP and the satisfaction index regardless of the cause proposed. It is possible to test (albeit in a fairly crude way) whether the cause and the likely mix of use- and nonuse-related motives affected the relationship between the stated WTP and their satisfaction index. Any differences in the WTP/satisfaction index offer a counterargument to the good cause argument (i.e., indiscriminating expressions of value for good causes).

V. KERRY SMITH

TABLE II

The WTP/Moral Satisfaction Relationship[a]

Independent variables[b]	Median WTP		Mean WTP	
	(1)	(2)	(3)	(4)
Intercept	−35.66	−33.34	−107.11	−94.81
	(−2.53)	(−2.23)	(−1.54)	(−1.30)
	[−7.12]	[−5.81]	[−1.99]	[−1.98]
Satisfaction index	8.96	8.59	38.58	36.48
	(3.96)	(3.60)	(3.46)	(3.14)
	[11.43]	[9.49]	[4.84]	[5.08]
Inclusive good	−0.97	−1.03	−46.15	−45.29
	(−0.21)	(−0.21)	(−2.01)	(−1.86)
	[−0.36]	[−0.36]	[−1.34]	[−1.39]
Existence of species	−6.51	−40.51	−24.44	−173.94
	(−0.94)	(−0.52)	(−0.74)	(−0.46)
	[−2.29]	[−2.56]	[−1.53]	[−1.37]
Type of pollution	12.01	−116.04	−9.57	−870.93
	(1.60)	(−0.65)	(−0.26)	(−1.01)
	[2.20]	[−1.06]	[−0.36]	[−1.58]
Recreation related	−6.51	−6.59	8.80	8.38
	(−0.95)	(−0.93)	(0.26)	(0.24)
	[−1.83]	[−1.91]	[0.58]	[0.55]
Satisfaction index × existence		5.38		23.69
		(0.44)		(0.39)
		[2.12]		[1.08]
Satisfaction index × type of pollution		17.29		116.24
		(0.72)		(1.00)
		[1.20]		[1.61]
R^2	0.60	0.61	0.44	0.47

[a]The numbers in parentheses below the coefficients are the t ratios for the null hypothesis of no association using the OLS standard errors. In brackets are t ratios using the Newey–West [43] version of the White [52] consistent covariance matrix for situations in which a general form of heteroscedasticity and autocorrelation may be present.

[b]The results from KK's Table II were reordered so that the adjoining responses from each of the subsets of the sample were entered in blocks. Correlation was assumed to be possible for up to 10 lags (the maximum number of estimates elicited from a single subsample). This estimator replaces $\hat{\sigma}^2(X^TX)^{-1}$ with $(X^TX)^{-1}X^T\hat{\Sigma}X(X^TX)^{-1}$, where X is a $T \times K$ matrix of observations on the independent variables (N is the number of observations and K the number of independent variables including a limit vector for the intercept). $\hat{\sigma}^2$ is the estimate for the error's variance based on OLS residues. $\hat{\Sigma}$ is the estimate of the nonspherical covariance matrix based on OLS residuals using the Newey–West format.

Table II reports the results from such an evaluation by comparing the results across causes and classifying them in several groups: maintaining the existence of one or more endangered species, improving the facilities or quality of recreation, and reducing pollution. In performing this exercise, my analysis accepts KK's premise and uses the simple summary statistics reported in their Table II. This requires the models to ignore the role of individual's characteristics and constraints. Because the sample subsets were asked multiple questions, I arranged the data following KK's description of the process so that responses from the same subsets followed each other in the sample. I report estimates of the coefficients' standard errors that allow for the heteroscedasticity and "autocorrelation" that the survey design may have introduced (see footnote b to Table II).

My findings are based on ordinary least-squares (OLS) estimates of linear models with KK's reported median and mean WTPs across the 14 causes considered. The analysis compares a sample that pools responses for the WTP and satisfaction index across questions and subsamples regardless of the inclusiveness of the cause description. They include a dummy variable to identify the inclusive descriptions. The models also include dummy variables based on whether the good cause involved the existence of one or more species, some improvement in recreation access or facilities, or the amount of pollution. The first might be expected to be primarily associated with nonuse values, the second might have both use and nonuse values (through the specific examples used would seem to imply little nonuse value), and the last might be argued to involve pollution-related impure public goods. The findings confirm KK's conclusion that inclusiveness did not significantly influence the median WTPs across causes.

Both the median and the mean responses are strongly associated with the satisfaction index. *However, differences in stated WTPs also arise from the character of the good causes, which is contrary to the expectations implied by interpreting CVM responses as generalized desires to do "good things."* Indeed, it appears in the case of the median WTP responses (KK's preferred summary statistic), based on the *t* ratios using standard errors adjusted for the heteroscedasticity and cross-observation correlation, that the nature of the causes does affect the relationship between the satisfaction index and the WTP. When the type of cause is treated as shifting the intercept, the findings indicate that causes associated with existence of species have effects different from those of pollution-related causes on the WTP/satisfaction relationship. Even in an interactive form, the type of cause influences both the intercept and the relationship between WTP and the satisfaction index for existence of species.

Given the limitations in the data and the crude nature of my classification of causes, these findings should be treated carefully. Nonetheless, they are consistent with other evidence in the literature that people express small WTPs for changes that they regard as unimportant and larger values for those that are important to them, *not* the same amount for all types of causes, provided that these are the first causes mentioned in an interview.

Even for unique natural environments, when small changes in quality are carefully described, the CVM estimates appear to be able to distinguish values for these small changes from concern about the overall resource. For example, the Grand Canyon is arguably a national treasure and would seem to qualify as an ideal example of an environmental good cause. Yet, a recent study on the value of visibility improvements at the Grand Canyon (see Balson *et al.* [5]) found clear differences between summer versus winter improvements, with less than 10% of respondents willing to pay any positive amount for large visibility improvements on 20 winter days—certainly not what Kahneman and Knetsch's arguments would predict.

4. ANOTHER VERDICT ON CVM

An important motivation for the renewed interest in CVM's accuracy and for a detailed evaluation of what the Kahneman–Knetsch results actually establish about its performance can be traced to CVM's use in natural resource damage assessment. This is especially true since the July 14, 1989 D.C. District Court of Appeals opinion on challenges to the Department of Interior's final rules for Type B assessments.[8] The Court ruled against petitioners who argued, for a variety of reasons, that CVM estimates should not be accorded rebuttable presumption. Some objections to CVM that motivated this case as well as those raised since the decision was issued identify two general questions: is CVM reliable, and is it accurate? Both issues are discussed as if some generally accepted thresholds in other areas of economics can be used to develop answers. This premise is simply not correct.

Accuracy is impossible to judge because economists can never know the "true" values people place on any commodity—marketed or nonmarketed. As a result, research attempting to evaluate the performance of CVM has focused on judging it by using a variety of standards, including:

(a) comparisons of indirect and CVM estimates of the value of some change in an environmental resource (Brookshire *et al.* [10] or Smith *et al.* [49] are examples);

(b) use of simulated markets in which commodities were offered for sale and the results compared with CVM estimates for the same commodity (see Bishop and Heberlein [6, 7], Dickie *et al.* [19], or Kealy *et al.* [31]);

(c) evaluation of CVM for measuring the demand for actual marketed commodities or programs in comparison with actual demands (see Smith *et al.* [51]);

(d) test/retest comparisons of CVM estimates from the same sample of respondents over time (see Loehman and De [36] and Loomis [38, 39]);

(e) creation of laboratory experiments in which hypothetical and actual sales of commodities were undertaken (see Brookshire and Coursey [8]); and

(f) surveys of purchase intentions and actual sales of commodities (see Seip and Strand [47]).

For the most part, these studies evaluated CVM based on what Mitchell and Carson [42] identified as criterion or convergent validity. The Kahneman and Knetsch analysis proposes a form of construct validity—testing whether prior hypotheses implied by the theory postulated to govern CMV responses are rejected. I have argued that their conclusions about CVM are incorrect. The framing of their questions does not satisfy the rudimentary criteria identified by Fischhoff and Furby for understandable valuation tasks. The implementation of the survey and the analysis of results do not conform to conventional practice with CVM research (see Mitchell and Carson [42]). Finally, even if these two problems are overlooked, their results fail to provide the test that they imply because their primary results *would be* consistent with standard value theory.

This is a strongly stated contradiction to their conclusions. It should not be misconstrued. It does *not* imply that the question of describing public goods and changes in them, as well as the role of alternative substitute or complementary commodities in that description, are unimportant. Research using and evaluating CVM methods has raised fundamental questions regarding the methods that economists have used to characterize environmental amenities. They are relevant

---

[8]For further discussion of this ruling, see Kopp *et al.* [35].

more generally to other public goods. Moreover, these issues are not unique to CVM; they apply to using all methods for estimating the values of nonmarketed goods.

Nothing in the evaluation record to date contradicts the D.C. Court of Appeals' decisions. Based on existing evidence, CVM is a "best available procedure" when applied properly to situations in which conventional protocols are used to ensure that people understand what has been asked of them.

REFERENCES

1. R. W. Anderson, Some theory of inverse demand for applied demand analysis, *European Econom. Rev.* **14**, 281–290 (1980).

2. J. Andreoni, Giving with impure altruism: Applications to charity and Ricardian equivalence, *J. Polit. Econom.* **97**, 1447–1458 (1989).

3. J. Andreoni, Impure altruism and donations to public goods: A theory of warm glow giving, *Econom. J.* **100**, 464–477 (1990).

4. M. A. Atlaf, H. Jamal, J. L. Liu, V. K. Smith, and D. Whittington, Prices and connection decisions for public water systems in developing countries: A case study of the Punjab, Pakistan, unpublished paper, Department of Economics, North Carolina State University (June, 1990).

5. W. E. Balson, R. T. Carson, M. B. Conaway, B. Fischhoff, W. M. Hanemann, A. Hulse, R. J. Kopp, K. Martin, R. C. Mitchell, S. Molenar, S. Presser, and P. A. Ruud, Development and design of a contingent valuation survey for measuring the public's value for visibility improvements at the Grand Canyon National Park, Draft Report (September 1990).

6. R. C. Bishop and T. A. Heberlein, Measuring values of extra market goods: Are indirect measures biased? *Amer. J. Agr. Econom.* **61**, 926–930 (1979).

7. R. C. Bishop and T. A. Heberlein, Does contingent valuation work? *in* "Valuing Environmental Goods" (R. G. Cummings, D. S. Brookshire, and W. D. Schulze, Eds.), Rowman and Allanheld, Totowa, NJ (1986).

8. D. S. Brookshire and D. L. Coursey, Measuring the value of a public good: An empirical comparison of elicitation procedures, *Amer. Econom. Rev.* **77**, 554–566 (1987).

9. D. S. Brookshire, L. S. Eubanks, and A. Randall, Estimating option prices and existence values for wildlife resources, *Land Econom.* **59**, 1–15 (1983).

10. D. S. Brookshire, M. A. Thayer, W. D. Schulze, and R. C. d'Arge, Valuing public goods: A comparison of survey and hedonic approaches, *Amer. Econom. Rev.* **72**, 165–177 (1982).

11. N. E. Bockstael and C. L. King, Valuing environmental quality: Weak complementarity with sets of goods, *Amer. J. Agr. Econom.* **70**, 654–662 (1988).

12. C. F. Camerer, Do biases in probability judgment matter in markets? Experimental evidence, *Amer. Econom. Rev.* **77**, 981–987 (1987).

13. J.-P. Chavas, The theory of mixed demand functions, *European Econom. Rev.* **24**, 321–344 (1984).

14. S. V. Ciriacy-Wantrup, Capital returns from soil-conservation practices. *J. Farm Econom.* **29**, 1181–1196 (1947).

15. M. L. Cropper, L. B. Deck, and K. E. McConnell, On the choice of functional form for hedonic price functions, *Rev. Econom. Statist.* **70**, 668–675 (1988).

16. Maureen L. Cropper, L. Deck, N. Kishor, and K. E. McConnell, "The Estimation of Consumer Preferences for Attributes: A Comparison for Hedonic and Discrete Choice Approaches, Discussion Paper QE90-20, Resources for the Future, Washington, DC (June 1990).

17. R. G. Cummings, Letter to the Office of Environmental Project Review, Department of the Interior (November 10, 1989).

18. R. G. Cummings, David S. Brookshire, and William D. Schulze, "Valuing Environmental Goods: An Assessment of the Contingent Valuation Method," Roman and Allanheld, Totowa, NJ (1986).

19. M. Dickie, A. Fisher, and S. Gerking, Market transactions and hypothetical demand data: A comparative study, *J. Amer. Statist. Assoc.* **82**, 69–75 (1987).

20. B. Fischhoff and L. Furby, Measuring values: A conceptual framework for interpreting transactions with special reference to contingent valuation of visibility, *J. Risk Uncertainty* **1**, 147–184 (1988).

21. W. M. Hanemann, Willingness to pay and willingness to accept: How much can they differ? *Amer. Econom. Rev.* **81**, 635–647 (1991).

22. D. W. Harless, More laboratory evidence on the disparity between willingness to pay and compensation demanded, *J. Econom. Behav. Organiz.* **11**, 359–379 (1989).

23. J. A. Hausman, Individual discount rates and the purchase and utilization of energy-using durables, *Bell J. Econom.* **10**, 33–54 (1979).

24. J. J. Heckman, Sample selection bias as a specification error, *Econometrica* **47**, 153–161 (1979).

25. H. Hotelling, The general welfare in relation to problems of taxation and of railway and utility rates, *Econometrica* **6**, 242–269 (1938).

26. J. Irwin, W. Schulze, G. McClelland, D. Waldman, D. Schenk, T. Stewart, L. Deck, P. Slovic, S. Lichtenstein, and M. Thayer, "Valuing Visibility: A Field Test of the Contingent Valuation Method," Report to the U.S. Environmental Protection Agency, Cooperative Agreement CR-812054 (March 1990).

27. P. O. Johansson, Valuing public goods in a risky world: An experiment, in valuation methods and policy making in environmental economics, in "Studies in Environmental Science" (H. Folmer and E. van Ireland, Ed.), No. 36, Elsevier Science, Amsterdam (1989).

28. D. Kahneman and J. L. Knetsch, Valuing public goods: The purchase of moral satisfaction, *J. Environ. Econom. Management* **21** (1991).

29. D. Kahnemann and A. Tversky, The psychology of preferences, *Sci. Amer.* **January**, 160–180 (1982).

30. G. Kalton and H. Schuman, The effect of the question on survey responses: A review, *J. Roy. Statist. Soc. Part 1* **145**, 42–73 (1982).

31. M. J. Kealy, M. Montgomery, and J. F. Dovido, Reliability and predictive validity of contingent valuation: Does the nature of the good matter? *J. Environ. Econom. Management* **19**, 244–263 (1990).

32. C. L. Kling, Comparing welfare estimates of environmental quality changes from recreation demand models, *J. Environ. Econom. Management* **15**, 331–340 (1988).

33. C. L. Kling, The reliability of estimates of environmental benefits from recreation demand models, *Amer. J. Agri. Econom.* **70**, 892–901 (1988).

34. J. L. Knetsch, Environmental policy implications of disparities between willingness to pay and compensation demanded measures of values, *J. Environ. Econom. Management* **18**, 227–237 (1990).

35. R. J. Kopp, P. R. Portney, and V. K. Smith, The economics of natural resource damages after *Ohio v. U.S. Department of the Interior*, *Environ. Law Reporter* **20** (4), 10,127–10,131 (1990).

36. E. Loehman and V. H. De, Application of stochastic choice modeling to policy analysis of public goods: A case study of air quality improvements, *Rev. Econom. Statist.* **64**, 474–480 (1982).

37. J. B. Loomis, Expanding contingent valuation sample estimates to aggregate benefit estimates: Current practices and proposed solutions, *Land Econom.* **63**, 396–402 (1987).

38. J. B. Loomis, Test–retest reliability of the contingent valuation method: A comparison of general population and visitor response, *Amer. J. Agri. Econom.* **71**, 76–84 (1989).

39. J. B. Loomis, Comparative reliability of the dichotomous choice and open-ended contingent valuation techniques, *J. Environ. Econom. Management* **18**, 78–85 (1990).

40. K. E. McConnell, Indirect methods for assessing natural resource damages under CERCLA, in "Valuing Natural Assets" (R. J. Kopp and V. K. Smith, Eds.), Resources for the Future, Washington, DC, to appear.

41. G. McClelland, W. Schulze, D. Waldman, J. Irwin, and D. Schenk. "Sources of Error in Contingent Valuation," Paper presented at the Association of Environmental and Resource Economists Meetings, Washington, DC (December 1990).

42. R. C. Mitchell and R. T. Carson, "Using Surveys to Value Public Goods—The Contingent Valuation Method," Resources for the Future, Washington, DC (1989).

43. W. K. Newey and K. D. West, A simple positive semi-definite heteroskedasticity and autocorrelation consistent covariance matrix, *Econometrica* **55**, 703–708 (1987).

44. A. Randall and J. Hoehn, Benefit estimation for complex policies, in "Valuation Methods and Policy Making in Environmental Economics" (H. Folmer and E. van Ierland, Eds.), Elsevier, Amsterdam (1989).

45. P. A. Samuelson, Aspects of public expenditure theories, *Rev. Econom. Statist.* **40**, 332–338 (1958).

46. W. D. Schulze, Use of direct methods for valuing natural resource damages, in "Valuing Natural Assets" (R. J. Kopp and V. K. Smith, Eds.), Resources for the Future, Washington, DC, to appear.

47. K. K. Seip and J. Strand, Willingness to pay for environmental goods in Norway: A contingent valuation study with real payment, Unpublished paper, Energy and Society Research Program, SAF Center for Applied Research, Department of Economics, University of Oslo (1990).
48. V. K. Smith and W. H. Desvousges, An empirical analysis of the economic value of risk changes, *J. Polit. Econom.* **95**, 89–114 (1987).
49. V. K. Smith, W. H. Desvousges, and Ann Fisher, A comparison of direct and indirect methods for estimating environmental benefits, *Amer. J. Agr. Econom.* **68**, 280–289 (1986).
50. V. K. Smith and Y. Kaoru, Signals or noise? Explaining the variation in recreation benefit estimates, *Amer. J. Agr. Econom.* **72**, 419–433 (1990).
51. V. K. Smith, J. L. Liu, M. A. Altaf, H. Jamal, and D. Whittington, How reliable are contingent valuation surveys for policies in developing economies? Draft under revision, Department of Economics, North Carolina State University (1991).
52. H. White, A heteroscedasticity-consistent covariance matrix estimator and a direct test for heteroscedasticity, *Econometrica* **48**, 817–838 (1980).

[25]

JOURNAL OF ENVIRONMENTAL ECONOMICS AND MANAGEMENT 22, 90–94 (1992)

Contingent Valuation and the Value
of Public Goods: Reply*

DANIEL KAHNEMAN[†] AND JACK L. KNETSCH[‡]

[†]Department of Psychology, University of California, Berkeley, Berkeley, California 94720; and
[‡]School of Resource and Environmental Management, Simon Fraser University, Burnaby,
British Columbia, Canada V5A 1S6

Received March 26, 1991; revised April 15, 1991

We reported survey results in an experimental design that (i) showed little sensitivity of people's willingness to pay (WTP) to the inclusiveness of a public good and (ii) illustrated an embedding effect; WTP for a particular good varied greatly depending on whether it was assessed on its own or embedded in a more inclusive good [3]. The implications of embedding effects for the contingent valuation method (CVM) are potentially serious. Smith [4] does not deny—nor does anyone else to our knowledge—that a contingent valuation assessment that is demonstrably susceptible to manipulation by embedding is essentially meaningless as a measure of resource value.

Our study was intended to illustrate a simple test for the presence of embedding effects, which can be included in any individual contingent valuation study or added to it after the fact. Our demonstration was less elaborate than most contingent valuations, because it was designed as an experiment and because we had the freedom to pick a commodity that could be easily explained. The application of this design to more elaborate problems is straightforward. For example, it will usually be possible for a defendant in an environmental damages action to replicate a contingent valuation study in every detail, but also to add several alternative versions that systematically vary levels of embedding. If the various versions yield widely different assessments of value, and in the absence of a persuasive principle for choosing one over the others, any obtained estimate will be too arbitrary to provide either a basis for legal actions for damages or a useful guide to resource allocation policies. For example, if the estimated value of a group of sea otters varies by a sizable multiple depending on whether the assessments are derived from people's responses to questions about all otters, all sea mammals, or a single otter, none of the conflicting estimates can be used with confidence to assess the compensable loss for the destruction of any specific number of sea otters, or to determine the resources that should be devoted to avoiding such losses. This is the issue that our study raises.

Smith acknowledges the importance of the issue, but does not deal with it and devotes his article entirely to an unusually close scrutiny of the study itself. The

*We thank Ralph d'Arge, Baruch Fischhoff, George Loewenstein, and Richard Thaler for their comments and advice.

reasoning appears to be that if sufficient doubts can be raised about this particular demonstration, the urgency of the issue will be somehow diminished. Probably because he did not find any fatal flaw in our argument, Smith offers a long list of points at which an alternative interpretation could perhaps be offered and a long list of alternative design choices that could perhaps alter the results. We find none of the alternative interpretations that are offered for our results compelling and are surprised by the extraordinary burden of proof that Smith would impose on a study that is critical of the CVM: the method is apparently to be judged innocent unless found guilty beyond any reasonable doubt, and the entire burden of removing all doubt lies on our study. This criterion is inappropriate to a debate in social science, where single studies are rarely conclusive. It is also worthy of note that Smith offers no definite prediction that the embedding effect will disappear if any particular improvement is adopted in further research. The refinements of method that he proposed are welcome as suggestions for future research on embedding, not as reasons to drop the subject. How Smith intended them is not clear.

To avoid both tedium and escalation, we restrict our response to Smith's discussion of the central point of our study, which is the demonstration of embedding. It is useful to recognize a distinction between two types of embedding effects: embedding can be called *perfect* if the same WTP is observed for nested commodities. To demonstrate *regular* embedding it is sufficient to show that WTP for a particular commodity varies depending on whether it is assessed on its own or as part of a more inclusive commodity. Perfect embedding, of course, implies regular embedding. We obtained perfect embedding in our study, but the argument against contingent valuation does not depend on this strong result. The weaker result of regular embedding suffices to label estimates of value as potentially arbitrary, and the weaker result is likely to be much more common. Thus, raising questions about our demonstration of perfect embedding does nothing to overcome the difficulty that regular embedding poses for the interpretation of contingent valuation. There are only two ways to defend CVM against a demonstration of regular embedding: (i) by offering improved survey techniques that reliably yield similar estimates of value for a commodity regardless of its level of embedding; (ii) by providing a rationale to select one of the competing estimates where they disagree. As far as we can tell, Smith did neither. Many of his observations are concerned with reasons for questioning the generality of the perfect embedding that we observed—but this is not the core of the problem.

The critique introduces our paper with a somewhat misleading description of its conclusions, to the effect that CVM-based estimates are "largely arbitrary and consequently useless for practical purposes." This phrase is taken from the statement that one of the objectives of our study was to "examine the proposition that CVM results are susceptible to an embedding effect that *could* render them largely arbitrary and consequently useless for practical purposes..." (emphasis added). Our key conclusion was clearly stated elsewhere. Following a comment noting that no single study could demonstrate that the embedding effect is universal, we wrote, "The conservative conclusion from our findings is that future applications of CVM should incorporate an experimental control: the contingent valuation of any public good should routinely be supported by adequate evidence that the estimate is robust to manipulations of embedding...." We stand by this conclusion.

Section 2 compares the method of our survey to the criteria laid out by Fischhoff and Furby [2] and finds it wanting. The main conclusion is that "it is not clear that respondents understood the inclusive commodities . . . as KK intended." There is little force to this criticism. First, our experiment was designed to minimize the problem of ambiguity by using a commodity that is easily described. Second, the definition of "disaster preparedness" given to group 2 explicitly included "availability of equipment and trained personnel for rescue operations" as a constituent of preparedness—this removed the ambiguity about which Smith complains, but did not eliminate the embedding effect.

We do not claim that all our subjects understood the problem exactly as we do; no survey researcher can make that claim. Our point is that there is no reason to believe that ambiguity was particularly severe in our study. The ambiguity issue can be raised about any inclusive public commodity that is described without technical specifications and a detailed budget. Contingent valuation surveys are also notoriously vague about the critical issue of payment vehicle. It is inappropriate to hold a study that is critical of CVM to methodological standards that the targets of the critique do not, and probably could not meet: the Fischhoff–Furby criteria describe an unattainable ideal, not the current state of the art in contingent valuation (Fischhoff's review of the Mitchell–Carson book [1] makes this evident).

Smith suggests that a large bias was introduced by our procedure, in which respondents who indicated zero WTP for an inclusive good were assumed to have zero WTP for its constituents. We agree that the procedure could be tightened (see footnote 1 in the original paper). However, the possible bias was surely small in our study: the proportion of respondents indicating positive WTP for "improved availability of equipment and trained personnel" was 56, 58, and 61%, respectively, for the three groups in the study, in descending order of inclusiveness. Thus, the higher bound of the percentage of respondents to whom zero WTP could have been incorrectly imputed is 5%, clearly too little to change any conclusion of the study.

We disagree with Smith's insistence on the desirability of within-subject analyses. This suggestion misses the point of the study. We start from the premise that the current standards for CVM do not specify the appropriate level of embedding at which questions should be framed. Indeed, Smith never tells us what level of embedding would be appropriate in the study that we reported. We point out that this indeterminacy can have significant consequences, because different levels of embedding can yield systematically different estimates of value. Because a respondent in a CVM study is exposed only to a single framing, a between-subject design is most appropriate.

As we review Section 2 of Smith's article we are struck by what it does not say. Smith does not explain how the wording that we chose might have caused our results and provides no answer to the critical question: is there a wording of the requests presented to our groups 1 and 2 that would yield the same WTP as that which we observed in group 3? He commits himself to no predictions and offers no suggestions about empirical research that could lay the issue to rest. The logic of the criticism of our work is worth noting, because if pursued further it would tend to make CVM immune to empirical critique. In effect, the argument is that our study could have been done differently, that the outcome might then have been different, and that our results are therefore inconclusive. The problem with this mode of criticism is that it is too easy: it is true of every study that it could have been done differently. If you will only allow a completely conclusive study to change your mind, you will rarely have to do so.

Section 3 is mostly concerned with an attempt to show that our demonstrations of embedding are not necessarily incompatible with standard value theory. The broad lines of the argument are familiar and were anticipated in our article, where we discussed examples in which apparent embedding effects arise as a result of substitution and income effects. The critical task is not to show that substitution and income effects *could* produce the result, but to provide a plausible account, preferably supported by evidence, of their role in particular cases. This section does not do so, and it provides no answers to several critical questions. Does Smith endorse the hypothesis that the approximate constancy of WTP is caused by a particular pattern of income and substitution effects? How would this hypothesis be tested? Which level of embedding would be the appropriate one for a study of WTP for rescue equipment and personnel? Which specification of the timing of payments is appropriate for a contingent valuation? How should payment streams be described, if people do not spontaneously apply a consistent discounting model? Here again, the main claim is that our results are not fully conclusive, but there is no commitment to particular predictions, nor much evidence of interest in seeing the issues resolved by future research.

In summary, Smith's article does not lay to rest the question which our results brought into sharp focus and which had troubled many students of contingent valuation over the years: could embedding effects have been demonstrated in many —and perhaps all—of the "several hundred applications . . . completed to date" in which CVM was used to measure economic value? The results of a single study do not, of course, demonstrate that the valuation of every good will be susceptible to an embedding effect. However, together with earlier observations cited in our article, our results suggest that the likelihood of observing embedding effects is high, especially when the respondents have had no relevant market experience. In our view, the evidence appears sufficiently strong to impose on users of CVM the burden of demonstrating that their estimate of the value of a good is immune to manipulations of embedding. In the absence of such a demonstration of robustness, any assessment based on CVM should remain suspect. If embedding effects can be removed by improved survey techniques, the experiment that we have proposed will show this to be the case. The required tests are easily done, and their cost will usually be small relative to the stakes. The question of whether an estimate of the value of a particular public good is robust or arbitrary can be and should be settled by research, not by statements of faith.

Contrary to the implication of Smith's title, we did not propose a premature verdict against CVM. We do believe, however, that the premature verdict in its favor should be carefully reconsidered in a spirit of impartial scientific inquiry. We must voice our concern: it would be a truly appalling state of affairs if the wish to protect the rebuttable presumption of validity that CVM now enjoys in the courts were allowed to have a chilling effect on research.

REFERENCES

1. B. Fischhoff, Using surveys to value public goods: The contingent valuation method, *Public Opinion Quart.* **54**, 286–289 (1990).

2. B. Fischhoff and L. Furby, Measuring values: A conceptual framework for interpreting transactions with special reference to contingent valuation of visibility, *J. Risk Uncertainty* **1**, 147–184 (1988).
3. D. Kahneman and J. L. Knetsch, Valuing public goods: The purchase of moral satisfaction, *J. Environ. Econom. Management* **22**, 57–70 (1992).
4. V. K. Smith, Arbitrary values, good causes, and premature verdicts, *J. Environ. Econom. Management* **22**, 71–89 (1992).

discharge kills fish and thereby reduces the incomes of commercial fishermen, their losses can reasonably be calculated by the reduce catch multiplied by the market price(s) of the fish (less, of course, any costs they would have incurred). Similarly, if the discharge of oil discourages tourist travel to an area, the lost incomes of those owning and/or operating motels, cottages, or other facilities can be reasonably represented by the difference in revenues between the affected period and a "normal" season. Even the losses to recreational fishermen, boaters, swimmers, hikers, and others who make active use of the areas affected by the discharge can be included in the estimate of diminished value, although these losses will generally be somewhat more difficult to value than the more obvious out-of-pocket losses.

The losses described above have come to be known as lost "use values" because they are experienced by those who, in a variety of different ways, make active use of the resources adversely affected by the discharge. But for at least the last twenty-five years, economists have recognized the possibility that individuals who make no active use of a particular beach, river, bay, or other such natural resource might, nevertheless, derive satisfaction from its mere existence, even if they never intend to make active use of it.

This concept has come to be known as "existence value" and it is the major element of what are now referred to as "non-use" or "passive-use" values (the latter term is employed in the balance of this report). In regulations promulgated by the Department of the Interior in 1986 under the Comprehensive Environmental Response, Compensation, and Liability Act—regulations that also pertained to natural resource damage assessments—passive-use values were included among the losses for which trustees could recover. The inclusion of passive-use values was recently upheld by the D.C. Court of Appeals (*State of Ohio* v. *Department of the Interior*, 880 F.2d 432 (D.C. Cir. 1989)), as long as they could be reliably measured.

This begs an interesting and important question, however. If passive-use values are to be included among the compensable losses for which trustees can make recovery under the Oil Pollution Act, how will they be estimated? Unlike losses to commercial fishermen or recreational property owners, there are no direct market transactions that can be observed to provide information on which estimates can be based. Unlike losses to boaters, swimmers, recreational fishermen and

Appendix I—Report of the NOAA Panel on Contingent Valuation

January 11, 1993.

I. Introduction

Under the Oil Pollution Act of 1990, the President—acting through the Under Secretary of Commerce for Oceans and Atmosphere—is required to issue regulations establishing procedures for assessing damages to or destruction of natural resources resulting from a discharge of oil covered by the Act. These procedures are to ensure the recovery of restoration costs as well as the diminution in value of the affected resources and any reasonable costs of conducting the damage assessment.

At least some of the values that might be diminished by such a discharge are relatively straightforward to measure through information revealed in market transactions. For instance, if the

Federal Register / Vol. 58, No. 10 / Friday, January 15, 1993 / Proposed Rules   **4603**

others, there exist no indirect methods through which market data can provide at lest some clues as to lost values. In other words, there appear to be neither obvious nor even subtle behavioral trails that can provide information about lost passive-use values.

Some experts believe that there exists an approach than can provide useful information about the economic significance of the lost passive-use values individuals may suffer when oil discharges damage natural resources. Known as the contingent valuation (or CV) technique, this approach is based on the direct elicitation of these values from individuals through the use of carefully designed and administered sample surveys. Its appeal lies in its potential to inform damage assessment in an area (lost passive-use values) where there appear to be no behavioral trails to be followed.

Typically, CV studies provide respondents with information about a hypothetical government program that would reduce the likelihood of a future adverse environmental event such as an oil spill, chemical accident, or the like. Respondents are usually given some specific information about the exact nature of the damages that the program in question would prevent. And they are also confronted in the study with a question or questions that provide information about the economic sacrifice they would have to make to support the environmental program. This may take the form of an open-ended question asking what is the maximum amount they would be willing to pay for the program in question: it may involve a series of questions confronting them with different prices for the program depending on their previous answers; or it may take the form of a hypothetical referendum (like a school bond issue) in which respondents are told how much each would have to pay if the measure passed and are then asked to cast a simple "yes" or "no" vote. (The conceptually correct measure of lost passive-use value for environmental damage that has already occurred is the minimum amount of compensation that each affected individual would be willing to accept. Nevertheless, because of concern that respondent would give unrealistically high answers to such questions, virtually all previous CV studies have described scenarios in which are asked to pay to prevent future occurrences of similar accidents. This is the conservative choice because willingness to accept compensation should exceed willingness to pay, if only triviality; we say more about other biases below.)

The CV technique has been used for twenty years or so to estimate passive-use values. In the last five years, however, there has been a dramatic increase in the umber of academic papers and presentations related to the CV technique. This is due in part to the availability of comprehensive reference texts on the subject (Mitchell and Carson (1989), for instance), and to the growing interest both nationally and internationally in environmental problems and policies. But it is also attributable to the growing use of the CV technique in estimating lost passive-use values in litigation arising from state and federal statutes designed to protect natural resources. Since *Ohio* v. *Department of the Interior* admitted the concept of passive-use values in damage assessments, this can only give added impetus to the use of CV in such litigation.

The CV technique is the subject of great controversy. Its detractors argue that respondents give answers that are inconsistent with the tenets of rational choice, that these respondents do not understand what it is they are being asked to value (and, thus, that stated values reflect more than that which they are being asked to value), that respondents fail to take CV questions seriously because the results of the surveys are not binding and raise other objections as well. Proponents of the CV technique acknowledge that its early (and even some current) applications suffered from many of the problems critics have noted, but believe that more recent and comprehensive studies have already or soon will be able to deal with these objections.

This (sometimes acrimonious) debate has put the National Oceanic and Atmospheric Administration (NOAA) in a very difficult spot. NOAA must decide in promulgating the regulations under the Oil Pollution Act whether the CV technique is capable of providing reliable information about lost existence or other passive-use values. Toward this end, NOAA appointed the Contingent Valuation Panel to consider this question and make recommendations to it.

This report is the product of the Panel's deliberations and is organized in the following way. Following this introduction, the drawbacks to the CV technique are discussed in Section II. Section III discusses several key issues concerning the design of CV surveys, including use of the referendum format to elicit individual values, ways of addressing the so-called "embedding" problem, and the evaluation of damages that last for some period but not forever. Section IV presents guidelines to which

the Panel believes any CV study should adhere if the study is to produce information useful in natural resource damage assessment. (These are elaborated upon in an Appendix.) In Section V a research agenda is described; it is the Panel's belief that future applications of the CV technique may be less time-consuming and contentious if the research described in the agenda is carried out. Section VI presents the Panel's conclusions.

II. Criticisms of the Contingent Valuation Method

The contingent valuation method has been criticized for may reasons and the Panel believes that a number of these criticisms are particularly compelling. Before identifying and discussing these problems, however, it is worth pointing out that they all take on added importance in light of the impossibility of validating externally the results of CV studies. It should be noticed, however, that this same disadvantage must inhere in any method of assessing damages from deprivation of passive-use. It is not special to the CV approach although, as suggested in Section I, there are currently no other methods capable of providing information on these values.

One way to evade this difficulty, as least partially, is to construct experiments in which an artificial opportunity is created to pay for environmental goods. The goods in question can perfectly well involve passive use. Then the results of a CV estimate of willingness to pay can be compared with the "real" results when the opportunity is made available to the same sample or an analogous sample.

A few such experiments have been attempted. The most recent, due to Seip and Strand (1992), used CV to estimate willingness to pay for membership in a Norwegian organization devoted to environmental affairs, and compared this estimate with actual responses when a number of the same respondents were presented with an opportunity actually to contribute. The finding was that self-reported willingness to pay was significantly greater than "actual" willingness to pay. A recent study by Duffield and Patterson (1991) took as the environmental amenity in question the maintenance of stream flow in two Montana rivers. The rivers in question provided spawning grounds for two rare species of fish; passive use was believed to be the main motivation for respondents. One of two parallel samples was asked about hypothetical willingness to contribute to the Montana Nature Conservancy which would then maintain stream flow; the other was offered an opportunity actually to

4604 **Federal Register** / Vol. 58, No. 10 / Friday, January 15, 1993 / Proposed Rules

contribute to the same organization for the same purpose. It was found that response rates and expressed willingness to contribute were significantly higher when the contribution was hypothetical than when "expressed willingness" meant an immediate cash contribution. On the other hand, the size of contributions, hypothetical in one case and actual in the other, was not much different as between those who said they would contribute and those who did so.

These studies suggest that the CV technique is likely to overstate "real" willingness to pay. Duffield and Patterson, however, hold out hope that the differences are small enough and predictable enough that CV estimates could be discounted for possible overstatement and then used as a conservative estimate of willingness to pay. Clearly more such experiments would be useful.

A less direct test of the "reality" of CV estimates of lost passive use values is to use the technique to estimate willingness to pay for ordinary market goods and then to compare the results with actual purchases. This has been tried by Dickie, Fisher, and Gerking (1987) using the demand for strawberries. When the data were re-analyzed by Diamond, Hausman, Leonard, and Denning (1992), it was found that the CV approach tended systematically to overestimate quantity demanded at each price, sometimes by as much as 50 percent. This result has to be qualified in two ways. First, the original CV study seems to have been fairly casual by the standards now proposed by practitioners; pre-testing and improvement of the survey instrument might (perhaps) have narrowed the gap. And second, it seems to go too far to conclude from systematic over-estimation that the CV study, even as conducted, provides no information about the demand for strawberries. Much of the same could be said about a study submitted to the Panel by Cummings and Harrison (1992) comparing hypothetical and demonstrated willingness to pay for small household goods. (See also Bishop and Heberlein (1979).)

External validation of the CV method remains an important issue. A critically important contribution could come from experiments in which state-of-the-art CV studies are employed in contexts where they can in fact be compared with "real" behavioral willingness to pay for goods that can actually be bought and sold.

Of the other problems arising in CV studies, the following are of most concern to the Panel: (i) The contingent valuation method can produce results that appear to be inconsistent with assumptions of rational choice; (ii) responses to CV surveys sometimes seem implausibly large in view of the many programs for which individuals might be asked to contribute and the existence of both public and private goods that might be substitutes for the resource(s) in question; (iii) relatively few previous applications of the CV method have reminded respondents forcefully of the budget constraints under which all must operate; (iv) it is difficult in CV surveys to provide adequate information to respondents about the policy or program for which values are being elicited and to be sure they have absorbed and accepted this information as the basis for their responses; (v) in generating aggregate estimates using the CV technique, it is sometimes difficult determining the "extent of the market;" and (vi) respondents in CV surveys may actually be expressing feelings about public spiritedness or the "warm glow" of giving, rather than actual willingness to pay for the program in question. We discuss each of these briefly.

Inconsistency With Rational Choice

Some of the empirical results produced by CV studies have been alleged to be inconsistent with the assumptions of rational choice. This raises two questions: What requirements are imposed by rationality? Why are they relevant to the evaluation of the reliability of the CV method?

Rationality in its weakest form requires certain kinds of consistency among choices made by individuals. For instance, if an individual chooses some purchases at a given set of prices and income, then if some prices fall and there are no other changes, the goods that the individual would now buy would make him or her better off. Similarly, we would expect an individual's preferences over public goods (i.e., bridges, highways, air quality) to reflect the same kind of consistency.

Common notions of rationality impose other requirements which are relevant in different contexts. Usually, though not always, it is reasonable to suppose that more of something regarded as better is better so long as an individual is not satiated. This is in general translated into a willingness to pay somewhat more for more of a good, as judged by the individual. Also, if marginal or incremental willingness to pay for additional amounts does decline with the amount already available, it is usually not reasonable to assume that it declines very abruptly.

This point assumes importance in view of some empirical evidence from CV studies that willingness to pay does not increase with the good. In one study, Kahneman (1986) found that willingness to pay for the cleanup of all lakes in Ontario was only slightly more than willingness to pay for cleaning up lakes in just one region. Evidence of this kind has multiplied (see Kahneman and Knetch (1992), Desvousges, *et al.* (1992), and Diamond *et al.* (1992)). Desvousges' result is very striking; the average willingness to pay to take measures to prevent 2,000 migratory birds (not endangered species) from dying in oil-filled ponds was as great as that for preventing 20,000 or 200,000 birds from dying. Diminishing marginal willingness to pay for additional protection could be expected to result in some drop. But a drop to zero, especially when the willingness to pay for the first 2,000 birds is certainly not trivial, is hard to explain as the expression of a consistent, rational set to choices.

It has been argued on a more technical level that the studies finding such apparent inconsistencies are defective, that the choices are not presented clearly to the respondents. In the study referred to immediately above, for instance, respondents were told that 2,000 birds was "* * * much less than 1%" of the total migratory bird population while 200,000 birds was "* * * about 2%" of the total. This may have led respondents to evaluate the programs as being essentially the same. But on the face of it, the evidence certainly raises some serious questions about the rationality of the responses.

It could be asked whether rationality is indeed needed. Why not take the values found as given? There are two answers. One is that we do not know yet how to reason about values without some assumption of rationality, if indeed it is possible as all. Rationality requirements impose a constraint on the possible values, without which damage judgments would be arbitrary. A second answer is that, as discussed above, it is difficult to find objective counterparts to verify the values obtained in the response to questionnaires. Therefore, some form of internal consistency is the least we would need to feel some confidence that the verbal answers corresponded to some reality.

Implausibility of Responses

The CV method is generally used to elicit values for a specific program to prevent environmental damage, whether it be dead animals, spoilage of a pristine wilderness area, or loss of visibility in some very unusually clear area. Though

Federal Register / Vol. 58, No. 10 / Friday, January 15, 1993 / Proposed Rules   **4605**

in each case, individuals often express zero willingness to pay, average willingness to pay over the whole sample is often at least a few dollars and frequently $20 to $50. With 100,000,000 households in the United States, these responses result in very large totals, frequently over $1 billion. Some have argued that these large sums are in themselves incredible and cast doubt on the CV method. The Panel is not convinced by this argument, since it is hard to have an intuition as to a reasonable total.

But there is a different problem with these answers. One can envision many possible types of environmental damage—oil spills or groundwater contamination in many different locations, visibility impairment in a variety of places, and so on. Would the average individual or household really be willing to pay $50 or even $5 to prevent each one? This seems very unlikely, since the total resulting willingness to pay for all such programs could easily become a very large fraction of one's income or perhaps even exceed it.

In other words, even if the willingness to pay responses to individual environmental insults are correct if only one program is to be considered, they may give overestimates when there are expected to be a large number of environmental problems. Similarly, if individuals fail to consider seriously the public or private goods that might be substitutes for the resources in question, their responses to questions in a CV survey may be unrealistically large.

Absence of a Meaningful Budget Constraint

Even if respondents in CV surveys take seriously the hypothetical referendum (or other type of) questions being asked them, they may respond without thinking carefully about how much disposable income they have available to allocate to all causes, public and private (see Kemp and Maxwell (1992), for instance). Specifically, respondents might reveal a willingness to pay of, say, $100 for a project that would reduce the risk of an oil spill; but if asked what current or planned expenditures they would forgo to pay for the program, they might instead re-evaluate their responses and revise them downward. This is similar to the problem identified immediately above where individuals fail to think of the possible multiplicity of environmental projects or policies they might be asked to support. To date, relatively few CV surveys have reminded respondents convincingly of the very real economic

constraints within which spending decisions must be made.

Information Provision and Acceptance

If CV surveys are to elicit useful information about willingness to pay, respondents must understand exactly what it is they are being asked to value (or vote upon) and must accept the scenario in formulating their responses. Frequently, CV surveys have provided only sketchy details about the project(s) being valued and this calls into question the estimates derived therefrom.

Consider the following example. Suppose information is desired about individuals' willingness to pay to prevent a chemical leak into a river. Presumably, their responses would depend importantly on how long it would take for the chemical to degrade naturally in the river (if it would at all), what ecological and human health damage the chemical would do until it had degraded, and so on. Absent information about such matters, it is unreasonable to expect even very bright and well-informed respondents to place meaningful values on a program to prevent leaks.

Even if detailed information were supplied, there are limits on the ability of respondents to internalize and thus accept and proceed from the information given. It is one thing to tell respondents matter-of-factly that complete recovery will occur in, say, two years. It is another thing for them to accept this information completely and then incorporate it in their answers to difficult questions.

To return to the example above, respondents who take a pessimistic view of the probable consequences of a chemical leak are likely to report relatively high willingness to pay to prevent the contamination—too high, in fact if in actuality such an event had less serious effects. On the other hand, respondents with an exaggerated sense of the river's assimilative capacity or regenerative power could be expected to report a willingness to pay that understates their "true" valuation if provided with a more complete description of likely consequences.

To repeat, even when CV surveys provide detailed and accurate information about the effects of the program being valued, respondents must accept that information in making their (hypothetical) choices. If, instead, respondents rely on a set of heuristics ("these environmental accidents are seldom as bad as we're led to believe," or "authorities almost always put too good a face on these things"), in effect they will be answering a different question from that being asked; thus, the

resulting values that are elicited will not reliably measure willingness to pay.

Extent of the Market

Suits for environmental damages are brought by trustees on behalf of a legally definable group. This group limits the population that is appropriate for determining damages even though individuals outside of this group may suffer loss of passive and active use. Undersampling and zero sampling of a subgroup of the relevant population may be appropriate if the subgroup has a predictably low valuation of the resource. For example, the authors of the CV study conducted in connection with the Nestucca oil spill limited their sample to households in Washington and British Columbia possibly because the individuals living elsewhere were presumed to have values too low to justify examination (or possibly because the sponsors of the study were agencies of the State of Washington and the province of British Columbia and so defined the legally appropriate population) (Rowe, Shaw, and Schulze, 1992).

"Warm Glow" Effects

Some critics of the CV technique (e.g., Diamond and Hausman (1992)) have observed that the distribution of responses to open-ended questions about willingness to pay often is characterized by a significant proportion of "zeros"—people who would pay nothing for the program—and also a number of sizable reports. This bi-modal distribution also characterizes individual giving: Most of us give nothing to most charities, but give non-trivial amounts to the ones we do support (at least $10 or $20, say). This has led these critics to conclude that individuals' responses to CV questions serve the same function as charitable contributions—not only to support the organization in question, but also to feel the "warm glow" that attends donating to worthy causes (see Andreoni (1989)). If this is so, CV responses should not be taken as reliable estimates of true willingness to pay, but rather as indicative of approval for the environmental program in question.

III. Key Issues in the Design of Contingent Valuation Instruments

In the course of its deliberations, the Panel discussed many issues surrounding the design of CV surveys. Here we provide our views on several issues that are especially important. In Section IV and in an Appendix to this report, we provide much greater detail on the characteristics of a valid application of the CV method.

4606   **Federal Register** / Vol. 58, No. 10 / Friday, January 15, 1993 / Proposed Rules

The Referendum Format

Considered as a survey, a CV instrument is descriptive rather than explanatory. Description may be as simple as reporting univariate averages of one kind or another, such as the percentages of those employed, seeking work, and not seeking work in the United States, the mean number of rooms occupied by American households, or the proportion of "likely" voters favoring one or another candidate in an upcoming election. A CV study seeks to find the average willingness to pay for a specific environmental improvement. Nevertheless, as will be seen later, it is often desirable to ask respondents to specify the reasons for their reported choices.

Univariate descriptive results are meaningful mainly when the alternative responses to a question are simple and can be well specified and there is a high consensus among both respondents and investigators about the precise meaning of the questions and answers. In some cases where consensus would initially not be adequate, simple definitions can be added to a questionnaire to attain satisfactory agreement—e.g., in asking people how many rooms they have in their homes, one states whether bathrooms, basements, etc. are to be included in the count; most respondents will conform to this specification.

With questions about subjective phenomena, such as attitudes and values, treating answers as simply descriptive is seldom meaningful. Too much depends on how questions are worded, and there is neither sufficient social consensus about precise meaning, nor an external reference to facilitate such consensus. There are many examples in the survey literature of how changes in wording or context will affect results based on questions about subjective phenomena (see Schuman and Presser (1981)). For example, in national surveys close to a quarter of the population will choose the "don't know" response to most attitude questions if it is explicitly offered; yet these same people will select a substantive alternative if "don't know" is not specifically provided, even though accepted when asserted spontaneously. More puzzlingly, a question about "forbidding" a particular action tends to elicit less agreement than a question about "not allowing" the same action, although the two questions are logically equivalent. Beyond these examples, most attitude objects are simply too complex to be summarized by a single survey question, e.g., attitudes toward abortion are too

dependent on the reasons for abortion and the time in pregnancy to be adequately captured by a single question; attitudes toward "gun control" vary enormously depending on the exact framing of the issue (e.g., handguns vs. all guns, registration vs. banning, and other concrete policy distinctions).

Contingent valuation studies seek descriptive information, yet call for a response similar to those elicited by questions about subjective phenomena. Thus they risk many of the same response effects and other wording difficulties that turn up regularly in attitude surveys. Minimizing these effects presents a considerable challenge to anyone wishing to elicit reliable CV estimates. The simplest way to approach the problem is to consider a CV survey as essentially a self-contained referendum in which respondents vote on whether to tax themselves or not for a particular purpose. Since real referenda are exposed to most of the response effects that occur with attitude surveys, and since we take the result of referenda as telling us something about "true" preferences, it is not necessary to claim they can be eliminated completely in a CV study.

The Panel is of the opinion that open-ended CV questions—e.g., "What is the smallest sum that would compensate you for environmental damage X?" or, "What is the largest amount you would be willing to pay to avoid (or repair) environmental damage X?"—are unlikely to provide the most reliable valuations. There are at least two reasons for this conclusion. In the first place, the scenario lacks realism since respondents are rarely asked or required in the course of their everyday lives to place a dollar value on a particular public good. There responses to such questions are therefore likely to be unduly sensitive to trivial characteristics of the scenario presented. In the second place, an open-ended request for willingness to pay or willingness to accept compensation invites strategic overstatement. The more seriously the respondent takes the question, the more likely it is that he or she will see that reporting a large response is a costless way to make a point. Both experience and logic suggest that responses to open-ended questions will be erratic and biased.

However, the referendum format, especially when cast in the willingness to pay mode—"Would you be willing to contribute (or be taxed) D dollars to cover the cost of avoiding or repairing environmental damage X?"—has many advantages. It is realistic: referenda on the provision of public goods are not

uncommon in real life. There is no strategic reason for the respondent to do other than answer truthfully, although a tendency to overestimate often appears even in connection with surveys concerning routine market goods. The fact that market surveys continue to be used routinely suggests that this tendency is not a insuperable obstacle. Of course, the respondent in a CV survey understands that the referendum is hypothetical; there is no implication that the tax will actually be levied and the damage actually repaired or avoided. This suggests that considerable efforts should be made to induce respondents to take the question seriously, and that the CV instrument should contain other questions designed to detect whether the respondent has done so. Although Carson, *et al.* (1992), included a useful question to determine whether respondents believed the survey was biased in any direction, they did not sufficiently test whether the completeness of, and time period for, restoration stated in the survey were fully accepted by respondents. But, as far as strategic reasons go, a respondent who would not be willing to pay D dollars has no reason to answer "Yes," and a respondent who would be willing to pay D dollars has no reason to answer "No."

There are, however, several other reasons why one's response to a hypothetical referendum question might be the opposite of one's actual vote on a real ballot. On one hand, a respondent unwilling to pay D dollars in reality might feel pressure to give the "right" or "good" answer when responding to an in-person or telephone interviewer. This could happen if the respondent believes that the interviewer would herself favor a yes answer. On the other hand, a respondent actually willing to pay the stated amount might answer in the negative for several reasons: (i) Belief that the proposed scenarios distributed the burden unfairly; (ii) doubt of either the feasibility of the proposed action, so that any contribution would be wasted, or the ability of the relevant agency to carry out the action efficiently; or (iii) refusal to accept the hypothetical choice problem, because of either a generalized aversion to taxes or a view that someone else—the "oil industry", for example—should pay for repair or avoidance as the responsible party. The same considerations suggest that a CV instrument should include questions designed to detect the presence of these sources of bias. This is in fact often done, but we do not know how successfully.

There are two further problems that could detract from the reliability of CV responses without producing any determinate bias: (i) A feeling that one's vote will have no significant effect on the outcome of the hypothetical referendum, leading to no reply or an unconsidered one; and (ii) poor information about the damage being valued. Of course, either of these could occur in real referenda.

Here we must decide on the standard of knowledgeability of the respondents that we went to impose on a CV study. It is clear that it should be at least as high as that which the average voter brings to a real referendum on the provision of a specific public good, but should it be higher? A "conservative" CV study, i.e., one that avoids overestimating true willingness to pay, will no doubt exceed the minimum standard of information and will also lean over backwards to avoid providing information in a way that might bias the response upwards. In particular, a conservative study will provide the respondent with some perspective concerning the overall frequency and magnitude of oil spills, the amount of money currently being spent on preventing and remedying them, the overall scale of their consequences, the peculiar features of the spill in question, and similar relevant information. Placing the choice problem in a broader context helps the respondent to arrive at a realistic or even conservative valuation.

Most of the provision of public goods in this country is decided by representatives and bureaucrats rather than by direct vote of the citizens. It is presumed that these agents are more "expert" or at least draw on more knowledge than the citizens themselves. The agent's expertise, if it really exists, is about the means and cost of providing public goods, though elected officials may sometimes be presumed to "represent" judgments of ultimate value to the citizens. Nevertheless, to increase one's confidence that a CV study is conservatively reliable, one might want to compare its outcome with that provided by a panel of experts. This will help check whether respondents and those conducting the study or studies are reasonably well-informed and well-motivated. This comparison could be made on a sample of CV studies to give an idea of their reliability in general.

The above considerations suggest that a CV study based on the referendum scenario can produce more reliably conservative estimates of willingness to pay, and hence of compensation required in the aftermath of environmental impairment, provided

that a concerted effort is made to motivate the respondents to take the study seriously, to inform them about the context and special circumstances of the spill or other accident, and to minimize any bias toward high or low answers originating from social pressure within the interview. This implies that, in the present state of the art, a reliably conservative CV study should be conducted with personal interviews of significant duration and will therefore be relatively costly. If follows therefore that, in order that the cost of the study not be disproportionately large compared to the amount of damages, the CV approach would likely be used only in relatively major spills, at least until further improvements in methodology can be developed and accepted. (A suggestion for doing so is offered in Section V.)

The referendum format offers one further advantage for CV. As we have argued, external validation of elicited lost passive-use values is usually impossible. There are however real-life referenda. Some of them, at least, are decisions to purchase specific public goods with defined payment mechanisms, e.g., an increase in property taxes. The analogy with willingness to pay for avoidance or repair of environmental damage is far from perfect but close enough that the ability of CV-like studies to predict the outcomes of real-world referenda would be useful evidence on the validity of the CV method in general.

The test we envision is not an election poll of the usual type. Instead, using the referendum format and providing the usual information to the respondents, a study should ask whether they are willing to pay the average amount implied by the actual referendum. The outcome of the CV-like study should be compared with that of the actual referendum. The Panel thinks that studies of this kind should be pursued as a method of validating and perhaps even calibrating applications of the CV method (see Magleby, 1984).

Addressing the Embedding Problem

Perhaps the most important internal argument against the reliability of the CV approach (as against general criticisms about vagueness, lack of information, or unreality of the scenario) is the observation of the "embedding" phenomenon (see the discussion in Section II). Different but similar samples of respondents are asked about their willingness to pay for prevention of environmental damage scenarios that are identical except for their scale: different numbers of seabirds saved, different numbers of

forest tracts preserved from logging, etc. It is reported that average willingness to pay is often substantial for the smallest scenario presented but is then substantially independent of the size of the damage averted, rising slightly if at all for large changes in size.

The usual interpretation proposed by critics of the CV method is that the responses are not measuring the equivalent dollar value of the utility of the environmental assets preserved, because that would certainly be measurably larger for substantially larger programs of preservation. Instead, the fixed sum offered is the value of a feeling of having done something praiseworthy; a "warm glow" is the phrase often used.

This is potentially a very damaging criticism of the method. CV studies almost always seek to measure willingness to pay to avoid a particular incident rather then compensation that would be required for damage that has already occurred. This is because respondents are more likely to exaggerate the compensation they would require than their willingness to pay, and because the latter is expected to be less than the former and so is conservative. If reported willingness to pay accurately reflected actual willingness to pay, then, under the "warm glow" interpretation, willingness to pay might well exceed compensation required because the former contains an element of self-approbation. It might be real but not properly compensable.

Defenders of the CV approach reply to this criticism in various ways. Sometime it is argued that the evidence used to support "embedding" simply indicates diminishing marginal utility of the asset in question. In many cases, however, the constancy or near-constancy of willingness to pay does not appear consistent with the large reported amounts for the first small increment of environmental preservation.

A second defense of CV against the embedding phenomenon is that CV questions have to be posed carefully and in context. It is argued that carelessly formulated CV instruments leave respondents with the impression that they are being asked, "Would you pay $X to avert a certain small environmental harm?" In a very large population of birds, the death of 1,000 is not seen as noticeably different from the death of 100,000—and may not actually be very different—so that respondents simply answer the question just asked.

This second response leads to the obvious question: how should a CV instrument be framed to elicit an answer that responds to the precise scenario and not to a generalized "warm glow" effect? We must reject one possible approach, that of asking each respondent to express willingness to pay to avert incidents of varying sizes; the danger is that embedding will be forcibly avoided, still without realism. This issue is best considered as part of the broader question: How much context about the incident itself and about the respondent's circumstances and choices should be included in the CV instrument?

We are recommending a high standard of richness in context to achieve a realistic background. Our proposed guidelines regarding this issue are embodied in Section IV below.

Time Dimension of Passive Use Losses

Typically, environmental damages from oil spills or similar accidents are severe for some period of time—weeks, months, or sometimes a few years—and gradually are reduced by natural forces and human efforts to a low or possibly even zero steady state level. In some circumstances, passive-use losses derive only or mostly from the steady state conditions; thus, if passive use value derives from species diversity, even a considerable loss of birds or mammals which does not endanger any species will give rise to no loss. If, on the contrary considerable passive-use value is attached to the interim state of the natural resource, then respondents have to do a very difficult present value calculation properly to compute their current *willingness* to pay for the difference between the fully restored state of the resource and the actual state as the level of restoration varies over time. *CV surveys accordingly* have to be carefully designed to allow respondents to differentiate interim from steady state passive-use loss, and, if there is interim passive-use loss, to report its present value correctly.

It is reasonable to assume that interim passive-use values are additive over time. Hence, we need a calculation of present values of the interim losses. The discounting and the estimation of the rate of recovery of the resource should be done by technical experts and not by the respondents, who are unlikely to handle these tasks adequately. Respondents should be asked only their willingness to pay to eliminate the difference between some partially restored level of the resource and the pristine state for a specific period of time, say a year, on the assumption that after that time full restoration is assured. Technical experts would estimate how the state of the resource will vary from year to year as the restoration takes

place. The technical information about the state of the resource, together with the respondent's assessments of the flow valuation of the resource, can be used to construct a time series of passive-use losses which can be discounted to the present at an appropriate rate of interest to determine the present value of the damages.

IV. Survey Guidelines

In this section we try to lay down a fairly complete set of guidelines compliance with which would define an ideal CV survey. A CV survey does not have to meet each of these guidelines fully in order to qualify as a source of reliable information to a damage assessment process. Many departures from the guidelines or even a single serious deviation would, however, suggest unreliability *prima facie*. To preserve continuity, we give only a bald list of guidelines here. They are repeated together with further explanatory comments in the Appendix to this Report.

General Guidelines

• *Sample Type and Size:* Probability sampling is essential for a survey used for damage assessment.[1] The choice of sample specific design and size is a difficult, technical question that requires the guidance of a professional sampling statistician.

• *Minimize Nonresponses:* High nonresponse rates would make the survey results unreliable.

• *Personal Interview:* The Panel believes it unlikely that reliable estimates of values could be elicited with mail surveys. Face-to-face interviews are usually preferable, although telephone interviews have some advantages in terms of cost and centralized supervision.

• *Pretesting for Interviewer Effects:* An important respect in which CV surveys differ from actual referenda is the presence of an interviewer (except in the case of mail surveys). It is possible that interviewers contribute to "social desirability" bias, since preserving the environment is widely viewed as something positive. In order to test this possibility, major CV studies should incorporate experiments that assess interviewer effects.

---

[1] This need not preclude use of less adequate samples, including quota or even convenience samples, for preliminary testing of specific experimental variations, so long as order of magnitude differences rather than univariate results are the focus. Even then, obvious sources of bias should be avoided (e.g., college students are probably too different in age and education from the heterogeneous adult population to provide a trustworthy basis for wider generalization).

• *Reporting:* Every report of a CV study should make clear the definition of the population sampled, the sampling frame used, the sample size, the overall sample non-response rate and its components (e.g., refusals), and item non-response on all important questions. The report should also reproduce the exact wording and sequence of the questionnaire and of other communications to respondents (e.g., advance letters). All data from the study should be archived and made available to interested parties (see Carson *et al.* (1992), for an example of good practice in inclusion of questionnaire and related details; as of this date, however, the report has not been available publicly and the data have not been archived for open use by other scholars).

• *Careful Pretesting of a CV Questionnaire:* Respondents in a CV survey are ordinarily presented with a good deal of new and often technical information, well beyond what is typical in most surveys. This requires very careful pilot work and pretesting, plus evidence from the final survey that respondents understood and accepted the main description and questioning reasonably well.

Guidelines for Value Elicitation Surveys

The following guidelines are met by the best CV surveys and need to be present in order to assure reliability and usefulness of the information that is obtained.

• *Conservative Design:* Generally, when aspects of the survey design and the analysis of the responses are ambiguous, the option that tends to underestimate willingness to pay is preferred. A conservative design increases the reliability of the estimate by eliminating extreme responses that can enlarge estimated values wildly and implausibly.

• *Elicitation Format:* The willingness to pay format should be used instead of the compensation required because the former is the conservative choice.

• *Referendum Format:* The valuation question should be posed as a vote on a referendum.

• *Accurate Description of the Program or Policy:* Adequate information must be provided to respondents about the environmental program that is offered. It must be defined in a way that is relevant to damage assessment.

• *Pretesting of Photographs:* The effects of photographs on subjects must be carefully explored.

• *Reminder of Undamaged Substitute Commodities:* Respondents must be reminded of substitute commodities, such as other comparable natural resources or the future state of the same natural resource. This reminder should be introduced forcefully and directly prior to the main valuation question to assure that respondents have the alternatives clearly in mind.

• *Adequate Time Lapse from the Accident:* The survey must be conducted at a time sufficiently distant from the date of the environmental insult that respondents regard the scenario of complete restoration as plausible. Questions should be included to determine the state of subjects' beliefs regarding restoration probabilities.

• *Temporal Averaging:* Time dependent measurement noise should be reduced by averaging across independently drawn samples taken at different points in time. A clear and substantial time trend in the responses would cast doubt on the "reliability" of the finding.

• *"No-answer" Option:* A "no-answer" option should be explicitly allowed in addition to the "yes" and "no" vote options on the main valuation (referendum) question. Respondents who choose the "no-answer" option should be asked nondirectively to explain their choice. Answers should be carefully coded to show the types of responses, for example: (i) Rough indifference between a yes and a no vote; (ii) inability to make a decision without more time or more information; (iii) preference for some other mechanism for making this decision; and (iv) bored by this survey and anxious to end it as quickly as possible.

• *Yes/no Follow-ups:* Yes and no responses should be followed up by the open-ended question: "Why did you vote yes/no?" Answers should be carefully coded to show the types of responses, for example: (i) It is (or isn't) worth it; (ii) Don't know; or (iii) The oil companies should pay.

• *Cross-tabulations:* The survey should include a variety of other questions that help to interpret the responses to the primary valuation question. The final report should include summaries of willingness to pay broken down by these categories. Among the items that would be helpful in interpreting the responses are:

Income
Prior Knowledge of the Site
Prior Interest in the Site (Visitation Rates)
Attitudes Toward the Environment
Attitudes Toward Big Business
Distance to the Site
Understanding of the Task
Belief in the Scenarios
Ability/Willingness to Perform the Task

• *Checks on Understanding and Acceptance:* The above guidelines must be satisfied without making the instrument so complex that it poses takes that are beyond the ability or interest level of many participants.

Goals for Value Elicitation Surveys

The following items are not adequately addressed by even the best CV surveys. In the opinion of the Panel, these issues will need to be convincingly dealt with in order to assure the reliability of the estimates.

• *Alternative Expenditure Possibilities:* Respondents must be reminded that their willingness to pay for the environmental program in question would reduce their expenditures for private goods or other public goods. This reminder should be more than perfunctory, but less than overwhelming. The goal is to induce respondents to keep in mind other likely expenditures, including those on other environmental goods, when evaluating the main scenario.

• *Deflection of Transaction Value:* The survey should be designed to deflect the general "warm-glow" of giving or the dislike of "big business" away from the specific environmental program that is being evaluated. It is possible that the referendum format limits the "warm glow" effect, but until this is clear the survey design should explicitly address this problem.

• *Steady State or Interim Losses:* It should be made apparent that respondents can distinguish interim from steady-state losses.

• *Present Value Calculations of Interim Losses:* It should be demonstrated that, in revealing values, respondents are adequately sensitive to the timing of the restoration process.

• *Advance Approval:* Since the design of the CV survey can have a substantial effect on the responses, it is desirable that—if possible—critical features be preapproved by both sides in a legal action, with arbitration and/or experiments used when disagreements cannot be resolved by the parties themselves.

• *Burden of Proof:* Until such time as there is a set of reliable reference surveys, the burden of proof of reliability must rest on the survey designers. They must show through pretesting or other experiments that their survey does not suffer from the problems that these guidelines are intended to avoid. Specifically, if a CV survey suffered from any of the following maladies, we would judge its findings "unreliable":

—A high nonresponse rate to the entire survey instrument or to the valuation question.
—Inadequate responsiveness to the scope of the environmental insult.
—Lack of understanding of the task by the respondents.
—Lack of belief in the full restoration scenario.
—"Yes" or "no" votes on the hypothetical referendum that are not followed up or explained by making reference to the cost and/or the value of the program.

• *Reliable Reference Surveys:* In order to alleviate this heavy burden of proof, we strongly urge the government to undertake the task of creating a set of reliable reference surveys that can be used to interpret the guidelines and also to calibrate surveys that do not fully meet the conditions.

V. Recommendations for Future Research

The Panel's major research recommendation goes toward a drastic reform of the CV procedure, extending beyond the guidelines suggestion in Section IV.

The problem of estimating the demand for highly innovative commercial products, including some that have not yet actually been produced, is much like the problem faced in CV research. It is the problem of estimating willingness to pay for a necessarily unfamiliar product. The field of market research has developed methods—"conjoint analysis," for example—that are very similar to the CV approach. (One important difference is that a new product may eventually reach the market, and projections of expected sales can be checked. Survey responses are usually found to be moderate overestimates of actual willingness to pay.) Practitioners have found that survey methods are better at estimating relative demand than absolute demand. There is an anchoring problem, even with private goods—that is, absolute willingness to pay is hard to pin down. This leads to the following suggestion.

The federal government should produce standard damage assessments for a few specific reference oil spills, either hypothetical or actual, ranging from small to large. These standard valuations could be generated by any method. One possibility would be through a jury of experts. Such a jury of experts might wish to conduct a series of CV studies, satisfying the guidelines laid out above. These CV studies would be inputs into the jury process, to be combined with other information and expert judgment. Once these

4610 **Federal Register** / Vol. 58, No. 10 / Friday, January 15, 1993 / Proposed Rules

benchmarks were available, they could serve as reference points for later CV studies. When a damage assessment is required, surveys could be used to elicit answers to questions like: "Would you pay (much more, more, about the same, less, much less) to prevent this spill than you would to prevent Standard Spill A?" "Would you pay an amount to avoid this spill that is between the amounts you would pay to avoid Standard Spill B and Standard Spill C? If so, is the amount much closer to B than C, closer to B than C, halfway between B and C, closer to C than B, much closer to C than B?" These questions presumably would not be asked so schematically. Responses to such a study could then serve as one reliable source of information in the damage assessment.

We recognize that this technique would require that respondents be made familiar with the reference spills as well as the particular spill whose damage is being assessed. We expect that the additional effort would be more than offset by the greater simplicity and reliability in estimating relative willingness to pay.

This possibility suggests a slightly more radical extension of the CV method. Respondents could be asked to compare their willingness to pay to avoid a specific case of environmental damage to their willingness to pay for a range of fairly familiar private goods. It would no doubt be best if the private goods were to bear some similarity to the environmental good in question, but that is not necessary. The anchoring purpose would be served if respondents could measure their willingness to pay in units of articles of clothing or small household appliances forgone.

This latter is a suggestion for research in the CV method, not necessarily a recommendation for current practical use.

The guidelines proposed in Section IV themselves suggest areas for further research, this time within the contingent valuation community. In particular, we emphasize the urgency of studying the sensitivity of willingness to pay responses to the number and extent of budgetary substitutes mentioned in survey instruments (that is, reminders of other things on which respondents could spend their money). In such research it would be helpful if parallel studies were conducted on the sensitivity of stated intentions to buy ordinary market goods—both familiar and unfamiliar—to reminders of alternative uses of those resources. The point is to discover the extent to which the valuation of environmental public goods is intrinsically more difficult than

similar exercises with respect to market goods.

A closely-related line of research is the sensitivity of responses in CV surveys to the number and extent of undamaged substitute commodities mentioned explicitly in the survey instrument (miles of nearby shoreline, miles of shoreline elsewhere, similarity for animal or bird life, alternative recreation possibilities and so on). This could be extended to variations in the way in which the budget constraint is presented to respondents. Here again, comparisons with market goods would be useful.

Finally, having urged that the availability of a no-vote option is an important component of the ability of the CV technique to mimic an actual referendum, we recommend further research into alternative ways of presenting and interpreting the no-vote option. In this respect, too, comparative studies with familiar public and private goods (local parks, school facilities, housing for the homeless, food distributions) would be enlightening. Real referenda always allow the option of not voting, in a natural way. CV studies have to achieve the same result more deliberately, so there is a need to know if the precise formulation matters very much to the result.

VI. Conclusions and Recommendations

The Panel starts from the premise that passive-use loss—interim or permanent—is a meaningful component of the total damage resulting from environmental accidents. A problem arises because passive-use losses have few or no overt behavioral consequences. The faintness of the behavioral trail means that a well-designed and adequately sensitive measuring instrument is needed to substitute for conventional observations of behavior. In particular, can the CV method provide a sufficiently reliable estimate of total loss—including passive-use loss—to play a useful role in damage assessment?

It has been argued in the literature and in comments addressed to the Panel that the results of CV studies are variable, sensitive to details of the survey instrument used, and vulnerable to upward bias. These arguments are plausible. However, some antagonists of the CV approach go so far as to suggest that there can be no useful information content to CV results. The Panel is unpersuaded by these extreme arguments.

In Section IV above, we identify a number of stringent guidelines for the conduct of CV studies. These require that respondents be carefully informed

about the particular environmental damage to be valued, and about the full extent of substitutes and undamaged alternatives available. In willingness to pay scenarios, the payment vehicle must be presented fully and clearly, with the relevant budget constraint emphasized. The payment scenario should be convincingly described, preferably in a referendum context, because most respondents will have had experience with referendum ballots with less-than-perfect background information. Where choices in formulating the CV instrument can be made, we urge they lean in the conservative direction, as a partial or total offset to the likely tendency to exaggerate willingness to pay.

The Panel concludes that under those conditions (and others specified above), CV studies convey useful information. We think it is fair to describe such information as reliable by the standards that seem to be implicit in similar contexts, like market analysis for new and innovative products and the assessment of other damages normally allowed in court proceedings. As in all such cases, the more closely the guidelines are followed, the more reliable the result will be. It is not necessary, however, that every single injunction be completely obeyed; inferences accepted in other contexts are not perfect either.

Thus, the Panel concludes that CV studies can produce estimates reliable enough to be the starting point of a judicial process of damage assessment, including lost passive-use values. To be acceptable for this purpose, such studies should follow the guidelines described in Section IV above. The phrase "be the starting point" is meant to emphasize that the Panel does not suggest that CV estimates can be taken as automatically defining the range of compensable damages within narrow limits. Rather, we have in mind the following considerations.

The Panel is persuaded that hypothetical markets tend to overstate willingness to pay for private as well as public goods. The same bias must be expected to occur in CV studies. To the extent that the design of CV instruments makes conservative choices when alternatives are available, as urged in Section IV, this intrinsic bias may be offset or even over-corrected. All surveys of attitudes or intentions are bound to exhibit sensitivity of response to the framing of questions and the order in which they are asked. No automatic or mechanical calibration of responses seems to be possible.

The judicial process must in each case come to a conclusion about the degree to which respondents have been induced to consider alternative uses of funds and take the proposed payment vehicle seriously. Defendants will argue that closer attention to substitute commodities would have yielded lower valuations. Trustees will argue that they have already leaned over backwards to ensure conservative responses. Judges and juries must decide as they do in other damage cases. The Panel's conclusion is that a well-conducted CV study provides an adequately reliable benchmark to begin such arguments. It contains information that judges and juries will wish to use, in combination with other evidence, including the testimony of expert witnesses.

The Panel's second conclusion is that the appropriate federal agencies should begin to accumulate standard damage assessments for a range of oil spills, as described in Section V. That process should further improve the reliability of CV studies in damage assessment. It should thus contribute to increasing the accuracy and reducing the cost of subsequent damage assessment cases. In that sense, it can be regarded as an investment.

The proposals for further research outlined in Section V are an integral part of our recommendations. The Panel believes that the suggestions put forward there could lead to more reliable and less controversial damage assessment at reduced cost. It is not to be expected that controversy will disappear, however. There will always be controversy where intangible losses have to be evaluated in monetary terms.

Appendix—General Guidelines

• *Sample Type and Size:* Probability sampling is essential for a survey used for damage assessment.[1] The choice of sample specific design and size is a difficult, technical question that requires the guidance of a professional sampling statistician.

If a single dichotomous question of the yes-no type is used to elicit valuation responses, then a total sample size of 1000 respondents will limit sampling error to about 3% plus or minus on a single dichotomous question, assuming simple random sampling. However, this or any other sample size needs to be reconceptualized for three reasons.

First, if face-to-face interviewing is used, as we suggest above, clustering and stratification must be taken into account. Second, if dichotomous valuation questions are used (e.g., hypothetical referenda), separate valuation amounts must be asked of random sub-samples and these responses must be unscrambled econometrically to estimate the underlying population mean or median. Third, in order to incorporate experiments on interviewer and wording effects, additional random sub-sampling is required. For all these reasons, it will be important to consult sampling statisticians in the design of a CV survey intended for legal or policy-making purposes.

• *Minimize Nonresponses:* High nonresponse rates would make the survey results unreliable.

To the extent that a CV study is expected to represent the adult population of the United States or a portion of it, minimizing both sample non-response and item non-response are important. The former is unlikely to be below 20% even in very high quality surveys; the latter has also been large in some CV surveys because of the difficulty of the task respondents are being asked to perform. These sources of potential bias can be partially justified on the grounds that they also occur with official referenda, in both cases with the loss especially of the least educated parts of the population. The further reduction of the final sample by elimination of "protest zeros," "unrealistic high values," and other problematic responses may lead to effective final total response rates so low as to imply that the survey population consists of interested and specially instructed quasi-experts. This consideration reinforces the desirability of combining a reasonable response rate with a high but not forbidding standard of information as discussed in Section III above.

• *Personal Interview:* The Panel believes it unlikely that reliable estimates of values could be elicited with mail surveys. Face-to-face interviews are usually preferable, although telephone interviews have some advantages in terms of cost and centralized supervision.

Assuming a CV survey is to represent a natural population, such as all adults in the United States, or those in a single urban area or a state, it is desirable that it be carried out using either face-to-face or telephone interviews. Mail surveys typically employ lists that cover too small a part of the population (e.g., samples based on telephone directories omit approximately half the U.S.

population because of non-listed numbers, incorrect numbers, and non-phone households), and then miss another quarter or more of the remainder through non-response. In addition, since the content of a mail questionnaire can be reviewed by targeted respondents before deciding to return it, those most interested in a natural resource issue or in one side or the other can make their decision on that basis. It is also impossible using mail surveys to guarantee random selection within households or to confine answering to a single respondent, and it is difficult (though not impossible) to control question-order effects. Thus, mail surveys should be used only if another supplementary method can be employed to cross-validate the results on a random sub-sample of respondents.

The choice between telephone and face-to-face administration is less clear. Face-to-face surveys offer practical advantages in maintaining respondent motivation and allowing use of graphic supplements. Both coverage and response rates are also usually somewhat higher than with telephone surveys. However, telephone surveys can cut interviewing costs by between a third and a half; for CV purposes, it may be a disadvantage that most survey investigators believe telephone interviews need to be kept shorter in length than face-to-face interviews because respondent attention and cooperation are more difficult to maintain. In addition, random-digit-dial telephone surveys approximate simple random sampling. Face-to-face surveys must be based on cluster sampling and, therefore, the results provide less precise estimates than do telephone surveys of the same size.

• *Pretesting for Interviewer Effects:* An important respect in which CV surveys differ from actual referenda is the presence of an interviewer (except in the case of mail surveys). It is possible that interviewers contribute to "social desirability" bias, since preserving the environment is widely viewed as something positive. In order to test this possibility, major CV studies should incorporate experiments that assess interviewer effects.

To test for interviewer effects, two modifications might be made to a standard face-to-face CV survey. In one variant on current practice, respondents would stop when they came to the valuation question, write their "vote" on a ballot, and fold and deposit it in a sealed box. However, since this practice would not mimic the complete anonymity of the voting booth, for a subsample of respondents a second

---

[1] This need not preclude use of less adequate samples, including quota or even convenience samples, for preliminary testing of specific experimental variations, so long as order of magnitude differences rather than univariate results are the focus. Even then, obvious sources of bias should be avoided (e.g., college students are probably too different in age and education from the heterogeneous adult population to provide a trustworthy basis for wider generalization).

modification should be made. Respondents would be allowed to mail their "ballots" in unmarked envelopes directly to the survey organization, even though that will preclude any but the simplest analysis of responses. Tests of the effect of both these modifications of current practice will indicate whether they are needed routinely or whether at least some calibration should be introduced to compensate for interviewer effects. (The more modest of these proposed modifications—a simulated ballot box, or even voting on a portable computer—has few if any disadvantages and might be made standard if it shows any reliable departure at all from answers given orally to the interviewer.)

• *Reporting:* Every report of a CV study should make clear the definition of the population sampled, the sampling frame used, the sample size, the overall sample non-response rate and its components (e.g., refusals) and item non-response on all important questions. The report should also reproduce the exact wording and sequence of the questionnaire and of other communications to respondents (e.g., advance letters). All data from the study should be archived and made available to interested parties (see Carson *et al.* (1992)), for an example of good practice in inclusion of questionnaire and related details; as of this date, however, the report has not been available publicly and the data have not been archived for open use by other scholars).

• *Careful Pretesting of a CV Questionnaire:* Respondents in a CV survey are ordinarily presented with a good deal of new and often technical information, well beyond what is typical in most surveys. This requires very careful pilot work and pretesting, plus evidence from the final survey that respondents understood and accepted the main description and questioning reasonably well.

Parenthetically, the claim sometimes made by CV proponents that particular methods of piloting, such as focus groups, are essential should be viewed with skepticism, since these claims are unsupported by any systematic evidence. Nor is it clear that what are called "state-of-the-art" CV surveys constitute something entirely new or different from other types of serious survey investigations. Thus, although evidence that questionnaire development has been carried out carefully is certainly important, it cannot be taken as a self-sufficient basis of validity—the more so because we know that many people will answer survey questions without apparent

difficulty, even when they do not understand them well. A way of reducing pressure to give answers of questionable meaningfulness would be to provide respondents an explicit "no opinion" type of alternative when a key valuation question is posed.

Guidelines for Value Elicitation Surveys

The following guidelines are met by the best CV surveys and need to be present in order to assure reliability and usefulness of the information that is obtained.

• *Conservative Design:* Generally, when aspects of the survey design and the analysis of the responses are ambiguous, the option that tends to underestimate willingness to pay is preferred. A conservative design increases the reliability of the estimate by eliminating extreme responses that can enlarge estimated values wildly and implausibly.

• *Elicitation Format:* The willingness to pay format should be used instead of compensation required because the former is the conservative choice.

In experimental settings, the gap between stated intentions to support a particular referendum and actual behavior in the voting booth can be very great (see Magleby, 1984). This gap might be treated by "calibration" if there were historical data on the relationship between such intentions and behavior. Unfortunately, we are aware of no data that is close enough to the CV context that could be used to calibrate CV responses. In the absence of historical data that can be used to calibrate the intentions reported in the CV surveys, the survey instrument has to be designed with extraordinary care so that it can stand on its own.

• *Referendum Format:* The valuation question should be posed as a vote on a referendum.

As is now generally recognized by most CV proponents, asking respondents to give a dollar valuation in response to an open-ended question presents them with an extremely difficult task. At the same time, CV proponents also recognize that presenting respondents a set of dollar amounts from which they are to choose is likely to create anchoring and other forms of bias. Thus, we recommend as the most desirable form of CV elicitation the use of a dichotomous question that asks respondents to vote for or against a particular level of taxation, as occurs with most real referenda. As already noted, such a question form also has advantage in terms of incentive compatibility. (If a double-bounded dichotomous choice or some other

question form is used in order to obtain more information per respondent, experiments should be developed to investigate biases that may be introduced.)

• *Accurate Description of the Program or Policy:* Adequate information must be provided to respondents about the environmental program that is offered. It must be defined in a way that is relevant to damage assessment.

Ideally a CV survey would elicit attitudes toward three alternative (future) recovery scenarios: (A) "immediate" restoration, (b) accelerated restoration, and (c) natural restoration. Damages would be the difference between (a) and (b) on the assumption that accelerated restoration is provided by the responsible party. Unfortunately, respondents may not find "immediate" restoration very plausible and they may resist the notion that they should be expected to contribute to accelerated restoration when it is an oil company that is at fault. If respondents are unable or unwilling to deal hypothetically with the most relevant "clean-up" scenarios, alternative "prevention" scenarios will have to be used in the survey instrument. For example, respondents may be asked to vote for a referendum that offers reduced risk of another spill for a specified period of time.[2] The weaker is the linkage between the "prevention" scenarios and the "clean-up"scenarios, the more unreliable are the survey results. Rhetorically: Is a decade of prevention equal in value to the difference in value between accelerated and immediate clean-up?

• *Pretesting of Photographs:* The effects of photographs on subjects must be carefully explored.

One effective means for conveying information and holding interest in a CV interview has been the use of large and impressive photographs. However, this technique is a two-edged sword because the dramatic nature of a photograph may have much more emotional impact than the rest of the questionnaire. Thus it is important that photographs be subjected to even more careful assessment than verbal material if the goal is to avoid bias in presentation.[3]

• *Reminder of Undamaged Substitute Commodities:* Respondents must be reminded of substitute commodities, such as other comparable natural resources or the future state of the same natural resource. This reminder should

---

[2] As in the survey actually performed by the State of Alaska after the Valdez spill (See Carson et al. (1992)).

[3] Failure to test the effects of photographs on responses is one shortcoming of Carson et al. (1992).

Federal Register / Vol. 58, No. 10 / Friday, January 15, 1993 / Proposed Rules   **4613**

be introduced forcefully and directly prior to the main valuation question to assure that respondents have the alternatives clearly in mind.

• *Adequate Time Lapse from the Accident:* The survey must be conducted at a time sufficiently distant from the date of the environmental insult that respondents regard the scenario of complete restoration as plausible. Questions should be included to determine the state of subjects' beliefs regarding restoration probabilities.

Survey respondents who would not suffer interim passive-use loss may not regard full restoration as very plausible; therefore, they may report substantial passive-use loss even if told that full restoration in some reasonable amount if time is certain. Misunderstanding of the restoration probability is most acute when the accident has recently occurred and before any substantial restoration takes place. It would be ideal to assess steady state passive-use loss after natural and human restoration is complete or nearly so, since then presumably respondents would believe in the restoration. If that is not a possibility, surveys might be conducted over time until the reported willingness to pay settles down (assuming that it does), as the respondents come to believe more and more in the probable success of the restoration effort. Alternatively, respondents might be asked to value a menu of alternative possible scenarios, without being told explicitly which is applicable for the environmental insult under study. The menu should be designed to force them to consider the difference between interim and steady-state passive-use value.

• *Temporal Averaging:* Time dependent measurement noise should be reduced by averaging across independently drawn samples taken at different points in time. A clear and substantial time trend in the responses would cast doubt on the "reliability" of the finding.

• *"No-answer" Option:* A "no-answer" option should be explicitly allowed in addition to the "yes" and "no" vote options on the main valuation (referendum) question. Respondents who choose the "no-answer" option should be asked nondirectively to explain their choice. Answers should be carefully coded to show the types of responses, for example: (i) Rough indifference between a yes and a no vote; (ii) inability to make a decision without more time or more information; (iii) preference for some other mechanism for making this decision; and (iv) bored by this survey and anxious to end it as quickly as possible.

• *Yes/no Follow-ups:* Yes and no responses should be followed up by the open-ended question: "Why did you vote yes/no?" Answers should be carefully coded to show the types of responses, for example: (i) It is (or isn't) worth it; (ii) Don't know; or (iii) The oil companies should pay.

• *Cross-tabulations:* The survey should include a variety of other questions that help to interpret the responses to the primary valuation question. The final report should include summaries of willingness to pay broken down by these categories. Among the items that would be helpful in interpreting the responses are:

Income
Prior Knowledge of the Site
Prior Interest in the Site (Visitation Rates)
Attitudes Toward the Environment
Attitudes Toward Big Business
Distance to the Site
Understanding of the Task
Belief in the Scenarios
Ability/Willingness to Perform the Task

We believe that these cross tabulations will prove useful in interpreting and lending credibility to the responses and possibility also in forming adjustments that can enhance reliability.

• *Checks on Understanding and Acceptance:* The above guidelines must be satisfied without making the instrument so complex that it poses tasks that are beyond the ability or interest level of many participants.

Since CV interviews often present information that is new to respondents, the questionnaire should attempt at the end to determine the degree to which respondents accept as true the descriptions given and assertions made prior to the valuation question. Such an inquiry should be carried out in detail but non-directively, so that respondents feel free to reject any part of the information they were given at earlier points.

Goals for Value Elicitation Surveys

The following items are not adequately addressed by even the best CV surveys. In the opinion of the Panel, these issues will need to be convincingly dealt with in order to assure the reliability of the estimates.

• *Alternative Expenditure Possibilities:* Respondents must be reminded that their willingness to pay for the environmental program in question would reduce their expenditures for private goods or other public goods. This reminder should be more than perfunctory, but less than overwhelming. The goal is to induce

respondents to keep in mind other likely expenditures, including those on other environmental goods, when evaluating the main scenario.

Consumers can be expected to make expenditure decisions that are adequately sensitive to other expenditure possibilities with which they are familiar. But environmental referenda of the type presented in CV surveys are unfamiliar and respondents may not be aware of the large set of other expenditure possibilities that might be offered in future CV surveys or future referenda. Unless informed otherwise, respondents may suppose that there is only one environmental scenario that will ever be offered and they may overspend on it.

It is not at all clear how exhaustive should be the list of alternative public goods that are explicitly presented. If the list is too brief, overspending can be expected. If the list is too long, respondents will be encouraged to spread expenditures to public goods for which there is not adequate total demand and which therefore cannot really be offered to them. Also, if the list gets large enough to encompass a significant fraction of income, the gap between willingness to pay and willingness to accept may widen.

It is also not clear what form the reminder should take. It does not seem enough merely to list other environmental goods since respondents would then have to guess the level of expenditure that would be necessary to pay for the alternatives.

The survey should probably include some statement about the price of alternatives, for example, the per capita expenditure that would be required to provide the items.

• *Deflection of Transaction Value:* The survey should be designed to deflect the general "warm-glow" of giving or the dislike of "big business" away from the specific environmental program that is being evaluated. It is possible that the referendum format limits the "warm glow" effect, but until this is clear the survey design should explicitly address this problem.

Economic models of consumer behavior generally are based on the assumption that value derives from the goods and services that are consumed, not from the process by which these goods are allocated. But happiness that derives from charitable giving may come mostly from the act of giving rather from the material changes that follow from the gift. To give another example, consumers may get pleasure from the act of shopping as well as from ownership of the goods they purchase. Words that might be useful to

4614 Federal Register / Vol. 58, No. 10 / Friday, January 15, 1993 / Proposed Rules

distinguish between these utility-producing events as "consumption value" and "transaction value," the latter referring to the process or transaction that establishes ownership.

We do not question the validity of "transaction value" or differentiate it from "consumption value" as far as damage assessment is concerned. But for both forms of value, respondents need to be thinking clearly about the substitutes, since the closer are the substitute the less there are a damage that is done. In the case of "transaction value," there are many close substitutes to cleaning up oil spills since there are many other charitable activities that can generate the same—the "warm glow" and there are many other ways to express hostility toward big business and modern technology.

• *Steady State or Interim Losses:* It should be made apparent that respondents can distinguish interim from steady-state losses.

The quality of any natural resource varies daily and seasonally around some "equilibrium" or "steady state" level. Active-use value of a resource depends on its actual state at the time of use (and at other times), not on its equilibrium. But passive-use value of a natural resource may derive only or mostly from its steady state and not from its day-to-day state. If so, full restoration at some future date eliminates or greatly reduces passive-use loss. Surveys accordingly need to be carefully designed to allow respondents to differentiate interim from steady state passive-use loss.

• *Present Value Calculations of Interim Losses:* It should be demonstrated that, in revealing values, respondents are adequately sensitive to the timing of the restoration process.

As discussed in section III above, the time profile of restoration following an accident potentially is an important determinant of active-use loss and interim passive-use loss, but respondents may have little ability to distinguish between and to evaluate different profiles.

• *Advanced Approval:* Since the design of the CV survey can have a substantial effect on the responses, it is desirable that—if possible—critical features be preapproved by both sides in a legal action, with arbitration and/or experiments used when disagreements cannot be resolved by the parties themselves.

• *Burden of Proof:* Until such time as there is a set of reliable reference surveys, the burden of proof of reliability must rest on the survey designers. They must show through pretesting or other experiments that their survey does not suffer from the

problems that these guidelines are intended to avoid. Specifically, if a CV survey suffered from any of the following maladies, we would judge its findings "unreliable":

—A high nonresponse rate to the entire survey instrument or to the valuation question

—Inadequate responsiveness to the scope of the environmental insult.

—Lack of understanding of the task by the respondents.

—Lack of belief in the full restoration scenario.

—"Yes" or "no" votes on the hypothetical referendum that are not followed up or explained by making reference to the cost and/or the value of the program.

• *Reliable Reference Surveys:* In order to alleviate this heavy burden of proof, we strongly urge the government to undertake the task of creating a set of reliable reference surveys that can be used to interpret the guidelines and also to calibrate surveys that do not fully meet the conditions.

Table of References

Andreoni, James; "Giving With Impure Altruism: Applications to Charity and Ricardian Equivalence;" Journal of Political Economy 97 (1989): pp. 1447–1458.

Bishop, Richard C., and Thomas A. Heberlien: "Measuring Values of Extra-Market Goods: Are Indirect Measures Biased?" American Journal of Agricultural Economics 61 (1979): 926–930.

Carson, Richard T. Robert Cameron Mitchell, W. Michael Hanemann, Raymond J. Kopp, Stanley Presser, and Paul A. Ruud: "A Contingent Valuation Study of Lost Passive Use Values Resulting from the Exxon Valdez Oil Spill;" A report for the Attorney General of the State of Alaska; November 19, 1992.

Cummings, Ronald G., and Glenn W. Harrison: "Homegrown Values and Hypothetical Surveys: Is the Dichotomous Choice Approach Incentive Compatible;" Department of Economics, University of New Mexico, submitted to Office of General Counsel, National Oceanic and Atmospheric Administration, 1992, 18 pp.

Desvousges, William H., F. Reed Johnson, Richard W. Dunford, Kevin J. Boyle, Sara P. Hudson, and K. Nicole Wilson: "Measuring Natural Resource Damages with Contingent Valuation: Tests of Validity and Reliability;" Paper presented to the Cambridge Economics, Inc., Symposium, Contingent Valuation: A Critical Assessment; Washington, D.C., April 1992.

Diamond, P.A., and J.A. Hausman: "On Contingent Valuation Measurement of Nonuse Values;" Paper presented at the Cambridge Economics, Inc. Symposium, Contingent Valuation: A Critical Assessment; Washington, D.C., April 1992.

Diamond, P.A., J.A. Hausman, G.K. Leonard, and M.A. Denning: "Does Contingent Valuation Measure Preferences? Experimental Evidence;" Paper presented at the Cambridge Economics, Inc. Symposium, Contingent Valuation: A Critical Assessment; Washington, D.C., April 1992.

Dickie, Mark, Ann Fisher, and Shelby Gerking: Market Transactions and Hypothetical Demand Data: A Comparative Study; Journal of American Statistical Association, Vol. 82, March 1987, pp. 69–75.

Duffield, John W., and David A. Patterson; "Field Testing Existence Values: An Instream Flow Trust Fund for Montana Rivers;" Paper presented at the annual meeting of the American Economic Association; New Orleans, January 1991.

Kahneman, Daniel; "Comments" in Valuing Environmental Goods, edited by Ronald G. Cummings, David S. Brookshire and William D. Schulze; Totowa, N.J.: Rowman and Allanheld, 1986.

Kahneman, Daniel, and Jack Knetch; "Valuing Public Goods: The Purchase of Moral Satisfaction;" 22 JEEM 57–70; 1992.

Kemp, M.A., and C. Maxwell: "Exploring a Budget Context for Contingent Valuation Estimates;" Paper presented at the Cambridge Economics, Inc. Symposium, Contingent Valuation: A Critical Assessment; Washington, D.C., April 1992.

Magleby, David B.: Direct Legislation, Johns Hopkins Press, 1984.

Mitchell, Robert Cameron, and Richard T. Carson; Using Surveys to Value Public Goods: The Contingent Valuation Method; Resources for the Future: Washington, DC, 1989; 499 pp.

Rowe, Robert D., W. Douglass Shaw, William Shulzer; "Nestucca Oil Spill;" Chapter 20 in Natural Resource Damages: Law and Economics (eds. Kevin M. Ward and John W. Duffield); New York: John Wiley & Sons; 1992.

Schuman, Howard, and Stanley Presser; Questions and Answers in Attitude Surveys: Experiments on Question Form Working, and Context; New York Academic Press, 1981.

Seip, Kalle, and Jon Strand; Willingness to Pay for Environmental Goods in Norway: A Contingent Valuation Study with Real Payment; Paper prepared for the SAP Center for Applied Research, Department of Economics, University of Oslo, 26 pp.

State of Ohio v. Department of the Interior, 880 V. 2d 432 (D.C. Cir. 1969).

[FR Doc. 93–1018 Filed 1–14–93; 8:45 am]

BILLING CODE 3210–13–14.

Journal of Economic Perspectives—Volume 8, Number 4—Fall 1994—Pages 19–43

Valuing the Environment Through Contingent Valuation

W. Michael Hanemann

T he ability to place a monetary value on the consequences of pollution discharges is a cornerstone of the economic approach to the environment. If this cannot be done, it undercuts the use of economic principles, whether to determine the optimal level of pollution or to implement this via Pigouvian taxes or Coase-style liability rules. Sometimes, the valuation involves a straightforward application of methods for valuing market commodities, as when sparks from a passing train set fire to a wheat field. Often, however, the valuation is more difficult. Outcomes such as reducing the risk of human illness or death, maintaining populations of native fish in an estuary, or protecting visibility at national parks are not themselves goods that are bought and sold in a market. Yet, placing a monetary value on them can be essential for sound policy.

The lack of a market to generate prices for such outcomes is no accident. Markets are often missing in such cases because of the nonexcludable or nonrival nature of the damages: for those affected by it, pollution may be a public good (or bad). The public good nature of the damages from pollution has several consequences. It explains, for example, why the damages are sometimes large—only a few people may want to own a sea otter pelt, say, but many may want this animal protected in the wild. It also explains why market prices are inappropriate measures of value. In the presence of externalities, market transactions do not fully capture preferences. Collective choice is the more relevant paradigm.

This is precisely what Ciriacy-Wantrup (1947) had in mind when he first proposed the contingent valuation method. Individuals should be interviewed

■ *W. Michael Hanemann is Associate Professor of Agricultural and Resource Economics, University of California, Berkeley, California.*

and "asked how much money they are willing to pay for successive additional quantities of a collective extra-market good." If the individual values are aggregated, "the result corresponds to a market-demand schedule" (p. 1189). Thus, surveys offered a way to trace the demand curve for a public good that could not otherwise be gleaned from market data. Schelling (1968) made a similar point in his paper on valuing health. While the price system is one way to find out what things are worth to people, he wrote, another way is to ask people, whether through surveys or votes. Answering surveys may be hypothetical, but no more than buying unfamiliar or infrequent commodities. "In any case, relying exclusively on market valuations and denying the value of direct enquiry in the determination of government programs would depend on there being for every potential government service, a close substitute available in the market at a comparable price. It would be hard to deduce from first principles that this is bound to be the case" (pp. 143–4).

Schelling's point was not that indirect methods using market transactions have no role, but rather that they cannot always be counted on to provide a complete measure of value. Analysts can often capture some effects of a change in air quality or a change in risk to human health through a hedonic analysis that looks for evidence to property values or wage rates (Rosen, 1974). But people may also value those items in ways not reflected in wages or property values. Similarly with averting expenditures and household production models (Freeman, 1993), which rely on the demand for market commodities that are complements to, or surrogates for, the nonmarket good. If people value that good at least partly for reasons unrelated to their consumption of the complementary private goods, those methods capture just part of people's value—what is called the "use value" component, following Krutilla (1967).[1] They fail to measure the "non-use value" or "existence value" value component, which contingent valuation can capture.

An alternative is to turn to the political system, for example using collective choice models to estimate demands for local public goods (Oates, 1994). However, Cropper (1994) suggests this is unlikely to be useful for the environment because, in the United States, there are few cases where local governments actually set environmental quality. Moreover, as Chase (1968) noted, the method contains an element of circularity: a major reason for the spread of benefit-cost analysis is legislators' desire to obtain information on the public's value for government programs. While it may sometimes be desirable to leave the assessment of value to the legislative process, it is not obvious that this is always so. Measuring liability for damages from pollution is an example. In some cases one wants to ascertain how the public values something, and contingent valuation may be the only way to measure this short of a plebiscite.

Ciriacy-Wantrup (1947) recognized that surveys are not foolproof. The degree of success depends on the skill with which the survey is designed and

[1] For a formal definition, see Hanemann (1994a).

implemented. But it was time, he felt, that economics took advantage of developments in social psychology and the newly emerging academic field of survey research: "Welfare economics could be put on a more realistic foundation if a closer cooperation between economics and certain young branches of applied psychology could be established" (p. 1190). This finally occurred in the 1980s, and contingent valuation came of age. Two landmarks were an EPA conference in 1984 that brought together leading practitioners, other economists, and psychologists to assess the state-of-the-art (Cummings et al., 1986), and the publication of what has become the standard reference on contingent valuation, Mitchell and Carson (1989), which puts it in a broader context involving elements from economics, psychology, sociology, political science, and market research.

Contingent valuation is now used around the world (Navrud, 1992; Bateman and Willis, forthcoming), both by governments agencies and the World Bank for assessing a variety of investments. A recent bibliography lists 1600 studies and papers from over 40 countries on many topics, including transportation, sanitation, health, the arts and education, as well as the environment (Carson et al., 1994c). Some notable examples are Randall, Ives and Eastman (1974) on air quality in the Four Corners area, the first major non-use value study; Brookshire et al. (1982) on air pollution in Southern California; Carson and Mitchell (1993) on national water quality benefits from the Clean Water Act; Smith and Desvousges (1986) on cleaning up the Monongahela River, Jones-Lee, Hammerton and Phillips (1985) on highway safety; Boyle, Welsh and Bishop (1993) on rafting in the Grand Canyon; Briscoe et al. (1990) on drinking water supply in Brazil; and the study on the *Exxon Valdez* oil spill I helped conduct for the State of Alaska (Carson et al., 1992).

This paper focuses generally on the use of contingent valuation to measure people's values for environmental resources, rather than specifically on natural resource damages. It will describe how researchers go about conducting reliable surveys. It then addresses some common objections to surveys and, lastly, considers the compatibility between contingent valuation and economic theory.

Conducting Reliable Surveys

In all research, details matter. How a contingent valuation survey is conducted is crucial. While there is no panacea, various procedures have been developed in recent years that enhance the credibility of a survey and make it more likely to produce reliable results. These touch all aspects, including sampling, instrument development, formulation of the valuation scenario, questionnaire structure, and data analysis. The main ways of assuring reliability are summarized here.

Suppose one approached people in a shopping mall, made them put their bags down for a moment, and asked them what was the most they would be willing to pay for a sea otter in Alaska or an expanse of wilderness in Montana. This is how the President of American Petroleum Institute and other critics have characterized contingent valuation (DiBona, 1992). The essence of their argument is summarized in titles such as "Ask a Silly Question" and "Pick a Number" (Anon., 1991; Bate, 1994). It does not require any unusual perspicacity to see that this approach is unlikely to produce reliable results. For precisely this reason, it is *not* what good contingent valuation researchers do, and it is *not* what was recommended by the NOAA Panel on Contingent Valuation (Arrow et al., 1993) described in Portney's paper in this issue.

Serious surveys of the general public avoid convenience sampling, such as stopping people in the street; they employ statistically based probability sampling.[2] They also avoid self-administered surveys, such as mail surveys or questionnaires handed out in a mall, because of the lack of control over the interview process. For a major study, the NOAA Panel recommended in-person interviews for their superior reliability. Furthermore, interviews should occur in a setting that permits respondents to reflect and give a considered opinion, such as their home. Unless the study deals with consumer products, shopping malls are a poor choice. Indeed, the only contingent valuation study where people were stopped for a few minutes in a mall was one performed for Exxon (Desvousges et al., 1992).

The crux is how one elicits value. The two key developments have been to confront subjects with a specific and realistic situation rather than an abstraction, and to use a closed-ended question which frames the valuation as voting in a referendum.

A common temptation is to characterize the object of valuation in rather general terms: "What would you pay for environmental safety?" "What would you pay for wilderness?" The problem is that these are abstractions. People's preferences are not measured in the abstract but in terms of specific items. "Paying for wilderness" is meaningless; what is meaningful is paying higher taxes or prices to finance particular actions by somebody to protect a particular wilderness in some particular manner. Therefore, one wants to confront respondents with something concrete. Moreover, one should try to avoid using counterfactuals. "What would you pay not to have had the *Exxon Valdez* oil spill?" is utterly hypothetical because one cannot undo the past. By contrast, "What would you pay for this new program that will limit damage from any future oil spills in Prince William Sound?" offers something that is tangible.

The goal in designing a contingent valuation survey is to formulate it around a specific commodity that captures what one seeks to value, yet is plausible and meaningful. The scenario for providing the commodity may be real; if not, the key is to make it seem real to respondents. They are not actually

---

[2]DiBona's scenario actually was the practice in the 1930s when most surveys were "brief encounters" on the street or in stores (Smith, 1987). The 1940s saw the adoption of probability sampling, standardized survey techniques, longer and more complex survey instruments, and in-depth focused interviews (Merton and Kendall, 1946).

making a payment during the interview, but they are expressing their intention to pay. The vaguer and less specific the commodity and payment mechanism, the more likely respondents are to treat the valuation as symbolic. To make the payment plausible, one needs to specify the details and tie them to provision of the commodity so this cannot occur without payment. There should be a clear sense of commitment; for example, if the program is approved, firms will raise prices, or the government taxes, so there is no avoiding payment once a decision is made.[3]

Until the mid-1980s, most contingent valuation surveys used some version of an open-ended question, like "What is the most you would be willing to pay for . . . ?" Since then, most major contingent valuation studies have used closed-ended questions like "If it cost x, would you be willing to pay this amount?" or "If it cost x, would you vote for this?" Different people are confronted with different dollar amounts. Plotting the proportion of "yes" responses against the dollar amount traces out the cumulative distribution function of willingness-to-pay.[4]

Of course, if people carried utility functions engraved in their brains, the question format would not matter. But they don't, and it does matter. In this country, posted prices are the norm rather than bargaining. In market transactions people usually face discrete choices: here is an item, it costs x, will you take it? Similarly in voting. Moreover, there is abundant evidence that respondents find the open-ended willingness-to-pay question much more difficult to answer than the closed-ended one; for market and nonmarket goods alike, people can generally tell you whether they would pay some particular amount, but they find it much harder to know what is the *most* that they would possibly pay. Indeed, the experience with open-ended willingness-to-pay questions for market goods is that people are more likely to tell you what the good costs than what it is worth to them. In addition to being less realistic and harder to answer, the open-ended format creates incentives which are different from those in the closed-ended format. With the open-ended format, as with an oral auction, there are strategic reasons for stating less than one's full value—a theoretical result strongly supported by experimental evidence. This is not so with a closed-ended format; there, the NOAA Panel held, there is no strategic reason for the respondent to do other than answer truthfully.[5]

For these reasons, the NOAA Panel considered the closed-ended format combined, where possible, with a voting context the most desirable for

---

[3]To underscore this, the interviewer may tell respondents that the government uses surveys like this to find out whether taxpayers are willing to pay for new programs it is considering.

[4]The methodology here is to assume a random utility model for individual preferences. This can be estimated using standard techniques for binary choices. Bishop and Heberlein (1979) were the first to use this format; the link with utility theory was developed in Hanemann (1984).

[5]With auctions, it is well documented that formal matters and that oral auctions generate lower prices than posted-price auctions. Why the surprise when the same holds true for open- versus closed-ended payment questions?

contingent valuation: "The simplest way to approach the valuation problem," it held, "is to consider a contingent valuation survey as essentially a self-contained referendum in which respondents vote to tax themselves for a particular purpose" (p. 20). This is a rather different conception of contingent valuation from asking silly questions of passers-by.

In his introduction to this symposium, Portney describes other ways to make a contingent valuation questionnaire more reliable: providing adequate and accurate information; making the survey balanced and impartial; insulating it from any general dislike of big business; reminding respondents of the availability of substitutes, and of their budget constraint; facilitating "don't know" responses; allowing respondents to reconsider at the end of the interview. Several steps can be taken to eliminate any perception of interviewer pressure. At the outset, the interviewer can assure respondents that there are no "right" answers. Before asking the voting question, to legitimate a negative response, the interviewer could say something like: "We have found that some people vote for the program and others vote against. Both have good reasons for voting that way," and then list some reasons for saying "no."[6] Another possibility is if the interviewer does not actually see the respondents' votes, for example by having them write on a ballot placed in a sealed box.

A recent innovation, considered essential by the NOAA Panel, is a "debriefing" section at the end of the survey. This checks respondents' understanding and acceptance of key parts of the contingent valuation scenario. For example, was the damage as bad as described? Did you think the program would work? Did you think you really would have to pay higher taxes if the program went through? This also probes the motives for their answer to the willingness-to-pay question. What was it about the program that made you decide to vote for it? Why did you vote no? Moreover, throughout the survey, all spontaneous remarks by the respondent are recorded verbatim as they occur. After the survey, the interviewer is debriefed and asked about the circumstances of the interview, how attentive the respondent was, whether the respondent seemed to understand the questions and appeared confident in his responses. In this way, one creates a rich portrait of the interview. This information can be exploited in the data analysis. One can monitor for the misunderstandings, measure statistically how they affected respondents' willingness-to-pay, and adjust accordingly. For example, if a subject who voted "yes" appeared to be valuing something different than the survey intended, this case can be dropped or the "yes" converted to a "no."

With any data, different statistical procedures can produce different results. The closed-ended format raises several statistical issue, for example, one might summarize the willingness-to-pay distribution by using its mean, or its

---

[6]For example, the interviewer might note that some people prefer to spend the money on other social or environmental problems instead, or they find the cost is more than they can afford or than the program is worth, or they cannot support the program because it would benefit only one area (Carson et al., 1992).

median, or another quantile. The mean is extremely sensitive to the right tail of the distribution; that is, to the responses of the higher bidders. For this reason, if the mean is to be used, a nonparametric or bounded influence approach is highly recommended for fitting the willingness-to-pay distribution. The median, by contrast, is usually very robust (Hanemann, 1984). Another issue is that the choice of dollar bids affects the precision with which the parameters of the willingness-to-pay distribution are estimated; significant improvements can be achieved by using optimal experimental designs (Kanninen, 1993). Statistical techniques can also be used to probe for yea-saying or other response effects, and correct for them if they are present (Hanemann and Kanninen, forthcoming).

While none of these alone is decisive, taken together they are likely to produce a reliable measure of value. Apart from the expense of in-person interviews, they are all eminently feasible.[7] Other essential ingredients are relentless attention to detail and rigorous testing of the instrument, usually in collaboration with survey experts, so that the researcher understands exactly how it works in the field and is sure it communicates what was intended.

It is no coincidence that the handful of studies that Diamond and Hausman select from the contingent valuation literature in their companion paper in this issue violate most of these precepts, as do the Exxon surveys reported in Hausman (1993). None uses in-person interviews. Many are self-administered. Most use open-ended questions. None is cast as voting.[8] Many ask questions with a remarkable lack of detail.[9] Several seem designed to highlight the symbolic aspects of valuation at the expense of substance.[10] The Exxon surveys were designed and fielded in great haste, with little pretesting, just at a time when federal agencies were gearing up for natural resource damage regulations.[11] The only way to justify this is to make the tacit assumption that, if

---

[7] Is there an acceptable alternative to in-person surveys? The NOAA Panel felt mail surveys have significant problems rendering them unsuitable. Telephone surveys avoid these problems, but preclude the use of visual aids and need to be short. The most promising alternative is a mail/telephone combination in which an information package is mailed to respondents who are then interviewed by phone (Hanemann, Loomis and Kanninen, 1991). This permits an extensive phone interview which seems to provide many of the benefits of an in-person survey at much lower cost.

[8] Two studies Diamond and Hausman cite as showing a lack of commitment in contingent valuation, Seip and Strand (1992) and Duffield and Patterson (1991), used open-ended questions about payment to an environmental charity. Most of Seip and Strand's subjects who were followed up afterwards said that they had been expressing their willingness-to-pay for environmental problems generally, rather than the particular environmental group. Careful pretesting would have discovered this beforehand.

[9] This is notably a problem in Diamond et al. (1993).

[10] Including Kahneman and Ritov (1993), Kahneman and Knetsch (1992), and Kemp and Maxwell (1993). The last two employ a "top-down" procedure in which respondents are given details of the item only *after* they value it. They are first confronted with something broad, like "preparedness for disasters." After stating their willingness-to-pay for the broad category, they are told what it comprises and asked their willingness-to-pay for *one* of those components. Then, they are told what *this* comprises, and so on. The *change* in the *quantity* of any item is never specified.

[11] Hanemann (1994a, b) critiques these studies.

contingent valuation is valid, details of its implementation should not matter. This is fundamentally wrong: measurement results are not invariant with respect to measurement practice in *any* science.

Objections to Surveys

McCloskey (1985, p. 181) observes that economists generally dislike surveys: "Economists are so impressed by the confusions that might possibly arise from questionnaires that they have turned away from them entirely, and prefer the confusions resulting from external observation." In this section, I discuss four common objections to surveys.

Surveys are Vulnerable to Response Effects

Small changes in question wording or order sometimes cause significant changes in survey responses (Schuman and Presser, 1981). Since virtually all data used in economics come from surveys (including experiments, which are a form of survey), and all surveys are vulnerable to response effects, it is important to understand why these arise and how they can be controlled. A consensus is beginning to emerge based on insights from psychology and linguistics. Answering survey questions requires some effort, usually for no apparent reward. Respondents must interpret the meaning of the question, search their memory for pertinent information, integrate this into a judgment, and communicate the judgment to the interviewer. Although some are motivated to make the effort, others may become impatient, disinterested, or tired. Instead of searching for an accurate and comprehensive answer, they satisfice, just aiming for some response that will be accepted. Furthermore, interviews are interactions governed by social and linguistic norms that shape assumptions and expectations. Viewing respondents as satisficing agents following norms of conversation has proved helpful in interpreting survey data, explaining response effects, and designing more effective surveys (Groves, 1989; Krosnick, 1991).

Not all response phenomena are equally intractable. Some, such as order effects (for example, bias towards the first item in a list), can be detected and controlled, either by choosing the sequence that produces a conservative result or by randomizing the order of items across interviews.

A second type of effect is where there is a shift in meaning. This is substance, not noise. For example, similar words turn out to mean different things: "allow" is not the same as "not forbid," nor "higher prices" the same as "higher taxes."[12] Or there are framing effects, where subjects respond differ-

---

[12]And different words can mean the same thing, as in the movie *Annie Hall* where Woody Allen and Diane Keaton are asked by their psychiatrists how often they have sex. He says: "Hardly ever, maybe three times a week." She says: "Constantly, I'd say three times a week." With consumer expenditure surveys, Miller and Guin (1990) attest that life imitates art.

ently to situations the researcher saw as equivalent. It has been shown through debriefings that the subjects perceived the situations as substantively different, because either the researcher induced an unintended change in meaning or context, or the subjects made inferences that went beyond the information given (Frisch, 1993).[13] In each case, the shift in meaning is a source of error only if the researcher is unaware of it. Through rigorous testing with cognitive techniques, the researcher can come to understand exactly what the instrument means to people, and what they mean in response.[14]

A third phenomenon arises from the inherent difficulty of the task assigned the respondent. In recalling past events or behavior, for example, respondents resort to rounding, telescoping (time compression) and other inferential strategies that yield inaccurate reports of magnitudes and frequencies.[15] Bradburn et al. (1987) emphasize that factual and attitudinal surveys share many similar cognitive processes and errors. There is no easy solution for recall errors. This continues to be a problem for many data used by economists,[16] though not for contingent valuation data since there is no recall.

One cannot avoid the fact that surveys, like all communication, are sensitive to nuance and context and are bound by constraints of human cognition. One tries to detect discrepancies and repair them, but they cannot be entirely ruled out. It is important to keep a sense of proportion. As far as I know, nobody has stopped using data from the Current Population Survey, Consumer Expenditure Survey, Monthly Labor Survey, or Panel Study on Income Dynamics because there are response effects in such surveys. The same should apply to contingent valuation surveys.

The Survey Process Creates the Values

It has been asserted that contingent valuation respondents have no real value for the item, but just make one up during the course of the interview: the process creates the values that it seeks to measure. Debriefings can identify

---

[13]When there is incomplete information in a survey, respondents may go ahead and make their own assumptions. Consequently, the researcher loses control over his instrument. Diamond et al. (1993) is a contingent valuation example.

[14]On testing by federal survey agencies, see Tanur (1992). Lack of adequate testing can explain some notable violations of procedural invariance—respondents saw cues or meaning which the researcher didn't intend and failed to detect. An example is the base rate fallacy where "when no specific information was given, prior probabilities are properly utilized; when worthless evidence is given prior probabilities are ignored" (Tversky and Kahneman, 1974). A norm of conversation is to present information one believes relevant. That this was the expectation of subjects could have been detected through debriefings. On violations of conversational norms in base-rate experiments, see Krosnick, Li and Lehman (1990).

[15]Some pronounced telescoping errors are to be found in the Alaska recreation survey conducted by Hausman, Leonard and McFadden (1993).

[16]Juster and Stafford (1991) and Mathiowetz and Duncan (1988) discuss biases in labor supply estimates due to problems with bunching and misreporting in Current Population Survey data. Atkinson and Micklewright (1983) discuss errors in Family Expenditure Survey reports of income and its components. Other inconsistencies between micro- and macro-data sets for the household sector are discussed in Maki and Nishiyama (1993).

whether subjects were inattentive or unfocused and offered hasty or ill-considered responses, and these can be discarded if desired. But, the issue raised here is more fundamental. Diamond and Hausman feel they know real preferences when they see them, and they do not see them in contingent valuation. Based on the debriefing statements in Schkade and Payne (1993) that show most subjects, faced with an open-ended willingness-to-pay question, think about either what the item could cost or what they have spent on something remotely similar, Diamond and Hausman conclude that these people are just making up their answer rather than evincing "true economic preferences." But, what are "true economic preferences"? If a subject responds thoughtfully to a question about voting to raise taxes for a public good, by what criterion is that not a valid preference?

It is true that economists often assume consumer choice reflects an individual's global evaluation of alternatives, a "top-down" or "stored-rule" decision process. The stored-rule notion traces back to Hobbes and the English empiricists who conceived of cognition in terms of storing and retrieving "slightly faded copies of sensory experiences" (Neisser, 1967). Wilson and Hodges (1992) call this the "filing cabinet" concept of the mind. It long dominated not only economics but also psychology. But it is now being abandoned in the face of accumulating evidence from the neurosciences (Rose, 1992) and elsewhere that all cognition is a constructive process—people construct their memories, their attitudes, and their judgments. The manner of construction varies with the person, the item, and the context. A general principle is that people are cognitive misers: they tend to resolve problems of reasoning and choice in the simplest way possible. This is the emerging consensus not only in survey research, but also in social psychology, political psychology, and market research (Martin and Tesser, 1992; Sniderman, Brody and Tetlock, 1991; Payne, Bettman and Johnson, 1988).

For non-habituated and complex consumer choices, people often make "bottom-up" decisions; that is, they make up a decision rule at the moment they need to use it (Bettman, 1988). Olshavsky and Granbois (1979, p. 98) found that "for many purchases a decision process never exists, not even on first purchase." Bettman and Zins (1977) found that grocery shoppers construct a choice heuristic "on the spot" about 25 percent of the time; bottom-up construction of preferences occurred especially for meat and produce "as might be expected, since consumers cannot really rely on brand name for most choices of this type," less often for beverages and dairy products "where either strong taste preferences may exist or only a limited number of brands are available" (p. 81). This calls to mind a remark by Robert Solow that the debriefings in Schkade and Payne "sound an awful lot like Bob Solow in the grocery store." I suppose critics of contingent valuation would consider that Solow does not have true economic preferences, or that he has true economic preferences when buying milk but not meat.

The real issue is not whether preferences are a construct but whether they are a *stable* construct. While this surely varies with circumstances, the evidence for contingent valuation is quite strong. There is now a number of test-retest studies in the contingent valuation literature, and these show both consistency in value over time and a high correlation at the individual level (Carson et al., 1994b). These levels of consistency are comparable to the most stable social attitudes such as political party identification.

Ordinary People are Ill-Trained For Valuing the Environment

If, as the NOAA Panel suggests, the goal of a contingent valuation survey is to elicit people's preferences as if they were voting in a referendum, then prior experience or training are irrelevant. These are not a criterion for voting.[17] Nor is their absence an argument against contingent valuation per se. Through direct questioning, one can readily identify which respondents knew of the issue before the interview, or before the oil spill, and determine whether they hold different values from those who did not. How one proceeds in calculating aggregate willingness-to-pay is something that can be decided separately from the survey. Who has standing, and whose values should count, are questions that we as economists have no special competence to judge.

Survey Responses Can't Be Verified

There are three ways to validate contingent valuation results: replication, comparison with estimates from other sources, and comparison with actual behavior where this is possible. Replication is useful even on a small scale both to see if results hold up and to check whether the instrument is communicating as intended. This is the single best way for a researcher to determine whether somebody's survey instrument works as claimed.

When contingent valuation measures direct use values, it may be possible to make a comparison with estimates obtained through indirect methods. Knetsch and Davis (1966) conducted the first test, comparing contingent valuation and travel demand estimates (a method described in Portney's paper) of willingness-to-pay for recreation in the Maine woods. The difference was less than 3 percent. There are now over 80 studies, offering several hundred comparisons between contingent valuation and indirect methods. The results are often fairly close; overall, the contingent valuation estimates are slightly

---

[17]Voter ignorance is a constant refrain for Diamond and Hausman. They use it to form a syllogism: voters are ill-informed, contingent valuation is like a referendum, therefore contingent valuation respondents are ill-informed. Both parts are false. Contingent valuation researchers take pains to ensure their samples are representative and their questionnaires intelligible, informative, and impartial, thus avoiding the vagaries of turnout and biased advertising in election campaigns. This is why political scientists are becoming interested in "deliberative polling"—in effect, extended contingent valuation surveys (Fishkin, 1991). Many analysts see a substantial core of rationality in voter behavior. Cronin (1989) finds Magleby's (1984) assessment of voter ignorance in referenda overblown. Fiorina (1981) and McKelvey and Ordeshook (1986) emphasize how campaign protagonists use signals to inform voters. Lupia (1993) analyzes the insurance reform battle in the 1988 California ballot and finds that informational "short cuts" enabled poorly informed voters to act as though they were well informed. What Sniderman (1993) calls "the new look in public opinion research" stresses how ordinary citizens use the information at hand to make sense of politics.

lower than the revealed preference estimates and highly correlated with them (Carson et al., 1994a).

The ideal is direct testing of contingent valuation predictions against actual behavior. There are about ten such tests in the literature. Diamond and Hausman mention only five of these. The ones not mentioned yield results quite favorable to contingent valuation.

Bohm (1972) conducted the first test, where subjects in Stockholm were asked their willingness-to-pay to see a new TV program. In five treatments, the program was shown if the group raised 500 Kr, with actual payment based in various ways on stated willingness-to-pay. A sixth treatment asked subjects what was the highest amount they would have given *if* they had been asked to pay an individual admission fee. The mean response was 10.2 Kr (about $2) when the group was asked a hypothetical question, versus an overall average of 8.1 Kr when the group actually paid. The difference between contingent valuation and non-contingent valuation means was not statistically significant in four of the five cases.

Bishop and Heberlein (1990) conducted a series of experiments with hunters who had applied for a deer-hunting permit in a favored game preserve run by the state of Wisconsin. The most relevant for current practice is an experiment in which they wrote to two groups of hunters offering to sell them a permit at a specified price. In one case, this was a real offer; in the other, it was asked as a hypothetical question. Estimated willingness-to-pay was $31 in the real sale versus $35 in the hypothetical sale, a statistically insignificant difference.

Dickie, Fisher and Gerking (1987) offered boxes of strawberries door-to-door at different prices. One treatment was a real offer—the household could buy any number of boxes at this price. The other asked how many boxes they *would* buy if these were offered at the given price. The resulting two demand curves were not significantly different. The parameter estimates were actually more robust over alternative model specifications for the hypothetical than the actual data (Smith, 1994).

Carson, Hanemann and Mitchell (1986) tested the accuracy of voting intentions in a water quality bond election in California in 1985. Closed-ended contingent valuation questions were placed on the Field California Poll a month before the vote, using different figures for the household cost. Adjusted for "don't know" responses, the predicted proportion of yes votes at the actual cost was 70–75 percent. The ballot vote in favor was 73 percent.

Cummings, Harrison and Rutstrom (1993) offered subjects small commodities at various prices. For one group, it was a real sale. A second group was first asked a hypothetical contingent valuation question—this item is not actually for sale but, if it were, would you buy it now? The experimenter then announced that, after all, she *would* sell the item, but they should feel free to revise their answer. When juicers were the item, 11 percent actually bought them in the real sale; with the second treatment, 41 percent said they would buy it if it were on sale, but then only 16 percent did. The 41 percent and 11

percent are significantly different. With calculators, 21 percent would buy in
the hypothetical sale, versus 8 percent in the real sale. One wonders whether
some respondents interpreted the question as "*if you needed a juicer*, would you
buy this one?" Smith (1994) shows that the calculator responses do not generate a downward sloping demand curve for either the actual or hypothetical
data. The experimental procedure contained nothing to emphasize commitment or counteract yea-saying in the hypothetical treatment. Cummings and
his colleagues have recently added wording like the "reasons to say no"
mentioned earlier. In one case, this reduced the hypothetical yes for calculators
from 21 percent to 10 percent, not significantly different from the real 8
percent; in another there was no effect (Cummings, 1994).

Other contingent valuation tests have used open-ended payment questions,
with predictable difficulties. Boyce et al. (1989) measured willingness-to-pay
and willingness-to-accept for a house plant, with mixed results; Neill et al.
(1994) measured willingness-to-pay for a map and a picture, with negative
results. Both confound the issue by comparing contingent valuation responses
to an experimental auction, begging the question of whether auction behavior
understates willingness-to-pay. Duffield and Patterson (1991) and Seip and
Strand (1992) compare actual and hypothetical contributions to an environmental cause. Diamond and Hausman focus on these studies because they
showed a significant difference. But, soliciting an intention to make a charitable
donation is a poor test of contingent valuation, because it invites less commitment than soliciting an intention to vote for higher taxes. To make things
worse, Seip and Strand used members of the environmental group as the
interviewers in their hypothetical treatment, thus increasing pressures for
compliance. They compared hypothetical phone responses with responses to an
actual mail solicitation. Duffield and Patterson compared hypothetical mail
solicitations from the University of Montana with actual mail solicitations from
the Nature Conservancy. In both studies, the difference in survey administration introduces a confounding factor which undermines the comparison.[18]

A cleaner test is provided by Sinden (1988) who conducted a series of 17
parallel experiments soliciting actual and hypothetical monetary donations to a
fund for assisting soil conservation or controlling eucalypt dieback. In all 17
cases, there was no statistical difference between actual and hypothetical
willingness-to-pay.

Thus, there is some substantial evidence for the validity of contingent
valuation survey responses, although more studies are certainly needed. Many
existing studies do not incorporate the refinements in contingent valuation

---

[18]The problem with mail surveys is that people may think the survey is junk mail and throw it out
unopened. Duffield and Patterson made no allowance for the difference in sponsor identity on the
envelope, which could explain the difference in response rates (Schuman, 1992). Response rates
apart, the pattern of contributions was similar in the two treatments. Seip and Strand made no
allowance for the fact that phone and mail solicitations generally have different response rates.
Infosino (1986) found a sales rate three times higher with telephone than mail in an AT&T
marketing effort.

method, described earlier, that emphasize realism and commitment. In this respect, the test by Carson, Hanemann and Mitchell (1986) points in the right direction because it deals directly with expression of voting intentions. The positive results in that study are consistent with other evidence showing that polls in this country reliably indicate public sentiment at the time they are taken, and polls close to an election are generally accurate predictors of the outcome.[19] Kelley and Mirer (1974) found voting intentions correctly predicted the actual vote in four presidential elections for 83 percent of those respondents who voted.[20] Surveys of purchase intentions in market research may not be accurate predictors of subsequent purchase behavior, but surveys of voting intentions are.[21]

Contingent Valuation and Economic Theory

Critics of contingent valuation like Diamond and Hausman, and their coauthors in Hausman (1993), reject contingent valuation as a method of economic valuation because the results of contingent valuation studies are inconsistent with economic theory as they see it. These assertions have become quite widely known. However, careful examination shows that in some cases the claims are not supported by the findings in the contingent valuation literature, and in others they rest on unusual notions about what economic theory does or does not prescribe. I briefly review these issues here, leaving a more detailed treatment to Hanemann (1994a).

Diamond and Hausman, and Milgrom (1993), make a number of statements about what is a permissible argument in a utility function. They argue that people should care about outcomes, not about the process whereby these are generated. People should not care whether animals are killed by man or die naturally. They should not care about details of provision or payment for a

---

[19]Diamond and Hausman seem troubled that voters change their minds during the course of an election campaign. They cite a 1976 electricity rate proposition in Massachusetts where support went from 71 percent in February to 25 percent in the November ballot. They fail to mention the reasons. Magleby (1984, p. 147) identifies opposition spending as the chief cause of such opinion reversals, and that certainly occurred in 1976—opponents outspent supporters more than threefold. In May, the Dukakis administration came out against it, as eventually did businesses, the unions, hospitals, colleges, and major newspapers.

[20]Ajzen and Fishbein (1980) offer some reasons to expect a high level of attitude-behavior correspondence for voting in terms of their theory of reasoned action.

[21]One reason for the difference is timing: unlike elections, people generally control the timing of their market purchases. The result is they may end up buying the commodity, but later than they said (Juster, 1964). This is especially likely for durables, the focus of much literature, since their durability permits delay in replacement. This is consistent with findings that purchase intentions are significantly more accurate for nondurables than durables (Ferber and Piskie, 1965); intentions *not* to purchase durables are highly accurate (Theil and Kosobud, 1968); and predictions of the brand selected when the purchase *does* occur tend to be highly accurate (Ajzen and Fishbein, 1980; Warshaw, 1980).

commodity, only price. Above all, they should value things for purely selfish motives. In their accompanying piece, Diamond and Hausman phrase this argument by saying that respondents should not contemplate "what they think is good for the country," because that reflects "warm glow" rather than "true economic preferences."[22] From this perspective, contingent valuation is unacceptable because it picks up existence values; for those to be allowed in a benefit-cost analysis, Milgrom (1993, p. 431) argues, "it would be necessary for people's individual existence values to reflect only their own personal economic motives and not altruistic motives, or sense of duty, or moral obligation."[23]

This criticism hardly comports with the standard view in economics that decisions about what people value should be left up to them. For example, Kenneth Arrow (1963, p. 17) wrote: "It need not be assumed here that an individual's attitude toward different social states is determined exclusively by the commodity bundles which accrue to his lot under each. The individual may order all social states by whatever standards he deems relevant." Or as Gary Becker (1993, p. 386) writes: "[I]ndividuals maximize welfare *as they conceive it*, whether they be selfish, altruistic, loyal, spiteful, or masochistic." When estimating demand functions for fish prior to Vatican II, no economist ever proposed removing Catholics because they were eating fish out of a sense of duty. Nor, when estimating collective choice models, do we exclude childless couples who vote for school bonds because they lack a personal economic motive.

A more substantive matter is how willingness-to-pay varies with factors that could reasonably be expected to influence it. This has been raised in connection with the embedding effect and the income elasticity of willingness-to-pay. Regarding the latter, Diamond and Hausman assert in this issue that the income effects measured in typical contingent valuation surveys are lower than would be expected if true preferences are measured. McFadden and Leonard (1993, p. 185) make the more specific claim that an income elasticity of willingness-to-pay less than unity constitutes grounds for doubting the validity of the contingent valuation method. There is no basis for either assertion. In the literature on the demand for state and local government services in the United States, the income elasticities generally fall in the range 0.3 to 0.6 (Cutler, Elmendorf and Zeckhauser, 1993). With charitable giving by individuals, the income elasticities generally fall in the range of 0.4 to 0.8. (Clotfelter, 1985). The income elasticities in the contingent valuation literature vary with

---

[22]"Warm glow" is simply a red herring. I have seen no empirical evidence that people get a warm glow from voting to raise their own taxes, whether in real life or in a contingent valuation study.
[23]Milgrom (1993) also asserts that using contingent valuation to measure altruistic preferences creates double counting. His analysis has three flaws. First, it depends on the particular specification of the utility function, as Johansson (1992) notes; if the argument of the utility function is another's consumption rather than his utility, there is no double counting. Second, it derives its force from the auxiliary assumption that the respondent *does not realize* that the other people for whom he cares will have to pay, too; this is not a problem in a referendum format. Third, in many contingent valuation studies the object of the altruism is often wildlife—sea otters, for example. Since those creatures are *not* surveyed, the issue of double counting is moot.

the item being valued, but are generally in this same range (Kristrom and Riera, 1994).

The term "embedding effect," introduced by Kahneman and Knetsch (1992), has come to mean several different things. The general notion is captured in the (mis)conception that, with contingent valuation, you get the same willingness-to-pay if you value one lake, two lakes, or ten lakes.[24] This combines three distinct notions. One assertion, which arises when the object of preference is thought to be simply the number of lakes, is that willingness-to-pay varies inadequately with changes in the scale or scope of the item being valued. This is a scope effect. Alternatively, if each lake is seen as a separate argument in the utility function, then the assertion is that a given lake has quite different value if it is first, second or tenth in a set of items to be valued—it gets a high value when the first, but it adds little or nothing to total value when second or tenth. This is a sequencing effect. Thirdly, with either preference structure, the willingness-to-pay for a composite change in a group of public goods may be less than the sum of the willingnesses-to-pay for the individual changes separately. This is a sub-additivity effect.

The question of how willingness-to-pay varies with the scale or scope of the item being valued in a contingent valuation survey has long been considered, starting with Cicchetti and Smith (1973) who elicited hiker's values for trips in a Montana wilderness area and found that the willingness-to-pay for trips where other hikers were encountered on two nights was 34 percent lower than the willingness-to-pay for trips with no encounters. Many other studies have since reported comparable findings using both internal (within-subject) and external (split-sample) scope tests, including meta-analyses by Walsh, Johnson and McKean (1992) covering over 100 contingent valuation studies of outdoor recreation, and Smith and Osborne (1994) on 10 contingent valuation studies of air quality. Carson (1994) reviews 27 papers with split-sample tests of scope and finds a statistically significant effect of scope on willingness-to-pay in 25 of them.

The two exceptions are Kahneman and Knetsch (1992) and Desvousges et al. (1992). Critics of contingent valuation rely heavily on these two studies when asserting the absence of scope effects in contingent valuation.[25] Some of the problems with these two studies have already been noted, including their failure to use a closed-ended voting format, the after-the-fact provision of information in Kahneman and Knetsch's "top-down" procedure, and the use of

---

[24] Though widely believed, this is a myth. It may be traced to Kahneman (1986), which is usually cited as showing that respondents were willing to pay the same amount to clean up fishing lakes in one region of Ontario as in all of Ontario. His data actually show a 50 percent difference. Moreover, the survey involved a brief telephone interview using an open-ended willingness-to-pay question. It provided no detail on how and when the cleanup would occur. Respondents may not have seen cleaning up *all* the lakes as something likely to happen soon.

[25] Also, in their contingent valuation survey, Diamond et al. (1993, pp. 45–46) mention that, using a Kruskal-Wallis test, they found no difference in willingness-to-pay for three wilderness areas ranging in size from 700,000 to 1.3 million acres. If they had run a simple regression of willingness-to-pay on acreage, they would have found a significant scope effect.

brief shopping mall intercepts by Desvousges et al.[26] The latter elicited people's willingness-to-pay for preventing the deaths of migratory waterfowl. Three separate versions of the questionnaire said that 2,000, 20,000, and 200,000 out of 85 million birds die each year from exposure to waste-oil holding ponds that could be sealed under a new program. Respondents were told that the deaths amounted to *much less than* 1 *percent* of the bird population, to *less than* 1 *percent*, and to *about* 2 *percent*. If respondents focused on the relative impact on the population, it is hard to believe that they would have perceived any real difference among these percentages. The results of the scope test depend crucially on how much one trims the data to remove what are clearly outliers. With a 10 percent trim, one obtains a highly significant scope effect.[27] At any rate, even if one regards these two studies as highly credible evidence that respondents were insensitive to scope, they certainly do not represent the majority finding in the contingent valuation literature regarding the variation of willingness-to-pay with scope.

How much should willingness-to-pay vary with scope? Diamond (1993) asserts that economic theory requires it to increase *more than proportionately* with the number of bird deaths. The variables in his model are the number of birds originally in the population, q_0, the number at risk of dying, q_R, and the number of those that are saved, q_S. Let $q_F \equiv q_0 - q_R + q_S$. Diamond assumes that people should care only about q_F, the ultimate number of birds, not how many were alive initially, at risk, or saved. He also assumes preferences are quasiconcave in q_0. The two assumptions together imply *quasiconvexity* in q_R, which is what makes the elasticity of willingness-to-pay with respect to q_R greater than unity. The conclusion depends critically on the assumption of perfect substitution between q_0, q_S and $-q_R$. When contingent valuation data disconfirm this, Diamond dismisses the method. Others might be more inclined to believe the data and drop the assumption.[28]

With regard to sequencing and sub-additivity effects, these effects are certainly present in contingent valuation responses, but one expects them to occur, and they can be explained in terms of substitution effects and diminish-

---

[26]Other questions about Kahneman and Knetsch are raised by Harrison (1992) and Smith (1992).
[27]How the survey was administered clearly affected the results. Schkade and Payne (1993) used the same questionnaire as Desvouges et al., but slowed respondents down and made them think about their answer. Their data show a different pattern of willingness-to-pay responses, and a significant relationship between willingness-to-pay and the percentage of birds killed (Haneman, 1994b).
[28]Some, while not sharing Diamond's extreme position on the elasticity of willingness-to-pay, still hold that contingent valuation responses vary inadequately with scale. People's perceptions undoubtedly differ from objective measures of attributes. But this is not just a feature of contingent valuation. In psychophysics, it has been known since the 1880s that there is a general tendency for judgments of magnitude to vary inadequately. Observers standing at a distance overestimate the height of short posts, and underestimate that of tall ones; people reaching quickly for an object overestimate small distances and angles, and underestimate large ones; subjects matching loudness of a tone to a duration overestimate the loudness of short tones, and underestimate the loudness of long ones; people overestimate infrequent causes of death, and underestimate frequent ones; small probabilities are overestimated, large ones underestimated (Poulton, 1989). This "response contraction bias" in judgment or rating is an authentic feature of how people perceive the world, not an artifact of contingent valuation.

ing marginal rates of substitution. When the quality of one lake improves, you value an improvement in a second lake *less* if the lakes are what Madden (1991) calls *R*-substitutes, and *more* if they are *R*-complements. Far from being inconsistent with economic preferences (Diamond et al., 1993, pp. 48–49), sub-additivity is likely to be the norm: while all goods cannot be *R*-comple-ments, Madden shows they *can* all be *R*-substitutes.[29] Similarly, *R*-substitution explains sequence effects: if the lakes are *R*-substitutes, the willingness-to-pay for an improvement in one lake is *lower* when it comes at the end of a sequence of changes in lake improvements than at the beginning while the willingness-to-accept for the change in the lake is *higher* when it comes later in a sequence (Carson, Flores and Hanemann, 1992).[30] It should come as no surprise that the value of one commodity changes when the quantity of another varies: in other words, that willingness-to-pay depends on economic context.[31]

For many economists, the ultimate argument against contingent valuation is that it violates the habitual commitment of the profession to revealed preference. Three points should be noted. First, one must distinguish between private market goods and public goods. Revealed preference is harder to apply to the latter, especially when they are national rather than local public goods (Cropper, 1994). Second, revealed preference is not foolproof, either. It in-volves an extrapolation from observation of particular choices to general conclusions about preference. One relies on various auxiliary assumptions to rule out factors that might invalidate the extrapolation. Those assumptions are not themselves verifiable if one is restricted to observed behavior. This can sometimes make revealed preference a relatively hypothetical undertaking.[32]

---

[29] If the intention of the Diamond et al. (1993) contingent valuation survey was to test the adding-up of willingness-to-pay, it was strangely designed for the purpose. The survey stated that there were 57 federal wilderness areas in the Rocky Mountain states, without identifying them, and said that there now was a proposal to open these to commercial development. In one version, respondents were told that seven unidentified areas had already been earmarked for development, and were asked their willingness-to-pay to protect an eighth area, identified as the Selway Bitterroot Wilderness. In another, respondents were told that eight unnamed areas had been earmarked for development and asked their willingness-to-pay to protect a ninth area, identified as the Washakie Wilderness. In a third version, respondents were told that seven unnamed areas had been earmarked for development and asked their willingness-to-pay to protect two areas identified as Selway and Washakie. In all three cases, respondents were not told the identity or fate of the other 48 or 49 areas. Given that respondents were not indifferent among wilderness areas, as evidenced by the regression mentioned in note 25, I leave it to the reader to decide whether the surveys constitute a sensible basis for testing the adding up of willingness-to-pay.

[30] In natural resource damages, where willingness-to-accept is the relevant welfare measure, this implies that the usual practice of taking the injured resource as the first item in any possible valuation sequence is a conservative procedure.

[31] The practical implications are that, when one values a program, it be placed in whatever sequence applies under the circumstances, and that one take care when extrapolating results in a benefits transfer exercise because the values might change with the difference in circumstances (Hoehn and Randall, 1989).

[32] Revealed preference estimates are sensitive to the measurement of price, which is often uncertain and precarious for disaggregated commodities (Pratt, Wise and Zeckhauser, 1979; Randall, 1994). The price at which demand falls to zero, needed to estimate consumer's surplus, may lie outside the range of the observed data and be estimated inaccurately (for example, one knows travel cost only for participants, or one believes that participants and nonparticipants have different preferences). This can cause revealed preference to produce a less reliable estimate of use value than contingent

Third, there is no reason why observing people's behavior and asking them about behavioral intentions and motives should be mutually exclusive. Fathoming human behavior is never easy; one should utilize every possible source of information.

Above all, one should take a balanced view of the difficulties with each approach. As Sen (1973, p. 258) wrote, "we have been too prone, on the one hand, to overstate the difficulties of introspection and communication and, on the other, to underestimate the problems of studying preferences revealed by observed behavior." In the debate on contingent valuation, critics have shown a tendency to employ simplistic dichotomies. Surveys of attitudes are fallible and subject to the vagaries of context and interpretation; surveys of behavior are unerring. In the market place, people are well informed, deliberate, and rational. Outside it, they are ignorant, confused, and illogical. As consumers, people can be taken seriously; as voters, they cannot. In particular instances, these assertions may be correct. As generalizations, however, they are a caricature.

Conclusions

When cost-benefit analysis started in the United States in the 1930s, economic valuation was generally perceived in terms of market prices. To value something, one ascertained an appropriate market price, adjusted for market imperfections if necessary, and then used this to multiply some quantity. Two things changed this. The first was the recognition, prompted by the "new welfare economics" of the 1940s and especially Hotelling's paper on public utility pricing, that the appropriate welfare criterion is maximization of aggregate consumers' plus producers' surplus. While market prices can safely be used to value marginal changes for market commodities, the impact of non-marginal changes is measured by the change in areas under demand and supply curves. The second development was Samuelson's theory of public goods and his finding that their valuation must be based on vertical aggregation of individual demand curves.

Together, these developments led to an important paradigm shift—one that contributed directly to the emergence of nonmarket valuation and is still evident in the current debate on contingent valuation.[33] This shift changed the focus of valuation away from market prices towards demand and supply functions as the underlying repositories of value. These functions are behavioral relations, and the implication of the paradigm shift was that economics is

---

valuation (Hanemann, Chapman and Kanninen, 1993). With other variables there may be inadequate variation in the data (for example, attributes are correlated across brands). Hence, revealed preference data alone may yield a less reliable estimate of demand functions than contingent valuation choice data, and one may need to combine both types of data for best results (Adamowicz, Louviere and Williams, 1994).

[33] For an account of the development of nonmarket valuation generally, see Hanemann (1992).

not just the study of markets, but more generally the study of human preferences and behavior.

The conceptual link to nonmarket valuation is the recognition that, while a demand curve is not observable if there is no market for a commodity, there still exists a latent demand curve that perhaps can be teased out through other means. Indirect methods are one approach to doing this, and contingent valuation is another. In both cases, the details of implementation have a large impact on the quality of the results.

Faced with the assertion that contingent valuation surveys can *never* be a reliable source of information either for benefit cost analysis or for damage assessment, the NOAA Panel rejected this as unwarranted. Two years later, there is now even more evidence from recent studies and literature analyses to support the Panel's conclusion. However, it would be misleading for me to suggest that contingent valuation surveys can be made to work well in all circumstances. I am sure situations could exist where a contingent valuation researcher might be unable to devise a plausible scenario for the item of interest. Nor would I wish to argue that all contingent valuation surveys are of high quality. The method, though simple in its directness, is in fact difficult to implement without falling into various types of design problems that require effort, skill and imagination to resolve. Each particular study needs to be scrutinized carefully. But the same is true of any empirical study.

While I believe in the feasibility of using contingent valuation to measure people's value for the environment, I do not mean to advocate a narrow benefit-cost analysis for all environmental policy decisions, nor to suggest that everything can or should be quantified. There will be cases where the information is inadequate, the uncertainties too great, or the consequences too profound or too complex to be reduced to a single number. I am well aware of the fallacy of misplaced precision. But this cuts both ways. It also applies to those who suggest that it is better not to measure nonuse values at all than to measure them through contingent valuation. I reply to such critics by quoting Douglass North: "The price you pay for precision is an inability to deal with real-world issues" (*Wall Street Journal*, 7/29/94).

Is expert judgment an alternative to contingent valuation? Experts clearly play the leading role in determining the physical injuries to the environment and in assessing the costs of clean-up and restoration. Assessing what things *are worth* is different. How the experts know the value that the public places on an uninjured environment, without resort to measurement involving some sort of survey, is unclear. When that public valuation is the object of measurement, a well-designed contingent valuation survey *is* one way of consulting the relevant experts—the public itself.

■ *I want to thank Richard Carson, Jon Krosnick, Robert Mitchell, Stanley Presser and Kerry Smith for their helpful comments, and Nicholas Flores and Sandra Hoffmann for excellent assistance. I also thank the editors, without whom this paper would be far longer.*

References

Adamowicz, W., J. Louviere, and M. Williams, "Combining Revealed and Stated Preference Methods for Valuing Environmental Amenities," *Journal of Environmental Economics and Management*, 1994, *26*, 271–92.

Ajzen, Icek, and Martin Fishbein, *Understanding Attitudes and Predicting Social Behavior*. New Jersey: Prentice-Hall, Inc., 1980.

Anonymous, "'Ask a Silly Question...' Contingent Valuation of Natural Resource Damages," *Harvard Law Review*, June 1992, *105*, 1981–2000.

Arrow, Kenneth, J., *Social Choice and Individual Values*, 2nd ed., New Haven: Yale University Press, 1963.

Arrow, Kenneth, et al., *Report of the NOAA Panel on Contingent Valuation*, Washington, D.C.: January 1993, p. 41.

Atkinson, A. B., and J. Micklewright, "On the Reliability of Income Data in the Family Expenditure Survey, 1970–1977," *Journal of the Royal Statistical Society* (A), 1983, *146(1)*, 33–53.

Bate, Roger, "Pick a Number: A Critique of Contingent Valuation Methodology and Its Application in Public Policy." Competitive Enterprise Institute, Environmental Studies Program, Washington, D.C., January 1994.

Bateman, Ian, and Ken Willis (eds.), *Valuing Environmental Preferences: Theory and Practice of the Contingent Valuation Method in the US, EC and Developing Countries*. Oxford, UK: Oxford University Press, forthcoming.

Becker, Gary S., "Nobel Lecture: The Economic Way of Looking at Behavior," *Journal of Political Economy*, June 1993, *101(3)*, 385–409.

Bettman, James R., "Processes of Adaptivity in Decision Making," *Advances in Consumer Research*, 1988, *15*, 1–4.

Bettman, J. R., and M. A. Zins, "Constructive Processes in Consumer Choice," *Journal of Consumer Research*, September 1977, *4*, 75–85.

Bishop, Richard C., and Thomas A. Heberlein, "Measuring Values of Extramarket Goods: Are Indirect Measures Biased?" *American Journal of Agricultural Economics*, December 1979, *61*, 926–30.

Bishop, Richard C., and Thomas A. Heberlein, "The Contingent Valuation Method." In Johnson, Rebecca L., and Gary V. Johnson, eds., *Economic Valuation of Natural Resources: Issues, Theory, and Applications*, Boulder: Westview Press, 1990, 81–104.

Bohm, Peter, "Estimating Demand for Public Goods: An Experiment," *European Economic Review*, 1972, *3*, 111–30.

Boyce, R. R., et al., "Experimental Evidence of Existence Value in Payment and Compensation Contexts." Paper presented at the USDA W-133 Annual Meeting, San Diego, California, February 1989.

Boyle, Kevin J., Michael P. Welsh, and Richard C. Bishop, "The Role of Question Order and Respondent Experience in Contingent-Valuation Studies," *Journal of Environmental Economics and Management*, 1993, *25*, S-80-S-99.

Bradburn, Norman M., Lance J. Rips, and Steven K. Shevell, "Answering Autobiographical Questions: The Impact of Memory and Inference on Surveys," *Science*, April 1987, *236*, 157–161.

Briscoe, John, et al., "Toward Equitable and Sustainable Rural Water Supplies: A Contingent Valuation Study in Brazil," *World Bank Economic Review*, May 1990, *4*, 115–34.

Brookshire, David S., Mark A. Thayer, William D. Schulze, and Ralph C. d'Arge, "Valuing Public Goods: A Comparison of Survey and Hedonic Approaches," *American Economic Review*, 1982, *72*, 165–77.

Carson, Richard T., "Contingent Valuation Surveys and Tests of Insensitivity to Scope." Paper presented at the International Conference on Determining the Value of Nonmarketed Goods: Economic Psychological, and Policy Relevant Aspects of Contingent Valuation Methods, Bad Hamburg, Germany, July 1994.

Carson, Richard T., and Nicholas E. Flores, "Another Look at 'Does Contingent Valuation Measure Preferences: Experimental Evidence'—How Compelling is the Evidence?" Economics Department, University of California, San Diego, December 1993.

Carson, R., N. Flores, and W. M. Hanemann, "On the Creation and Destruction of Public Goods: The Matter of Sequencing," working paper 690, Agricultural and Resource Economics, University of California, Berkeley, 1992.

Carson, Richard T., Nicholas E. Flores, Kerry Martin and Jennifer Wright, "Contingent Valuation and Revealed Preference Methodologies: Comparing the Estimates for Quasi-Public Goods," Discussion Paper 94-07, University of California, San Diego, May 1994a.

Carson, Richard T., W. Michael Hanemann, and Robert Cameron Mitchell, "The Use of Simulated Political Markets to Value Public Goods," Economics Department, University of California, San Diego, October 1986.

Carson, Richard T., Kerry Martin, Jennifer Wright, "A Note on the Evidence of the Temporal Reliability of Contingent Valuation Estimates," working paper, University of California, San Diego, Economics Department, July 1994b.

Carson, Richard T., and Robert Cameron Mitchell, "The Value of Clean Water: The Public's Willingness to Pay for Boatable, Fishable, and Swimmable Quality Water," *Water Resources Research*, 1993, *29*, 2445–54.

Carson, R., et al., *A Contingent Valuation Study of Lost Passive Use Values Resulting from the Exxon Valdez Oil Spill*, Report to the Attorney General of Alaska, Natural Resource Damage Assessment, Inc. La Jolla, CA, November 1992.

Carson, Richard T., et al., *A Bibliography of Contingent Valuation Studies and Papers*, Natural Resource Damage Assessment, Inc., La Jolla, CA, March 1994c.

Chase, S. B., ed., *Problems in Public Expenditure Analysis.* Washington, D.C.: Brookings Institution, 1968.

Cicchetti, Charles J., and V. Kerry Smith, "Congestion, Quality Deterioration, and Optimal Use: Wilderness Recreation in the Spanish Peaks Primitive Area," *Social Science Research*, 1973, *2*, 15–30.

Ciriacy-Wantrup, S. V., "Capital Returns from Soil-Conservation Practices," *Journal of Farm Economics*, November 1947, *29*, 1188–90.

Clotfelter, Charles T., *Federal Tax Policy and Charitable Giving.* Chicago: The University of Chicago Press, 1985.

Cronin, Thomas E., *Direct Democracy: The Politics of Initiative, Referendum, and Recall.* Cambridge: Harvard University Press, 1989.

Cropper, Maureen L., "Comments on Estimating the Demand for Public Goods: The Collective Choice and Contingent Valuation Approaches." Paper presented at the DOE/EPA Workshop on "Using Contingent Valuation to Measure Non-Market Values," Herndon, VA, May 19–20, 1994.

Cummings, Ronald G., "Relating Stated and Revealed Preferences: Challenges and Opportunities." Paper presented at the DOE/EPA Workshop on "Using Contingent Valuation to Measure Non-Market Values," Herndon, VA, May 19–20, 1994.

Cummings, Ronald G., David S. Brookshire, and William D. Schulze, et al., eds. *Valuing Environmental Goods: An Assessment of the Contingent Valuation Method.* Totowa, New Jersey: Rowman and Allanheld, 1986.

Cummings, Ronald G., Glenn W. Harrison, and E. E. Rustström, "Homegrown Values and Hypothetical Surveys: Is the Dichotomous Choice Approach Incentive Compatible?" Economics Working Paper Series, B-92-12, Division of Research, College of Business Administration, The University of South Carolina, February 1993.

Cutler, David, Douglas W. Elmendorf, and Richard J. Zeckhauser, "Demographic Characteristics and the Public Bundle," National Bureau of Economic Research, Cambridge, NBER Working Paper No. 4283, February 1993.

Desvousges, William H., et al., *Measuring Nonuse Damages Using Contingent Valuation: An Experimental Evaluation of Accuracy.* North Carolina: Research Triangle Institute Monograph, 1992.

Diamond, Peter A., Jerry Hausman, Gregory K. Leonard, and Mike A. Denning, "Does Contingent Valuation Measure Preferences? Experimental Evidence." In Hausman, J. A., ed., *Contingent Valuation: A Critical Assessment.* New York: North-Holland, 1993, 41–89.

DiBona, Charles J., "Assessing Environmental Damage," *Issues in Science and Technology*, Fall 1992, *8*, 50–54.

Dickie, M. A. Fisher, and S. Gerking, "Market Transactions and Hypothetical Demand Data: A Comparative Study," *Journal of American Statistical Association*, March 1987, *82*, 69–75.

Duffield, John W., and David A. Patterson, "Field Testing Existence Values: An Instream Flow Trust Fund for Montana Rivers." Presented at the American Economics Association Annual Meeting, New Orleans, Louisiana, January 4, 1991.

Ferber, Robert, and Robert A. Piskie, "Subjective Probabilities and Buying Intentions," *Review of Economics and Statistics*, August 1965, *47*, 322–25.

Fiorina, Morris P., *Retrospective Voting in American National Elections.* New Haven: Yale University Press, 1981.

Fishkin, J. S., *Democracy and Deliberation: New Directions for Democratic Reform.* New Haven: Yale University Press, 1991.

Freeman, A. Myrick, *The Measurement of Environment and Resource Values: Theory and*

Method. Washington, D.C.: Resources for the Future, 1993.

Frisch, Deborah, "Reasons for Framing Effects," *Organizational Behavior and Human Decision Processes*, 1993, *54*, 399–429.

Groves, Robert M., *Survey Errors and Survey Costs*. New York: John Wiley and Sons, 1989.

Hanemann, W. Michael, "Welfare Evaluations in Contingent Valuation Experiments with Discrete Responses," *American Journal of Agricultural Economics*, August 1984, *66*, 332–41.

Hanemann, W. Michael, "Preface: Notes on the History of Environmental Valuation in the USA." In Navrud, Stale, ed., *Pricing the Environment: The European Experience*. Oxford, UK: Oxford University Press, 1992.

Hanemann, W. Michael, "Contingent Valuation and Economics," Working Paper No. 697, Giannini Foundation of Agricultural and Resource Economics, University of California, Berkeley, February 1994a. To appear in Willis, Ken, and John Corkindale, eds., *Environmental Valuation: Some New Perspectives*, Wallingford, Oxon, UK: CAB International, forthcoming.

Hanemann, W. Michael, "Strictly For the Birds: A Re-examination of the Exxon Tests of Scope in CV," working paper, Giannini Foundation of Agricultural and Resource Economics, University of California, Berkeley, August 1994b.

Hanemann, W. Michael, and B. J. Kanninen, "Statistical Analysis of CV Data." In Bateman, I., and K. Willis, eds. *Valuing Environmental Preferences: Theory and Practice of the Contingent Valuation Method in the US, EC and Developing Countries*. Oxford: Oxford University Press, forthcoming.

Hanemann, W. Michael, David Chapman, and Barbara Kanninen, "Non-Market Valuation Using Contingent Behavior: Model Specification and Consistency Tests." Presented at the American Economic Association Annual Meeting, Anaheim, California, January 6, 1993.

Hanemann, W. M., J. Loomis, and B. Kanninen, "Statistical Efficiency of Double-Bounded Dichotomous Choice Contingent Valuation," *American Journal of Agricultural Economics*, 1991, *73*, 1255–63.

Harrison, Glenn W., "Valuing Public Goods with the Contingent Valuation Method: A Critique of Kahneman and Knetsch," *Journal of Environmental Economics and Management*, 1992, *23*, 248–57.

Hausman, J. A., ed., *Contingent Valuation: A Critical Assessment*. New York: North-Holland, 1993.

Hoehn, J. P., and A. Randall, "Too Many Proposals Pass the Benefit Cost Test," *American Economic Review*, June 1989, *79*, 544–51.

Infosino, William J., "Forecasting New Product Sales from Likelihood of Purchase Ratings," *Marketing Science*, Fall 1986, *5*, 372–384.

Johansson, Per-Olov, "Altruism in Cost-Benefit Analysis," *Environmental and Resource Economics*, 1992, *2*, 605–13.

Jones-Lee, Michael W., M. Hammerton, and P. R. Philips, "The Value of Safety: Results of a National Sample Survey," *Economic Journal*, March 1985, *95*, 49–72.

Juster, F. Thomas, *Anticipations and Purchases: An Analysis of Consumer Behavior*. Princeton: Princeton University Press, 1964.

Juster, F. Thomas, and Frank P. Stafford, "The Allocation of Time: Empirical Findings, Behavioral Models, and Problems of Measurement," *Journal of Economic Literature*, 1991, *29*, 471–522.

Kahneman, Daniel, "Valuing Environmental Goods: An Assessment of the Contingent Valuation Method: The Review Panel Assessment." In Cummings, R. G., D. S. Brookshire, W. D. Schulze, et al., eds., *Valuing Environmental Goods: An Assessment of the Contingent Valuation Method*. Totowa, New Jersey: Rowman & Allanheld, 1986, 185–94.

Kahneman, Daniel, and Jack L. Knetsch, "Valuing Public Goods: The Purchase of Moral Satisfaction," *Journal of Environmental Economics and Management*, 1992, *22*, 57–70.

Kahneman, Daniel, and Ilana Ritov, "Determinants of Stated Willingness to Pay for Public Goods: A Study in the Headline Method," unpublished, Department of Psychology, University of California, Berkeley, 1993.

Kanninen, B. J., "Optimal Experimental Design for Double-Bounded Dichotomous Choice Contingent Valuation," *Land Economics*, May 1993, *69*, 128–46.

Kelly, S., and T. W. Mirer, "The Simple Act of Voting," *American Political Science Review*, 1974, *68*, 572–91.

Kemp, Michael A., and Christopher Maxwell, "Exploring a Budget Context for Contingent Valuation Estimates." In Hausman, J. A., ed., *Contingent Valuation: A Critical Assessment*. New York: North-Holland, 1993, 217–69.

Knetsch, J. L., and R. K. Davis, "Comparisons of Methods for Recreation Evaluation." In Kneese A. V., and S. C. Smith, eds., *Water Research*, Baltimore: Resources for the Future Inc., Johns Hopkins Press, 1966, 125–42.

Kriström, Bengt, and Pere Riera, "Is the Income Elasticity of Environmental Improvements Less Than One?" Paper presented at the Second Conference on Environmental Economics, Ulvöng, Sweden, June 2–5, 1994.

Krosnick, Jon A., "Response Strategies for Coping with the Cognitive Demands of Attitude Measures in Surveys," *Applied Cognitive Psychology*, 1991, *5*, 213–36.

Krosnick, Jon A., Fan Li, and Darrin R. Lehman, "Conversational Conventions, Order of Information Acquisition, and the Effect of Base Rates and Individuating Information on Social Judgments," *Journal of Personality and Social Psychology*, 1990, *59*, 1140–52.

Krutilla, John V., "Conservation Reconsidered," *American Economic Review*, September 1967, *57*, 777–86.

Lupia, Arthur, "Short Cuts versus Encyclopedias: Information and Voting Behavior in California Insurance Reform Elections," working paper, Department of Political Science, University of California, San Diego, April 1993.

Madden, Paul, "A Generalization of Hicksian *q* Substitutes and Complements with Application to Demand Rationing," *Econometrica*, September 1991, *59*, 1497–1508.

Magleby, David B., *Direct Legislation, Voting on Ballot Propositions in the United States*. Baltimore and London: The John Hopkins University Press, 1984.

Maki, Atsushi, and Shigeru Nishiyama, "Consistency Between Macro- and Micro-Data Sets in the Japanese Household Sector," *Review of Income and Wealth*, 1993, *39*, 195–207.

Martin, Leonard L., and Abraham Tesser, eds., *The Construction of Social Judgments*. New Jersey: Lawrence Erlbaum Associates, chapter 2, 1992, 37–65.

Mathiowetz, Nancy A., and Greg J. Duncan, "Out of Work, Out of Mind: Response Errors in Retrospective Reports of Unemployment," *Journal of Business & Economic Statistics*, 1988, *6*, 221–29.

McCloskey, Donald, *The Rhetoric of Economics*. Madison: The University of Wisconsin Press, 1985.

McFadden, Daniel, and Gregory K. Leonard, "Issues in the Contingent Valuation of Environmental Goods: Methodologies for Data Collection and Analysis." In Hausman, J. A., ed., *Contingent Valuation: A Critical Assessment*. New York: North-Holland, 1993, 165–215.

McKelvey, Richard D., and Peter C. Ordeshook, "Information, Electoral Equilibria and the Democratic Ideal," *Journal of Politics*, 1986, *48*, 909–37.

Merton, Robert K., and Patricia L. Kendall, "The Focused Interview," *American Journal of Sociology*, 1946, *51*, 541–57.

Milgrom, Paul, "Is Sympathy an Economic Value? Philosophy, Economics, and the Contingent Valuation Method." In Hausman, J. A., ed., *Contingent Valuation: A Critical Assessment*. New York: North-Holland, 1993, 417–41.

Miller, Leslie A., and Theodore Downes-Le Guin, "Reducing Response Error in Consumers' Reports of Medical Expenses: Application of Cognitive Theory to the Consumer Expenditure Interview Survey," *Advances in Consumer Research*, 1990, *17*, 193–206.

Mitchell, Robert Cameron, and Richard T. Carson, *Using Surveys to Value Public Goods: The Contingent Valuation Method*. Washington, D. C.: Resources for the Future, 1989.

Navrud, Ståle, *Pricing the European Environment*. New York: Oxford University Press, 1992.

Neill, Helen R., et al., "Hypothetical Surveys and Real Economic Commitments," *Land Economics*, May 1994, *70*, 145–54.

Neisser, Urlic, *Cognitive Psychology*. Appleton-Century-Crofts, Educational Division, New York: Meredith Corporation, 1967.

Oates, W., "Comments on Estimating the Demand for Public Goods: The Collective Choice and Contingent Valuation Approaches." Paper presented at the DOE/EPA Workshop on Using Contingent Valuation to Measure Non-Market Values, Hemdon, VA, May 19–20, 1994.

Olshavsky, Richard W., and Donald H. Granbois, "Consumer Decision Making—Fact or Fiction?" *Journal of Consumer Research*, September 1979, *6*, 93–100.

Payne, J. W., J. R. Bettman, and E. J. Johnson, "Adaptive Strategy Selection in Decision Making," *Journal of Experimental Psychology: Learning, Memory, and Cognition*, 1988, *14*, 534–52.

Poulton, E. C., *Bias in Quantifying Judgments*. Hove, UK: Lawrence Erlbaum Associates, 1989.

Pratt, John W., David A. Wise, and Richard Zeckhauser, "Price Differences in Almost

Competitive Markets," *Quarterly Journal of Economics*, May 1979, *93*, 189–212.

Randall, Alan, "A Difficulty with the Travel Cost Method," *Land Economics*, February 1994, *70*, 88–96.

Randall, Alan, Berry C. Ives, and Clyde Eastman, "Bidding Games for Valuation of Aesthetic Environmental Improvements," *Journal of Environmental Economics and Management*, 1974, *1*, 132–49.

Rose, Steven, *The Making of Memory: From Molecules to Mind*. New York: Anchor Books, Doubleday, 1992.

Rosen, S., "Hedonic Prices and Implicit Markets: Product Differentiation in Pure Competition," *Journal of Political Economy*, January-February 1974, *82*, 34–55.

Schelling, Thomas, "The Life You Save May Be Your Own." In Chase, S., ed., *Problems in Public Expenditure Analysis*. Washington, D.C.: Brookings Institution, 1968, 143–4.

Schkade, David A., and John W. Payne, "Where Do the Numbers Come From? How People Respond to Contingent Valuation Questions." In Hausman, J. A., ed., *Contingent Valuation: A Critical Assessment*. New York: North-Holland, 1993, 271–303.

Schuman, H., remarks in transcript of Public Meeting of the National Oceanic and Atmospheric Administration, Contingent Valuation Panel, Washington, D.C.: NOAA, Department of Commerce, August 12, 1992, p. 101.

Schuman, H., and S. Presser, *Questions and Answers in Attitude Surveys*. New York: Academic Press, 1981.

Seip, K., and J. Strand, "Willingness to Pay for Environment Goods in Norway: A Contingent Valuation Study with Real Payment," *Environmental and Resource Economics*, 1992, *2*, 91–106.

Sen, A. K., "Behavior and the Concept of Preference," *Economica*, August 1973, *40*, 241–59.

Sinden, J. A., "Empirical Tests of Hypothetical Biases in Consumers' Surplus Surveys," *Australian Journal of Agricultural Economics*, 1988, *32*, 98–112.

Smith, Tom W., "The Art of Asking Questions, 1936–1985," *Public Opinion Quarterly*, 1987, *51*, 21–36.

Smith, V. Kerry, "Arbitrary Values, Good Causes, and Premature Verdicts," *Journal of Environmental Economics and Management*, 1992, *22*, 71–89.

Smith, V. Kerry, "Lightning Rods, Dart Boards and Contingent Valuation," *Natural Resources Journal*, forthcoming 1994.

Smith, V. Kerry, and William H. Desvousges, *Measuring Water Quality Benefits*. Boston: Kluwer-Nijhoff Publishing, 1986.

Smith, V. Kerry, and Laura Osborne, "Do Contingent Valuation Estimates Pass a 'Scope' Test?: A Preliminary Meta Analysis." Presented at the American Economics Association Annual Meeting, Boston MA, January 5, 1994.

Sniderman, Paul M., "The New Look in Public Opinion Research." In Finifter, Ada W., ed., *Political Science: The State of the Discipline II*. Washington, D.C.: The American Political Science Association, 1993, 219–45.

Sniderman, Paul M., Richard A. Brody, and Phillip E. Tetlock, *Reasoning and Choice, Explorations in Political Psychology*. Cambridge: Cambridge University Press, 1991.

Tanur, Judith M., ed., *Questions about Questions: Inquiries into the Cognitive Bases of Surveys*. New York: Russell Sage Foundation, 1992.

Theil, Henri, and Richard F. Kosobud, "How Informative Are Consumer Buying Intentions Surveys?" *Review of Economics and Statistics*, February 1968, *50*, 50–59.

Tversky, Amos, and Daniel Kahneman, "Judgment under Uncertainty: Heuristics and Biases," *Science*, 1974, *185*, 124–31.

Walsh, Richard G., Donn M. Johnson, and John R. McKean, "Benefits Transfer of Outdoor Recreation Demand Studies: 1968–1988," *Water Resources Research* 1992, *28*, 707–13.

Warshaw, Paul R., "Predicting Purchase and Other Behaviors from General and Contextually Specific Intentions," *Journal of Marketing Research*, February 1980, *17*, 26–33.

Wilson, Timothy D., and Sara D. Hodges, "Attitudes as Temporary Constructions." In Martin, L., and A. Tesser, eds., *The Construction of Social Judgments*. New Jersey: Lawrence Erlbaum Associates, chapter 2, 1992, 37–65.

Name Index

The International Library of Critical Writings in Economics